P9-BVV-941

D0020370

THE PO...

Each volume in The Viking Portable Library either presents a representative selection from the works of a single outstanding writer or offers a comprehensive anthology on a special subject. Averaging 700 pages in length and designed for compactness and readability, these books fill a need not met by other compilations. All are edited by distinguished authorities, who have written introductory essays and included much other helpful material.

"The Viking Portables have done more for good reading and good writers than anything that has come along since I can remember."

—Arthur Mizener

Eugene Kamenka was born in Cologne, Germany. He emigrated to Australia in 1937 and is now head of the History of Ideas Unit at the Australian National University, Canberra. He has written many books and articles, including *The Ethical Foundations of Marxism*, and has lectured at Columbia University in New York City; Trinity College, Oxford; the University of Singapore; the Hebrew University of Jerusalem; and numerous other schools and universities.

The Portable

KARL MARX

*Selected, translated in part,
and with an Introduction by
Eugene Kamenka*

PENGUIN BOOKS

PENGUIN BOOKS
Published by the Penguin Group
Viking Penguin Inc., 40 West 23rd Street, New York, New York 10010, U.S.A.
Penguin Books Ltd, 27 Wrights Lane, London W8 5TZ, England
Penguin Books Australia Ltd, Ringwood, Victoria, Australia
Penguin Books Canada Ltd, 2801 John Street, Markham, Ontario, Canada L3R 1B4
Penguin Books (N.Z.) Ltd, 182–190 Wairau Road, Auckland 10, New Zealand

Penguin Books Ltd, Registered Offices:
Harmondsworth, Middlesex, England

First published in the United States of America
in simultaneous hardcover and paperback editions by
Viking Penguin Inc. 1983

9   11   13   15   14   12   10   8

Copyright © Viking Penguin Inc., 1983
All rights reserved

ISBN 0 14 015.096 X
(CIP data available)

Printed in the United States of America
Set in CRT Janson

Grateful acknowledgment is made to the following for permission to reprint copyrighted material from other sources.

Fondazione Giangiacomo Feltrinelli, Italy: Selections from "Lettres et documents de Karl Marx, 1856–1883," edited by E. Bottigelli, in *Annali Feltrinelli I*. Selections from Wolfgang Schwerbrock, *Karl Marx privat*, Munich, 1962. Courtesy of Archives and Annali della Fondazione Feltrinelli.

International Publishers: Selections from *The German Ideology* by Karl Marx and Friedrich Engels, edited by R. Pascal. New York: International Publishers, 1947.

Lawrence & Wishart Ltd, London: Selections from *Selected Works of Karl Marx and Friedrich Engels*, 3 volumes, Moscow, 1969. Selections from *Selected Works of Karl Marx and Friedrich Engels*, 2 volumes, Moscow, 1951.

K. J. Kenafick: Selections from *Michael Bakunin and Karl Marx*, translated by K. J. Kenafick, Melbourne, 1948.

Except in the United States of America,
this book is sold subject to the condition
that it shall not, by way of trade or otherwise,
be lent, re-sold, hired out, or otherwise circulated
without the publisher's prior consent in any form of
binding or cover other than that in which it is
published and without a similar condition
including this condition being imposed
on the subsequent purchaser

CONTENTS

Contents

INTRODUCTION

I

Karl Marx confronts us as a thinker of world-historical dimensions. Nineteenth-century European socialism and social theory found in him their greatest and most penetrating mind. Our own century has run much of its course in the shadow of his teaching. The two great revolutions that succeeded, rivalled, and partly eclipsed the rise of European socialism—the Bolshevik Russian and the Communist Chinese—were launched or consolidated under the banner of 'Marxism'. Today half the population of the world is led and governed in his name. On every continent, radical movements find inspiration in his forecasts and programmes in his theories.

Practical political impact and ideological persuasiveness are not necessarily related to intellectual power. The position of Marx as the greatest of the socialist ideologists and as the posthumously proclaimed founder of one of the world's great religions is no guarantee of his stature as a thinker and as a theorist of modern society. Nevertheless, Marx has such stature. Few would now seriously contest the proposition that he was the greatest thinker in the history of socialism. He gave socialism its intellectual respectability and its theoretical self-confidence. From diverse sources and materials, from phrases in radical pamphlets and slogans at socialist meetings, from German philosophy, French politics, and English economics, he created a socialist system of thought, a total socialist critique of modern society. He refined and systematized the language of socialism; he explained and expounded the place of socialism in history; he reconciled, or seemed to reconcile, its conflicting hopes and theoretical contradictions. His work—itself a process of self-clarification—set the seal upon the transition from the romantic revolutionism of the 1840s to the working-class movement of the 1860s, 70s, and 80s. It fused into a single body of connected doctrine moral criticism and economic analysis, revolutionary activism and social science, the longing for community and the acceptance of economic rationality and industrial progress. It clothed the interests and demands of a still largely nascent and despised working class in the dignity of a categorical imperative pronounced by history itself.

Marx's attempt to explain socialism to itself thus laid the foundations for a critical account of the birth and development of modern society. For Marx correctly recognized the world-historical importance of the French Revolution and the Industrial Revolution. He saw that, in Europe at least, they were part and parcel of one development. He realized that they had inaugurated a new era in history, an era in which civil society—the world of industry and trade—had moved to the center of the stage and was being driven by violent internal compulsions to ever more rapid change and expansion. Marx recognized more clearly than others the birth of modern society and the tensions and conflicts involved in its internal dynamic. Since the Napoleonic wars set the seal of destruction upon the old order and the old regime in Europe, we have been living through a continuing crisis which has spread outward from Europe until it engulfs the world. Marx was the first and in many respects greatest student of that crisis. His predictions have proved at least partly false; his presentation of the issues may now seem far too simple; but he saw where the issues lay, not only of his time but of ours. The study of modern society still begins with the work of Karl Marx.

II

Karl Marx was born Carl Heinrich Marx in the ancient Rhenish city of Trier at two o'clock in the morning of 5 May 1818. His father, the Trier lawyer and public notary Heinrich Marx, born Hirschl or Herschel Halevi Marx, came from a long line of distinguished rabbis, many of whom had officiated in Trier. Hirschl himself left home at an early age, struggled through his university studies in jurisprudence without his parents' support, or even approval, and became an enlightened Deist and liberal Kantian, mixing an admiration for Voltaire and Rousseau with Prussian nationalism and veneration for the philosopher-king Frederick the Great. Nevertheless, he came back to practise law in Trier, where his father and then his elder brother Samuel were rabbis of the community. Formally, he remained a Jew. On 30 November 1813, he married, in a Jewish ceremony, Henriette Pressborck (Pressburg), the twenty-six-year-old daughter of a rabbi from Nijmegen in Holland, whose ancestors had been rabbis in Hungary. Between 1815 and 1826 she bore him nine children—four sons and five daughters. The eldest of them died almost immediately after birth. Four others died young from tuberculosis. Karl, the third child and oldest surviving son, was the only male child to attain middle age.

In Trier, recently 'liberated' by the Prussians from the French, the family lived comfortably. Heinrich Marx was a respected citizen; the family had rents from land and houses as well as the income from his lawyer's practice; they lived in a well-appointed house in a fashionable part of town. Nevertheless, at least one shadow must have hung over the young Karl's earliest years. At some time between the autumn of 1816 and the summer of 1817 his father, Heinrich, was baptized into the Evangelical established church of the kingdom of Prussia. His wife,

Henriette, stayed at home that day. Some seven years later, on 24 August 1824, the six-year-old Karl Marx (with his five sisters) stood at the baptismal font. In 1825, after both her parents had died, Marx's mother finally went through the ceremony of baptism. Some of Karl Marx's earlier biographers have presented Heinrich's baptism as the logical outcome of his Deist convictions and his identification with the Enlightenment, and have glossed over the time-lag between Heinrich's baptism and that of his children. More recent researches have made it clear that Heinrich entered into baptism only because Prussian legislation forced him to choose between remaining a Jew and remaining a State Legal Counsellor in the city of Trier. In 1815, when the Rhineland was re-attached to the Prussian crown, Heinrich had addressed a memorandum to the Governor-General respectfully asking that the laws applying exclusively to Jews be annulled. In the memorandum he spoke of his 'fellow believers' and fully identified himself with the Jewish community. In 1816 the President of the provincial Supreme Court interviewed Heinrich Marx and recommended that Heinrich and two other Jewish officials be retained in their posts and that the King grant them the special exception made necessary by the decision to apply Prussian legislation to the Rhineland. The Prussian Minister of Justice failed to recommend such an exception, and Heinrich Marx was baptized.

Sympathetic socialist biographers have generally ignored or played down Marx's Jewish origins and the rather hostile attitude that he took up, through much of his life, to both Jews and Judaism. Others have written a great deal of nonsense about the blood of his ancestors and his 'rabbinical' brain. We have no reputable evidence about the extent of 'Jewishness' in the Marx household. But in Marx's childhood character, in his sharp tongue, strong ambition, and frequent aloofness—characteristics that stayed with him for much of his life—we do find some evidence of an underlying insecurity and distress, so frequently linked with equivocal status.

The young Karl was a strong character—we must not picture him shrinking from his school-fellows, holding his head in shame, or crying with frustration at the fact that he was different. His sisters, later in life, recalled that he bullied them mercilessly, but made up for everything by reading them wonderful stories. In 1830, at the age of twelve, Karl entered the Friedrich-Wilhelm-Gymnasium, originally a Jesuit foundation, which had become a first-rate high school with a liberal Kantian headmaster. Karl gained a reputation and a somewhat fearful respect, though little love, among his school-fellows as a skilful lampooner and writer of satirical verses. In his childhood as in his later life, he was a leader, less capable of inspiring easy friendship than the devotion of a disciple. He graduated from school in 1835, with excellent marks in Greek, Latin, and German, but much weaker results in mathematics, French, and especially history.

In the same year Karl Marx committed as great an audacity as the son of a baptized Jewish lawyer might then commit: he fell in love with Jenny, the daughter of Trier's leading citizen, the Government Councillor Baron Ludwig von Westphalen. The Baron, an educated liberal aristocrat, partly of Scottish origin, could recite Homer and Shakespeare by heart and had an interest in Saint-Simon. He befriended the young Karl, who was a school-fellow of Westphalen's son Edgar and obviously had enormous influence upon him. Nevertheless, neither the Marxes nor the Westphalens could be expected to welcome this union. Karl and Jenny became engaged secretly in the summer of 1836. It was to take them seven years to overcome family opposition and to improve Karl's lack of definite prospects and become married.

In the autumn of 1835 Karl entered the University of Bonn as a student of jurisprudence. The family intention was that he should become a lawyer like his father. His conduct at Bonn was not exemplary; he was arrested by the police and punished by the University authorities for 'nocturnal noisiness and drunkenness'; he was involved in a duel in Cologne and investigated for possessing 'forbidden weapons' (i.e., duelling pistols instead of swords). By October 1836 he had persuaded his father to allow him to transfer to the great center of critical thought, the University of Berlin, where the intellectual legacy of Hegel, dead five years earlier, weighed, as Marx put it later, heavily on the living. There Marx studied law, philosophy, and history, attending lectures by Gans and Savigny. After the death of his father in 1838, Karl abandoned any intention of embarking on a legal or administrative career and turned frankly to philosophy. He identified himself with the left wing of the Young Hegelians, became an atheist, a democrat, and a radical critic of the Prussian authoritarian state. Between 1839 and 1841 he worked on his doctoral thesis, a study of the philosophy of nature in Epicurus and Democritus; earlier he had written a great deal of romantic poetry and a fragment of a bad play. His dissertation was completed in 1841 and successfully submitted for the doctorate of the University of Jena. He hoped to join his friend and mentor Bruno Bauer, a radical Young Hegelian, in an academic post, lecturing in philosophy.

Marx's own reputation as a Young Hegelian critic of religion, censorship, and monarchy, coupled with Bauer's dismissal from the Faculty of Theology in the University of Bonn, dashed his hopes for a university career. He became instead, in 1842, editor of a new newspaper founded by liberal businessmen in Cologne, the *Rheinische Zeitung*, but had to resign in March 1843 in a vain attempt to stave off the newspaper's threatened suppression. Later that year he and Jenny were married. They promptly began what was virtually a lifelong exile from Germany. First they settled in Paris, where Marx became better acquainted with socialist and radical literature, and where he formed a friendship with the great German poet

Heinrich Heine and an even more important friendship with a young German from the Wuppertal, Friedrich Engels, who was working as a clerk in a Manchester cotton mill partly owned by his family. The latter friendship was to develop into probably the most momentous literary partnership in history. It began when they collaborated in an attack on Marx's erstwhile mentor, Bruno Bauer, 'and his consorts', entitled *The Holy Family or Critique of Critical Critique*, published in 1845. In Paris, too, Marx's first daughter, Jenny, was born, and here Marx met Proudhon, Bakunin, and other revolutionaries. Here he began his studies of English political economy, sketching, in his *Economico-Philosophical Manuscripts of 1844*, the first, metaphysical, version of his critique of modern society.

Expelled from France at the request of the Prussian Government, Marx made a brief visit to London in the company of Engels and then settled with his family in Brussels. Here he continued his economic studies—discovering, or inventing, in 1845, the 'materialist conception of history'. He made more serious contact with working-class movements and again collaborated with Engels in what is perhaps the first statement of his new 'materialist' view of society, an attack on Feuerbach, Max Stirner, and German 'true socialism' under the heading *The German Ideology*. In Brussels Marx and his family were joined by Helene Demuth, a young servant in the Westphalen household sent to Jenny by her mother to lighten the load of bohemian living with an arrogant but impecunious intellectual and revolutionary. Helene was to become a devoted member of the household, whose practical good sense held the family together and earned the deep affection of the children—though she was also to bear Marx an illegitimate son.

In 1847 Marx, who had been attacking the German working-class Communist Wilhelm Weitling for irresponsible romanticism, was asked to draft, in collaboration with Engels, a program and statement of principles for the small but revolutionary Communist League. The famous *Communist Manifesto*, published in February 1848, was the result. It appeared just as the abortive February revolution broke out in Paris. Marx, arrested in Brussels on suspicion of supplying arms to revolutionaries, was expelled, and he left for Paris. He stayed there less than a month. By June he was in Cologne, editing the radical *Neue Rheinische Zeitung*, the voice of extreme democracy in Germany's abortive experiment in parliamentary government. Upon the defeat of the 1848 revolution, Marx was arrested, tried for sedition, acquitted, and expelled. On 26 August 1849 he arrived, via Paris, in London. He was to spend the rest of his life there, much of it in serious poverty, supported financially by Engels, who had returned to his family's prosperous textile business in Manchester.

Apart from some journalism for Horace Greeley's *New York Tribune* and occasional poor commissions from other well-disposed papers, Marx never had regular work. He lived a life of poverty, complicated, as Neil McInnes has put it, 'by his own notions of respectability, worsened by chronic illness, and saddened by the death of three children'. From 1850 to 1856 he and his family lived in crowded quarters at 28 Dean Street in Soho—a situation no doubt made much more unpleasant by the birth of Helene's child, Frederick. It is now certain that the child was Marx's, though it appears to have been given out at the time as an indiscretion of Engels's. (The boy, called Fred, was placed in the care of foster parents in London and, according to material gathered by Robert Payne, became a mechanic, a good unionist, and moderate labour man, who never married and who died in 1929.)

The 1850s were perhaps Marx's worst years: years of uncertainty, of constant financial worry, of scenes with bailiffs and tradesmen, and of the death of his two sons in infancy and childhood. Marx himself lived the life of an émigré, forming virtually no significant contacts with Englishmen or the English working class, moving among radical émigrés, spending his time between the British Museum, an occasional pub crawl, and his home. In 1856, it is true, he delivered a fiery speech to a Chartist gathering—though all who knew him agreed that he was no orator—but his only really significant political activity was his participation in the International Working Men's Association (the First International) formed by French, German, and Italian workers in 1864. It was finally scuttled by Marx himself in 1872 (a year after the Paris Commune) because of prolonged factional strife, especially between himself and Bakunin. In 1856, too, Marx had moved his family to a somewhat more comfortable house in Grafton Terrace; and in 1864, when his wife Jenny gave her first ball in England, Marx was able to move to still better quarters in Maitland Park Road. But he spent most of the 1850s and 1860s gathering material for his great economic and historical analysis of capitalism, *Das Kapital.* His other writings, apart from the *Contribution to the Critique of Political Economy* that had appeared in 1859 and the important and voluminous notes that he took for *Capital,* were mostly essays in political pamphleteering.

Das Kapital was Karl Marx's—unfinished—*magnum opus.* The first volume, the only one published in Marx's lifetime, was issued by a small publisher of radical literature, Otto Meissner of Hamburg, on or about September 2, 1867, in an edition of 1000 copies. At first, there was virtually no scholarly and very little political reaction to what seemed a heavy and pretentious tome published by an obscure German émigré living in poverty in London. Marx fretted over the silence with which his work was received; Engels and Marx's Hanover friend Kugelmann tried, fairly unethically, to 'drum up some noise' by placing 'reviews' and notices prepared by Engels in any newspaper and journal prepared to take them. Few were. The German academic state socialist Eugen Dühring, whose ethical, philosophical, and economic views Engels was soon to hold up to ridicule, published a not unsympathetic review in one of the supplements to Meyer's well-known *Encyclopaedia*. It was clear, however, that Dühring was more concerned to carry on his feud with German academics than to understand or expound Marx. For the rest, independent comment came almost exclusively from socialist radicals, especially Russians, and from the men who had known Marx in the Young Hegelian movement of the 1840s. The oldest of the Young Hegelians, Arnold Ruge, had by then quarrelled with Marx and in any case had a profound dislike of Communism. Nevertheless his comment was by far the most perceptive. He wrote:

> It is an epoch-making work and it sheds a brilliant, sometimes dazzling, light on the development, decline, birth-pangs and horribly painful maladies of social periods. The passages on the production of surplus-value by unpaid labour, the expropriation of the workers who work for themselves, and the approaching expropriation of the expropriators are classic. Marx's knowledge is wide and scholarly, and he possesses splendid dialectical talent. The book is far beyond the intellectual horizon of many people and many newspaper writers, but it will certainly make its way despite the breadth of its plan, or perhaps it will exercise a powerful influence for just this reason.

Ludwig Feuerbach, the by then forgotten idol of the German radicals of the 1840s, spent the 1860s working on quasi-utilitarian ethical papers not published till after his death. In a footnote he praised *Capital* for its valuable presentation 'of undeniable facts of the most interesting, though horrible, nature' concerning the life of workers in factory society, facts which Feuerbach took to illustrate one of the slogans of his new moral philosophy—'where the necessities of life are absent, moral necessity (obligation) is also absent' Yet Marx's former friend and fellow

Communist, the German poet Freiligrath, missed the point completely. He wrote from Germany to congratulate Marx, and added: 'I know that many young merchants and manufacturers in the Rhineland are enthusiastic about the book, and in such circles it will fulfil its real aim and, besides, it will prove an indispensable work for scholars.'

In the latter half of the 1860s Marx's life was becoming somewhat easier, less bitter and isolated, though hardly crowned with the political success or the intellectual acclaim he thought he deserved. In the 1870s his reputation did begin to 'take', at least in radical circles in Western Europe and Russia. The general rise of the labour movement in the 1860s, coupled with the subsequent notoriety achieved by the Paris Commune, did a great deal to spread the reputation of Marx and his 'scientific' Communism. He was widely, if wrongly, believed to be the instigator and shadowy *éminence grise* behind the Commune. By November 1871 the stocks of the first German edition of *Capital, Volume I,* were almost exhausted. The next year saw the publication of a second German edition; of the first part of a serialized French translation (prepared by J. Roy and revised by Marx), brought out in 10,000 copies and completed in 1875; and of a Russian translation by Lopatin and Danielson, also issued serially in an edition of 3000. It also saw a new edition, the first since 1848, of the *Communist Manifesto.* Marx, taking heart, sent inscribed copies of *Capital* to the two great Englishmen of the age, Charles Darwin and Herbert Spencer. Both responded courteously but noncommittally. In Russia, however, Marx's thought was making obvious impact on real—and not mere fantasy—revolutionaries. Marx had already begun to study Russian and the Russian situation, while keeping up connections with members of German social democracy and the revolutionary movement in Europe.

Meanwhile, however, Marx's health was giving way. He had been troubled for years by carbuncles and a liver complaint, ascribed to his irregular mode of life, heavy pipe-smoking, and constant overwork. In 1873 he came close to complete nervous collapse, plagued by insomnia, constant headaches, fits of trembling. He began taking the cure at Karlsbad, often accompanied by his youngest daughter, Eleanor. As always, he continued to read and take voluminous notes, but he was incapable of further serious creative work. His short *Critique of the Gotha Programme* of 1875, which had been formulated by German socialists in an attempt to heal the split between the 'Marxists' and the Lassalleans, was his last important statement. For the main part he spent his last years living quietly in London, receiving occasional visits from socialists and other admirers. His wife, Jenny, by 1875 already a shrunken figure, was dying from cancer of the liver and endeavouring, as long as possible, to conceal this from Karl. She died in 1881. Marx, himself in ill health, shattered by this blow and the death of his oldest daughter, Jenny, in the same year, sought to recuperate by travelling to Algiers, Monte Carlo, and France. He died in London, on 14 March 1883. There were eleven people to attend his funeral; the eulogy was read by Engels.

Marx had founded no lasting political party, had led no successful—or unsuccessful—revolution, and had produced no major finished work that amounted to a systematic exposition of the critique of capitalist civilization to which he intended to devote his life and a six-volume work. Yet his thought was to shake the world.

III

Karl Marx, it is often said, 'combined' German philosophy, French politics, and English economics. The variety of interpretations of Marx, to be discussed below, has been historically or politically conditioned. But it also reflects the richness and variety of his thought, the number of elements he synthesized into a single logical structure Marx began as an heir of the eighteenth-century Enlightenment, of the German Idealist philosophy of Kant, Fichte, and Hegel, and of the critique of Kant, Fichte, and Hegel himself at the hands of Feuerbach and the Left Hegelians. In the early 1840s, in his last year as a student and during his brief employment as editor of the liberal *Rheinische Zeitung*, Marx stood for a rational society, in which man would be self-determined, cooperating rationally and spontaneously with his fellows, mastering nature and social life instead of being mastered by them. He thus shared and extended the Enlightenment's belief in personal liberty as human self-determination. He accepted the Enlightenment's faith in science and rationality and their connection with progress; he had its optimistic conviction that man must and can mould the universe (both nature and society) to his requirements. Throughout his life Marx was to have nothing but the deepest contempt for nihilism, for the denial of culture and rationality, for the nameless authoritarianism of terroristic individuals or terroristic groups. He loathed the German radical egoist Max Stirner and his cult of the individual's egoistic 'self-expression', just as he was always to loathe that crude 'barracks-communism' which pretends to achieve equality by forcing men into an undifferentiated mass, by rejecting talent, education, all that which for Marx makes men human and not animal. In 1843–1844 Marx began to call himself a Communist, because he saw 'true Communism' as the fullest possible development of human potentialities, of human self-determination, of human culture, and because he was reinforcing his philosophical attack on alienation by making the proletariat as a 'universal class' the center and point of his critique of modern society. 'The criticism of religion', he wrote in 1844, 'ends in the teaching that *man is the highest being for man*, it ends, that is, with the categorical imperative to overthrow all conditions in which man is a debased, forsaken, contemptible being forced into servitude.' For Marx, from the early

1840s onward, 'every emancipation consists of leading the human world and human relationships back to man himself'; every social revolution thus becomes for him 'the protest of man against the dehumanised life'. In the famous concluding sentence of the Preface to his doctoral dissertation Marx announced that Prometheus was the chief saint and martyr in the human calendar, because he had defied the Gods on behalf of man. To the vindication of man, to the creation of a society that would reflect human requirements, and to the critique of man's present alienation and servitude, Marx devoted the whole of his adult life. But man for Marx was always *social* man, bound and shaped in social relationships, disciplined by production and social life. It was not Marx's humanism but his grasp of social movements and social life, his *rejection* of moralism and social and ethical individualism, that made him the greatest of the socialists.

The French Revolution of 1789, as Alexis de Tocqueville wrote,

> has given the impression of striving for a renewal of mankind and not merely for the reform of France. It has therefore kindled a passion such as even the most violent political revolutions have hitherto not been able to produce. It started a proselytizing campaign and brought propaganda into the world. In this way, it eventually assumed a religious character which astonished contemporaries. Even more, it became itself a kind of religion . . . one which has flooded the world with its fighters, its apostles and its martyrs.

The French Revolution consummated and symbolized the political birth of the modern era. It gave the world the very idea of Revolution, an idea that has proved perhaps even more powerful than that other eighteenth-century invention, the idea of Happiness. The world that followed the French upheaval of 1789 stood, as Hegel saw, under the category of the *Incomplete*. Countries and kingdoms were entering upon a new *Becoming*. The implications of the slogan 'Liberty, Equality, Fraternity', of socialism, of democracy and of the nation-state, of the violent change-over from the concept of subject to that of citizen, are indeed not yet exhausted. Coupled with the Industrial Revolution, they provide the key to the dynamic of the modern world.

The importance of the French Revolution for an understanding of modern society lay in the forces it liberated, in the hopes it awakened *and then failed to fulfil*. It swept aside the oppressive government and law associated with monarchy, feudal privileges, and estates. In the name of Liberty, Equality, and the Fraternity of all mankind, it proclaimed the Rights of Man and the Citizen in a pretendedly egalitarian and universal political constitution. It freed man—for a period at least—from slavery, religious oppression, political hierarchies, and social castes. It appeared to herald a new reign of social and political freedom.

In eighteenth- and early nineteenth-century Germany, as Marx put it in a famous passage, the French Revolution took place only in the realm of ideas. What the French did in the streets and on the barricades the Germans did in philosophy. In this comment we find the key to Marx's ability to *fuse* and not merely to 'combine' German philosophy, French politics, and English economics. Already before the French Revolution, Immanuel Kant had proclaimed in his three great *Critiques* that the knowing mind provides the synthetic *a priori* propositions on the basis of which all knowledge is organized and connected, that man creates the concept of God as a 'regulative idea' of reason, that human understanding is the standard of beauty, and that morality rests on the fundamental principle that men must be treated only as ends and never as means. Kant's disciple, the young Fichte, in his *Critique of All Revelation*, had argued that religion was *immoral* because it rested on the *heteronomy* (external determination) and not on the *autonomy* (self-determination) of man. (In another work, Fichte did plead with the Princes of Europe to honour the dignity of man by restoring the lost liberties of their subjects.) Kant and Fichte were thus, in this aspect of their work, proclaiming the Rights of Man—at least in metaphysics. But one of the laws of politics, as Marx saw, provides that tendencies toward radical extremism, metaphysics, and romantic utopianism grow in direct proportion to the lack of practical success and practical involvement of a political or cultural movement. The French achieved the Fall of the Bastille, the inauguration of the Republic, the Declaration of the Rights of Man; the Germans, first powerless to make a real revolution, then disillusioned by Napoleon, wrote philosophical books devoted to increasingly pretentious claims on behalf of the active, knowing mind and the role of reason in history.

The philosophy of Hegel dominated German intellectual life in the 1830s and early 1840s. It represented both the culmination and the dissolution of this Promethean elevation of the *ego cogitans* in German philosophy. The Hegelian system was a vindication of the claims of reason and of philosophy in world history and world politics. It placed logic and rationality above traditional authority, custom, religion, princes, and historical States. But in Hegel Reason had become an unfolding spiritual totality of which all else was but an aspect; it had become an *inhuman* Absolute Idea, ultimately suspiciously like the pantheist God in whom we live and move and have our being. Extremely conscious of the 'formlessness', conflict, and insecurity of the Hobbesian 'civil society' of atomic individuals engaged in the war of all against all, Hegel increasingly stressed the roles of the State, law, custom, and the family in binding men into a rational whole and thus doing the work of reason. His personal convictions became ever more conservative. His position on Christianity and the claims of the Church established in Prussia was at best equivocal. His support of the Prussian monarchy became strong. One of his last acts, as he lay on his deathbed with cholera in Berlin in 1831, was to denounce the proposed English Reform Bill, enacted a year later, as introducing formlessness into what should be a political order held together by the undivided rational will of the Sovereign.

The Hegelian legacy, thus, was ambiguous. Hegel's disciples split into a Right and Left (or Young) Hegelian wing. The Right Hegelians endeavoured to use the Hegelian system, in which everything is subordinated to the 'rational' whole, to support the claims of religion and the State. They tried to pull Hegel's logic back into the service of political conservatism and theology. The Left Hegelians emphasized the Hegelian method, its dialectic and exposure of 'contradictions', including those of autocracy, censorship, religion, and theology. Hegel's elevation of the Monarch and the State as representing true freedom and reason in history seemed to them inconsistencies in his system and lapses from his critical method. The Right Hegelians saw in Hegel the basis for a new and more rational justification of established religion and established authority; the Left or Young Hegelians saw in his elevation of reason and in his dialectical method the most potent weapon of criticism. If the Hegelian Absolute Idea was manifest only in human thinking, they argued, then the Absolute Idea was nothing but a 'theological' fantasy, a projection of human thinking. In reality, there was no Absolute Idea, no spiritual totality or organizing principle, above and beyond Man. In Hegel, religion had been a façade for the Absolute Idea; in truth, then, it must be a façade—for Man. The Left Hegelians thus stressed that freedom and rationality were forms of self-determination, of the autonomy of man. A truly rational society, for them, would be a universal kingdom of ends, a free republic of reason in which 'contradictions'—the mark of abstraction, of separation, of external determination—had completely disappeared. Their attack in the 1830s and early 1840s was centered on religion, but its political implications were clear.

These implications received their fullest development before Marx in the work of Ludwig Feuerbach, in his *Essence of Christianity* (1841) and his writings on the 'Philosophy of the Future' in 1842 and 1843. The qualities ascribed to God, Feuerbach sought to show, are in reality the qualities and potentialities of man, which now could and should be further developed in the cooperative, free democratic society. In conscious reference to Feuerbach's work and as a continuation of it, Marx proclaimed in 1843 that the criticism of religion 'ends in the teaching that man is the highest being for man'.

This is not the place to discuss in detail Marx's debt to Hegel and to German Idealism generally. The debt extends not only to Marx's conception of history and his use of logic, but to a whole series of concepts, from 'self-determination' and 'contradiction' to 'civil society' and 'alienation'. These will be referred to in some of the prefaces to the selections that follow. There is a sense in which German philosophy underlies the whole of Marx's intellectual development, moulding his basic attitudes, giving his work direction and thrust. But in 1842 and 1843, when Marx began reading French political pamphlets and French histories of the Great Revolution of 1789, he was not merely mechanically supplementing his German philosophical training with French political thought. He was also recognizing the inadequate limits within which that German philosophical 'criticism' still moved; he was recognizing that it had failed to penetrate to the roots of the problem. German Idealist philosophy was the German metaphysical version of the French Revolution, enthroning abstract reason in place of gods and kings. The Left

Hegelians in Germany were attempting to criticize Hegelianism from within, on the basis of Hegel's own assumptions, drawn as these partly were from the philosophy of Kant and of the Enlightenment. The socialist and pre-socialist sects in France, as Marx came to realize, were making a similar but more radical and far-reaching criticism of the French Revolution in terms of *its* own assumptions, also drawn from the Enlightenment and thus paralleling some of Hegel's and Kant's assumptions. The real problems, however, were obscured in the German development and made clear in the French. The Great Revolution of 1789 that swept aside the government and law associated with a system of feudal privileges and estates had proclaimed liberty, equality, and fraternity—but only in the *political* sphere. This political liberation resulted in a thoroughgoing economic 'liberation'. Capitalism, the sway of property, the 'civil society' of Ferguson and Hobbes and the British economists, the 'material world' of industry and trade, were freed from the political, social, and moral restraints that feudalism had always imposed on them. The abstract slogan 'Liberty, Equality, Fraternity' thus could and did lead to a social order that was profoundly individualistic, weighted in favour of a minority of property owners. As George Lichtheim has put it in his *Origins of Socialism* (p. 4):

For the bulk of society, then made up of peasants and artisans, economic freedom—in the sense of an uncontrolled market in commodity values, operating in accordance with its own impersonal 'laws'—held danger as much as promise. To the proletariat, already in existence on the eve of the industrial revolution in the shape of a mass of paupers deprived of 'active' citizenship, this kind of freedom signified virtually nothing beyond the bare right to sell one's labor to the highest bidder. Economic liberalism thus conflicted with social democracy, unless it could be shown that all members of society stood an equal chance of attaining to ownership of property. Such an assertion was more plausible in the America of Jefferson and Jackson than in the France of the July Monarchy, or the England of the 1832 Reform Bill, whence the decisive impact of socialist doctrines in Western Europe and their relative failure to attract attention in the United States.

From the disenchantment of the French *sansculottes* and the radical demands of those who identified with them, from the English social and economic critics of the miseries of the new industrial revolution, from the Saint-Simonian cult of the *industriels*, grew the movement that came later to see itself as the class ideology of the industrial proletariat. The term 'socialism' made its first appearance in the early 1830s, among radical sects in France. It defined itself through its criticism of bourgeois society, of bourgeois rights, and of the economic liberalism associated with these. It brought together, as aspects of one movement, the beginnings of workers' associations and workers' protests in Germany, the abortive 1830 revolution in France, and the Chartist agitations in Britain. It fused, or held in loose relation, the Ricardian labour theory of value, the doctrines of Fourier or Saint-Simon, and the radical egalitarianism of the extreme democrats of the French Revolution. Socialism, thus, was a critique—made in the light of the industrial revolution—of bourgeois society, of the hopes and assumptions of the Enlightenment, and of the political theory enshrined in the (bourgeois) Republic. It shared with the prophets, utopians, radical reformers, and rebels of earlier days a common hostility to private property, to the inequalities of economic position and of social opportunity that resulted from the uneven distribution of property, and to the power that this gave some men over others. Unlike the Left Hegelians, thus, it saw man as Hegel himself had done—*in a concrete social context.*

With the rise of the industrial system the attack on property gained a new impetus. It was helped by the concentration of the propertyless in the new industrial towns and barracks, but it rested, above all, on the perception that ownership, now of capital and of machines, had, in these new conditions, vast social ramifications. These ramifications stood in direct contradiction to the egalitarian hopes and pretensions of the French Revolution and to the scientific and economic optimism surrounding the industrial revolution. The machines that were to make man rich and free were in fact making or keeping thousands poor and dependent. By the late 1820s some of the followers of Saint-Simon had developed his unflattering contrast between the 'bourgeois' and the *'industriels'* into a far-reaching attack on the role of bourgeois private property in industry. To make the ownership of industrial capital and of the means of production a private concern was *immoral* because it enabled one man to exploit the labour of others; it was *uneconomic* because it failed to provide for the proper planning of industry, for the optimal allocation of resources throughout that vast industrial workshop into which each nation was being turned. Bourgeois society treated property as a private function, when the industrial system was converting it into a social function. The Saint-Simonian Bazard, in the lectures later assembled in the *Exposition* of Saint-Simonian doctrine, was the first to use the phrase 'the exploitation of man by man'; he combined the moral and economic attacks on private property in the industrial system in a broad indictment:

If, as we proclaim, mankind is moving toward a state in which all individuals will be classed according to their work, it is evident that the right of property, as it exists, must be abolished, because, by giving to a certain class of men the chance to live on the labour of others and in complete idleness, it preserves the exploitation of one part of the population, the most úseful one, that which works and produces, in favour of those who only destroy.

This was the crucial respect in which the socialism of the 1830s and its revolutionary consummation—Marxism—went beyond the ideology of the French Revolution, just as the concept of the role of the proletariat was the crucial respect in which Marxism went beyond the idle chatter of the Left Hegelians and beyond the equally idle terrorist acts and demonstrations of the anarchists.

There was an important difference between Marx and the German philosophical radicals from whom he learnt so much in the years 1837–1843: Ludwig Feuerbach, Bruno Bauer, Arnold Ruge, and Moses Hess. Marx, besides vastly superior ability, had enormous intellectual and practical drive as well as a genuine understanding of society and social forces. The romantic reaction launched by Frederick William IV in 1841, the expulsion of Hegelians from university posts, the subsequent suppression of the *Rheinische Zeitung,* and the increasing evidence of the physical and political helplessness of the 'party of criticism' drove most of the Young Hegelians into ever more empty verbalizing. It drove Marx into the study of economics and politics and the search for *practical,* 'material' support for his hopes. It made him a revolutionary.

IV

'My writings, whatever shortcomings they may have, have one characteristic: they form an artistic whole', Marx wrote to Engels as he was preparing the first volume of *Capital* for publication. This is true not only of Marx's writing taken individually; it is true of his creative output taken in its entirety. The outstanding thing about Marx's career as a thinker was the powerful logical thrust lying at the center of his work, the way in which he expanded and developed his views, assimilating the most diverse materials and remoulding them to suit his system and his purposes.

In the early 1840s Marx, as we have seen, was under the influence of Feuerbach and the Left Hegelians. He stood for a rational society, in which man would be free and self-determined as a *social* being, cooperating rationally and spontaneously with his fellows, mastering nature and social life instead of being mastered by them. In 1843, on becoming more seriously aware of (French) socialism and of Moses Hess's work on money, Marx proclaimed that such a transformation of society had for its prime targets the two fundamental conditions (and expressions) of human *alienation:* money and the state. The struggle against these required not only philosophy but also 'a material weapon'—the proletariat—the class outside existing society and its existing system of property which was fitted by its very deprivation to overcome the whole apparatus of social and economic coercion and to inaugurate the society of freedom.

In his *Economico-Philosophical Manuscripts of 1844,* and somewhat more concretely and less philosophically in the *German Ideology* a few years later, Marx spelled out his view that the division of labour, accompanied by private property, made men the slaves of a social system of production instead of being its masters; forced each man to play out a certain role, to subordinate himself to his needs and to the abstract economic role of money necessary to satisfy those needs; brought man into conflict with other men, forced men to live at each other's expense. This alienation was monstrous and dehumanizing, but it was also a necessary step in the history of mankind. If the division of labour made men slaves to the process of production, it also enabled them to realize and perfect their powers. The process of production, developing by its own logic, was the great moulder and educator of mankind. The 'material' life of men, Marx discovered between the spring and autumn of 1845, shaped their political institutions, ideas, conceptions, and legal systems. The history or 'pre-history' of man in the period of alienation and consequent class struggle was to be understood through economic history or, at least, through the history of material production.

By 1848, when Marx and Engels published the *Communist Manifesto*, Marx had worked out the outlines of a general view that has come to be almost inextricably linked with his name. The introduction of tools, the division of labour, and the rise of private property divide men into social classes, primarily into the class of exploiters, who own and administer means of production, and the class or classes of the exploited, who actually work and produce. Each class of exploiters—slave owners, feudal lords, capitalist merchants and manufacturers—comes upon the arena of history as the bearer of economic enterprise, as a class developing new techniques of production and increasing human capacities. But the class relationships in a social system tend to be rigid, whereas the forces of production are constantly developing. There comes a time, at each stage, when the class that inaugurated and developed a given mode of production becomes a fetter upon further development and is swept aside by revolutionary change. Thus slave owners give way to feudal landlords and feudal landlords give way to the bourgeoisie. The state that pretends to represent the *general* social interest is in fact representing a *sectional* interest, safeguarding the social and political conditions congenial to the ruling class.

The alienation and 'contradiction' expressed in the class struggles of history is oppressive and dehumanizing, but it is nevertheless *necessary* for the development of economic and human potentialities, for *progress*. Thus, in the *Communist Manifesto*, Marx and Engels recognize fully the historic role of the bourgeoisie in developing human productivity and capacities, in tearing down privileges, superstitions, and national barriers:

The bourgeoisie, by the rapid improvement of all instruments of production, by the immensely facilitated means of communication, draws all, even the most barbarian, nations into civilisation. The cheap prices of its commodities are the heavy artillery with which it batters down all Chinese walls, with which it forces the barbarians' intensely obstinate hatred of foreigners to capitulate. It compels all nations, on pain of extinction, to adopt the bourgeois mode of production; it compels them to introduce what it calls civilisation into their midst, i.e., to become bourgeois themselves. In one word, it creates a world after its own image. . . .

The bourgeoisie, during its rule of scarce one hundred years, has created more massive and more colossal productive forces than have all preceding generations together. Subjection of nature's forces to man, machinery, application of chemistry to industry and agriculture, steam navigation, railways, electric telegraphs, clearing of whole continents for cultivation, canalisation of rivers, whole populations conjured out of the ground—what earlier century had even a presentiment that such productive forces slumbered in the lap of social labour?

The bourgeoisie, however, is also doomed. The 'inner logic of capitalism'—economic forces independent of the will of man—will produce the breakdown of the whole system of private property and production for a market; it will raise in its stead the socialist-communist society of conscious cooperation and rational planning. Then production will be *socially* controlled and directed toward use instead of profit. Man will cease to be the *object* of history, the slave of a productive process that he himself created, and will become master of himself, society, and nature. Human relations, instead of being determined by forces beyond man's individual control, will assume the aspect of rational and intelligible relations; they will no longer be 'mystified'—concealed from the consciousness of the actors involved through their abstraction from their real context and their real purpose. Men will act as conscious and cooperative members of a *community* and will cease to live and act as individuals existing at each other's expense.

The process by which the collapse of capitalism would come about was sketched by Marx in a number of earlier works—in the *Communist Manifesto*, in *Wage-Labour and Capital*, and in the *Contribution to the Critique of Political Economy*—but it was in the first volume of *Capital* that Marx presented what seemed to many to be the *scientific proof* that capitalism must collapse. Economic systems have their own laws; those who participate in them must play out their allotted roles or perish. The function of the capitalist is to make a profit; if he ceases to make a profit, he ceases to be a capitalist and is replaced by another. But the capitalist can make profit only out of the exploitation of labour, and Marx thought he could show, from Ricardo's labour theory of value, that this search for profit, in capitalist conditions, would lead to collapse.

Value, Marx argued, was congealed labour. The capitalist's profit—surplus value—therefore could only be created by the labour he employed. The worker, in capitalist society, does not sell the *product* of his labour, but his *capacity* to work. What the labourer produces belongs to his master; what he is paid for is his *labour* and that alone. The capitalist therefore does not pay the worker the value of what he produces; he pays the worker only what is needed to keep the worker alive to produce. The difference between the subsistence wage paid to the worker and the values produced by him is surplus value, on which the capitalist's profit depends. If in a ten-hour day the worker works for six hours to produce the equivalent of his subsistence, then in the remaining four hours he produces surplus value, profit for the capitalist. The fierce competition of capitalism and what Marx believed to be a falling rate of profit due to the increased use of machinery will force the capitalist to exploit the worker even more viciously, to bring his wages nearer and nearer to the level of bare subsistence. The capitalist will be able to do this because the increased use of machines and the increasing proletarianization of middle-men and artisans create a growing reserve army of the unemployed—a miserably dependent potential labour pool that helps to depress wages and to prevent palliative action by trade unions. Meanwhile, however, capitalist competition leads to the concentration of capital in fewer and fewer hands through the bankruptcy of the weaker, less ruthless, and less efficient. Society is split and simplified into two classes, each recognizing its interests with increasing clarity:

> Along with the steady decrease in the number of capitalist magnates who usurp and monopolize all the advantages of this development, there grows the extent of misery, oppression, servitude, degradation and exploitation, but at the same time, there arises the rebellious indignation of the working class which is steadily growing in number, and which is being disciplined, unified, and organized by the very mechanism of the capitalist method of production. Ultimately, the monopoly of capital becomes a fetter upon the mode of production which has flourished with it, and under it. Both the centralization in a few hands of the means of production, and the social organization of labour, reach a point where their capitalist cloak becomes a strait-jacket. It bursts asunder. The hour of capitalist private property has struck. The expropriators are expropriated.

The collapse of capitalism, Marx appeared to be saying, was inevitable. The very steps that capitalists took to overcome their difficulties only deepened and intensified the crisis. As the rate of profit falls, the capitalist attempts to overcome his difficulties by extending the scope of production and by making ever-increasing use of machinery. He squeezes out the middle-man and reduces the number of workers in his employment; he thus extends production at the same time as he contracts the market. The upshot is overproduction and underconsumption—crisis, the paralysis of productive forces, and the wastage of capital. It becomes evident that the bourgeoisie can no longer produce the goods and can no longer feed its slaves. Revolution—the seizure of the means of production by the workers themselves and the placing of production under social control—ensues.

The immediate motive force of all this, in Marx's mature system, is the class struggle. The concept of class moved to the forefront of Marx's work in 1843–1844 and remained there to the end of his life.

V

Karl Marx's position as the greatest of the socialist ideologists and as the posthumously proclaimed founder of one of the world's great religions, of course, has not prevented his greatness from being questioned, as it no doubt will continue to be, at least by some. More important is the fact that his admirers and followers have differed sharply in their characterizations of his claim to greatness. Marx has been hailed as the founder of scientific socialism, as the great theorist who discovered the 'laws of motion' of history and society and was thus able to chart the future of capitalism and industrial civilization as it came to envelop the whole of mankind. More recently, he has been reinterpreted as an existentialist philosopher and radical moral critic, exposing the alienation and dependence that characterize modern man. Some have seen him as an embittered émigré, living in a fantasy world of revolutionary cliques, as an alienated eternal student with neurotically grandiose views about building a society fit for man to live in, or as a fervent Hebrew prophet denouncing oppression, injustice, and the cash-nexus while heralding the inevitable coming of the Kingdom of Man. Others have acclaimed him as the most relevant and far-seeing of the classical economists, as the initiator and presiding genius of the whole subject of economic history, and as one of the founding fathers of modern sociology.

The very variety of interpretations, as we have said, is an indication of the richness and fertility of Marx's thought, of the number of profound insights and great questions that can be found in his work. Truly great men and truly great works have something to say to each generation. They do not come back as unrecognized elements of a cultural inheritance; they come back, as Schumpeter has put it, 'in their individual garb, with their personal scars which people may see and touch'. Each generation will find in them new features, new sources of illumination, while recognizing the strength and integrity of the original work.

Those politically, intellectually, or temperamentally unsympathetic to Marx's style of thinking have tended to see Marx's work as primarily a *moral* onslaught, exposing the vices and evils of capitalism, calling on men to strive for a perfection that a more realistic thinker would have known to be beyond them, or, alternatively, to smash the existing order in an existentialist act of self-assertion. Yet the rejection of 'voluntarism' and of any abstract appeal to moral principles was for many decades one of the best-known features of the work of Marx and Engels, emphasized by all of their serious disciples. Marxism was distinguished from utopian socialism and revolutionary anarchism by reference to its *scientific* character, to its refusal to confront society with moral principles and moral appeals. 'Communists preach no *morality* at all', Marx wrote in the *German Ideology* in 1845–1846. 'They do not put to people the moral demand: Love one another, be not egoists, etc.; on the contrary, they know very well that egoism, like sacrifice, *is* under specific conditions a necessary form of the individual's struggle for survival.' Throughout the remainder of his life—in his famous *Critique of the Gotha Programme*, for instance—Marx objected bitterly to any attempt to base a socialist platform on 'abstract' moral demands expressed by such terms as 'justice', 'equality', etc. Marxism was a science: it did not abstractly advocate socialism; it showed that socialism was inevitable. It did not ask for a 'just' wage; it showed that the wage system was dehumanizing and self-destructive. Marxism did not tell the proletariat what it *ought* to do; it showed the proletariat what it would be *forced* to do, by its own character and situation, by its position in industry and in history.

In recent years it has become fashionable to reject the sharp dichotomy between an obviously crude moral-psychological interpretation of Marx, often designed to discount much of his achievement, and a less obviously crude, but still inadequate, empiricist or 'positivist', 'scientific' interpretation of Marx that falsifies his conception of social criticism and at the same time puts emphasis on those aspects of his thought that have proved the most time-bound. As against Marx the moral prophet and Marx the scientist of society, the 1960s gave us Marx the philosopher of the human condition, whose early concern with freedom and with the Hegelian concept of alienation was taken to underlie the whole of his thought. This more scholarly approach was made possible by the rediscovery and publication, in the late 1920s and 1930s, of a number of Marx's most important theoretical and philosophical writings. Marx's incomplete *Critique of Hegel's Philosophy of Right*, jotted down in Kreuznach in 1843, when Marx was twenty-five, was published for the first time in 1927; the full text of the *German Ideology* was not printed until 1932; Marx's *Economico-Philosophical Manuscripts of 1844* were also discovered and printed in 1932. The ex-

tremely important and revealing drafts for *Capital* that
Marx wrote in 1857 and 1858, known as the *Grundrisse
der Kritik der politischen Ökonomie*, were not published
until 1939. The careful study of these writings, delayed
by the Nazis, the Stalinist domination of the world Communist movement, and the Second World War, has made
it possible to determine much more accurately Karl
Marx's intellectual antecedents and assumptions, as well
as his precise place in the history of ideas. It has clarified
his relation to Hegel and Feuerbach, and has shown up
as nonsense much of the more traditional Marxist and
non-Marxist accounts of these matters. It has enabled the
modern student to see more clearly the philosophical presuppositions and logical and ethical beliefs underlying his
mature system, to trace in detail the evolution of his
thought, to grasp its logical structure and the subtle inter-
dependence of its categories. It has established, once and
for all, that Marx was a much more subtle and complex
thinker than old-fashioned Communist and Kautskyist
Marxists, potted Marx-Engels selections, and crude 'bourgeois' critics suggested.

In his introduction to the Soviet Communist-
sponsored English translation of Parts I and III of the
German Ideology, R. Pascal wrote:

The *German Ideology*, the joint work of Marx and
Engels, is their first and most comprehensive statement of historical materialism. Many of their smaller,
separate articles of the years 1844 and 1845, and their
earlier composite work, *The Holy Family*, fore-
shadow their later views; but this work, the product
of a period of undisturbed co-operation, is almost
completely free of idealistic traces of Hegel or Feuerbach. Despite the technical imperfectness of the text
it is the first systematic account of their view of the
relationship between the economic, political and intellectual activities of man, the first full statement of
Marxism.

This is still the official Soviet Communist line: that the year. 1845 saw a radical break in Marx's thinking, a rejection of his earlier Young Hegelian, thoroughly philosophical way of dealing with social problems and the inauguration of scientific Marxism, in which the history of material production and the class struggle replaced the earlier appeal to rationality and the overcoming of alienation. Serious scholarly work in the West has thrown doubt on this proposition. The continuity of Marx's thought has been emphasized by a number of recent writers and backed up with detailed references to Marx's published works and unpublished drafts and notes. The contrast between the rational free cooperation of Communism and the alienation enshrined in a society based on private property and the division of labour still remains the keynote of Marx's mature work. The concept of alienation, it is true, is no longer appealed to specifically as a key concept in terms of which the Marxian system is to be organized and understood. It is in fact mentioned only once or twice, in passing. Nevertheless, the positive content which the young Marx gave to that concept remained central to the position that the mature Marx expounds in economic and political terms in his *Wage-Labour and Capital*, in his *Contribution to the Critique of Political Economy*, and in his *Capital*. The process of objectifying man's own product and allowing it to dominate man himself Marx now calls the fetishism of commodities; it remains the same process throughout. Man's loss of identification with and subjective control over his labour-power Marx calls dehumanization; this too is the same process—a process that for Marx remains of central importance for the understanding of capitalism. Man's loss of objective control over the product of his work and over his labour-time Marx now calls exploitation. Exploitation does not mean, for Marx, that the capitalist is getting too much—more than is 'reasonable'. It expresses Marx's insistence that under capitalism, and in class society generally, one man appropriates that which is produced by another man or is part of that man (his labour or labour-power). Fetishism, dehumanization, and exploitation—in a word, alienation—continue to play a key role in the work of the mature Marx, as they did for him in 1844. They are still shown as following inevitably from the division of labour and from the elevation of private property.

Despite this important element of continuity, a marked change of style and a marked shift toward empirical interests do take place in Marx's work at the end of 1844. His concern now is with economics and economic history, and with concrete political analysis. The Marxist system is now presented (by Marx himself and even more bluntly by Engels) as a *science of society*, relying on economics and history rather than on moral or philosophical categories in the abstract. The discussion of philosophy, jurisprudence, and moral and political ideology thus becomes, for Marx, a matter of only incidental interest: civil society, the world of industry and trade, is the real arena of history. Marx busies himself entirely with 'civil society', its economics and its political reflexes; Engels, not Marx, becomes the 'philosopher' of scientific Marxism. He does so largely *by the way* through the accident of polemical requirements. He does so—for the most part—in the last years of his life. Of course, even in his mature period, Marx's conception of science remains much closer to an idealist logician's conception of *Wissenschaft* than to the Comtean positivist's or the British empiricist's conception of science as the mechanical collection of facts. 'If the appearance of things coincided with their essence all science would be superfluous,' Marx wrote in *Capital*, and no one can read Marx seriously without recognizing his elevation of the role of logical analysis and logical organization, of the search for categories and for coherence and consistency in his analysis of empirical material. In that sense, Marx remained a philosopher: he had no time whatever for any concept of science as the passive summation of 'facts', as generalization from 'induction'. But, like Feuerbach, he now emphasized, even more strongly, that we must *begin* and *end* with the empirical and not abstract from it; for it is our only possible point of departure and the real content of everything we say.

Superficially, both Marx's importance and the possibility of understanding him well would seem to be enhanced rather than obscured by the worldly success of a political faith that claims to express and further Marx's vision of history, society, and government. Yet the relation of that faith to Marx's own work is the subject of bitter and quite fundamental dispute. Like Christianity (as I have written in my *Ethical Foundations of Marxism*) both Marxism and Marxism-Leninism speak in the name of their founder more often than they speak with his voice. Their sacred texts are not confined to the writings of Marx. Their most general conclusions and simplified catechisms were not formulated by him. Engels—the true founder of 'Marxism'—was elevated, partly by himself, to the status of co-prophet and intellectual *alter ego* of Marx. Lenin—the true founder of Marxism-Leninism and of revolutionary Communism—Stalin, and Mao, have been proclaimed 'disciples of genius', clarifying the thought of the Master and building on its foundations. For some forty years, a disciplined international Communist movement, led by the Communist Party of the Soviet Union, claimed to be the sole repository of orthodox Marxism and the final arbiter of what Marx 'really meant'. Its impact on our conception of Marx and Marxism has been enormous, even if we are all too often unaware of it. As the number of Marxist pronouncements and 'classics' increased, as more and more heresies were invented or denounced, Marx himself steadily slipped from one's grasp. The abundance of followers and interpreters obscured as much as it illuminated his thought. 'Joint founders' and 'inspired disciples' may carry the prestige of numbers; they do not make for a single view.

The treatment of 'Marxism' as a religion would be regarded by many of his followers as pejorative. Marx himself once proclaimed that he was no 'Marxist'; there is a great deal of evidence that he would have repudiated completely the role of a religious prophet or of a political saint. The historic mission of the proletariat in liberating mankind, he hoped, would be accomplished by the proletariat itself. No leaders could do the work on its behalf; no dogmas could act as a substitute for theoretical understanding and practical insight. To approach Marx through the simple catechisms of what used to be known as the World Marxist Movement or through the tortured and conflicting exegeses of men seeking only to find practical inspiration or *justification* in his work is seriously to distort Marx's aims, Marx's methods, and the content of his thought. The volume before the reader therefore deliberately separates Marx from his interpreters, including Engels, and eschews any attempt to seek a single theme or a simple quintessence of his work. Marx was a complex man and a complex thinker. He confronts us at various levels of generality and provides us with signposts that point in conflicting directions. This volume, perhaps more so than other Marx anthologies, attempts to present the man with his individual scars, to provide the material for an understanding of Marx himself. He and his work have already inspired a host of Marxisms and may yet inspire a number more. But in their own right they still stand—as we have argued—at the very center of all serious social thinking today.

EUGENE KAMENKA

Institute of Advanced Studies,
Australian National University,
Canberra
September 1981

BIBLIOGRAPHICAL NOTE AND ACKNOWLEDGMENTS

~~~~~~~~~~~~~~~~~~~~~~~~~~

It is now one hundred years since Marx died. There is still no single scholarly and complete collection of the works published in his lifetime, not to speak of a historical-critical *variorum* edition. There is no complete standard collection of his correspondence and no scholarly biography that commands the general approbation of the learned. When Marx died in 1883 he left behind him a large quantity of unsorted papers, among them numerous drafts and whole copybooks of excerpts and notes, and a large library, including books with marginal annotations. Engels, assisted by Marx's youngest daughter, Eleanor, spent three and a half months bringing the papers into some sort of order. At the end of that period he reported in a letter to Friedrich Adolf Sorge:

> Almost everything from the period before 1848 has been saved. Not only are the manuscripts which he and I worked on then almost complete (in so far as not eaten by mice), but also the correspondence. Naturally after 1849 all complete, and from 1862 half-way orderly. Also very far-reaching written material on the International, I think enough for its complete history but I haven't been able to look at it closely. Of mathematical works there are three to four copybooks.

On Engels's death in 1895, Marx's *Nachlass*—his literary remains—passed into the keeping of August Bebel and

Eduard Bernstein, though many of the letters in the collection were returned to their senders. Bebel and Bernstein acted as representatives of the German Social Democratic Party, but the papers were kept in London until the last legal restrictions on socialism in Germany were lifted in 1900. Then they were transferred to the archives of the Social Democratic Party in Berlin.

Engels, in the last years of his life, had published the second volume of *Capital*, constructing it out of four separate drafts, each of more than one thousand pages. It was sent to the printer in May 1885, and Engels, assisted by Bernstein and Karl Kautsky, had gone on to complete the publication of the third volume of *Capital*, for which Marx had left only a first draft. In Berlin, the socialist historian Franz Mehring published a four-volume selection based on Marx's *Nachlass* in 1902, including some of the early works, and between 1905 and 1910 Kautsky published the three volumes of Marx's notes on the history of theories of surplus value under the title *Theories of Surplus Value*. Then, between 1910 and 1913, Bernstein played the major part in preparing for publication four thick volumes of the correspondence between Marx and Engels, covering forty years. Marx's surviving daughter, Laura Lafargue, however, insisted that sections of the correspondence compromised her father's memory, and both she and Bernstein made significant alterations and omissions. These omissions were not indicated in the published volumes, and there is some evidence that actual erasures and corrections were made on the manuscripts themselves.

Seventy years later much of Marx's *Nachlass* has still not been published. The Marx papers lodged in the archives of the Social Democratic Party in Berlin were taken to Paris in 1933 and are now in the Institute of Social History in Amsterdam, where they are freely available to scholars. The German Social Democratic Party and the Institute of Social History, however, have made no attempt to publish any major part of the *Nachlass* or to arrange for a scholarly and complete edition of Marx's works.

The Russian revolution did initially produce more serious and more sustained attempts to publish at least the corpus of Marx's work. In 1918 the Bolshevik Party set up a special commission to translate the works of Marx and Engels into Russian. It was hoped to produce a twenty-eight-volume edition, which, it was believed, would be complete. The edition, hampered by the civil war and by the lack of Marx and Engels manuscripts and even works in the Soviet Union, had to be abandoned in 1922, after only four volumes had been produced. In 1920, however, Soviet emissaries in London had begun purchasing rare copies of Marx's and Engels's works. In January 1921 the Marx-Engels Institute was set up in Moscow under the directorship of the serious Marx scholar and former Menshevik, David Ryazanov. That Institute has now also built up a very substantial collection of Marx's and Engels's documents, books, and personal items, making photostat copies of manuscripts in the Social Democratic archives and purchasing other material from abroad. The collection is not open to unapproved scholars.

Nevertheless, the most serious attempts to produce major editions of the works of Marx and Engels have come from the Communist Party of the Soviet Union and, more recently, from the German Democratic Republic. In 1929, under the directorship of David Ryazanov, the Marx-Engels Institute in Moscow began issuing the first substantial scholarly edition of the works of Marx and Engels: the *Marx-Engels Gesamtausgabe*, published in Frankfurt, Berlin, and Moscow between 1927 and 1935. It began as a historical-critical *variorum* edition, arranging chronologically everything by Marx and Engels that was extant, and publishing it in the original language of composition. The edition lost its serious scholarly character when Ryazanov was recalled to Moscow (he subsequently died in a Stalinist prison). He was replaced by V. Adoratski, a much less serious scholar, who gave up the attempt to produce a *variorum* edition; the work as a whole was discontinued in 1935. Since then Russian and Communist editions of the works of Marx and Engels have been subject to political censorship and political selection. The nearest thing to a complete edition mostly in the original language now available is that of the Marx-Engels *Werke*, published in East Berlin since 1957 in forty volumes, the last of which appeared in 1968. The *Werke* volumes do not claim to be a complete edition and do not satisfy fully the criteria of scholarship. They do contain all of the major works published in Marx's lifetime, with the exception of the strongly Russophobic *Secret Diplomatic History of the Eighteenth Century*, which is not republished in Communist countries. Certain of the earlier works and the important drafts that Marx made for *Capital* in 1857 to 1858, first published in 1939 as the *Grundrisse der Kritik der politischen Ökonomie*, have been republished as separate volumes associated with the edition, though not included among the numbered volumes. Far more serious is the fact that omissions and alterations are not indicated in the *Werke*. The text of the first volume of *Capital*, for instance, is the text of the fourth edition published in 1890, which incorporates both Marx's revisions and Engels's editorial corrections. It differs substantially from the first (German) edition of 1867, which even the professional scholar still finds extremely difficult to obtain. The *Werke* volumes, then, though the best single edition that we have, are very far from being a satisfactory scholarly edition.

The Marx-Engels Institute in Moscow and various editorial committees have now begun issuing the most complete edition of the works of Marx and Engels ever published. It is projected to appear in fifty volumes and to be published simultaneously in Russian, German, and English. The first volume of the English edition, prepared jointly by Progress Publishers, Moscow; International Publishers Co. Inc., New York; and Lawrence and Wishart Ltd., London, appeared in 1975 and more than a dozen volumes have appeared since. According to the planning committee, it will contain all the works of Marx and Engels published in their lifetimes, their correspondence, and most of their unpublished hand-written manuscripts, including manuscript variants of *Capital.* Much of this material, as well as a number of letters, will be published for the first time in any language, and more than half for the first time in English. The edition could be completed before 1990.

Until it is completed, the student of Marx must be prepared to move from one edition to another, to consult single volumes, to make use of several languages. That is what I have done for this selection. The sources from which the selections are taken are indicated at the end of each text. I have used the standard abbreviation *MEGA* for the *Marx-Engels Gesamtausgabe* of 1927 to 1935 and the abbreviation *MEW* for the Marx-Engels *Werke* published in East Berlin from 1957 onward. The numerals that follow indicate section, volume, and page numbers in the case of *MEGA*, and volume and page numbers in the case of the *Werke*. All translations, unless otherwise indicated, are my own and those of Mrs E. Y. Short.

A student and critic who has lived with Marx's writings for a long time will owe many debts that he is hardly conscious of. In recent years I have been most strongly influenced by the writings of Mr George Lichtheim. Portions of the Introduction owe a great deal to the splendid series of books that has come from his pen. His death was to many a personal loss and a sad blow to Marx scholarship and to cultural life generally. I have also profited over many years from the work of Dr. Maximilien Rubel of Paris, and more recently from that of Professor Shlomo Avineri of Jerusalem.

The publishers of this *Portable Karl Marx*, The Viking Press and Penguin Books, inspired the venture and then displayed unusual (and undeserved) patience with an author and editor who, for one reason and another, took a very long time to deliver. It is pleasant to have worked with them and to thank Mr Edwin Kennebeck for his perceptive and courteous revision of the manuscript.

The excellent conditions for research that I have so long enjoyed in the Institute of Advanced Studies of the Australian National University have done much to make this at least a better book than it might have been. The Research Institute on Communist Affairs at Columbia University, New York, generously proffered me a second invitation and a senior fellowship grant for part of 1970, enabling me to work at the Institute and to visit libraries in the eastern United States. Even so, the book would have taken even longer to complete if the president and fellows of Trinity College, Oxford, had not, in Michaelmas Term, 1978, generously allowed me to work in their midst as a Visiting Fellow. Mrs E. Y. Short, research assistant in the Australian National University's History of Ideas Unit, has helped me in numerous ways, in Canberra, in the Bodleian Library in Oxford, and in the British Museum. She has collected material, assisted in and prepared translations, checked the manuscript and proofs, and prepared a draft bibliography and index of names. I am very grateful to her; for any errors that remain I am responsible.

It remains to acknowledge the kindness of Mr K. J. Kenafick, the author of *Michael Bakunin and Karl Marx*, Melbourne, 1948, in permitting me to cite his translation of Bakunin's comments of Marx, of International Publishers, New York, and of the Archives and Annali della Fondazione Feltrinelli in permitting me to translate letters and reports first published by them.

E.K.

1818 May 5	Karl Marx born in Trier.
1824 August 26	Karl, together with the remaining Marx children, baptized into the Evangelical Church.
1830 October	Karl enters the Friedrich-Wilhelm-Gymnasium in Trier.
1834 March 23	Karl confirmed in the Evangelical Church.
1835 September	Karl completes his final high-school examinations.
October	Moves to Bonn and enrols in the Faculty of Jurisprudence in the University of Bonn; attends lectures on legal subjects, Greek and Roman mythology, Homer, and history of modern art.
1836 January– August	Marx active in student poetic circle and in the 'Trier' student fraternity in Bonn; becomes one of its five-man Presidium; attends lectures on legal subjects and Schlegel's course on the

Elegies of Propertius; involves himself in debts and is punished by University authorities for disorderly
conduct.

August–
October

Spends summer holidays in Trier
and becomes secretly engaged to
twenty-two-year-old Jenny von
Westphalen.

October

Moves to Berlin and enrols in the
Faculty of Jurisprudence in the University of Berlin; attends lectures by
Savigny and Gans and a course on
'anthropology'.

1837

Works on a philosophical critique of
Roman law and studies Hegelian
philosophy; writes a dialogue,
'Kleanthes', some poems, the fragments of a novel called 'Scorpio and
Felix', and a drama, 'Oulanem'; attends lectures on legal subjects in the
summer semester, reads Savigny on
possession and other textbooks; studies Aristotle and Bacon and becomes
a frequenter at the Doctors' Club, a
circle of Hegelian university lecturers and literary figures, where he
meets Bruno and Edgar Bauer, Adolf
Rutenberg, Friedrich Koeppen, and
others.

1838
February

Marx, suffering from an enlarged
heart, receives exemption from military service on that ground.

May 10

Marx's father, Heinrich, dies in
Trier.

May–December	Marx attends lectures on logic, general geography, and the Prussian code in the summer semester, and only one course of lectures (on succession) in the winter semester.
1839	Marx continues to frequent the Doctors' Club and becomes a regular visitor in the house of the brothers Bruno, Edgar, and Egbert Bauer; collects an album of folk songs copied in his own hand for Jenny von Westphalen and begins work on his doctoral dissertation, first planned as a study of Epicurean philosophy, and, later in the year, as a study of Epicurean, Stoic, and sceptical philosophy in its totality. Attends Bruno Bauer's course of lectures on 'Isaiah'.
1840	Continues to be active in the Doctors' Club and becomes especially friendly with Friedrich Koeppen, whose panegyric *Frederick the Great and His Opponents* appears in April dedicated to 'My Friend Karl Heinrich Marx of Trier'. Marx works on philosophy of religion and plans to publish a book attacking the Professor of Roman Catholic Theology at Bonn, Georg Hermes.
1841 January–March	Marx begins to look more thoroughly at modern philosophy, reading and making excerpts from Spinoza, Leibniz, Hume, and Rosenkranz's *History of Kantian Philosophy;* decides

to narrow his doctoral dissertation to the Democritean and the Epicurean philosophy of nature, with an appendix criticizing Plutarch's polemic against Epicurus' theology; studies Italian and becomes active in a circle of radical litterateurs connected with the periodical *Athenäum;* plans to establish a philosophical periodical devoted to atheism, in collaboration with Bruno Bauer.

April

Marx, having concluded his studies in the University of Berlin, sends his dissertation on 'The Difference Between the Democritean and the Epicurean Philosophy of Nature' to the Dean of the Philosophy Faculty in Jena and receives the doctorate of that university; he leaves for Trier and remains there until the beginning of July.

July–December

Marx moves to Bonn for closer contact with Bruno Bauer, with whom he collaborates in an anonymous pamphlet bringing out in an ironic way the anti-religious message of Hegel's work; Georg Jung and Moses Hess draw Marx into plans for establishing a liberal newspaper, *Die Rheinische Zeitung,* in Cologne.

1842

Marx writes comments on the latest Prussian censorship instructions for Arnold Ruge's *Deutsche Jahrbücher* (ultimately published a year later in Ruge's *Anekdota* in Switzerland).

He further plans articles on religious art, romanticism, the historical school of law, and philosophical positivism. In April he begins to contribute to the *Rheinische Zeitung,* and on 15 October, when he has moved to Cologne, he becomes its editor-in-chief. As editor, Marx finds himself under pressure from the shareholders, anxious to avoid radicalism and confrontation with the censors, and a group of anarchist intellectuals in Berlin, 'The Free Ones' (then including Max Stirner, Edgar Bauer, and Friedrich Engels), whose intransigent atheism and determination to shock the bourgeoisie were causing public concern. By November, Marx is rejecting what he regards as superficial and aggressive contributions on Communism and atheism submitted by 'The Free Ones', who respond outraged because they see themselves as the successors to the Doctors' Club.

November 24   Friedrich Engels visits the editorial offices of the *Rheinische Zeitung* and meets Marx for the first time. The meeting is cool because of Engels's association with 'The Free Ones'.

1843
January–
March   Marx writes articles on poverty in the Moselle district for the *Rheinische Zeitung;* receives copies of Ruge's *Anekdota,* which contains Feuerbach's 'Preliminary Theses on

the Reform of Philosophy' as well as Marx's contribution.

March 18   Marx resigns from the editorship of the *Rheinische Zeitung*, which has had increasing difficulties with censorship and has been served with formal notice of closure.

June 19   Marx marries Jenny von Westphalen at Kreuznach, where she has been living with her mother since her father, Baron von Westphalen, died in March 1842; resumes the study of Hegel's *Philosophy of Right*.

October   Having rejected an offer of employment in the Prussian Civil Service, Marx moves to Paris with Jenny. Begins to collaborate with Arnold Ruge in the production of the new radical periodical, the *Deutschfranzösische Jahrbücher*.

December   In Paris Marx meets and forms a friendship with Heinrich Heine; writes his critique of Hegel's *Philosophy of Right* for the *Deutschfranzösische Jahrbücher*, in which he proclaims that the proletariat is the class destined to bring about the total redemption of humanity. (In September, in a letter to Ruge, he was still dismissing the actual Communism of Cabet, Weitling, and Dezamy as a 'dogmatic abstraction'.)

1844
January–
March   Marx reads histories and contemporary records of the French Revolu-

tion, plans to write a history of the Convention.

February

Publication of the only issue of the *Deutsch-französische Jahrbücher*, containing Marx's contributions and an important article by Engels, 'Outlines of Political Economy'; copies of the journal seized in Prussia and warrants issued for the arrest of Marx, Ruge, Heine, and Bernays if they should set foot in Prussia.

March

Marx enters into correspondence with Engels. Excited by Engels's article, Marx begins to study political economy, making notes on and from Adam Smith, Ricardo, J. B. Say, Sismondi, Pecqueur, Buret, James Mill, Skarbek, Schulz, and McCulloch, reading the English authors in French translation. Marx attends an international democratic banquet where Ruge, Leroux, Louis Blanc, Pyat, and Bakunin are present. Marx quarrels and breaks with Ruge.

April

Marx forms contact with leaders of the League of the Just and with some secret French workers' associations.

April–
June

Composes his (incomplete) *Economico–Philosophical Manuscripts*.

May 1

Marx's first child, his daughter Jenny, born.

July

Marx in personal contact with Proudhon, with whom he discourses on Hegel; Marx gives up his plan to write a substantial critique of Hegel's *Philosophy of Right* and proposes instead to treat in several independent brochures the critique of law, of morality, and politics and then to sum up their interrelation; meanwhile Marx publishes an attack on Ruge's article on the Silesian weavers' revolt, thus consummating his break with the Young Hegelians, and enters into collaboration with the radical socialist group publishing *Vorwärts* in Paris.

August–December

Marx has frequent meetings with Bakunin; at the end of August he spends ten days with Engels, who is visiting from England; Engels finds that he and Marx 'reach complete agreement on all theoretical matters'. Their collaboration dates from this time, and they begin work on their first joint publication, *The Holy Family*, an attack on Bruno Bauer. The manuscript, written largely by Marx, is sent to Frankfurt for publication at the end of November.

1845
January 11

French Ministry of the Interior orders that Marx and other members of the *Vorwärts* editorial group should leave France.

February 3

Marx leaves Paris for Brussels, followed by his wife and daughter.

March–May

Marx sets down in his notebook his Eleven Theses on Feuerbach; Engels joins Marx in Brussels to find that

Marx has worked out the main lines of his 'materialist conception of history'. Marx and Engels plan to publish, in collaboration with Moses Hess, a history of socialism and communism in France and England from the eighteenth century onward, including translations from the works of Buonarotti, Fourier, Godwin, Mably, Morelly, etc. The publisher, Leske in Darmstadt, rejects the proposal. At the demand of the Belgian police, Marx undertakes not to publish in Belgium any comments on current political affairs. Helene Demuth joins the family in April as a maid.

July

Marx receives 1500 francs from Leske as an advance on royalties for Marx's planned 'Critique of Politics and Political Economy' to be ready by 1846; Marx and Engels leave to spend six weeks in England, returning at the end of August.

September

Marx's daughter Laura born; Marx and Engels begin work on a critique of Bauer and Max Stirner, ultimately to become *The German Ideology*, and set out in it their 'materialist conception of history'.

December

Marx relinquishes citizenship of the Prussian Union.

1846
February–
March

Marx and Engels, still in Brussels, found a Communist Correspondence Committee that would engage in international propaganda and lay the foundation for a Communist organization, continuing the work of the League of the Just. Its members, almost entirely young German émigrés with a sprinkling of artisans, include Marx's wife, Jenny, and her brother, Edgar von Westphalen, Moses Hess, the poet Ferdinand Freiligrath, the proletarian German Communist Wilhelm Weitling, and the revolutionary agitator Wilhelm Wolff ('Lupus'), to whom Marx was to dedicate *Capital*. By the end of March Marx is denouncing the sectarian 'artisan communism' of Weitling, with its rejection of political struggle, and the 'philosophical communism' of Karl Grün and the 'true socialists' and demanding a 'sorting-out' of the 'party', as he calls it. The publisher Leske cancels Marx's contract for the 'Critique of Politics and Political Economy'.

May   Marx, in the name of the Correspondence Committee, writes to Proudhon in Paris asking for regular reports on France and warning Proudhon against Karl Grün; Proudhon declines and defends Karl Grün. Weitling, a lone dissenting voice, is defeated in a Brussels Correspondence Committee discussion that ends with a denunciation of the 'empty communism' of Hermann Kriege and his New York German radical paper, *Volkstribun;* the Brussels Committee also demands that a London Communist Correspondence Committee be formed by the German émigrés there, who make up the London League of the Just and its associated organization, the German Workers' Educational Association. London in reply complains about the 'academic arrogance' of the Brussels Committee and suggests that attitudes to 'sentimental' communism be discussed at the proposed Communist Congress in London.

June   Marx, Engels, and others take steps to establish contact with Communists in the Wuppertal but reject as premature the Wuppertal suggestion of a General Communist Congress.

July   Plans to publish *The German Ideology* fall through, the manuscript left 'to the mice'; Marx suffers from chest cramps; Marx, Engels, and Gigot, in the name of German Communists in Brussels, send an address to the Chartist Feargus O'Connor, congratulating him on his electoral victory in Nottingham; the address is published in the *Northern Star*.

August   Brussels Committee forms contact with Communists in Silesia.

December   Marx's son Edgar born; Marx reads in the French original Proudhon's just published book, *The System of Economic Contradictions, or the Philosophy of Poverty*.

1847

January

Marx begins work on a reply to Proudhon's book, to be published in French, *The Poverty of Philosophy*.

February

Leske, threatening 'unpleasant steps', demands the return of the 1500 francs advance paid to Marx to write the 'Critique of Politics and Political Economy'. Discussions with representatives of the League of the Just, who invite Marx and his Brussels circle to join their organization and offer to rewrite the program in the light of the 'critical communism' expounded in Brussels.

June

First Congress of Communists in London; Marx, unable to raise the fare, is represented by Engels and Wilhelm Wolff. The Congress resolves to reorganize the League of the Just, to adopt the title 'The Communist League', to draft a Communist credo for the next congress, and to expel the followers of Weitling.

August

Brussels Correspondence Committee becomes the Brussels chapter of the Communist League; Marx elected president. Engels arrives in Brussels, and he and Marx form a German Workers' Association to work under the direction of the Communist League.

September

Marx attends the Brussels Congress of Economists; fails in a bid to be called on to speak; Marx, in financial trouble, leaves to visit his relatives in

Holland, who approach his mother regarding his so far unsuccessful attempts to get a portion of the inheritance from his father; his brother-in-law in Maastricht ultimately lends him 150 francs.

October

Marx, in a series of articles in the *Deutsche-Brüsseler Zeitung*, with which he has become associated, emphasizes the importance of the bourgeois revolution as a precondition for the working-class revolution and denounces his admirer, the revolutionary Carl Heinzen, for attacking princes instead of the bourgeoisie.

November

Marx elected vice-president of the *Association démocratique*; travels to London for the Second Congress of the Communist League, is commissioned, with Engels, to prepare a statement of principles for the League under the title *Manifesto of the Communist Party*; addresses a rally on behalf of Poland and proposes, in the name of the *Association démocratique*, the holding of an international democratic congress in 1848.

December

Discussions with Harney, Jones, and other English Chartists; Marx, in great financial difficulties, seeks a loan of 100–200 francs from his friend Annenkov, then in Paris; back in Brussels gives a number of lectures to the German Workers' Association on wage-labour and capital.

| December 26 | Marx takes part in a Brussels meeting of the *Association démocratique*, in which Bakunin is admitted to membership. |

1848

| January | Marx completes the manuscript of the *Communist Manifesto*. |

| February | Marx receives 6000 francs from his mother as his share of the inheritance from his father; Engels, expelled from Paris, arrives in Brussels; Marx takes an active part in preparations for an armed republican uprising in Brussels and encourages similar preparations in Cologne. Revolution in Paris, followed (in March) by revolution in Germany. |

| March 3 | Marx receives an invitation from the Provisional Government of France to return to French soil followed, at 5:00 p.m., by an order issued on behalf of the King of Belgium, that he leave Belgium within twenty-four hours. |

| March 4 | Marx and his wife arrested at 1:00 a.m., released after a few hours, and brought under police supervision with their children to the French border, where they travel to Paris. |

| March | Marx, as secretary, participates in a meeting of the four Paris sections of the Communist League and busies himself in the founding of a German workers' club; makes arrangements for German exiles to return to Ger- |

many; prepares, together with Schapper, Engels, Wilhelm Wolff, and others, a leaflet embodying the Demands of the Communist Party of Germany, to be distributed in Germany together with the *Communist Manifesto*, published a month earlier; sharp conflicts between Marx and the leaders of Herwegh's Legion.

April 10–11   Marx arrives in Cologne and takes over the organization of the planned radical democratic newspaper, the *Neue Rheinische Zeitung*.

May 11   Meeting, in Cologne, of the Communist League; sharp conflict between Marx and his followers on the one hand and Gottschalk and his Cologne Workers' Association on the other over the latter's determination not to take part in indirect elections for a Prussian National Assembly.

May 31   First number of the *Neue Rheinische Zeitung*, 'Organ of Democracy' (dated 1 June); Karl Marx listed as editor-in-chief and Engels and Wilhelm Wolff among the six editors. A number of shareholders withdraw in consequence of an article by Engels criticizing the National Assembly in Frankfurt.

June   The *Neue Rheinische Zeitung* rejects the federalist program of the left in the Frankfurt National Assembly and of the radical democratic party; demands a single undivided German

Republic as a result of a decisive resolution of internal and external conflict; prints *verbatim* the decree of the French National Convention sentencing Louis XVI to death; hails the June uprising in Paris as a revolution of the proletariat against the bourgeoisie. More shareholders withdraw.

July 3–5

Gottschalk and others arrested; Marx and Engels attack the judicial authorities in Cologne in the *Neue Rheinische Zeitung* and, in an article entitled 'Arrests', call on the Left in the Berlin National Assembly to act more energetically and to take part in an extra-Parliamentary struggle.

July 6

Interrogations and search of editorial offices in connection with a claim that the *Neue Rheinische Zeitung* has, in its articles, insulted public officials.

July 11

The *Neue Rheinische Zeitung* supports war against Russia as the war in which 'revolutionary' Germany can free itself internally through freeing itself externally.

August 3

Marx, who has printed several of Bakunin's explanations in answer to suspicions raised by his conduct, prints in the *Neue Rheinische Zeitung* a letter from George Sand rejecting the rumour that Bakunin is an agent of the Russian Government.

August–
September

Marx active in the Democratic Association, opposing Weitling's policy of separating the social from the political struggle; protests to the Cologne authorities against their refusal to restore his citizenship; visits Berlin and Vienna; tries to raise money for the *Neue Rheinische Zeitung;* the newspaper editors sponsor a mass meeting in Cologne, with delegates from other Rhenish cities, to discuss the situation produced by the crises in Berlin and Frankfurt; the meeting declares itself for a 'democratic-social, red republic'; further meeting to express solidarity with those fighting on the barricades in Frankfurt; the *Neue Rheinische Zeitung* opens appeal for the insurgents and their families.

September 26
State of siege declared in Cologne; the *Neue Rheinische Zeitung* suppressed; Engels, Wilhelm Wolff, and other editors leave Cologne to escape arrest; Marx remains to reestablish the *Neue Rheinische Zeitung.*

October 11
State of siege ended; the *Neue Rheinische Zeitung* resumes publication under the same editorial committee, together with Freiligrath.

October 31
The *Neue Rheinische Zeitung* calls for the formation of a volunteer corps to aid revolutionary Vienna.

November 12
Marx, in an editorial, calls for a refusal to pay taxes until the Prussian National Assembly is reconvened.

November 13–14
Marx brought before the Cologne Investigatory Tribunal; addresses

crowd outside Court House after second day of the hearing.

December 20	Marx brought before the assizes on a charge of insulting the Procurator Zweiffel and a gendarme in articles in the *Neue Rheinische Zeitung*; hearing adjourned.

1849

February 7	The *Neue Rheinische Zeitung* in severe financial difficulties; Marx, Engels, and Korff charged before the assizes with printing material insulting officials; Marx speaks in his own defence; the accused are all acquitted.
February 8	Marx, Schapper, and Schneider charged before the assizes with inciting to rebellion; Marx speaks in his own defence; the accused are all acquitted.
March	The *Neue Rheinische Zeitung* declares that it will not celebrate the anniversary of the March Revolution, but that of the June Uprising, on 25 June.
May 9–16	Marx publishes in the *Neue Rheinische Zeitung* attacks on the German Royal House of Hohenzollern; uprising in Elberfeld sympathetically reported in the *Neue Rheinische Zeitung*; Marx ordered to leave Prussian territory on the grounds that the latest number of the *Neue Rheinische Zeitung* calls for violent overthrow of the government.

May 18	The last issue of the *Neue Rheinische Zeitung,* printed in red, appears in several editions with a poem of Freiligrath's, a call to the workers of Cologne warning them against any useless *putsch* in Cologne, and an editorial attacking the expulsion order against Marx and stressing that the *Neue Rheinische Zeitung* stands for a red democratic-social republic, for solidarity with the June Uprising in Paris, and for the emancipation of the working classes.
May 19–20	Marx and Engels leave for Frankfurt and vainly try to persuade the left delegates to the National Assembly to lead the uprising in southwest Germany by bringing in revolutionary forces from Baden and the Pfalz.
May 24– June 1	Marx and Engels journey to Baden, then to the Pfalz and Bingen; arrested by soldiers in Hessen, brought back to Frankfurt, but then allowed to continue to Bingen.
June 3	Marx leaves for Paris as representative of German revolutionary parties; Engels takes part in revolutionary campaigns in Baden-Pfalz, which are crushed by 13 June, when he leaves for Switzerland.
August 24	Marx leaves Paris for London, where he is to make his home for the rest of his life.
September	Marx and others reconstitute the London Central Committee of the

Communist League, and Marx joins
the German Workers' Educational
Association, run by the London section of the League; Marx's wife and
three children join him on 17 September. The family takes a furnished
room in Leicester Square and then
moves to 4 Anderson Street, Chelsea.

November 5   Marx's second son, Guido, born.

November 11   Engels arrives in London by ship
              from Genoa.

1850
January–
June   Marx and Engels active in writ-
              ing on recent experiences for the
              *Neue Rheinische Zeitung–Politisch-
              Ökonomische Revue,* published in
              Hamburg as a periodical, delayed by
              Marx's illness and financial difficul-
              ties; Marx lectures to German Work-
              ers' Educational Association and
              participates in seeking material help
              for German refugees in London and
              reorganizing the Communist League;
              sharp conflicts with a number of
              German émigrés; Marx establishes
              contact with French Blanquists in
              London; attends international meet-
              ing in London called to celebrate
              Robespierre's birthday, where En-
              gels and Harney are among the
              speakers; the social-democratic com-
              mittee of émigrés, of which Marx has
              become president, denies charges of
              political favoritism in distributing
              relief; in April Marx has his house-

hold articles seized in Chelsea for arrears of rent; the family moves briefly to a hotel and then to 64 Dean Street, Soho.

July–December

Marx begins systematic study of economic conditions, prices, and economic crises over the previous ten years; decides that the economic crisis has ended and that there is no immediate prospect for revolution in the new conditions of general prosperity and rapid expansion of the means of production; sharp conflicts in the Communist League and the German Workers' Educational Association between Marx's followers and those of Willich and Schapper; the League splits in September, when Marx leaves the German Workers' Educational Association, where the Willich group has a majority. The Communist League Central Committee splits and the headquarters are transferred to Cologne, thus deliberately ending its effectiveness. In October Marx resumes work on a Critique of Political Economy; in November the *Red Republican*, organ of the Chartist Left, begins to print an English translation of the *Communist Manifesto*, and Engels moves to Manchester to work in the family textile mill; his main motive is to be able to support Marx materially while Marx continues his economic studies.

November 19	Marx's one-year-old son, Guido, dies suddenly from convulsions.
December	The Marx family moves to 28 Dean Street, mainly to get Marx's wife, Jenny, much affected by Guido's death, out of the rooms where he died. They remain in these rooms for the next five years.
1851 January–June	Marx, urged by Engels to complete his economic writing, works in the British Museum, studying books on money and credit, the economic writings of Hume and Locke, the works of Malthus, Carey, Jones, and Ramsay, and rereading Ricardo. Marx requests and receives the seven volumes of Feuerbach's collected works from Cologne.
March–April	Marx, in serious financial straits, draws a note on his mother at Trier, resulting in a bitter correspondence between them; Engels comes to the rescue with money. The *Collected Works of Karl Marx* advertised by the Cologne publisher Becker; one brochure, containing some of Marx's writings from 1842, actually published, project then abandoned because of financial difficulties.
March 28	Marx's daughter Franziska born.
May	Marx develops friendly contact with Lassalle after defending him against the Cologne Communists, who have refused him admission.

June 23	Helene Demuth gives birth to an illegitimate son, Frederick, who is given out to foster care. Engels, on his deathbed in 1895, declared the child to be Marx's.
August	Marx begins to write commissioned articles on European affairs for the *New York Daily Tribune*, and continues to do so until 1862 (though the first series of articles on Revolution and Counter-Revolution in Germany, and many others signed by Marx, were written for him by Engels, while Marx was busy with economic studies); Marx meanwhile reads Wakefield and various works on colonies and the slave trade.
September–October	Marx accused in German newspapers of having betrayed Communists arrested in 1850, deliberately or by his 'indiscretions' to the Hungarian Baroness Beck; documents seized from the Willich-Schapper group, arrested in Paris, cited in evidence.
November 11	Marx, deep in debt, sued for £5 in Magistrate's Court and ordered to pay; Engels, Weerth, and Freiligrath help him with small sums.
December	Coup d'état of Louis Napoleon in France; Marx begins writing *The Eighteenth Brumaire of Louis Bonaparte*.
1852	Marx family in extreme poverty and distress; financial help (£10) from

Freiligrath, but by end of February Marx has pawned his coat and cannot go out; in March £3 from Lassalle and £9 as the first payment from the *New York Daily Tribune* for articles 'Revolution and Counter-Revolution in Germany', ghosted by Engels.

April 14

Franziska Marx dies at the age of one; Marx has to borrow money for the funeral from a neighbour, a French exile.

July

Marx offers the publisher Brockhaus, for his periodical *Die Gegenwart* (*The Present*), a study of modern economic literature in England; offer refused.

October

Trial of Cologne Communists begins; Marx involved in refuting various slanders; Marx's landlord threatens legal action for arrears of rent; Marx pawns coat to buy writing paper.

November 17

Marx dissolves the Communist League in London, noting that on the Continent, in consequence of the Cologne arrests in May 1851, it has factually ceased to exist.

1853
January

Marx's work on the Communist trial in Cologne, published in Basel, confiscated by police, published afresh in Boston on 24 April; Marx writes his first article in English, for the *New York Daily Tribune*, 'Capital Punishment—Mr Cobden's Pamphlets. Regulations of the Bank of

England'; earlier articles have been translated for him. The Marx family's destitution and illness continue.

April
: Publishes, in various papers, articles criticizing Gladstone's financial policies.

May
: Marx concerned with the problem of 'Oriental Despotism' and the special characteristics of historical development based on the Asiatic mode of production, where private property is insignificant and the State appropriates the overwhelming proportion of surplus value; corresponds with Engels on this; studies history of East India Company; writes articles on India and China for the *Tribune*.

June
: Marx receives from the radical American economist Henry Charles Carey a copy of his book, *Slavery at Home and Abroad*, where Marx's *Tribune* article on 'The Duchess of Sutherland and Slavery' is cited.

August
: Marx publicly denies the suspicion, voiced by Herzen and Golovin, that an article in *The Morning Advertiser* portraying Bakunin as a Russian spy was inspired by him or represents the attitude taken to Bakunin by the *Neue Rheinische Zeitung* in 1848–1849.

October
: Marx publishes six articles attacking Palmerston in the *Tribune* and the *People's Paper*; inquires fruitlessly

	whether Dana, the editor of the *Tribune*, could place articles on the history of German philosophy from Kant to the present.
1854 January– April	Marx writes articles on Austrian economic affairs, English finances, the Greek insurrection, Christians in Turkey; interested in Napoleon III's preparation for war with Russia; reads material on the Ottoman Empire; argues in correspondence with Lassalle, who rejects Marx's view that Lord Palmerston is a Russian agent.
May	Marx studies Spanish; reads Calderón and Cervantes.
June	Marx's wife, Jenny, dangerously ill; Marx unable to pay doctor's bill.
August	Marx studies the history of Spain in connection with the revolution there.
December	Marx, through Lassalle's good offices, offered work as contributor to the *Neue Oder Zeitung;* continues until end of 1855.
1855 January– February	Lassalle and Countess Hatzfeld send Marx financial help; Marx rereads his economic notebooks of 1844–1847 and 1850–1851 to prepare himself for a reworking of the material; studies Roman history.
January 16	Marx's daughter Eleanor born.
April 6	Marx's eight-year-old son Edgar dies.

September	Marx's wife receives a legacy on the death of her uncle.
1856 April 14	Marx addresses the anniversary gathering of the Chartist *People's Paper* on the coming proletarian revolution.
May	Jenny Marx receives a further sum from her uncle's estate; travels with her three daughters to Trier to visit her sick mother, who dies on 23 July. The female Marxes return to London in September.
July–August	Marx works on his Russophobic *Secret Diplomatic History of the Eighteenth Century*.
September	Jenny Marx receives a small legacy from her mother.
October	The Marxes move to better quarters at 9 Grafton Terrace, Maitland Park, Hampstead Road, Haverstock Hill.
1857 January–March	Dispute with the *New York Daily Tribune* over payment for articles; Marx family's financial and health worries continue. Marx at work on his critique of political economy; compiles in 1857 and 1858 the manuscripts first published in 1939 as the *Grundrisse* (Outlines) of the Critique of Political Economy.
July 8	Jenny Marx delivered of a stillborn child.
December 21	Marx refuses an offer, made through

the influence of Lassalle, to contribute to the Viennese *Presse*.

1858
February

Lassalle offers to find a publisher for Marx's *Contribution to the Critique of Political Economy;* more financial crises and illness; Marx reopens the question of contributing to the *Presse*, but the editor does not reply.

1859
January 21

Manuscript of Marx's *Contribution to the Critique of Political Economy* completed and sent off to the publisher.

March–
April

Marx's mother refuses him further money; Lassalle helps out.

May–
August

Marx and Engels work for the paper *Das Volk;* Marx becomes editor at the beginning of July.

August 20

Last issue of *Das Volk* published; Marx quarrels with Freiligrath and Lassalle.

1860
January–
April

Marx continues his economic studies, for the work that becomes *Capital, Volume I;* reads Montesquieu, Locke, Hobbes, Aristotle's *Politics,* and Plato; becomes aware of a brochure by Karl Vogt, being widely quoted and reprinted in German newspapers, which accuses Marx of blackmail and forgery; Marx responds with a 'Public Explanation'; collects material for his more extended reply, *Herr Vogt,* published later in the year, and threatens legal action against several newspapers that have printed the accusations, including the Berlin *National Zeitung* and the London *Daily Telegraph*; quarrels with Freiligrath, who refuses to make Marx's cause against Vogt his own because of 'a feeling for cleanliness'; Lassalle also holds back from support; further attacks on Marx's probity in various German newspapers; Engels gives Marx £100.

June — Berlin City Court rejects Marx's defamation suit against the *National Zeitung* on the ground that those of its editorial assertions and comments which did not consist of quotations were 'within the limits of permissible criticism'. Marx's subsequent appeal rejected.

September — Marx, unable to find a printer in Germany for his *Herr Vogt*, lets the pamphlet be printed in London; Engels, Lassalle, and Countess Hatzfeld contribute to the printing costs.

November — Marx's wife seriously ill with smallpox; Marx studies mathematics, 'the only occupation that enables [him] to maintain the necessary quietness [*sic*] of mind'.

December — Marx reads Darwin's *Origin of Species* and tells Engels that it provides the foundation in natural history for their theory of class struggle.

1861
January–
February

Marx, in great financial need, unable to pay taxes, debts, or rent; Dana, editor of the *New York Daily Tribune*, protests against Marx drawing a note on the newspaper for £30.

February–
April

Marx, in search of further funds, visits his uncle Lion Philips in Holland, Lassalle in Berlin, and his mother in Trier.

July

Lassalle makes efforts to have Marx's renunciation of Prussian citizenship (in 1845) cancelled.

October 20

Marx accepted as a contributor to the Viennese paper *Die Presse*.

November

Lassalle reports Prussian government's refusal to renew Marx's citizenship; Marx active on behalf of the imprisoned French revolutionary Auguste Blanqui; in desperate financial straits again, is sued for unpaid balance of printing bill for *Herr Vogt;* Marx's wife seriously ill with worry.

1862

Ill health and financial distress continue; Marx spends the whole year intensively at work on rough drafts of the continuation (the second part) of his Critique of Political Economy, which he decides at the end of the year to treat as a separate work, to be called *Das Kapital;* he fills fourteen thick notebooks with writings on the problem of the production of relative surplus value, on the history of theories of surplus value, and on his theory of land rent; he writes chapters on capital and profit, surplus value and profit, the rate of profit, mercantile capital, and money capital.

January

Writes a number of articles for the Vienna *Presse,* of which only five are printed, on the danger of war between England and North America (the *Trent* affair).

February

Marx's daughter Jenny tries unsuccessfully to go on the stage, to relieve the family's financial distress.

April

Marx's connection with the *New York Daily Tribune* ended.

July

Lassalle visits Marx and gives him financial help; Marx writes for the *Presse* on the Taiping rebellion in China and, in August, on events in America.

August–
September

Marx travels to Holland and Trier in a fruitless search for financial help. An effort through his Dutch cousin August Philips to get Marx a job as a clerk in the English railways fails as a result of Marx's bad handwriting. In October Philips gives him £20.

1863
January

Marx family in extreme need, lack of food and fuel, children lack clothes and shoes to attend school; Marx begins the final version of *Capital* for the printer; attends a practical course on technology given by Professor Willis. Marx's cold reception of the death of Engels's mistress, Mary Burns, leads to a cold reply from Engels; Marx apologizes; Engels sends Marx £100. Marx reads Lassalle's 'Workers' Program' and dubs it a bad vulgarization of the *Communist Manifesto*.

February	Marx plans a pamphlet in connection with the uprising in Poland.
March	Beginning of friendship with Kugelmann; Marx family still dogged by illness and money troubles.
May–July	Marx increasingly critical of Lassalle's political agitation on behalf of the working class; studies mathematics and integral and differential calculus; commences final editing of *Capital* and expands the material considerably, so that it grows to three volumes, the rough draft of which is not completed until December 1865, and does not include the material on theories of surplus value.
November 30	Marx's mother dies in Trier; Engels provides money for Marx to travel to Trier to settle her affairs; returning via Holland, Marx falls ill and remains there until February 1864.
1864 February 29	Marx returns to London; suffers from boils and is unable to work until April.

March	Marx receives a share of his mother's estate from Trier; the Marx family moves to better quarters in 1 Modena Villas, Maitland Park, Haverstock Hill.
May 9	Wilhelm Wolff dies in Manchester; leaves Marx £800 in his will.
June	Marx's friend and comrade Wilhelm Liebknecht has left London and become active in the Berlin section of the General Association of German Workers founded by Lassalle in 1863; he keeps Marx informed of the situation there and receives Marx's instructions not to identify himself with Lassalle's policies, but not to oppose them openly yet.
August 31	Lassalle dies as the result of a duel.
September 28	The International Working Men's Association (the First International) founded at a meeting in St Martin's Hall, London, attended by English, Italian, French, Swiss, and Polish workers and members of the Communist German Workers' Educational Association. The meeting was chaired by the Comtian positivist and socialist Professor Edward Spencer Beesly, of University College, London; Marx, who had taken no part in the preparations for the meeting, was respectfully invited to attend as a socialist scholar and writer known in London refugee circles and among a section of former

Chartists. He sat, as he wrote to Engels, as a 'mute figure on the platform', while the refugee tailor Eccarius spoke on behalf of the German Workers' Educational Association; Marx and Eccarius were the two elected as German representatives on the thirty-two-member provisional central committee; the English trade unionist George William Wheeler moved the resolution that called the International into existence.

October–November

Provisional Central Committee of the International, later called the General Council, meets several times; it elects the English shoemaker George Odgers as chairman and Marx, representing Germany, to a subcommittee commissioned to draft the rules and principles of the International. The Central Committee finally (on 1 November) adopts a version drafted by Marx in preference to an English translation of the Statutes of Mazzini's Italian Workers' Societies proffered by Luigi Wolff and another declaration drafted by the old Owenite John Weston. Marx gives copies of the address and rules to Bakunin, whom he meets for the first time in sixteen years in London on 5 November, and asks him to transmit a copy to Garibaldi. Bakunin, who is on his way to Italy, agrees to act as representative of the International there.

November 17   Marx begins to write for the *Social-Demokrat* in Berlin.

November 22–29   Marx, on behalf of the International, writes an Address to Abraham Lincoln on the occasion of Lincoln's re-election as President.

1865
January–
February   Marx protests over accusations, in the Paris correspondence of Moses Hess, that the Paris members of the International are Bonapartists; begins to attack the dead Lassalle for 'scientific charlatanism and political opportunism' after learning of Countess Hatzfeld's reports that Lassalle planned to mobilize German workers to support Bismarck's belligerence over Schleswig-Holstein; contract for the publication of *Capital* sent by Meissner of Hamburg. Marx meets the French medical student and radical Paul Lafargue; declines an offer of the editorship of *The Bee-Hive;* ends his connection with the *Social-Demokrat.*

May–
July   Marx suffers from boils and liver attacks and is in financial straits; on behalf of the International, Marx writes to President Johnson calling on him to continue Lincoln's work.

September   Marx takes part in the first conference of the International Working Men's Association in London; Jenny Marx, during the summer, completes her *Short Sketch of an Eventful*

	Life, first published in 1965; Engels sends Marx £95.
December	Rough draft of three volumes of *Capital* completed.
1866	
	Marx continues to suffer from ill health and financial embarrassments; receives about £60 from Engels during February.
March	Corresponding secretaries of the International (Marx is Corresponding Secretary for Germany and later also Russia) meet to discuss tactics against Mazzini and his sympathizers.
April	Marx demands a four-month postponement of the forthcoming first Congress of the International to September, because of the situation created in the General Council when he was absent through illness and because of the threat of Proudhonian domination if the Congress were held in May.
May	Italian Workers' Association in Naples announces its adherence to the International.
July–August	Marx wants London to be kept as the seat of the General Council of the International; spends a good deal of time preparing for the September Congress.
August 6	Laura Marx becomes engaged to Paul Lafargue.
September 3–8	First Congress of the International in

	Geneva, for which Marx writes the 'Instructions', but which, like all other congresses except the last, he does not attend.
September–November	Marx in great financial need; creditors threaten to sue; Marx's wife pawns clothes; in October and November he receives a total of £75 from Engels; Marx sends the first portions of *Capital* to Meissner.
December 31	Marx receives news of the death of his uncle, Lion Philips.
1867 January	Marx in great financial need, threatened with eviction, owes the baker alone £20.
February	Marx addresses the German Workers' Educational Association in London on wage-labour and capital and advocates war against Russia as a way of forcing the workers' party into a revolutionary stance; suffers from boils, in financial need, receives £60 from Engels; the International makes its first significant impact on the working class through its support of the Paris bronze-workers, locked out by their employers until they renounced their union.
April	Marx receives another £35 from Engels for his fare to Germany; takes the completed manuscript of *Capital I* to Hamburg; goes on to stay in Hanover as a guest of Kugelmann; Marx visited by a 'satrap of Bismarck's' (the advocate Warnebold)

who wishes to 'employ Marx's great talent in the interests of the German nation'.

May	Marx returns to London; revises proofs of *Capital*.
July	The German 'Communist Club' in New York joins the International.
August	Marx warns the General Council of the International of the Russian danger and the danger of standing armies as instruments of oppression.
September	Marx campaigns for support for the Irish Independence movement; Second Congress of the International meets in Lausanne, but Marx has refused an offer to attend as representative of the General Council in London.
October–November	Marx in dire financial distress; suffers from insomnia, incapable of work; declines an offer to participate in the Committee of the Central Association of Freethinkers in London.
December	Marx borrows £150 from a life insurance company on the guarantee of Engels and Borkheim.
1868	Throughout the year Marx is in constant financial need, and frequently considers moving to Geneva, where the cost of living is lower; Engels provides him with about £400 during this period.
January–March	Marx suffers from boils and constant headaches, but continues his eco-

nomic studies and reads with great interest Maurer's *Introduction to the History of the Constitution of the Mark, the Village and the Town*, finding there renewed evidence that Asiatic forms of property constitute the beginning everywhere in Europe.

April	Marx undergoes arsenic cure for his boils.
April 2	Laura Marx marries Paul Lafargue in a civil ceremony in London.
August	Marx suffers from gall-bladder attacks; works on material for the projected third volume of *Capital*; writes reports of the General Council of the International.
September 6–13	Third Congress of the International in Brussels.
November	Marx's daughter Jenny takes a post as governess, unbeknown to her father.
November 25	Engels offers to pay all of Marx's outstanding debts and to make him an annual allowance of £350.
December	Laura Lafargue's first child born; Bakunin's International Alliance of Socialist Democracy, founded a few months earlier, applies to affiliate with the International, and Bakunin writes to Marx saying that he is Marx's disciple and proud to be one.
1869 January– March	Marx ill, but works on revisions for the projected new German edition

of the *Eighteenth Brumaire*, to be published by Meissner; cannot find a French publisher for the book; resumes work on material for the second volume of *Capital.*

March– July 6	Marx's wife and daughter visit the Lafargues in Paris; Marx studies the official United Kingdom report on child labour in agriculture; Marx, in an address adopted by the General Council of the International, calls on the National Labor Union in America to oppose the threatened war between England and the United States, since it will enable the American government to crush the young labour movement; at the July meeting of the Council he attacks the 'petty bourgeois' standpoint of the Proudhonians.
July 7–12	Marx visits the Lafargues in Paris, using the cover-name 'A. Williams'.
August	Engels sends Marx £100 to clear up old debts that Marx's wife had concealed in November 1868 when the Marxes were drawing up an account of their debts; Marx reports to the Council of the International on the formation of the German Social Democratic Workers' Party at Eisenach.
September– October	Marx writes the annual report of the International, and treats the persecution of its members by governments in France, Austria, and Hungary as signs of its growing importance; re-

port presented to the Fourth Congress of the International in Basel;
Marx does not attend but he and his
daughter Jenny visit his Philips cousins in Aachen and the Kugelmanns
in Hanover; soon after the Congress
Bakunin begins his attack on the
General Council of the International
and produces splits in France and
Switzerland by April 1870.

November–   Marx studies the Russian language in
December   order to read the Russian socialist
                   writer N. Flerovski (pseudonym of
                   V. V. Bervii), whose *Position of the
                   Working Class in Russia* has just
                   been published in St Petersburg;
                   Marx first reads Herzen's *Prison and
                   Exile* and then (in February 1870)
                   Flerovski; Marx seeks amnesty for
                   the imprisoned Fenians in a speech
                   to the General Council of the Inter-
                   national on 16 November; attacks
                   Gladstone's Irish policy; sends re-
                   sulting resolution to the Irish Work-
                   ingmen's Association.

1870
March   Marx, in the General Council, suc-
                   cessfully moves that the Paris So-
                   ciety of Proletarian Positivists be
                   admitted to the International as 'pro-
                   letarian' but not as 'positivist'; cam-
                   paigns for the release of the Fenians;
                   complains, in correspondence, of Ba-
                   kunin's elevation of the nihilist Ne-
                   chaev and of the 'Lassalle-cult'
                   developing in Germany.

April	Marx receives a full report from Lafargue on the activities of Bakuninists and Proudhonians in Paris; receives the first Russian edition of the *Communist Manifesto*, published in 1869.
May	The General Council resolves to issue a public explanation, drafted by Marx, that the so-called French branch of the International has had no relation with the International for two years; Marx receives newspapers and official statistics concerning the position of workers in the United States.
July	France declares war on Prussia; Marx, who has been suffering from continued liver attacks, writes the First Address of the General Council on the Franco-Prussian War.
September 1–2	Napoleon III surrenders to the Prussians at Sedan.
September 9	Marx writes the Second Address of the General Council.
September 18	Engels moves permanently from Manchester to London.
1871 January–March	Marx in regular correspondence with Serraillier on events in France.
February 28	General Council of the International hears first-hand report from Serraillier on conditions in Paris.
March 18–May 28	The Paris Commune; General Council of the International in London expresses support on 21 March.

April	Marx begins to be widely—and falsely—regarded in Europe as the instigator of the Commune, giving him his first wide public reputation; Marx, in a letter to *The* (London) *Times*, denies the French report printed in *The Times* that he had organized the Paris insurrection from London.
May 11	Nikolai Danielson, the Russian populist economist who is preparing the Russian translation of *Capital*, asks Marx to supply any revisions or corrections he wishes to make, and (in a subsequent letter) to send copies of all publications of the International.
May 30	Marx's address on the Commune (*The Civil War in France*) commissioned by the General Council on 28 March, as an address to the people of Paris, completed and approved for publication.
June 13	Address on the Civil War in France published; second edition three weeks later.
May–August	Marx's daughters Jenny and Eleanor visit the Lafargues in Bordeaux; they are placed under temporary arrest while Paul Lafargue flees to Spain; Marx active in aiding Communard refugees; German translation by Engels of Marx's address on the Commune published in the *Volksstaat*.
September 7	Various newspapers report the death of Marx.

September 9–22 | Conference of the International in London in which Marx is a leading figure; Marx proposes a series of resolutions aimed against anarchists (Bakuninists and Proudhonians) and the 'trade-unionists', emphasizing that the proletariat must wage political struggles and capture political power; Marx also proposes the formation of a women's section of the International, noting the part played by women in the Paris Commune, Marx reelected as Corresponding Secretary for Russia.

November | The Bakuninists controlling the French-Swiss Federation within the International, now calling themselves the Jura Federation, hold a separate Congress and attack the General Council of the International for exercising usurped and dictatorial power as though it were a kind of government; a London agent of the Russian secret police, working in Polish émigré circles as 'Count Albert Potockij', seeks information on the International from Marx; Marx's brief replies are sent on to St Petersburg.

December | Marx informs the General Council of factions fighting in the International in New York and in Geneva, where the Bakuninists have been routed; together with Mazzini and Garibaldi, Marx is made an honorary member of the Associazione Democratica in Macerata.

1872

February | Marx continues his attacks on the Bakuninist anarchists in the International, especially in Switzerland; personal conflicts break out in the General Council in London.

April | Marx receives a copy of the Russian translation of *Capital;* works on revisions for the second German edition and the French translation being done by J. Roy.

August | First instalment of the French translation of *Capital* published.

September 1–7 | Fifth Congress of the International in The Hague; Marx attends as an official delegate, accompanied by his wife, Eleanor, and Engels; bitter struggle with Bakuninists; Marx, after challenging decisions of the Credentials Committee, helps to put through the resolution to transfer the General Council to New York, moved by Engels. The International is now purely Marxist and has support only from a section of the socialist movement in Germany, from German Switzerland, and from Blanquist refugees from Paris.

October 10 | Marx's daughter Jenny marries the (Proudhonian) French revolutionary journalist and former Communard Charles Longuet.

1873

January– February | Marx reads, in Russian, reports of the trial of Nechaev; collects material for an attack on Bakunin; finishes the preface for the second German edition of *Capital;* reads several books on Russia.

May–July   Marx in very poor health from overwork; suffers from insomnia and blood rushing to the head; ordered by physician to work no more than four hours a day.

July–
October   Marx studies Russian land-holding, especially the peasant commune; refuses invitation of the New York section of the International to act as their representative at the planned Geneva Congress of the International, which turns out to be a fiasco; sends copies of the second edition of Capital to Darwin and Spencer, and meets Edward Aveling.

November   Marx, suffering from chronic headache, takes mineral water cure at Harrogate with Eleanor; ordered by physician to cease all work.

1874

Lissagaray in close relationship with the Marx family until 1877; considered to be Eleanor's future husband, Marx in January reads Bakunin's book *Statism and Anarchism;* Marx totally incapable of work from February to April, but begins to collect and study the official Blue Books on the English economy and British economic policy; Marx loses in an arbitrated commercial-legal dispute over money he has invested in marketing a patent.

June–July	Marx and Engels, who have been advising 'Marxist' anti-Lassalleans in Germany, turn their attention to combating the influence of Eugen Dühring.
August 1	Marx applies for British citizenship, refused on 29 August.
August 15– September 21	Marx in Karlsbad with his daughter Eleanor, taking a cure. At first on terms of close friendship with the Kugelmanns, later quarrels with them and ends the connection. Marx and Eleanor return to London via Dresden, Leipzig, Berlin, and Hamburg.
October– December	The Lassallean German Workers' Party offers to discuss a merger with the 'Marxist' or 'Eisenach' Social-Democratic Workers' Party.
1875 January 23	Marx addresses a meeting commemorating the Polish Uprising of 22 January 1863, at which Lavrov and other Russian populists are present.
May	Marx writes his critical marginal comments on the proposed (Gotha) unity program for uniting Lassalleans and Eisenachers in Germany; reads Haxthausen's book on Russian land-holding; enters into regular contact with Lavrov.
August– September	Cure at Karlsbad; Marx sees a good deal of the Russian sociologist M. M. Kovalevski.

October–December	Back in London Marx reads Slavophile brochures and studies the social and economic position of Russia; says, in a letter to Dietzgen, that at the conclusion of his economic work he would like to write a book on dialectic.
1876 March–May	Marx reads books on human and plant physiology; resolves to study land-holding in Hungary.
May 10	Birth of Jenny Longuet's second son—the first of Marx's grandchildren to survive infancy.
June	Marx begins intensive study of primitive land-holding among various peoples, especially the Slavs, reading Maurer, Hanssen, Demelič, Cardenas, and others; also studies Russian history throughout the year.
August–September	Marx takes the cure at Karlsbad with Eleanor again; has social contact there with the Jewish historian Heinrich Graetz, with whom he discusses the weaknesses of Tsarism.
November	Marx, working on the second volume of *Capital,* suffers badly from rheumatism and bronchitis.
1877 January–March	Marx writes anonymously—in the *Whitehall Review* and *Vanity Fair*—against Gladstone's pro-Russia policy; corresponds with Heinrich Graetz; writes the chapter

on Dühring's 'Critical History of Political Economy' for Engels's *Anti-
Dühring*.

May–July

Marx suffers from insomnia and nervous disorders; finds return to Karlsbad too expensive, receives £100
from Engels to go to Neuenahr.

August–
September

Marx, his sick wife, and Eleanor take
a cure at Bad Neuenahr, then, on
medical advice, visit the Black Forest
for more rest.

November

Marx drafts a reply to an article by
the Russian populist Mikhailovski,
who ascribes to Marx the view that
Russia must dissolve the peasant
commune and enter into a capitalist
phase before it can become socialist;
Marx's draft, which did not become
publicly known until Engels sent it
to Vera Zasulich in March 1884, rejects the view that his own analysis
of Western European capitalism implies that all peoples must pass
through the capitalist stage.

1878
April

Liebknecht visits Marx in London.

July

Jenny Marx's health deteriorates
markedly.

November

Marx reads books on the relations
between Leibniz and modern science.

1879

Marx's health and his wife's deteriorate further.

August–September 1880	Marx visits Jersey and Ramsgate for his health, together with Eleanor.
	Marx reads books on Central Australia, Australia's economic future, etc.; agrees to a Dutch abridgement of *Capital;* in July Marx meets H. M. Hyndman and forms a close relationship.
September	Annenkov's recollections of his meeting with Marx in the 1840s published in *Vestnik Evropy.*
1881 February	Marx receives a letter from Vera Zasulich, writing in the name of socialists in Russia, asking for his opinion on the economic development of Russia, and especially on the future of the peasant commune; Marx drafts four versions of a reply and finally sends a letter on 8 March saying that his studies of Russia suggest that under certain conditions the peasant commune 'could become the point of departure for the social regeneration of Russia'.
April–June	Kautsky a frequent visitor to the Marx household.
June	Marx quarrels with Hyndman and ends all contact; both Marx and his wife in even poorer health.
July–August	Marx and his wife visit Eastbourne and then their daughter Jenny at Argenteuil; return suddenly to London on account of the serious illness of Eleanor.

December 21	Marx's wife dies of cancer.
1882 February–October	Marx travels for his health, visiting his daughter Jenny in Argenteuil, going on to Algiers and Monte Carlo, and then to Cannes and Switzerland with Laura Lafargue.
November–January 1883	Marx goes to the Isle of Wight for the winter, where Eleanor and his grandson Jean Longuet visit him.
1883 January 11	Jenny Longuet dies in Paris.
March 14	Marx dies in London.
March 17	Marx buried in Highgate Cemetery.
1895 August 5	Death of Friedrich Engels.
1898 March 31	Suicide of Eleanor Marx.
1911 November 26	Suicide of Laura and Paul Lafargue.

Note: Brief biographical details of persons mentioned in this chronology, together with those for other persons mentioned in this volume, will be found in the Index.

CHRONOLOGY: MARX'S CHIEF WORKS

1836

Three books of poems for his fiancée, Jenny von Westphalen. MS, first published in MEGA (*Marx-Engels Gesamtausgabe*), 1927.

1841

Doctoral dissertation 'Differenz der demokritischen und epikureischen Naturphilosophie' ('The Difference Between the Democritean and the Epicurean Philosophy of Nature'); first published in F. Mehring: *Aus dem literarischen Nachlass von Karl Marx . . .*, Stuttgart, 1902, and again in MEGA, 1927; French translation in the collected French edition of Marx's works, 1946.

'Wilde Lieder' ('Wild Songs'), in *Athenäum*, Berlin, no. 4, 23.1.1841; reprinted in MEGA, 1927.

1842–1843

Articles and editorial notes in the *Rheinische Zeitung;* articles published in Arnold Ruge's *Anekdota* (Zurich), nos. I and II, 1843. (A number of articles from both *Rheinische Zeitung* and *Anekdota* were included in Mehring, 1902, and all were published in MEGA, 1927. The second, anonymous *Anekdota* article, *'Luther als Schiedsrichter zwischen Strauss und Feuerbach,'* there attributed to Marx, is now known to have been written by Feuerbach himself.)

1843

Unfinished Kreuznach manuscript 'Kritik des Hegelschen Staatsrechts' ('Critique of Hegelian Constitutional Law'), first published in MEGA, 1927; French translation in 1935; full English translation by J. O'Malley and A. Jolin, published as K. Marx, *Critique of Hegel's Philosophy of Right*, Cambridge, 1970, edited by J. O'Malley.

1811

'Zur Judenfrage' ('On the Jewish Question') and 'Zur Kritik der Hegelschen Rechtsphilosophie, Einleitung' ('Contribution to the Critique of Hegel's Philosophy of Right, Introduction'), published in the first (and only) issue of the *Deutsch-französische Jahrbücher*, Paris, 1844. The first of these reprinted in *Der Sozialdemokrat*, Zurich, 1881, and included complete in Mehring, 1902, and MEGA; French translation appeared in 1850 and 1903, an Italian translation in 1899. The second was reprinted in the *Berliner Volksblatt*, December 1890 and appears complete in Mehring, 1902 and MEGA, 1927. Portions of both works were translated into English in H. J. Stenning: *Selected Essays*, 1926; complete translation in *Karl Marx: Early Writings*, translated and edited by T. B. Bottomore, London, 1963. The Hegel critique is also included in O'Malley, *op. cit.*, 1970.

The incomplete Paris Manuscripts known as the 'Economico-philosophical manuscripts of 1844' or as 'Zur Kritik der Nationalökonomie, mit einem Schlusskapitel über die Hegelsche Philosophie'; first published in MEGA, 1932; important German edition by E. Thier in 1950; complete English translation in Bottomore, 1963.

1845
Die heilige Familie, oder, Kritik der kritischen Kritik, gegen Bruno Bauer und Consorten (The Holy Family, etc.), by Friedrich Engels and Karl Marx, Frankfurt, a.M., 1845; reprinted in Mehring, 1902, and MEGA, 1932; French translation 1927–1928 and an English translation in 1957.

'Thesen über Feuerbach' ('Theses on Feuerbach'), jotted down in Marx's notebook and first published as an appendix to F. Engels: *Ludwig Feuerbach und der Ausgang der klassischen deutschen Philosophie*, 1888; reprinted MEGA, 1932; facsimile of MS, differing from Engels's version, in *Marx-Engels Archiv*, I, 1926; first English translation, with commentary, in Sidney Hook, *From Hegel to Marx*, London, 1936.

1845–1846
Die deutsche Ideologie (The German Ideology) by Marx and Engels, first published in MEGA, 1932, though extracts had appeared in 1902–1903, 1921, and 1927, and variants are still being published for the first time; French translation 1937–1947, and English translation of parts I and III by W. Louch and C. P. Magill, edited by R. Pascal, London, 1938.

1847

Misère de la philosophie: réponse à la Philosophie de la misère de M. Proudhon, Brussels-Paris, 1847; enlarged French editions published in Paris, 1896, 1908, 1935; German translation, *Das Elend der Philosophie*, by E. Bernstein and K. Kautsky, published in Stuttgart, 1885, and the first English translation, *The Poverty of Philosophy*, by H. Quelch, in London, 1900; Spanish translation published Madrid, 1891, and Italian translation, Rome, 1901; new English translation published New York, 1963.

1848

Discours sur la question du libre échange, Brussels, 1848; German translation the same year; English translation, *Free Trade*, published Boston, 1888.

Manifest der kommunistischen Partei (Manifesto of the Communist Party) by Marx and Engels, London, February 1848; Swedish translation Stockholm, 1848, projected versions in French, Italian, Spanish, Polish, Danish, etc., having been suppressed for political reasons; English translation by Helen Macfarlane published in *The Red Republican*, London, 1850, and reprinted in New York in 1871; authorized English translation by S. Moore was published London, 1888; a translation by E. and C. Paul in 1930, and an edition with a lengthy introduction by H. J. Laski, London, 1948; Russian version by Bakunin appeared in Geneva, 1859, and another, by Vera Zasulich, in Geneva in 1882; first authorized French translation, by Laura Lafargue, published in *Le Socialiste*, Paris, 1885. For original text and variants, see MEGA, 1932.

1848–1849

Articles for *Neue Rheinische Zeitung*, including 'Lohnarbeit und Kapital' ('Wage-Labour and Capital'), published there in April 1849, and reprinted as a separate pamphlet with revisions and modifications by Engels in Zurich, 1884, and Berlin, 1891; English translation, *Wage-Labour and Capital*, by J. L. Joynes, published 1885, one by

H. E. Lothrop in New York in 1902, and one by F. Baldwin in 1925. The original is reprinted in MEGA, 1932.

1850

'Die Klassenkämpfe in Frankreich' ('Class Struggles in France'), a series of articles published in *Neue Rheinische Zeitung–Politischökonomische Revue*, Hamburg, 1850; published in one volume by Engels, Berlin, 1895, and in a new edition in 1911; English translation, *The Class Struggles in France, 1848–1850*, by H. Kuhn, published New York, 1924; Serbian and Hungarian translation same year; French translation, Paris, 1900.

1851

Publication of the *Gesammelte Aufsätze von Karl Marx*, hrsg. von H. Becker, Cologne, 1851, halted abruptly (after the publication of Heft 1), by police action against the Communist League, of which Becker is a member; the first volume (or brochure) contains writings from 1842.

1852

Der Achtzehnte Brumaire des Louis Napoleon (The Eighteenth Brumaire of Louis Bonaparte), published in *Die Revolution*, New York, May 1852; second edition, with foreword by Marx, published Hamburg, 1869, third edition, by Engels, in 1885; French translation based on the third edition appeared in Lille, c. 1888, and another in Paris in 1900; English translation by Daniel de Leon, New York, 1898, and one by E. and C. Paul in London in 1926; Russian translation St Petersburg, 1905.

1852–1862

Articles for the *New York Daily Tribune;* reprinted in various thematic selections such as *The Eastern Question:* a reproduction of letters written 1853–1856, dealing with the events of the Crimean War, edited by E. M. Aveling and E. Aveling, London, 1897, and *Revolution in Spain*, articles by Marx and Engels reproduced from the *New York Daily Tribune*, 1939. A series of articles contributed to the *New York Daily Tribune*, in Marx's name between

October 1851 and December 1852, and republished as his work by E. M. Aveling in *Revolution and Counter-Revolution*, London, 1896, is now known to have been principally the work of Engels. The articles dealing with Russia, India, and China have been tampered with in most Communist editions.

1853

Enthüllungen über den Kommunistenprozess zu Köln (Revelations of the Communist Trial in Cologne), Basel, 1853 and Boston, 1853 (the former was confiscated, and the second achieved only limited distribution); new edition in *Volksstaat*, Leipzig, 1874–1875; an edition by Engels in Zurich, 1885; French translation, Paris, 1949, English translation, London, 1971.

1856

'Revelations of the Diplomatic History of the Eighteenth Century', appeared in much-shortened form in *The Sheffield Free Press*, June–August 1856. In consequence of a protest by Marx the complete text was published by *The Free Press*, London, August 1856–April 1857; published as *The Secret Diplomatic History of the Eighteenth Century*, edited with some omissions by Eleanor Marx Aveling, London, 1899; new edition by Lester Hutchinson, London, 1969, which adds *The Story of the Life of Lord Palmerston*, originally published by Marx in the *New York Daily Tribune* in 1853, and with additions in *The Free Press*, London, 1855–1856. This text was published as a separate pamphlet by E. M. Aveling in London, 1899.

1857–1858

Grundrisse der Kritik der politischen Ökonomie (Rohentwurf). *Anhang 1850–59;* published for the first time from the German MSS now in Moscow, in two volumes, Moscow, 1939–1941 ('Introduction and one other extract had previously been published by Kautsky in *Die Neue Zeit*, Stuttgart, 1903–1904), complete one-volume edition published in Berlin, 1953; a section translated into English as K. Marx, *Precapitalist Economic Formations*, edited by E. J. Hobsbawm, London, 1964; a fuller selection in English translation is *Marx's Grundrisse*, by D. McLellan, London, 1971.

1859

Zur Kritik der politischen Ökonomie, Erstes Heft, Berlin, 1859; reprinted with Marx's 'Introduction' of 1857 (above) by Karl Kautsky, Stuttgart, 1897 and 1907; Russian translation by Rumiantsev, Moscow, 1896; French translation at Paris in 1899 and another, by Laura Lafargue, Paris, 1909; an Italian translation in 1914 in Milan; first English translation was *A Contribution to the Critique of Political Economy*, translated from the second German edition by N. I. Stone, Chicago, 1904; second revised edition of this in New York and London in the same year.

1860

Herr Vogt, London, 1860. Some chapters were reprinted in the *Demokratisches Wochenblatt*, 1869. A photographic reprint of original edition published in Leipzig, 1927, and a full modern edition in Berlin, 1953. A French translation published in Paris, 1927–1928.

During the following years Marx was much involved in work for the International Working Men's Association, and for Polish refugees.

1864

Address and Provisional Rules of the Working Men's International Association, London, by the Association at the *Bee-Hive* Newspaper Office, 1864 (written by Marx); reprinted in *The Miner and Workmen's Advocate*, London, 1864: ratified at the First Congress of the International, Geneva, 1866, and revised at the London Conference, 1871; German translation of the *Address* appeared in *Der Social-Demokrat*, Berlin, 1864, and in *Der Vorbote*, Geneva, 1866; included in W. Eichhoff: *Die internationale Arbeiter-Assoziation*, Berlin, 1868; French translation by Charles Longuet, Brussels, 1866, Italian translation Rome, 1901, Russian translation in Geneva, 1903; new edition *General Rules and Administrative Regulations of the International Working Men's Association.* Official Edition, revised ... London, 1871; French, German, and Italian editions of this edited by Marx and Engels.

1865

Value, Price and Profit, an address to the General Council of the I.W.M.A., published by E. M. Aveling, London, 1898, reprinted Edinburgh, 1908, and published in a new edition by International Publishers, New York, 1935; German translation by E. Bernstein appeared in *Die Neue Zeit,* 1898, and a French translation by Charles Longuet was published in Paris, 1899.

1867

Das Kapital: Kritik der politischen Ökonomie, I.Bd., Buch I, Hamburg and New York, 1867. (Second edition published in Hamburg, 1872; third edition by Engels, in 1883; fourth edition, which incorporates Marx's own second thoughts and Engels's editorial labours, in 1890. It is this edition that is used for most modern editions of the work.) Until 1966 the text of the original (1867) first chapter was available only in the first edition and in a Japanese reprint. It is now included in a four-volume paperback edition of selections edited by Iring Fetscher, published by Fischer Verlag, Frankfurt a.M., 1966; an important French translation by J. Roy, supervised by Marx himself, appeared in Paris, 1872–1875; Russian translation by H. Lopatin and N. Danielson, St Petersburg, 1872; Italian translation based on the French of J. Roy, in 1886. An English translation, *Capital: a Critical Analysis of Capitalist Production,* by Samuel Moore and Edward Aveling, two volumes, London, 1887, and another, translated from the fourth German edition by E. and C. Paul, London, 1928.

1867–1887

Drafts of later volumes of *Capital,* first published posthumously, and variants of first volume, extant but not yet published. The later volumes appeared as follows: 2.*Bd.,* *Buch II,* edited by Engels, Hamburg, 1885; a second, much revised and shortened edition appeared 1893, which was translated into English as *Capital Vol. II: The Process of Circulation of Capital* by E. Untermann, Chicago, 1907; revised English translation appeared in 1957; a Russian translation by N. Danielson was published 1885, and a French translation by J. Borchardt and H. Vanderrydt, in Paris, 1900. Popular German editions by K. Kautsky, Berlin, 1926, and by the Marx-Engels-Lenin Institute, Moscow, 1933. 3.*Bd., Buch III,* edited by Engels, Hamburg, 1894; popular editions by Kautsky, Berlin, 1926, and the Marx-Engels-Lenin Institute, Zurich, 1933; translated as *Capital Vol. III: The Process of Capitalist Production as a Whole* by E. Untermann, Chicago, 1907; revised English translation in 1959; French translation by J. Borchardt and H. Vanderrydt was published Paris, 1901–1902, and another by J. Molitor, Paris, 1928–1929, *Theorien über den Mehrwert* ... Aus dem nachgelassenen Manuskript 'Zur Kritik der politischen Ökonomie' ... hrsg. von Karl Kautsky, Stuttgart, 1905–1910, 3 Bde. (Engels had planned to publish this as the fourth volume of *Capital*); French translation in eight volumes by J. Molitor, Paris, 1924–1925; English translation of the first volume of this, *A History of Economic Theories,* by T. McCarthy, New York, 1952. *Theories of Surplus Value: a selection from* ... *Theorien über den Mehrwert* ... Translated by G. A. Bonner and E. Burns, published London, 1951.

1867

Aufruf des Generalraths der Internationalen Arbeiterassoziation an die Sektionen ..., of which Marx was a signatory and certainly a coauthor, appeared in *Der Vor-*

bote, Geneva, 8 August 1867, and in *La Tribune du Peuple*, 31 August 1867.

'Report to the General Council of the International Working Men's Association, Lausaune, 1867', of which Marx was a signatory, was published in the *Procès-verbaux du Congrès de Lausanne*, Lausanne, 1867.

1868

'Report of the General Council to the Third Congress of the I.W.M.A.', Brussels, 1868, was edited by Marx and was adopted as the official report. Published in *The Times*, 9 September 1868; in *Le Peuple Belge* (in French), 6 September 1868; and in *Der Vorbote* (in German), 9 September 1868.

1869

'Report to the Fourth Annual Congress of the I.W.M.A.', Basel, 1869, was again edited by Marx, and published in London in 1869. A French translation appeared in *Compte rendu du IVe Congrès international* ..., Brussels, 1869, and a German translation in *Der Vorbote*, Geneva, 1869, and in *Demokratisches Wochenblatt*, 1869. An Italian translation appeared in *Eguaglianza*, 1869.

1870–1871

The Civil War in France: the work generally known by this title includes the following addresses of the I.W.M.A.:
(i) *The General Council of the I.W.M.A. on the War* (or First Address of the General Council of the I.W.M.A. on the Franco-Prussian War), London, 1870. An incomplete German translation appeared in *Volksstaat*, Leipzig, 1870, and another translation in *Der Vorbote*, Geneva, 1870. A French version was published in O. Testut: *L'Internationale et le jacobinisme au ban de l'Europe*, Paris, 1872.
(ii) *Second Address of the General Council of the I.W.M.A. on the Franco-Prussian War*, London, 1870.
(iii) *Address of the General Council of the I.W.M.A. on the Civil War in France, 1871*, London, 1871. This pamphlet went through three editions in as many months. A

German translation by Engels appeared in *Volksstaat*, Leipzig, July 1871. A French translation was published in *L'Internationale*, Brussels, 1871, and in pamphlet form in Brussels in 1872. A new French translation by J. Longuet, entitled *La Commune de Paris* appeared in Paris, 1901. Engels wrote a long introduction for the third German edition, Berlin, 1891, which is usually included in editions of *The Civil War in France;* two important preliminary drafts by Marx of the third *Address* are not always included; the most convenient English-language edition containing these drafts is that published by the Foreign Languages Press in Peking, 1966, and frequently reprinted.

1875

'Randglossen zum Programm der deutschen Arbeiterpartei', written in May 1875, but first published by Engels in *Die Neue Zeit*, Stuttgart, 1891; French translation was published in Paris in 1894, and another translation by G. Platon, in Paris in 1901; German edition *Zur Kritik des sozialdemokratischen Programms von Gotha*, by K. Kreibich, Reichenberg, 1920, and another, edited by K. Korsch, Berlin, in 1922; translated by E. and C. Paul, *The Socialist Programme*, Glasgow, in 1919, another translation, called *Critique of the Gotha Programme* (the name by which it is usually known in English), London, 1933, and in an edition by C. Palme Dutt in 1936.

1877

'Aus der "Kritischen Geschichte" '. This became chapter 10 of Engels's book *Anti-Dühring*, and appeared in *Vorwärts*, Leipzig, 1877. The first complete edition of Engels's work was published Leipzig, 1878.

1880

'Enquête ouvrière'. Original published in *Revue Socialiste*, Saint-Cloud, April 1880. A full translation is included in Bottomore and Rubel, 1956.

I. Marx the Man: Documents, Letters, and Reminiscences

EDITOR'S NOTE

Karl Marx was a strong, stubborn, outstandingly gifted and intellectually ambitious man, who could, at his worst, be childish, petty, morose, treacherous, and vain. He was endowed, as Isaiah Berlin has put it, 'with a powerful, active, concrete, unsentimental mind, an acute sense of injustice and exceptionally little sensibility'. To his father and to many of those who knew him, he seemed a man with more brains and brilliance than heart, driven by a Faustian demon and not by a divine compassion. Pride, a fierce love of independence, intellectual arrogance, and a firm conviction of moral superiority were his outstanding character traits: he was less than generous to those from whom he learnt and bitterly jealous of those who achieved political success or intellectual standing in threatened competition to his own. He hated the stupidity and complacency of the bourgeoisie, the moral hypocrisy that concealed its worship of Mammon, with a bitter, personal hate. He was no less bitter in his contempt for the rhetoric and emotionalism of his fellow intellectuals, for their radical posturing, their empty verbalizing, their lack of practical sense and theoretical incisiveness.

'Great letters', says Philip Rieff in his *Freud: The Mind of the Moralist*, 'are written by great characters; they must be intensely personal and revealing, yet make us feel that, however familiarly we lean across the shoulder of the writer, we are in the presence of greatness. . . . Only great characters can survive this test of intimacy. Marx, for example, does not survive; his letters do not move us to respect him more as we get to know him better'. There is an obvious sense in which this is true: Marx's letters are often embarrassing in their pettiness, their malice, their self-justification and petulance. They are the letters of a Prometheus whose rock has turned out to be a crowded flat in Soho, with wife, children, doctors' bills, landlords threatening eviction, and butchers refusing further credit. They are the letters of a man who spent much of his life and energy in the squabbles of small émigré sects—of a man contemptuous of most of his allies and adversaries, yet suspicious, touchy, and always ready to sniff a conspiracy against him. But they also show a mind constantly at work—reading, thinking, seeking information over an extraordinary range of issues in contemporary politics, science, and intellectual learning.

Marx, then, was a proud man, much concerned with his sense of dignity, impatient of fools, displaying all the quarrelsomeness and willingness to exaggerate minor differences that characterize the member of a sect or faction. Intellectually, he was an immensely ambitious man. Personally, some found him gentle, warm-hearted, and good-natured. He was patient, it is said, with children, with his own family, and with workers who had come seeking instruction. Most people, nevertheless, found the man himself impressive—and intolerable.

In the documents, letters, and reminiscences that follow, I have endeavoured to bring out Marx's style of life and some of his main character traits, and to indicate how differently various people reacted to him.

[BIRTH CERTIFICATE]

~~~~~~~~~~~~~~~~~~~~~~~~~~~~~~~~~~~~

NO. 231 OF THE REGISTRY OF BIRTHS

In the year eighteen hundred and eighteen on the seventh day of the month of May at four o'clock in the afternoon there appeared before me, the Registrar of Civil Status of the Burgomaster's Office of Trier, Mr Heinrich Marx, resident of Trier, thirty-seven years of age, an Advocate in the Higher Court of Appeal, and brought before me a child of the male sex and declared that the same child had been born in Trier on the fifth day of May at two o'clock in the morning, being the issue of Mr Heinrich Marx, Advocate, resident in Trier, and his wife, Henriette Presborck, and that these latter wished to name their child Carl. After the child had been brought before me and the above declaration had been made in the presence of two witnesses, namely of Mr Karl Petrasch, thirty-two years of age, senior civil servant, resident in Trier, and Mathias Kropp, twenty years of age, employee, resident in Trier, I recorded these events in this document, in two original copies, doing so in the presence of the person bringing the child before me and of the witnesses, and after reading it to them, I signed it together with the person presenting the child and the witnesses.

This took place at Trier on the day, month and year indicated above.

(Signatures) Karl Petrasch
Mathias Kropp
Heinrich Marx
E. Grach

MEGA I, l-ii, l63.
Original, Standesamt der Stadt Trier.

1835

CERTIFICATE OF MATRICULATION OF A PUPIL AT THE HIGH SCHOOL AT TRIER

KARL MARX

of Trier, 17 *years old*, Lutheran *by religion, son of the* Advocate and Solicitor Herr Justizrat Marx *of* Trier, *spent 5 years in the High School at Trier and 2 years in the senior class*

I. Conduct toward his teachers and fellow pupils was good

II. Abilities and Application. He has good abilities; he showed very satisfactory application in classical languages, in German and in history, satisfactory application in mathematics and only some application in French

III. Knowledge and Accomplishments

    1. Languages:

      (a) *In German* his grammatical knowledge, as well as his composition, very good

      (b) *In Latin* he translates and explicates at sight the easier passages in the classical texts read in High School accurately and fluently; after appropriate preparation or with some aid he can often also translate the more difficult passages, especially those where the difficulty lies in the subject-matter and the train of thought rather than in peculiarities of language. His composition, in terms of content, shows richness of thought and an attempt to go seriously into the subject-matter, but is often overloaded with the irrelevant; so far as language expression is concerned, he evinces considerable practice and a striving toward genuine Latinity, although he does make grammatical mistakes. In the Latin oral he showed reasonably satisfactory fluency.

(c) *In Greek,* so far as the classical texts read in High School are concerned, he shows knowledge and abilities similar to those that he displays in Latin

(d) *In French* his grammatical knowledge is fairly good; with help he can read difficult passages and he has some fluency in oral expression

(e) *In Hebrew*

2. *Sciences*

(a) *Religion.* His knowledge of Christian theology and ethics is reasonably clear and well-founded; he also knows something of the history of the Christian Church

(b) *Mathematics.* In mathematics his knowledge is good

(c) *In History and Geography* he is in general reasonably proficient

(d) *Physics (and the Natural Sciences).* In physics his knowledge is mediocre

(e) (*Philosophical Propaedeutics*)

3. *Accomplishments*

(a) (Drawing)

(b) (Singing)

The undersigned members of the Royal Examining Commission, in view of the fact that he is now leaving this High School in order to study jurisprudence, *issue to him this Certificate of Matriculation and give him permission to leave,* expressing the hope that he will fulfil the favourable expectations aroused by his abilities.

Trier 24 September 1835

Royal Examining Commission

Brüggemann, Royal Commissioner.

Wyttenbach, Headmaster.

Loers.

Hamacher.

Schwendler.   Küpper.

Steininger.   Schneemann.

MEGA I, 1-ii, 182-84.

1836

[MARX'S RECORD OF STUDIES ISSUED BY THE UNIVERSITY OF BONN]

We the Rector and Senate of the Royal Prussian Rhenish Friedrich-Wilhelm University at Bonn certify by means of this Record of Studies, that Mr Carl Heinrich Marx, born at Trier, son of the Justizrat Marx of the same city, who was prepared for academic studies at the High School in Trier, was accepted by us as a matriculated student on the basis of the Certificate of Matriculation issued by the said High School on 15 October 1835 and that he has since then been a student in this University occupying himself with juridical sciences.

During his period at this University, as the reports below indicate, he attended the following lectures:

I. In the Winter Semester 1835–36

1. Encyclopaedia of the Legal Sciences, by Prof. Puggé, very industriously and attentively.
2. The Institutes [of Justinian], by Prof. Böcking, very industriously and with constant attention.
3. History of Roman Law, by Prof. Walter, ditto.
4. Mythology of the Greeks and Romans, by Prof. Welcker, with exemplary industry and attention.
5. Homeric Problems, by Prof. v. Schlegel, industriously and attentively.
6. Modern Art History, by Prof. d'Alton, industriously and attentively.

II. In the Summer Semester 1836

7. The History of German Law, by Prof. Walter, industriously.
8. The Elegies of Propertius, by Prof. v. Schlegel, industriously and attentively.
9. European Legal Systems and
10. Natural Law, by Prof. Puggé. Because of the sud-

den death of Prof. Puggé on 5 August no comment can be made on the latter two.

So far as his conduct is concerned, it should be noted that he was sentenced to one day's imprisonment for drunkenness and causing a disturbance at night; in moral and economic connections nothing else discreditable to him is known. Subsequently a complaint was lodged against him, claiming that he carried forbidden weapons in Cologne. The investigation is still under way.

He is not suspected of taking part in illegal organisations amongst students.

In witness whereof, this Record has been prepared under the Seal of the University and signed by the present Rector and by the present Deans of the Faculties of Law and of Philosophy with their own hand.

Bonn, 22 August 1836.

The Rector

Freytag.

The Dean of the Faculty of Law
Walter.

The University Judge

v. Salomon.

The Dean of the Faculty of Philosophy
Loebell.

Oppenhoff.
U.S.

Seen by the Extraordinary Governmental Representative and Curator *v. Rehfues.*

MEGA I, 1-ii, 194-95.

1836

[FROM MARX'S SISTER SOPHIE]

Trier, 28 December 1836

[Added to a letter from Heinrich]

Your last letter, dear Karl, brought forth bitter tears; how could you think that I would forget to give you news of your Jenny? I dream and think only of the two of you. Jenny loves you; if she is worried by the difference in your years, this is only because of her parents. She will now attempt gradually to prepare them; later write to them yourself; they do, after all, think highly of you. Jenny visits us frequently. She came to our place yesterday and wept tears of joy and pain on receiving your poems. Our parents and our sisters love her very much, the latter above all measure; she is never allowed to leave our home before ten o'clock at night—how do you like that? Adieu, dear, good Karl, my most deep-felt wishes for the success of your most deep-felt wish.

MEGA, I, 1-ii, 199.

1837

[HEINRICH MARX TO HIS SON]

Trier, 2 March 1837

... My heart often leaps at the thought of you and your future. Yet at times I cannot rid myself of sadder, more fearful ideas and intimations, when I suddenly have the thought: does your heart correspond to your head, to your talents? Does it have room for the softer feelings of this world, which provide such essential comfort for the man of feeling in this vale of woe? Your soul is obviously animated and ruled by a demon not given to all men; is this demon a heavenly or a Faustian one? Will you ever—and this is the doubt that causes me the most pain—be receptive to true human happiness—domestic happiness? Will you ever . . . be able to spread happiness to your immediate surroundings? . . .

> Your loving father
> Marx.

> MEGA I, 1-ii, 202-05.

1837

[KARL MARX TO HIS FATHER]

Berlin, 10 November [1837]

Dear Father,

There are moments in life which manifest themselves as boundary posts, marking the close of a period, but at the same time definitely pointing in a new direction.

At such a moment of transition, we feel compelled to survey the past and present with the eagle eye of thought and so to come to a consciousness of our actual position. . . .

When I left you, a new world had opened before me, the world of love, at first a love full of longing and void of hope. Even the journey to Berlin . . . depressed me profoundly, for the rocks I saw were no rougher, no harsher, than the sensation of my soul; the large cities no more lively than my blood; the tables in the hostelries no more overladen, the food no more indigestible, than the contents of my imagination; in short, art was not as beautiful as Jenny.

Having arrived in Berlin, I broke all existing ties, made few and reluctant visits, and sought to immerse myself in learned studies and art.

In my then state of mind, lyrical poetry inevitably became my first concern, at any rate the most agreeable and deeply felt concern; but my position and my whole previous development made this poetry purely idealistic. A beyond as remote as my love became my heaven, my art. Everything real grew misty, and everything misty was without boundaries. Onslaughts on the present, broad and shapeless feelings, nothing natural, everything constructed out of the blue, everything the precise opposite of what is and what ought to be, rhetorical reflections in place of poetic thought—but perhaps also a certain warmth of sentiment and a struggle for movement: this is what characterises all the poems in the first three volumes I sent to Jenny. . . .

But poetry could and should only be an avocation. I had to study jurisprudence and above all I felt the urge to wrestle with philosophy. Both became closely intertwined, so that I read Heineccius, Thibaut and the sources schoolboy fashion, quite uncritically. Thus, I translated for instance the first two books of the pandects into German, attempting to work out a philosophy of law through a study of law. I prefixed some metaphysical propositions to serve as an introduction and developed this ill-starred work up to the topic of public law, making a work of nearly three hundred pages.

In the course of this work the conflict between what is and what ought to be emerged in a very disturbing fashion. This conflict, peculiar to idealism, initially gave rise to the following hopelessly inadequate classifications. First came what I gratuitously called the metaphysics of law, that is, principles, reflections, fundamental concepts—all severed from any actual law and from any actual forms of law, just as they are in the writing of Fichte, except that my treatment was more modern and less substantial. Here, the unscientific form of mathematical dogmatism—where the subject wanders around the topic, arguing hither and thither, while the topic itself never emerges as something rich in content, something alive—

became from the very start a hindrance to comprehending the truth.

The nature of the triangle permits the mathematician to treat it as, and to demonstrate that it is, a pure idea in space, developing into nothing further. Only when the triangle is put next to something else does it assume various positions; only when such two shapes are compared does the comparison endow the triangle with various relational properties and truths. In contrast with this, when we express concretely the living world of thought, that of law, the state, nature, philosophy as a whole, we must observe the object in its development, we cannot inject arbitrary classifications. The rationale of the thing itself must appear before us with all its contradictions and find an internal unity.

As the second part of my manuscript there follows the philosophy of law, that is, as I then conceived it to be, the study of the development of ideas in positive Roman law, as if the development of ideas in positive law (I do not mean in their purely finite determinations) could be anything but the structure of the concept of law, which I was supposed to treat in the first part.

On top of this, I had divided this part into formal doctrine of law and material doctrine of law. The former was to describe the pure form of the system, its order and internal connection, its classification and scope. The latter, on the other hand, was to describe its content, the condensation of the form into content. This was an error that I shared with Herr von Savigny, as I discovered later when reading his scholarly work on possession, but while he speaks of formal determination of concepts as 'finding the place which this or that doctrine occupies in the (posited) Roman system' and of material concepts as the doctrine 'of the positive which the Romans connect with a concept established in this way' I understood by form the necessary architectonic of the formulations of the concept and by matter the necessary quality of these formulations.

My mistake lay in believing that one could and had to develop the one apart from the other, with the result that I achieved no genuine form, but only a desk with a number of drawers that I subsequently littered with sand.

After all, the concept is that which mediates between form and content. In a philosophical discussion of law, therefore, the one must arise out of the other because form cannot be anything but the continuation of content. . . .

On coming to the end of the discussion of material private law, I saw the fallacy of the whole which in its fundamental structure borders on the Kantian, though it totally departs from Kant in matters of execution. It again became clear to me that I could not get any further without philosophy. Thus I was again able, with good conscience, to throw myself into the arms of philosophy and I wrote a new fundamental metaphysical system. On coming to the end, I again had to recognise its futility and the futility of all my previous endeavours.

In the course of this work, I had acquired the habit of making excerpts from all the books I was reading, from Lessing's *Laocoön*, Solger's *Erwin*, Winckelmann's *History of Art*, Luden's *German History*. In the process, I scribbled down some reflections. At the same time I translated Tacitus's *Germania*, Ovid's *Tristium libri*. Privately, that is with the aid of grammar books, I began to study English and Italian, but there I have not yet achieved anything. I read Klein's book on criminal law and his *Annals*, and a lot of the most recent literature, but the latter only by the way.

At the end of the semester, I once more sought out the dance of the Muses and the music of the Satyrs. In the last notebook that I sent you, idealism manifests itself in forced humour (Scorpio and Felix), in an unsuccessful, fantastic drama (Oulanem), until it finally takes a completely different direction and changes into purely formal art, for the most part without any inspiring objects and without any surge of ideas.

These last poems, however, are the only ones in which the realm of true poetry suddenly flashed before me like a distant fairy palace, as if by the wave of a magician's wand—the suddenness was shattering at the beginning— and all my creations collapsed into nothing.

These various occupations kept me awake many a night during the first semester; I went through many struggles and experienced much excitement from within and from without. Yet I found in the end that my mind had not been greatly enriched while I had thus been neglecting nature, art, and the world and alienating my friends. My body also reached this conclusion: a physician advised a stay in the country and for the first time I crossed the whole large city and went through the gate to Stralow. . . .

A curtain had fallen, my holy of holies had been shattered and new gods had to be found.

Setting out from idealism—which, by the way, I compared and nourished with that of Kant and Fichte—I came to the point of seeking the Idea in the real itself. If the gods had formerly dwelt above the world, they had now become its centre.

I had read fragments of Hegelian philosophy and had found its grotesque craggy melody uncongenial. But I wished to dive into the sea once more, now with the particular intention of finding our intellectual nature to be just as necessary, concrete, and firmly established as our physical. . . .

I wrote a dialogue of about twenty-four pages, entitled 'Cleanthes, or the Starting Point and the Necessary Progress of Philosophy'. Here I reunited, to some extent, art and science, which had wholly diverged. Now, an energetic wanderer, I set to the work itself, a philosophical-dialectical discussion of the godhead as a concept per se, as religion, as nature, and as history. My final sentence was the beginning of the Hegelian system, and this task—in preparation for which I had to some extent made myself acquainted with natural science, Schelling and history, and which (since it was to be a new logic) is written in so confused a manner and caused me so many headaches, that I can scarcely make head or tail of it—this darling child of mine, nurtured in moonlight, bears me like a false siren into the clutches of the enemy.

My vexation was such that for several days I was quite unable to think. Like a lunatic I ran around in the garden by the dirty waters of the Spree. . . .

Soon thereafter I immersed myself in purely positive studies—Savigny's study of possession, Feuerbach's and Grolmann's works on criminal law, Cramer's *De verborum significatione*, Wenning-Ingenheim's system of the pandects and Mühlenbruch's *Doctrina Pandectarum* (which I am still reading), and finally some of Lauterbach's works, books on civil law and especially on ecclesiastical law... Then I translated part of Aristotle's *Rhetoric* and read the *De dignitate et augmentis scientiarum* of the famous Bacon of Verulam. I then occupied myself intensively with Reimarus, whose work on the mechanical instincts of animals I followed through with delight. Next I turned to German law, concerning myself mainly with the capitularies of the Frankish kings and the letters of the Popes to them.

Upset by Jenny's illness and the futility of my lost labours, consumed by anger at having to make an idol of a view I detest, I fell sick. . . . Recovered, I burned all my poems, my sketches, four novellas, etc., in the mad belief that I could refrain from writing things of that kind. So far, I must admit there is no evidence to the contrary.

While I was ill, I worked through Hegel from beginning to end and through most of his disciples as well. In consequence of several meetings with friends in Stralow, I became a member of a Doctors' Club to which some lecturers and my most intimate friend in Berlin, Dr Rutenberg, belong. Here, in the course of argument, one heard many conflicting opinions and I became more and more attached to the current world philosophy from which I had thought to escape. . . .

Concerning the question of a fiscal career, dear father, I have recently made the acquaintance of an assistant judge, Schmidthänner, who advises me to enter upon the first stage of a judicial career after passing the third of my law examinations. This rather appeals to me, since I really prefer jurisprudence to any study of administration. This gentleman told me that he and many others had, from the Münster Provincial Court of Appeal, attained the position of assistant judge in three years. This, he says, is not diffi-cult—provided, of course, that one works hard—since in Münster the steps for promotion are not as rigidly marked out as they are in Berlin and elsewhere. If, as assistant judge, one attains the doctorate, there are excellent chances of quick appointment as professor extraordi-nary. . . .

I remain always your loving son,
Karl.

MEGA I, 1-ii, 213–21.

1837

[HEINRICH MARX TO HIS SON]

Trier, 9 December 1837

Dear Karl,

. . . My son, as though we were made of gold, spends in one year almost 700 taler, contrary to all dissuasion, con-trary to all custom, while the richest do not even spend 500. And why? I admit, in justice, that my son is no high-liver, no spendthrift. But how can a man who finds it nec-essary to invent a new system every eight or fourteen days and who has to tear up all the work he has achieved with great labour, how can such a son, I ask, bother himself with trivialities? How can he subject himself to a petty ordered existence? Everybody has his hand in my son's pocket? Everybody makes use of him ... and it is easy to pen yet another order to pay. Let petty people like G. R. and Evers bother about these things. They are common fellows....

> Your father
> Marx.

> MEGA I, 1-ii, 223–28.

1840

[BRUNO BAUER TO MARX]

Bonn, 25 July 1840

The letter, dear Marx, which you gave me for Marcus was so bad that I could not possibly pass it on. You can write in roughly that fashion to your washerwoman but not to a publisher, whom you have first to win to your side. I therefore went to visit him, to discuss the proposal with him personally, or rather, since I knew a priori that he will not be in the least interested, so as to carry out your commission. Marcus, who has never heard of you, who does not know me personally, who does not much engage in ventures and then only in ventures with very well known authors, was not in the least interested. . . .

There is no bookseller here that I know better. I cannot take the proposal to my new publisher, since I must first wait to see how my own book succeeds with him. . . .

> Your
> B. Bauer.

> MEGA I, 1-ii, 244–45.

1841

[MARX'S RECORD OF STUDIES IN THE UNIVERSITY OF BERLIN]

We the Rector and the Senate
of the Royal Friedrich Wilhelms University
in Berlin

let it be known by means of this Record of Studies, that Mr Carl Heinrich Marx, born at Trier, son of the late Advocate Marx, who has already attained his majority, and who was prepared for academic studies in the High School at Trier, was accepted as a matriculated student in this University on the basis of his Certificate of Matriculation from the above-mentioned High School and his Record of Studies from the University of Bonn dated 22 October 1836 and that he has since then until the end of the Winter Semester 1840/41 attended the University as a student and occupied himself with juridical sciences.

During his period in this University, he attended the lectures shown below in the manner indicated:

I. In the Winter Semester 1836/7
1. Pandects, with Prof. v. Savigny, industriously,
2. Criminal Law, with Prof. Gans, especially industriously,
3. Anthropology, with Prof. Steffens, industriously.

II. In the Summer Semester 1837
1. Ecclesiastical Law
2. Common German Civil Procedure,   with Prof. Helffter, industriously.
3. Prussian Civil Procedure

III. In the Winter Semester 1837/38
1. Criminal Procedure, with Prof. Helffter, industriously.

IV. In the Summer Semester 1838

1. Logic, with Prof. Gabler, with exemplary industry.
2. General Geography, with Prof. Ritter, registered.
3. The Prussian Civil Code, with Prof. Gans, with excellent industry.

V. In the Winter Semester 1838/9

1. Succession, with Prof. Rudorff, industriously.

VI. In the Summer Semester 1839

1. Isaiah, with Lecturer Bauer, attended.

VII and VIII. In the Winter Semester 1839/40 and the Summer Semester 1840
No courses.

IX. In the Winter Semester 1840/41

1. Euripides, with Dr. Geppert, industriously.

v. Medem
23.3.41.

So far as his conduct at this University is concerned, there has been nothing to his detriment in disciplinary matters, and in economic matters we have only to note that he has frequently been complained of regarding debts.

Hitherto he has not been accused of taking part in forbidden associations among students in this University.

In witness whereof this Record has been prepared under the Seal of the University and signed by the current Rector and the Judge, as well as by the current Deans of the Faculties of Law and of Philosophy in their own hands.

Berlin, the 30th March 1841
Lichtenstein. Krause. Lancizolle. Zumpt.
Seen by the acting Representatives of the Royal Government.

Lichtenstein. Krause.

MEGA I, 1-ii, 247–48.

1841

[LETTER OF PROFESSOR C. F. BACHMANN, DEAN OF THE FACULTY OF PHILOSOPHY IN THE UNIVERSITY OF JENA, PRESENTING MARX'S DOCTORAL THESIS TO THE FACULTY FOR CONSIDERATION]

Senior Venerande,
Assessores Gravissimi,

I herewith present to you a very worthy candidate, Mr Carl Heinrich Marx of Trier, who has forwarded (1) an application; (2) two University Certificates relating to his academic studies in Bonn and Berlin: the disciplinary lapses noted in these we may ignore; (3) an application in Latin, a curriculum vitae and a dissertation: 'Concerning the Difference Between the Democritean and the Epicurean Philosophy of Nature', together with a declaration of authorship in Latin; (4) twelve Friedrichs d'or, the excess contained therein to be returned to the candidate. The dissertation shows as much spirit and incisiveness as scholarship, wherefore I consider the candidate to be especially deserving. Since the candidate's German letter indicates that he seeks only the degree of Doctor, we may take it to be an error, arising from lack of acquaintance with the Statutes of the Faculty, that the candidate in his Latin letter speaks of the degree of Master. He probably believed that the two go together. I am quite convinced that he only needs an explanation of this point to be satisfied.

Seeking from you your wise decision

I remain, with great respect
Dr Carl Friedrich Bachmann
Dean

Jena
13 April 1841
Ordinis philosophorum Decane maxime spectabilis

Luden F. Hand. E. Reinhold. Döbereiner.
J. F. Fries. Goettling. Schulze.

MEGA I, 1-ii, 254–55.

1841

[MOSES HESS ON KARL MARX]

Cologne, 2 September 1841

Dear Auerbach,

... You will be glad to meet here a man who is now also one of our friends, even though he lives in Bonn, where he is shortly to become a lecturer ... He is a phenomenon that has made an enormous impression on me, even though I am active in the same field. You can prepare yourself to meet the greatest, perhaps the only real, philosopher now living. Soon, when he makes his public *debut* (both as a writer and as an academic), he will draw the eyes of all of Germany upon himself. He has gone, in the line of his thinking as well as in his philosophical education, not only beyond Strauss, but even beyond Feuerbach, which is saying not a little! If I could be in Bonn when he lectures on logic, I should be his most attentive listener. ...

Dr Marx—that is the name of my idol—is still a very young man (about 24 years old at most), who will give mediaeval religion and politics their death blow. He combines with the deepest philosophical earnestness the most biting wit. Imagine Rousseau, Voltaire, Holbach, Lessing, Heine and Hegel united in one person, I say *united*, not thrown together—and you have Dr Marx.

Moses Hess to Berthold Auerbach, First published in *Grünberg's Archiv*, Vol. 10, 1922, pp. 411–12; MEGA I, 1-ii, 260–61.

Nine years later, in a letter to Alexander Herzen, Moses Hess added:

What a pity, what a terrible pity, that the vanity of this man, unquestionably the ablest man in our party, is not satisfied with the respect which he quite justifiably receives from all those who know his achievements and understand how to honor them, but that he should appear to demand a degree of personal submission that I, for one, will never condescend to give to another.

Moses Hess, *Briefwechsel*, The Hague, 1959, p. 256, cited in A. Künzli, *Karl Marx*, Vienna, 1966, p. 402.

1842

[MARX TO ARNOLD RUGE]

Trier, 9 July 1842

Dear Friend,

If events did not speak for me, I would give up every attempt to make an excuse. Naturally, I regard being a contributor to the *Anekdota* as a great honour, and only the most unpleasant external circumstances have prevented me from sending my contributions.

Since April until now I have not been able to work for more than four weeks at the most, and this not even uninterruptedly. I had to spend six weeks in Trier because of a new death; the remaining time was broken up and spoilt by the most repulsive family controversy. My family has put difficulties in my way which have exposed me at the moment to the most pressing circumstances, even though my family is very well off. I cannot possibly burden you with a recital of these private vulgarities; it is really fortunate that public vulgarities make it impossible for a man of character to become irritated over the private. . . .

Do you know any more about the so-called 'Free Ones'? The article in the *Königsberger* was at the very least undiplomatic. It is one thing to declare one's emancipation, which is to act according to one's conscience; it is another thing to yell oneself out in propaganda beforehand, which sounds like empty boastfulness and brings the Philistines onto one's head. . . .

Your Marx.

MEGA I, 1-ii, 277–78.

1843

[MARX TO ARNOLD RUGE]

Cologne, 13 March 1843

Dear Friend,

. . . I should like to tell you something about my private plans . . . I shall travel to Kreuznach and get married, and spend a month or more with the mother of my bride. . . .

I can assure you without any trace of romanticism, that I am head over heels and most earnestly in love. I have been engaged for more than seven years, and my bride has had to wage the bitterest fight on my behalf, a fight that has almost undermined her health, partly with her pietistic-aristocratic relatives, for whom the Lord in Heaven and the Lord in Berlin are equally objects of idolatry, and partly with my own family, in which a few clerics and other enemies of mine have made themselves at home. For years, therefore, I and my bride have lived through more unnecessary and bitter conflicts than many others who are three times as old as we are and constantly speak of their 'experience of life' . . .

Your Marx.

MEGA I, 1-ii, 306–8.

1843

[JENNY VON WESTPHALEN TO MARX]

Kreuznach, March 1843.

... I think you were never dearer or sweeter or closer to my heart; indeed, I was in a state of rapture each time you left and would have called you back again and again just to tell you once more how much, how very much I love you. But the last time was really your triumphal departure; I scarcely know how much I loved you in my heart of hearts, when I could no longer see you in the flesh and only your one true image stood so vividly before my soul in all its angelic mildness and goodness, its noble love and spiritual splendour. If only you were here now, my dear Karlchen, what capacity for joy you would find in your brave little wife; however wicked a purpose, whatever *evil* intentions you might display, I would still not take any retaliatory measures; I would patiently lay down my head as a sacrifice to my naughty boy.... Do you still remember our talks at twilight, how we used to wave and wave to one another, our hours of rest? Dear heart, how good, how dear, how indulgent, how happy you were! ...

Jenny to Karl Marx, March 1843, in M. Müller, ed., *Familie Marx in Briefen*, Berlin, 1966, pp. 39–44.

1844

[ARNOLD RUGE TO LUDWIG FEUERBACH ON MARX]

His is a peculiar nature, very well suited to a learned man or an author, but totally useless for a journalist. He reads a great deal, he works with unusual intensity ..., but he does not complete anything, he is constantly breaking off and plunging anew into an endless sea of books ... If it were possible, Marx is even more excited and impressive when he has worked himself ill and has not been to bed for three or even four nights in succession.

Ruge, in a letter to Feuerbach of 15 May 1844, from A. Ruge, *Briefwechsel und Tagebuchblätter aus den Jahren 1825-1880*, Bd. 1, Berlin, 1886, as cited in A. Künzli: *Karl Marx*, p. 234.

1845

[BAKUNIN'S REMINISCENCE]

Marx was then much more advanced than I was, and he still remains today incomparably more advanced than I—as far as learning is concerned. I knew nothing at that time of political economy, I still had not got rid of metaphysical abstractions, and my Socialism was only instinctive. He, although younger than I, was already an Atheist, an instructed Materialist, and a conscious Socialist. It was precisely at this time that he elaborated the first bases of his system as it is today. We saw each other pretty often, for I greatly respected him for his learning and for his passionate and serious devotion—though it was always mingled with vanity—to the cause of the proletariat, and I eagerly sought his conversation, which was always instructive and witty, when it was not inspired by petty hate, which alas! was only too often the case. There was, however, never any frank intimacy between us—our temperaments did not permit. He called me a sentimental Idealist, and he was right; I called him vain, perfidious, and sly, and I was right too.

Bakunin, writing in 1871, as translated and cited in K. J. Kenafick, *Michael Bakunin and Karl Marx*, Melbourne, 1948, pp. 25-26.

1846

[P. ANNENKOV: KARL MARX IN 1846]

Marx was the sort of man who is packed with energy, force of character and unshakable conviction—a type highly remarkable in outward appearance as well. In spite of the thick black mane of hair on his head, his hairy hands and his crookedly buttoned frock coat, he gave the impression of a man who has the right and the power to command respect, no matter how he appears before you or what he does. All his movements were angular, but bold and confident; his manners directly violated all accepted social conventions. They were proud and somehow contemptuous, while his sharp, metallic voice matched remarkably well the radical judgments he was continually passing on men and things. Marx never spoke at all except to pronounce judgments which permitted no appeal, and he said everything in a painfully harsh tone. This tone expressed his firm conviction that he had a mission to rule men's minds, to legislate for them, to compel them to follow him. Before me stood the personification of a democratic dictator, as one might imagine it in a moment of fantasy.

From P. Annenkóv, 'A Wonderful Ten Years', in *Vestnik Evropy*, no. 4, April 1880, p. 497.

1847

[MARX TO ENGELS IN PARIS]

Brussels, 15 May 1847

Dear Engels,

You know that Vogler has been under arrest in Aachen since May. For the moment that makes the printing of the brochure which you sent impossible. I liked the first third of it very much. The other two thirds will in any case have to be altered. I shall write more about this next time.

I enclose a copy of your caricature. I sent it to the *Brüsseler Zeitung*.

So far as the truly revolting article by Grün or his accomplices in the *Triersche Zeitung* is concerned, it is now too late; originally you would have done well to publish a counter-explanation in two lines in the same dirty rag.

I can't come to London. My financial position does not allow it. We hope to be able to get Wolff there. That will be enough, since you will both be there.

Concerning money:

You remember that Hess owes me and my brother-in-law Edgar money in connection with the *Gesellschafts-spiegel*. I am therefore drawing a note on him here, payable at thirty days on sight. Bernays also owes me 150 francs since May of last year. He will also have a demand presented to him.

I ask you for the following:

1. Let me know the address of these two;
2. Tell both of them what I have said and tell both these idiots
3. that, if they don't believe that they will be able to pay the monies owing by 15 June, they should nevertheless not repudiate the notes. I shall then arrange to have them covered in Paris. Naturally you will tell the idiots this only if there is no other way of arranging matters.

I am in such financial troubles at the moment, that I have to take refuge in drawing notes on people and I don't intend to present the idiots with anything for nothing. If the two asses should only pretend that they will accept the notes let me know this immediately.

Since the matter is very urgent, I expect that you will

waste not a single day in putting everything in order and letting me know the outcome . . .

Yours,
Marx.

MEGA III, 1, 70–71.

1848

[CARL SCHURZ ON MARX IN COLOGNE, SUMMER 1848]

. . . Karl Marx . . . could not have been much more than thirty years old at that time, but he was already the recognized head of the advanced socialistic school. The somewhat thick-set man, with broad forehead, very black hair and beard and dark sparkling eyes, at once attracted general attention. He enjoyed the reputation of having acquired great learning, and as I knew very little of his discoveries and theories, I was all the more eager to gather words of wisdom from the lips of the famous man. This expectation was disappointed in a peculiar way. Marx's utterances were indeed full of meaning, logical and clear, but I have never seen a man whose bearing was so provoking and intolerable. To no opinion which differed from his own did he accord the honor of even condescending consideration. Everyone who contradicted him he treated with abject contempt; every argument that he did not like he answered either with biting scorn at the unfathomable ignorance that had prompted it, or with opprobrious aspersions upon the motives of him who had advanced it. I remember most distinctly the cutting disdain with which he pronounced the word "bourgeois"; and as a "bourgeois"—that is, as a detestable example of the deepest mental and moral degeneracy—he denounced everyone who dared to oppose his opinion. . . . it was very evident that not only had he not won any adherents, but he had repelled many who otherwise might have become his followers.

From Carl Schurz, *Reminiscences*, New York, 1913, Vol. 1, pp. 138–39.

1848

[MARX TO ENGELS IN BRUSSELS]

Paris, 16 March 1848

Dear Engels,

These days I have not a moment's time to write in greater detail. I confine myself to what is necessary.

Flocon is very much on your side.

The local journeymen all more or less hate you. . . .

So far as my things are concerned, take them with you as far as Valenciennes and let them be put in bond there. I shall get everything out. So far as the silver is concerned, it has already been stamped here in Paris. In Valenciennes you must however go to the man whose address I enclose. My wife, on the advice of Vogler, sent him the keys of the suitcases (which are in Brussels), but without any accompanying letter. You must get these keys from him, since otherwise everything will be broken open in the customs here.

So far as money is concerned, explain to Cassel that he should return the promissory note to you if he does not want to pay on it. Perhaps Baillut will then pay on it.

Let Gigot settle his accounts and at least pay the remainder.

So far as Breyer is concerned, you must go to him again

and explain to him how contemptible it would be if he made my bad luck an excuse not to pay. He must at least give you part of it. The revolution has not cost him a single sou.

Here the bourgeoisie is again becoming more horribly impudent and reactionary, but it will learn its mistake.

Bornstedt and Herwegh behave like blackguards. They have founded a black, red and gold society directed against us. The former is to be expelled from the League today.

Your

M.

MEGA III, 1, 96–97.

1848

[MARX TO ENGELS IN LAUSANNE]

Cologne, November 1848

Dear Engels,

I am really surprised that you have still not received any money from me. I sent you ages ago 61 Thaler, 11 in notes and 50 in promises to pay. They were sent to Geneva to the address you gave me. . . . I later sent 20 Thaler to Gigot and a further 50 to Dronke for you, out of my own pocket. Altogether about 130 Thaler. . . .

I am short of money. I brought 1850 Thaler with me from the journey; I received 1950 from the Poles: I needed 100 on the journey and I advanced 1000 Thaler to the newspaper and to you and other refugees. I have to pay 500 for the machine this week; 350 are left On top of that I have not received a single cent from the newspaper.

So far as your editorship is concerned, I (1) indicated

in the first number that the committee remains the same, (2) explained to the idiotic reactionary shareholders that they have the right to regard you as no longer belonging to the editorial personnel, but that I still have the right to pay contributors as much as I like, and that they will therefore not gain anything financially.

If I had any sense, I would not have advanced this large sum for the newspaper, since I have three or four suits relating to the newspaper hanging over my head, may be arrested any day and can then whistle for money. . . .

The thought that I might for one moment abandon you is pure fantasy. You remain my most intimate friend, as I hope I remain yours.

K. Marx

Your old man is a pig, to whom we shall write a swinish letter.

MEGA III, 1, 102–3.

1849

[MARX TO ENGELS IN LAUSANNE]

Paris, 23 August 1849

Dear Engels,

I have been banished to the Département of Morbihan, the Pontine Marshes of Brittany. You will understand that I cannot accept this veiled attempt to murder me. I am leaving France.

I cannot get a passport to Switzerland. I must therefore go to London and go tomorrow. Switzerland will in any case soon be hermetically sealed and all the mice would be trapped at one stroke.

Besides that, I have *positive* hopes of founding a German journal in London. I am *sure* of part of the money.

You must therefore immediately come to London . . . in London we will go into business together. . . .

Your

K.M.

MEGA III, 1, 113.

1850

[JENNY MARX TO JOSEPH WEYDEMEYER]

London, 20 May 1850

Dear Herr Weydemeyer,

. . . Circumstances, however, force me to take up my pen. I beg you to *send us as soon as possible any money that has been or will be received* from the *Revue.*[1] *We need it very, very much.* Certainly nobody can reproach us with ever having made much case of the sacrifices we have been making and bearing for years, the public has never or almost never been informed of our circumstances; my husband is very sensitive in such matters and he would rather sacrifice his last than resort to democratic begging like officially recognized "great men". But he could have expected active and energetic support for his *Revue* from his friends, particularly those in Cologne. He could have expected such support above all from those who knew his sacrifices for the *Neue Rheinische Zeitung*. But instead of that the business has been completely ruined by negligent and disorderly management, and one cannot say whether the delays of the bookseller or of the business managers or acquaintances in Cologne or the attitude of the Democrats as a whole were the most ruinous.

1. *Neue Rheinische Zeitung: Politisch-ökonomische Revue*, see Chronology, Jan.–June 1850.[E.K.]

Here my husband has been almost overwhelmed with the paltry worries of bourgeois life in so revolting a form that it has taken all his energy, all his calm, clear, quiet self-confidence to maintain him in that daily, hourly struggle. You know, dear Herr Weydemeyer, the sacrifices my husband has made for the paper. He put thousands in cash into it, he took over proprietorship, talked into it by worthy Democrats who would otherwise have had to answer for the the debts themselves, at a time when there was already little prospect of success. To save the paper's political honour and the civic honour of his Cologne acquaintances he took upon himself the whole responsibility; he sacrificed his printing-press, he sacrificed all income, and before he left he even borrowed 300 thaler to pay the rent of the newly hired premises and the outstanding salaries of the editors, etc. And he was turned out by force.

You know that we kept nothing for ourselves. I went to Frankfurt to pawn my silver—the last that we had—and I sold my furniture in Cologne because I was in danger of having my linen and everything sequestrated. At the beginning of the unhappy period of the counter-revolution my husband went to Paris and I followed him with my three children. Hardly had he settled down in Paris when he was expelled and even my children and I were refused permission to reside there any longer. I followed him again across the sea. A month later our fourth child was born. You have to know London and conditions here to understand what it means to have three children and give birth to a fourth. For rent alone we had to pay 42 thaler a month. We were able to cope with this out of money which we received, but our meagre resources were exhausted when the *Revue* was published. Contrary to the agreement, we were not paid, and later only in small sums, so that our situation here was desperate.

I shall describe to you just *one* day of that life, exactly as it was, and you will see that few fugitives, perhaps, have gone through anything like it. As wet-nurses here are too expensive I decided to feed my child myself in spite of continual terrible pains in the breast and back. But the poor little angel drank in so much anxiety and silent grief that he was always poorly and suffered horribly day and night. Since he came into the world he has not slept through a single night, but only two or three hours at the most. Recently he has had violent convulsions, too, and has been constantly at death's door. In his pain he sucked so hard that my breast was chafed and the skin cracked and the blood often poured into his trembling little mouth. I was sitting with him like that one day when our landlady came in. We had paid her more than 250 thaler during the winter and had an agreement to give the money in the future not to her but to her landlord, who had a bailiff's warrant against her. She denied the agreement and demanded five pounds that we still owed her. As we did not have the money at the time (Naut's letter came too late) two bailiffs came and sequestrated all my few possessions—beds, linen, clothes—everything, even my poor child's cradle and the better toys of my daughters, who stood there weeping bitterly. They threatened to take everything away in two hours. I would then have had to lie on the bare floor with my freezing children and my painful breast. Our friend Schramm hurried to town to get help for us. He got into a cab, but the horses bolted, he was thrown out and was brought bleeding back to the house, where I sat crying with my poor shivering children.

We had to leave the house the next day. It was cold, rainy and dull. My husband looked for accommodation for us. When he mentioned the four children nobody would take us in. Finally a friend helped us, we paid our rent and I hastily sold all my beds to pay the chemist, the baker, the butcher and the milkman who, alarmed by the report of the sequestration, suddenly besieged me with their bills. The beds which we had sold were taken out and put on a cart—but then what happened? It was well after sunset; we were contravening English law! The landlord pushed his way in with constables, maintaining that there might be some of his belongings among the things, and that we wanted to make away abroad. In less than five minutes there were two or three hundred persons loitering around our door—the whole Chelsea mob. The beds were brought in again—they could not be delivered to the buyer until after sunrise next day. When we had sold all our possessions we were in a position to pay what we owed to the last farthing. I went with my little darlings to the two small rooms we are now occupying in the German Hotel, 1 Leicester St., Leicester Square. There for £5½ a week we were given a human reception.

Forgive me, dear friend, for being so long and wordy in describing a single day of our life here. It is presumptuous, I know, but my heart is full to overflowing this evening, and I must at least once pour it out to one of our oldest, best and truest friends. Do not think that these paltry worries have bowed me down: I know only too well that our struggle is not an isolated one and that I, in particular, am one of the chosen, happy, favoured ones, for my dear husband, the prop of my life, is still at my side. What really tortures my very soul and makes my heart bleed is that he had to suffer so much from paltry things, that so little could be done to help him, and that he who willingly and gladly helped so many others was so helpless himself. But do not think, dear Herr Weydemeyer, that we make demands on anybody; if we *receive advances from anybody*, my husband is *still in a position to repay it from his possessions*. The only thing that my husband could have asked of those to whom he gave his ideas, his encouragement and his support was to show more energy in business and more support for his *Revue*. I am proud and bold to make that assertion. That little was his due. Nor do I know whether my husband has not with perfect right, earned for his labours ten silver groschen [about 3 thaler].

I do not think that was unfair to anybody. That is what grieves me. But my husband is of a different opinion. Never, not even in the most frightful moments, has he lost his confidence in the future or even his high spirits, and he was satisfied when he saw me cheerful and our loving children cuddling close to their dear mother. He does not know, dear Herr Weydemeyer, that I have written to you in such detail about our situation. That is why I ask you not to refer to these lines. All he knows is that I have asked you in his name to hasten as much as you can the collection and sending of our money ...

Die Neue Zeit, Vol. 2, 1906–7, translated from *Mohr und General,* Berlin, 1970, pp. 237–44.

1850
[GUSTAV TECHOW TO A FRIEND]

First we drank port, then claret which is red Bordeaux, then champagne. After the red wine Marx was completely drunk. ... In spite of his drunkenness Marx dominated the conversation up to the last moment.

The impression he made on me was that of someone possessing an unusual intellectual superiority, and he was obviously a man of outstanding personality. If his heart had matched his intellect, and if he had possessed as much love as hate, I would have gone through fire for him, even though at the end he expressed his complete and open contempt for me, and though he had earlier already indicated his contempt in passing. He was the first and only one among us whom I would trust to lead, for he was a man who never lost himself in small matters while dealing with great events.

In view of our aims, it is nevertheless a pity that this man with his fine intellect lacks all nobility of soul. I am convinced that a most dangerous personal ambition has eaten away all the good in him. He laughs at the fools who parrot his proletarian catechism, just as he laughs over the communists à la Willich and over the bourgeoisie. The only people he respects are the aristocrats, the genuine ones, those who are well aware of their aristocracy. To prevent them from governing, he needs his own source of power, and he can find this only in the proletariat. Accordingly he has tailored his system to them. In spite of all his assurances to the contrary, and perhaps because of them, I took away with me the impression that the acquisition of personal power was the aim of all his endeavours.

E[ngels] and all his old associates, despite their very real gifts, are all far inferior to him, and if they dare to forget it for a moment, he puts them in their place with a shameless impudence worthy of a Napoleon.

Gustav Techow, writing to a friend in Switzerland, reproduced by Marx's detractor, Karl Vogt, in *Mein Prozess gegen die Allgemeine Zeitung*, Geneva, 1859.

1851

[MARX TO ENGELS]

28 Dean Street,
Soho.
31 March 1851

Dear Engels,

While you occupy yourself with military history, I am waging a little war which threatens me by and by with defeat, and from which neither Napoleon nor even Willich—the communist Cromwell—could have found a way out.

You know that on 23 March I was to pay old Bamberger thirty-one pounds, ten shillings and on 16 March I was to pay ten pounds to the Jew Stiebel, all on notes of mine that were in circulation. I first had Jenny turn directly to my mother-in-law. The answer was that Mr Edgar had once again been sent off to Mexico with the remainder of Jenny's money and I could not get a centime from them.

Then I wrote to my mother, threatened her that I would draw notes on her and that, if these were not paid, I would go to Prussia and allow myself to be arrested. I really meant to go through with this if it came to the point, but this became impossible when the asses in the newspapers began to noise it abroad that the workers were deserting me, that my popularity was disappearing, etc. This would have made the whole matter look like a political coup-de-théâtre. . . . I had told my mother that 20 March was the final date.

On 10 March she wrote to me that she would write to her relatives; on 18 March she wrote that the relatives had not replied, which was to say, the whole matter had come to an end. I immediately answered that I stuck to my first resolution.

I paid Stiebel his ten pounds on 16 March with the help of Pieper. On 23 March, after I had tried various expedients without success I had to tell old Bamberger that I could not pay the IOU. I had a terrible scene with the old man, who cursed me most horribly to the worthy Seiler as well. The idiot had asked his bankers in Trier to make enquiries about me from the banker Lautz. This fellow, my mother's banker and my personal enemy, naturally wrote the greatest nonsense about me and on top of it, stirred my mother up against me.

I had no choice but to give old Bamberger two more promissory notes, one payable to him in London four weeks after 24 March, the other payable in three weeks in Trier by my mother, meant to cover the first. I immediately informed my mother. Today, together with your letter, I receive a letter from her in which she is most impertinent and full of moral indignation and positively declares that she will repudiate every note that I draw on her.

I can therefore expect the worst on 21 April from a furious old Simon Bamberger. . . .

> Your
> K.M.

> MEGA III, 1, 177–79.

1851

[MARX TO ENGELS]

5 May 1851

Dear Engels,

I am sending you with this the following copy of an article on the use of electricity in agriculture, written in English. Will you be so good as to write by return

1. what you think of this
2. explain the business to me in plain German, as I don't quite understand it . . .

> Your
> K.M.

> MEGA III, 1, 191–93.

1853

[A PRUSSIAN POLICE AGENT'S REPORT]

Marx is of middling height, 34 years old; despite his being in the prime of life, he is already turning grey. He is powerfully built, and his features distinctly remind one of Szemere [the Prime Minister of the short-lived Hungarian revolutionary government in 1848, who was a friend of

Marx], but his complexion is darker and his hair and beard are quite black. The latter he does not shave; his large piercing fiery eyes have something demoniacally sinister about them. However, one can tell at the first glance that this is a man of genius and energy. His intellectual superiority exercises an irresistible force on his surroundings. In his private life he is a highly disorderly, cynical human being and a bad manager. He lives the life of a gypsy, of an intellectual Bohemian; washing, combing and changing his linen are things he does rarely, he likes to get drunk. He is often idle for days on end, but when he has work to do, he will work day and night with tireless endurance. For him there is no such thing as a fixed time for sleeping and waking. He will often stay up the whole night and then lie down on the sofa, fully dressed, around midday and sleep till evening, untroubled by the fact that the whole world comes and goes though his room.

His wife is the sister of the Prussian Minister, von Westphalen, a cultured and pleasant woman who has accustomed herself to this Bohemian existence out of love for her husband and now feels perfectly at home in such misery. She has two girls and one son; all three children are truly handsome and have the intelligent eyes of their father. —As a husband and a father, Marx is the gentlest and mildest of men in spite of his wild and restless character. Marx lives in one of the worst, and therefore one of the cheapest, quarters of London. He occupies two rooms. One of them looks out on the street—that is the salon. The bedroom is at the back. There is not one clean and solid piece of furniture to be found in the whole apartment: everything is broken, tattered and torn; there is a thick coat of dust everywhere; everywhere, too, the greatest disorder. In the middle of the salon stands a large old-fashioned table covered with oil cloth. On it lie his manuscripts, books and newspapers, then the children's toys, his wife's mending and patching, together with several cups with chipped rims, dirty spoons, knives, forks,

lamps, an ink-pot, glasses, dutch clay pipes, tobacco ash—
in one word everything is topsy turvy, and all on the same
table. A rag-and-bone man would step back ashamed from
such a remarkable collection. When you enter Marx's
room, smoke and tobacco fumes make your eyes water so
badly, that you think for a moment that you are groping
about in a cave. Gradually your eyes become accustomed
to the fog and you can make out a few objects. Everything
is dirty and covered with dust. It is positively dangerous
to sit down. One chair has only three legs. On another
chair, which happens to be whole, the children are playing
at cooking. This one is offered to the visitor but the children's cooking has not been wiped away: if you sit down,
you risk a pair of trousers. None of this embarrasses Marx
or his wife. You are received in the friendliest of fashions;
pipes and tobacco and whatever else there might happen
to be are offered to you most cordially. Intellectually
spirited and agreeable conversation makes amends for the
domestic deficiencies, at least in part. One even grows accustomed to the company, and finds this circle interesting,
even original. This is the true picture of the family life of
the communist chief, Marx . . .

Published in G. Mayer, 'Neue Beiträge zur Biographie von
Karl Marx', in *Grünberg's Archiv*, Vol. 10, pp. 56–63.

1853

[MARX TO ENGELS]

28 Dean Street,
Soho.
7 September 1853

Dear Frederic,
        . . . The miserable Russians, in the *Tribune*, as well as
in the London *Advertiser* (although by different persons

and in different form) are riding their hobby horse, that the Russian people are democratic through and through and that only official Russia (Czar and bureaucracy) is German and that the nobility is also German.

In other words, we must fight Germany in Russia and not Russia in Germany.

You know more about Russia than I do, and if you can make the time to answer this nonsense (it is as though the Teutonic idiots were to blame the despotism of Frederick II on to the French, as if backward serfs did not always need civilised serfs to tame them) I should be much obliged to you. . . .

Your
K.M.

MEGA III, 1, 499–501.

1855

[MARX TO ENGELS]

28 Dean Street,
Soho.
8 March 1855

Dear Engels,

The £5 received . . .

A very happy event, the death of my wife's 90 year old uncle, became known to us yesterday. My mother-in-law thereby saves an annual expenditure of 200 Thaler and my wife gains £100; more if the old dog doesn't leave that part of his money, which was not in trust, to his housekeeper. There will also be a decision concerning the manuscript of the Duke of Brunswick on the Seven Years War, for which old Scharnhorst offered large sums. My wife has entered a protest against any attempt by her brother to give it as a present to his 'Most Gracious Majesty'. The Prussian state can acquire it for cash, but not otherwise.

Another possible source of money has appeared. My wife deposited 1300 Thaler with a banker, Grach, in Trier. This fellow went bankrupt, and, with respect to her, fraudulently, since he was already insolvent (although not to the knowledge of the public) when he accepted her deposit. At the urging of the wife of this Grach, my wife allowed herself to be 'softened' and refrained from prosecuting the matter. The senior procurator had explained that if she did proceed Grach would come before the assizes. Now the wife of this Grach has inherited a large fortune, and if she remains true to her promises we can count on recouping at least part of the loss . . .

Your
K.M.

MEGA III, 2, 82–83.

1855

[MARX TO ENGELS]

28 Dean Street,
Soho.
6 April 1855

Dear Engels,

Poor Musch is no more. He went to sleep (literally) in my arms today between five and six o'clock. I shall never forget how much your friendship has helped us through this terrible time. You will understand my anguish for the child. My wife sends you her warmest greetings. Possibly, when I come to Manchester, I shall bring her with me for a week, in which case we shall naturally stay in a guest

house or in a private lodging. I must look for some means
of helping her through the first few days.

Your
K.M.

MEGA III, 2, 87.

1856

[KARL MARX TO HIS WIFE]

Manchester, 21 June 1856

Dearest Heart,

I am writing to you again because I am alone, and because I find it embarrassing always to hold conversations
with you in my head, without your knowing anything
about them or hearing them or being able to answer me.
Bad as your portrait is, it serves me very well and I can
now understand how even the 'black madonnas', the most
vulgar portraits of the Mother of God, find the most devoted admirers, and even more admirers than the good
portraits. In any case, no such black madonna has been
kissed more often, has been eyed and adored more often,
than your photograph which is admittedly not black, but
which is sour, and does not, by any means, reflect your
dear, sweet, kissable, 'dolce' face. But I myself improve
on the sun, which has painted falsely, and I find that my
eyes, so ruined by lamplight and tobacco, can still paint
your face, not only in dreams, but even when I am
awake. I have you before me in the flesh, I carry you on
my hands and I kiss you from head to toe and I fall on
my knees before you and I groan: 'Madam, I love you'.
And I really love you, more than the Moor of Venice
ever loved . . .

There are indeed many women in the world and some

of them are beautiful. But where shall I again find a face of which every lineament, every wrinkle even, reminds me of the greatest and sweetest memories of my life. Even my never-ending pains, my irreplaceable losses I read in your sweet face and I kiss until I have forgotten my pain when I kiss your sweet face . . .

Your Karl.

Cited from 'Lettres et documents de Karl Marx, 1856–1883', ed., E. Bottigelli in *Annali Feltrinelli*, Vol. 1, 1958, pp. 153–54.

1857

[MARX TO ENGELS]

18 December 1857

Dear Frederick,

I am writing a few lines in all haste. I have just had a third and last warning from the lousy tax collector that if I do not pay before Monday, the broker will be sent into the house on Monday afternoon. If possible, therefore, send me a few pounds before Monday. The pressure of money is currently greater than usual, since I have had to pay everything in cash for the last three weeks, and anything like credit has ceased. At the same time, two thirds of the money that I receive has to go out immediately to cover floating debts. On top of that, the money coming in is very little . . .

I am working splendidly, mostly until four in the morning. The work is of two sorts: 1. Working out the outlines of economics. (It is essential, from the point of view of the public, to get to the heart of the matter, and for me, individually, to get rid of this nightmare.)

2. The present crisis. On this—apart from the articles

for the *Tribune*, I am simply keeping notes, which takes up considerable time however. . . .

Your
K.M.

MEGA III, 2, 257–58.

1858

[MARX TO ENGELS]

28 January 1858

Dear Frederick,

The bitter cold, which has broken out here, and the very real lack of coals in our house, forces me to press you once again—even though I find that the most painful of all things. I decided to do it only as a result of heavy pressure from without. My wife has demonstrated to me, that in consequence of the money from Jersey arriving earlier than usual, you have made an error in your accounts and would therefore not send us anything this month unless I specially write to you. She has already pawned her shawl, etc. etc. and does not know what to do next. In other words, I *must* write and therefore I am writing. In truth, if these conditions are to go on, I would sooner be one hundred fathoms under the earth, than go on vegetating. To be a constant burden to others and to be continually plagued by the most petty filth cannot be borne for long. I personally can escape this misery by immersing myself in public affairs. My wife of course does not have the same resources, etc.

Lassalle's book arrived today. It cost two shillings, not the price of the book but the cost of transportation. This assured it of an unfriendly welcome. . . . In the preface the fellow lies to the public and says that he has been pregnant with it since 1846 ...

Your
K.M.

MEGA III, 2, 279.

1858

[ELEANOR MARX ON HER FATHER]

... For those who knew Marx, no legend is funnier than that which portrays him as a morose, embittered, unbending and unapproachable person, a sort of Jupiter Tonans, ceaselessly hurling his thunderbolts with never a smile on his lips, enthroned alone and aloof in Olympus. Such a description of the merriest, gayest person who ever lived, the man bubbling over with fun, whose laughter irresistibly won one's heart, the most friendly, gentle and sympathetic of all companions, is a constant source of amazement and amusement to all who knew him.

In his family circle, as among friends and acquaintances, his goodness of heart was most evident ...

But the most delightful aspects of Marx's character were displayed above all in his dealings with children. Children could wish for no better playmate. I recall when I was about three years old, how Mohr [the Moor] (his old nickname always comes to mind) used to carry me around on his shoulders in our little garden in Grafton Terrace, and stick convolvulus flowers in my brown curls. Mohr was certainly a splendid steed; I was often told how my older sisters, together with my brother, whose death shortly after I was born was a lifelong source of deep grief to my parents, used to harness Mohr to some chairs, which they mounted, and which he had to pull. In fact, some chapters of the *Eighteenth Brumaire* were written, in Dean Street, Soho, while he was acting as draughthorse for his three little children who sat behind him on chairs, cracking their whips. For my part, perhaps because I had no sisters of my own age, I preferred Mohr as a riding-horse. Sitting on his shoulder, firmly clutching his thick hair, which at that time was still black with only a trace of grey, I loved to gallop around in our little garden and over the fields, which in those days were not yet built up. A few words, in passing, concerning the name 'Mohr'. In our family everyone had a nickname. Mohr was Marx's regular, almost official name, used not only by us but by close friends as well. He was also called 'Challey' (probably a corruption of Charley, from Charles, i.e. Karl) and 'Old Nick' . . . Our mother was always known as 'Möme', our dear old friend Helene Demuth was finally called 'Nim' . . . Engels, after 1870, was our 'General'. My sister Jenny was known as 'Qui-qui, Emperor of China' and 'Di', my sister Laura as 'Hottentot' and 'Kakadu'. I was called 'Quo-quo, Crown Prince of China' and 'Dwarf Alberich' from the Nibelungenlied; finally I became 'Tussy' which I remain today.

Mohr was not only an excellent horse, but (a still higher commendation) a unique and unrivalled story-teller. My aunts have often told me that Mohr as a boy was a terrible tyrant; he forced them to pull him down the Marxberg in Trier at full gallop, and, still worse, to eat the cakes which he made himself with dirty hands out of dirtier dough. But they did it all without a murmur for Karl told them such wonderful stories as reward. Many many years later he told stories to his children. To my sisters—I was still too little—he told stories during their walks together, stories not reckoned in chapters but in miles. 'Tell us another mile' the two girls would beg. For my part, of all the countless wonderful stories which Mohr told me, I loved most the story of Hans Röckle. It went on for months, for it was a long long story and never came to an end. Hans

Röckle was a magician, like those in Hoffmann's Tales, who had a toyshop and many debts. His shop was full of wonderful things: wooden men and women, giants, dwarves, kings, queens, workmen and masters, animals and birds as numerous as in a Noah's Ark, tables, chairs, carriages, boxes large and small. But alas! although he was a magician he was always short of money and most reluctantly had to sell all his pretty toys to the devil. But after many adventures and wanderings these things always came back to his shop. Some of the adventures were as gruesome and hair-raising as anything in Hoffmann's Tales, some were comic, but all were told with inexhaustible invention, wit and humour.

Mohr also read aloud to his children. To me, as to my sisters, he read the whole of Homer, the Nibelungenlied, Gudrun, Don Quixote, The Thousand and One Nights. Shakespeare was our family Bible, and before I was six I knew whole scenes from Shakespeare by heart.

For my sixth birthday Mohr gave me my first novel—the immortal *Peter Simple*. Then followed Marryat and Cooper. My father read all these books with me and discussed the contents very seriously with his little girl. And when the child, fired by Marryat's sea-stories, declared that she wanted to be a Post-Captain, and asked her father whether it would not be possible to dress as a boy and join the crew of a man-of-war, he assured her that this could very well be done but warned her to say nothing to anybody till all her plans were complete. But before this happened, the Walter Scott craze had set in, and I heard with horror that I was myself distantly related to the hated Clan Campbell. Plans followed for the raising of the Highlands and a revival of the '45'. I should add that Marx read and reread Walter Scott; he admired him and knew him almost as well as he knew Fielding and Balzac . . .

In the same way, this 'bitter' and 'embittered' man would discuss politics and religion with his children. I remember clearly once as a child having religious scruples. We had been to a Roman-Catholic church to hear the splendid music, which had made such a deep impression on me that I confided in Mohr. He quietly explained everything to me in such a clear and lucid fashion that from that day to this no doubt could ever cross my mind again. And how simply and sublimely he told me the story of the carpenter's son who was put to death by rich men! Often and often I heard him say: 'After all, we can forgive Christianity much, since it taught us to love children'.

Marx himself could have said: 'Suffer the little children to come unto me', for wherever he went he was surrounded by children. Whether he sat on Hampstead Heath (a large open space north of London, near our old home) or in one of the parks, a swarm of children gathered round the big man with the long hair and beard and the kindly brown eyes. Perfectly strange children came up to him too, and stopped him in the street, and animals showed the same trust in him. I remember once, how a completely strange ten-year-old boy unceremoniously stopped the Chief of the International in Maitland Park and asked him to 'swop knives'. After he had explained to Marx that 'swop' was schoolboy slang for 'exchange', the two knives were produced and compared. The boy's knife had only one blade, Marx's two, which were however dreadfully blunt. After some discussion the deal was concluded, the knives exchanged, and the 'dreaded Chief of the International' added a penny as compensation for the bluntness of his blades.

With what patience and sweetness, too, Marx answered all my questions, when American war-reports and Blue Books had temporarily ousted Marryat and Scott. I brooded for days over English government reports and maps of America. Mohr never complained about my interruptions, though it must have distracted him to have a chatterbox around while he was at work on his great book.

At about this time, I distinctly remember, I had an un-shakeable conviction that Abraham Lincoln (President of the U.S.A.) could not possibly get on without my advice, so I wrote long letters to him, which Mohr then had to read and post. Many years later he showed me these child-ish letters which had so much amused him that he had kept them.

And so throughout my youth Mohr was an ideal friend. At home we were all good friends, and he was the best and gayest of all, even during those years when he suffered such pain from boils, until the very end ...

Eleanor Marx-Aveling, 'Karl Marx—Lose Blätter', in *Österreichischer Arbeiter-Kalender für das Jahr 1895*, pp. 51–54, cited in *Mohr und General*, pp. 269–79.

1860

[MARX TO ENGELS IN MANCHESTER]

London, 14 June 1860

Dear Engels,

Can you send me some money till Monday? Up to now I have spent altogether about £13 on the business with Vogt and the trial and my being unwell has prevented me from conducting any correspondence for the last three weeks ...

Many thanks for your portrait.

I have something politically *very important* to tell you (tomorrow). A visitor waiting for me downstairs makes it impossible to write more.

Yours,
K.M.

MEW 30, p. 62.

1865

[CONFESSIONS OF MARX]

These confessions were Marx's replies, in English, to a set of questions given him by Jenny and Laura as part of a parlor game and recorded in English by Laura in 1865.

Your favourite virtue ....Simplicity.
Your favourite virtue in man ....Strength.
Your favourite virtue in woman ....Weakness.
Your chief characteristic .....Singleness of purpose.
Your idea of happiness ....To fight.
Your idea of misery ....Submission.
The vice you excuse most ....Gullibility.
The vice you detest most ....Servility.
Your aversion ....Martin Tupper.
Favourite occupation ....Book-worming.
Favourite poet .....Shakespeare, Aeschylus, Goethe.
Favourite prose-writer ....Diderot.
Favourite hero ....Spartacus, Kepler.
Favourite heroine ...Gretchen [Heroine of Goethe's
                                    Faust].
Favourite flower ....Daphne.
Favourite colour ....Red.
Favourite name ....Laura, Jenny.
Favourite dish ....Fish.
Favourite maxim.*Nihil humani a me alienum puto.*
                  [Nothing human is alien to me.]
Favourite motto ....*De omnibus dubitandum.*
                  [To doubt of everything.]

1866

[KARL MARX TO LAURA MARX]

Margate, 20 March 1866

My dear Cacadou,

... I am right glad that I have taken my lodgings in a private House, and not in an Inn or Hotel where one could hardly escape being pestered with local politics, vestry scandals, and neighbourly gossip. But still I cannot sing with the miller of the Dee, that I care for nobody and nobody cares for me. For there is my landlady, who is deaf like a post, and her daughter, who is afflicted with chronic hoarseness, but they are very nice people, attentive, and not intruding. As to myself, I have turned into a perambulating stick, running about the greatest part of the day, airing myself, going to bed at 10 o'clock, reading nothing, writing less, and altogether working up my mind to that state of nothingness which Buddhaism considers the element of human bliss ...

On Sunday I made up my mind to walk per pedes to Canterbury ... As to Canterbury, you know, of course, all about it, and more than I can boast, from your Eves [author of a series of widely-used schoolbooks] ... Happily, I was too tired, and it was too late to look out for the celebrated cathedral. Canterbury is an old, ugly, mediaeval sort of town, not mended by large modern English barracks at the one, and a dismal dry Railway Station at the other end of the oldish thing. There is no trace of that poetry about it, which you find in continental towns of the same age. The swaggering of the private soldiers and the officers in the streets, reminded me somewhat of 'Vaterland'. In the inn, where I was scantily purveyed with some slices of cold beef, I caught the newest scandal. Captain Le Merchant, it seems, had been taken up by the police on Saturday night, fo. systematically knocking at the doors of all the most respectable citizens. And a summons will be taken out against the Captain because of this innocent pastime. And the redoubtable Captain will have to bend down his diminished head before aldermanic majesty. This is my whole packet of 'Canterbury Tales'.

And now, Cacadou, pay my compliments to Elly to whom I shall write one of these days, and whose little letter was very welcome. As to Möhmchen, she will hear of me by the by.

That damned boy Lafargue pesters me with his Proudhonism, and will not rest, it seems, untill I have administered to him a sound cudgelling of his Creole pate. My good wishes to all

Your master.

English original as given in 'Lettres et documents de Karl Marx, 1856–1883', in *Annali Feltrinelli*, Vol. 1, 1958, pp. 160–62.

1866

[KARL MARX TO FRANÇOIS LAFARGUE]

London, 12 November 1866.

My dear Mr. Lafargue,

I hope that Monsieur il amoroso [Paul Lafargue] will have excused to you my unpardonable silence. On the one hand I was plagued by continual recurrences of my illness, on the other, so absorbed in a lengthy work that I neglected writing to my most intimate friends. If I did not include you in this category, I should never have dared to flout convention in such a manner. I thank you warmly for the wine. As I come from a wine-growing country and am a former vine-grower, I know how to value wine justly. I am inclined to agree with old Luther, that a man who does not love wine will never be good for much. (No general rule without exceptions.) But one cannot deny, for instance, that political activity in England has been accelerated by the trade agreement with France and the importation of French wine. That is one of the good things which L. Bonaparte was in a position to do, whereas poor Louis-Philippe was so intimidated by the industrialists of the north that he did not dare to make trade agreements with England. It is only to be regretted that such régimes as the Napoleonic, which rest on the fatigue and impotence of the two opposed classes of society, buy some material advances at the cost of general demoralisation. Happily the mass of the workers cannot be demoralised. Manual labour is the great antidote to all social infection.

You will have been as pleased as I was at the defeat of President Johnson in the last elections. The workers of the north have at last clearly understood that work, as long as it is oppressed in a black skin, will never become free in a white skin.

I received on Saturday evening, through citizen Dupont, a letter addressed to Paul by the Secretary of the College of Surgeons. He asked for papers which (except for the Baccalaureate certificate) are neither with my daughter nor with those who are looking after your son's belongings. It is therefore necessary to send these documents *immediately*.

Would you please tell your son that he would oblige me greatly by making no propaganda in Paris. The time is *dangerous*. The best thing that he can do in Paris is to make good use of his time and to profit by his contact with Dr. Moilin. He will lose nothing by saving his polemical powers. The more he holds back now, the better a fighter will he be at the right moment.

My daughter asks me to beg you to send her, through Paul, photographs of Madame Lafargue and yourself.

All my family joins me in expressing our friendship for the whole family Lafargue.

> Wholly yours,
> Karl Marx.

French original reproduced in 'Lettres et documents de Karl Marx, 1856–1883', in *Annali Feltrinelli*, Vol. 1, 1958, pp. 163–64.

1870
[KARL MARX TO PAUL LAFARGUE]

18 April 1870

Dear Paul-Laurent,

. . . I am now forced to say a few words which Paul-Laurent will a little fret at, but I cannot help doing so.

Your father wrote me a letter to Hanover which I have not yet answered, because I did not know what to say.

I feel quite sure that Paul has discarded all notion of finishing, or occupying himself with, his medical studies. When at Paris I wrote to his father in a different sense, and I was warranted in doing so by Paul's own promises. Thus I am placed in quite a false position towards M. Lafargue the elder. I cannot remain in that fix, I see no other prospect of getting out of it but by writing to him that I have as little influence with his beloved son as himself. If you see any other way of escape for me, any other means of clearing my position, please communicate it to me.

In my opinion, which however I neither pretend nor hope to see accepted and acted upon, Paul-Laurent cum filio ought to pay a visit to their parents at Bordeaux and try to coax them by the many means personal intercourse permits of.

> Yours truly.

English original, as given in 'Lettres et documents de Karl
Marx, 1856–1883', in *Annali Feltrinelli*, Vol. 1, 1958,
pp. 171–72.

1871

[*From* R. LANDOR'S INTERVIEW WITH MARX]

LONDON, July 3.—You have asked me to find out something about the International Association, and I have tried
to do so. . . . I have called on two of their leading members, have talked with one freely, and I here give you the
substance of my conversation. I have satisfied myself of
one thing, that it is a society of genuine working-men, but
that these workmen are directed by social and political
theorists of another class. One man whom I saw, a leading
member of the council, was sitting at his workman's
bench during our interview, and left off talking to me from
time to time to receive a complaint, delivered in no courteous tone, from one of the many little masters in the
neighborhood who employed him. . . . This man helped
me to a glimpse of one side of the nature of the International, the result of labor against capital, of the workman
who produces against the middleman who enjoys. Here
was the hand that would smite hard when the time came,
and as to the head that plans, I think I saw that, too, in my
interview with Dr Karl Marx.

Dr Karl Marx is a German doctor of philosophy with a
German breadth of knowledge derived both from observation of the living world and from books. I should conclude that he has never been a worker in the ordinary
sense of the term. His surroundings and appearance are
those of a well-to-do man of the middle class. The draw-
ing-room into which I was ushered on the night of my interview would have formed very comfortable quarters for

a thriving stockbroker who had made his competence and was now beginning to make his fortune. It was comfort personified, the apartment of a man of taste and of easy means, but with nothing in it peculiarly characteristic of its owner. A fine album of Rhine views on the table, however, gave a clue to his nationality. I peered cautiously into the vase on the side-table for a bomb. I sniffed for petroleum, but the smell was the smell of roses. I crept back stealthily to my seat, and moodily awaited the worst.

He has entered and greeted me cordially, and we are sitting face to face. . . . Do you remember the bust of Socrates, the man who dies rather than profess his belief in the gods of the time—the man with the fine sweep of profile for the forehead running meanly at the end into a little snub, curled-up feature like a bisected pothook that formed the nose? Take this bust in your mind's eye, colour the beard black, dashing it here and there with puffs of grey; clap the head thus made on a portly body of the middle height, and the Doctor is before you. Throw a veil over the upper part of the face and you might be in the company of a born vestryman. Reveal the essential feature, the immense brow, and you know at once that you have to deal with that most formidable of all composite forces—a dreamer who thinks, a thinker who dreams. . . .

I went straight to my business. The world, I said, seemed to be in the dark about the International, hating it very much, but not able to say clearly what thing it hated. Some . . . declared that they had made out a sort of Janus figure with a fair, honest workman's smile on one of its faces, and on the other a murderous, conspirator's scowl. . . .

The professor laughed, chuckled a little I fancied, at the thought that we were so frightened of him. 'There is no mystery to clear up, dear sir', he began . . . 'except perhaps the mystery of human stupidity in those who perpetually ignore the fact that our association is a public one and that the fullest reports of its proceedings are published for all who care to read them. You may buy our rules for a penny, and a shilling laid out in pamphlets will teach you almost as much about us as we know ourselves.'

R.—Almost—yes, perhaps so; but will not the something I shall not know constitute the all-important reservation? To be quite frank with you, and to put the case as it strikes an outside observer, this general claim of depreciation of you must mean something more than the ignorant ill-will of the multitude. And it is still pertinent to ask even after what you have told me, what is the International Society?

Dr. M—You have only to look at the individuals of which it is composed—workmen.

R.—Yes, but the soldier need be no exponent of the statecraft that sets him in motion. I know some of your members, and I can believe that they are not of the stuff of which conspirators are made. Besides, a secret shared by a million men would be no secret at all. But what if these were only the instruments in the hands of a bold, and I hope you will forgive me for adding, not over-scrupulous conclave?

Dr. M—There is nothing to prove it.

R.—The last Paris insurrection?

Dr. M—I demand firstly the proof that there was any plot at all—that anything happened that was not the legitimate effect of the circumstances of the moment; or the plot granted, I demand the proofs of the participation in it of the International Association.

R.—The presence in the communal body of so many members of the association.

Dr. M—Then it was a plot of the Freemasons, too, for their share in the work as individuals was by no means a slight one. I should not be surprised, indeed, to find the Pope setting down the whole insurrection to their account. But try another explanation. The insurrection in Paris was made by the workmen of Paris. The ablest of the workmen must necessarily have been its leaders and administrators; but the ablest of the workmen happen also to be members of the International Association. Yet the association as such may in no way be responsible for their action.

R.—It will still seem otherwise to the world. People talk of secret instructions from London, and even grants of money. Can it be affirmed that the alleged openness of the association's proceedings precludes all secrecy of communications?

Dr. M—What association ever formed carried on its work without private as well as public agencies? But to talk of secret instruction from London, as of decrees in the matter of faith and morals from some centre of Papal domination and intrigue is wholly to misconceive the nature of the International. This would imply a centralized form of government of the International, whereas the real form is designedly that which gives the greatest play to local energy and independence. In fact the International is not properly a government for the working class at all. It is a bond of union rather than a controlling force.

R.—And of union to what end?

Dr. M—The economical emancipation of the working class by the conquest of political power. The use of that political power to the attainment of social ends. It is necessary that our aims should be thus comprehensive to include every form of working class activity. To have made them of a special character would have been to adapt them to the needs of one section—one nation of workmen alone. But how could all men be asked to unite to further the objects of a few? To have done that the association must have forfeited its title of International. The association does not dictate the form of political movements; it only requires a pledge as to their end. It is a network of affiliated societies spreading all over the world of labor. In each part of the world some special aspect of the problem presents itself, and the workmen there address themselves to its consideration in their own way. Combinations among workmen cannot be absolutely identical in detail in New-castle and in Barcelona, in London and in Berlin. In England, for instance, the way to show political power lies open to the working class. Insurrection would be madness where peaceful agitation would more swiftly and surely do the work. In France a hundred laws of repression and a moral antagonism between classes seem to necessitate the violent solution of social war. The choice of that solution is the affair of the working classes of that country. The International does not presume to dictate in the matter and hardly to advise. But to every movement it accords its sympathy and its aid within the limits assigned by its own laws.. . . .

R. LANDOR

The New York *World*, 18 July 1871, reprinted in *Science & Society*, Vol. 36, 1972, pp. 6–16.

1875

[REPORT ON KARL MARX IN KARLSBAD]

Charles Marx, Doctor of Philosophy, of London, an outstanding leader of the Democratic-Social Democratic Party, is in Karlsbad taking the cure. Since he also took the cure in Karlsbad last year and gave no cause for suspicion, I permit myself obediently to confine myself to adding to this report the information that so far Marx has conducted himself quietly, has had no great contact with other persons taking the cure and frequently goes for long walks alone.

Karlsbad.
1 September 1875
The Imperial and Royal Government-Councillor and Regional Director Veith.

Cited in Wolfgang Schwerbrock, *Karl Marx Privat*, Munich, 1962, p. 70.

1878
[*From* THE *CHICAGO TRIBUNE*'S INTERVIEW WITH MARX]

LONDON, Dec. 18.—In a little villa at Haverstock Hill, in the northwest portion of London, lives Karl Marx, the corner-stone of modern Socialism. . . .

Your correspondent has called upon him twice or thrice, and each time the Doctor was found in his library, with a book in one hand and a cigarette in the other. He must be over 70 years of age.[1] His physique is well-knit, massive, and erect. He has the head of a man of intellect, and the features of a cultivated Jew. His hair and beard are long, and iron-gray in color. His eyes are glittering black, shaded by a pair of bushy eyebrows. To a stranger he shows extreme caution. A foreigner can generally gain admission: but the ancient-looking German woman[2] who waits upon visitors has instructions to admit none who hail from the Fatherland, unless they bring letters of introduction. Once into his library, however, and, having fixed his one eye-glass in the corner of his eye, in order to take your intellectual breadth and depth, so to speak, he loses that self-restraint, and unfolds to you a knowledge of men and things throughout the world apt to interest one. And his conversation does not run in one groove, but is as varied as are the volumes upon his library shelves. A man can generally be judged by the books he reads, and you can form your own conclusions when I tell you a casual glance revealed Shakespeare, Dickens, Thackeray,

1. Marx was then 60. [E.K.]
2. Helene Demuth. [E.K.]

Molière, Racine, Montaigne, Bacon, Goethe, Voltaire, Paine; English, American, French bluebooks; works political and philosophical in Russian, German, Spanish, Italian, etc., etc. During my conversations I was struck with his intimacy with American questions, which have been uppermost during the past twenty years. His knowledge of them, and the surprising accuracy with which he criticised our National and State legislation, impressed upon my mind the fact that he must have derived his information from inside sources. But, indeed, this knowledge is not confined to America, but is spread over the face of Europe. When speaking of his hobby—Socialism—he does not indulge in those melodramatic flights generally attributed to him, but dwells upon his utopian plans for 'the emancipation of the human race' with a firm conviction in the realization of his theories, if not in this century, at least in the next.

(signed) H.

Chicago Tribune, 5 January 1879, reprinted in *Science & Society*, Vol. 36, 1972, pp. 16–28.

1879

[SIR MOUNTSTUART ELPHINSTONE GRANT-DUFF[1] TO EMPRESS FREDERICK[2]]

Febr. 1, 1879

Madam,

Your Imperial Highness, when I last had the honor of seeing you, chanced to express some curiosity about Carl

---

1. Balliol man, Liberal M.P. for Elgin Burghs 1857–1881, who had been Under-Secretary for India in Gladstone's first administration. [E.K.]
2. Eldest daughter of Queen Victoria. [E.K.]

Marx and to ask me if I knew him. I resolved accordingly to take the first opportunity of making his acquaintance, but that opportunity did not arise till yesterday when I met him at luncheon and spent three hours in his company.

He is a short, rather small man with grey hair and beard which contrasts strangely with a still dark moustache. The face is somewhat round: the forehead well shaped and filled up—the eye rather hard but the whole expression rather pleasant than not, by no means that of a gentleman who is in the habit of eating babies in their cradles—which is I daresay the view which the Police takes of him.

His talk was that of a well-informed, nay learned man—much interested in Comparative Grammar which had led him into the Old Slavonic and other out-of-the-way studies and was varied by many quaint turns and little bits of dry humour, as when speaking of Hezechiell's 'Life of Prince Bismarck', he always referred to it, by way of contrast to Dr Busch's book, as the *Old* Testament.

It was all very *positif*, slightly cynical—without any appearance of enthusiasm—interesting and often, as I thought, showing very correct ideas when he was conversing of the past and the present, but vague and unsatisfactory when he turned to the future.

He looks, not unreasonably, for a great and not distant crash in Russia, thinks it will begin by reforms from above which the old bad edifice will not be able to bear and which will lead to its tumbling down altogether. As to what would take its place he had evidently no clear idea, except that for a long time Russia would be unable to exercise any influence in Europe.

Next he thinks that the movement will spread to Germany taking there the form of a revolt against the existing military system.

To my question, 'But how can you expect the army to rise against its commanders', he replied—you forget that in Germany now the army and the Nation are nearly identical. These Socialists you hear about are trained soldiers like anybody else. You must not think of the standing army only. You must think of the Landwehr—and even in the standing army there is much discontent. Never was an army in which the severity of the discipline led to so many suicides. The step from shooting oneself to shooting one's officer is not long and an example of the kind once set is soon followed.

But supposing I said the rulers of Europe came to an understanding amongst themselves for a reduction of armaments which might greatly relieve the burden on the people, what would become of the Revolution which you expect it one day to bring about?

Ah was his answer they can't do that. All sorts of fears and jealousies will make that impossible. The burden will grow worse and worse as science advances for the improvements in the Art of Destruction will keep pace with its advance and every year more and more will have to be devoted to costly engines of war. It is a vicious circle— there is no escape from it. But I said You have never yet had a serious popular rising unless there was really great misery. You have no idea he rejoined how terrible has been the crisis through which Germany has been passing in these last five years.

Well I said supposing that your Revolution has taken place and that you have your Republican form of Government—it is still a long long way to the realization of the special ideas of yourself and your friends. Doubtless he answered but all great movements are slow. It would merely be a step to better things as your Revolution of 1688 was—a mere step on the road.

The above will give Your Imperial Highness a fair idea of the kind of ideas about the near future of Europe which are working in his mind.

They are too dreamy to be dangerous, except just in so far as the situation with its mad expenditure on armaments is obviously and undoubtedly dangerous.

If however within the next decade the rulers of Europe have not found means of dealing with this evil without any warning from attempted revolution I for one shall despair of the future of humanity at least on this continent.

In the course of conversation Carl Marx spoke several times both of Your Imperial Highness and of the Crown Prince and invariably with due respect and propriety. Even in the case of eminent individuals of whom he by no means spoke with respect there was no trace of bitterness or savagery—plenty acrid and dissolvent criticism but nothing of the Marat tone.

Of the horrible things that have been connected with the International he spoke as any respectable man would have done.

One thing which he mentioned showed the dangers to which exiles who have got a revolutionary name are exposed. The wretched man Nobiling, he had learned, had when in England intended to come to see him. If he had done so, he said, I should certainly have admitted him for he would have sent in his card as an employé of the Dresden Bureau of Statistics and as I occupy myself with Statistics, it would have interested me to talk with him—What a pleasant position I should have been in he added if he *had* come to see me!!

Altogether my impression of Marx, allowing for his being at the opposite pole of opinion from oneself was not at all unfavourable and I would gladly meet him again. It will not be he, who whether he wishes it or not, will turn the world upside down. . . .

(signed) M. E. GRANT-DUFF.

As first printed in the *Times Literary Supplement*, 15 July 1949.

1882

[KARL MARX TO LAURA LAFARGUE]

Ventnor (Isle of Wight)
14 December 1882

Dear Cacadou,

... *Some recent Russian publications*, printed in Holy Russia, not abroad, show the great run of my theories in that country.

Nowhere my success is some more delightful; it gives me the satisfaction that I damage a power, which, besides England, is the true bulwark of the old society.

Yours,
Nick.

English original as given in 'Lettres et documents de Karl Marx, 1856–1883', in *Annali Feltrinelli*, Vol 1, 1958, pp. 214–15.

1883

[ENGELS'S SPEECH AT THE GRAVESIDE OF KARL MARX]

On the 14th of March, at a quarter to three in the afternoon, the greatest living thinker ceased to think. He had been left alone for scarcely two minutes, and when we came back we found him in his armchair, peacefully gone to sleep—forever.

An immeasurable loss has been sustained both by the militant proletariat of Europe and America, and by historical science, in the death of this man. The gap that has been left by the departure of this mighty spirit will soon enough make itself felt.

Just as Darwin discovered the law of development of organic nature, so Marx discovered the law of development of human history: the simple fact, hitherto concealed by an overgrowth of ideology, that mankind must first of all eat, drink, have shelter and clothing, before it can pursue politics, science, art, religion, etc.; that therefore the production of the immediate material means of subsistence and consequently the degree of economic development attained by a given people or during a given epoch form the foundation upon which the state institutions, the legal conceptions, the ideas on art, and even on religion, of the people concerned have been evolved, and in the light of which they must, therefore, be explained, instead of *vice versa*, as had hitherto been the case.

But that is not all. Marx also discovered the special law of motion governing the present-day capitalist mode of production and the bourgeois society that this mode of production has created. The discovery of surplus value suddenly threw light on the problem, in trying to solve which all previous investigations, of both bourgeois economists and socialist critics, had been groping in the dark.

Two such discoveries would be enough for one lifetime. Happy the man to whom it is granted to make even one such discovery. But in every single field which Marx investigated—and he investigated very many fields, none of them superficially—in every field, even in that of mathematics, he made independent discoveries.

Such was the man of science. But this was not even half the man. Science was for Marx a historically dynamic, revolutionary force. However great the joy with which he welcomed a new discovery in some theoretical science whose practical application perhaps it was as yet quite impossible to envisage, he experienced quite another kind of joy when the discovery involved immediate revolutionary changes in industry, and in historical development in general. For example, he followed closely the development of the discoveries made in the field of electricity and recently those of Marcel Deprez.

For Marx was before all else a revolutionist. His real mission in life was to contribute, in one way or another, to the overthrow of capitalist society and of the state institutions which it had brought into being, to contribute to the liberation of the modern proletariat, which *he* was the first to make conscious of its own position and its needs, conscious of the conditions of its emancipation. Fighting was his element. And he fought with a passion, a tenacity and a success such as few could rival. His work on the first *Rheinische Zeitung* (1842), the Paris *Vorwärts* (1844), the *Deutsche Brüsseler Zeitung* (1847), the *Neue Rheinische Zeitung* (1848–49), the *New York Tribune* (1852–61), and in addition to these a host of militant pamphlets, work in organizations in Paris, Brussels and London, and finally, crowning all, the formation of the great International Working Men's Association—this was indeed an achievement of which its founder might well have been proud even if he had done nothing else.

And, consequently, Marx was the best hated and most calumniated man of his time. Governments, both absolutist and republican, deported him from their territories. Bourgeois, whether conservative or ultra-democratic, vied with one another in heaping slanders upon him. All this he brushed aside as though it were cobweb, ignoring it, answering only when extreme necessity compelled him. And he died beloved, revered and mourned by millions of revolutionary fellow workers—from the mines of Siberia to California, in all parts of Europe and America—and I make bold to say that though he may have had many opponents he had hardly one personal enemy.

His name will endure through the ages, and so also will his work!

Delivered in English, retranslated from the printed German version in *Der Sozialdemokrat,* 22 March 1883.

II. Karl Marx's
Writings

1. The Formation of a Young Radical: Early Writings, 1841–1844

~~~~~~~~~~~~~~~~~~~~~~~~~~~~~~~~~~~~~~

EDITOR'S NOTE

Karl Marx's early writings are not easy reading. They do not provide the most painless introduction to his work. Often philosophical in subject matter, always philosophical in style and underlying conception, they make constant use of the esoteric terms, concepts, and arguments of Hegelian and Young Hegelian philosophy. Hegelianism as a public philosophy had died by 1848; to later generations of students, and of Marxists, Marx's philosophical writings seemed at worst tortured, at best unnecessarily metaphysical adumbrations of positions developed more clearly and more empirically in Marx's later work. Readers studied them, if at all, in the light of Marx's mature system as presented, say, in the *Communist Manifesto* and *Das Kapital.* They studied them as parts of Marx's intellectual biography, not as self-standing contributions to thought.

In recent years, especially in the 1950s and 1960s, the early philosophical writings have once more had substantial independent impact on modern thought and acquired a substantial independent following. To some, Marx's philosophical critique of modern society—his concern with freedom, universality, and rationality, his treatment of the distinction between the social and the political, and his development of the concept of alienation—seems more interesting and perhaps more lasting than his subsequent analysis of the social and economic ramifications of private property in the means of production or his associated doctrines of class struggle, of the economic contradictions of capitalism, and of the coming expropriation of the expropriators. Be that as it may, it is certainly true that Marx's early philosophical concern with freedom and alienation provides a *leitmotif* for the whole of his work, enabling us to see its structure and thrust more clearly, deepening our appreciation of the complex assumptions and ramifications of his thought, and at the same time explaining some aspects of the renewed crisis of our times, with its demand that political emancipation become genuine social emancipation.

In the four years from 1841 to the end of 1844, Marx moved rapidly from philosophical democratic radicalism to revolutionary socialism, from the 'party of the concept' to the proletariat, from political philosophy to studying the anatomy of civil society, of the world of industry and trade. He did so as part of a process of intellectual self-clarification, conducted, until 1844, in Hegelian terms, and seen by Marx himself as a process of recognizing and overcoming the internal contradictions in the social philosophy of Hegel.

The young Marx is philosophical not only in style, but also in his concerns. His point of departure as a radical is not the existence of poverty, but the existence of domination, privilege, and 'contradictions'. His ethical inspiration comes from Aristotle, Spinoza, and Rousseau; his methodology comes from Hegel and, in a subsidiary but nevertheless important way, from Bruno Bauer and Feuerbach. This gives him the basic assumptions that underlie all his early writings, including the selections presented here, the technically defined concepts of 'freedom', 'universality', and 'rationality', which Marx sees as man's highest and implicit ethical ends and as the essential conditions of true humanity. For Marx all three are closely related, interdependent conceptions. To be free, for him, is to be self-determined, that is, to be determined by one's essence, by one's inner nature and constitution, instead of being determined from without, by the nature and essence of other things. It is to be autonomous and not heteronomous. But the true nature or essence of a thing is always universal; it combines the members of the species or class by seeing what is common to them instead of separating them, seeing them as individuals. The essence, as universal, expresses itself in harmony, cooperation, instead of conflict, for conflict, contradiction, division, rest on separation, on particularity as opposed to universality, and are therefore irrational, one-sided, and incomplete conditions of unfreedom. The realization of philosophy, with which Marx is initially much concerned, is the bringing to actuality of essences and thus of this concept of freedom, universality, and rationality; it is the overcoming of the empirical division, separation, conflict, and 'contradiction' that we find in the empirical world of particulars.

For Marx, as for Hegel, however, there is no ultimate difference in logical status, no dualism, as between the world of thought and the world of things, activities, etc. 'Philosophy' and 'the world' are two aspects of the one process. Contradictions in philosophy will be paralleled by contradictions in the world; philosophical strivings are also worldly strivings. The real conflict is not between philosophy and the world but between the essence, the universal, the rational, on the one hand, and the particular, the partial, the incomplete, on the other. The progress of that conflict, in Marx as in Hegel, is itself logically necessary and determined. It is to be understood by going to the essence of things, by grasping the 'contradictions', partialities, and one-sidedness of specific theories and empirical realities, something that can only be done by grasping the fundamental essence or energizing principle behind the development.

All this is what Marx means by *criticism*, a word that he habitually uses with the philosophical overtones sketched above, thus making the philosophical rendering 'critique' much more appropriate when translating into English. A critique is more than a criticism—it brings out the logical foundations of error and thus shows it to be determined logically, to be a consequence of fundamental 'contradictions' or misconceptions. Thus, in his doctoral dissertation, Marx had endeavoured to show that Epicurus, though at first sight more inconsistent than Democritus, had in fact developed the concept of the atom to a much higher level because, in his doctrine of the swerve, Epicurus had given it 'speculative development' as *free*, self-determined, just as he had overcome vulgar empiricism in his theory of the ultimate unknowability of the causes that determine the movements of heavenly bodies. In a note to the dissertation, reproduced here, Marx set out his conception of philosophy as criticism, as measuring the individual existence against the universal essence, and as therefore necessarily striving to become worldly, to make the world rational and reason actual.

A year later, in 1842 and part of 1843, Marx was writing for and then editing the *Rheinische Zeitung*, turning his main attention to censorship, new laws forbidding the collection of dead wood by the poor, the discussion of material hardship in the Moselle district, and the projected, somewhat 'liberalized', divorce law drafted by Savigny. The articles tend to be written in a somewhat rambling Hegelian debating style; they constantly and often tediously and sophistically search for 'contradictions', whether in speech or reality. But they are again a polemic on behalf of the essence, which is free and universal, against the appearance, which is externally determined, partial, one-sided, and full of contradiction. Thus freedom of the press is for Marx a rational, coherent concept; censorship is necessarily incoherent, contradictory, and parasitic. The article on the draft Divorce Law reproduced here is a particularly clear and unusually succinct example of Marx's approach and style of argumentation at this stage of his development.

In the Kreuznach manuscripts, set down in mid-1843, Marx wrestled for his own satisfaction and intellectual clarification with those sections of Hegel's *Philosophy of Right* that deal with the constitutional law of the state, the princely power, the executive power, and the legislative power. They mark an important further stage in Marx's development. His critique makes use of arguments he had used constantly in the *Rheinische Zeitung,* e.g., that morality and law—freedom, universality, and rationality—cannot be based upon the feudal recognition of privileges and estates, cannot be based on principles of separation, or on arbitrary will. He also insists that the criteria of freedom, universality, and rationality cannot be satisfied when the part is treated as though it were the whole, when the general interest falls into the hands of particular persons or groups—the monarch, the bureaucracy, etc. In the Kreuznach manuscripts, however, he develops his position further into a fundamental internal critique of Hegel. He emphasizes Hegel's failure to resolve the contradiction between the particularity and division of his civil society and the universality and consequent abstractness of his political state and thus brings the 'contradiction' between 'civil society' and the 'political state' to the centre of his own political thinking.

In his contributions to the *Deutsch-französische Jahrbücher,* completed later in 1843 and published in February 1844, Marx presents his new conclusions: the fundamental contradiction of modern society is the contradiction between egoistic civil society and the universal pretensions of the political state, between the egoistic man of economic life and the universal but abstract citizen of political life. The political revolution against feudalism split man into two, consummated man's alienation, divorced man's social but egoistic being in civil society from his political being in the state. Only the proletariat, Marx discovered at the end of 1843—only the proletariat, which stands outside the whole system of private property and of private rights, can overcome this contradiction and bring about a true social emancipation, as distinct from a partial and abstract political emancipation.

From DOCTORAL DISSERTATION, THE DIFFERENCE BETWEEN THE DEMOCRITEAN AND THE EPICUREAN PHILOSOPHY OF NATURE

[FROM THE NOTE TO PART I, CHAPTER 4]

... It is a psychological law that the theoretical spirit which has become internally free is turned into practical energy. Emerging as *will* from the shadow kingdom of Amenthes, it turns against the mundane reality that exists without it. ... The *practice* [*praxis*] of philosophy, however, is itself *theoretical.* It is *criticism,* which measures individual existence against essence, particular reality against the Idea. But this *direct realization* of philosophy is burdened by contradiction in its innermost essence, an essence which manifests itself in the appearance and puts its stamp upon it.

Inasmuch as philosophy as will turns toward the world of appearances, the [philosophical] system is reduced to an abstract totality and thus becomes one side of the world confronted by another side. Its relation to the world is a reflexive relation. Caught up in the drive to realize itself it comes into tension with everything else. Its inner self-sufficiency and rounded completeness is destroyed. What was an inner light becomes a consuming flame, turned outward. We thus arrive at the consequence that the world's becoming philosophical is at the same time philosophy's becoming worldly, that the realization of philosophy is at the same time its loss, that what it struggles against outside is its own inner defect, that it is precisely in this struggle that it falls into the defects which it fights in its opponents, and that it can transcend these defects only by falling victim to them. That which opposes philosophy and that which philosophy struggles against is always the same thing as philosophy, only with the factors reversed.

This is one side, when we treat the matter *purely objectively* as the immediate realization of philosophy. But there is also a *subjective* side, which is only a different form of the matter. This is *the relation of the philosophical system* brought into actuality *to its intellectual bearers*, to the individual self-consciousnesses through which its progress manifests itself. The relation involved in the realization of philosophy in opposition to the world implies that these individual self-consciousnesses always have a *double-edged demand*, one edge turning against the world and the other against philosophy itself. For what is in fact a relation turned on itself appears in those self-consciousnesses as a dual, self-contradictory demand and action. Their freeing the world from non-philosophy is at the same time their freeing themselves from that philosophy which, as a particular system, held them in fetters. Themselves involved in the action and the immediate energy of development and therefore theoretically not yet able to transcend that system, they sense only the contradiction with the plastic self-identity of the system and do not know that in turning against it they only actualize its particular moments.

Finally we have this duality of the philosophical self-consciousness manifesting itself in dual directions diametrically opposed to each other. One of these directions, which we may call generally the *liberal party*, takes as its mainstay adherence to the Concept and to the Principle of Philosophy; the other adheres to its having *No-Concept*, to taking the element of reality as its mainstay. This second direction is *positive philosophy*. The act of the first direction is criticism—that is, exactly, the turning outward of philosophy; the act of the second is the attempt to philosophize—that is, the turning inward of philosophy. The second direction sees deficiency as immanent in philosophy, while the first conceives deficiency as deficiency in a world that has to be made philosophical. Each of these parties does precisely what the other would like to do and what it itself does not want to do. But the first party, with its inner contradiction, is conscious of principle in general and of its own aims. In the second party we have perversity, madness so to speak, as such. According to its content, only the liberal party, the party of the Concept, can bring about real progress, while positive philosophy can achieve only demands and tendencies whose form contradicts their meaning.

MEGA I, 1-i, 64–65; MEW *Ergänzungsband*, Part 1, 326–30.

1842
'THE DRAFT DIVORCE LAW'

COLOGNE, Dec. 18 [1842]. The *Rheinische Zeitung* has taken a *totally isolated* stand on the *Divorce Bill*, but no one has yet shown it that this stand is untenable. The *Rheinische Zeitung* agrees with the Bill in so far as it considers Prussian matrimonial legislation up to now to have been inconsonant with morality, the innumerable quantity and frivolity of the grounds for divorce to be inadmissible, and the current procedure to be unsuited to the dignity of the cause, a point, incidentally, which applies to all Old Prussian court proceedings. On the other hand, the *Rheinische Zeitung* urges the following main objections to the Bill: (1) that instead of *reform* there has been mere *revision*, so that the Prussian Law remains the fundamental law, producing a piecemeal effect and creating considerable uncertainty; (2) that the Legislature has treated marriage as a *religious* institution, as an *ecclesiastical* institution, instead of treating it as a *moral* one, and has missed the *secular* nature of marriage; (3) that the procedure is imperfect and brings together contradictory elements in a [purely] external way; (4) that on the one hand there are police severities contradicting the concept of marriage, and on the other, excessive concessions to so-called equitable grounds; (5) that the entire drafting of the Bill leaves much to be desired in terms of logical connection, precision, clarity and guiding principles.

In so far as the opponents of the Bill denounce any of these shortcomings, we agree with them, but we cannot possibly accept their unconditional apology for the previous system. We repeat a statement we have uttered before: 'If legislation cannot enact public morality, still less can it accept immorality as law.' If we ask on what *these* opponents (who are not opponents of the ecclesiastical treatment and of the other shortcomings indicated) rest their reasoning, we are met with constant talk of the unhappiness of the marriage partners, bound against their will. These opponents adopt a eudaemonistic standpoint, they think only of the two individuals, they forget the *family*, they forget that almost every dissolution of a marriage is the dissolution of a family, and that even from a purely legal standpoint the children and their expectations cannot be made dependent on caprice and its whims. If marriage were not the basis of the family, it would no more be the object of legislation than friendship is, for instance. The opponents, therefore, consider *only* the individual will, or rather, the *arbitrary will*, of the marriage partner; they do not consider the *will of the marriage*, the moral substance of this relationship. The legislator, however, has to regard himself as a scientist. He does not *make* laws, he does not invent them, he only formulates them, he expresses as conscious positive laws the inner laws of intellectual and spiritual [*geistiger*] relationships. Just as the legislator is accused of gross arbitrariness the moment he replaces the essential nature of the matter with his own whims and fancies, so the legislator has a corresponding right to regard it as gross arbitrariness when private persons seek to uphold their caprices against the essential nature of the matter. No one is forced to contract a marriage; but everyone must be forced, the moment he contracts a marriage, to resolve upon obedience to the laws of marriage. A person who contracts a marriage no more *makes* or *invents* marriage than a swimmer invents nature and the laws of water and of gravity. Marriage, therefore, cannot adapt itself to his caprice, to his arbitrary will, but his caprice, his arbitrary will, must adapt itself to marriage. The person who arbitrarily breaks a marriage maintains: *Caprice, lawlessness, is the law of marriage*, for no rational person would have the presumption to regard his actions as privileged actions, as actions appropriate for *him only*. On the contrary, he will claim that they are lawful actions, *appropriate for everyone*. What then are you opposing? You oppose arbitrary legislation, but you cannot seek to make caprice into law in the very moment that you accuse the legislator of capriciousness.

Hegel says that *in itself*, according to its concept, marriage is indissoluble, but *only* in itself, i.e., only according to its concept. This lays down nothing *peculiar* to marriage. All moral relationships are indissoluble *according to their concept*, as one can easily convince one's self by postulating their *truth*. A *true* state, a *true* marriage, a *true* friendship, are indissoluble. But no state, no marriage, no friendship corresponds completely to its concept, and just like actual friendship even in the family, just like the actual state in world history, so the actual marriage in the state is *dissoluble*. No moral *existence* corresponds to its *essence*, or at least, *needs* to correspond to its essence. Just as in nature dissolution and death appear spontaneously when a particular existing thing no longer corresponds fully to its definition, just as world history decides whether a state has departed so far from the idea of the state that it no longer deserves to exist, so the state decides under what conditions an *existing* marriage has ceased to be a marriage. The dissolution of a marriage is nothing but the declaration: This marriage is a *dead* marriage, whose existence is only a snare and a delusion. It is self-evident, of course, that neither the capricious will of the legislator nor the capricious will of the private person, but only the *nature of the case*, can decide whether a marriage is dead or not, for it is well-known that a declaration of death depends on the factual evidence and not on the *wishes* of the parties concerned. But if in the case of *physical* death you demand precise and unmistakeable proofs, must not a legislator lay down a *moral death* only after the most incontestable symptoms, since the conservation of moral relationships is not only his right, but also his *duty*, the duty of his self-preservation?

The *guarantee* that the *conditions* under which the *existence* of a moral relationship no longer corresponds with its *essence* will be laid down truly, in accordance with the state of knowledge and of universal opinion, without preconceptions, can be found only when law is the conscious expression of the will of the people, created with it and through it. As far as making divorce easier or more difficult is concerned, we will say only one more word: Do you regard a natural organism as sound, healthy, correctly organised if every external knock, every injury, destroys it? Would you not consider yourself slighted if it were assumed as an axiom that your friendship could not withstand the slightest mishap and would *necessarily* dissolve before every worry? In respect of marriage, however, the legislator can only determine when a marriage *may* be dissolved, i.e., when according to its essence it already has been dissolved. The judicial dissolution can only be a formal recording of the inner dissolution. The standpoint of the legislator is the standpoint of necessity. The legislator thus *honours* marriage, recognizes its deep moral essence, when he considers it powerful enough to withstand many collisions without suffering internal damage. Yielding to the wishes of individuals would be intransigence toward the essential nature of individuals, toward their moral rationality as embodied in moral relationships.

Finally, we can only say that it is rash to accuse the States with *strict notions of divorce*, to which the Rhineland is *proud* to belong, of *hypocrisy*. Only someone who cannot see beyond the moral degeneration surrounding him could dare such accusations, which are regarded as laughable in the Rhine Province, and taken at most as proof that the very *conception* of moral relationships is being lost and that every moral fact can be treated as a lie and a *fairy tale.* Such is the direct consequence of laws not dictated by respect for man, a mistake which is not erased by passing from material contempt to intellectual contempt and putting a demand for thoughtless obedience to super-moral and supernatural authority in place of the demand for conscious submission to natural-moral powers.

MEGA I, 1-i, 317–20; MEW 1, 148–51.

1843
From THE KREUZNACH MANUSCRIPTS: CRITIQUE OF HEGEL'S *PHILOSOPHY OF RIGHT*

[FROM DISCUSSION OF THE PRINCELY POWER, COMMENTS ON HEGEL'S § 279]

. . . Democracy is the truth of monarchy; monarchy is not the truth of democracy. Monarchy is forced to be democracy as a *non sequitur* within itself, whereas the monarchical moment is not a *non sequitur* within democracy. Democracy can be understood in its own terms; monarchy cannot. In democracy, none of its moments acquires a meaning other than that which is appropriate to it. Each is actually only a moment within the whole demos. In monarchy, a part determines the character of the whole. The whole constitution has to take shape on this firm foundation. Democracy is the type or species of the constitution. Monarchy is a variety, and indeed a bad variety. Democracy is 'form and content'. Monarchy is *supposed* to be only form, but it falsifies the content.

In monarchy, the whole, the people, is subsumed under one of its particular modes of existence, that of the political constitution. In democracy, on the other hand, the *constitution itself* appears as only *one* determination, and indeed, as the self-determination of the people. In monarchy we have the people of the constitution; in democracy, we have the constitution of the people. Democracy is the *riddle* of all constitutions solved. In democracy the constitution is always based on its actual foundation, on *actual man* and the *actual people*, not only *in itself*, according to its essence, but in its *existence* and actuality; it is postulated as autonomous. The constitution is seen as what it is, the freely-created product of man. One could say that in some respects this is also true of constitutional monarchy, but what specifically differentiates democracy is the fact that in democracy the *constitution* is only one particular moment in the existence of the people, that the *political constitution* does not itself constitute the state.

Hegel begins with the state and turns man into the state subjectivized; democracy begins with man and makes the state into man objectivized. Just as religion does not create man but man creates religion, so the constitution does not create the people but the people create the constitution. In certain respects, democracy bears the same relation to all other forms of state as Christianity bears to all other religions. Christianity is religion *par excellence*, the *essence of religion*, man deified as a *particular* religion. Similarly, democracy is the *essence of* every constitution; it is socialized man as a particular constitution. Democracy is related to other constitutions as a species is related to its varieties. But in democracy the species itself appears as a particular [form of] existence, as one therefore that appears as a particular type *vis-à-vis* other particular [individual] existences that do not correspond to their essence. Democracy is the Old Testament in relation to all other forms of state. Man does not exist for the law, but the law exists for man. In democracy law is the existence of man, while in other forms of state man is the existence of law. This is the fundamental distinguishing mark of democracy.

All other *state formations* are specific, definite, *particular forms of state*. In democracy the *formal* principle is at the same time the *material* principle. Only democracy, therefore, is the true unity of the universal and the particular. In monarchy, for instance, in a republic as merely a particular form of state, political man has a specific existence next to the unpolitical man, the private man. Property, contract, marriage, civil society here appear as particular modes of existence along side the political state. (Hegel develops this with complete correctness for these *abstract* forms of state, but he is under the impression that he is unfolding the idea of the state.) These particular modes of existence appear as the *content* in respect of which the *political state* constitutes the *organizing form*, but in actuality only as a content that determines and limits understanding, that is itself without content, that approves at the one time and denies at another. In democracy the political state, in so far as it puts itself beside this content and distinguishes itself from it, is itself only a *particular* content and a particular *form of existence* of the people. In monarchy, for example, this particularity, this political constitution, signifies the *universal* which dominates and determines everything particular. In democracy the state as particular is *only* particular, while as universal it is the actual existing universal, i.e. it is nothing determinate in contrast with the remaining content. Modern French thinkers have understood this in such a way, that they see the *political state disappearing* in true democracy. This is correct to the extent that the political state as political state, as constitution, no longer has significance for the whole.

In all states other than democracy the *state*, the *law*, the *constitution* is dominant without actually dominating, i.e. without penetrating materially the content of the remaining non-political spheres. In democracy the constitution, the law, the state itself as a political constitution is only a self-determination of the people, a particular content of theirs.

It is self-evident, incidentally, that all forms of state have democracy as their truth, and are therefore untrue in so far as they are not democratic.

MEGA I, 1-i, 434–36; MEW 1, 230–32.

[FROM DISCUSSION OF THE EXECUTIVE POWER, HEGEL'S § 287ff.]

... 'Bureaucracy' is the *'étatist formalisation'* [*Staatsformalismus*] of civil society. It is the 'state's consciousness', the 'state's will', the 'state's power' as made into a *corporation*, hence into a *particular*, *closed* society within the state. (The 'universal interest' can confront the particular only as itself a 'particular' so long as the particular confronts the universal as itself a 'universal'. Bureaucracy must therefore protect the *imaginary* universality of the particular interest, namely the spirit of the corporation, in order to protect the *imaginary* particularity of the universal interest, namely its own spirit. The state has to be a corporation so long as the corporation wants to be a state.) ...

The 'étatist formalisation' which is the bureaucracy is the 'state as formalism', and Hegel has described it as such a formalism. Since this 'étatist formalisation' constitutes itself into an actual power and becomes its own *material* content, it is obvious that the 'bureaucracy' is a web of *practical* illusions or the 'illusion of the state'. The bureaucratic spirit is thoroughly Jesuitical and theological. The bureaucrats are the Jesuits and theologians of the state. Bureaucracy is the republic of priests.

. . . The spirit of bureaucracy is the 'formal spirit of the state'. Bureaucracy makes the formal spirit of the state or the state's *actual* lack of spirit its categorical imperative. Bureaucracy sees itself as the ultimate final purpose of the state. Since bureaucracy everywhere converts its 'formal' purposes into its content, it everywhere comes into conflict with 'real' purposes. It is therefore false to pretend that the formal is the content and that the content is the formal. The purposes of the state are transformed into the purposes of bureaux and the purposes of bureaux are transformed into purposes of the state. Bureaucracy is a circle from which no one can escape. Its hierarchy is a *hierarchy of knowing*. The top echelon leaves insight into details to the lower circles, while the lower circles leave insight into the universal to the top; they thus mutually deceive each other.

Bureaucracy is the imaginary state next to the real state; it is the spiritualism of the state. Everything therefore has a double meaning, a real meaning and a bureaucratic one, just as knowledge (and the will) are something double, both real and bureaucratic. But the real is dealt with according to its bureaucratic nature, according its other-worldly, spiritual essence. The bureaucracy has the essence of the state, the spiritual essence of society, in its possession; this is its *private property*. The universal spirit of bureaucracy is the *secret*, the mystery, sustained within bureaucracy itself by hierarchy and protected externally as a closed corporation. The openly public-spirited and the feeling for the state therefore appear to bureaucracy as a betrayal of its mystery. *Authority* is therefore the principle of the bureaucracy's knowledge, and the deification of authority is its *sentiment*. Within bureaucracy itself, however, its *spiritualism* becomes a *crass materialism*, the materialism of passive obedience, of faith in authority, of the *mechanical nature* of fixedly formal activity, fixed fundamental principles, views and traditions. So far as the individual bureaucrat is concerned, the purpose of the state becomes his private purpose, *hunting for higher positions, making a career*. In the first place, he sees real life as *material*, since the spirit of this life *has a separate existence of its own* in bureaucracy. Bureaucracy must therefore strive to make life as material as possible. In the second place, life for the individual bureaucrat himself is actually material insofar as it becomes the object of bureaucratic treatment, for the bureaucratic spirit is prescribed for him, his purpose lies outside him, his existence is the existence of his bureau.

MEGA I, 1-i, 455–57; MEW 1, 248–49.

From A CORRESPONDENCE OF 1843

[An exchange of letters between Marx, Ruge, and Bakunin concerning the prospects of social and political emancipation was published in lieu of an editorial statement in the first and only issue of *Deutsch-französische Jahrbücher* in February 1844, to indicate the *raison d'être* of the journal. The passages that follow are from letters by Marx.]

... Man's self-esteem, freedom, must be awakened once more in the heart of these men. Only this feeling, which disappeared from the world with the Greeks and vanished into the blue mists of heaven with Christianity, can once more transform society into a fellowship of men working for their highest purposes, a democratic state.

Those people, on the other hand, who do not feel themselves to be men become appendages of their masters, like a herd of slaves or horses. The hereditary masters are the point of this whole society. This world belongs to them. They take it as it is and as it feels. They take themselves as they find themselves and stand where their feet have grown, on the necks of these political animals who know no other destiny than to be subject, loyal and at their master's service.

The world of the philistines is the *political kingdom of animals;* if we have to recognize its existence then we have no alternative but simply to accept the *status quo.* Centuries of barbarism created and shaped it and it now exists as a consistent system, whose principle is the *dehumanized world.* The perfected world of the philistine, our Germany, naturally had to lag far behind the French Revolution, which restored man to himself. A German Aristotle, who would take his *Politics* from our conditions, would write on the first page: 'Man is a social, but a completely apolitical, animal.'

... In Germany everything is forcibly suppressed: a real anarchy of the spirit, the regime of stupidity itself, has set in and Zurich obeys the orders that come from Berlin. It is becoming clearer and clearer therefore that we must seek a new meeting place for the genuinely thoughtful and independent. I am convinced that our plan [to found the radical journal, the *Deutsch-französische Jahrbücher*] will answer a real need and real demands must be met ... The internal difficulties seem almost greater than the external obstacles. Even if there is no doubt about the 'whence', there is only all the more confusion about the 'whither'. Not only has general anarchy broken out among reformers, each will have to admit to himself that he has no exact idea of what is to be. But that is precisely the advantage of the new direction, namely that we do not anticipate the world dogmatically, but seek to find a new world through criticism of the old. Up to now philosophers had the solution to all riddles lying in their desks, and the stupid outside world had only to open its mouth to let the roast pigeons of absolute science fly in. Philosophy has become worldly, and the most striking proof of this is the fact that the philosophical consciousness has been drawn into the torment of the fray—not only externally, but internally as well. If the building of the future and its consummation for all time is not to be our work, then it is still clearer what we have to accomplish at this time—I mean *the relentless criticism of all existing conditions*, relentless in the sense that the criticism must not be afraid of its results and just as little afraid of conflict with the powers that be.

I am not in favour, therefore, of setting up a dogmatic standard; on the contrary. We must try to help the dogmatists make their propositions clear to themselves. Thus *communism* especially is a dogmatic abstraction. When I say this I do not have in mind some imagined or possible communism, but the actual existing one, as taught by Cabet, Dezamy, Weitling, etc. This communism is only a manifestation of the humanistic principle which holds itself separate and is infected by its opposite, private being. The dissolution and transcendence of private property, therefore, is in no way identical with communism, and the confrontation between communism and other socialist teachings—such as those of Fourier, Proudhon, etc.— is not accidental but necessary, because communism itself is only a particular, one-sided realization of the socialist principle.

And the entire socialist principle in turn is only one aspect of the *reality* of the truly human existence. We must be just as concerned with the other aspect, the theoretical existence of man. We must make religion, science, etc. the object of our criticism. Moreover, we wish to influence our contemporaries, and especially our German contemporaries. The question is, how does one go about this? Two facts cannot be denied. Religion first, and then politics, constitute the chief interest of Germany today. Whatever state these may be in, we must take our departure from them and not simply set up against them some finished system, such as, for instance, [Cabet's] *Voyage to Icaria.*

Reason has always existed, but not always in a rational form. The critic can therefore begin with any form of the theoretical and practical consciousness and develop, out of the forms *inherent* in existing actuality, that true reality which is existing actuality's ought-to-be and final aim. So far as actual life is concerned, it is precisely the *political state*, even where it is not consciously permeated by socialist demands, which contains in all its *modern* forms the demands of reason. And the political state does not rest there. Everywhere it assumes the realization of reason. Equally, however, it falls everywhere into the contradiction between its ideal character and its real presuppositions.

Out of this conflict of the political state with itself, therefore, it is possible to develop everywhere the social truth. Just as *religion* is the table of contents of the theoretical struggles of mankind, so the *political state* is that of the practical ones. The political state therefore expresses within its form, *sub specie rei publicae*, all social struggles, needs and truths. It is therefore in no way below the level of our principles to take as the object of our criticism the most specific political problem, e.g., the difference between a system of estates and a representative system. For this question only expresses in a *political* way the difference between the sovereignty of man and the sovereignty of private property ... Nothing therefore prevents us from tying our criticism to the criticism of politics, from taking sides in politics, from becoming involved in real struggles and identifying with them. Then we do not face the world in doctrinaire fashion with a new principle, declaring, 'Here is truth, kneel here!' We develop new principles for the world out of the world's principles. We do not tell the world, 'Cease your struggles, they are stupid;

we want to give you the true watchword for the struggle', we shall only show the world why it actually struggles. The consciousness of this is something which the world *must* acquire even if it does not want to.

MEGA I, 1-i, 561–62, 572–75; MEW 1, 338–39, 343–45.

1844
From 'ON THE JEWISH QUESTION'

I

[Comment on *Die Judenfrage* (*The Jewish Question*) by Bruno Bauer, Braunschweig, 1843; published in *Deutsch-französische Jahrbücher*, February 1844.]

The Jews of Germany want emancipation. What sort of emancipation do they want? *Civil, political* emancipation.

Bruno Bauer gives them the reply: No one in Germany is politically emancipated. We ourselves are not free. How shall we emancipate you? You Jews are *egoists* if you demand a special emancipation for yourselves as Jews. You should work as Germans for the political emancipation of Germany and as men for the emancipation of mankind. You should regard the particular form in which you are oppressed and shamed not as an exception to the rule, but rather as its confirmation ... The *Christian* state knows only *privileges*. In it the Jew has the privilege of being a Jew. As a Jew he has rights that Christians do not have. Why does he want rights which he does not have and which Christians enjoy?

If the Jew wants to be emancipated from the Christian state, then he is demanding that the Christian state abandon its *religious* prejudice. But does the Jew abandon *his* religious prejudice? Has he then the right to demand this rejection of religion from another?

The Christian state by *its very nature* cannot emancipate the Jew but, Bauer adds, the Jew by his nature cannot be emancipated. So long as the state remains Christian and the Jew Jewish, both remain equally incapable of either giving or receiving emancipation ...

On what basis then do you Jews want emancipation? On the basis of your religion? It is the mortal enemy of the state religion. As citizens? There are no citizens in Germany. As men? You are not men, just as those to whom you appeal are not men either.

Bauer, after criticizing previous formulations and solutions, has put the question of Jewish emancipation in a new way. What, he asks, is the nature of the Jew who is to be emancipated and of the Christian state that is to emancipate him? He replies with a critique of the Jewish religion, he analyses the *religious* contradiction between Judaism and Christianity and he explains the essence of the Christian state. All this he does with élan, acuteness, wit and thoroughness, in a style as precise as it is energetic and charged with content.

How, then, does Bauer solve the Jewish question? What is the result? To formulate a question is to solve it. The critique of the Jewish question is the answer to the Jewish question ...

On the one hand, Bauer demands that the Jew give up Judaism and that man generally give up religion so that he might be emancipated *as a citizen.* On the other hand, Bauer regards the political abolition of religion as logically implying the abolition of religion altogether. The state that presupposes religion is not yet a true, a real state. 'To be sure religious conceptions reinforce the state. But which state? *What kind of state?*' (p. 97.)

At this point the one-sidedness of Bauer's formulation of the Jewish question becomes apparent. It is by no means sufficient to ask: Who is to emancipate? Who is to be emancipated? Criticism has yet a third task. It must ask: *What kind of emancipation* is involved? What underlying conditions are involved in the very nature of the sought-for emancipation? The ultimate critique of the Jewish question is the critique of *political* emancipation itself and the true resolution of that question into the *'universal question of the age'*.

Because Bauer does not raise the question to this level, he falls into contradictions. He imposes conditions that are not based on the essential nature of *political* emancipation. He throws up questions irrelevant to his problem and he solves problems that leave his question unresolved. Of the opponents of Jewish emancipation, Bauer says: 'Their mistake lay simply in this, that they assumed the Christian state to be the only true state and that they have not subjected it to the same critique as they apply to Judaism' (p. 3). But Bauer's mistake here lies in the fact that he criticizes only the 'Christian state' and not the state as such, in the fact that he fails to examine *the relation between political emancipation and human emancipation* and that he therefore imposes conditions that can be explained only as the product of his uncritical confusion of political emancipation and universal human emancipation. Bauer asks the Jews: Have you the right, from your standpoint, to demand *political emancipation?*, while we ask the contrary: Has the standpoint of *political* emancipation the right to demand from the Jews abolition of Judaism and from man the abolition of religion?

The Jewish question presents itself in different ways according to the state in which the Jew finds himself. In Germany, where there is no political state, no state as state, the Jewish question is a purely *theological* question. The Jew finds himself in *religious* opposition to a state that acknowledges Christianity as its foundation. This state is a theologian by profession. Here, critique is critique of theology, a double-edged critique, critique of

Christian theology and of Jewish theology. We still move within theology, no matter how *critically* we may move within it.

In France, in a *constitutional* state, the Jewish question is the question of constitutionalism, the question of the *incompleteness of political emancipation*. Here the *semblance* of a state religion is preserved, even if only in an empty and self-contradictory formula, in the formula of the *religion of the majority* and the relation of the Jew to the state therefore also retains the *semblance* of a religious or theological contradiction.

Only in the free states of North America—or at least in some of them—does the Jewish question lose its *theological* significance and become a truly *secular* question. The Jew's relationship toward the political state, and that of the religious man generally—in other words, the relationship between religion and the state—can appear in its pure form only where the political state has reached its full development. The critique of this relationship ceases to be theological as soon as the state abandons a *theological* posture toward religion, as soon as it deals with religion as a state, i.e., *politically*. Then critique becomes the *critique of the political state*. At this point, where the question ceases to be *theological*, Bauer's critique ceases to be critical. In the United States there is neither a state religion, nor a religion officially declared to be that of the majority nor a pre-eminence of one form of worship over another. The state is a stranger to all forms of worship (G. de Beaumont, *Marie ou l'esclavage aux Etats-Unis* [*Marie or Slavery in the United States*], Paris, 1835, p. 214). There are even some North American states where 'the constitution imposes no form of religious faith and no specific religious practice as a precondition for political rights' (*loc. cit.*, p. 225). Yet 'people in the United States do not believe that a man professing no religion can be an honest man' (*loc. cit.*, p. 224).

North America, further, is pre-eminently the land of religiosity, as Beaumont, Tocqueville and the Englishman Hamilton unanimously assure us. The North American states serve us only as an example. The question is: What is the relation of consummated political emancipation to religion? If we find, even in the country of perfected political emancipation, that religion not only *exists* but leads a *fresh* and *vital* existence, then we have proof that the existence of religion does not contradict the perfection of the state. But since the existence of religion is the existence of a defect, the source of this defect has to be sought in the *essential nature* of the state itself. We no longer take religion to be the *basis* of secular narrowness, but only as its *manifestation.* We therefore explain the religious inhibition of free citizens out of their secular inhibition. We do not claim that they must give up their religious limitations in order to transcend their secular limitations. We claim that they will transcend their religious limitations once they have transcended their secular limits. We do not convert secular questions into theological ones. We convert theological questions into secular ones. History has been resolved into superstitions long enough; we can now resolve superstition into history. For us the question of the *relation between political emancipation and religion* becomes the question of the *relation between political emancipation and human emancipation* ...

The political emancipation of the Jew, of the Christian, of the *religious* man generally is the *emancipation of the state* from Judaism, from Christianity, from *religion* in general ...

The limits of political emancipation immediately become evident in the fact that the *state* can free itself of a limitation without men really being free of it, that a state can be a *free state* without men becoming *free men* ...

It is possible for the state to have emancipated itself from religion even though the *overwhelming majority* is still religious. And the overwhelming majority does not cease to be religious simply because it is religious *in private*.

... Man frees himself from a limitation *politically*, *through the state*, by overcoming the limitation in an *abstract, limited* and partial manner, in a manner that stands in contradiction with himself. Further, when man frees himself *politically*, he frees himself *indirectly*, through an *intermediary*, even if that *intermediary* be a *necessary* one. It follows finally that man is still captive to religion when he proclaims himself an atheist through the mediation of the state, i.e., when he proclaims the state to be an atheist, because man recognizes himself only indirectly, through a *mediator*. The state is the mediator between man and the freedom of man. Just as Christ is the mediator onto whom man loads all his divinity and his religious limitations, so the state is the mediator to which man surrenders all his unholiness and all his *human lack of limitation*.

The *political* elevation of man over religion shares in all the defects and all the advantages of political elevation generally. The state as state, e.g., abolishes *private property;* man proclaims that private property has been *overcome politically* once the *property qualification* for the right to vote or to be elected has been abolished, as has been done in many North American states. Politically, *Hamilton* interprets this fact correctly when he says '*The great majority of the people have gained a victory over property owners and financial wealth*'. Has not private property been abolished in idea when the have-nots become the legislators for the haves? The *property qualification* is the last *political* form of recognition of private property.

Nevertheless, the political annulment of private property does not abolish private property; on the contrary, it presupposes it. The state abolishes distinctions of *birth, rank, education* and *occupation* according to its fashion when it takes distinctions of birth, rank, education and occupation to be *non-political* distinctions, when it proclaims that every member of the community participates *equally* in popular sovereignty without regard to these distinctions, and when it deals with all elements of the actual life of the nation from the standpoint of the state. For all that, the state permits private property, education and occupation to *act* and to make their *specific* being felt in *their* own way, i.e., as private property, as education, as occupation. Far from overcoming these *factual* distinctions, the political state exists only by presupposing them; it sees itself as a *political state* and makes its *universality* effective only in opposition to these, its elements . . .

The perfected political state is in its essence the *species-life* of man in *opposition* to his material life. All the presuppositions of this egoistic life remain in *civil society*, as properties of civil society, *outside* the sphere of the state. Where the political state has reached its true form, man leads a double life, a heavenly life and an earthly one, not only in thought, in consciousness, but in *reality*, in life itself. He leads a life within the *political community* [*politisches Gemeinwesen*], in which he is himself a *communal being* [*Gemeinwesen*] and he leads a life in *civil society* in which he acts as a *private individual*, regarding other people as means and degrading himself to the level of a means, so that he becomes the football of alien powers. The political state is as spiritual in its relation to civil society as heaven is in relation to earth. It stands in the same opposition to civil society; it overcomes civil society in the same way as religion overcomes the limitations of the profane world, i.e. by recognizing and reestablishing that world and allowing itself to be dominated by it. Man in his *innermost* actuality, in civil society, is a profane being. Here, where he is regarded as a real individual by himself and by others, he is an *illusory* [*lit. 'untrue'*] appearance. In the state, on the other hand, where he counts as a species-being, he is an imaginary member of an imagined sovereignty. He is divested of his real individual life and endowed with an unreal universality. The conflict in which man as believer in a *particular* religion finds himself—a conflict with its own citizenship with other men as members of the community—reduces itself to the *secular* split between the *political* state and *civil society*. For man as a *bourgeois* 'life in the state is only appearance or a momentary exception from the rule and real nature of things'. Of course, the *bourgeois*, like the Jew, participates in the life of the state only sophistically, just as the *citoyen* is only sophistically a Jew or a *bourgeois:* but his sophistry is not personal. It is the *sophistry of the political state* itself. The difference between the religious man and the citizen is the difference between the shopkeeper and the citizen, between the day-laborer and the citizen, between the landowner and the citizen, between the *living individual* and the *citizen*. The contradiction between the religious man and the political man is the same as the contradiction between the *bourgeois* and the *citoyen*, between the member of civil society and his *political lion skin*.

The Jewish question then, is finally reducible to a secular conflict, to the relationship between the political state and its presuppositions, whether these presuppositions be material elements, such as private property, or spiritual elements, such as education and religion. It is reducible to the conflict between the *general* interest and the *private* interest, to the split between the *political state* and *civil society*. These secular contradictions Bauer leaves as they are, while he attacks their *religious* expression . . .

Political emancipation is indeed a great step forward. It is not, to be sure, the final form of human emancipation in general, but it is the final form of human emancipation *within* the prevailing order. Naturally, we speak here of real, practical emancipation.

Man emancipates himself from religion *politically* by banishing it from the sphere of public law into that of private right. Religion is no longer the spirit of the *state* where man behaves as a species-being in community with other men, even if he does so in a limited way, under a particular form and in a specific sphere. It has become the spirit of *civil society*, of the sphere of egoism, of the *bellum omnium contra omnes*. It is no longer the essence of *community*, but the essence of *distinction*. Religion has become what it was *originally*, an expression of the *separation* of man from his *communal* nature, from himself and from other men. It now remains only an abstract recognition of a particular oddity, of a *private whim*, of caprice. The endless proliferation of religious sects in North America, e.g., already gives religion the *external* form of a purely individual concern. It has been relegated to its place among numerous private interests and exiled from the communal being as communal being. But one must not deceive oneself about the limits of political emancipation. The splitting of man into the *public* man and the *private* man, the *displacement* of religion from the state into civil society, is not a step in political emancipation but its *completion*. Political emancipation does not abolish man's *actual* religiosity any more than it seeks to abolish it.

. . . To be sure, in times when the political state as such is born, violently, out of civil society, when men strive to liberate themselves under the form of political self-liberation, the state can and must go on to *abolish* and destroy religion. But it does so only in the way that it abolishes private property, by setting a maximum, providing for confiscation and progressive taxation, just as it abolishes life by establishing the guillotine. In moments when political life has a specially strong feeling for its own importance, it seeks to repress its presuppositions, civil society and its elements, and to constitute itself as the real, harmonious species-life of man. It can do this only by entering into *violent* contradiction with its own conditions of existence; it can do so only by declaring the revolution

to be *permanent;* and the political drama therefore necessarily ends with the restoration of religion, of private
property, and of all the elements of civil society, just as
war ends with peace ...

We have shown, then, that political emancipation from
religion leaves religion standing, even if not as privileged
religion. The contradiction in which the follower of a specific religion finds himself in relation to his citizenship is
only *one aspect* of the universal secular *contradiction between the political state and civil society.* The consummation of the Christian state is a state that recognizes itself as
state and abstracts itself from the religion of its members.
The emancipation of the state from religion is not the
emancipation of actual man from religion.

We thus do not join with Bauer in saying to the Jews:
You cannot be politically emancipated without radically
emancipating yourselves from Judaism. We tell them,
rather: Because you can be emancipated politically without renouncing Judaism completely and unprotestingly,
therefore *political emancipation* by itself cannot be
human emancipation. If you Jews want to be politically
emancipated without emancipating yourselves humanly,
then the half-heartedness and contradiction lies not only
in you: it lies in the *essence* and in the *category* of political
emancipation. If you are caught in the confines of this category, you share a general confinement. Just as the state
evangelizes when, in spite of being a state, it behaves toward the Jew in a Christian way, so the Jew *acts politically* when, in spite of being a Jew, he demands civil
rights.

But if a man can be emancipated politically and acquire
civil rights even though he is a Jew, can he claim and acquire the so-called *rights of man?* Bauer denies this ...

According to Bauer, man must sacrifice the 'privilege of
faith' to be able to acquire the universal rights of man. Let
us consider for a moment these so-called rights of man and
consider them in their most authentic form, in the form

they have among their *discoverers*, the North Americans and the French. In part these rights of man are *political* rights, rights than can be exercised only in community with others. Indeed, participation in the *community*, in the *political* community or *state*, makes up their substance. They come under the category of *political freedom*, of *civil rights*, which, as we have seen, in no way presuppose the consistent and positive transcendence of religion, and therefore also not of Judaism. It remains for us to consider the other part of human rights, the *droits de l'homme* in so far as they are distinguished from the *droits du citoyen*. These rights include freedom of conscience, the right to practise one's chosen religion. The *privilege of faith* is expressly recognized, either as a right of man or as a consequence of one of the rights of man—the right of freedom.

Declaration of the Rights of Man and of Citizens, 1791, Art. 10: 'No one is to be caused unease on account of his beliefs, even of his religious beliefs.' Chapter I of the Constitution of 1791 guarantees as a right of man 'the liberty of every man to practise the form of religious worship to which he is attached'.

Declaration of the Rights of Man etc. 1793, includes among the rights of man, Art. 7: 'Freedom of Worship'. Further, in regard to the right to express one's thoughts and opinions, to assemble and to worship it maintains: 'The necessity for proclaiming these *rights* presupposes the presence or the recent memory of despotism.' Compare the Constitution of 1795, Chapter XIV, Art. 354.

Constitution of Pennsylvania, Art. 9. para. 3. 'All men have a natural and indefeasible *right* to worship Almighty God according to the dictates of their own consciences; no man can of right be compelled to attend, erect, or support any place of worship, or to maintain any ministry against his consent; no human authority can, in any case whatever, interfere with the rights of conscience and control the prerogatives of the soul.'

Constitution of New Hampshire, Arts. 5 & 6: 'Among the natural rights, some are in their very nature unalienable, because no equivalent can be conceived for them. Of this kind are the *rights* of conscience.' (Beaumont, *loc. cit.*, pp. 213, 214.)

The incompatibility between religion and the rights of man is so little part of the concept of the rights of man that the right to be *religious* in the fashion that pleases one and to practise a particular form of worship is explicitly included among the rights of man. The *privilege of faith* is a *universal human right*.

The *droits de l'homme*, the rights of man, are distinguished *as such* from the *droits du citoyen*, from the rights of the citizen. Who is the *homme* as distinguished from the *citoyen*? None other than the member of civil society. Why is the member of civil society called 'man', man without qualification, and why are his rights called the *rights of man*? How shall we explain this fact? By the relationship of the political state to civil society, by the essential character of political emancipation.

Let us first note the fact that the so-called *rights of man*, the *droits de l'homme* as distinguished from the *droits du citoyen*, are nothing but the rights of the *member of civil society, i.e.*, of egoistic man, of man separated from other men and from the community. The most radical constitution, the Constitution of 1793, can be cited:

Declaration of the Rights of Man and of Citizens, Art. 2. 'These rights (natural and imprescriptible rights) are: *equality, liberty, security, property*.'

What does *liberty* consist of?

Art. 6. 'Liberty is the right vested in every man to do anything which does not impair the rights of others,' or, according to the Declaration of the Rights of Man of 1791: 'Liberty consists in the right to do anything which does not harm others.'

Liberty is hence the right to do everything that does not harm others. The limits within which every man can move without *harming* others are determined by the law, just as the boundary between two fields is determined by a fence-post. This is the liberty of man as an isolated monad withdrawn into itself. Why, according to Bauer, is the Jew incapable of having the rights of man conferred on him? 'As long as he remains a Jew, that limited nature which makes him a Jew must triumph over that human nature which should link him as a man with other men and must separate him from non-Jews.' But liberty as one of the rights of man is not based on the linking of man with man but rather on the separation of man from man. It is the right of this separation, the right of the *limited* individual, limited to himself.

The practical application of the right of liberty as one of the rights of man is the right of *private property*. What does the right of private property consist of?

Art. 16 (*Constitution of 1793*): 'The right of *property* is the right vested in every citizen to enjoy and to dispose of his goods, his revenues, the fruit of his labour and of his industry *according to his will*.'

Man's right to private property is therefore the right to enjoy one's property and to dispose over it arbitrarily *à son gré* [according to one's will], without considering other men, independently of society. It is the right of self-interest. That individual freedom, like this application of it, constitutes the basis of civil society. It allows every man to find in other men not the *realization* of his freedom, but rather the *limitation* of it. It proclaims above all man's right 'to enjoy and dispose of his goods, his revenues, the fruit of his labor and of his industry *according to his will*'.

There still remain the other rights of man, equality and security.

Equality, here used in its non-political sense, is nothing but the equality implicit in the *liberty* described above, namely that every man is equally regarded as a self-sufficient monad. The Constitution of 1795 treats the significance of the concept of equality thus: Art. 3 (*Constitution of 1795*): 'Equality consists in the fact that the same law applies to all, whether that law protects or punishes'.

And security?

Art. 8. (*Constitution of 1793*): 'Security consists in the protection which society affords to each of its members for the preservation of his person, his rights and his property.'

Security is the supreme social concept of civil society, the concept held by the police that the whole of society exists only in order to guarantee to each of its members the preservation of his person, his rights and his property . . .

Civil society does not rise above egoism through the concept of security. Security is rather the *guarantee* of its egoism.

None of these so-called rights of man goes beyond the egoistic man, beyond man as a member of civil society, as man separated from life in the community and withdrawn into himself, into his private interest and his private arbitrary will. These rights are far from conceiving man as a species-being. They see, rather, the life of the species itself, society, as a frame external to individuals, as a limitation of their original independence. The only bond that keeps men together is natural necessity, need and private interest, the preservation of their property and of their egoistic person.

It is a curious problem that a nation which is just beginning to free itself, to tear down all barriers between various sections of the people and to found a political community, should solemnly proclaim (*Declaration of 1791*) the vindication of the egoistic man, severed from his fellow men and from the community, and that it should even repeat this proclamation at the moment when only the most heroic sacrifices can save the nation and are therefore urgently required, when the sacrifice of all the interests of civil society has become the main order of the day and when egoism must be punished as a crime (*Declaration of the Rights of Man of 1793*). This fact becomes even more curious when we observe that the political emancipators reduce citizenship, the *political community*, to a mere means for preserving these so-called rights of man, so that the *citoyen* is proclaimed to be the servant of the egoistic *homme*. The sphere in which man conducts himelf as a communal being is degraded, put below the sphere in which he conducts himself as a sectional being. Finally man as a *bourgeois* and not man as a *citoyen* is taken to be the *essential* and *true* man.

> 'The *goal* of all *political association* is the *preservation* of the natural and imprescriptible rights of man' (*Declaration of the Rights of Man*, etc *of 1791*, Art. 2). 'Government is instituted to guarantee man's enjoyment of his natural and imprescriptible right' (*Declaration*, etc. *of 1793*, Art. 1).

Thus even at the time when its enthusiasm is still youthful and brought to its highest pitch through the urgency of circumstances, political life proclaims itself to be a mere *means*, whose end is life in civil society. To be sure, revolutionary practice flagrantly contradicts its theory. While security, e.g., is proclaimed to be one of the rights of man, invasion of the privacy of correspondence is publicly made part of the order of the day. While the *'unlimited* freedom of the press' (*Constitution of 1791*, Art. 122) is guaranteed as a consequence of the rights of man and of individual freedom, freedom of the press is completely abolished because 'the freedom of the press should not be permitted to compromise public freedom' ('Robespierre jeune', *Histoire parlementaire de la révolution française* [*Parliamentary History of the French Revolution*] by Buchez and Roux, vol. 28, p. 159). Man's right to liberty, in other words, ceases to be a right when it comes into conflict with *political* life. According to the theory, on the other hand, political life is only the guarantee of the rights of man, of the rights of the individual man, and should therefore be abandoned as soon as it comes into contradiction with its *end*, the rights of man. But practice is only the exception, theory is the rule. Even if we took revolutionary practice as correctly expressing the relationship [between political life and the rights of man], we still have to explain why the relationship is turned on its head in the consciousness of the emancipators, so that the end appears as means and the means appear as end. The optical illusion in their consciousness poses the same problem, though as a psychological, a theoretical problem.

The problem is easily solved. Political emancipation is also the *dissolution* of the old society, on which the sovereign power, the alienated political life of the people, rests. The political revolution is the revolution of civil society. What was the character of the old society? One word describes it. *Feudalism*. The old civil society had a *directly* political character, i.e., the elements of civil life, such as property or the family or the mode or manner of working, e.g., were made into elements of political life in the form of landlordism, estates and corporations. In this form they determine the relationship of the particular individual to the *state as a whole*, i.e., they determine his *political* relationship, his separation and exclusion from other component parts of society. For the feudal organization of the life of the people did not raise property or labor to the level of social elements; it rather completed their *separation* from the totality of the state and established them as *particular* societies within society. The functions and conditions of life in civil society thus always remained political, but political in the feudal sense. They excluded the individual, i.e., from the totality of the state, they transformed the *particular* relation between his corporation and the state totality into his universal relation to the life of the people, just as they transformed his specific civil activity and situation into his general activity and situation. As a consequence of such organization, the unity of the state and the consciousness, will and activity of this unity, the general power of the state, appear as the *particular* business of a ruler and his servants, separated from the people.

The political revolution which overthrew this power of the rulers and made affairs of state affairs of the people, i.e., which made it a true state, necessarily smashed all estates, corporations, guilds and privileges as just so many expressions of the separation of the people from its communal life. The political revolution thereby *abolished* the *political character of civil society*. It shattered civil society into its simple constituents: on the one hand, individuals, on the other, the *material* and *spiritual elements* which constitute the life-content, the social situation, of these individuals. It released the political spirit, which had been broken up, fragmented, and lost in the various *culs-de-sac* of feudal society. It gathered it up where it lay scattered, liberated it from its entanglement with civil life and constituted it into the sphere of the common communal life [*Gemeinwesen*], the sphere of *universal* public affairs separated in idea, from the *particular* elements of civil life. The *specific* activity and situation in life sank to merely individual significance. They no longer formed the general relationship of the individual to the state as a totality. Public affairs as such became the general affairs of every individual and the political function became his general function.

This consummation of the idealism of the state, however, was at the same time the consummation of the materialism of civil society. Throwing off the political yoke meant at the same time throwing off those bonds which had held fast the egoistic spirit of civil society. Political emancipation was at the same time the emancipation of civil society from politics, from the *appearance* even of a universal content.

Feudal society was dissolved into its basic element, into *man*, but into man in the form in which he really was its basic element, into *egoistic* man.

This *man*, the member of civil society, is now the basis and presupposition of the *political state*. The political state recognizes him as such in the rights of man.

The freedom of egoistic man and the recognition of this freedom is rather the recognition of the unbridled movement of the spiritual and material elements which form the content of his life.

Man was therefore not freed from religion; he received religious freedom. He was not freed from property. He received freedom of property. He was not freed from the egoism of trade, but received freedom to trade.

The *constitution of the political state* and the dissolution of civil society into independent *individuals* (the relationship between these individuals is *law* just as the relationship between men belonging to estates and guilds was *privilege*) is accomplished in *one and the same act.* But man as a member of civil society, as the *non-political* man, necessarily appears to be *natural* man. The *rights of man* appear as *natural rights*, because self-conscious activity has concentrated on the *political act.* The *egoistic* man is the passive *datum* that results from the dissolved society, an object of *direct certainty* and hence a *natural* object. The *political revolution* dissolves civil life into its constituent elements without *revolutionizing* these elements and subjecting them to criticism. It treats civil society—the realm of needs, labor, private interests, and private right—as the *foundation of its existence*, as a *presupposition* needing no further justification, and therefore as its *natural basis*. Finally, man as a member of civil society is regarded as the *authentic* man, as *man* distinguished from the citizen, since he is man in his sensuous, individual, and *most intimate* existence while *political* man is only the abstract, artificial man, man as an *allegorical moral* person. Man as he actually is is recognized only in the form of the egoistic individual, *true man* only in the form of an *abstract citizen*.

This abstraction of political man was correctly portrayed by Rousseau:

> Whoever dares to undertake the founding of a nation must feel himself capable of *changing*, so to speak, *human nature* and of *transforming* each individual who is in himself a complete but isolated whole into a *part* of something greater than himself from which he somehow derives his life and existence, substituting a *limited* and *moral existence* for physical and independent existence. *Man* must be deprived of his *own powers* and given alien powers which he cannot use without the aid of others. (*Contrat social* [*The Social Contract*] Book II, London, 1782, p. 67—Marx's italics.)

All emancipation is the *leading back* of the human world and of human relationships and conditions, to *man himself*.

Political emancipation is the reduction of man to a member of civil society, to an *egoistic independent* individual, on the one hand and to a *citizen*, a moral person, on the other. Only when actual, individual man has taken back into himself the abstract citizen and has become a *species-being* in his everyday life, in his individual work and his individual circumstances, only when he has recognized and organized his own powers as *social* powers so that social power is no longer separated from him as *political* power, only then is human emancipation complete.

MEGA I, 1-i, 576–99; MEW 1, 347–70.

1844

From 'CONTRIBUTION TO THE CRITIQUE OF HEGEL'S PHILOSOPHY OF RIGHT: INTRODUCTION'

PUBLISHED IN DEUTSCH-FRANZÖSISCHE JAHRBÜCHER, *FEBRUARY 1844*

For Germany the *criticism of religion* is in essence complete, and the criticism of religion is the premise of all criticism. . . .

The basis of irreligious criticism is: *man makes religion*, religion does not make man. Religion, indeed, is the self-consciousness and the self-esteem of the man who has not yet found himself or who has already lost himself. But *man* is not an abstract being crouching outside the world. Man is man's *world*, the state, society. This state and this society produce religion, which is an *inverted consciousness* of the world because state and society are an *inverted world*. Religion is the general theory of this world, its encyclopedia, its logic in popular form, its spiritualistic *point d'honneur*, its enthusiasm, its moral sanction, its solemn complement, and the general ground for the consummation and justification of this world. It is the *ghostly realization* of the human essence, ghostly because the *human essence* possesses no true reality. The struggle against religion is therefore indirectly the struggle against *that world* whose spiritual aroma is religion.

Religious suffering is at once the *expression* of real suffering and the *protest* against real suffering. Religion is the sigh of the oppressed creature, the heart of a heartless world, just as it is the spirit of spiritless conditions. It is the *opium* of the people.

The overcoming of religion as the *illusory* happiness of the people is the demand for their real happiness. The demand that they should abandon illusions about their conditions is the *demand to give up conditions that require illusions.* The critique of religion is therefore in embryo a *critique of the vale of tears,* whose *halo* is religion.

... Thus the critique of heaven turns into the critique of earth, the *critique of religion* into the *critique of law* and the *critique of theology* into the *critique of politics.*

... German history preens itself on a development that no nation under the skies of history has ever previously exhibited or will ever imitate. We have, in fact, shared in the restorations of modern nations without having shared in their revolutions. We have suffered restorations, first, because other nations were bold enough to make revolutions and, second, because other nations underwent counter-revolutions—in the first instance, we suffered because our masters were afraid, and in the second instance, because they were not afraid. With our shepherds at the head, we always found ourselves in the company of freedom only once, *on the day of its burial.*

A school of thought that justifies the infamy of today by the infamy of yesterday, a school of thought that regards the serf's every cry against the knout as rebellion the moment the knout is a time-honoured, ancestral, historical knout, a school to which history shows only its *a postiori,* as the god of Israel showed it to his servant Moses—this school, the *historical school of law,* might have invented German history if the school itself were not an invention of history. This school—a Shylock, but a servile Shylock—swears on its bond, on its historical bond, on its Christian-Germanic bond, for every pound of flesh cut from the heart of the people.

Well-disposed enthusiasts, on the other hand, German chauvinists by instinct and liberals by reflection, seek to find the history of our freedom somewhere beyond our history, in the primeval Teutonic forests. But how are we to distinguish the history of our freedom from the history of the wild boar's freedom if it can be found only in the forests? As the proverb has it, what is shouted into the forest the forest echoes back. So let the primeval Teutonic forest be.

War on German conditions! By all means! They are *below the level of history*, they are *beneath all criticism*, but they remain an object for criticism just as the criminal who stands below the level of humanity remains an object of the *executioner*. In struggling against these conditions, criticism is not a passion of the head, but the head of passion. It is not a scalpel; it is a weapon. Its object is its *enemy*, whom it does not want to refute but to *destroy*. For the spirit of these conditions has already been refuted. In essence they are not objects worthy of *thought* but *existences* as despicable as they are despised. Criticism does not even need to seek self-clarification in the matter, for it is already clear about it. Critique is no longer *an end in itself* but now only a *means*. Its essential pathos is *indignation*, its essential task is *denunciation*.

What is needed is a description of the pervasive suffocating pressure which all social spheres exert on one another, of the general passive dejection, of a narrowness that recognizes itself but misunderstands itself and which is framed within a system of government that lives on the conservation of poverty of spirit and is itself nothing but the *poverty of spirit in government*. . . .

Once *modern* political-social reality is itself subjected to criticism, once criticism raises itself to considering truly human problems, it either finds itself outside the German *status quo* or else has to deal with its objects at a level below its objects. An example! The major problem of modern times is the relationship of industry and of the world of wealth in general to the world of politics. In what form does this problem begin to occupy the Germans? In the form of *protective tariffs*, of the *system of prohibition*, of *national political economy*. German chauvinism has passed from man to matter and suddenly one morning our cotton barons and heroes of iron find themselves transformed into patriots ... In Germany we are about to begin where France and England are about to end. Those old decayed conditions against which these countries revolt in theory and which they put up with only in the sense in which one puts up with chains, are greeted in Germany as the dawn of a glorious future ...

Just as the peoples of antiquity lived out their prehistory in imagination, in mythology, so we Germans have lived out our post-history in thought, in *philosophy*. We are *philosophical* contemporaries of the present without being its *historical* contemporaries. German philosophy is the *ideal extension* of German history. If instead of criticizing the *oeuvres incomplètes* of our real history, we criticize the posthumous works of our ideal history—*philosophy*—then our critique stands in the midst of those questions of which the present says: *That is the question.* What in progressive nations is a *practical* break with modern political conditions is in Germany, where these conditions do not yet even exist, in the first instance a *critical* break with the philosophical reflection of those conditions.

... The critique of the German philosophy of *state and law*, of a philosophy which reached its most consistent, its richest and ultimate formulation with *Hegel*, consists in the critical analysis of the modern state and of the reality surrounding it and in the decisive negation of all the *forms of German political and legal consciousness* that have existed up to now, forms whose most distinguished and universal expression at the level of science is precisely the *speculative philosophy of law.* If the speculative philosophy of law (that abstract and extravagant *thinking* about the modern state whose reality remains in the beyond, if only beyond the Rhine) was possible only in Germany, the *German* conception of the modern state as abstracted from actual man was conversely possible only because and to the extent that the modern state abstracts itself from the *actual man* or satisfies the *whole man* only in an illusory way. In politics the Germans have *thought* what other nations have *done*. Germany has been their *theoretical conscience*. The abstraction and presumption of German thought has kept constant pace with the one-sided and stunted character of Germany's actual conditions . . .

As the resolute gainsayer of the present mode of German political consciousness, the critique of the speculative philosophy of law does not continue within the same system, but proceeds to *tasks* that can be solved only in one way—through *praxis*.

There is the question: Can Germany attain to a practice *in keeping with its high principles*, i.e., to a *revolution* . . . The weapon of criticism, it is true, cannot replace the criticism of weapons. Material force must be overthrown by material force. But theory also becomes a material force when it takes hold of the masses. Theory is capable of taking hold of the masses as soon as it makes its demonstrations *ad hominem*, and it makes its demonstrations *ad hominem* when it becomes radical. To be radical is to take things by the root. The root for man, however, is man himself. The clear proof of the radicalism of German theory, and of its practical energy, therefore, is the fact that it proceeds from a decisive, *positive* dissolution and transcendence of religion. The criticism of religion ends in the teaching that *man is the highest being for man*, hence in the *categorical imperative to overthrow all those conditions* in which man is a debased, enslaved, abandoned, contemptible being—conditions that cannot be better described than by the exclamation of a Frenchman on hearing of a proposed tax on dogs: Poor dogs! They want to treat you like men.

Theoretical emancipation has a specific practical significance for Germany even in a historical way. Germany's *revolutionary* past is itself theoretical—it is the *Reforma-*

tion. It was then the *monk*, it is now the *philosopher*, in whose brain the revolution begins. . . .

But a major difficulty seems to confront a *radical* German revolution.

Revolutions require a *passive* element, a *material* base. Theory becomes concrete in a people only to the extent that it is the concretization of their needs. Will the enormous discrepancy between the demands of German thought and the answers furnished by German reality be accompanied by a corresponding discrepancy between civil society and the state and a corresponding split within civil society itself? Will theoretical needs be direct practical needs? It is not enough that the thought should seek realization; reality must itself strive toward the thought. . . .

If Germany has joined in the development of modern nations only through the abstract activity of thought, without taking any active part in the real struggles involved in this development, it has also shared in the sufferings of this development without sharing in its enjoyments or partial satisfactions. Abstract suffering on the one side parallels abstract activity on the other. One fine day, therefore, Germany will find itself having reached the level of European decadence before it has even reached the level of European emancipation. One can compare this with the fetish-worshipper who is wasting away from the diseases of Christianity . . . As the *gods* of all nations were found in the Roman Pantheon, so the *sins* of all forms of state will be found in the German Holy Roman Empire . . . *Germany is the deficiency of the political present erected into a political system* and it will therefore not be able to overthrow the limitations specific to Germany without overthrowing the universal limitations of the political present.

Radical revolution, *universal human* emancipation, is not a utopian dream for Germany. What is utopian is the partial, *merely* political revolution, the revolution that leaves the pillars of the house standing. What does a partial, merely political revolution rest on? On the fact that a *part of civil society* emancipates itself and attains universal dominion, on the fact that a specific class undertakes the general emancipation of society on the basis of its *particular situation.* This class emancipates all of society, but only on the condition that all of society is in the same position as this class, e.g., that it has money and education or can easily acquire them.

No class in civil society can play this role without arousing a moment [*Moment,* energizing impulse or element] of enthusiasm in itself and in the masses, a moment which leads it to fraternize and merge with society at large, to identify itself with it, to be regarded and acknowledged as society's *general representative.* In this moment of enthusiasm, the demands and rights of the class really become the demands and claims of society itself, of the society of which this class is the social head and the social heart. Only in the name of the general rights of society can a particular class pretend to general supremacy. Revolutionary energy and intellectual self-confidence are not themselves sufficient for a class to be able to seize this emancipation position and thus to gain political control over all spheres of society in the interests of its own sphere. For a *popular revolution* to coincide with the *emancipation of a particular class* of civil society, for one estate to stand for the whole state of society, all the defects of society must conversely be concentrated in another class. A particular class must be the class giving general offence, must be the concretization of a general limitation. A particular social sphere must stand for the *notorious crime* of society as a whole, so that emancipation from this social sphere appears as general self-emancipation. For one class to be *par excellence* the class of emancipation, another must conversely be the obvious class of oppression. The universally negative significance of the French nobility and the French clergy brought about and determined the universally positive significance of the class that was immediately next to them, but opposed them—the *bourgeoisie.*

In Germany, however, every class lacks the consistency, penetration, courage and ruthlessness which could stamp it the negative representative of society. And more, in every estate there is equally lacking that breadth of soul which identifies itself with the soul of the people, even if only momentarily. There is lacking that genius which inspires material force toward political power, that revolutionary boldness which flings at its adversary the defiant slogan: *I am nothing, and I should be everything. . . .*

In France it is enough that man be something, for him to want to be everything. In Germany no one can be anything unless he is prepared to renounce everything. In France partial emancipation is the basis of universal emancipation. In Germany universal emancipation is the *conditio sine qua non* of any partial emancipation. In France it is the reality, in Germany the impossibility, of progressive emancipation which must give birth to complete freedom. In France every class of the population is *politically idealistic* and considers itself first of all, not as a particular class, but as the representative of the general needs of society. The role of emancipator, therefore, passes in a dramatic movement to different classes in the population successively, until it finally reaches the class which achieves social freedom, which no longer assumes certain conditions external to man which are none the less created by human society, but which organizes all the conditions of human life on the basis of social freedom. In Germany, by contrast, where practical life is as mindless as mental life is impractical, no class of civil society feels the need for, or the ability to achieve, a general emancipation, until it is forced to it by its *immediate* situation, by *material* necessity and by its *fetters themselves.*

Where, then, the *positive* possibility of emancipation in

Germany? *Answer:* In the formation of a class with *radical chains,* a class in civil society which is not a class of civil society, a class which is the dissolution of all classes, a sphere of society which has a universal character because its sufferings are universal, and which does not claim a *particular redress* because the wrong which is done to it is not a *particular wrong* but *wrong as such.* There must be formed a sphere of society which claims no *traditional* title but only a human title, which is not partially opposed to the consequences but is totally opposed to the assumptions of the German political system; a sphere, finally, which cannot emancipate itself without emancipating itself from all the other spheres of society, and thereby emancipating all of them; a sphere, in short, which is the *total loss* of humanity and which can only redeem itself by a *total redemption of humanity.* This dissolution of society, as a particular class, is the *proletariat.*

Only the intrusion of industrial development is beginning to create a proletariat in Germany. For the proletariat is not being formed by a *natural growth* of poverty, but by *artificially produced* poverty. It does not consist of the masses of men mechanically oppressed by the weight of society, but of the masses that result from the *acute disintegration* of society, and particularly of the middle-class—though gradually, needless to say, naturally conditioned poverty and Christian-Germanic serfdom will enter the proletariat's ranks.

If the proletariat heralds the *dissolution of the order that has existed hitherto,* it thereby merely announces the *secret of its own existence,* since it is the *factual* dissolution of this order. If the proletariat demands the *negation of private property,* the proletariat thereby elevates as a *principle of society* what society has made into the principle of *the proletariat* . . .

Just as philosophy finds its *material* weapons in the proletariat, so the proletariat finds its *intellectual* weapons in philosophy. Once the lightning of thought has struck deeply into this naive popular soil, the emancipation of the German into a man will take place.

Let us summarize the result: the emancipation of Germany is only possible *in practice* if one adopts the point of view of *that* theory according to which man is the highest being for man. Germany will not be able to emancipate itself from the *Middle Ages* unless it emancipates itself at the same time from the *partial* victories over the *Middle Ages*. In Germany *no* type of enslavement can be abolished unless *all* enslavement is destroyed. Germany, which likes to get to the bottom of things, can only make a revolution which upsets *the whole order* of things. The *emancipation of Germany* will be an *emancipation of man*. *Philosophy* is the *head* of this emancipation and the *proletariat* is its *heart*. Philosophy can only be realized by the abolition of the proletariat, and the proletariat can only be abolished by the realization of philosophy. . . .

MEGA I, 1-i, 607–21; MEW 1, 378–91.

2. Beyond Philosophy to Communism, Political Economy, and the Materialist Conception of History: Transitional Writings, 1844–1847

EDITOR'S NOTE

The period 1844–1847 is a period of some of Marx's most intense and imaginative intellectual activity. He makes the transition from radical philosophical criticism to Communism and the concrete world of politics, economics, and history, thereby initiating a sharp breach with the Young Hegelians, on whom he now pours nothing but scorn; he begins his lifelong collaboration with Friedrich Engels, 'discovers' (or invents) the materialist conception of history, establishes—uneasy—links with French and German workers and intellectuals of the extreme socialist left, and forges that great Marxian synthesis of German philosophy, French socialism, and English economics, which is to receive its first popular programmatic expression in the *Communist Manifesto* of 1848.

The incomplete *Economico-Philosophical Manuscripts of 1844*, substantial portions of which are reproduced below, stand at the centre of that transition and illuminate the manner in which it was accomplished. Marx's critique of politics—of Hegel's *Philosophy of Right*, of Bruno Bauer's plea for the *political* emancipation of the Jews, and of the rights guaranteed by the French Revolution—had led him to the conclusion that the universal *pretensions* of the political state and of the demand for political emancipation were contradicted by the egoistic *facts* of economic life. In 1843 and 1844 Marx does not yet treat politics or the political state as a mere reflection of productive activity and relations, but he already ascribes to them a certain impotence. They are fantasy-constructions that mask the reality of the naked, competitive greed of civil society. It is to the study of that civil society that Marx now turns.

During 1843 and 1844 Marx had absorbed the Feuerbachian 'genetic-critical' method, Feuerbach's extension of the Fichtean-Hegelian concept of alienation and its application to religion in the endeavour to expose the real secret of Christianity—the secret that man made God out of the hopes, characteristics, and achievements of the human species, as an escape from need and dependence, but then fell into dependence on his own creation, mortified himself before his own fantasy, gave to God what he sorely needed for himself and what he must now take back into himself. In the *Economico-Philosophical Manuscripts* Marx now seeks to show the same mechanism at work in economic life and thus to subject the political economy of capitalism and of all societies based on private property and the division of labour to a fundamental logico-ethical critique—to bring out their theoretical, practical, and moral 'contradictions', summed up in the phrase 'The more riches the worker produces, the poorer he becomes.' Private property and the division of labour, Marx seeks to show, separate man from the tools he needs, which belong to another, from the product of his work, which he does not make for his own use, but for that of another, and finally—under capitalism—from his very capacity to work, which, for a fixed period each day, is purchased by his employer. Man is separated, estranged, from the preconditions of his work, from the products of his work, from his very labour-power, and hence from his own humanity, from other men, from society, and from nature. He is *alienated*, reduced to the dependence of an animal, but a dependence that is infinitely more pervasive and horrible in so far as it is the self-created dependence of a conscious and potentially universal being, capable of mastering the universe. Money infinitely intensifies this dependence and at the same time 'mystifies' all economic relationships, conceals their fundamentally *human* content and purpose. Communism, in abolishing private property, money, and the division of labour, overcomes this alienation, restores or unveils the human content of labour and economic activity—but it can do so only in so far as it finally becomes a genuine humanist Communism which totally overcomes the whole conception of property and replaces it by free, conscious, creative social activity, in which man is not dominated by need, envy, or the desire to possess.

In a passage of his critical note on Arnold Ruge's article 'The King of Prussia and Social Reform', reproduced here, Marx again draws the consequences of his critique of political emancipation and the political State: the key to the political is the socioeconomic, before which the former is powerless. By the spring of 1845, he has developed this theory of the impotence of the State and the inadequacy of political emancipation into the 'materialist conception of history'—the proposition that 'the mode of production of material life conditions the general process of social, political and intellectual life'. In the process, he has also finally broken with Feuerbach and the Young Hegelians. In the *Economico-Philosophical Manuscripts* he had presented man as a being who shapes himself in a continuous, active relationship with nature, in a practical *transaction* with surrounding reality, which he fashions and which fashions him. In the *Theses on Feuerbach*—jotted down in Brussels in the spring of 1845—perhaps his last 'philosophical' statement, and itself a very slender base for the elaborate ontologies, epistemologies, and dialectical philosophies often ascribed to Marx—he rejects sharply both sides of the traditional idealist-materialist controversy: the materialism that reduces man to nature, that therefore excludes human history and fails to recognize the extent to which nature is shaped and fashioned and given significance by man, and the idealism that sees nature as a spiritual construct and history as the story of consciousness. Feuerbach, in affirming the reality of both man and nature, of both consciousness and matter, fails to see the active interaction between them. He makes man's relationship to nature purely passive, a relationship of contemplation and feeling. He has no conception of *praxis*, of human *activity*, which shapes and is shaped by the objects that it works on.

Philosophy, however, is no longer one of Marx's significant concerns. Man is to be understood not through philosophy but through history, and history is to be understood not through the development of politics or of ideologies, but through the development of production. This is the view that Marx describes himself as reaching in the period 1844–1845 in the famous Preface to the *Contribution to the Critique of Political Economy*, published in 1859 but reproduced here to portray his views at the time they were formed; this is the view he sets out in his letter to Annenkov and elaborates in the opening chapters of *The German Ideology*. That would-be book was written, in collaboration with Engels, as a critique of Feuerbach and the Young Hegelians and in an attempt to set out more fully the real, historical development of man as seen in the light of the materialist conception of history. The sections here do just that and complete Marx's transition to the Marxism of his maturity. It is a Marxism still destined to undergo elaboration and modifications, to exhibit shifts of emphasis and more frequently to reveal vacillation between component doctrines and attitudes that conflict, but at Marx's hands it was not to undergo any further significant change in style, in its logical structure, or in its principal categories.

From ECONOMICO-PHILOSOPHICAL MANUSCRIPTS OF 1844

~~~~~~~~~~~~~~~~~~~~~~~~~~~~~~~~~~~~

FROM THE FIRST MANUSCRIPT: *'ALIENATED LABOUR'*

We have set out from the presuppositions of political economy. We have accepted its terminology and its laws. We presupposed private property; the separation of labor, capital and land and therefore of wages, profit of capital and rent of land; the division of labor; competition, the concept of exchange value, etc. From political economy itself, in its own words, we have shown that the worker sinks to the level of a commodity and, indeed, of the most miserable commodity; that the worker's misery is inversely proportional to the power and scope of his production; that the necessary result of competition is the accumulation of capital in a few hands and thus the most frightful restoration of monopoly; and finally, that the distinction between the capitalist and the land owner, like that between agricultural laborer and industrial worker, disappears and the whole of society must fall apart into two classes—those of property *owners* and of propertyless *workers.*

Political economy proceeds from the fact of private property. It does not explain private property. It expresses the *material* process through which private property actually passes in general abstract formulas and then takes these formulas to be *laws.* It does not *comprehend* these laws, i.e. it does not show how they arise from the very nature of private property. Political economy does not show us the source of the division between labor and capital, and between capital and land. When it determines the relationship of wages to profit, for example, its final principle of explanation is the interest of the capitalist, i.e. it assumes what it is supposed to explain. Similarly, competition is referred to at every point and explained in terms of external conditions. Political economy tells us nothing about the extent to which these external, apparently accidental conditions are simply the expression of a necessary development. We have seen how political economy regards exchange itself as an accidental fact. The only wheels which political economy sets in motion are *greed* and the *war among the greedy—competition.*

Precisely because political economy does not grasp the interconnections within the movement, it could oppose, for instance, the doctrine of competition to the doctrine of monopoly, the doctrine of the freedom of the crafts to the doctrine of the guild, the doctrine of the division of landed property to the doctrine of the big estate. Competition, freedom of the crafts and division of landed property were explained and conceived only as accidental, deliberate, violent consequences of monopoly, of the guild system, and of feudal property, not as their necessary, inevitable, natural consequences.

We now, therefore, have to grasp the real connection between private property, greed, the division of labor, capital and land ownership, and the connection between exchange and competition, between value and the devaluation of men, between monopoly and competition etc.— the connection between all of this alienation and the system of money.

Let us not go back to a fictitious primordial state, as the political economist does when he tries to explain. Such a primordial state explains nothing. It only pushes the issue back into a grey, nebulous distance. It asserts as a fact, as an event, what it should deduce, namely the necessary relation between two things—between, for example, division of labor and exchange. Theology explains the origin of evil in this manner, by means of the fall of man; i.e., it assumes as a fact, it presents as history, what has to be explained.

We proceed from an economic, *contemporary* fact.

The more wealth the worker produces, the more his production increases in power and scope, the poorer he becomes. The more commodities the worker produces, the cheaper a commodity he becomes. The *extinction of value* from the world of things is directly proportional to the *devaluation* of the world of men. Labor does not only produce commodities; it produces itself and the worker as a *commodity* and it does so to the same extent as it produces commodities in general.

This fact expresses nothing but this: the object which labor produces—the product of labor—confronts it as an *alien being*, as a *power independent* of the producer. The product of labor is labor embodied and made material in a thing; it is the *objectification* of labor. The realization of labor is its objectification. Within political economy, this realization of labor appears as the *loss of reality* of the worker, objectification appears as the *loss of the object* and *bondage to* it; appropriation appears as *alienation* [*Entfremdung*], as *externalization* [*Entäusserung*].

The realization of labor appears as the loss of reality by the worker to such an extent that he loses reality to the point of starvation. Objectification appears as loss of the object to such an extent that the worker is robbed of the most essential objects, not only for life but also for work. Indeed, work itself becomes an object which he can obtain only with the greatest effort and with the most unpredictable interruptions. The appropriation of the object appears as alienation to such an extent that the more objects the worker produces the fewer he can own and the more he falls under the domination of his product, capital.

All these consequences are contained in the fact that the

worker is related to the *product of his labor* as to an *alien* object. For on this premise it is clear that the more the worker exhausts himself, the more powerful the alien world of objects which he creates over and against himself becomes, the poorer he and his inner world become, the less there is that belongs to him as his own. The same is true in religion. The more man puts into God, the less he retains in himself. The worker puts his life into the object; but now it no longer belongs to him, it belongs to the object. The greater this activity, therefore, the greater the worker's lack of objects. What the product of his work is, he is not. The greater the product, therefore, the less is he himself. The *externalization* of the worker into his product does not only mean that his work becomes an object, an *external* existence, but that it exists *outside him* independently, as something alien to him, as confronting him as an autonomous power. It means that the life which he has given to the object confronts him as something hostile and alien.

Let us now look more closely at *objectification*, at the worker's production and at the *alienation*, the *loss* of the object, of the product, within it.

The worker cannot create anything without *nature*, without the *external world of the senses*. It is the material in which his labor realizes itself, in which it is active, out of which and by means of which it produces.

But just as nature furnishes labor with the *means of life* in the sense that labor cannot *live* without objects on which to operate, so, on the other hand, nature also furnishes the *means of life* in the narrower sense, i.e. the means for the physical subsistence of the *worker* himself.

The more therefore, the worker *appropriates* the external world and hence sensuous nature through his labor, the more he deprives himself of the *means of life* in two respects: first, in that the external world of the senses more and more ceases to be an object belonging to his labor, a *means of life* of his work; second, in that it more and more ceases to be a *means of life* in the direct sense, a means of physical subsistence for the worker.

In these two respects, therefore, the worker becomes a slave to his object: first, in that he receives an *object of labor*, that is, he receives *labor*, and second, in that he receives the *means of subsistence*. The first, therefore, enables him to exist as a *worker* and the second as a *physical subject*. The high point of this bondage lies in the fact that he can maintain himself as a *physical subject* only in so far as he is a *worker* and that only as a *physical subject* is he a worker.

(The alienation of the worker in his object is expressed within the laws of political economy thus: the more the worker produces, the less he has to consume; the more values he creates, the less value, the less dignity, he has; the better shaped his product, the more mis-shapen the worker; the more civilized his object, the more barbaric the worker; the more powerful the work, the more powerless the worker; the more intelligent the work, the more witless the worker, the more he becomes a slave of nature.)

Political economy conceals the alienation inherent in the nature of labor by not considering the direct relationship between the worker (labor) *and production.* To be sure, labor produces marvels for the rich but it produces deprivation for the worker. It produces palaces, but hovels for the worker. It produces beauty, but deformity for the worker. It replaces labor by machines, but it throws one section of the workers back to barbaric labor, and it turns the remainder into machines. It produces intelligence, but imbecility and cretinism for the worker.

The direct relationship of labor to its product is the relationship of the worker to the objects of his production. The relationship of the man of means to the objects of production and to production itself is only a *consequence* of this first relationship and confirms it. We shall consider this latter aspect below.

When we ask 'What is the essential relationship of labor', then we ask about the relationship of the *worker* to production.

So far we have considered the worker's alienation, externalization, only from one side: his *relationship to the products of his work*. But alienation manifests itself not only in the result, but in the *act of production*, in the *producing activity* itself. How could the worker confront the product of his activity as an alien if he did not alienate himself from himself in the very act of production? The product is after all only the résumé of the activity of production. If the product of labor is externalization, then production itself must be active externalization, the externalization of activity, the activity of externalization. The alienation of the object of labor merely recapitulates the alienation, the externalization, in the activity of labor itself.

What, then, constitutes the alienation of labor?

First, in the fact that labor is *external* to the worker, that is, that it does not belong to his essential being; that in his work, therefore, he does not affirm himself but denies himself, does not feel well but unhappy, does not freely develop his physical and mental energy but mortifies his body and ruins his mind. The worker, therefore, feels himself only outside his work, and feels beside himself in his work. He is at home when he is not working, and when he is working he is not at home. His work therefore is not voluntary, but coerced; it is *forced labor*. It is therefore not the satisfaction of a need, but only a *means* for satisfying needs external to it. Its alien character emerges clearly in the fact that labor is shunned like the plague as soon as there is no physical or other compulsion. External labor, labor in which man is externalized, is labor of self-sacrifice, of mortification. Finally, the external nature of labor for the worker appears in the fact that it is not his own, but someone else's, that it does not belong to him, that in that labor he does not belong to himself but to someone else. Just as in religion, the spontaneous activity of human imagination, of the human brain and the human heart, operates independently of the individual, i.e. as an alien divine or diabolical activity, so the worker's activity is not his spontaneous activity. It belongs to another; it is the loss of his self.

The result, therefore, is that man (the worker) feels that he is acting freely only in his animal functions—eating, drinking, procreating, or at most in his shelter and his finery—while in his human functions he feels himself nothing more than an animal. What is animal becomes human and what is human becomes animal.

Eating, drinking, procreating, etc. are, of course, also genuinely human functions. But taken in abstraction, separated from the remaining sphere of human activities and turned into sole and ultimate ends, they are animal.

We have considered labor, the act of alienation of practical human activity, in two aspects: (1) the relation of the worker to the *product of labor* as an alien object that dominates him. This relationship is at the same time the relation to the sensuous external world, to natural objects as an alien world confronting him in a hostile way. (2) The relation of labor to the *act of production* within *labor*. This relation is the relationship of the worker to his own activity as an alien activity that does not belong to him; activity as suffering, strength as weakness, procreation as emasculation, the worker's *own* physical and spiritual energy, his personal life—for what is life but activity—as an activity turned against him, independent of him, and not belonging to him. Here we have *self-alienation*, as above we had the alienation of the *thing*.

We have now only to infer a third aspect of *alienated labor* from the two previous ones.

Man is a species-being, not only in that practically and theoretically he makes his own species as well as that of other things into his object, but—and this is only another way of putting the same thing—also in that he treats himself as the actual, living species, treats himself as a *universal* and therefore a free being.

The life of the species, in man as in animals, physically consists in the fact that man (like the animal) lives on inorganic nature; and the more universal man is in comparison with an animal, the more universal the sphere of inorganic nature on which he lives. Just as plants, animals, stones, air, light, etc. on the theoretical side form part of human consciousness, partly as objects of natural science, partly as objects of art, just as they are his spiritual inorganic nature, spiritual nourishment which he must first prepare for enjoyment and digestion, so they also form a part of human life and of human activity on the practical side. Physically man lives only by these products of nature, whether they appear in the form of food, heating, clothing, housing, etc. The universality of man appears in practice precisely in that universality which makes the whole of nature his *inorganic* body, insofar as nature is (1) a direct means to life, and (2) the material, object and instrument of his life activity. Nature is man's *inorganic body*,—nature, i.e., in so far as it is not the human body. Man *lives* by nature. This means that nature is his *body*, with which he must constantly remain in step if he is not to die. That man's physical and spiritual life is tied to nature means no more than that nature is tied to itself, for man is a part of nature.

In alienating (1) nature and (2) man himself, his own active function, his life activity, from man, alienated labor alienates the *species* from man. It converts the *life of the species*, for him, into a means of individual life. First, it alienates the species—life and the individual life and secondly it makes the individual life, in its abstract form, the purpose of the species-life, also in abstract and alienated form.

Labor, *life activity* and *productive life*, indeed, first appear to man only as a *means* to satisfy a need, the need of maintaining physical existence. Productive life, however, is species-life. It is life-begetting life. The whole character of a species—its species-character—is contained in the character of its life activity; and free conscious activity is the species-character of man. Life itself appears only as a *means* to life.

The animal is immediately one with its life activity. It does not distinguish itself from it. The animal is *its life activity*. Man makes his life activity itself into an object of his will and of his consciousness. He has conscious life activity. It is not a determination with which he merges directly. Conscious life activity distinguishes man directly from the life activity of the animal. It is only thereby that he is a species-being. Or rather he is only a conscious being—that is, his own life is an object for him—precisely because he is a species-being. Only for that reason is his activity free activity. Alienated labor reverses this relationship in such a way that man, just because he is a conscious being, makes his life activity, his *essence*, a mere means for his *existence*.

His creation, in practice, of an *objective world*, his *working upon* inorganic nature, is the proof that man is a conscious species-being, that is a being which is related to the species as its own essence or to itself as a species-being. To be sure, animals also produce. They build themselves nests, dwelling places, as the bees, beavers, ants, etc. do. But the animal produces what it needs directly for itself or its young. It produces one-sidedly, while man produces universally. It produces under the domination of direct physical need while man produces even when he is free from physical need and produces truly, indeed, only in freedom from such need. The animal produces only itself, while man reproduces the whole of nature. The animal's product is directly part of its physical body, while man steps out freely to confront his product. The animal builds only according to the standard and the need of the species to which it belongs, while man knows how to produce according to the standard of every species and always knows how to apply the intrinsic standard to the object. Man, therefore, creates according to the laws of beauty.

It is precisely in his working over of the objective world, therefore, that man proves himself to be really a *species-being*. This production is his active species-life. In and through such production, nature appears as *his* work and his reality. The object of labor, therefore, is the *objectification* of the species-life of man: for man duplicates himself not only intellectually, as in consciousness, but also actively, in reality, and therefore contemplates himself in a world that he has created. In so far as alienated labor tears the object of his production away from man, therefore, it tears away from him his *species-life*, his actual objectivity as a member of the species and transforms his advantage over the animal into the disadvantage that his inorganic body, nature, is taken away from him.

Similarly, in degrading spontaneous activity, free activity, to the level of a means, alienated labor makes man's species-life a means for his physical existence.

Alienation thus transforms the consciousness which man has of his species, in such a way, that the species-life becomes a means for man.

Alienated labor therefore makes:

(3) *man's species-being,* his nature as well as his generic intellectual ability, into an existence *alien* to him, into a *means* to his *individual existence*. It alienates from man his own body, as well as nature outside him, as well as his spiritual being, his *human* being.

(4) A direct consequence of man's alienation from the product of his labor, from his life activity, from his species-being, is the *alienation of man* from *man*. When man confronts himself, he confronts *another* man. What is true of man's relationship to his work, to the product of his work, and to himself, is also true of man's relationship to

the other man, and to that man's labor and the object of his labor.

Generally, the proposition that man's species-being is alienated from him means that one man is alienated from another, just as each of them is alienated from human nature.

The alienation of man, indeed every relationship in which man stands to himself, is realized and expressed only in the relationship in which man stands to other men.

In the relationship of alienated labor, therefore, every man sees others in accordance with the standard and the relationship in which he finds himself as a worker.

We began with an economic fact, the alienation of the worker and of his production. We have formulated the concept of this fact: *alienated, externalized* labor. We have analyzed this concept, that is we have analyzed a mere fact of political economy.

Let us now see, further, how the concept of alienated, externalized labor must express and present itself in real life.

If the product of labor is alien to me, if it confronts me as an alien power, to whom then does it belong? If my own activity does not belong to me, if it is an alien, a forced activity, to whom, then, does it belong?

To a being *other* than me.

Who is this being?

The *gods???* To be sure, in earliest times, the principal production (for example the building of temples, etc., in Egypt, India, Mexico) appears to be in the service of the gods, and the product belongs to the gods. But the gods themselves were never the lords of labor. Neither was *nature.* And what a contradiction it would be if the more man subjugated nature through his labor and the more the miracles of the gods were rendered superfluous by the marvels of industry, the more man were to renounce his joy in production and the enjoyment of the product in favor of these powers.

The *alien* being to whom labor and the product of labor belong, whom labor serves and for whose satisfaction the product of labor is provided, can only be *man* himself.

If the product of labor does not belong to the worker, if it is an alien power that confronts him, then this is possible only because it belongs to *a man other than the worker.* If the worker's activity is torment for him, it must be *pleasure* and a joy of life for another. Neither the gods, nor nature, but only man himself can be this alien power over man.

We must remember the proposition previously put forward, that man's relationship to himself only becomes *objective* and *actual* for him through his relationship to the other man.

If he relates himself to the product of his labor, to his objectified labor, as to an *alien,* hostile, powerful object independent of him, then his position toward it is such that someone else is master of this object, someone who is alien, hostile, powerful and independent of him. If he treats his own activity as an unfree one, then he treats it as an activity performed in the service, under the domination, coercion and yoke of another man.

Every self-alienation of man from himself and from nature appears in the relationship in which he places himself and nature toward other men, men distinguished from him. . . . In the real practical world self-alienation can become manifest only through the real practical relationship to other men. The means whereby alienation takes place is itself *practical.* Through alienated labor man creates not only his relationship to the object and to the act of production as to an alien and hostile man, he also creates the relation in which other men stand to his production and to his product, and the relationship in which he stands to these other men. Just as he creates his own production as a loss of his own reality, as his punishment; just as he creates his own product as a loss, as a product not belonging to him; so he creates the domination of the non-producer over production and over the product. Just as he alienates his own activity from himself, so he confers upon the stranger an activity which is not his own.

Up to now, we have looked at this relationship only from the standpoint of the worker and we shall later look at it also from the standpoint of the non-worker.

Through *alienated, externalized labor*, then, the worker creates the relationship to this work of a man alien to work and standing outside it. The relation of the worker to labor produces the relation of the capitalist (or whatever one chooses to call the master of labor) to labor. *Private property* is therefore the product, the result, the necessary consequence of *externalized labor*, of the worker's external relation to nature and to himself.

Private property is thus arrived at through analysis of the concept of *externalized labor*, that is of *externalized man*, of alienated labor, of alienated life, and of *alienated* man.

True, it is as a result of the *movement of private property* that we have obtained the concept of *externalized labor* (*externalized life*) from political economy. But analysis of this concept shows that although private property appears to be the basis, the cause of externalized labor, it is rather its consequence, just as the gods are *originally* not the cause but the effect of man's intellectual confusion. Later this relationship becomes reciprocal.

Only when the development of private property reaches its final, culminating point does this, its secret, appear again—namely, that it is the *product* of externalized labor on the one hand and that it is, on the other, the *means* by which labor externalizes itself, that it is the *realization* of this externalization.

This account at the same time throws light on several conflicts hitherto unresolved.

(1) Political economy takes its departure from labor as the real soul of production; yet it gives nothing to labor and everything to private property. Proudhon, faced by this contradiction, has decided in favor of labor against

private property. We, however, recognize that this apparent contradiction is the contradiction of *alienated labor* with itself and that political economy has merely given expression to the laws of alienated labor.

We also recognize, therefore, that *wages* and *private property* are identical: for wages, like the product, the object of labor, labor itself remunerated, are but a necessary consequence of the alienation of labor. After all, in wages labor does not appear as an end in itself, but as the servant of wages. We shall develop this point later and meanwhile only bring out some of its consequences.

An enforced *increase of wages* (disregarding all the other difficulties, including the fact that such an anomaly could only be maintained by force) would therefore be nothing but *better remuneration for the slaves,* and would have won, neither for the worker nor for labor, their human significance and worth.

Indeed, even the *equality of incomes* as demanded by Proudhon only transforms the relationship of the present-day worker to his labor into the relationship of all men to labor. Society is then conceived as an abstract capitalist.

Wages are a direct result of alienated labor, and alienated labor is the direct cause of private property. If one falls therefore, the other must fall.

(2) From the relationship of alienated labor to private property it further follows that the emancipation of society from private property etc., from servitude, expresses itself *politically* as the *emancipation of the workers;* not that *their* emancipation alone is at stake, but because the emancipation of the workers contains within it universal human emancipation. Such human emancipation is contained within it, because the whole of human servitude is involved in the relation of the worker to production and every relation of servitude is only a modification and consequence of this relation.

Just as we have arrived at the concept of *private property* by an *analysis* of the concept of *alienated labor* so with the help of these two factors we can arrive at the *cat-egories* of political economy, and in every category, e.g. trade, competition, capital, money, we shall find only *par-ticular* and *developed* expression of these first elements.

Before considering this structure, however, let us seek to solve two problems.

(1) To determine the general nature of *private prop-erty* as it has resulted from alienated labor in its relation-ship to *genuine human and social property.*

(2) We have taken the *alienation of labor* as a fact and analyzed it. How does it happen, we ask now, that *man alienates his labor?* How is this alienation grounded in the nature of human development? We have already come a considerable way toward the solution in so far as we have *transformed* the question regarding *origin of private property* into a question regarding the relationship be-tween alienated labor and the process of development of mankind. For when one speaks of private property one believes oneself to be dealing with something external to mankind. But when one speaks of labor one deals directly with mankind itself. This new formulation of the problem already contains its solution.

Ad (1): *The general nature of private property and its relationship to truly human property.*

Alienated labor has resolved itself for us into two ele-ments which mutually determine one another, or which are but different expressions of one and the same relation-ship. *Appropriation* appears as *alienation* and *alienation* appears as *appropriation.* Alienation appears as the true induction into civil life.

We have considered one aspect—*alienated* labor in re-lation to the *worker* himself, i.e., the *relation of alienated labor to itself.* We have found the *property relation of the non-worker to the worker and to labor* to be the product, the necessary consequence of this relationship. *Private property,* as the material, summarized expression of alien-ated labor, embraces both relations—the *relation of*

*the worker to labor, to the product of his labor and to the
non-worker,* and the relation of the *non-worker to the
worker and to the product of the latter's labor.*

We have already seen that in relation to the worker who
appropriates nature by means of his labor, this appropriation appears as alienation; the worker's spontaneous activity appears as activity for another and as the activity of
another, living appears as a sacrifice of life, production
of the object as loss of the object to an alien power, to an
alien person. Let us now consider the relation to the
worker, to labor and to its object of this person, *alien* to
labor and the worker.

It should be noted first that everything which appears
in the worker as an *activity of alienation, of externalization,* appears in the non-worker as a *state of alienation, of
externalization.*

Secondly, that the *real, practical attitude* (as a state of
mind) of the worker in production and to the product appears in the non-worker who confronts him as a *theoretical* attitude.

Thirdly, the non-worker does everything against the
worker which the worker does against himself; but he
does not do against himself what he does against the
worker.

Let us examine these three relations more closely.

[*At this point the first manuscript breaks off unfinished.*]

MEGA I, 3, 81–94; MEW *Ergänzungsbd* I, 510–22.

FROM THE THIRD MANUSCRIPT: 'PRIVATE PROPERTY AND COMMUNISM'

... The supersession of self-estrangement follows the
same course as self-estrangement. *Private property* is first
considered only from its objective aspect, but with labor

conceived as its essence. Its mode of existence is, therefore, *capital* which it is necessary to abolish "as such"
(Proudhon). Or else the *specific form* of labor (labor
which is brought to a common level, subdivided, and thus
unfree) is regarded as the source of the *harmfulness* of
private property and of its existence alienated from man.
Fourier, in accord with the Physiocrats, regards *agricultural labor* as being at least the exemplary kind of labor.
Saint-Simon asserts on the contrary that *industrial labor*
as such is the essence of labor, and consequently he desires
the *exclusive* rule of the industrialists and an amelioration
of the condition of the workers. Finally, *communism* is
the positive expression of the abolition of private property, and in the first place of universal private property. In
taking this relation in its *universal aspect* communism is,
in its first form, only the generalization and fulfilment of
the relation. As such it appears in a double form; the domination of material property looms so large that it aims to
destroy everything which is incapable of being possessed
by everyone as private property. It wishes to eliminate talent, etc. by *force*. Immediate physical possession seems to
it the unique goal of life and existence. The role of *worker*
is not abolished, but is extended to all men. The relation
of private property remains the relation of the community
to the world of things. Finally, this tendency to oppose
general private property to private property is expressed
in an animal form; *marriage* (which is incontestably a
form of *exclusive private property*) is contrasted with the
community of women, in which women become communal and common property. One may say that this idea of
the *community of women* is the *open secret* of this entirely crude and unreflective communism. Just as women
are to pass from marriage to universal prostitution, so the
whole world of wealth (i.e. the objective being of man) is
to pass from the relation of exclusive marriage with the
private owner to the relation of universal prostitution with
the community. This communism, which negates the *per-

sonality of man in every sphere, is only the logical expression of private property, which is this negation. Universal *envy* setting itself up as a power is only a camouflaged form of cupidity which re-establishes itself and satisfies itself in a different way. The thoughts of every individual private property are *at least* directed against any *wealthier* private property, in the form of envy and the desire to reduce everything to a common level, so that this envy and levelling in fact constitute the essence of competition. Crude communism is only the culmination of such envy and levelling-down on the basis of a *preconceived* minimum. How little this abolition of private property represents a genuine appropriation is shown by the abstract negation of the whole world of culture and civilization, and the regression to the *unnatural* simplicity of the poor, rough man without wants, who has not only not surpassed private property but has not yet even attained to it.

The community is only a community of *work* and of *equality of wages* paid out by the communal capital, by the *community* as universal capitalist. The two sides of the relation are raised to a *supposed* universality; *labor* as a condition in which everyone is placed, and *capital* as the acknowledged universality and power of the community.

In the relationship with *woman*, as the prey and the handmaid of communal lust, is expressed the infinite degradation in which man exists for himself; for the secret of this relationship finds its *unequivocal*, incontestable, open and revealed expression in the relation of man to woman and in the way in which the *direct* and *natural* species-relationship is conceived. The immediate, natural and necessary relation of human being to human being is also the *relation* of *man* to *woman*. In this *natural* species-relationship man's relation to nature is directly his relation to man, and his relation to man is directly his relation to nature, to his own *natural* function. Thus, in this relation is *sensuously revealed*, reduced to an observable *fact*, the extent to which human nature has become nature for man and to which nature has become human nature for him. From this relationship man's whole level of development can be assessed. It follows from the character of this relationship how far *man* has become, and has understood himself as, a *species-being*, a *human being*. The relation of man to woman is the *most natural* relation of human being to human being. It indicates, therefore, how far man's *natural* behaviour has become *human*, and how far his *human* essence has become a *natural* essence for him, how far his *human nature* has become *nature* for him. It also shows how far man's needs have become *human* needs, and consequently how far the other person, as a person, has become one of his needs, and to what extent he is in his individual existence at the same time a social being.

The first positive annulment of private property, crude communism, is therefore only a *manifestation* of the infamy of private property representing itself as positive community.

2. Communism (*a*) still political in nature, democratic or despotic; (*b*) with the abolition of the state, yet still incomplete and influenced by private property, that is, by the alienation of man. In both forms communism is already aware of being the reintegration of man, his return to himself, the supersession of man's self-alienation. But since it has not yet grasped the positive nature of private property, or the *human* nature of needs, it is still captured and contaminated by private property. It has well understood the concept, but not the essence.

3. *Communism* is the *positive* abolition of *private property*, of *human self-alienation*, and thus the real *appropriation* of *human* nature through and for man. It is therefore the return of man himself as a *social*, i.e. really human, being, a complete and conscious return which assimilates all the wealth of previous development. Communism as a fully developed naturalism is humanism and as a fully developed humanism is naturalism. It is the *defini-*

tive resolution of the antagonism between man and nature, and between man and man. It is the true solution of the conflict between existence and essence, between objectification and self-affirmation, between freedom and necessity, between individual and species. It is the solution of the riddle of history and knows itself to be this solution.

Thus the whole historical development, both the *real* genesis of communism (the birth of its empirical existence) and its thinking consciousness, is its comprehended and conscious process of becoming; whereas the other, still undeveloped, communism seeks in certain historical forms opposed to private property a *historical* justification founded upon what already exists, and to this end tears out of their context isolated elements of this development (Cabet and Villegardelle etc., in particular, ride this hobby-horse) and asserts them as proofs of its historical pedigree. In doing so, it makes clear that by far the greatest part of this development contradicts its own assertions, and that if it has ever existed its past existence refutes its pretension to *essential being*.

It is easy to understand the necessity which leads the whole revolutionary movement to find its empirical, as well as its theoretical, basis in the development of *private property*, and more precisely of the economic system.

This material, directly *perceptible* private property is the material and sensuous expression of *alienated human* life. Its movement—production and consumption—is the *sensuous* manifestation of the movement of all previous production, i.e the realization or reality of man. Religion, the family, the state, law, morality, science, art, etc. are only *particular* forms of production and come under its general law. The positive supersession of *private property*, as the appropriation of *human* life, is, therefore, the positive supersession of all alienation, and the return of man from religion, the family, the state, etc. to his *human*, i.e. social life. Religious alienation as such occurs only in the sphere of *consciousness*, in the inner life of man, but economic alienation is that of *real life* and its supersession, therefore, affects both aspects. Of course, the development in different nations has a different beginning according to whether the actual and *established* life of the people is more in the realm of mind or more in the external world, is a real or ideal life. Communism begins where atheism begins (Owen), but atheism is at the outset still far from being *communism;* indeed it is still for the most part an abstraction. . . .

Private property has made us so stupid and one-sided that an object is only *ours* when we have it, when it exists for us as capital or when it is directly eaten, drunk, worn, inhabited, etc., in short, *utilized* in some way But private property itself only conceives these various forms of possession as *means of life*, and the life for which they serve as means is the *life* of *private property*—labor and creation of capital.

Thus *all* the physical and intellectual senses have been replaced by the simple alienation of *all* these senses, the sense of *having*. The human being had to be reduced to this absolute poverty in order to be able to give birth to all his inner wealth. (On the category of *having* see Hess in *Einundzwanzig Bogen*.)

The supersession of private property is, therefore, the complete *emancipation* of all the human qualities and senses. It is such an emancipation because these qualities and senses have become *human*, from the subjective as well as the objective point of view. The eye has become a *human* eye when its *object* has become a *human*, social object, created by man and destined for him. The senses have, therefore, become directly theoreticians in practice. They relate themselves to the thing for the sake of the thing, but the thing itself is an *objective human* relation to itself and to man, and vice versa. Need and enjoyment have thus lost their *egoistic* character and nature has lost its mere *utility* by the fact that its utilization has become *human* utilization.

MEGA I, 3, 111–15, 118–19; MEW *Ergänzungsbd* I, 533–37, 540.

1844

From CRITICAL NOTES ON THE ARTICLE 'THE KING OF PRUSSIA AND SOCIAL REFORM. BY A PRUSSIAN'

The article, which appeared in *Vorwärts*, the German radical periodical published in Paris, on 27 July 1844, was written by Arnold Ruge; Marx's reply— the Critical Notes—appeared in the same periodical on 7 August 1844.

... *The state* will *never* find the cause of *social ills* in the "*state* and the *organization of society*" as the "Prussian" demands of his King. Where there are political parties, each finds the cause of *every* evil in the fact that its antagonist, instead of itself, is at the *helm of state*. Even radical and revolutionary politicians seek the cause of the evil not in the *nature* of the state but in a specific *form of state*, which they want to replace by *another* form.

The *state* and the *organization of society* are not, from the *political* standpoint, *two* different things. The state is the organization of society. So far as the state admits the existence of *social* evils, it attributes them either to *natural laws*, which no human power can command, or to *private life*, which is independent of the state, or to the *inadequacy of administration*, which is dependent on it. Thus England finds poverty rooted in the *natural law* according to which population must constantly exceed the means of subsistence. From another side, England explains *pauperism* as a consequence of the *ill will of the poor*, just as the King of Prussia explains it by the *unchristian spirit of the rich* and the Convention explains it by the *counter-revolutionary and equivocal attitude of property owners*. Hence England punishes the poor, the King of Prussia admonishes the rich, and the Convention beheads property owners.

In the end, *every* state seeks the cause of its ills in *accidental* or *intentional defects* of *administration* and therefore seeks the remedy in laying down rules for the administration. Why? Precisely because the *administration* is the *organizing* activity of the state.

The state cannot overcome and transcend the *contradiction* between the good intentions of the administration on the one hand and its means and resources on the other without overcoming and transcending itself, for the state is based on this contradiction. It is based on the contradiction between public and private life, between universal interest and special interests. The administration therefore has to confine itself to formal and negative action, for where civil life and its work begin there the power of the administration ends. Impotence *vis-à-vis* the consequences which spring from the unsocial nature of civil life, from private ownership, trade, industry and the mutual plundering engaged in by the various bourgeois circles is the natural law governing the administration. This fragmentation, this oppression, this slavery to civil society, is the natural foundation on which the modern state rests, just as the civil society of slavery was the natural foundation on which the ancient state rested. The existence of the state and the existence of slavery are inseparable. The state and slavery of antiquity—open *classical* antitheses—were not more closely welded together than are the modern state and the modern world of bargaining—sanctimonious *Christian* antitheses. If the modern state wanted to overcome and transcend the *impotence* of its administration, it would have to overcome and transcend the present mode of *private life*. If it wanted to transcend this private life, it would have to transcend itself, for it exists *only* in contrast to that life. No *living person*, however, believes that the defect of his specific existence is rooted in the *principle* or essence of his life, but rather in circumstances *outside* his life. *Suicide* is unnatural. Thus the state cannot believe in the *innate* impotence of its administration, that is, of its own self. It can recognize *only* formal, accidental defects of administration and seek to remedy them. If these modifications are fruitless, then the social ill is a natural imperfection independent of mankind, a *law of God*, or else the will of private individuals is too corrupted to respond to the good aims of the administration. And what perverse private individuals! They grumble against the government whenever it restricts freedom, and they demand that the government prevent the necessary consequences of this freedom.

The more powerful the state and hence the more *political* a country is, the less is it inclined to seek the basis and to grasp the *general* principle of *social* ills in the *principle of the state* itself, thus in the *existing organization of society* of which the state is the active, self-conscious, and official expression. *Political* thought is *political* precisely because it takes place *within* the bounds of politics. The more acute, the more vigorous it is, the more *incapable* it is of comprehending social ills. The *classical* period of political thought is the *French Revolution*. Far from perceiving the source of social defects in the principle of the state, the heroes of the French Revolution rather saw the source of political evils in social defects. Thus *Robespierre* saw in great poverty and great wealth only an obstacle to *pure democracy*. Hence he wanted to establish a general *Spartan* frugality. The principle of politics is *will*. The more one-sided and thus the more perfected *political* thought is, the more it believes in the *omnipotence* of will, the blinder it is to *natural* and spiritual *restrictions* on the will, and the more incapable it is of discovering the source of social ills.

MEGA I, 3, 14–16; MEW 1, 400–2.

'THESES ON FEUERBACH'

Jotted down by Marx in his notebooks in Brussels, c. March 1845, first published by Engels, in a slightly revised version, in 1888 as an appendix to his *Ludwig Feuerbach and the End of German Philosophy*.

I

The chief defect of all previous materialism (including Feuerbach's) is that the object, reality, what we apprehend through our senses, is understood only in the form of *object* or *contemplation;* but not as *sensuous human activity,* as *practice;* not subjectively. Hence in opposition to materialism the *active* side was developed abstractly by idealism, which of course does not know real sensuous activity as such. Feuerbach wants sensuous objects, really distinguished from the objects of thought: but he does not understand human activity itself as *objective* activity. Hence, in *The Essence of Christianity*, he sees only the theoretical attitude as the true human attitude, while practice is understood and established only in its dirty Jewish manifestation. He therefore does not comprehend the significance of "revolutionary," of "practical-critical" activity.

II

The question whether human thought can attain to objective truth is not a theoretical but a *practical* question. Man must prove the truth, i.e. the reality and power, the this-sidedness of his thinking in practice. The dispute over the reality or non-reality of thinking which is isolated from practice is a purely *scholastic* question.

III

The materialistic doctrine concerning the changing of [men's] circumstances and education forgets that circumstances are changed by men and that the educator himself must be educated. This doctrine therefore has to divide society into two parts, one of which is superior to society.

The coincidence of the changing of circumstances and of human activity or self-change can be comprehended and rationally understood only as *revolutionary practice*.

IV

Feuerbach takes his departure from the fact of religious self-estrangement, from the duplication of the world into a religious and a secular one. His work consists in resolving the religious world into its secular basis. But the fact that the secular basis raises itself above itself and establishes for itself an independent realm in the clouds can be explained only through the cleavage and self-contradictoriness of this secular basis. The latter must therefore be understood, both in itself and in its contradiction, as revolutionized in practice. Therefore after the earthly family, e.g., is discovered to be the secret of the heavenly family, one must proceed to destroy the former both in theory and in practice.

V

Feuerbach, not satisfied with *abstract thought*, wants contemplation: but he does not understand sensuousness as *practical*, human-sensuous activity.

VI

Feuerbach resolves the essence of religion into the essence of *man*. But the essence of man is no abstraction inherent in each separate individual. In its reality it is the *ensemble* (aggregate) of social relations.

Feuerbach, who does not enter more deeply into the criticism of this real essence, is therefore forced:

1. To abstract from the process of history and to establish the religious temperament as something self-contained, and to postulate an abstract—*isolated*—human individual.

2. The essence of man can therefore be understood only as "species", the inward, dumb generality which *naturally* unites the many individuals.

VII

Feuerbach therefore does not see that the "religious temperament" itself is a social product and that the abstract individual whom he analyses belongs to a particular form of society.

VIII

All social life is essentially *practical*. All the mysteries which lead theory into mysticism find their rational solution in human practice and in the comprehension of this practice.

IX

The highest point attained by contemplative materialism, i.e. by that materialism which does not comprehend sensuousness as practical activity, is the contemplation of separate individuals and of civil society.

X

The standpoint of the old type of materialism is civil society, the standpoint of the new materialism is human society or social humanity.

XI

Philosophers have only *interpreted* the world in various ways; the point is to *change* it.

MEGA I, 5, 533–35; MEW 3, 5–7.

1859

From A CONTRIBUTION TO THE CRITIQUE OF POLITICAL ECONOMY

PREFACE

... I am omitting a general introduction which I had projected. . . . A few indications of the course of my own politico-economic studies may, on the other hand, appear not out of place here.

I was taking up law, which study, however, I only pursued as a subordinate subject along with philosophy and history. In the year 1842–43, as editor of the *Rheinische Zeitung*, I experienced for the first time the embarrassment of having to take part in discussions on so-called material interests. The proceedings of the Rhenish Landtag on thefts of wood and the parcelling of landed property, the official polemic which Herr von Schaper, then *Oberpräsident* of the Rhine Province, opened against the *Rheinische Zeitung* on the conditions of the Moselle peasantry, and finally the debates on free trade and protective tariffs gave the first incentive to my occupation with economic questions. On the other hand, at that time when the good will "to go further" frequently outweighed special-ized knowledge, a philosophically weakly tinged echo of French socialism and communism made itself audible in the *Rheinische Zeitung*. I declared myself against this bungling, but frankly confessed at the same time in a con-troversy with the *Allgemeine Augsburger Zeitung* that my previous studies did not permit me to venture for my-self any judgment on the content of the French tenden-cies. Instead, I eagerly seized on the illusion of the managers of the *Rheinische Zeitung*, who thought that by a weaker attitude on the part of the paper they could se-cure a remission of the death sentence passed upon it, to effect my withdrawal from the public stage into the study.

The first work which I undertook for a solution of the doubts which assailed me was a critical review of the Hegelian philosophy of law, a work the introduction to which appeared in 1844 in the *Deutsch-französische Jahrbücher*, published in Paris. My investigation led to the result that legal relations such as forms of state are to be grasped neither from themselves nor from the so-called general development of the human mind, but rather have their roots in the material conditions of life, the sum total of which Hegel, following the example of the Englishmen and Frenchmen of the eighteenth century, combines under the name of "civil society," that however the anat-omy of civil society is to be sought in political economy. The investigation of the latter, which I began in Paris, I continued in Brussels, whither I had emigrated in conse-quence of an expulsion order of M. Guizot. The general result at which I arrived and which, once won, served as a guiding thread for my studies, can be briefly formulated as follows: In the social production of their life, men enter into definite relations that are indispensable and indepen-dent of their will; these relations of production correspond to a definite stage of development of their material forces of production. The sum total of these relations of produc-tion constitutes the economic structure of society—the real foundation, on which rises a legal and political super-structure and to which correspond definite forms of social consciousness. The mode of production of material life determines the social, political and intellectual life process in general. It is not the consciousness of men that determines their being, but, on the contrary, their social being that determines their consciousness. At a certain stage of their development, the material productive forces in society come in conflict with the existing relations of production, or—what is but a legal expression for the same thing—with the property relations within which they have been at work before. From forms of development of the productive forces these relations turn into their fetters. Then begins an epoch of social revolution. With the change of the economic foundation the entire immense superstructure is more or less rapidly transformed. In considering such transformations a distinction should always be made between the material transformation of the economic conditions of production, which can be determined with the precision of natural science, and the legal, political, religious, aesthetic or philosophic—in short, ideological forms in which men become conscious of this conflict and fight it out. Just as our opinion of an individual is not based on what he thinks of himself, so can we not judge of such a period of transformation by its own consciousness; on the contrary, this consciousness must be explained rather from the contradictions of material life, from the existing conflict between the social productive forces and the relations of production. No social order ever disappears before all the productive forces for which there is room in it have been developed; and new, higher relations of production never appear before the material conditions of their existence have matured in the womb of the old society itself. Therefore, mankind always sets itself only such tasks as it can solve; since, looking at the matter more closely, we will always find that the task itself arises only when the material conditions necessary for its solution already exist or are at least in the process of formation. In broad outlines we can designate the Asiatic,[1] the ancient, the feudal, and the modern bourgeois modes of production as so many progressive epochs in the economic formation of society. The bourgeois relations of production are the last antagonistic form of the social process of production—antagonistic not in the sense of individual antagonism, but of one arising from the social conditions of life of the individuals; at the same time the productive forces developing in the womb of bourgeois society create the material conditions for the solution of that antagonism. This social formation constitutes, therefore, the closing chapter of the prehistoric stage of human society.

Frederick Engels, with whom, since the appearance of his brilliant sketch on the criticism of the economic categories (in the *Deutsch-französische Jahrbücher*), I maintained a constant exchange of ideas by correspondence, had by another road (compare his *The Condition of the Working Class in England*) arrived at the same result as I, and when in the spring of 1845 he also settled in Brussels, we resolved to work out together the opposition of our view to the ideological view of German philosophy, in fact, to settle accounts with our previous philosophical conscience. The resolve was carried out in the form of a criticism of post-Hegelian philosophy. The manuscript, two large octavo volumes, had long reached its place of publication in Westphalia when we received the news that altered circumstances did not allow of its being printed. We abandoned the manuscript to the gnawing criticism of the mice all the more willingly since we had achieved our main purpose—self-clarification.

MEW 13, 7–10, as translated in Karl Marx and Frederick Engels, *Selected Works*, 2 vols., Moscow, 1947, I, pp. 299–302.

---

1. This concept of the Asiatic mode of production was not introduced into Marx's work until 1853. [E.K.]

1845–1846

From *THE GERMAN IDEOLOGY*, VOLUME ONE

PREFACE

Hitherto men have constantly made up for themselves false conceptions about themselves, about what they are and what they ought to be. They have arranged their relationships according to their ideas of God, of normal man, etc. The phantoms of their brains have gained the mastery over them. They, the creators, have bowed down before their creatures. Let us liberate them from the chimeras, the ideas, dogmas, imaginary beings under the yoke of which they are pining away. Let us revolt against the rule of thoughts. Let us teach men, says one,[1] to exchange these imaginations for thoughts which correspond to the essence of man; says the second,[2] to take up a critical attitude to them; says the third,[3] to knock them out of their heads; and—existing reality will collapse.

These innocent and childlike fancies are the kernel of the modern Young-Hegelian philosophy, which not only is received by the German public with horror and awe, but is announced by our philosophic Heroes with the solemn consciousness of their cataclysmic dangerousness and criminal ruthlessness. The first volume of this present publication has the aim of uncloaking these sheep, who take themselves and are taken for wolves; of showing how their bleating merely imitates in a philosophic form the conceptions of the German middle class; how the boasting of these philosophic commentators only mirrors the wretchedness of the real conditions in Germany. It is its aim to discredit the philosophic struggle with the shadows

---

1. Ludwig Feuerbach. [E.K.]
2. Bruno Bauer. [E.K.]
3. Max Stirner. [E.K.]

of reality, which appeals to the dreamy and muddled German nation.

Once upon a time an honest fellow had the idea that men were drowned in water only because they were possessed with the idea of gravity. If they were to knock this idea out of their heads, say by stating it to be a superstition, a religious idea, they would be sublimely proof against any danger from water. His whole life long he fought against the illusion of gravity, of whose harmful results all statistics brought him new and manifold evidence. This honest fellow was the type of the new revolutionary philosophers in Germany.

MEGA I, 5, 3; MEW 3, 13–14, as translated in K. Marx and F. Engels, *The German Ideology*, ed. R. Pascal, New York, 1947 (repr. 1968), pp. 1–2.

[THE MATERIALIST CONCEPTION OF HISTORY]

... The premises from which we begin are not arbitrary ones, not dogmas, but real premises from which abstraction can only be made in the imagination. They are the real individuals, their activity and the material conditions under which they live, both those which they find already existing and those produced by their activity. These premises can thus be verified in a purely empirical way.

The first premise of all human history is, of course, the existence of living human individuals. Thus the first fact to be established is the physical organization of these individuals and their consequent relation to the rest of nature. Of course, we cannot here go either into the actual physical nature of man, or into the natural conditions in which man finds himself—geological, orohydrographical, climatic and so on. The writing of history must always set out from these natural bases and their modification in the course of history through the action of man.

Men can be distinguished from animals by consciousness, by religion or anything else you like. They themselves begin to distinguish themselves from animals as soon as they begin to *produce* their means of subsistence, a step which is conditioned by their physical organization. By producing their means of subsistence men are indirectly producing their actual material life.

The way in which men produce their means of subsistence depends first of all on the nature of the actual means they find in existence and have to reproduce. This mode of production must not be considered simply as being the reproduction of the physical existence of the individuals. Rather it is a definite form of activity of these individuals, a definite form of expressing their life, a definite *mode of life* on their part. As individuals express their life, so they are. What they are, therefore, coincides with their production, both with *what* they produce and with *how* they produce. The nature of individuals thus depends on the material conditions determining their production.

This production only makes its appearance with the increase of population. In its turn this presupposes the intercourse of individuals with one another. The form of this intercourse is again determined by production.

The relations of different nations among themselves depend upon the extent to which each has developed its productive forces, the division of labour and internal intercourse. This statement is generally recognized. But not only the relation of one nation to others, but also the whole internal structure of the nation itself depends on the stage of development reached by its production and its internal and external intercourse. How far the productive forces of a nation are developed is shown most manifestly by the degree to which the division of labour has been carried. Each new productive force, in so far as it is not merely a quantitative extension of productive forces already known (for instance the bringing into cultivation of fresh land), brings about a further development of the division of labour.

The division of labour inside a nation leads at first to the separation of industrial and commercial from agricultural labour, and hence to the separation of town and country and a clash of interests between them. Its further development leads to the separation of commercial from industrial labour. At the same time through the division of labour there develop further, inside these various branches, various divisions among the individuals cooperating in definite kinds of labour. The relative position of these individual groups is determined by the methods employed in agriculture, industry and commerce (patriarchalism, slavery, estates, classes). These same conditions are to be seen (given a more developed intercourse) in the relations of different nations to one another.

The various stages of development in the division of labour are just so many different forms of ownership; i.e. the existing stage in the division of labour determines also the relations of individuals to one another with reference to the material, instrument, and product of labour.

The first form of ownership is tribal ownership. It corresponds to the undeveloped stage of production, during which a people lives by hunting and fishing, by the rearing of beasts or, in the highest stage, agriculture. In the latter case it presupposes a great mass of uncultivated stretches of land. The division of labour is at this stage still very elementary and is confined to a further extension of the natural division of labour imposed by the family. The social structure is therefore limited to an extension of the family; patriarchal family chieftains; below them the members of the tribe; finally slaves. The slavery latent in the family only develops gradually with the increase of population, the growth of wants, and with the extension of external relations, of war or of trade.

The second form is the ancient communal and state

ownership which proceeds especially from the union of several tribes into a city by agreement or by conquest, and which is still accompanied by slavery. Beside communal ownership we already find movable, and later also immovable, private property developing, but as an abnormal form subordinate to communal ownership. It is only as a community that the citizens hold power over their labouring slaves, and on this account alone, therefore, they are bound to the form of communal ownership. It is communal private property which compels the active citizens to remain in this natural form of association over against their slaves. For this reason the whole structure of society based on this communal ownership, and with it the power of the people, decays in the same measure as immovable private property evolves. The division of labour is already more developed. We already find the antagonism of town and country; later the antagonism between those states which represent town interests and those which represent country, and inside the towns themselves the antagonism between industry and maritime commerce. The class relation between citizens and slaves is now completely developed.

With the development of private property, we find here for the first time the same conditions which we shall find again, only on a more extensive scale, with modern private property. On the one hand the concentration of private property, which began very early in Rome (as the Licinian agrarian law proves), and proceeded very rapidly from the time of the civil wars and especially under the Emperors; on the other hand, coupled with this, the transformation of the plebeian small peasantry into a proletariat, which, however, owing to its intermediate position between propertied citizens and slaves, never achieved an independent development.

The third form of ownership is feudal or estate-property. If antiquity started out from the town and its little territory, the Middle Ages started out from the country. This different starting-point was determined by the sparseness of the population at that time, which was scattered over a large area and which received no large increase from the conquerors. In contrast to Greece and Rome, feudal development therefore extends over a much wider field, prepared by the Roman conquests and the spread of agriculture at first associated with them. The last centuries of the declining Roman Empire and its conquest by the barbarians destroyed a number of productive forces; agriculture had declined, industry had decayed for want of a market, trade had died out or been violently suspended, the rural and urban population had decreased. From these conditions and the mode of organization of the conquest determined by them, feudal property developed under the influence of the Germanic military constitution. Like tribal and communal ownership, it is based again on a community; but the directly producing class standing over against it is not, as in the case of the ancient community, the slaves, but the enserfed small peasantry. As soon as feudalism is fully developed, there also arises antagonism to the towns. The hierarchical system of land-ownership, and the armed bodies of retainers associated with it, gave the nobility power over the serfs. This feudal organization was, just as much as the ancient communal ownership, an association against a subjected producing class; but the form of association and the relation to the direct producers were different because of the different conditions of production.

This feudal organization of land-ownership had its counterpart in the towns in the shape of corporative property, the feudal organization of trades. Here property consisted chiefly in the labour of each individual person. The necessity for association against the organized robber-nobility, the need for communal covered markets in an age when the industrialist was at the same time a merchant, the growing competition of the escaped serfs swarming into the rising towns, the feudal structure of the whole country: these combined to bring about the guilds. Further, the gradually accumulated capital of individual craftsmen and their stable numbers, as against the growing population, evolved the relation of journeyman and apprentice, which brought into being in the towns a hierarchy similar to that in the country.

Thus the chief form of property during the feudal epoch consisted on the one hand of landed property with serf-labour chained to it, and on the other of individual labour with small capital commanding the labour of journeymen. The organization of both was determined by the restricted conditions of production—the small-scale and primitive cultivation of the land, and the craft type of industry. There was little division of labour in the heyday of feudalism. Each land bore in itself the conflict of town and country and the division into estates was certainly strongly marked; but apart from the differentiation of princes, nobility, clergy and peasants in the country, and masters, journeymen, apprentices and soon also the rabble of casual labourers in the towns, no division of importance took place. In agriculture it was rendered difficult by the strip-system, beside which the cottage industry of the peasants themselves emerged as another factor. In industry there was no division of labour at all in the individual trades themselves, and very little between them. The separation of industry and commerce was found already in existence in older towns; in the newer it only developed later, when the towns entered into mutual relations.

The grouping of larger territories into feudal kingdoms was a necessity for the landed nobility as for the towns. The organization of the ruling class, the nobility, had, therefore, everywhere a monarch at its head.

The fact is, therefore, that definite individuals who are productively active in a definite way enter into these definite social and political relations. Empirical observation must in each separate instance bring out empirically, and without any mystification and speculation, the connection of the social and political structure with production. The social structure and the state are continually evolving out of the life-process of definite individuals, but of individuals, not as they may appear in their own or other people's imagination, but as they really are; i.e. as they are effective, produce materially, and are active under definite material limits, presuppositions and conditions independent of their will.

The production of ideas, of conceptions, of consciousness, is at first directly interwoven with the material activity and the material intercourse of men, the language of real life. Conceiving, thinking, the mental intercourse of men, appear at this stage as the direct efflux of their material behaviour. The same applies to mental production as expressed in the language of the politics, laws, morality, religion, metaphysics of a people. Men are the producers of their conceptions, ideas, etc.—real, active men, as they are conditioned by a definite development of their productive forces and of the intercourse corresponding to these, up to its furthest forms. Consciousness can never be anything else than conscious existence, and the existence of men is their actual life-process. If in all ideology men and their circumstances appear upside down as in a *camera obscura*, this phenomenon arises just as much from their historical life-process as the inversion of objects on the retina does from their physical life-process.

In direct contrast to German philosophy, which descends from heaven to earth, here we ascend from earth to heaven. That is to say, we do not set out from what men say, imagine, conceive, nor from men as narrated, thought of, imagined, conceived, in order to arrive at men in the flesh. We set out from real, active men, and on the basis of their real life-process we demonstrate the development of the ideological reflexes and echoes of this life-process. The phantoms formed in the human brain are also, necessarily, sublimates of their material life-process, which is empirically verifiable and bound to material premises. Morality, religion, metaphysics, all the rest of ideology and their corresponding forms of consciousness, thus no longer retain the semblance of independence. They have no history, no development; but men, developing their material production and their material intercourse, alter, along with this their real existence, their thinking and the products of their thinking. Life is not determined by consciousness, but consciousness by life. In the first method of approach the starting-point is consciousness taken as the living individual; in the second it is the real living individuals themselves, as they are in actual life, and consciousness is considered solely as *their* consciousness.

This method of approach is not devoid of premises. It starts out from the real premises and does not abandon them for a moment. Its premises are men, not in any fantastic isolation or abstract definition, but in their actual, empirically perceptible process of development under definite conditions. As soon as this active life-process is described, history ceases to be a collection of dead facts as it is with the empiricists (themselves still abstract), or an imagined activity of imagined subjects, as with the idealists.

Where speculation ends—in real life—there real, positive science begins: the representation of the practical activity, of the practical process of development of men. Empty talk about consciousness ceases, and real knowledge has to take its place. When reality is depicted, philosophy as an independent branch of activity loses its medium of existence. At the best its place can only be taken by a summing-up of the most general results, abstractions which arise from the observation of the historical development of men. Viewed apart from real history, these abstractions have in themselves no value whatsoever. They can only serve to facilitate the arrangement of historical material, to indicate the sequence of its separate strata. But they by no means afford a recipe or schema, as does philosophy, for neatly trimming the epochs of history. On the contrary, our difficulties begin only when we set about the observation and the arrangement—the real depiction—of our historical material, whether of a past epoch or of the present. The removal of these difficulties is governed by premises which it is quite impossible to state here, but which only the study of the actual life-process and the activity of the individuals of each epoch will make evident. We shall select here some of these abstractions, which we use to refute the ideologists, and shall illustrate them by historical examples . . .

[ON HISTORY]

Since we are dealing with the Germans, who do not postulate anything, we must begin by stating the first premise of all human existence, and therefore of all history, the premise namely that men must be in a position to live in order to be able to "make history." But life involves before everything else eating and drinking, a habitation, clothing and many other things. The first historical act is thus the production of the means to satisfy these needs, the production of material life itself. And indeed this is a historical act, a fundamental condition of all history, which to-day, as thousands of years ago, must daily and hourly be fulfilled merely in order to sustain human life. Even when the sensuous world is reduced to a minimum, to a stick as with Saint Bruno,[4] it presupposes the action of producing the stick. The first necessity therefore in any theory of history is to observe this fundamental fact in all its significance and all its implications and to accord it its due importance. This, as is notorious, the Germans have never done, and they have never before had an earthly basis for history and consequently never a historian. The

---

4. Bruno Bauer. [E.K.]

French and the English, even if they have conceived the relation of this fact with so-called history only in an extremely one-sided fashion, particularly as long as they remained in the toils of political ideology, have nevertheless made the first attempts to give the writing of history a materialistic basis by being the first to write histories of civil society, of commerce and industry.

The second fundamental point is that as soon as a need is satisfied (which implies the action of satisfying, and the acquisition of an instrument), new needs are made; and this production of new needs is the first historical act. Here we recognize immediately the spiritual ancestry of the great historical wisdom of the Germans who, when they run out of positive material and when they can serve up neither theological nor political nor literary rubbish, do not write history at all, but invent the "prehistoric era." They do not, however, enlighten us as to how we proceed from this nonsensical "prehistory" to history proper; although, on the other hand, in their historical speculation they seize upon this "prehistory" with especial eagerness because they imagine themselves safe there from interference on the part of "crude facts," and, at the same time, because there they can give full rein to their speculative impulse and set up and knock down hypotheses by the thousand.

The third circumstance which, from the very first, enters into historical development, is that men, who daily remake their own life, begin to make other men, to propagate their kind: the relation between man and wife, parents and children, the FAMILY. The family which to begin with is the only social relationship, becomes later, when increased needs create new social relations and the increased population new needs, a subordinate one (except in Germany), and must then be treated and analysed according to the existing empirical data, not according to "the concept of the family," as is the custom in Germany. These three aspects of social activity are not of course to be taken as three different stages, but just, as I have said, as three aspects or, to make it clear to the Germans, three "moments," which have existed simultaneously since the dawn of history and the first men, and still assert themselves in history to-day.

The production of life, both of one's own in labour and of fresh life in procreation, now appears as a double relationship: on the one hand as a natural, on the other as a social relationship. By social we understand the co-operation of several individuals, no matter under what conditions, in what manner and to what end. It follows from this that a certain mode of production, or industrial stage, is always combined with a certain mode of co-operation, or social stage, and this mode of co-operation is itself a "productive force." Further, that the multitude of productive forces accessible to men determines the nature of society, hence that the "history of humanity" must always be studied and treated in relation to the history of industry and exchange. . . .

[CONSCIOUSNESS AND THE DIVISION OF LABOUR]

Only now, after having considered four moments, four aspects of the fundamental historical relationships, do we find that man also possesses "consciousness"; but, even so, not inherent, not "pure" consciousness. From the start the "spirit" is afflicted with the curse of being "burdened" with matter, which here makes its appearance in the form of agitated layers of air, sounds, in short, of language. Language is as old as consciousness, language is practical consciousness, as it exists for other men, and for that reason is really beginning to exist for me personally as well; for language, like consciousness, only arises from the need, the necessity, of intercourse with other men. Where there exists a relationship, it exists for me: the animal has no "relations" with anything, cannot have any. For the animal, its relation to others does not exist as a relation. Consciousness is therefore from the very beginning a social product, and remains so as long as men exist at all. Consciousness is at first, of course, merely consciousness concerning the immediate sensuous environment and consciousness of the limited connection with other persons and things outside the individual who is growing self-conscious. At the same time it is consciousness of nature, which first appears to men as a completely alien, all-powerful and unassailable force, with which men's relations are purely animal and by which they are overawed like beasts; it is thus a purely animal consciousness of nature (natural religion).

We see here immediately: this natural religion or animal behaviour towards nature is determined by the form of society and *vice versa*. Here, as everywhere, the identity of nature and man appears in such a way that the restricted relation of men to nature determines their restricted relation to one another, and their restricted relation to one another determines men's restricted relation to nature, just because nature is as yet hardly modified historically; and, on the other hand, man's consciousness of the necessity of associating with the individuals around him is the beginning of the consciousness that he is living in society at all. This beginning is as animal as social life itself at this stage. It is mere herd-consciousness, and at this point man is only distinguished from sheep by the fact that with him consciousness takes the place of instinct or that his instinct is a conscious one.

This sheep-like or tribal consciousness receives its further development and extension through increased productivity, the increase of needs, and, what is fundamental to both of these, the increase of population. With these there develops the division of labour, which was originally nothing but the division of labour in the sexual act, then that division of labour which develops spontaneously or "naturally" by virtue of natural predisposition (e.g. physical strength), needs, accidents, etc., etc. Division of labour only becomes truly such from the moment when a division of material and mental labour appears. From this moment onwards consciousness *can* really flatter itself that it is something other than consciousness of existing practice, that it is *really* conceiving something without conceiving something *real;* from now on consciousness is in a position to emancipate itself from the world and to proceed to the formation of "pure" theory, theology, philosophy, ethics, etc. But even if this theory, theology, philosophy, ethics, etc. comes into contradiction with the existing relations, this can only occur as a result of the fact that existing social relations have come into contradiction with existing forces of production; this, moreover, can also occur in a particular national sphere of relations through the appearance of the contradiction, not within the national orbit, but between this national consciousness and the practice of other nations, i.e. between the national and the general consciousness of a nation.

Moreover, it is quite immaterial what consciousness starts to do on its own; out of all such muck we get only the one inference that these three moments, the forces of production, the state of society, and consciousness, can and must come into contradiction with one another, because the division of labour implies the possibility, nay the fact that intellectual and material activity—enjoyment and labour, production and consumption—devolve on different individuals, and that the only possibility of their not coming into contradiction lies in the negation in its turn of the division of labour. It is self-evident, moreover, that "spectres," "bonds," "the higher being," "concept," "scruple," are merely the idealistic, spiritual expression, the conception apparently of the isolated individual, the image of very empirical fetters and limitations, within which the mode of production of life, and the form of intercourse coupled with it, move.

With the division of labour, in which all these contradictions are implicit, and which in its turn is based on the natural division of labour in the family and the separation of society into individual families opposed to one another, is given simultaneously the distribution, and indeed the unequal distribution (both quantitative and qualitative), of labour and its products, hence property: the nucleus, the first form, of which lies in the family, where wife and children are the slaves of the husband. This latent slavery in the family, though still very crude, is the first property, but even at this early stage it corresponds perfectly to the definition of modern economists who call it the power of disposing of the labour-power of others. Division of labour and private property are, moreover, identical expressions: in the one the same thing is affirmed with reference to activity as is affirmed in the other with reference to the product of the activity.

Further, the division of labour implies the contradiction between the interest of the separate individual or the individual family and the communal interest of all individuals who have intercourse with one another. And indeed, this communal interest does not exist merely in the imagination, as "the general good," but first of all in reality, as the mutual interdependence of the individuals among whom the labour is divided. And out of this very contradiction between the interest of the individual and that of the community the latter takes an independent form as the STATE, divorced from the real interests of individual and community, and at the same time as an illusory communal life, always based, however, on the real ties existing in every family and tribal conglomeration (such as flesh and blood, language, division of labour on a larger scale, and other interests) and especially, as we shall enlarge upon later, on the classes, already determined by the division of labour, which in every such mass of men separate out, and of which one dominates all the others. It follows from this that all struggles within the state, the struggle between democracy, aristocracy and monarchy, the struggle for the franchise, etc., etc., are merely the illusory forms in which the real struggles of the different classes are fought out among one another. . . .

And finally, the division of labour offers us the first example of how, as long as man remains in natural society, that is as long as a cleavage exists between the particular and the common interest, as long therefore as activity is not voluntarily, but naturally, divided, man's own deed becomes an alien power opposed to him, which enslaves him instead of being controlled by him. For as soon as labour is distributed, each man has a particular, exclusive sphere of activity, which is forced upon him and from which he cannot escape. He is a hunter, a fisherman, a shepherd, or a critical critic, and must remain so if he does not want to lose his means of livelihood; while in communist society, where nobody has one exclusive sphere of activity but each can become accomplished in any branch he wishes, society regulates the general production and thus makes it possible for me to do one thing to-day and another to-morrow, to hunt in the morning, fish in the afternoon, rear cattle in the evening, criticize after dinner, just as I have a mind, without ever becoming hunter, fisherman, shepherd or critic.

This crystallization of social activity, this consolidation of what we ourselves produce into an objective power above us, growing out of our control, thwarting our expectations, bringing to naught our calculations, is one of the chief factors in historical development up till now. The social power, i.e. the multiplied productive force, which arises through the co-operation of different individuals as it is determined by the division of labour, appears to come about naturally, not as their own united power, but as an alien force existing outside them, of the origin and goal of which they are ignorant, which they thus cannot control, which on the contrary passes through a peculiar series of phases and stages independent of the will and action of man, nay even being the prime governor of these. . . .

This "estrangement" [or "alienation"] (to use a term which will be comprehensible to the philosophers) can, of course, only be abolished given two *practical* premises. For it to become an "intolerable" power, i.e. a power against which men make a revolution, it must necessarily have rendered the great mass of humanity "propertyless," and produced, at the same time, the contradiction of an existing world of wealth and culture, both of which conditions presuppose a great increase in productive power, a high degree of its development. And, on the other hand, this development of productive forces (which itself implies the actual empirical existence of men in their *world-historical,* instead of local, being) is absolutely necessary as a practical premise: firstly, for the reason that without it only *want* is made general, and with want the struggle for necessities and all the old filthy business would necessarily be reproduced; and secondly, because only with this universal development of productive forces is a *universal* intercourse between men established, which produces in all nations simultaneously the phenomenon of the "propertyless" mass (universal competition), makes each nation dependent on the revolutions of the others, and finally has put *world-historical,* empirically universal individuals in place of local ones. Without this, (1) Communism could only exist as a local event; (2) The forces of intercourse themselves could not have developed as universal, hence intolerable powers: they would have remained home-bred superstitious conditions; and (3) Each extension of intercourse would abolish local communism. Empirically, communism is only possible as the act of the dominant peoples "all at once" or simultaneously, which presupposes the universal development of productive forces and the world-intercourse bound up with them.

Moreover, the world-market is presupposed by the mass of propertyless workers—labour-power cut off as a mass from capital or from even a limited satisfaction—and therefore no longer by the mere precariousness of labour, which, not giving an assured livelihood, is often lost through competition. The proletariat can thus only exist *world-historically*, just as communism, its movement, can only have a "world-historical" existence. World-historical existence of individuals, i.e. existence of individuals which is directly linked up with world history.

Communism is for us not a stable state which is to be established, an *ideal* to which reality will have to adjust itself. We call communism the *real* movement which abolishes the present state of things. The conditions of this movement result from the premises now in existence.

The form of intercourse determined by the existing productive forces at all previous historical stages, and in its turn determining these, is *civil society*. This, as is clear from what we have said above, has as its premises and basis the simple family and the multiple, the so-called tribe, the more precise determinants of which are enumerated in our remarks above. Already here we see how this civil society is the true source and theatre of all history, and how nonsensical is the conception of history held hitherto, which neglects the real relationships and confines itself to high-sounding dramas of princes and states. [Civil society embraces the whole material intercourse of individuals within a definite stage of the development of productive forces. It embraces the whole commercial and industrial life of this stage and, in so far, transcends the state and the nation, though, on the other hand again, it must assert itself towards foreign peoples as nationality, and inwardly must organize itself as state.

The word "civil society" emerged in the eighteenth century, when property relationships had already extricated themselves from the ancient and medieval communal society. Civil society as such only develops with the bourgeoisie; the social organization evolving directly out of production and commerce, which in all ages forms the basis of the State and of the rest of the idealistic superstructure, has, however, always been designated by the same name.][5] . . .

MEGA I, 5, 10–12, 13–26; MEW 3, 20–23, 24–36, as translated in Marx and Engels, *The German Ideology*, ed. cit., pp. 6–27, but rearranged—save for the passage noted above—according to the revised ordering of the manuscript by the Institute of Marxism-Leninism, believed to be closer to the original, and published in *Voprosy filosofii*, nos. 10 and 11, for 1965.

History is nothing but the succession of the separate generations, each of which exploits the materials, the forms of capital, the productive forces handed down to it by all preceding ones, and thus on the one hand continues the traditional activity in completely changed circumstances and, on the other, modifies the old circumstances with a completely changed activity. This can be speculatively distorted so that later history is made the goal of earlier history, e.g. the goal ascribed to the discovery of America is to further the eruption of the French Revolution. Thereby history receives its own special aims and becomes "a person ranking with other persons" (to wit: "self-consciousness, criticism, the Unique," etc.), while what is designated with the words "destiny," "goal," "germ," or "idea" of earlier history is nothing more than an abstraction formed from later history, from the active influence which earlier history exercises on later history.

---

5. The passage in square brackets is now believed to belong to a later part of the manuscript version of Chapter One. [E.K.]

The further the separate spheres, which interact on one another, extend in the course of this development, the more the original isolation of the separate nationalities is destroyed by the developed mode of production and intercourse and the division of labour naturally brought forth by these, the more history becomes world-history. Thus, for instance, if in England a machine is invented, which in India or China deprives countless workers of bread, and overturns the whole form of existence of these empires, this invention becomes a world-historical fact. Or again, take the case of sugar and coffee which have proved their world-historical importance in the nineteenth century by the fact that the lack of these products, occasioned by the Napoleonic Continental system, caused the Germans to rise against Napoleon, and thus became the real basis of the glorious Wars of Liberation of 1813. From this it follows that this transformation of history into world-history is not indeed a mere abstract act on the part of the "self-consciousness," the world-spirit, or of any other metaphysical spectre, but a quite material, empirically verifiable act, an act the proof of which every individual furnishes as he comes and goes, eats, drinks and clothes himself. . . .

MEGA I, 5, 34–35; MEW 3, 45–46, as translated in Marx and Engels, *The German Ideology,* ed. cit., pp. 38–39.

This conception of history depends on our ability to expound the real process of production, starting out from the material production of life itself, and to comprehend the form of intercourse connected with this and created by this mode of production (i.e., civil society in its various stages), as the basis of all history; and to show it in its action as state, to explain all the different theoretical products and forms of consciousness, religion, philosophy, ethics, etc., etc., and trace their origins and growth from that basis; by which means, of course, the whole thing can be depicted in its totality (and therefore, too, the reciprocal action of these various sides on one another). It has not, like the idealistic view of history, in every period to look for a category, but remains constantly on the real *ground* of history; it does not explain practice from the idea but explains the formation of ideas from material practice and accordingly it comes to the conclusion that all forms and products of consciousness cannot be dissolved by mental criticism, by resolution into "self-consciousness" or transformation into "apparitions," "spectres," "fancies," etc., but only by the practical overthrow of the actual social relations which give rise to this idealistic humbug; that not criticism but revolution is the driving force of history, also of religion, of philosophy and all other types of theory. It shows that history does not end by being resolved into "self-consciousness" as "spirit of the spirit," but that in it at each stage there is found a material result: a sum of productive forces, a historically created relation of individuals to nature and to one another, which is handed down to each generation from its predecessor; a mass of productive forces, capital funds and conditions, which, on the one hand, is indeed modified by the new generation, but also on the other prescribes for it its conditions of life and gives it a definite development, a special character. It shows that circumstances make men just as much as men make circumstances.

This sum of productive forces, capital funds and social forms of intercourse, which every individual and generation finds in existence as something given, is the real basis of what the philosophers have conceived as "substance" and "essence of man," and what they have deified and attacked: a real basis which is not in the least disturbed, in its effect and influence on the development of men, by the fact that these philosophers revolt against it as "self-consciousness" and the "Unique." These conditions of life, which different generations find in existence, decide also whether or not the periodically recurring revolutionary convulsion will be strong enough to overthrow the basis of the entire existing system. And if these material elements of a complete revolution are not present (namely, on the one hand the existing productive forces, on the other the formation of a revolutionary mass, which revolts not only against separate conditions of society up till then, but against the very "production of life" till then, the "total activity" on which it was based), then, as far as practical development is concerned, it is absolutely immaterial whether the *idea* of this revolution has been expressed a hundred times already, as the history of communism proves.

MEGA I, 5, 27–28; MEW 3, 37–39, as translated in Karl Marx and Frederick Engels, *Selected Works*, 3 vols., Moscow, 1969, I, pp. 41–43.

[LAW AND THE MATERIALIST CONCEPTION OF HISTORY]

The first form of property, in the ancient world as in the Middle Ages, is tribal property, determined with the Romans chiefly by war, with the Germans by the rearing of cattle. In the case of the ancient peoples, since several tribes live together in one town, the tribal property appears as state property, and the right of the individual to it as mere *"possession"* which, however, like tribal property as a whole, is confined to landed property only. Real private property began with the ancients, as with modern nations, with personal movable property—(slavery and community) (*dominium ex jure Quiritium*). In the case of the nations which grew out of the Middle Ages, tribal property evolved through various stages—feudal landed property, corporative movable property, manufacture-capital—to modern capital, determined by big industry and universal competition, i.e. pure private property, which has cast off all semblance of a communal institution and has shut out the state from any influence on the development of property. To this modern private property corresponds the modern state, which, purchased gradually by the owners of property by means of taxation, has fallen entirely into their hands through the national debt, and its existence has become wholly dependent on the commercial credit which the owners of property, the bourgeois, extend to it in the rise and fall of state funds on the stock exchange. By the mere fact that it is a *class* and no longer an *estate*, the bourgeoisie is forced to organize itself no longer locally, but nationally, and to give a general form to its mean average interest. Through the emancipation of private property from the community, the state has become a separate entity, beside and outside civil society; but it is nothing more than the form of organization which the bourgeois necessarily adopt both for internal and external purposes, for the mutual guarantee of their property and interests. The independence of the state is only found nowadays in those countries where the estates have not yet completely developed into classes, where the estates, done away with in more advanced countries, still have a part to play, and where there exists a mixture; countries, that is to say in which no one section of the population can achieve dominance over the others. This is the case particularly in Germany. The most perfect example of the modern state is North America. The modern French, English and American writers all express the opinion that the state exists only for the sake of private property, so that this fact has penetrated into the consciousness of the normal man.

Since the State is the form in which the individuals of a ruling class assert their common interests, and in which the whole civil society of an epoch is epitomized, it follows that in the formation of all communal institutions the State acts as intermediary, that these institutions receive a political form. Hence the illusion that law is based on the will, and indeed on the will divorced from its real basis—

on free will. Similarly, the theory of law is in its turn reduced to the actual laws.

Civil law develops simultaneously with private property out of the disintegration of the natural community. With the Romans the development of private property and civil law had no further industrial and commercial consequences, because their whole mode of production did not alter. With modern peoples, where the feudal community was disintegrated by industry and trade, there began with the rise of private property and civil law a new phase, which was capable of further development. The very first town which carried on an extensive trade in the Middle Ages, Amalfi, also developed maritime law. As soon as industry and trade developed private property further, first in Italy and later in other countries, Roman civil law was adopted again in a perfected form and raised to authority. When later the bourgeoisie had acquired so much power that the princes took up their interests in order to overthrow the feudal nobility by means of the bourgeoisie, there began in all countries—in France in the sixteenth century—the real development of law, which in all countries except England proceeded on the basis of the Roman Codex. In England too, Roman legal principles had to be introduced to further the development of civil law (especially in the case of personal movable property). It must not be forgotten that law has just as little an independent history as religion.

In civil law the existing property relationships are declared to be the result of the general will. The *jus utendi et abutendi*[8] itself asserts on the one hand the fact that private property has become entirely independent of the community, and on the other the illusion that private property itself is based on the private will, the arbitrary disposal of the thing. In practice, the *abuti* has very defi-

---

8. 'The right of using and consuming', a restrictive right that the owner, in Roman law, can confer without passing title. [E.K.]

nite economic limitations for the owner of private property, if he does not wish to see his property and hence his *jus abutendi* pass into other hands, since actually the thing, considered merely with reference to his will, is not a thing at all, but only becomes true property in intercourse, and independently of the right to the thing (a *relationship*, which the philosophers call an idea). This juridical illusion, which reduces law to the mere will, necessarily leads, in the further development of property relationships, to the position that a man may have a title to a thing without really having the thing. If, for instance, the income from a piece of land is lost owing to competition, then the proprietor has certainly his legal title to it along with the *jus utendi et abutendi.* But he can do nothing with it; he owns nothing as a landed proprietor if he has not enough capital besides to cultivate his ground. This illusion of the jurists also explains the fact that for them, as for every codex, it is altogether fortuitous that individuals enter into relationships among themselves (e.g. contracts); it explains why they consider that these relationships can be entered into or not at will, and that their content rests purely on the individual free will of the contracting parties. Whenever, through the development of industry and commerce, new forms of intercourse have been evolved (e.g. assurance companies etc.), the law has always been compelled to admit them among the modes of acquiring property. . . .

MEGA I, 5, 51–54; MEW 3, 61–65, as translated in Marx and Engels, *The German Ideology*, ed. cit., pp. 58–62.

[THE ROLE OF VIOLENCE IN HISTORY]

This whole interpretation of history appears to be contradicted by the fact of conquest. Up till now violence, war, pillage, rape and slaughter, etc. have been accepted as the driving force of history. Here we must limit ourselves to the chief points and take therefore only a striking example—the destruction of an old civilization by a barbarous people and the resulting formation of an entirely new organization of society. (Rome and the barbarians; Feudalism and Gaul; the Byzantine Empire and the Turks.) With the conquering barbarian people war itself is still, as hinted above, a regular form of intercourse, which is the more eagerly exploited as the population increases, involving the necessity of new means of production to supersede the traditional and, for it, the only possible, crude mode of production. In Italy it was, however, otherwise. The concentration of landed property (caused not only by buying-up and indebtedness but also by inheritance, since loose living being rife and marriage rare, the old families died out and their possessions fell into the hands of a few) and its conversion into grazing-land (caused not only by economic forces still operative to-day but by the importation of plundered and tribute-corn and the resultant lack of demand for Italian corn) brought about the almost total disappearance of the free population. The very slaves died out again and again, and had constantly to be replaced by new ones. Slavery remained the basis of the whole productive system. The plebeians, mid-way between freemen and slaves, never succeeded in becoming more than a proletarian rabble. Rome indeed never became more than a city, its connection with the provinces was almost exclusively political and could therefore easily be broken again by political events.

MEGA I, 5, 12–13; MEW 3, 23, as translated in Marx and Engels, *The German Ideology*, ed. cit., pp. 10–11.

Nothing is more common than the notion that in history up till now it has only been a question of *"taking."* The barbarians "take" the Roman Empire, and this fact of "taking" is made to explain the transition from the old world to the feudal system. In this taking by barbarians, however, the question is, whether the nation which is conquered has evolved industrial productive forces, as is the case with modern peoples, or whether their productive forces are based for the most part merely on their association and on the community. Taking is further determined by the object taken. A banker's fortune, consisting of paper, cannot be taken at all, without the taker's submitting to the conditions of production and intercourse of the country taken. Similarly the total industrial capital of a modern industrial country. And finally, everywhere there is very soon an end to taking, and when there is nothing more to take, you have to set about producing. From this necessity of producing, which very soon asserts itself, it follows that the form of community adopted by the settling conquerors must correspond to the stage of development of the productive forces they find in existence; or, if this is not the case from the start, it must change according to the productive forces. By this, too, is explained the fact, which people profess to have noticed everywhere in the period following the migration of the peoples, namely that the servant was master, and that the conquerors very soon took over language, culture and manners from the conquered. The feudal system was by no means brought complete from Germany, but had its origin, as far as the conquerors were concerned, in the martial organization of the army during the actual conquest, and this only evolved after the conquest into the feudal system proper through the action of the productive forces found in the conquered countries. To what an extent this form was determined by the productive forces is shown by the abortive attempts to realize other forms derived from reminiscences of ancient Rome (Charlemagne, etc.). . . .

MEGA I, 5, 54; MEW 3, 64–65; as translated in Marx and Engels, *The German Ideology*, ed. cit., pp. 62–63.

[COMMUNISM AS THE END OF HISTORY]

Communism differs from all previous movements in that it overturns the basis of all earlier relations of production and intercourse, and for the first time consciously treats all natural premises as the creatures of men, strips them of their natural character and subjugates them to the power of individuals united. Its organization is, therefore, essentially economic, the material production of the conditions of this unity; it turns existing conditions into conditions of unity. The reality, which communism is creating, is precisely the real basis for rendering it impossible that anything should exist independently of individuals, in so far as things are only a product of the preceding intercourse of individuals themselves. Thus the communists in practice treat the conditions created by production and intercourse as inorganic conditions, without, however, imagining that it was the plan or the destiny of previous generations to give them material, and without believing that these conditions were inorganic for the individuals creating them.

The difference between the individual as a person and what is accidental to him, is not a conceptual difference but a historical fact. This distinction has a different significance at different times—e.g. the estate as something accidental to the individual in the eighteenth century, the family more or less too. It is not a distinction that we have to make for each age, but one which each age makes itself from among the different elements which it finds in existence, and indeed not according to any theory, but compelled by material collisions in life. Of the elements handed down to a later age from an earlier, what appears accidental to the later age as opposed to the earlier, is a form of intercourse which corresponded to a less developed stage of the productive forces. The relation of the productive forces to the form of intercourse is the relation of the form of intercourse to the occupation or activity of the individuals. . . . The conditions under which individuals have intercourse with each other, so long as the above-mentioned contradiction is absent, are conditions appertaining to their individuality, in no way external to them; conditions under which these definite individuals, living under definite relationships, can alone produce their material life and what is connected with it; are thus the conditions of their self-activity and are produced by this self-activity. The definite condition under which they produce, thus corresponds, as long as the contradiction has not yet appeared, to the reality of their conditioned nature, their one-sided existence, the one-sidedness of which only becomes evident when the contradiction enters on the scene and thus only exists for the later individuals. Then this condition appears as an accidental fetter, and the consciousness that it is a fetter is imputed to the earlier age as well.

These various conditions, which appear first as conditions of self-activity, later as fetters upon it, form in the whole evolution of history a coherent series of forms of intercourse, the coherence of which consists in this: that in the place of an earlier form of intercourse, which has become a fetter, a new one is put, corresponding to the more developed productive forces and, hence, to the advanced mode of the self-activity of individuals—a form which in its turn becomes a fetter and is then replaced by another. Since these conditions correspond at every stage to the simultaneous development of the productive forces, their history is at the same time the history of the evolving productive forces taken over by each new generation, and is therefore the history of the development of the forces of the individuals themselves.

Since this evolution takes place naturally, i.e. is not subordinated to a general plan of freely combined individuals, it proceeds from various localities, tribes, nations, branches of labour, etc., each of which to start with develops independently of the others and only gradually enters into relation with the others. Furthermore, it takes place only very slowly; the various stages and interests are never completely overcome, but only subordinated to the interest of the victor, and trail along beside the latter for centuries afterwards. It follows from this that within a nation itself the individuals, even apart from their pecuniary circumstances, have quite different developments, and that an earlier interest, the peculiar form of intercourse of which has already been ousted by that belonging to a later interest, remains for a long time afterwards in possession of a traditional power in the illusory community (state, law), which has won an existence independent of the individuals; a power which in the last resort can only be broken by a revolution. This explains why, with reference to individual points which allow of a more general summing-up, consciousness can sometimes appear further advanced than the contemporary empirical relationships, so that in the struggles of a later epoch one can refer to earlier theoreticians as authorities.

On the other hand, in countries which, like North America, begin in an already advanced historical epoch, their development proceeds very rapidly. Such countries have no other natural premises than the individuals, who settled there and were led to do so because the forms of intercourse of the old countries did not correspond to their wants. Thus they begin with the most advanced individuals of the old countries, and therefore with the correspondingly most advanced form of intercourse, before this form of intercourse has been able to establish itself in the old countries.[9] This is the case with all colonies, in so far

---

9. Personal energy of the individuals of various nations—Germans and Americans—energy merely through cross-breeding—hence the cretinism of the Germans—in France and England, etc., foreign peoples transplanted to an already developed soil, in America to an entirely new soil—in Germany the natural population quietly stayed where it was. [Note by Marx and Engels.]

as they are not mere military or trading stations. Carthage, the Greek colonies, and Iceland in the eleventh and twelfth centuries, provide examples of this. A similar relationship issues from conquest, when a form of intercourse which has evolved on another soil is brought over complete to the conquered country: whereas in its home it was still encumbered with interests and relationships left over from earlier periods, here it can and must be established completely and without hindrance, if only to assure the conquerors' lasting power. (England and Naples after the Norman Conquest, when they received the most perfect form of feudal organization.)

Thus all collisions in history have their origin, according to our view, in the contradiction between the productive forces and the form of intercourse. But also, to lead to collisions in a country, this contradiction need not necessarily come to a head in this particular country. The competition with industrially more advanced countries, brought about by the expansion of international intercourse, is sufficient to produce a similar contradiction in countries with a backward industry (e.g. the latent proletariat in Germany brought into view by the competition of English industry).

This contradiction between the productive forces and form of intercourse, which, as we saw, has occurred several times in past history, without however endangering its basis, necessarily on each occasion burst out in a revolution, taking on at the same time various subsidiary forms, such as all-embracing collisions, collisions of various classes, contradiction of consciousness, battle of ideas, etc., political conflict, etc. . . .

The transformation, through the division of labour, of personal powers (relationships) into material powers, cannot be dispelled by dismissing the general idea of it from one's mind, but only by the action of individuals in again subjecting these material powers to themselves and abolishing the division of labour. This is not possible without the community. Only in community with others has each individual the means of cultivating his gifts in all directions; only in the community, therefore, is personal freedom possible. In the previous substitutes for the community, in the state, etc., personal freedom has existed only for the individuals who developed within the relationships of the ruling class, and only in so far as they were individuals of this class. The illusory community, in which individuals have up till now combined, always took on an independent existence in relation to them, and was at the same time, since it was the combination of one class over against another, not only a completely illusory community, but a new fetter as well. In the real community the individuals obtain their freedom in and through their association.

It follows from all we have been saying up till now that the communal relationship into which the individuals of a class entered, and which was determined by their common interests over against a third party, was always a community to which these individuals belonged only as average individuals, only in so far as they lived within the conditions of existence of their class—a relationship in which they participated not as individuals but as members of a class. With the community of revolutionary proletarians on the other hand, who take their conditions of existence and those of all members of society under their control, it is just the reverse; it is as individuals that the individuals participate in it. It is just this combination of individuals (assuming the advanced stage of modern productive forces, of course) which puts the conditions of the free development and movement of individuals under their control—conditions which were previously abandoned to chance and had won an independent existence over against the separate individuals just because of their separation as individuals, and because their combination had been determined by the division of labour, and through their separation had become a bond alien to them.

Combination up till now (by no means an arbitrary one, such as is expounded for example in the *Contrat Social*, but a necessary one) was permitted only upon these conditions, within which the individuals were at the mercy of chance (compare, e.g. the formation of the North American state and the South American republics). This right to the undisturbed enjoyment, upon certain conditions, of fortuity and chance has up till now been called personal freedom: but these conditions are, of course, only the productive forces and forms of intercourse at any particular time. . . .

This subsuming of individuals under definite classes cannot be abolished until a class has taken shape, which has no longer any particular class interest to assert against the ruling class.

Individuals have always built on themselves, but naturally on themselves within their given historical conditions and relationships, not on the "pure" individual in the sense of the ideologists. But in the course of historical evolution, and precisely through the inevitable fact that within the division of labour social relationships take on an independent existence, there appears a division within the life of each individual, in so far as it is personal and in so far as it is determined by some branch of labour and the conditions pertaining to it. (We do not mean it to be understood from this that, for example, the rentier, the capitalist, etc., cease to be persons; but their personality is conditioned and determined by quite definite class relationships, and the division appears only in their opposition to another class and, for themselves, only when they go bankrupt.) . . .

For the proletarians, on the other hand, the condition of their existence, labour, and with it all the conditions of existence governing modern society, have become something accidental, something over which they, as separate individuals, have no control, and over which no *social* organization can give them control. The contradiction be-

tween the individuality of each separate proletarian and
labour, the condition of life forced upon him, becomes
evident to him himself, for he is sacrificed from youth upwards and, within his own class, has no chance of arriving
at the conditions which would place him in the other class.
Thus, while the refugee serfs only wished to be free to develop and assert those conditions of existence which were
already there, and hence, in the end, only arrived at free
labour, the proletarians, if they are to assert themselves as
individuals, will have to abolish the very condition of their
existence hitherto (which has, moreover, been that of all
society up to the present), namely, labour. Thus they find
themselves directly opposed to the form in which, hitherto, individuals have given themselves collective expression, that is, the state. In order, therefore, to assert
themselves as individuals, they must overthrow the state.

MEGA I, 5, 60–67; MEW 3, 70–77, as translated in Marx
and Engels, *The German Ideology*, ed. cit., pp. 70–78.

3. Revolution and Counter-Revolution: Political Writings, 1848–1852

~~~~~~~~~~~~~~~~~~~~~~~~~~~~~~~~

EDITOR'S NOTE

Between April 1844, when Marx, in Paris, made contact with the Communist revolutionary leaders of the League of the Just and with some clandestine French workers' associations, and the end of January 1848, when he sent the manuscript of the *Communist Manifesto* to the London Communist League, Marx had moved from being a mere philosopher of the human condition, or even a scientist of society, to becoming an active revolutionary. In Brussels, in February to March 1846, he and Engels had founded a Communist Correspondence Committee that would engage in international propaganda and lay the foundation for an international Communist organization to continue the work of the League of the Just. By June 1847, the first Congress of Communists met in London; Marx, unable to raise the fare from Brussels, was represented by Engels and Wilhelm Wolff. The Congress resolved to reorganize the League of the Just as the Communist League, to expel the allegedly anarchist and unscientific followers of Weitling, and to draft a Communist credo for the next Congress

The Second Congress, held in London in November 1847, commissioned Marx and Engels to draft that statement of principles and the *Communist Manifesto*, published in February 1848, just before the revolution broke out, was the result. Engels had prepared a draft in catechism form, under the title 'Principles of Communism', but had himself suggested that Marx redraft the whole, abandoning the question-and-answer method of presentation. Though Marx drew on a number of passages in Engels, the final version of the *Communist Manifesto* was written by Marx. It differed significantly from Engels's preparatory work in its much sharper emphasis on class struggle as opposed to Engels's elevation of an Enlightenment-based conception of progress and its greater caution about elevating abundance as the material foundation of the classless society.

The revolution of 1848, as Sir Lewis Namier has reminded us, 'was universally expected, and it was supernational as none before or after; it ran through, and enveloped, the core of Europe, "the world" of the continental Europeans, which extended from the Channel ports to the frontiers of Russia, from Paris to Vienna'. Insurrection at Palermo, barricades in Paris, Vienna, and Berlin; disturbances in Cologne; street riots, National Guards, 'Academic Legions', Committees of Public Safety; Metternich's house in flames and the Prince himself forced to flee; revolution in Hungary, Bohemia, Milan, Venice, the Kingdom of the two Sicilies, the minor German states, Denmark, and Holland; ministers dismissed, constitutions granted, national assemblies, democratic and supra-national congresses convoked; kings and emperor, Pope and princes trembling and uncertain. Progress, it seemed in the first few months of 1848, was on the march: constitutional democracy and the principle of national self-determination as steps toward the conversion of all men from subjects into citizens and from serfs or oppressed and despised workers and nationalities into free men and free nations could not be resisted.

The revolution that was so universally expected and that appeared to rest so firmly on every principle that enlightened, progressive Europeans held dear, proved, within one year, to be a momentous failure. The overthrow of Louis Philippe's bourgeois monarchy in France in February 1848 was followed by a crushing defeat, first for both democratic and revolutionary socialism and then for republicanism. The working-class revolt was suppressed; the victory of the 'party of order' in June 1848 ended, by 1852, in the elevation of Louis Bonaparte, through universal or at least greatly extended suffrage, to plebiscitory dictator and Emperor of France. The German-speaking lands, despite or because of their welter of diets, assemblies, parliaments, and congresses, came out of their upheavals neither unified nor democratized, neither as Little Germany nor as Greater Germany. Poland remained divided under foreign rule, the remaining western and southern Slavs unfree and Italy fragmented; the Roman Republic collapsed and the Pope returned to Rome less liberal than he had left it; the Austrian Empire, like the Russian, lived on in fact if not quite in name into the twentieth century. Revolution had called forth successful counter-revolution: by 1852, Switzerland was the only democratic republic in Europe and Sardinia—whose King Charles Albert had skilfully averted internal revolution by granting a liberal Constitution, making nationalist war on Austria, and abdicating, in defeat, in favour of his son Victor Emmanuel—the only constitutional and liberal state in Italy. The Dutch Netherlands, Denmark, and Prussia had made some gains toward constitutional government compared with their situation before 1848, but the abolition of serfdom in Hungary, Bohemia, and Austria itself was the only immediate major and irrevocable gain of a revolution that hoped to emancipate not only the backward peasant areas but whole nations, cultures, and classes. With very little cost—a few minor constitutional reforms here and there—the revolution had made reaction secure for another generation.

The twenty years after 1848 were to be, depending on one's point of view, periods of unparalleled peaceful progress or of reactionary stability; certainly there were not the products of revolutionary slogans or revolutionary achievement, a consummation of constitutionalism or a liberation of nations. The uprisings of 1848–1849 had driven revolutionaries almost everywhere into exile and political outer darkness. They had retarded, in many ways, the development of democracy in Europe by revealing the weakness of its democrats and the competing allegiances of its middle classes.[1]

The *Communist Manifesto* today may strike us as a historic landmark; in 1848 it attracted no significant attention, even though it appeared, as it were, at a good time. It neither produced the revolutions of 1848 nor significantly influenced their progress. Marx and Engels, it is true, on their return to Germany in April 1848, founded a reasonably important radical newspaper, the *Neue Rheinische Zeitung*—important enough to be suppressed and to lead to Marx's trial at the end of 1848 and the beginning of 1849 on a charge of printing material insulting to officials. But mass radicalism in Cologne was led and represented by the physician Gottschalk and his Cologne Workers Association, with which Marx had quarrelled by May 1848. As usual, it is not Marx's actions, but his words, that live. It is not his ability to build up followers or movements, but his ability to analyse events and produce theoretically coherent policies that makes his work significant. Between

---

1. For a fuller discussion of the revolutions of 1848 and the role that Marx and Engels played in them, see Eugene Kamenka and F. B. Smith (eds.), *Intellectuals and Revolution: Socialism and the Experience of 1848*, in the series 'Ideas and Ideologies', Edward Arnold, London, 1979. [E.K.]

1848 and the Paris Commune of 1871, the *Communist Manifesto* was virtually forgotten. Its revival was based on a mistake—the belief that Marx was the *éminence grise* behind the events in Paris in 1871 and that the *Communist Manifesto* represented the creed of the communards. Today, we read that *Manifesto* for three things: its clear, if extremely simplified, summary of the Marxian view, on which the world Communist movement long based itself; its once again clear, if crude, differentiation of Marxian socialism from other socialisms and communisms; and its indication of Marx's conception of proletarian power immediately after the revolution, his proclamation of a—surprisingly moderate—Communist programme which most of the world's Communist parties have taken very seriously indeed. That programme was condensed into a leaflet embodying the demands of the Communist Party of Germany, published in March 1848, after the revolution had broken out; it is also reprinted here, as are parts of the interesting Address of the Central Committee to the Communist League, written by Marx and Engels in March 1850. In that address, one of the classical texts for the theory of the permanent revolution, Marx and Engels discussed the role of the proletariat in a revolution that begins as a bourgeois democratic revolution but can be driven further.

The revolutionary hopes that Marx and Engels had in the spring of 1848 had been dashed firmly by the combination of reaction and economic upswing and stability that followed the defeat of the revolution. The years 1848 and 1849 left Marx with a bitter hatred of the Russian Tsarist autocracy, which had successfully become the gendarme of Europe—a hatred that led him to childish excesses of racism and paranoia in his Russophobic *Secret Diplomatic History of the Eighteenth Century,* a work that Communists have understandably excluded from the canon. Of much greater importance—and presented here—are his attempts, in retrospect, to understand the proletarian defeat of 1848 in *The Class Struggles in France* and the rise of a new type of politician, Louis Bonaparte, an adventurer without class base who had turned universal suffrage in the form of the plebiscite into a weapon against socialism and who used the state for his personal ends. For a critical understanding of Marx's view of classes and the state *The Eighteenth Brumaire of Louis Bonaparte* is of crucial importance.

MANIFESTO OF THE COMMUNIST PARTY

A spectre is haunting Europe—the spectre of communism. All the powers of old Europe have entered into a holy alliance to exorcise this spectre: Pope and Tsar, Metternich and Guizot, French Radicals and German police-spies.

Where is the party in opposition that has not been decried as communistic by its opponents in power? Where is the opposition that has not hurled back the branding reproach of communism, against the more advanced opposition parties, as well as against its reactionary adversaries?

Two things result from this fact:

I. Communism is already acknowledged by all European powers to be itself a power.

II. It is high time that Communists should openly, in the face of the whole world, publish their views, their aims, their tendencies, and meet this nursery tale of the spectre of communism with a manifesto of the party itself.

To this end, Communists of various nationalities have assembled in London and sketched the following manifesto, to be published in the English, French, German, Italian, Flemish and Danish languages.

I. BOURGEOIS AND PROLETARIANS

The history of all hitherto existing society is the history of class struggles.

Freeman and slave, patrician and plebeian, lord and serf, guild-master and journeyman, in a word, oppressor and oppressed, stood in constant opposition to one another, carried on an uninterrupted, now hidden, now open fight, a fight that each time ended, either in a revolutionary reconstitution of society at large, or in the common ruin of the contending classes.

In the earlier epochs of history, we find almost everywhere a complicated arrangement of society into various orders, a manifold gradation of social rank. In ancient Rome we have patricians, knights, plebeians, slaves; in the Middle Ages, feudal lords, vassals, guild-masters, journeymen, apprentices, serfs; in almost all of these classes, again, subordinate gradations.

The modern bourgeois society that has sprouted from the ruins of feudal society has not done away with class antagonisms. It has but established new classes, new conditions of oppression, new forms of struggle in place of the old ones.

Our epoch, the epoch of the bourgeoisie, possesses, however, this distinctive feature: It has simplified the class antagonisms. Society as a whole is more and more splitting up into two great hostile camps, into two great classes directly facing each other—bourgeoisie and proletariat.

From the serfs of the Middle Ages sprang the chartered burghers of the earliest towns. From these burgesses the first elements of the bourgeoisie were developed.

The discovery of America, the rounding of the Cape, opened up fresh ground for the rising bourgeoisie. The East-Indian and Chinese markets, the colonisation of America, trade with the colonies, the increase in the means of exchange and in commodities generally, gave to commerce, to navigation, to industry, an impulse never before known, and thereby, to the revolutionary element in the tottering feudal society, a rapid development.

The feudal system of industry, in which industrial production was monopolised by closed guilds, now no longer sufficed for the growing wants of the new markets. The manufacturing system took its place. The guild-masters were pushed aside by the manufacturing middle class; division of labour between the different corporate guilds vanished in the face of division of labour in each single workshop.

Meantime the markets kept ever growing, the demand ever rising. Even manufacture no longer sufficed. Thereupon, steam and machinery revolutionised industrial production. The place of manufacture was taken by the giant, modern industry, the place of the industrial middle class by industrial millionaires, the leaders of whole industrial armies, the modern bourgeois.

Modern industry has established the world market, for which the discovery of America paved the way. This market has given an immense development to commerce, to navigation, to communication by land. This development has, in its turn, reacted on the extension of industry; and in proportion as industry, commerce, navigation, railways extended, in the same proportion the bourgeoisie developed, increased its capital, and pushed into the background every class handed down from the Middle Ages.

We see, therefore, how the modern bourgeoisie is itself the product of a long course of development, of a series of revolutions in the modes of production and of exchange.

Each step in the development of the bourgeoisie was accompanied by a corresponding political advance of that class. An oppressed class under the sway of the feudal nobility, an armed and self-governing association in the medieval commune; here independent urban republic (as in Italy and Germany), there taxable "third estate" of the monarchy (as in France); afterwards, in the period of manufacture proper, serving either the semi-feudal or the absolute monarchy as a counterpoise against the nobility, and, in fact, cornerstone of the great monarchies in general—the bourgeoisie has at last, since the establishment of modern industry and of the world market, conquered for itself, in the modern representative state, exclusive political sway. The executive of the modern state is but a committee for managing the common affairs of the whole bourgeoisie.

The bourgeoisie, historically, has played a most revolutionary part.

The bourgeoisie, wherever it has got the upper hand, has put an end to all feudal, patriarchal, idyllic relations. It has pitilessly torn asunder the motley feudal ties that bound man to his "natural superiors," and has left no other nexus between man and man than naked self-interest, than callous "cash payment." It has drowned the most heavenly ecstasies of religious fervour, of chivalrous enthusiasm, of philistine sentimentalism, in the icy water of egotistical calculation. It has resolved personal worth into exchange value, and in place of the numberless indefeasible chartered freedoms, has set up that single, unconscionable freedom—Free Trade. In one word, for exploitation, veiled by religious and political illusions, it has substituted naked, shameless, direct, brutal exploitation.

The bourgeoisie has stripped of its halo every occupation hitherto honoured and looked up to with reverent awe. It has converted the physician, the lawyer, the priest, the poet, the man of science, into its paid wage labourers.

The bourgeoisie has torn away from the family its sentimental veil, and has reduced the family relation to a mere money relation.

The bourgeoisie has disclosed how it came to pass that the brutal display of vigour in the Middle Ages, which reactionaries so much admire, found its fitting complement in the most slothful indolence. It has been the first to show what man's activity can bring about. It has accomplished wonders far surpassing Egyptian pyramids, Roman aqueducts, and Gothic cathedrals; it has conducted expeditions that put in the shade all former exoduses of nations and crusades.

The bourgeoisie cannot exist without constantly revolutionising the instruments of production, and thereby the relations of production, and with them the whole relations of society. Conservation of the old modes of production in unaltered form was, on the contrary, the first condition of existence for all earlier industrial classes. Constant revolutionising of production, uninterrupted disturbance of all social conditions, everlasting uncertainty and agitation distinguish the bourgeois epoch from all earlier ones. All fixed, fast frozen relations, with their train of ancient and venerable prejudices and opinions, are swept away, all new-formed ones become antiquated before they can ossify. All that is solid melts into air, all that is holy is profaned, and man is at last compelled to face with sober senses his real conditions of life and his relations with his kind.

The need of a constantly expanding market for its products chases the bourgeoisie over the whole surface of the globe. It must nestle everywhere, settle everywhere, establish connections everywhere.

The bourgeoisie has through its exploitation of the world market given a cosmopolitan character to production and consumption in every country. To the great chagrin of reactionaries, it had drawn from under the feet of industry the national ground on which it stood. All old-established national industries have been destroyed or are daily being destroyed. They are dislodged by new industries, whose introduction becomes a life and death question for all civilised nations, by industries that no longer work up indigenous raw material, but raw material drawn from the remotest zones; industries whose products are consumed, not only at home, but in every quarter of the globe. In place of the old wants, satisfied by the production of the country, we find new wants, requiring for their satisfaction the products of distant lands and climes. In place of the old local and national seclusion and self-sufficiency, we have intercourse in every direction, universal inter-dependence of nations. And as in material, so also in intellectual production. The intellectual creations of individual nations become common property. National one-sidedness and narrow-mindedness become more and more impossible, and from the numerous national and local literatures there arises a world literature.

The bourgeoisie, by the rapid improvement of all instruments of production, by the immensely facilitated means of communication, draws all, even the most barbarian, nations into civilisation. The cheap prices of its commodities are the heavy artillery with which it batters down all Chinese walls, with which it forces the barbarians' intensely obstinate hatred of foreigners to capitulate. It compels all nations, on pain of extinction, to adopt the bourgeois mode of production; it compels them to introduce what it calls civilisation into their midst, i.e., to become bourgeois themselves. In one word, it creates a world after its own image.

The bourgeoisie has subjected the country to the rule of the towns. It has created enormous cities, has greatly increased the urban population as compared with the rural, and has thus rescued a considerable part of the population from the idiocy of rural life. Just as it has made the country dependent on the towns, so it has made barbarian and semi-barbarian countries dependent on the civilised ones nations of peasants on nations of bourgeois, the East on the West.

The bourgeoisie keeps more and more doing away with the scattered state of the population, of the means of production, and of property. It has agglomerated population, centralised means of production, and has concentrated property in a few hands. The necessary consequence of this was political centralisation. Indepen-

dent, or but loosely connected provinces, with separate interests, laws, governments, and systems of taxation, became lumped together into one nation, with one
government, one code of laws, one national class interest,
one frontier and one customs tariff.

The bourgeoisie, during its rule of scarce one hundred
years, has created more massive and more colossal productive forces than have all preceding generations together. Subjection of nature's forces to man, machinery,
application of chemistry to industry and agriculture,
steam navigation, railways, electric telegraphs, clearing
of whole continents for cultivation, canalisation of rivers,
whole populations conjured out of the ground—what earlier century had even a presentiment that such productive
forces slumbered in the lap of social labour?

We see then: the means of production and of exchange,
on whose foundation the bourgeoisie built itself up, were
generated in feudal society. At a certain stage in the development of these means of production and of exchange, the
conditions under which feudal society produced and exchanged, the feudal organisation of agriculture and manufacturing industry, in one word, the feudal relations of
property became no longer compatible with the already
developed productive forces; they became so many fetters.
They had to be burst asunder; they were burst asunder.

Into their place stepped free competition, accompanied
by a social and political constitution adapted to it, and by
the economic and political sway of the bourgeois class.

A similar movement is going on before our own eyes.
Modern bourgeois society with its relations of production,
of exchange and of property, a society that has conjured
up such gigantic means of production and of exchange, is
like the sorcerer who is no longer able to control the
powers of the nether world whom he has called up by his
spells. For many a decade past the history of industry and
commerce is but the history of the revolt of modern pro-

ductive forces against modern conditions of production, against the property relations that are the conditions for the existence of the bourgeoisie and of its rule. It is enough to mention the commercial crises that by their periodical return put the existence of the entire bourgeois society on its trial, each time more threateningly. In these crises a great part not only of the existing products, but also of the previously created productive forces, are periodically destroyed. In these crises there breaks out an epidemic that, in all earlier epochs, would have seemed an absurdity—the epidemic of over-production. Society suddenly finds itself put back into a state of momentary barbarism; it appears as if a famine, a universal war of devastation had cut off the supply of every means of subsistence; industry and commerce seem to be destroyed. And why? Because there is too much civilisation, too much means of subsistence, too much industry, too much commerce. The productive forces at the disposal of society no longer tend to further the development of the conditions of bourgeois property; on the contrary, they have become too powerful for these conditions, by which they are fettered, and so soon as they overcome these fetters, they bring disorder into the whole of bourgeois society, endanger the existence of bourgeois property. The conditions of bourgeois society are too narrow to comprise the wealth created by them. And how does the bourgeoisie get over these crises? On the one hand, by enforced destruction of a mass of productive forces; on the other, by the conquest of new markets, and by the more thorough exploitation of the old ones. That is to say, by paving the way for more extensive and more destructive crises, and by diminishing the means whereby crises are prevented.

The weapons with which the bourgeoisie felled feudalism to the ground are now turned against the bourgeoisie itself.

But not only has the bourgeoisie forged the weapons that bring death to itself; it has also called into existence the men who are to wield those weapons—the modern working class—the proletarians.

In proportion as the bourgeoisie, i.e., capital, is developed, in the same proportion is the proletariat, the modern working class, developed—a class of labourers, who live only so long as they find work, and who find work only so long as their labour increases capital. These labourers, who must sell themselves piecemeal, are a commodity, like every other article of commerce, and are consequently exposed to all the vicissitudes of competition, to all the fluctuations of the market.

Owing to the extensive use of machinery and to division of labour, the work of the proletarians has lost all individual character, and, consequently, all charm for the workman. He becomes an appendage of the machine, and it is only the most simple, most monotonous, and most easily acquired knack, that is required of him. Hence, the cost of production of a workman is restricted, almost entirely, to the means of subsistence that he requires for his maintenance, and for the propagation of his race. But the price of a commodity, and therefore also of labour, is equal to its cost of production. In proportion, therefore, as the repulsiveness of the work increases, the wage decreases. Nay more, in proportion as the use of machinery and division of labour increases, in the same proportion the burden of toil also increases, whether by prolongation of the working hours, by increase of the work exacted in a given time, or by increased speed of the machinery, etc.

Modern industry has converted the little workshop of the patriarchal master into the great factory of the industrial capitalist. Masses of labourers, crowded into the factory, are organised like soldiers. As privates of the industrial army they are placed under the command of a perfect hierarchy of officers and sergeants. Not only are they slaves of the bourgeois class, and of the bourgeois state; they are daily and hourly enslaved by the machine, by the overseer, and, above all, by the individual bourgeois manufacturer himself. The more openly this despotism proclaims gain to be its end and aim, the more petty, the more hateful and the more embittering it is.

The less the skill and exertion of strength implied in manual labour, in other words, the more modern industry becomes developed, the more is the labour of men superseded by that of women. Differences of age and sex have no longer any distinctive social validity for the working class. All are instruments of labour, more or less expensive to use, according to their age and sex.

No sooner is the exploitation of the labourer by the manufacturer, so far at an end, that he receives his wages in cash, than he is set upon by the other portions of the bourgeoisie, the landlord, the shopkeeper, the pawnbroker, etc.

The lower strata of the middle class—the small tradespeople, shopkeepers, and retired tradesmen generally, the handicraftsmen and peasants—all these sink gradually into the proletariat, partly because their diminutive capital does not suffice for the scale on which modern industry is carried on, and is swamped in the competition with the large capitalists, partly because their specialised skill is rendered worthless by new methods of production. Thus the proletariat is recruited from all classes of the population.

The proletariat goes through various stages of development. With its birth begins its struggle with the bourgeoisie. At first the contest is carried on by individual labourers, then by the work people of a factory, then by the operatives of one trade, in one locality, against the individual bourgeois who directly exploits them. They direct their attacks not against the bourgeois conditions of production, but against the instruments of production themselves; they destroy imported wares that compete with their labour, they smash to pieces machinery, they set factories ablaze, they seek to restore by force the vanished status of the workman of the Middle Ages.

At this stage the labourers still form an incoherent mass scattered over the whole country, and broken up by their mutual competition. If anywhere they unite to form more compact bodies, this is not yet the consequence of their own active union, but of the union of the bourgeoisie, which class, in order to attain its own political ends, is compelled to set the whole proletariat in motion, and is moreover yet, for a time, able to do so. At this stage, therefore, the proletarians do not fight their enemies, but the enemies of their enemies, the remnants of absolute monarchy, the landowners, the non-industrial bourgeois, the petty bourgeoisie. Thus the whole historical movement is concentrated in the hands of the bourgeoisie; every victory so obtained is a victory for the bourgeoisie.

But with the development of industry the proletariat not only increases in number; it becomes concentrated in greater masses, its strength grows, and it feels that strength more. The various interests and conditions of life within the ranks of the proletariat are more and more equalised, in proportion as machinery obliterates all distinctions of labour, and nearly everywhere reduces wages to the same low level. The growing competition among the bourgeois, and the resulting commercial crises, make the wages of the workers ever more fluctuating. The unceasing improvement of machinery, ever more rapidly developing, makes their livelihood more and more precarious; the collisions between individual workmen and individual bourgeois take more and more the character of collisions between two classes. Thereupon the workers begin to form combinations (trade unions) against the bourgeois; they club together in order to keep up the rate of wages; they found permanent associations in order to make provision beforehand for these occasional revolts. Here and there the contest breaks out into riots.

Now and then the workers are victorious, but only for a time. The real fruit of their battle lies, not in the immediate result, but in the ever expanding union of the workers.

This union is helped on by the improved means of communication that are created by modern industry, and that place the workers of different localities in contact with one another. It was just this contact that was needed to centralise the numerous local struggles, all of the same character, into one national struggle between classes. But every class struggle is a political struggle. And that union, to attain which the burghers of the Middle Ages, with their miserable highways, required centuries, the modern proletarians, thanks to railways, achieve in a few years.

This organisation of the proletarians into a class, and consequently into a political party, is continually being upset again by the competition between the workers themselves. But it ever rises up again, stronger, firmer, mightier. It compels legislative recognition of particular interests of the workers, by taking advantage of the divisions among the bourgeoisie itself. Thus the Ten-Hours Bill in England was carried.

Altogether, collisions between the classes of the old society further in many ways the course of development of the proletariat. The bourgeoisie finds itself involved in a constant battle. At first with the aristocracy; later on, with those portions of the bourgeoisie itself, whose interests have become antagonistic to the progress of industry; at all times with the bourgeoisie of foreign countries. In all these battles it sees itself compelled to appeal to the proletariat, to ask for its help, and thus, to drag it into the political arena. The bourgeoisie itself, therefore, supplies the proletariat with its own elements of political and general education, in other words, it furnishes the proletariat with weapons for fighting the bourgeoisie.

Further, as we have already seen, entire sections of the ruling classes are, by the advance of industry, precipitated into the proletariat, or are at least threatened in their conditions of existence. These also supply the proletariat with fresh elements of enlightenment and progress.

Finally, in times when the class struggle nears the decisive hour, the process of dissolution going on within the ruling class, in fact within the whole range of old society, assumes such a violent, glaring character, that a small section of the ruling class cuts itself adrift, and joins the revolutionary class, the class that holds the future in its hands. Just as, therefore, at an earlier period, a section of the nobility went over to the bourgeoisie, so now a portion of the bourgeoisie goes over to the proletariat, and in particular, a portion of the bourgeois ideologists, who have raised themselves to the level of comprehending theoretically the historical movement as a whole.

Of all the classes that stand face to face with the bourgeoisie to-day, the proletariat alone is a really revolutionary class. The other classes decay and finally disappear in the face of modern industry; the proletariat is its special and essential product.

The lower middle class, the small manufacturer, the shopkeeper, the artisan, the peasant, all these fight against the bourgeoisie, to save from extinction their existence as fractions of the middle class. They are therefore not revolutionary, but conservative. Nay, more, they are reactionary, for they try to roll back the wheel of history. If by chance they are revolutionary, they are so only in view of their impending transfer into the proletariat; they thus defend not their present, but their future interests; they desert their own standpoint to place themselves at that of the proletariat.

The "dangerous class," the social scum, that passively rotting mass thrown off by the lowest layers of old society, may, here and there, be swept into the movement by a proletarian revolution; its conditions of life, however, prepare it far more for the part of a bribed tool of reactionary intrigue.

In the conditions of the proletariat, those of old society at large are already virtually swamped. The proletarian is without property; his relation to his wife and children has no longer anything in common with the bourgeois family relations; modern industrial labour, modern subjection to capital, the same in England as in France, in America as in Germany, has stripped him of every trace of national character. Law, morality, religion, are to him so many bourgeois prejudices, behind which lurk in ambush just as many bourgeois interests.

All the preceding classes that got the upper hand, sought to fortify their already acquired status by subjecting society at large to their conditions of appropriation. The proletarians cannot become masters of the productive forces of society, except by abolishing their own previous mode of appropriation, and thereby also every other previous mode of appropriation. They have nothing of their own to secure and to fortify; their mission is to destroy all previous securities for, and insurances of, individual property.

All previous historical movements were movements of minorities, or in the interest of minorities. The proletarian movement is the self-conscious, independent movement of the immense majority, in the interest of the immense majority. The proletariat, the lowest stratum of our present society, cannot stir, cannot raise itself up, without the whole superincumbent strata of official society being blown to pieces.

Though not in substance, yet in form, the struggle of the proletariat with the bourgeoisie is at first a national struggle. The proletariat of each country must, of course, first of all settle matters with its own bourgeoisie.

In depicting the most general phases of the development of the proletariat, we traced the more or less veiled civil war, raging within existing society, up to the point where that war breaks out into open revolution, and where the violent overthrow of the bourgeoisie lays the foundation for the sway of the proletariat.

Hitherto, every form of society has been based, as we have already seen, on the antagonism of oppressing and oppressed classes. But in order to oppress a class, certain conditions must be assured to it under which it can, at least, continue its slavish existence. The serf, in the period of serfdom, raised himself to membership in the commune, just as the petty bourgeois, under the yoke of feudal absolutism, managed to develop into a bourgeois. The modern labourer, on the contrary, instead of rising with the progress of industry, sinks deeper and deeper below the conditions of existence of his own class. He becomes a pauper, and pauperism develops more rapidly than population and wealth. And here it becomes evident that the bourgeoisie is unfit any longer to be the ruling class in society, and to impose its conditions of existence upon society as an overriding law. It is unfit to rule because it is incompetent to assure an existence to its slave within his slavery, because it cannot help letting him sink into such a state, that it has to feed him, instead of being fed by him. Society can no longer live under this bourgeoisie, in other words, its existence is no longer compatible with society.

The essential condition for the existence and for the sway of the bourgeois class, is the formation and augmentation of capital; the condition for capital is wage labour. Wage labour rests exclusively on competition between the labourers. The advance of industry, whose involuntary promoter is the bourgeoisie, replaces the isolation of the labourers, due to competition, by their revolutionary combination, due to association. The development of modern industry, therefore, cuts from under its feet the very foundation on which the bourgeoisie produces and appropriates products. What the bourgeoisie therefore produces, above all, are its own grave-diggers. Its fall and the victory of the proletariat are equally inevitable.

II. PROLETARIANS AND COMMUNISTS

In what relation do the Communists stand to the proletarians as a whole?

The Communists do not form a separate party opposed to other working-class parties.

They have no interests separate and apart from those of the proletariat as a whole.

They do not set up any sectarian principles of their own, by which to shape and mould the proletarian movement.

The Communists are distinguished from the other working-class parties by this only: (1) In the national struggles of the proletarians of the different countries, they point out and bring to the front the common interests of the entire proletariat, independently of all nationality. (2) In the various stages of development which the struggle of the working class against the bourgeoisie has to pass through, they always and everywhere represent the interests of the movement as a whole.

The Communists, therefore, are on the one hand, practically, the most advanced and resolute section of the working-class parties of every country, that section which pushes forward all others; on the other hand, theoretically, they have over the great mass of the proletariat the advantage of clearly understanding the lines of march, the conditions, and the ultimate general results of the proletarian movement.

The immediate aim of the Communists is the same as that of all other proletarian parties: Formation of the proletariat into a class, overthrow of the bourgeois supremacy, conquest of political power by the proletariat.

The theoretical conclusions of the Communists are in no way based on ideas or principles that have been invented, or discovered, by this or that would-be universal reformer.

They merely express, in general terms, actual relations springing from an existing class struggle, from a historical movement going on under our very eyes. The abolition of existing property relations is not at all a distinctive feature of communism.

All property relations in the past have continually been subject to historical change consequent upon the change in historical conditions.

The French Revolution, for example, abolished feudal property in favour of bourgeois property.

The distinguishing feature of communism is not the abolition of property generally, but the abolition of bourgeois property. But modern bourgeois private property is the final and most complete expression of the system of producing and appropriating products that is based on class antagonisms, on the exploitation of the many by the few.

In this sense, the theory of the Communists may be summed up in the single sentence: Abolition of private property.

We Communists have been reproached with the desire of abolishing the right of personally acquiring property as the fruit of a man's own labour, which property is alleged to be the groundwork of all personal freedom, activity and independence.

Hard-won, self-acquired, self-earned property! Do you mean the property of the petty artisan and of the small peasant, a form of property that preceded the bourgeois form? There is no need to abolish that; the development of industry has to a great extent already destroyed it, and is still destroying it daily.

Or do you mean modern bourgeois private property?

But does wage labour create any property for the labourer? Not a bit. It creates capital, i.e., that kind of property which exploits wage labour, and which cannot increase except upon conditions of begetting a new supply of wage labour for fresh exploitation. Property, in its present form, is based on the antagonism of capital and wage labour. Let us examine both sides of this antagonism.

To be a capitalist is to have not only a purely personal, but a social, *status* in production. Capital is a collective product, and only by the united action of many members, nay, in the last resort, only by the united action of all members of society, can it be set in motion.

Capital is therefore not a personal, it is a social power.

When, therefore, capital is converted into common property, into the property of all members of society, personal property is not thereby transformed into social property. It is only the social character of the property that is changed. It loses its class character.

Let us now take wage labour.

The average price of wage labour is the minimum wage, i.e., that quantum of the means of subsistence which is absolutely requisite to keep the labourer in bare existence as a labourer. What, therefore, the wage labourer appropriates by means of his labour merely suffices to prolong and reproduce a bare existence. We by no means intend to abolish this personal appropriation of the products of labour, an appropriation that is made for the maintenance and reproduction of human life, and that leaves no surplus wherewith to command the labour of others. All that we want to do away with is the miserable character of this appropriation, under which the labourer lives merely to increase capital, and is allowed to live only in so far as the interest of the ruling class requires it.

In bourgeois society, living labour is but a means to increase accumulated labour. In communist society, accumulated labour is but a means to widen, to enrich, to promote the existence of the labourer.

In bourgeois society, therefore, the past dominates the present; in communist society, the present dominates the past. In bourgeois society capital is independent and has individuality, while the living person is dependent and has no individuality.

And the abolition of this state of things is called by the bourgeois abolition of individuality and freedom! And rightly so. The abolition of bourgeois individuality, bourgeois independence, and bourgeois freedom is undoubtedly aimed at.

By freedom is meant, under the present bourgeois conditions of production, free trade, free selling and buying.

But if selling and buying disappears, free selling and buying disappears also. This talk about free selling and buying, and all the other "brave words" of our bourgeoisie about freedom in general, have a meaning, if any, only in contrast with restricted selling and buying, with the fettered traders of the Middle Ages, but have no meaning when opposed to the communist abolition of buying and selling, of the bourgeois conditions of production, and of the bourgeoisie itself.

You are horrified at our intending to do away with private property. But in your existing society, private property is already done away with for nine-tenths of the population; its existence for the few is solely due to its non-existence in the hands of those nine-tenths. You reproach us, therefore, with intending to do away with a form of property, the necessary condition for whose existence is the non-existence of any property for the immense majority of society.

In one word, you reproach us with intending to do away with your property. Precisely so; that is just what we intend.

From the moment when labour can no longer be converted into capital, money or rent, into a social power capable of being monopolised, i.e., from the moment when individual property can no longer be transformed into bourgeois property, into capital, from that moment, you say, individuality vanishes.

You must, therefore, confess that by "individual" you mean no other person than the bourgeois, than the middle-class owner of property. This person must, indeed, be swept out of the way, and made impossible.

Communism deprives no man of the power to appropriate the products of society; all that it does is to deprive him of the power to subjugate the labour of others by means of such appropriation.

It has been objected, that upon the abolition of private property all work will cease, and universal laziness will overtake us.

According to this, bourgeois society ought long ago to have gone to the dogs through sheer idleness; for those of its members who work, acquire nothing, and those who acquire anything, do not work. The whole of this objection is but another expression of the tautology: There can no longer be any wage labour when there is no longer any capital.

All objections urged against the communistic mode of producing and appropriating material products, have, in the same way, been urged against the communistic modes of producing and appropriating intellectual products. Just as to the bourgeois, the disappearance of class property is the disappearance of production itself, so the disappearance of class culture is to him identical with the disappearance of all culture.

That culture, the loss of which he laments, is, for the enormous majority, a mere training to act as a machine.

But don't wrangle with us so long as you apply, to our intended abolition of bourgeois property, the standard of your bourgeois notions of freedom, culture, law, etc. Your very ideas are but the outgrowth of the conditions of your bourgeois production and bourgeois property, just as your jurisprudence is but the will of your class made into a law for all, a will whose essential character and direction are determined by the economical conditions of existence of your class.

The selfish misconception that induces you to transform into eternal laws of nature and of reason the social forms springing from your present mode of production and form of property—historical relations that rise and disappear in the progress of production—this misconception you share with every ruling class that has preceded you. What you see clearly in the case of ancient property, what you admit in the case of feudal property, you are of course forbidden to admit in the case of your own bourgeois form of property.

Abolition of the family! Even the most radical flare up at this infamous proposal of the Communists.

On what foundation is the present family, the bourgeois family, based? On capital, on private gain. In its completely developed form this family exists only among the bourgeoisie. But this state of things finds its complement in the practical absence of the family among proletarians, and in public prostitution.

The bourgeois family will vanish as a matter of course when its complement vanishes, and both will vanish with the vanishing of capital.

Do you charge us with wanting to stop the exploitation of children by their parents? To this crime we plead guilty.

But, you will say, we destroy the most hallowed of relations, when we replaced home education by social.

And your education! Is not that also social, and determined by the social conditions under which you educate, by the intervention direct or indirect, of society, by means of schools, etc.? The Communists have not invented the intervention of society in education; they do but seek to alter the character of that intervention, and to rescue education from the influence of the ruling class.

The bourgeois claptrap about the family and education, about the hallowed correlation of parent and child, becomes all the more disgusting, the more, by the action of modern industry, all family ties among the proletarians are torn asunder, and their children transformed into simple articles of commerce and instruments of labour.

But you Communists would introduce community of women, screams the whole bourgeoisie in chorus.

The bourgeois sees in his wife a mere instrument of production. He hears that the instruments of production are to be exploited in common, and, naturally, can come to no other conclusion than that the lot of being common to all will likewise fall to the women.

He has not even a suspicion that the real point aimed at is to do away with the status of women as mere instruments of production.

For the rest, nothing is more ridiculous than the virtuous indignation of our bourgeois at the community of women which, they pretend, is to be openly and officially established by the Communists. The Communists have no need to introduce community of women; it has existed almost from time immemorial.

Our bourgeois, not content with having wives and daughters of their proletarians at their disposal, not to speak of common prostitutes, take the greatest pleasure in seducing each other's wives.

Bourgeois marriage is in reality a system of wives in common and thus, at the most, what the Communists might possibly be reproached with is that they desire to introduce, in substitution for a hypocritically concealed, an openly legalised community of women. For the rest, it is self-evident, that the abolition of the present system of production must bring with it the abolition of the community of women springing from that system, i.e., of prostitution both public and private.

The Communists are further reproached with desiring to abolish countries and nationality.

The working men have no country. We cannot take from them what they have not got. Since the proletariat must first of all acquire political supremacy, must rise to be the leading class of the nation, must constitute itself *the* nation, it is, so far, itself national, though not in the bourgeois sense of the word.

National differences and antagonism between peoples are daily more and more vanishing, owing to the development of the bourgeoisie, to freedom of commerce, to the world market, to uniformity in the mode of production and in the conditions of life corresponding thereto.

The supremacy of the proletariat will cause them to vanish still faster. United action of the leading civilised countries at least, is one of the first conditions for the emancipation of the proletariat.

In proportion as the exploitation of one individual by another is put an end to, the exploitation of one nation by another will also be put an end to. In proportion as the antagonism between classes within the nation vanishes, the hostility of one nation to another will come to an end.

The charges against communism made from a religious, a philosophical and, generally, from an ideological standpoint, are not deserving of serious examination.

Does it require deep intuition to comprehend that man's ideas, views, and conceptions, in one word, man's consciousness, change with every change in the conditions of his material existence, in his social relations and in his social life?

What else does the history of ideas prove, than that intellectual production changes its character in proportion as material production is changed? The ruling ideas of each age have ever been the ideas of its ruling class.

When people speak of ideas that revolutionise society, they do but express the fact that within the old society the elements of a new one have been created, and that the dissolution of the old ideas keeps even pace with the dissolution of the old conditions of existence.

When the ancient world was in its last throes, the ancient religions were overcome by Christianity. When Christian ideas succumbed in the eighteenth century to rationalist ideas, feudal society fought its death battle with the then revolutionary bourgeoisie. The ideas of religious liberty and freedom of conscience merely gave expression to the sway of free competition within the domain of knowledge.

"Undoubtedly," it will be said, "religious, moral, philosophical and juridical ideas have been modified in the course of historical development. But religion, morality, philosophy, political science, and law, constantly survived this change."

"There are, besides, eternal truths, such as Freedom, Justice, etc., that are common to all states of society. But communism abolishes eternal truths, it abolishes all religion, and all morality, instead of constituting them on a new basis; it therefore acts in contradiction to all past historical experience."

What does this accusation reduce itself to? The history of all past society has consisted in the development of class antagonisms, antagonisms that assumed different forms at different epochs.

But whatever form they may have taken, one fact is common to all past ages, viz., the exploitation of one part of society by the other. No wonder, then, that the social consciousness of past ages, despite all the multiplicity and variety it displays, moves within certain common forms, or general ideas, which cannot completely vanish except with the total disappearance of class antagonisms.

The communist revolution is the most radical rupture with traditional relations; no wonder that its development involves the most radical rupture with traditional ideas.

But let us have done with the bourgeois objections to communism.

We have seen above that the first step in the revolution by the working class is to raise the proletariat to the position of ruling class to win the battle of democracy.

The proletariat will use its political supremacy to wrest, by degrees, all capital from the bourgeoisie, to centralise all instruments of production in the hands of the state, i.e., of the proletariat organised as the ruling class; and to increase the total of productive forces as rapidly as possible.

Of course, in the beginning, this cannot be effected except by means of despotic inroads on the rights of property, and on the conditions of bourgeois production; by means of measures, therefore, which appear economically insufficient and untenable, but which, in the course of the movement, outstrip themselves, necessitate further inroads upon the old social order, and are unavoidable as a means of entirely revolutionising the mode of production.

These measures will of course be different in different countries.

Nevertheless, in the most advanced countries, the following will be pretty generally applicable.

1. Abolition of property in land and application of all rents of land to public purposes.

2. A heavy progressive or graduated income tax.

3. Abolition of all right of inheritance.

4. Confiscation of the property of all emigrants and rebels.

5. Centralisation of credit in the hands of the state, by means of a national bank with state capital and an exclusive monopoly.

6. Centralisation of the means of communication and transport in the hands of the state.

7. Extension of factories and instruments of production owned by the state; the bringing into cultivation of waste lands, and the improvement of the soil generally in accordance with a common plan.

8. Equal obligation of all to work. Establishment of industrial armies, especially for agriculture.

9. Combination of agriculture with manufacturing industries; gradual abolition of all the distinction between town and country by a more equable distribution of the population over the country.

10. Free education for all children in public schools. Abolition of children's factory labour in its present form. Combination of education with industrial production, etc.

When, in the course of development, class distinctions have disappeared, and all production has been concentrated in the hands of a vast association of the whole nation, the public power will lose its political character. Political power, properly so called, is merely the organised power of one class for oppressing another. If the proletariat during its contest with the bourgeoisie is compelled, by the force of circumstances, to organise itself as a class; if, by means of a revolution, it makes itself the ruling class, and, as such, sweeps away by force the old conditions of production, then it will, along with these conditions, have swept away the conditions for the existence of class antagonisms and of classes generally, and will thereby have abolished its own supremacy as a class.

In place of the old bourgeois society, with its classes and class antagonisms, we shall have an association in which the free development of each is the condition for the free development of all.

III. SOCIALIST AND COMMUNIST LITERATURE

1. REACTIONARY SOCIALISM

A. FEUDAL SOCIALISM

Owing to their historical position it became the vocation of the aristocracies of France and England to write pamphlets against modern bourgeois society. In the French Revolution of July, 1830, and in the English reform agitation, these aristocracies again succumbed to the hateful upstart. Thenceforth a serious political struggle was altogether out of the question. A literary battle alone remained possible. But even in the domain of literature the old cries of the Restoration[1] period had become impossible.

In order to arouse sympathy the aristocracy was obliged to lose sight, apparently, of its own interests, and to formulate its indictment against the bourgeoisie in the interest of the exploited working class alone. Thus the aristocracy took their revenge by singing lampoons on their new master and whispering in his ears sinister prophecies of coming catastrophe.

In this way arose feudal socialism: half lamentation, half lampoon; half echo of the past, half menace of the future; at times, by its bitter, witty and incisive criticism, striking the bourgeoisie to the very heart's core, but always ludicrous in its effect, through total incapacity to comprehend the match of modern history.

The aristocracy, in order to rally the people to them, waved the proletarian alms-bag in front for a banner. But the people, so often as it joined them, saw on their hindquarters the old feudal coats of arms, and deserted with loud and irreverent laughter

One section of the French Legitimists and "Young England" exhibited this spectacle.

In pointing out that their mode of exploitation was different to that of the bourgeoisie, the feudalists forget that they exploited under circumstances and conditions that were quite different and that are now antiquated. In showing that, under their rule, the modern proletariat never existed, they forget that the modern bourgeoisie is the necessary offspring of their own form of society.

For the rest, so little do they conceal the reactionary character of their criticism that their chief accusation against the bourgeoisie amounts to this, that under the

---

1. As Engels indicates in a footnote to the 1888 English edition of the *Manifesto*, the reference here is to the French Restoration of 1814–1830, not to the English Restoration of 1660–1689. [E.K.]

bourgeois régime a class is being developed which is destined to cut up root and branch the old order of society.

What they upbraid the bourgeoisie with is not so much that it creates a proletariat as that it creates a *revolutionary* proletariat.

In political practice, therefore, they join in all coercive measures against the working class; and in ordinary life, despite their high falutin' phrases, they stoop to pick up the golden apples dropped from the tree of industry, and to barter truth, love, and honour for traffic in wool, beetroot-sugar, and potato spirits.

As the parson has ever gone hand in hand with the landlord, so has clerical socialism with feudal socialism.

Nothing is easier than to give Christian asceticism a socialist tinge. Has not Christianity declaimed against private property, against marriage, against the state? Has it not preached in the place of these, charity and poverty, celibacy and mortification of the flesh, monastic life and Mother Church? Christian socialism is but the holy water with which the priest consecrates the heart-burnings of the aristocrat.

B. PETTY-BOURGEOIS SOCIALISM

The feudal aristocracy was not the only class that was ruined by the bourgeoisie, not the only class whose conditions of existence pined and perished in the atmosphere of modern bourgeois society. The medieval burgesses and the small peasant proprietors were the precursors of the modern bourgeoisie. In those countries which are but little developed, industrially and commercially, these two classes still vegetate side by side with the rising bourgeoisie.

In countries where modern civilisation has become fully developed, a new class of petty bourgeois has been formed, fluctuating between proletariat and bourgeoisie, and ever renewing itself as a supplementary part of bourgeois society. The individual members of this class, however, are being constantly hurled down into the proletariat by the action of competition, and, as modern industry develops, they even see the moment approaching when they will completely disappear as an independent section of modern society, to be replaced, in manufactures, agriculture and commerce, by overseers, bailiffs and shopmen.

In countries like France, where the peasants constitute far more than half of the population, it was natural that writers who sided with the proletariat against the bourgeoisie should use, in their criticism of the bourgeois régime, the standard of the peasant and petty bourgeois, and from the standpoint of these intermediate classes should take up the cudgels for the working class. Thus arose petty-bourgeois socialism. Sismondi was the head of this school, not only in France but also in England.

This school of socialism dissected with great acuteness the contradictions in the conditions of modern production. It laid bare the hypocritical apologies of economists. It proved, incontrovertibly, the disastrous effects of machinery and division of labour; the concentration of capital and land in a few hands; overproduction and crises; it pointed out the inevitable ruin of the petty bourgeois and peasant, the misery of the proletariat, the anarchy in production, the crying inequalities in the distribution of wealth, the industrial war of extermination between nations, the dissolution of old moral bonds, of the old family relations, of the old nationalities.

In its positive aims, however, this form of socialism aspires either to restoring the old means of production and of exchange, and with them the old property relations, and the old society, or to cramping the modern means of production and of exchange within the framework of the old property relations that have been, and were bound to be, exploded by those means. In either case it is both reactionary and utopian.

Its last words are: Corporate guilds for manufacture; patriarchal relations in agriculture.

Ultimately, when stubborn historical facts had dispersed all intoxicating effect of self-deception, this form of socialism ended in a miserable fit of the blues.

C. GERMAN OR "TRUE" SOCIALISM

The socialist and communist literature of France, a literature that originated under the pressure of a bourgeoisie in power, and that was the expression of the struggle against this power, was introduced into Germany at a time when the bourgeoisie in that country had just begun its contest with feudal absolutism.

German philosophers, would-be philosophers and men of letters eagerly seized on this literature, only forgetting that when these writings immigrated from France into Germany, French social conditions had not immigrated along with them. In contact with German social conditions this French literature lost all its immediate practical significance and assumed a purely literary aspect. Thus, to the German philosophers of the eighteenth century, the demands of the first French Revolution were nothing more than the demands of "Practical Reason" in general, and the utterance of the will of the revolutionary French bourgeoisie signified in their eyes the laws of pure will, of will as it was bound to be, of true human will generally.

The work of the German *literati* consisted solely in bringing the new French ideas into harmony with their ancient philosophical conscience, or rather, in annexing the French ideas without deserting their own philosophic point of view.

This annexation took place in the same way in which a foreign language is appropriated, namely, by translation.

It is well known how the monks wrote silly lives of Catholic saints *over* the manuscripts on which the classical works of ancient heathendom had been written. The German *literati* reversed this process with the profane French literature. They wrote their philosophical nonsense beneath the French original. For instance, beneath the French criticism of the economic functions of money, they wrote "alienation of humanity," and beneath the French criticism of the bourgeois state they wrote "dethronement of the category of the general," and so forth.

The introduction of these philosophical phrases at the back of the French historical criticisms they dubbed "Philosophy of Action," "True Socialism," "German Science of Socialism," "Philosophical Foundation of Socialism," and so on.

The French socialist and communist literature was thus completely emasculated. And, since it ceased in the hands of the German to express the struggle of one class with the other, he felt conscious of having overcome "French onesidedness" and of representing, not true requirements, but the requirements of truth; not the interests of the proletariat, but the interests of human nature, of man in general, who belongs to no class, has no reality, who exists only in the misty realm of philosophical phantasy.

This German socialism, which took its schoolboy task so seriously and solemnly, and extolled its poor stock-in-trade in such mountebank fashion, meanwhile gradually lost its pedantic innocence.

The fight of the German and especially of the Prussian bourgeoisie against feudal aristocracy and absolute monarchy, in other words, the liberal movement, became more earnest.

By this, the long-wished-for opportunity was offered to "True" Socialism of confronting the political movement with the socialist demands, of hurling the traditional anathemas against liberalism, against representative government, against bourgeois competition, bourgeois freedom of the press, bourgeois legislation, bourgeois liberty and equality, and of preaching to the masses that they had nothing to gain, and everything to lose, by this bourgeois movement. German socialism forgot, in the nick of time, that the French criticism, whose silly echo it was, presupposed the existence of modern bourgeois society, with its corresponding economic conditions of existence, and the political constitution adapted thereto, the very things whose attainment was the object of the pending struggle in Germany.

To the absolute governments, with their following of parsons, professors, country squires and officials, it served as a welcome scarecrow against the threatening bourgeoisie.

It was a sweet finish after the bitter pills of floggings and bullets, with which these same governments, just at that time, dosed the German working-class risings.

While this "True" Socialism thus served the governments as a weapon for fighting the German bourgeoisie, it, at the same time, directly represented a reactionary interest, the interest of the German philistines. In Germany the petty-bourgeois class, a relic of the sixteenth century, and since then constantly cropping up again under various forms, is the real social basis of the existing state of things.

To preserve this class is to preserve the existing state of things in Germany. The industrial and political supremacy of the bourgeoisie threatens it with certain destruction—on the one hand, from the concentration of capital; on the other, from the rise of a revolutionary proletariat. "True" Socialism appeared to kill these two birds with one stone. It spread like an epidemic.

The robe of speculative cobwebs, embroidered with flowers of rhetoric, steeped in the dew of sickly sentiment, this transcendental robe in which the German Socialists wrapped their sorry "eternal truths," all skin and bone, served wonderfully to increase the sale of their goods amongst such a public. And on its part German socialism recognised, more and more, its own calling as the bombastic representative of the petty-bourgeois philistine.

It proclaimed the German nation to be the model nation, and the German petty philistine to be the typical man. To every villainous meanness of this model man it gave a hidden, higher, socialistic interpretation, the exact contrary of its real character. It went to the extreme length of directly opposing the "brutally destructive" tendency of communism, and of proclaiming its supreme and impartial contempt of all class struggles. With very few exceptions all the so-called socialist and communist publications that now (1847) circulate in Germany belong to the domain of this foul and enervating literature.[2]

2. CONSERVATIVE OR BOURGEOIS SOCIALISM

A part of the bourgeoisie is desirous of redressing social grievances in order to secure the continued existence of bourgeois society.

To this section belong economists, philanthropists, humanitarians, improvers of the condition of the working class, organisers of charity, members of societies for the prevention of cruelty to animals, temperance fanatics, hole-and-corner reformers of every imaginable kind. This form of socialism has, moreover, been worked out into complete systems.

We may cite Proudhon's *Philosophie de la Misère* [*Philosophy of Poverty*] as an example of this form.

The socialistic bourgeois want all the advantages of modern social conditions without the struggles and dangers necessarily resulting therefrom. They desire the existing state of society minus its revolutionary and disintegrating elements. They wish for a bourgeoisie without a proletariat. The bourgeoisie naturally conceives the world in which it is supreme to be the best; and bourgeois socialism develops this comfortable conception into

---

2. The revolutionary storm of 1848 swept away this whole shabby tendency and cured its protagonists of the desire to dabble in socialism. The chief representative and classical type of this tendency is Mr. Karl Grün. [Note by F. Engels to the German edition of 1888.]

various more or less complete systems. In requiring the proletariat to carry out such a system, and thereby to march straightway into the social New Jerusalem, it but requires in reality that the proletariat should remain within the bounds of existing society, but should cast away all its hateful ideas concerning the bourgeoisie.

A second and more practical, but less systematic, form of this socialism sought to depreciate every revolutionary movement in the eyes of the working class by showing that no mere political reform, but only a change in the material conditions of existence, in economical relations, could be of any advantage to them. By changes in the material conditions of existence, this form of socialism, however, by no means understands abolition of the bourgeois relations of production, an abolition that can be effected only by a revolution, but administrative reforms, based on the continued existence of these relations; reforms, therefore, that in no respect affect the relations between capital and labour, but, at the best, lessen the cost, and simplify the administrative work of bourgeois government.

Bourgeois socialism attains adequate expression when, and only when, it becomes a mere figure of speech.

Free trade: for the benefit of the working class. Protective duties: for the benefit of the working class. Prison reform: for the benefit of the working class. This is the last word and the only seriously meant word of bourgeois socialism.

It is summed up in the phrase: the bourgeois is a bourgeois—for the benefit of the working class.

3. CRITICAL-UTOPIAN SOCIALISM AND COMMUNISM

We do not here refer to that literature which, in every great modern revolution, has always given voice to the demands of the proletariat, such as the writings of Babeuf and others.

The first direct attempts of the proletariat to attain its own ends, made in times of universal excitement, when feudal society was being overthrown; these attempts necessarily failed, owing to the then undeveloped state of the proletariat, as well as to the absence of the economic conditions for its emancipation, conditions that had yet to be produced, and could be produced by the impending bourgeois epoch alone. The revolutionary literature that accompanied these first movements of the proletariat had necessarily a reactionary character. It inculcated universal asceticism and social levelling in its crudest form.

The socialist and communist systems, properly so called, those of Saint-Simon, Fourier, Owen, and others, spring into existence in the early undeveloped period, described above, of the struggle between proletariat and bourgeoisie (see Section I. Bourgeois and Proletarians).

The founders of these systems see, indeed, the class antagonisms, as well as the action of the decomposing elements in the prevailing form of society. But the proletariat, as yet in its infancy, offers to them the spectacle of a class without any historical initiative or any independent political movement.

Since the development of class antagonism keeps even pace with the development of industry, the economic situation, as they find it, does not as yet offer to them the material conditions for the emancipation of the proletariat. They therefore search after a new social science, after new social laws, that are to create these conditions.

Historical action is to yield to their personal inventive action; historically created conditions of emancipation to fantastic ones; and the gradual, spontaneous class organisation of the proletariat to an organisation of society especially contrived by these inventors. Future history resolves itself, in their eyes, into the propaganda and the practical carrying out of their social plans.

In the formation of their plans they are conscious of caring chiefly for the interests of the working class, as being the most suffering class. Only from the point of view of being the most suffering class does the proletariat exist for them.

The undeveloped state of the class struggle, as well as their own surroundings, causes Socialists of this kind to consider themselves far superior to all class antagonisms. They want to improve the condition of every member of society, even that of the most favoured. Hence, they habitually appeal to society at large, without distinction of class; nay, by preference, to the ruling class. For how can people, when once they understand their system, fail to see in it the best possible plan of the best possible state of society?

Hence, they reject all political, and especially all revolutionary action; they wish to attain their ends by peaceful means, and endeavour, by small experiments, necessarily doomed to failure, and by the force of example, to pave the way for the new social gospel.

Such fantastic pictures of future society, painted at a time when the proletariat is still in a very undeveloped state and has but a fantastic conception of its own position, correspond with the first instinctive yearnings of that class for a general reconstruction of society.

But these socialist and communist publications contain also a critical element. They attack every principle of existing society. Hence they are full of the most valuable materials for the enlightenment of the working class. The practical measures proposed in them—such as the abolition of the distinction between town and country, of the family, of the carrying on of industries for the account of private individuals, and of the wage system, the proclamation of social harmony, the conversion of the function of the state into a mere superintendence of production—all these proposals point solely to the disappearance of class antagonisms which were, at that time, only just cropping up, and which, in these publications, are recognised in their earliest indistinct and undefined forms only. These proposals, therefore, are of a purely utopian character.

The significance of critical-utopian socialism and communism bears an inverse relation to historical development. In proportion as the modern class struggle develops and takes definite shape, this fantastic standing apart from the contest, these fantastic attacks on it, lose all practical value and all theoretical justification. Therefore, although the originators of these systems were, in many respects, revolutionary, their disciples have, in every case, formed mere reactionary sects. They hold fast by the original views of their masters, in opposition to the progressive historical development of the proletariat. They, therefore, endeavour, and that consistently, to deaden the class struggle and to reconcile the class antagonisms. They still dream of experimental realisation of their social utopias, of founding isolated *phalanstères*, of establishing "Home Colonies," or setting up a "Little Icaria"—pocket editions of the New Jerusalem—and to realise all these castles in the air they are compelled to appeal to the feelings and purses of the bourgeois. By degrees they sink into the category of the reactionary conservative socialists depicted above, differing from these only by more systematic pedantry, and by their fanatical and superstitious belief in the miraculous effects of their social science.

They, therefore, violently oppose all political action on the part of the working class; such action, according to them, can only result from blind unbelief in the new gospel.

The Owenites in England, and the Fourierists in France, respectively, oppose the Chartists and the *Réformistes*.

IV. POSITION OF THE COMMUNISTS IN RELATION TO THE VARIOUS EXISTING OPPOSITION PARTIES

Section II has made clear the relations of the Communists to the existing working-class parties, such as the Chartists in England and the Agrarian Reformers in America.

The Communists fight for the attainment of the immediate aims, for the enforcement of the momentary interests of the working class; but in the movement of the present they also represent and take care of the future of that movement. In France the Communists ally themselves with the Social-Democrats[3] against the conservative and radical bourgeoisie, reserving, however, the right to take up a critical position in regard to phrases and illusions traditionally handed down from the Great Revolution.

In Switzerland they support the Radicals, without losing sight of the fact that this party consists of antagonistic elements, partly of Democratic Socialists, in the French sense, partly of radical bourgeois.

In Poland they support the party that insists on an agrarian revolution as the prime condition for national emancipation, that party which fomented the insurrection of Cracow in 1846.

In Germany they fight with the bourgeoisie whenever it acts in a revolutionary way, against the absolute monarchy, the feudal squirearchy, and the petty-bourgeoisie.

But they never cease, for a single instant, to instil into the working class the clearest possible recognition of the

------

3. The party then represented in Parliament by Ledru-Rollin, in literature by Louis Blanc (1811–1882), in the daily press by the *Réforme.* The name of Social-Democracy signifies, with these its inventors, a section of the Democratic or Republican Party more or less tinged with socialism. [Note by F. Engels to the English edition of 1888.]

hostile antagonism between bourgeoisie and proletariat, in order that the German workers may straightway use, as so many weapons against the bourgeoisie, the social and political conditions that the bourgeoisie must necessarily introduce along with its supremacy, and in order that, after the fall of the reactionary classes in Germany, the fight against the bourgeoisie itself may immediately begin.

The Communists turn their attention chiefly to Germany, because that country is on the eve of a bourgeois revolution that is bound to be carried out under more advanced conditions of European civilisation and with a much more developed proletariat than that of England was in the seventeenth, and of France in the eighteenth century, and because the bourgeois revolution in Germany will be but the prelude to an immediately following proletarian revolution.

In short, the Communists everywhere support every revolutionary movement against the existing social and political order of things.

In all these movements they bring to the front, as the leading question in each, the property question, no matter what its degree of development at the time.

Finally, they labour everywhere for the union and agreement of the democratic parties of all countries.

The Communists disdain to conceal their views and aims. They openly declare that their ends can be attained only by the forcible overthrow of all existing social conditions. Let the ruling classes tremble at a communist revolution. The proletarians have nothing to lose but their chains. They have a world to win.

Working men of all countries, unite!

MEGA I, 6, 523–57; MEW 4, 459–93; as translated by S. Moore (authorized English edition, London, 1888).

1848

THE DEMANDS OF THE COMMUNIST PARTY IN GERMANY

[BY KARL MARX AND FRIEDRICH ENGELS]

These Demands were drawn up by Marx and Engels on behalf of the Central Committee of the Communist League in Paris during the last week of March 1848. They were published there as a leaflet on 31 March, and at the beginning of April in various democratic German newspapers. In summer 1848 the Demands were reprinted in Cologne.

Proletarians of all countries, unite!

1. The whole of Germany shall be declared a single, indivisible republic.
2. Every German over twenty-one years of age shall be able to vote and be elected, provided he has no criminal conviction.
3. Representatives of the people shall be paid, so that workers, too, will be able to sit in the parliament of the German people.
4. The whole population shall be armed. Armies in future are at the same time to be armies of workers, so that the military will not merely consume, as it did in the past, but will produce even more than the cost of its upkeep.
   Furthermore, this represents a means of organizing labour.
5. The provision of justice shall be free of charge.
6. All feudal dues, tributes, duties, tithes, etc., which have burdened the rural population up to now, shall be abolished, without compensation of any sort.

7. The estates of princes and other feudal estates and all mines, pits, etc., shall become state property. On these estates, large-scale agriculture will be carried on with the use of the most modern scientific aids for the benefit of the whole collectivity.

8. Mortgages on peasant lands shall be declared state property. The peasants are to pay the interest on these mortgages to the state.

9. In those regions where there is a developed system of lease-holding, the ground rent or the 'lease shilling' shall be paid to the state as tax.

All the measures listed in 6, 7, 8 and 9 are designed to reduce public and other burdens on peasants and small tenant farmers, without reducing the requisite means for paying the expenses of the state and without endangering production itself.

The actual owner of land who is neither a peasant nor a tenant plays no part in production. His consumption is therefore nothing but misuse.

10. One state bank shall replace all the private banks, and its note issue shall be legal tender.

This measure will make it possible to regulate credit in the interests of the *whole* population and thus undermine the domination of the big money-men. In so far as it gradually replaces gold and silver by paper money, it will reduce the cost of the indispensable instrument of bourgeois commerce, the universal means of exchange, and permit gold and silver to be used effectively abroad. Finally, this measure is needed in order to bind the interests of the conservative bourgeois to the revolution.

11. All means of transport: railways, canals, steamships, roads, posts, etc., shall be taken over by the state. They are to be transformed into state property and put at the free service of the needy.

12. There shall be no differentials in the payment of civil servants, save that those *with* a family, i.e. with more needs, will also receive a higher salary than the rest.

13. The complete separation of Church and State. Clergymen of all denominations are to be paid only by their voluntary congregations.

14. Restriction of the right of inheritance.

15. The introduction of severely progressive taxation and the abolition of taxes on consumption.

16. The establishment of national workshops. The state is to guarantee all workers their livelihood and to care for those unable to work.

17. Universal and free popular schooling.

It is in the interests of the German proletariat, petty bourgeoisie and peasantry to work energetically for the implementation of the above measures. For only through their realization can the millions who, in Germany up till now have been exploited by a small handful, and whom some will attempt to maintain in continued oppression, get their entitlement and the power that is their due as the producers of all wealth.

The Committee:

KARL MARX	F. ENGELS
KARL SCHAPPER	J. MOLL
H. BAUER	W. WOLFF

MEGA I, 7, 1–4; MEW 5, 3–5.

1850

ADDRESS OF THE CENTRAL COMMITTEE TO THE COMMUNIST LEAGUE, MARCH 1850

[BY KARL MARX AND FREDERICK ENGELS]

This address, printed in London, was illegally circulated among Communist League members within Germany and in exile. Seized by the Prussian police at the time of the arrest of the Cologne Central Committee of the League in April 1857, it was subsequently published in newspapers in Dresden and Cologne. It is here translated from the text as revised by Engels and published as appendix to the 1885 edition of Marx's *The Cologne Communist Trial*.

THE CENTRAL COMMITTEE TO THE LEAGUE

Brothers!

In the two revolutionary years of 1848–49 the League proved itself in two ways; once when its members everywhere participated energetically in the agitation, standing foremost in the ranks of the only resolutely revolutionary class, the proletariat, in the press, on the barricades and on the battlefields. The League further stood the test, since its interpretation of the movement, as set out in the circulars issued by the Congresses and the Central Committee of 1847 and in the *Manifesto of the Communist Party*, has proved to be the only correct one. The expectations given utterance in these documents have been completely fulfilled and the interpretation of present-day social conditions, previously only secretly propagated by the League, is now talked of everywhere and openly preached in the marketplace. At the same time the earlier strong organization of the League has been significantly broken up. A great part of the members, directly involved in the revolutionary movement, believed that the time for secret societies was past and that public action alone would suffice. Individual districts and communities allowed their connections with the Central Committee to weaken and gradually fall into abeyance. Thus, while the democratic party, the party of the petty bourgeoisie, became increasingly organized in Germany, the workers' party lost its only firm support, remaining organized at most in individual localities for local objects; in the movement as a whole it thereby fell completely under the leadership and direction of the petty bourgeois democrats. This situation must be ended; the independence of the workers must be restored. . . . Since the defeat of the revolutionary parties of Germany and France in July 1849 almost all the members of the Central Committee have come together again in London, have recruited new revolutionary forces and have pursued with renewed enthusiasm the reorganization of the League.

This reorganization can only be accomplished by an emissary, and the Central Committee deems it supremely important that the emissary should be sent at this precise moment, when a new revolution is in prospect and the workers' party must therefore present as organized, united and independent a front as possible, if it is not again to be exploited by the bourgeoisie as in 1848 and dragged along in its wake.

Brothers, already in 1848 we told you that the German liberal bourgeoisie would soon achieve control and at once turn its newly-won power against the workers. You have seen how this was fulfilled. In fact it was the bourgeoisie which, immediately after the revolutionary movement of March 1848, seized control of the administration and used this power to force the workers, its allies in the fight, back into their former state of oppression. Though not able to achieve this except by an alliance with the feudal party which had been thrust aside in March, and indeed in the end abdicating its control in favor of this feudal absolutist party, the bourgeoisie nevertheless secured for itself conditions which would in the long term, through the financial embarrassments of the government, ensure that control would come into its hands again and safeguard all its interests, were it possible that the revolutionary movement would henceforth follow a so-called peaceful course of development. In order to secure its control, the bourgeoisie would not even need to make itself hateful by violent measures against the people, since all these violent steps have already been taken by the feudal counterrevolution. Matters will not, however, develop in this peaceful way. On the contrary, the revolution which will hasten them is imminent, whether it be called forth by an independent rising of the French proletariat or by the intervention of the Holy Alliance against the revolutionary Babel.

And the part, the basely treacherous part, played by the German liberal bourgeoisie against the people in 1848 will be taken over in the approaching revolution by the democratic petty bourgeoisie, which now occupies the same position in the opposition as did the liberal bourgeoisie before 1848. This party, the democratic party, which is a far greater danger to the workers than the earlier progressive liberals were, is composed of three elements: 1) Of the most progressive sections of the greater bourgeoisie, whose aim is the immediate overthrow of feudalism and absolutism and which is represented by the former Berlin *Vereinbarer*[1] and by the tax-resisters; 2) of the democratic-constitutionalist petty bourgeoisie, whose chief aim in the agitation hitherto has been the establishment of a more or less democratic federal state, as was also the aim of their representatives, the party of the Left in the Frankfurt Assembly and later in the Stuttgart Parliament, and their own in the Constitutional Campaign; 3) of the republican petty bourgeoisie, whose ideal is a German federal republic on the Swiss model and which now calls itself 'red' and 'social-democratic' because it entertains the pious hope of doing away with the pressure of great capi-

---

1. This was the scornful term used by Marx and Engels for those delegates to the Prussian National Assembly at Berlin in 1848 who sought to solve the constitutional problem through an understanding with the crown and renounced the principle of the sovereignty of the people. The passive tax-resisters were those left-wing delegates whose answer to martial law and the dissolution of the National Assembly was passive resistance and a refusal to pay taxes. [E.K.]

tal on small, of the greater bourgeoisie on the petty bourgeois. The representatives of this party were the members of the democratic congresses and committees, the leaders of the democratic associations, the editors of democratic journals.

All these groups since their defeat claim to be republicans or 'reds,' just as in France the republican petty bourgeoisie now calls itself socialist. Where, as in Württemberg, Bavaria, etc., they still have opportunities for pursuing their aims constitutionally, they seize the occasion to retain their old slogans, hoping to prove thereby that they have not changed in the least. Moreover it is clear that the changed name of this party does not alter its position with regard to the workers at all but merely proves that it must, with the support of the proletariat, now form a front against the the union of bourgeoisie and absolutism.

The petty-bourgeois democratic party in Germany is very powerful, including not only the majority of bourgeois town-dwellers, small industrial tradesmen and factory bosses but also the peasants and rural proletariat, so long as the latter has not yet found support in the independent urban proletariat.

The relationship of the revolutionary workers' party to the petty-bourgeois democrats is this: it makes common cause with them against the party which it plans to overthrow, it opposes them wherever they seek to establish themselves.

The petty-bourgeois democrats, far from wanting to overturn the whole of society on behalf of the revolutionary proletariat, strive for a change in social conditions which will make existent society as bearable and comfortable for themselves as possible. Thus they demand above all a reduction in government spending through limitation of the bureaucracy and a transfer of the principal tax on to the great landowners and the bourgeoisie. They further demand relief from the pressure of great capital on small capital, by means of public credit institutions and laws against usury which would enable them and the peasants to borrow from the state on favorable terms instead of from capitalists, as well as the introduction of bourgeois conditions of ownership in the country through the total abolition of the feudal system. In order to achieve all this they need a democratic form of government, whether constitutional or republican, which would give them and their allies the peasants a majority, and a democratic system of local government, which would give them the direct control over municipal property and a number of offices, at present exercised by the bureaucrats.

The rule of capital and its rapid increase is to be further counteracted, in part by limiting the right of inheritance, in part by transferring as much employment as possible to the state. Concerning the workers one thing above all is determined: they are to remain, as in the past, wage-labourers. The democratic petty bourgeoisie do, however, wish for the workers better pay and more security, and hope to secure this by means of partial state employment and by welfare measures; in short, they hope to bribe the workers with more or less covert alms and to break their revolutionary force by making their present situation bearable. The demands of the petty-bourgeois democrats here summarized are not advocated equally by all sections of the party and are collectively the definite aim of very few of its members. The further individuals or groups of members proceed, the more of these demands will they adopt, and the few who see in the above their own program would believe themselves to have proposed by it the most that could be demanded of the revolution. These demands, however, can in no way satisfy the proletariat. While the democratic petty bourgeoisie would like to bring the revolution to an end as rapidly as possible with the realization of, at most, the foregoing demands, it is our interest and our duty to make the revolution permanent until all more or less propertied classes are forced out of power, control of the state has been won by the proletariat, and proletarians, not just of one country but in all leading countries throughout the world, have so far made common cause together that competition between proletarians in these countries has ceased and at least the critical productive forces are concentrated in the hands of the proletariat. For us it cannot be a question of changing private property but only of destroying it, not of smothering class antagonisms but only of wiping out classes, not of improving existing society but of founding a new one. That the petty-bourgeois democrats will, during the further development of the revolution, for a time exercise predominant influence in Germany does not admit of doubt. The question, therefore, is what the position of the proletariat, and more especially the League, toward them is to be: 1) while present conditions, under which the petty-bourgeois democrats are equally repressed, continue; 2) in the next revolutonary struggle which will give them supremacy; 3) after this struggle, during their supremacy over the defeated classes and the proletariat.

1. At the present time, when the democratic petty bourgeoisie is everywhere oppressed, it preaches general unification and reconciliation to the proletariat, offers friendship and aspires to the foundation of a great party in opposition which will embrace all shades of democratic opinion; that is, it seeks to entangle the workers in a party organization in which general social-democratic catchwords prevail, concealing its particular interests, and in which the positive demands of the proletariat may not, in the interests of peace, be advanced. Such an association would profit only it and wholly disadvantage the proletariat. The proletariat would lose its completely independent position, so hardly won, and relapse into a mere appendage of official bourgeois democracy. This association must be categorically repulsed. Instead of again demeaning themselves by acting as applauding chorus to the bourgeois democrats, the workers, and above all the League,

must work for the creation of an independent, both covert and overt, organization of the workers' party, alongside the official democrats, and aim to make every community a centre and nucleus of workers' associations in which the position and interests of the proletariat can be discussed independently of bourgeois influences. How little serious the bourgeois democrats are about an alliance in which the proletariat will stand by their side with equal power and equal rights is shown, for example, by the democrats of Breslau, who are waging a bitter campaign in their journal, the *Neue Oder-Zeitung*, against independent organized workers whom they dub socialists. In the event of a struggle against a common foe no particular association is necessary. As soon as such an opponent has to be combatted directly, the interests of both parties temporarily coincide, and such a temporary alliance will be produced of its own accord, in the future as in the past. Of course, in the bloody conflicts ahead, as in all earlier ones, the workers above all will have to win the victory by their courage, their resolution and their self-sacrifice. As in the past, so too in this struggle the mass of the petty bourgeoisie will hang back as long as possible, remaining irresolute and inactive, and then as soon as victory is secure they will claim it for themselves, direct the workers to retire and return to their labours, prevent so-called excesses and exclude the proletariat from all the fruits of victory. It is not in the power of the workers to forbid the petty-bourgeois democrats this, but it is in their power to render their rise against the armed proletariat more difficult and to dictate such conditions to them that the rule of the bourgeois democrats from the very beginning will carry within it the seeds of its downfall, making its subsequent displacement by proletarian rule significantly easier. The workers must, above all during the conflict and immediately after the struggle, as far as possible work against bourgeois appeasement and force the democrats to carry out their present terrorist slogans. They must work to ensure that direct revolutionary agitation is not suppressed again immediately after victory. They must, on the contrary, keep it alive as long as possible. Far from opposing the so-called excesses, examples of popular revenge against hated individuals or against public buildings with hateful associations, they must not only allow them but themselves undertake their direction. During and after the struggle the workers must seize every opportunity to publish their own demands beside the demands of the bourgeois democrats. They must seek guarantees for the workers as soon as the bourgeois democrats prepare to seize control of government. They must if necessary procure these guarantees by force and in general make sure that the new rulers commit themselves to all imaginable concessions and promises—the surest method of compromising them. Generally they must as far as possible restrain the delirium of victory, and the enthusiasm for the new state of affairs which follows every successful street fight, by every means, through calm and cold-blooded assessment of circumstances and through unconcealed distrust of the new administration. At the same time they must set up alongside the new official governments some revolutionary workers' administrations, whether in the form of local committees of management, local councils, or whether as workers' clubs or workers' committees, so that the bourgeois democratic administrations not only straightway lose the backing of the workers but find themselves from the start watched and threatened by authorities behind whom is ranged the entire mass of workers. In short, from the first moment of victory on, distrust must be directed no longer against the conquered reactionary party but against the workers' former allies, against the party which wants to exploit the common victory for its sole advantage.

2. However, in order energetically and menacingly to confront this party, whose treachery toward the workers will start in the first moment of victory, the workers must

be armed and organized. The arming of the whole proletariat with flintlocks, carbines, guns and ammunition must be put in hand directly, and the revival of the old citizens' militia, directed against the workers, must be opposed. Where this cannot be achieved, however, the workers must try to organize themselves independently as a proletarian guard, with leaders and a general staff elected by themselves, and to place themselves under the orders not of the state authority but of the revolutionary local councils set up by the workers. Where workers are employed by the state they must arrange to be armed and organized as a special corps with leaders elected by themselves or as a section of the proletarian guard. Arms and ammunition are on no account to be handed over; every attempt at disarmament must be frustrated, by force if need be. The destruction of bourgeois-democratic influence over the workers, their immediate independent, armed organization, and the imposition of conditions as burdensome and compromising as possible on the temporarily inescapable rule of bourgeois democracy, these are the principal points which the proletariat and also the League must bear in mind during and after the approaching insurrection.

3. As soon as the new administrations have to some extent established themselves, their struggle against the workers will begin. If then the workers are to confront the democratic petty bourgeoisie from a position of power, it is essential for them to be organized into independent and centralized clubs. As soon as may be possible after the overthrow of existing governments, the Central Committee is to set out for Germany, where it will immediately convene a congress and lay before it the necessary proposals for the centralization of workers' clubs under a board of control established at the movement's headquarters. The rapid organization of at least a provincial association of clubs is one of the most important points in strengthening and developing the workers' party; the direct consequence of the overthrow of existing govern-

ments will be the election of a national representative assembly. The proletariat must here watch out: 1) that local authorities and government commissioners do not by any underhand tricks exclude a number of workers on whatever pretext; 2) that workers' candidates are nominated everywhere alongside the bourgeois democratic candidates, that as far as possible they should be members of the League and their election should be pursued by all possible means. Even where there is no prospect of their election, the workers must nominate their own candidates, to preserve their independence, to estimate their strength and to publicize their revolutionary position and party standpoint. They must not allow themselves to be corrupted by democratic oratory, which will claim, for example, that this would split the democratic party and make possible the victory of reactionary forces. All such fine words mean, in the end, the swindling of the proletariat. The progress which the proletarian party must make through such an independent line of action is infinitely more important than the disadvantages arising from the presence of a few reactionaries in the representative assembly. If democracy from the first confronts the forces of reaction decisively and with terrorist methods, the latter's influence on the elections is destroyed at the start.

The first point giving rise to conflict between bourgeois democrats and workers will be the abolition of feudalism; as in the first French revolution, the petty bourgeoisie will give the feudal landed properties to the free ownership of the peasants, that is, they will permit the continuance of the rural proletariat and hope to create a petty-bourgeois peasant class which will suffer the same cycle of impoverishment and debt in which the French peasant is now caught.

The workers must oppose this plan both in their own interest and in the interest of the rural proletariat. They must demand that confiscated feudal properties remain the property of the state, to be used for workers' colonies and to be cultivated by rural proletarian collectives with all the advantages of large-scale agriculture; in this way the principle of common ownership will immediately acquire a firm foundation in the centre of the shaky system of bourgeois property relations. As the democrats ally themselves with the peasants, so the workers must ally themselves with the rural proletariat. The democrats will continue either to work directly toward a federal republic or at least, if they cannot avoid a single indivisible republic, will seek to cripple the central government by making the municipalities and provinces as autonomous and independent as possible. To counter this plan the workers must not only work for a single and indivisible German republic but must strive for the greatest possible centralization of power in the hands of its government. They must not allow themselves to be led astray by democratic talk of municipal freedom, self-government, etc. In a country like Germany, where so many traces of the Middle Ages still have to be done away with and where so much local and provincial self-will has to be broken, it must not under any circumstances be allowed that every village, every town, every province may put new obstacles in the path of revolutionary activity, whose full force can only proceed from a central point. The present situation, in which the Germans have to battle specially in each town, each province, for one and the same advance, must not be allowed to recur. Least of all can a so-called free system of local government be permitted to perpetuate a form of property which still stands behind modern private property and is everywhere necessarily absorbed into it: that is communal property, with its concomitant disputes between rich and poor communities, and also a system of communal civil law, with its underhand dealings toward the workers, which exists side by side with state civil law. As in France in 1793, the task of the true revolutionary party in Germany today is the establishment of the most rigid centralization.

We have seen how the next revolutionary movement will bring the democrats to power and how they will be forced to propose more or less socialist measures. It may be asked what measures the workers should propose in return. In the early stages of the movement the workers cannot, naturally, propose any directly communist measures. They can, however:

1) Compel the democrats to encroach upon as many aspects of the existing social order as possible, to interrupt its regular course and to compromise themselves, as well as concentrating in the hands of the state as many forces of production, means of transport, factories, railways, etc., as possible.

2) They must drive the proposals of the democrats, who will in any case appear as reformers rather than revolutionaries, to extremes and transform them into direct attacks on private property. For example, if the petty bourgeoisie proposes to purchase the railways and factories, the workers must demand that these railways and factories, as the property of reactionaries, be simply confiscated by the state without compensation. If the democrats propose proportional taxation, the workers must propose progressive taxation; if the democrats themselves suggest a moderate progressive tax, the workers must insist upon a tax whose rates rise so steeply that the great capitalists are thereby destroyed; if the democrats demand regulation of the national debt, the workers must demand national bankruptcy. The demands of the workers will thus in general have to be directed according to the concessions and measures of the democrats.

If the German workers cannot arrive at a position of authority and the fulfilment of their class interests without suffering a lengthy period of revolutionary development, they will at this time have at least the assurance that the first act of the ensuing revolutionary drama coincides with the direct victory of their own class in France and will thereby be greatly accelerated.

But they themselves must do the most for their eventual victory, by enlightening themselves as to their class interests, by adopting an independent political position as soon as possible, and by never for a moment allowing themselves to be misled concerning the independent organization of the proletarian party by the hypocritical phrases of the democratic petty bourgeoisie. Their battle-cry must be: Revolution Forever.

MEW 7, 244–54.

1850

From THE CLASS STRUGGLES IN FRANCE: 1848 TO 1850

The first three chapters of *The Class Struggles in France* were originally published in numbers 1, 2, and 3 of the *Neue Rheinische Zeitung. Politisch-ökonomische Revue*, Hamburg, 1850. The fourth chapter consists of two excerpts from the 'Review: May–October 1850' in the final double number 5/6 of the *Revue*, which were added by Engels to the earlier chapters as chapter IV when *The Class Struggles in France* was first published as a separate pamphlet in 1895. Chapter I is reproduced here in its entirety.

Except for a very few chapters, every significant section of the revolutionary annals of 1848 to 1849 bears the heading:

Defeat of the Revolution!

What was brought low by these defeats was not the revolution. It was the pre-revolutionary traditional trappings, the results of social relationships which had not yet intensified to sharp class antagonisms—persons, illusions, concepts, projects, from which the revolutionary party before the February revolution was not free and from which it could be freed not by the *victory of February* but only by a series of *reverses*.

In a word, revolutionary progress forced its way, not through its immediate tragicomic achievements, but conversely in creating a united and powerful counter-revolution, in creating an opponent, combat with whom brought the party of revolt to maturity as a true revolutionary party.

This the following pages undertake to show.

1. THE DEFEAT OF JUNE 1848

FROM FEBRUARY TO JUNE 1848

After the July Revolution [of 1830] as the liberal banker Laffitte was escorting his *compère* [accomplice], the Duke of Orléans, in triumph to the Hôtel de Ville, he let fall the remark: '*Henceforth the bankers will be in control*'. Laffitte had betrayed the secret of the revolution.

It was not the French bourgeoisie which ruled under Louis Philippe, but just *one section* of it, bankers, kings of the stock exchange and the railways, owners of coal and iron mines and of forests, and a group of landed proprietors who had rallied to them—the so-called *aristocracy of finance*. It sat on the throne, dictated laws in parliament and distributed official appointments, from ministerial rank down to the tobacco excise office.

The real industrial *bourgeoisie* formed part of the official opposition, that is, it had only minority representation in parliament. Its opposition intensified as the finance aristocracy grew more completely autocratic and as it felt its own control of the working classes increasingly secured by the bloodily repressed risings of 1832, 1834 and 1839. Grandin, a Rouen manufacturer and most fanatical voice of bourgeois reaction in both the Constituent and Legislative National Assemblies, was Guizot's most violent opponent in the Chamber of Deputies. In the last days of Louis Philippe, Léon Faucher, later known for his feeble attempts to gain prominence as the Guizot of the French counter-revolution, campaigned with his pen for industry against speculation and its train-bearer, the government. Bastiat agitated against the ruling system in the name of Bordeaux and the whole of wine-producing France.

The *petty bourgeoisie*, at all levels, and the *peasants* too, were completely excluded from political power. Finally, either in official opposition or entirely outside the *pays légal* [those with the right to vote] were the *ideological* representatives and spokesmen of the classes mentioned, their scholars, advocates, doctors, etc., in short their so-called authorities.

Because of its financial straits the July monarchy was from the first dependent on the upper middle classes and this dependence became the inexhaustible source of growing financial distress. It was impossible to subordinate the administration of the state to the interests of national productivity; without balancing the budget, without balancing the revenues and expenses of the state. And how was this balance to be achieved without restricting state expenditure, that is without damaging interests which were all supporters of the ruling system, and without a redistribution of taxes, that is without shifting a significant share of taxes on to the shoulders of the upper middle class themselves?

The *national debt* was rather the *direct interest* of that part of the bourgeoisie which ruled and legislated through parliament. The *state deficit* was indeed the real object of its speculation and the main source of its increasing wealth. At the end of each year a new deficit. Every four or five years a new loan. And every new loan gave the finance-aristocracy a new opportunity of swindling a state artificially maintained on the verge of bankruptcy, forced to negotiate with the bankers on the most unfavorable terms. Each new loan offered a fresh chance of cheating the public, whose capital was invested in government securities, by means of stock-exchange dealings whose secret was known only to the government and the parliamentary majority. Altogether, the fluctuations of state credit and the bankers' possession of state secrets offered these and their associates, both parliamentary and royal, the opportunity of creating sudden extreme fluctuations in the official rate of exchange, whereby a mass of small capitalists were regularly ruined while the big gamblers grew richer with amazing speed. That the state deficit was in the direct interests of the ruling bourgeois sector explains why the *extraordinary* state expenditure in the last years of Louis Philippe's reign amounted to more than double the extraordinary state expenditure under Napoleon, reaching almost annually the sum of 400 million francs, while the annual exports of France seldom averaged as much as 750 million francs. Moreover the enormous sums thus passing through the hands of the state gave opportunities for supply-contract swindles, bribery, embezzlement and all kinds of knavery. The wholesale defrauding of the state through loans was repeated retail in public works. The relationship between parliament and government was repeatedly copied in the relationship of individual departments and entrepreneurs.

The ruling class exploited the *building of railways* in the same way as it did state expenditure generally and state loans. Parliament threw the main burdens on the state and secured the golden fruit for the speculating finance-aristocracy. The scandals in the Chamber of Deputies may be remembered, when it was accidentally revealed that all members of the majority, including a number of ministers, were shareholders in the very railway construction schemes which, as legislators, they afterwards had carried out at state expense.

On the other hand, the smallest financial reform was

wrecked through the influence of the bankers. For example, on the question of *postal reform* Rothschild protested. Could the state be allowed to curtail sources of revenue from which the interest on its ever-increasing debt was to be paid?

The July monarchy was merely a joint-stock company for the exploitation of France's national wealth, whose dividends were shared out among ministers, parliament, 240,000 voters and their adherents. Louis Philippe was the company director ... Trade, industry, agriculture, shipping, the interests of the industrial bourgeoisie were bound to be continually endangered and prejudiced under this system. Cheap government, *gouvernement à bon marché*, was inscribed on its banner in the July days.

While the finance-aristocracy legislated, directed the administration of the state, controlled all organized public authorities and swayed public opinion through actual events and the press, the same prostitution, the same shameless fraud, the same feverish passion for wealth—achieved not through production but by juggling with the already available wealth of others—was repeated in every sphere from the court to the Café Borgne. Among the leaders of bourgeois society the unrestrained assertion of unhealthy and dissolute appetites broke out, appetites continually conflicting with the bourgeois laws themselves, in which the wealth derived from gambling seeks its natural satisfaction, where pleasure becomes *crapuleux* [debauched], in the confluence of money, filth and blood. The finance-aristocracy, in the way it acquires wealth as in its pleasures, is nothing more than the *Lumpenproletariat reborn at the top of bourgeois society*.

And the non-ruling sectors of the French bourgeoisie screamed '*Corruption!*' The people screamed '*A bas les grands voleurs! A bas les assassins!*' [Down with the master thieves! Down with the murderers!] when in 1847, on the most exalted platforms of bourgeois society, such similar scenes were publicly enacted as regularly bring the

Lumpenproletariat to brothels, workhouses, madhouses, to justice, the dungeon and the scaffold. The industrial bourgeoisie saw its interests endangered, the petty bourgeoisie was filled with moral indignation, popular imagination was incensed, Paris was flooded with pamphlets— *La Dynastie Rothschild, Les Juifs rois de l'époque,* etc.—in which the rule of the finance-aristocracy was denounced and stigmatized with more or less of wit.

Rien pour la gloire! Glory brings no profit! *La paix partout et toujours!* [Peace everywhere and forever.] War lowers the exchange rate of the three and four-per-cents!—this was inscribed on the banner of the France of the stock-exchange kings. Its foreign policy thereby disappeared in a string of insults to French national pride, which reacted all the more vigorously when the Austrian annexation of Cracow completed the rape of Poland and when Guizot actively sided with the Holy Alliance in the Swiss Sonderbund war. The victory of the Swiss liberals in this phoney war raised the self-respect of the bourgeois opposition in France, the bloody revolt of the people of Palermo acted like an electric shock on the paralysed nation and aroused their great revolutionary memories and passions.

Lastly, the outbreak of universal discontent was hastened, the revolutionary temper matured, by two *world-wide economic events.*

The *potato blight* and *crop failures* of 1845 and 1846 increased the general ferment among the people. The famine of 1847 called forth bloody conflicts, in France as in the rest of the continent. To the shameless orgies of the finance-aristocracy was contrasted the battle of the people for barest necessities. In Buzançais hunger-rioters were executed, in Paris bloated swindlers were snatched from justice by the royal family!

The second significant economic event which hastened the outbreak of revolution was a *general commercial and industrial crisis* in England. This, already heralded in the autumn of 1845 by the wholesale reverses of speculators in railway shares, arrested during 1846 by a number of secondary factors such as the impending abolition of the corn duties, finally broke in the autumn of 1847 in the bankruptcies of the great London wholesale grocers, closely followed by the failures of country banks and the closure of factories in the English industrial regions. The consequences to the continent of this crisis had not yet been exhausted when the February revolution broke out.

The devastation of trade and industry through the economic epidemic made the autocratic rule of the finance-aristocracy yet more intolerable. Throughout France the bourgeois opposition instituted *banquets agitating* for an *electoral reform* which was to win it a parliamentary majority and overthrow the Ministry of stock-brokers. In Paris the industrial crisis had the further special consequence that it threw a great number of manufacturers and wholesalers, who under existing conditions could no longer trade in foreign markets, on to the home market. They set up large establishments whose competition ruined masses of *épiciers* and *boutiquiers* [grocers and small shopkeepers]. Hence the innumerable bankruptcies in this section of the Parisian bourgeoisie, hence their revolutionary début in February. It is well known how Guizot and the Chambers countered the reform proposals with an unambiguous challenge, how Louis Philippe decided too late on a ministry led by Barrot, how it came to hand-to-hand fighting between the people and the army, how the army was disarmed through the passive attitude of the National Guard and how the July monarchy had to make way for a provisional government.

The *provisional government* which rose from the February barricades necessarily reflected in its composition the various parties that shared in the victory. It could not be other than a *compromise between the different classes*, which together had overthrown the July monarchy but whose interests were mutually antagonistic. The *great majority* consisted of representatives of the bourgeoisie. The republican petty bourgeoisie was represented by Ledru-Rollin and Flocon, the republican bourgeoisie by the people from the *National*, the dynastic opposition by Crémieux, Dupont de l'Eure, etc. The working-class had only two representatives, Louis Blanc and Albert. Lastly, Lamartine in the provisional government actually represented no real interest, no specific class, but rather the February revolution itself, the common uprising with its illusions, its poetry, its visionary content and its catch-words. Yet this spokesman of the February revolution, both in his position and in his opinions, belonged to the *bourgeoisie*.

If Paris because of political centralization rules France, the workers, in moments of revolutionary turmoil, control Paris. The first act in the life of the provisional government was the attempt to escape from this overpowering influence through an appeal from intoxicated Paris to sober France. Lamartine disputed the right of the fighters on the barricades to declare a republic, on the grounds that only a majority of the French had that right; their vote must be waited for, the Paris proletariat must not besmirch its victory through usurpation. The bourgeoisie allows the proletariat only a *single* usurpation—that of fighting.

By midday on 25 February the republic had not yet been proclaimed; against this, all the ministries had already been shared out among the bourgeois elements of the provisional government and the generals, bankers and lawyers of the *National*. But the workers were determined this time not to put up with any such skulduggery as that of July 1830. They were prepared to renew the fight and to compel a republic by force of arms. With this message Raspail betook himself to the Hôtel de Ville. In the name of the Paris proletariat he *commanded* the provisional government to proclaim a republic; if this command from the people were not executed within two hours he would return at the head of 200,000 men. The corpses of the fallen were barely cold, the barricades not yet taken away, the workers not disarmed, and the only force with which to oppose them was the National Guard. In these circumstances the politic misgivings and legal scruples of the provisional government suddenly vanished. The time limit of two hours had not yet expired, when all the walls of Paris displayed the historic and tremendous words:

République française! Liberté, Egalité, Fraternité!

With the proclamation of the republic founded on universal suffrage, the very memory of the limited aims and motives which had driven the bourgeoisie into the February revolution was wiped out. Instead of just a few sections of the bourgeoisie, all classes of French society were suddenly flung into the political ring, forced to leave the boxes, the pit, the gallery and play their own parts upon the revolutionary stage! With the constitutional monarchy the illusion of a despotic state power confronting bourgeois society, and the whole series of subordinate struggles summoned up by this semblance of power, had also vanished!

The proletariat, by dictating the republic to the provisional government and through the provisional government to the whole of France, directly moved into the foreground as an independent party but at the same time challenged the whole of bourgeois France to enter the lists against it. What it won was the battlefield for its revolutionary emancipation but by no means this emancipation itself.

The February republic had primarily rather *to complete the rule of the bourgeoisie,* by allowing *all the property-owning classes* to enter the orbit of political power alongside the finance-aristocracy. The majority of the great landowners, the Legitimists, were released from the political non-existence to which the July monarchy had condemned them. Not in vain had the *Gazette de*

France agitated together with the opposition papers, not in vain had La Rochejaquelein supported the revolutionary cause at the 24 February session of the Chamber of Deputies. Through universal suffrage the nominal property-owners, who constitute the great majority of the French people, *the peasants*, had been made arbiters of the fate of France. The February revolution finally revealed plainly the authority of the bourgeoisie by striking down the crown behind which it had lain concealed.

Just as the workers in the July days had fought for and won the *bourgeois monarchy*, so in the February days they fought for and won the *bourgeois republic*. Just as the July monarchy was compelled to declare itself a *monarchy surrounded by republican institutions*, so the February republic was compelled to declare itself a *republic surrounded by social institutions*. The proletariat of Paris enforced this concession too.

Marche, a worker, dictated the decree in which the newly formed provisional government pledged itself to guarantee the workers a livelihood through work, to provide work for all citizens, etc. And when, a few days later, it forgot its promises and seemed to have lost sight of the proletariat, a mass of 20,000 workers marched on the Hôtel de Ville with the cry: *We want organized labour! We want our own Ministry of Labour!* Reluctantly and after long debate the provisional government nominated a permanent special commission charged with *discovering* means of improving the lot of the working-classes! This commission was made up of delegates from the Paris trade associations and was presided over by Louis Blanc and Albert. The Luxembourg Palace was appointed as its meeting place. Thus the representatives of the working-class were banished from the seat of the provisional government, whose bourgeois section kept exclusive control of the real power of government and the reins of administration; and *alongside* the Ministries of Finances of Trade, of Public Works, *alongside* the Bank and Stock Exchange there arose a *socialist synagogue* whose high priests, Louis Blanc and Albert, had the task of discovering the promised land, proclaiming the new gospel and occupying the Paris proletariat. As distinct from every secular state authority, they had no budget, no executive power at their disposal. They were expected to bring down the pillars of bourgeois society by hitting their heads against them. While in the Luxembourg Palace the philosophers' stone was being sought, currency for circulation was being minted in the Hôtel de Ville.

And yet, the claims of the Paris proletariat, in so far as they went beyond the bourgeois republic, could achieve no other existence than the nebulous one of the Luxembourg.

The workers had made common cause with the bourgeoisie in the February revolution and they tried to advance their interests at the side of the bourgeoisie just as they had installed a worker alongside the bourgeois majority in the provisional government itself. *We want organized labour!* But wage labour is the existing bourgeois organization of labour. Without it there would be no capital, no bourgeoisie, no bourgeois society. Our own *Ministry of Labour!* But are not the Ministries of Finance, of Trade, of Public Works, the *bourgeois* ministries of labour? Beside these a *proletarian* Ministry of Labour had to be a ministry of impotence, a ministry of pious wishes, a Luxembourg Commission. Just as the workers believed they would be able to emancipate themselves side by side with the bourgeoisie, so they thought they could accomplish a proletarian revolution within the national boundaries of France, side by side with the remaining bourgeois nations. But French production relations are conditional upon France's foreign trade, its position on the world market and the laws of the latter, how could France break them without a European revolutionary war which would backfire on the despot of world trade, England?

As soon as a class has arisen in which the revolutionary

interests of society are concentrated, it immediately finds in its own situation the content and material of its revolutionary activity: enemies to be overthrown, measures dictated by the needs of the struggle to be taken, the consequences of its own deeds drive it on. It undertakes no theoretical investigations into its own task. The French working-class had not attained this position; it was still incapable of accomplishing its own revolution.

Generally speaking, the development of the industrial proletariat is conditioned by the development of the industrial bourgeoisie. Under its rule it first achieves the wider national character which can raise its revolution to a national level; under its rule does it first itself create the modern means of production which then themselves become the means of its revolutionary liberation. Bourgeois rule first tears up the material roots of feudal society and levels the terrain on which alone a proletarian revolution is possible. French industry is more advanced, the French bourgeoisie more revolutionary than that of the rest of the continent. But was not the February revolution clearly directed at the finance-aristocracy? This fact proved that the industrial bourgeoisie did not rule France. The industrial bourgeoisie can only rule where modern industry shapes all property relations to suit itself, and industry can only attain this power when it has conquered the world market, for national boundaries are not enough for its development. French industry, however, itself largely controls the national market through a more or less modified system of prohibitive duties. If therefore the French proletariat, at the moment of a revolution in Paris, possesses an actual power and an influence which spur it on to an attack beyond its means, yet in the rest of France it is crowded together in isolated scattered industrial centres, rapidly disappearing under a superfluity of peasants and petty bourgeois. The struggle against capital in its developed modern form, at its salient point, the struggle of the industrial wage-labourer against the industrial bourgeois, is in France a partial phenomenon which, after the February days, was the less able to furnish the national content of the revolution, since the struggle against secondary capitalist methods of exploitation, the struggle of the peasant against usury and mortgages, of the petty bourgeois against the wholesaler, banker and manufacturer, in short against bankruptcy, was still hidden in the general revolt against the finance-aristocracy. Nothing is more understandable, then, than that the Parisian proletariat should seek to further its interests alongside those of the *bourgeoisie* instead of promoting them as the revolutionary interests of society as a whole, and should lower the *red* flag before the *tricolor*. The French workers could not advance one step, or disarrange the bourgeois order by a single hair until the course of the revolution had aroused the mass of the nation, peasants and petty bourgeois, standing between the proletariat and the bourgeoisie, not against this order but against the rule of capital, and had forced them to attach themselves to the proletarians as their champions. Only with the tremendous defeat of June could the workers purchase this victory.

To the Luxembourg Commission, this creature of the Paris working-class, goes the credit of having betrayed the secret of the nineteenth-century revolution from a European platform: *the emancipation of the proletariat*. The *Moniteur universel* [the official French government paper] blushed at having officially to propagate the 'wild ravings' which up till then had lain buried in the apocryphal writings of the socialists and had only occasionally assailed the ears of the bourgeoisie as distant tales, half-terrifying, half-ridiculous. Europe was startled out of its bourgeois half-sleep. Thus, in the thought of the proletariat, who confused the finance-aristocracy with the bourgeoisie as a whole, in the imagination of republican worthies, who denied the very existence of classes or at most conceded it as a consequence of constitutional monarchy; in the hypocritical phrases of those sections of the citizenry which had previously been excluded from power, the *rule of the bourgeoisie* had been dismissed with the introduction of the republic. At that time all royalties became republicans and all the millionaires of Paris became workers. The phrase which represented this imaginary abolition of class distinctions was *fraternité*, universal fraternization and brotherhood. This comfortable abstraction from class antagonisms, this sentimental smoothing over of contradictory class interests, this fanatical exaltation above the class struggle, this fraternité, was the real watchword of the February revolution. A mere *misunderstanding* had divided the classes, and Lamartine on 24 February christened the provisional government 'un gouvernement qui suspende *ce malentendu terrible qui existe entre les differentes classes*' ['a government which removes *this terrible misunderstanding existing between the different classes*']. The proletariat of Paris luxuriated in this generous intoxication of brotherhood.

The provisional government, once forced to proclaim the republic, for its part did all it could to make it acceptable to the bourgeoisie and the provinces. The bloody terror of the first French revolution was repudiated in the abolition of the death penalty for political crimes, the press was made free to all opinions, the army, the law courts and the administration remained, with few exceptions, in the hands of their former officials, none of the chief culprits of the July monarchy was brought to account. The bourgeois republicans of the *National* amused themselves by exchanging monarchist titles and costumes for old republican ones. To them the republic was simply a new party dress for the old bourgeois society. The young republic sought its chief merit not in frightening others but rather in constantly alarming itself, in securing its existence and disarming opposition by gentle compliance and a conciliatory attitude. To the privileged classes at home and the despotic powers abroad it was loudly proclaimed that the republic was of a peaceful nature. Its motto was Live and let live. In addition, shortly after the February revolution, Germans, Poles, Austrians, Hungarians, Italians, every nation according to its particular situation, revolted too. Russia and England, the latter itself disturbed and the other intimidated, were unprepared. The republic therefore had no *national* enemy to face. Consequently there were no great foreign complications to inflame energy, hasten the revolutionary process, drive the provisional government on or throw it overboard. The Paris proletariat, which saw the republic as its own creation, naturally acclaimed every act of the provisional government which made easier its establishment in bourgeois society. It readily allowed itself to be employed by Caussidière for police duty, to protect property in Paris, just as it allowed Louis Blanc to arbitrate in wage disputes between workmen and employers. It was a *point d'honneur* for it to preserve the bourgeois honour of the republic unspotted in the eyes of Europe.

The republic met with no resistance, either externally or internally. This disarmed it. Its task was no longer the revolutionary transformation of the world but only to adapt itself to the circumstances of bourgeois society. With what fanaticism the provisional government undertook this task is most tellingly evidenced in its financial measures.

Public credit and *private credit* were, naturally, greatly shaken. *Public credit* is based on the firm belief that the state will allow itself to be exploited by Jewish financiers. But the old state had disappeared and the revolution was principally directed against the finance-aristocracy. The fluctuations of the last European commercial crisis had not yet worked themselves out. Bankruptcy still followed bankruptcy.

Private credit was thus paralysed, circulation restricted, production at a standstill, before the February revolution broke out. The revolutionary crisis heightened the commercial one. And if private credit rests on the confident belief that bourgeois production, in the entire compass of its relationships, and bourgeois order are inviolate and inviolable, what must have been the effect of a revolution which called in question the foundations of bourgeois production, the economic slavery of the proletariat, which raised the Sphinx of the Luxembourg Commission in opposition to the stock exchange? The proletarian revolt is the abolition of bourgeois credit; for it is the abolition of bourgeois production and its system. Public and private credit are the economic thermometer by which the intensity of a revolution may be measured. *The ardour and generative power of the revolution increase in proportion to their fall.*

The provisional government wanted to strip the republic of its antibourgeois appearance. It had therefore first of all to secure the *exchange value* of this new form of state, its *quotation* on the stock market. Private credit necessarily went up with the stock-market rating of the republic.

In order to allay the least *suspicion* that it would or could not honour the obligations assumed by the monarchy and to foster belief in the bourgeois morality and solvency of the republic, the provisional government had recourse to boasting as worthless as it was childish. *Before* the legal date of payment it paid its creditors the interest on the five-, four-and-a-half-, and four-per-cent bonds. Bourgeois assurance and capitalist self-confidence suddenly awoke when they remarked the anxious haste with which it sought to buy their confidence.

The pecuniary embarrassment of the provisional government was naturally not lessened by a theatrical gesture which robbed it of its stock of ready cash. Its financial straits could no longer be concealed and *petty bourgeois*, *servants* and *workers* had to pay for the pleasant surprise prepared for the state's creditors.

It was announced that *savings bank accounts* for sums over one hundred francs could no longer be drawn in cash. The sums deposited in savings banks were confiscated and transformed by decree into a non-repayable state debt. This embittered the already oppressed *petty bourgeois* against the state. Since he received state debt certificates in place of his savings bank account books he was forced to sell them on the stock exchange and so deliver himself directly into the hands of those stockjobbers against whom he had fought the February revolution.

The *Bank* was the high church of the finance-aristocracy which held sway under the July monarchy. As the stock exchange controls state credit, so the bank controls commercial credit.

Directly threatened, not just in its authority but in its very existence, by the February revolution, the bank from the very beginning sought to discredit the republic by creating a general lack of credit. It suddenly stopped credit to bankers, manufacturers, and merchants. Since it did not immediately produce a counter-revolution this move necessarily rebounded on the bank itself. Capitalists withdrew the sums which they had deposited in the bank's vaults. The possessors of banknotes rushed to the till to exchange them for gold and silver.

The provisional government could, legally and without violent interference, have forced the bank into bankruptcy; it had only to remain passive and leave the bank to its fate. The *bankruptcy of the bank* was the deluge which would in an instant have swept from French soil the finance-aristocracy, the most powerful and dangerous enemy of the republic, the golden pedestal of the July monarchy. And, the bank once bankrupt, the bourgeoisie itself would have viewed the government's creation of a national bank and its handing over of national credit to the control of the nation as a last desperate rescue attempt.

The provisional government, on the contrary, fixed a compulsory exchange rate for the bank's notes. It did more. It converted all provincial banks into branches of the Banque de France and allowed the latter to cast its net over the whole of France. Later it pledged the *state forests* as security for a loan which it negotiated with the bank. In this way the February revolution directly strengthened and extended the bankocracy which it was meant to overthrow.

Meanwhile the provisional government was bent double under the mountainous burden of a growing deficit. In vain it begged for patriotic sacrifices. Only the workers tossed it alms. A heroic measure, the imposition of a *new tax*, had to be taken. But who was to be taxed? The stock-exchange sharks, the princes of the bank, state-creditors, *rentiers*, industrialists? That was no way to ingratiate the republic with the bourgeoisie. It would have meant, on the one hand, endangering state and commercial credit, while on the other attempting to buy them with such great sacrifices and humiliations. But someone had to fork out. So who was sacrificed to bourgeois credit? *Jacques le bonhomme*, the *peasant*.

The provisional government imposed a supplementary tax of 45 centimes in the franc on the four direct taxes. The government press tried to fool the Paris proletariat into believing that this tax would fall rather on the great landed proprietors, on the possessors of the many millions paid in compensation at the Restoration [of 1825]. But above all it really hit the *peasant class*, that is the great majority of the French people. *They had to pay the costs of the February revolution*, in them the counter-revolution chiefly gained substance. The 45 centimes tax was of vital concern to the French peasant and he made it of vital concern to the republic. Henceforth the *republic* meant for the French peasant the *45 centimes tax* and in the proletariat of Paris he recognized the spendthrift who was leading a comfortable life at his expense.

Whereas the revolution of 1789 began by shaking off the feudal burdens of the peasant, the revolution of 1848, in order not to endanger capital and to keep the machinery of government in operation, announced itself to the rural population by a new tax.

There was only *one* expedient whereby the provisional government could set aside all these troubles and wrench the state out of its old courses—by *declaring the state bankrupt*. It may be remembered how subsequently, in the National Assembly, Ledru-Rollin instanced the virtuous indignation with which he rejected this imputation by the stock-exchange Jew Fould, now French Minister of Finance. Fould had handed him the apple from the tree of knowledge.

By honouring the bills of exchange drawn on the state by the old bourgeois society it became forfeit to the latter. It became the hard-pressed debtor of bourgeois society instead of confronting it as a threatening creditor who had to collect the revolutionary debts of many years. It had to strengthen the shaky bourgeois relationships, in order to fulfil obligations which are only to be fulfilled within these relationships. Credit became a condition of life for it, and the concessions and promises made to the proletariat became so many *fetters* which *had* to be broken. The emancipation of the workers—even as a *phrase*—became an insupportable threat to the new republic, for it was an ever-present protest against the restoration of credit which rests on the uninterrupted and untroubled recognition of existing economic class relationships. Therefore it was necessary *to have done with the workers*.

The February revolution had expelled the army from Paris. The National Guard, that is the bourgeoisie in its various gradations, represented the only power. On its own, however, it felt itself no match for the proletariat. Moreover it was forced, though only after the most obstinate resistance and after raising a hundred different objections, gradually and bit by bit to open its ranks and admit to them armed proletarians. Only one way out remained: *to set one section of the proletariat against the other*.

For this purpose the provisional government formed twenty-four battalions of *Mobile Guards*, each a thousand strong, of young men between the ages of fifteen and twenty. They mostly belonged to the *Lumpenproletariat* which in all large towns forms a body clearly differentiated from the industrial proletariat, a recruiting-ground for thieves and criminals of all sorts, living on the refuse of society, people with no definite trade, vagrants, *gens sans feu et sans aveu* [people without hearth or home], varying according to the cultural level of the region to which they belong, never disowning their beggarly character, and, in the youthful age at which the provisional government recruited them, in every way impressionable, apt to perform the most heroic deeds, the most exalted sacrifices, as well as the meanest forms of brigandage and the filthiest corruption. The provisional government paid them 1 franc 50 centimes a day, that is it bought them. It gave them their own uniform, thereby distinguishing them outwardly from the workers' blouse. As leaders they were assigned in part officers from the regular army and in part young sons of the bourgeoisie, whom they themselves elected and whose rodomontades about death for the fatherland and devotion to the republic corrupted them.

Thus the Paris proletariat was confronted by an army of 24,000 young, strong, foolhardy men drawn from its own midst. It called out *Vivats* to the Mobile Guard on its marches through Paris. It recognized in its members its champions on the barricades. It viewed it as the *proletarian* guard in contrast to the bourgeois National Guard. Its error was pardonable.

As well as the Mobile Guard the government resolved to rally round itself an army of industrial workers. Marie, the Minister, enrolled hundreds and thousands of workers, who had been thrown on the streets by the crisis and the revolution, in so-called National Workshops. This pompous title concealed nothing more than the use of the workers for boring, monotonous, unproductive earthworks at a wage of 23 sous. *Open-air English workhouses*—that was all these national workshops were. The provisional government believed it had created in them a

second proletarian army against the workers themselves.
In this the bourgeoisie was wrong about the national
workshops, just as the workers were wrong about the Mobile Guard. It had created an *army ripe for mutiny.*

But one purpose had been achieved.

National workshops—that was the name of the popular
workshops which Louis Blanc proclaimed in the Luxembourg Palace. Marie's workshops, conceived in direct *opposition* to the Luxembourg, yet bearing the same title,
offered occasion for a comedy of errors worthy of a Spanish servants' farce. The provisional government itself sur-
reptitiously spread the rumour that these national
workshops were the invention of Louis Blanc, which
seemed the more credible as Louis Blanc, the prophet of
the national workshop, was a member of the provisional
government. And in the half naive, half intentional confusion of the Paris bourgeoisie, in the artificially sustained
opinion of France and of Europe, these *workhouses*[1] were
the first realization of socialism, which was pilloried along
with them.

Not in their content but in their title, the *national
workshops* were the embodiment of proletarian protest
against bourgeois industry, bourgeois credit and the bourgeois republic. On them therefore descended all the hatred
of the bourgeoisie. In them it had at the same time found
the point on which to direct attack, as soon as it was strong
enough to break openly with the illusions of February.
Simultaneously all *petty bourgeois* uneasiness and discontent was directed against these national workshops, the
universal target. With real fury they reckoned up the
sums which the proletarian drones were devouring while
their own situation grew more intolerable every day. A
state pension for the semblance of work—that's socialism!
they growled to themselves. The national workshops, the
speechifying of the Luxembourg Commission, the work-

---

1 In English in the original. [E.K.]

ers' marches through Paris—in all these they sought the causes of their misery. And no-one was more fanatically opposed to the alleged machinations of the communists than the petty bourgeois, hovering helplessly on the brink of bankruptcy.

Thus in the approaching affray between the bourgeoisie and the proletariat all the advantages, all key positions, all the middle strata of society were in the hands of the bourgeoisie, at the same time as the waves of the February revolution broke high over the whole continent and every post brought a new revolutionary bulletin, now from Italy, now from Germany, now from the remotest parts of southeastern Europe, sustaining the general frenzy of the people by bringing them continual evidence of a victory they had already forfeited.

On 17 March and 16 April occurred the first skirmishes in the great class struggle concealed under the wings of the bourgeois republic.

17 March revealed the ambiguous situation of the proletariat, rendering impossible any decisive action. Its demonstration was originally intended to force the provisional government back on to its revolutionary course, to achieve, circumstances permitting, the exclusion of its bourgeois members and to compel the postponement of the election dates for the National Assembly and the National Guard. But on 16 March the bourgeois representation in the National Guard staged a demonstration hostile to the provisional government. Shouting '*A bas Ledru-Rollin!*' it forced its way to the Hôtel de Ville. And on 17 March the people were forced to shout: 'Long live Ledru-Rollin! Long live the provisional government!' They were forced to side with the apparently endangered bourgeois republic *against* the bourgeoisie. They strengthened the provisional government instead of subjugating it. 17 March misfired in a melodramatic scene and, although the proletariat of Paris once more on that day displayed its colossal bulk, the bourgeoisie both within and outside the

provisional government were all the more determined to break it.

16 April was a *misunderstanding* contrived by the provisional government together with the bourgeoisie. Great numbers of workers had assembled on the Champ de Mars and in the Hippodrome to prepare for the elections to the general staff of the National Guard. Suddenly the rumour spread like lightning from one end of Paris to the other, that the workers had assembled with arms on the Champ de Mars under the leadership of Louis Blanc, Blanqui, Cabet and Raspail, intending to march from there to the Hôtel de Ville, to overthrow the provisional government and proclaim a communist régime. The general alarm was sounded—Ledru-Rollin, Marrast and Lamartine later disputed the honour of having initiated this—and in one hour 100,000 men were under arms, the Hôtel de Ville was occupied at all points by the National Guard, the cry 'Down with the Communists! Down with Louis Blanc, with Blanqui, with Raspail, with Cabet!' echoed throughout Paris and the provisional government was honoured by countless deputations, all prepared to save the fatherland and society. When the workers finally appeared in front of the Hôtel de Ville, to hand over to the provisional government a patriotic collection taken up on the Champ de Mars, they learnt to their amazement that bourgeois Paris, in a most carefully staged mock battle, had defeated their shadow. The terrible outrage of 16 April provided the excuse for recalling the army to Paris—the real purpose of the clumsily performed comedy—and for reactionary federalist demonstrations in the provinces.

On 4 May the National Assembly, the result of the direct general elections, met. Universal suffrage did not possess the magic power with which it had been credited by republicans of the old stamp. Throughout France, at least among the majority of Frenchmen, they discovered *citoyens* with the same interests, the same view, etc. This was what their *cult of the common people* was. Instead of the people they had *imagined* the elections discovered the *real* people, that is representatives of the various classes of which it is composed. We have seen why peasants and petty bourgeois had to vote under the direction of a pugnacious bourgeoisie and of great landowners rabid for restoration. But although universal suffrage was not the miracle-working magic wand for which republican worthies had taken it, it possessed the incomparably higher merit of setting free the class struggle, of allowing the various middle sections of bourgeois society rapidly to get over their illusions and disappointments, of tossing all sections of the exploiting classes at one throw to the pinnacle of state power and so stripping them of their deceitful mask, whereas the monarchy with its census only allowed certain sections of the bourgeoisie to compromise themselves, leaving the rest concealed in the wings and surrounded with the aura of a common opposition.

In the constituent National Assembly, which met on 4 May, the *bourgeoisie republicans*, the republicans of the *National*, had the upper hand. Even Legitimists and Orléanists at first only dared to show themselves under the bourgeois republican mask. Only in the name of the republic could the struggle against the proletariat be undertaken.

The republic, that is the republic recognized by the French nation, *dates from 4 May, not from 25 February*; it is not the republic forced upon the provisional government by the proletariat of Paris, not the republic with social institutions, not the vision which inspired the fighters on the barricades. The republic proclaimed by the National Assembly, the sole legitimate republic, is the republic which is no revolutionary weapon against the bourgeois system but rather its political reconstruction, the political reconsolidation of bourgeois society, in short *the bourgeois republic*. This declaration resounded from the platform of the National Assembly and was echoed by the entire bourgeois press, republican and anti-republican alike.

We have seen, too, that the February revolution was and could be nothing but a *bourgeois* republic, but that the provisional government, under direct pressure from the proletariat, was forced to declare it a *republic with social institutions;* that the Paris proletariat was as yet incapable, except in *conception*, in *imagination*, of going beyond a bourgeois republic and, when it really came to acting, it acted throughout in the interests of such a republic; that the promises made to the proletariat became an intolerable threat to the new republic so that all the energies of the provisional government were devoted to a continuing fight against the demands of the proletariat.

In the National Assembly all France sat in judgement on the Paris proletariat. The Assembly at once broke with the social illusions of the February revolution and openly proclaimed a *bourgeois republic*, nothing but a bourgeois republic. It immediately excluded from its appointed executive commission the representatives of the proletariat, Louis Blanc and Albert; it turned down the suggestion of a special Ministry of Labour, and enthusiastically applauded the declaration by Minister Trélat that 'It is now just a matter of *restoring labour to its former conditions.*'

But all this was not enough. The February republic had been fought for by the workers with passive support from the bourgeoisie. The proletarians rightly regarded themselves as the victors of February and made the arrogant demands of victors. They had to be vanquished in the streets, had to be shown that they were beaten as soon as they fought *against* and not *with* the bourgeoisie. Just as the February republic with its socialist concessions needed a battle by the proletariat united with the bourgeoisie against the monarchy, so a second battle was necessary to detach the republic from its socialist concessions, to establish the bourgeois republic officially as predominant. The bourgeoisie, weapons in hand, had to reject the demands of the proletariat. Not the triumph of February but the defeat of June was the true birthplace of the bourgeois republic.

The proletariat hastened the decision by forcing its way into the National Assembly on 15 May in a vain attempt to recover its revolutionary influence, but which merely delivered its energetic leaders to the gaolers of the bourgeoisie. *Il faut en finir!* This situation must end! With this cry the National Assembly voiced its resolve to force the proletariat to a decisive contest. The Executive Commission issued a series of provocative decrees, such as that prohibiting public assemblies, etc. From the platform of the Constituent National Assembly the workers were directly provoked, reviled and laughed to scorn. But, as we have seen, the national workshops were the real focus of attack. The Constituent Assembly peremptorily brought these to the notice of the Executive Commission, which was only waiting to hear its own plan proclaimed as an order of the National Assembly.

The Executive Commission began by making admission to the National Workshops more difficult, by converting the daily wage into piece rates, and by banishing workers not natives of Paris to the Sologne, ostensibly for the construction of earthworks. These earthworks were only a rhetorical euphemism for their expulsion, as the disappointed workers told their comrades on their return. Finally on 21 June a decree was published in the *Moniteur*, ordering the expulsion of all unmarried workers from the national workshops by force, or their enlistment in the army.

The workers had no choice; they had either to starve or to attack. They replied on 22 June with the frightful insurrection in which the first great battle took place between the two classes which divide modern society. It was a battle for the survival or annihilation of the *bourgeois* order. The veil disguising the republic was torn asunder.

It is well known how the workers, with unexampled

bravery and ingenuity, without leaders, without a common plan, without materials, and for the most part without weapons, for five days held in check the army, the Mobile Guard, the Paris National Guard and the National Guard which streamed in from the provinces. It is well known how the bourgeoisie revenged itself for the mortal terror it had suffered by unheard-of brutality and the massacre of over 3,000 prisoners.

The official representatives of French democracy were so greatly engrossed by republican ideology that the meaning of the June struggle only began to dawn on them several weeks later. They were virtually stupefied by the shot and smoke in which their dream-republic vanished away.

The immediate impression made on us by the news of the June defeat, the reader will allow us to describe in the words of the *Neue Rheinische Zeitung*:

The last official remnant of the February Revolution, the Executive Commission, has faded away like an insubstantial shadow before the gravity of events. Lamartine's fireworks have turned into the incendiary rockets of Cavaignac. *Fraternité*, the brotherhood of hostile classes, of which one exploits the other, this *fraternité* was proclaimed in February, inscribed in capital letters on the brow of Paris, on every prison, on every barracks—but its true, unadulterated, unvarnished expression is *civil war*, civil war in its most terrible form, the war between labour and capital. This brotherhood blazed in front of all the windows of Paris on the evening of 25 June, as bourgeois Paris was illuminated while proletarian Paris burnt, bled and groaned in its deaththroes. Brotherhood lasted only as long as there was fraternity of interests between bourgeoisie and proletariat. Pedants of the old revolutionary tradition of 1793, socialist systematists who went begging to the bourgeoisie for the people and who were allowed to preach long sermons and to compromise themselves as long as the proletarian lion had to be lulled to sleep, republicans who wanted all the old bourgeois order except for the crowned head, dynastic supporters in opposition for whom chance had substituted the fall of a dynasty in place of a change of ministers, legitimists who did not want to cast off their livery but only to alter its cut, all these were the allies with whom the people created their February.... The February Revolution was the *splendid* revolution, the revolution of common sympathies, because the antagonisms which blazed in it against the monarchy remained undeveloped, slumbering peacefully side by side, because the social struggle forming its background had only achieved a vaporous existence, an existence of phrases and words. The June Revolution is the *base* revolution, the repulsive revolution, because events have taken the place of words, because the republic laid bare the head of the monster itself by striking off the crown that shielded and concealed it. *Order!* was Guizot's battle-cry. *Order!* cried Sebastiani, Guizot's follower, when Warsaw became Russian. *Order!* cries Cavaignac, the brutal echo of the French National Assembly and the republican bourgeoisie. *Order!* thundered his grapeshot as it tore to pieces the body of the proletariat. None of the numerous French bourgeois revolutions since 1789 was an attack on *order*, since it preserved class rule, the slavery of the workers and *bourgeois* order, no matter how often the political form of this rule and this slavery changed. The June revolution violated this order. Alas for June! [*N.Rh.Z.*, 29 June, 1848.]

Alas for June! comes back the echo from Europe.

The Paris proletariat was *forced* into the June uprising by the bourgeoisie. It was doomed from the start. It was neither driven by its immediate avowed need to attempt the overthrow by force of the bourgeoisie, nor was it equal to this task. The *Moniteur* had to inform it officially that the time was past when the republic felt obliged to defer to its illusions, and only its defeat convinced it of the truth that the slightest improvement in its position remains a *utopia within* the bourgeois republic, a utopia that becomes criminal as soon as it hopes to become a reality. In place of the demands, extravagant in form but petty and even bourgeois in content, satisfaction of which it had hoped to wrest from the February republic, appeared the bold revolutionary battle cry: *Down with the bourgeoisie! Dictatorship of the working-class!*

The proletariat, by making its grave the birthplace of the *bourgeois* republic, at once forced the latter to appear in its true colors as the state whose confessed aim is the perpetuation of the rule of capital and the slavery of labour. Having constantly in view its battle-scarred, irreconcilable and invincible foe—invincible since its existence is a precondition of the bourgeoisie's own life, bourgeois rule, freed of all restraints, necessarily and directly turned into *bourgeois terrorism*. With the proletariat for the present removed from the stage and the bourgeois dictatorship officially recognized, the middle sections of bourgeois society, the petty bourgeoisie and the peasant class, had to attach themselves more and more to the proletariat as their position became more unbearable, their antagonism to the bourgeoisie more acute. As they had previously found the cause of their misfortune in the rise of the proletariat, they had now to find it in its defeat.

If the June insurrection throughout the continent increased the self-confidence of the bourgeoisie and openly allied it with the feudal monarchy against the people, who was the first victim of this alliance? The continental bourgeoisie itself. The defeat of June prevented it from consolidating its rule and from halting the people, half satisfied, half resentful, on the lowest step of the bourgeois revolution.

Lastly, the June defeat betrayed to the despotic powers of Europe the secret that France must at all costs preserve peace abroad in order to be able to wage civil war at home. Thus the peoples who had begun their struggle for national independence were abandoned to the superior might of Russia, Austria and Prussia, while simultaneously the fate of these national revolutions, robbed of their apparent autonomy, their independence of the great social upheaval, was subordinated to the fate of the proletarian revolution. Neither Hungarian, Pole, nor Italian shall be free as long as the worker remains a slave!

Finally, with the victories of the Holy Alliance, Europe has developed in such a way that every new proletarian rising in France will immediately precipitate a *world war*. The new French revolution will be forced at once to leave its home ground in order to conquer the *European battlefield* on which alone the social revolution of the nineteenth century can be achieved.

Thus the June defeat alone created all the conditions under which France can seize the *initiative* in the European revolution. Once dipped in the blood of the *June insurgents*, the tricolor has become the banner of European revolution—*the red banner!*

And our cry is: *The revolution is dead! Long live the revolution!*

MEW 7, 11–34.

1852

From **THE EIGHTEENTH BRUMAIRE¹
OF LOUIS BONAPARTE**

I

Hegel observes somewhere that all great incidents and in-dividuals of world history occur, as it were, twice.² He forgot to add: the first time as tragedy, the second as farce. Caussidière takes the place of Danton, Louis Blanc of Robespierre, the Montagne of 1848–1851 that of the Mon-tagne of 1793–1795, the nephew that of the uncle. And the same caricature appears in the circumstances in which the second edition of the eighteenth brumaire is issued!

Men make their own history, but not spontaneously, under conditions they have chosen for themselves; rather on terms immediately existing, given and handed down to them. The tradition of countless dead generations is an incubus to the mind of the living. At the very times when they seem to be engaged in revolutionizing themselves and their circumstances, in creating something previously

---

1. The 'foggy month' in the new calendar adopted by the French Revolutionaries—the period between 21 October and 20 November. Napoleon's *coup d'état*, overthrowing the Directory and making him First Consul, took place on 18 Brumaire (9 November 1799). Marx's title draws an ironic parallel between the coup of 2 December 1851 by Napoleon's nephew Louis Bonaparte, who became Napoleon III, and the original Napoleonic coup. [E.K.]
2. Generations of scholars have been unable to find this remark in Hegel, though in his *Lectures on the Philosophy of History* (pub-lished 1837) Hegel refers to seemingly accidental events—such as a *coup d'état*, the defeat of Napoleon, or the driving out of the Bour-bons—gaining respectability and acceptance through their being re-peated. Marx was probably echoing, inaccurately, a remark made by Engels in a letter to Marx of 3 December 1851, where Engels writes: 'It really seems as if old Hegel in his grave were acting as World Spirit and directing history, ordaining most conscientiously that it should all be unrolled twice over, once as a great tragedy and once as a wretched farce.' [E.K.]

non-existent, at just such epochs of revolutionary crisis they anxiously summon up the spirits of the past to their aid, borrowing from them names, rallying-cries, costumes, in order to stage the new world-historical drama in this time-honoured disguise and borrowed speech. Thus Luther masqueraded as the Apostle Paul; the revolution of 1789–1814 camouflaged itself alternately as Roman republic or Roman empire and the revolution of 1848 could think of nothing better than to parody sometimes 1789 and sometimes the revolutionary tradition of 1793–1795. Just so does the beginner, having learnt a new language, always re-translate it into his mother-tongue; he has not assimilated the spirit of the new language, nor learnt to manipulate it freely, until he uses it without reference to the old and forgets his native language in using the new one.

Study of this world-historical necromancy reveals an immediate and obvious distinction. Camille Desmoulins, Danton, Robespierre, St. Just and Napoleon, the heroes as well as the factions and the general mass of the old French revolution, accomplished, in Roman dress and with Roman phrases, the taste of their time, the release and establishment of modern *bourgeois* society. The first group smashed to pieces the groundwork of feudalism and mowed down the feudal heads which had flourished on it; the last-named created within France the conditions in which for the first time free competition could be developed, a property system based on small-holdings be made profitable, and the industrial productivity of the nation, set free, could be put to use, while beyond the French borders he everywhere swept away feudal institutions, as far as was necessary to create for French bourgeois society a correspondingly up-to-date environment on the continent of Europe. Once the new model of society had been established, the antediluvian giants disappeared and with them the resurrected Roman figures—the Brutuses, Gracchi, Publicolas, the tribunes and senators, and Caesar himself. Bourgeois society in its prosaic reality had produced its true interpreters and speechmakers in the Says, Cousins, Royer-Collards, Benjamin Constants and Guizots; its actual military leaders sat behind office desks and the blubberheaded Louis XVIII was its political figurehead. Wrapped up as it was in the production of wealth and in peaceful competitive contests, it no longer realized that spectres of ancient Rome had guarded its cradle. But however unheroic bourgeois society may be, it still required heroism, sacrifice, terror, civil war and the slaughter of nations to bring it about. In the classically severe traditions of republican Rome, its gladiators found the ideals and art-forms, the illusions which they needed, to conceal from themselves the limited bourgeois substance of their struggles and to maintain their passions at the height of great historical tragedy. Thus, at another stage of development a century earlier, Cromwell and the English nation had taken over from the Old Testament the speech, passions and illusions of their bourgeois revolution. When the real goal had been reached, when the bourgeois reorganization of English society was complete, then Locke drove out Habakkuk.

The raising of the dead in those revolutions, therefore, served to glorify the new struggles, not to parody the old; it fostered in imagination an aggrandizement of the set task, not flight from its actual solution, a rediscovery of the spirit of revolution rather than a summoning up of its ghost.

But from 1848 to 1851 the ghost only of the old revolution walked, from Marrast, the *républicain en gants jaunes* disguised as old Bailly, to the adventurer hiding his commonplace unpleasing features behind the iron death-mask of Napoleon. An entire nation, believing itself to have achieved through revolution a more rapid power of motion, suddenly finds itself set back into a dead era, and, to avoid any possible illusion about the relapse, the old dates rise up again, the old chronology, the old names, the old edicts, long since become subjects for antiquarian scholarship, and the old agents of the law, long believed rotten. The nation sees itself like that mad Englishman in Bedlam, who believes himself to be living in the days of the ancient Pharaohs and daily complains of the hard labour which is his lot as a gold-digger in the Ethiopian mines, walled-up in this subterranean prison, a feeble lamp fastened to his head, behind him the overseer with a long whip and at the exits a confused throng of barbarian soldiers, who understand neither the forced labourers in the mines nor each other, since they have no common language. 'And all this,' sighs the mad Englishman, 'is exacted from me, a freeborn Briton, to make gold for the old Pharaohs.' 'To pay the debts of the Bonapartes,' sighs the French nation. The Englishman, as long as he was sane, could not shake off a passion for making gold. The French, as long as they were making revolutions, could not rid themselves of memories of Napoleon, as the election of 10 December [1848] demonstrated. They wished themselves delivered from the perils of revolution and back among the fleshpots of Egypt, and 2 December 1852 was the answer. They have not only the caricature of the old Napoleon, they have the old Napoleon himself, inevitably looking like a caricature in the middle of the nineteenth century.

The social revolution of the nineteenth century cannot draw its poetry from the past but only from the future. It cannot make a start on itself until it has stripped away all superstitions concerning the past. Earlier revolutions needed the recollections of world-history to render them insensible of their own significance. The nineteenth-century revolution must let the dead bury their dead if it is to appreciate its own significance. Then the rhetoric transcended the substance; now the substance transcends the rhetoric.

The February revolution was a sudden attack, taking the old society *by surprise* and the nation proclaimed this unforeseen *stroke* as an act of universal significance, inaugurating a new epoch. On 2 December the February revolution is fraudulently done away with by a cardsharper's trick and what seems to have been overthrown is no longer the monarchy but the liberal concessions wrung from it through centuries of struggle. Instead of *society* having achieved a new substance for itself, it seems only that the *state* has returned to its earliest form, the shameless open rule of sabre and cowl. Thus the *coup de main* of February 1848 is answered by the *coup de tête* of December 1851. Lightly come, lightly go. Meanwhile the time between has not been uselessly spent. In the years from 1848 to 1851 French society has made up, and that by a method shorter because revolutionary, those studies and experiences which in a regular, as it were prescribed, development should have preceded the February revolution if it were to be more than a superficial disturbance. Society now seems to have retreated behind its starting-point; in fact, it has first to create for itself the revolutionary starting-point, the situation, circumstances and conditions in which alone modern revolution can become a serious matter.

Bourgeois revolutions, like those of the eighteenth century, sweep on rapidly from success to success, surpassing one another in dramatic effects; men and things seem set in sparkling diamonds, ecstasy is the spirit of every day; but they are shortlived, soon reaching their climax, and a long hangover afflicts society until it learns soberly to assimilate the results of its periods of storm and stress. Proletarian revolutions, on the other hand, like those of the nineteenth century, constantly criticize themselves, continually interrupt their own progress, return to what seemed completed in order to start all over again, make a terrible and total mock of the half-measures, weaknesses and meannesses of their first attempts; they seem to overthrow their opponent only that he may draw new powers from the earth and rise up against them more gigantic than before, they recoil repeatedly from the indeterminate enormity of their own aims, till a situation is created from which retreat is impossible, and circumstances themselves cry: *Hic Rhodus, hic salta!*[3] Here is the rose, dance here!

Moreover, any average observer, even if he had not followed French developments step by step, must have suspected that an unheard-of disgrace lay in store for the revolution. It was enough to hear the self-satisfied buzz of victory with which the democratic gentlemen mutually wished each other joy of the beneficial effects of the second [Sunday in][4] May 1852. To them the second [Sunday in] May 1852 had become an obsession, a dogma, just as the day of Christ's second coming and the start of the millennium had to the Chiliasts. Weakness had as usual taken refuge in a belief in miracles, believed the enemy conquered when he was only conjured away in imagination, and lost all understanding of the present in a theoretical glorification of the future which lay ahead, and the actions it had *in petto* [in reserve] but just did not want to discharge as yet. Those heroes, who seek to refute their manifest incompetence by commiserating with one another and combining together in a body, had packed up their traps, pocketed their laurel-wreaths in advance and were at that moment employed in having discounted on the stock exchange those republics *in partibus*, for which they had already, in the secret recesses of their unpretending nature, thoughtfully organized the government personnel. The 2 December fell on them like a lightning-stroke out of a clear sky and the nations that in periods of faintheartedness and ill-humour readily allow their inward fears to be drowned by the loudest shouters may

---

3. 'Here is Rhodes, jump here!' from a Latin version of one of Aesop's fables, in which this reply is gvien to a man who boasts that he had once made an immense leap in Rhodes. The reference to the rose is Hegel's variant, in the Preface to the *Philosophy of Right*, based on the fact that the Greek *rhodos* can mean both Rhodes and a rose. [E.K.]

4. The date set for electing the President of the Republic. [E.K.]

perhaps have convinced themselves that those times are
past when the cackle of geese could save the Capitol.

The constitution, National Assembly, dynastic parties,
the blue and the red republicans, the heroes of Africa [i.e.
Generals Cavaignac, Lamoricière, and Bedeau], the thunder of the rostrum, the sheet lightning of the daily papers,
the whole literary body, political names and intellectual
reputations, civil and criminal law, *liberté, egalité, fraternité,* and the second [Sunday in] May 1852—all have
vanished like a mirage before the exorcism of a man whom
even his enemies do not pass off as a master magician.
Universal suffrage seems to have survived only for an instant, that it might, with its own hand and in the sight of
the whole world, make its last will and in the name of the
people themselves declare: 'Everything that exists is worthy of destruction.'

It is not enough to say, as the French do, that their nation was taken by surprise. A nation and a woman are not
forgiven the unguarded hour in which the first adventurer
to come along can ravish them. The puzzle is not solved
by such turns of expression, merely stated differently. It
has still to be explained how a nation of thirty-six million
could be surprised by three swindlers and unresistingly
led captive.

Let us recapitulate in broad outline the stages through
which the French revolution passed from 24 February
1848 to December 1851.

Three main periods are clearly marked: *the February
period;* 4 May 1848 to 28 May 1849, *the period of the establishment of the republic* or of *the Constituent National
Assembly;* 28 May 1849 to 2 December 1851, *the period of
the constitutional republic,* or of *the Legislative National
Assembly.*

The *first period,* from 24 February or the downfall of
Louis Philippe to 4 May 1848, the meeting of the Constituent Assembly, the real *February period,* may be defined
as the prologue to the revolution. Its character was offi-

cially demonstrated as the government which it had improvised declared itself to be *provisional* and anything proposed, attempted or uttered during this time declared itself to be, like the government, only *provisional.* No one and nothing dared to claim the right of existence and effective action. All elements which had prepared for or determined upon the revolution—the dynastic opposition, the republican bourgeoisie, the democratic-republican petty bourgeoisie and the social-democratic proletariat—found a provisional place in the February *government.*

It could not be otherwise. The February days originally had in view an electoral reform whereby the circle of the politically privileged in the propertied class itself was to be enlarged and the exclusive control of the finance aristocracy overthrown. But when it came to the actual conflict, when the people manned the barricades, the National Guard maintained a passive attitude, the army offered no serious resistance and the monarchy ran away, then the republic seemed to be an understood thing. Each party interpreted it in its own way. The proletariat, having secured it by armed defiance, put its stamp upon it and proclaimed it a *social republic.* In this way the general substance of modern revolution was indicated, a substance which most strangely contradicted everything that, with the resources available, with the level of education achieved by the masses and in the existing circumstances and conditions, could be translated into practice. On the other hand the claims of the remaining participant groups in the February revolution were recognized by the lion's share which they were given in the government. At no time, therefore, do we find a more motley combination of high-flown phrases with actual uncertainty and awkwardness, of more enthusiastic striving for the new with more thorough domination by the old system, of more apparent harmony in society in general with a deeper estrangement of its elements. While the Paris proletariat was still intoxicated by the vision of the great prospects which had opened to it and indulged in earnest discussions of social problems, the old forces of society organized and collected themselves, reflected and found unexpected support in the mass of the nation, the peasants and petty bourgeois, who all together rushed on to the political stage when the barriers of the July monarchy had fallen.

The *second period*, from 4 May 1848 to the end of May 1849, is the period of the *constitution, the founding of the bourgeois republic*. Immediately after the February days not only had the dynastic opposition been surprised by the republicans and the republicans by the socialists, but the whole of France had been surprised by Paris. The National Assembly, which met on 4 May 1848, was the result of national elections and represented the nation. It was an active protest against the demands of the February days and was to reduce the results of the revolution to the bourgeois scale. The Paris proletariat, immediately realizing the character of this National Assembly, vainly sought on 15 May, a few days after it met, to deny its existence by force, to disband it, to break up into its constituent parts the organic structure whereby the reactionary spirit of the nation threatened it. As is well known, the 15 May had no other result than to remove Blanqui and his associates, that is the real leaders of the proletariat, from the public scene for the duration of the cycle under consideration.

The *bourgeois monarchy* of Louis Philippe can only be followed by a *bourgeois republic;* that is, where formerly a limited section of the bourgeoisie ruled in the name of the King, today the whole of the bourgeoisie will rule in the name of the people. The demands of the Paris proletariat are utopian shams and must be stopped. To this declaration by the Constituent National Assembly the Paris proletariat responded with the *June insurrection*, the most significant event in the history of European civil wars. The bourgeois republic triumphed. With it stood the finance aristocracy, the industrial bourgeoisie, the middle class, the petty bourgeoisie, the army, the *Lumpenproletariat* organized as a Mobile Guard, the intellectuals, clergy and the rural population. The Paris proletariat stood alone. Over three thousand insurgents were massacred after the victory, and fifteen thousand were transported without trial. With this defeat the proletariat moves into the *background* on the revolutionary stage. Each time the movement seems to acquire fresh impetus it tries to press forward anew, but with ever feebler powers and ever slighter result. As soon as revolutionary ferment affects any social stratum above its own, it allies itself with this and so shares all the defeats which the different parties in turn suffer. But these additional blows grow ever weaker, the more they are spread over the whole surface of society. The more important leaders of the proletariat in the Assembly and in the press one after another fall victim to the courts and ever more dubious figures take control. In part the party throws itself into *doctrinaire experiments, exchange banks and workers' associations, that is into a movement in which it renounces the revolutionizing of the old world by means of its own great combined resources and rather seeks to accomplish its salvation behind society's back, privately, within its restricted conditions of existence, thereby inevitably coming to grief.* It seems unable either to rediscover its own revolutionary greatness or to gain new energy through forming new alliances, until *all the classes* against which it fought in June themselves lie prostrate at its side. But at least it goes down with the honours of the great world-historic struggle; not only France but all Europe shudders at the June earthquake while the subsequent defeats of the upper classes are so cheaply purchased that the impudent exaggeration of the victors is needed to enable them to pass for events at all and they become the more shameful, the further the defeated party is removed from the proletariat.

The defeat of the June insurgents had now at any rate

prepared and levelled the ground on which the bourgeois republic could be founded and built up; but at the same time it had demonstrated that in Europe other matters than that of 'republic v. monarchy' are at stake. It had revealed that *bourgeois republic* here stands for the unchecked despotism of one class over others. It had demonstrated that in long-civilized countries, with a developed class-structure, with modern conditions of production and an intellectual consciousness which in the course of centuries has absorbed all traditional ideas, *the republic really* represents *only the political transformation of the bourgeois society* and not its *conservative manifestation*, as for example in the United States of America, where classes, though indeed already existing, have not yet become fixed but, in continual flux, perpetually change and interchange their elements; where modern means of production, rather than coinciding with a stagnant overpopulation, compensate for a relative lack of heads and hands; and where, finally, the feverish youthful activity of material production, in taking possession of a new world, has left neither time nor opportunity for doing away with the old intellectual world.

In the June days all classes and parties had united as the *party of order* against the proletariat, the *party of anarchy*, of socialism, of communism. They had 'rescued' society from '*the enemies of society*'. They had distributed the slogans of the old society, '*Property, family, religion, order,*' as passwords to their army and had proclaimed to the counterrevolutionary crusade: 'In this sign you will conquer!' From that moment on, as soon as one of the countless parties, which had marshalled themselves under this sign against the June insurgents, sought mastery of the revolutionary battlefield in its own class interest, it was defeated by the cry: 'Property, family, religion, order.' Society is saved just as often as the circle of its rulers contracts, as a more exclusive interest is asserted against a wider one. Every demand for the simplest bourgeois financial reform, for the most petty liberalism, the most formal republicanism, the most trivial democracy is simultaneously punished as an 'outrage against society' and branded as socialism. Lastly the high priests of 'religion and order' themselves are driven with kicks from their Pythian seats, hauled from their beds under cover of darkness, thrust into Black Marias, thrown into prison or sent into exile, their temple is razed to the ground, their mouths sealed, their pens broken, their law torn in pieces, in the name of religion, of property, of the family and of order. Bourgeois fanatics for order are shot down on their balconies by drunken soldiery, their family shrine desecrated, their houses shelled to pass the time—in the name of property, the family, religion and order. At the close, the scum of bourgeois society forms the *sacred guard of order* and the hero Crapulinski[5] takes possession of the Tuileries as the 'saviour of society.' . . .

V

As soon as the revolutionary crisis had been surmounted and universal suffrage abolished, battle broke out afresh between the National Assembly and Bonaparte.

The constitution had fixed Bonaparte's salary at 600,-000 francs. Barely six months after his installation he succeeded in doubling this sum, for Odilon Barrot had wrested from the Constituent National Assembly an annual supplement of 600,000 francs for so-called official expenses. After 13 June [1849] Bonaparte had hinted at similar requests, but this time Barrot turned a deaf ear. Now, after 31 May [1850] he was prompt to seize the favourable moment and make his ministers propose a civil list

---

5. I.e. Louis Napoleon, here ironically identified with the spend-thrift Jewish nobleman of Heinrich Heine's poem 'Two Knights,' whose name derives from the French *crapule* (scoundrel). [E.K.]

of three million to the National Assembly. His long career as vagabond and adventurer had endowed him with the most sensitive feelers, to sense the weak moments for squeezing money from his bourgeois supporters. He practised downright *chantage* [blackmail]. The National Assembly had, with his complicity and cognizance, violated the sovereignty of the people. He threatened to denounce its crime to the people's tribunal unless it opened its purse and bought his silence with three million a year. It had robbed three million Frenchmen of their right to vote; for every Frenchman thus called in he demanded a franc in current coin, exactly three million francs. He had been elected by six million yet demanded compensation for the votes of which he subsequently said he had been cheated. The Commission of the National Assembly dismissed this importunate individual; the Bonapartist press grew threatening. Could the National Assembly break with the President of the Republic just when it had broken, in principle and definitively, with the mass of the people? It did indeed disallow the annual civil list but agreed to a once-only supplement of 2,160,000 francs, thereby becoming guilty of the double weakness of granting the money while at the same time demonstrating by its vexation its reluctance to do so. We shall see later on how Bonaparte used the money. After this annoying epilogue, following hard upon the abolition of universal suffrage, in which Napoleon exchanged his humble attitude during the crisis of March and April for one of impudent defiance of the usurping parliament, the National Assembly adjourned for three months from 11 August to 11 November. In its place it left a Standing Commission of twenty-eight members, including some moderate Republicans but no Bonapartist supporter. The Standing Commission of 1849 had contained only members of the Party of Order and Bonapartists. But at that time the Party of Order declared itself in permanent opposition to the revolution; this time the parliamentary republic declared itself in permanent opposition to the President. After the law of 31 May only this rival still confronted the Party of Order.

When the National Assembly reconvened in November 1850 it appeared that, instead of their former petty skirmishes with the President, a great and ruthless struggle, a life-and-death battle between the two forces, had become unavoidable.

As in 1849, the Party of Order had, during this year's recess, split up into its separate political parties, each occupied with its own restoration intrigues, which had been given fresh support by the death of Louis Philippe. The Legitimist monarch, Henri V, had even appointed a formal ministry, resident in Paris, on which members of the Standing Commission sat. Bonaparte was therefore justified, on his side, in making tours around the French departments, blabbing about his own restoration plans and canvassing for votes, more or less openly or covertly according to the mood of the town he was making happy with his presence. On these progresses, which the great official *Moniteur* and Bonaparte's little private newssheets naturally acclaimed as triumphal tours, he was continually escorted by members of the *Society of 10 December*. This Society dated from the year 1849. Under the pretext of founding a benevolent society, the Paris *Lumpenproletariat* had been organized into secret sections, each led by Bonapartist agents and at the head of the whole a Bonapartist general. Besides ruined *roués* of questionable means of subsistence and dubious origins, besides decayed adventurers, scions of the bourgeoisie, there were tramps, discharged soldiers, discharged convicts, fugitive galley slaves, sharpers, charlatans, *lazzaroni*, pickpockets, conjurors, gamblers, *maquereaux*, brothel-keepers, porters, literary drudges, organ-grinders, rag-pickers, knife-grinders, tinkers, beggars, in short the whole haphazard, dissolute, battered mass which the French call *la bohème*; of these kindred elements Bonaparte formed the main body of the Society of 10 December. A 'benevolent association'—to the extent that all members, like Bonaparte himself, felt the necessity of benefitting themselves at the expense of the nation's workers. This Bonaparte, who constitutes himself *leader of the Lumpenproletariat*, who only here can find again in the mass those interests which he personally pursues, who recognizes in this flotsam, refuse, dross of all classes the sole class on which he can unconditionally depend, this is the true Bonaparte, the Bonaparte *sans phrase*. An old and artful *roué*, he sees the historical life of nations and their grand historical events as comedy of the most vulgar sort, as a masquerade in which the splendid costumes, speeches and attitudes simply conceal the meanest chicanery. Thus on his progress to Strasbourg a trained Swiss vulture represented the Napoleonic eagle. For his descent upon Boulogne he put some London lackeys into French uniforms, to represent the army. In his Society of 10 December he gathered together 10,000 scoundrels to represent the people, as Snug the joiner represented the lion [in Shakespeare's *A Midsummer Night's Dream*]. At a moment when the bourgeoisie was acting the most perfect comedy, but in the most serious way in the world, without violating any of the pedantic conventions of French dramatic etiquette, and itself half taken in by, half convinced of the solemnity of its own grand historical actions, the adventurer who took the comedy as downright comedy was bound to win. Not until he has got rid of his pompous opponent, and first takes his imperial role seriously, thinking that with the Napoleonic mask he can act the real Napoleon, does he fall victim to his own world-view, the serious buffoon who no longer sees world history as a comedy but takes his comedy for world history. What the National Workshops were for the socialist workers and the Mobile Guard for the bourgeois republicans, the Society of 10 December was for Bonaparte, his personal party force. On his journeys sections of the Society, packed into the train, had to improvise an audience for him, display public enthusiasm, yell *Vive l'Empereur*, insult and soundly thrash the republicans, all with police protection, of course. On his return-trips to Paris they had to act as advance guard, forestalling or breaking up counter-demonstrations. The Society of 10 December belonged to him, it was *his* creation, his very own idea. Whatever else he appropriated fell to him by force of circumstance, whatever else he did circumstances did for him or he contented himself with copying the deeds of others; but it is Bonaparte himself as original author who appears in public to the citizens with official utterances on order, religion, the family and property, while at his back is the secret society of Schufterles and Spiegelbergs [thieves and murderers, from Schiller's play *The Robbers*], the society of lawlessness, prostitution and theft, and the history of the Society of 10 December is his own history. . . .

VI

. . . On 18 November an amendment to the law on municipal elections introduced by the Party of Order was moved, that one year's residence instead of three should be sufficient for the municipal vote. The amendment was defeated by a single vote, but this at once proved to be a mistake. The Party of Order, by splitting up into its hostile political factions, had long since lost its independent parliamentary majority. It now demonstrated that no majority whatever any longer existed in Parliament. The National Assembly had become incompetent to pass resolutions. Its atomized components were no longer held together by any cohesive power, it had exhausted its last breath, it was dead.

Finally, a few days before the catastrophe, the extra-parliamentary mass of the bourgeoisie was once again solemnly to declare its break with the parliamentary bourgeoisie. Thiers, who as parliamentary hero was suffering more than most from the incurable disease of parliamentary cretinism, had, after the death of the Parliament, hatched a new parliamentary plot with the Council of State, a law of responsibility which was meant to hold the President fast within the limits of the Constitution. As Bonaparte, when laying the foundation stone of the new market in Paris on 15 September, had bewitched the *dames des halles*, the fishwives, like a second Masaniello—and, indeed, in true power one fishwife outweighed seventeen feudal lords; as, after the introduction of the Quaestors bill, he filled with enthusiasm the lieutenants being entertained in the Elysée, so now on 25 November he swept along with him the industrial bourgeoisie assembled in the Circus to receive from his hands prize medals for the Great Exhibition of London. I give the relevant part of his speech, taken from the *Journal des Débats:*

> With such unhoped-for results, I am justified in repeating how great the French republic would be, were it allowed to pursue its true interests, to reform its institutions, instead of being constantly disturbed, on one hand by the demagogues and on the other by monarchist delusions. (*Loud and repeated storms of applause from all parts of the auditorium.*) The monarchist delusions hinder all progress and all significant branches of industry. Instead of progress we have only struggles. One sees men, formerly the most eager supporters of royal authority and prerogatives, become members of a convention, merely to weaken the authority deriving from universal suffrage. (*Loud and repeated applause.*) We see men, who have suffered most from the revolution and have deplored it most strongly, provoke a new one, solely to fetter the will of the people. . . . I promise you peace for the future etc., etc. (*Enthusiastic shouts of bravo.*)

Thus the industrial bourgeoisie servilely acclaimed the *coup d'état* of 2 December, the abrogation of parliament, the defeat of their own rule and the dictatorship of Bonaparte. The thunder of applause on 25 November was answered by the thunder of cannon on 4 December, and the house of M. Sallandrouze, who had applauded most loudly, was bombarded most heavily.

Cromwell, when he dissolved the Long Parliament, went alone into its midst, drew out his watch to ensure that it should exist not a minute longer than he had decreed, and chased out each individual member with good-natured and humorous abuse. Napoleon, smaller than his model, at least went to the Legislative Assembly on the 18 Brumaire and read out to it, though in a somewhat choked voice, its death-sentence. The second Bonaparte, who in any case found himself possessed of executive powers very different from those of Cromwell or Napoleon, did not seek a model in the annals of world history, but rather in the annals of the Society of 10 December, in the annals of the criminal jurisdiction. He robbed the Bank of France of 25 million francs, bought General Magnan with one million, the soldiers with fifteen francs and a dram apiece; stealthily got together with his accomplices, like a thief in the night, ordered the houses of the most dangerous parliamentary learders to be broken into and had Cavaignac, Lamoricière, Le Flô, Changarnier, Charras, Thiers, Baze, etc., dragged from their beds, had the main squares of Paris and the parliament buildings occupied by troops, and early in the morning had ostentatious posters put up on all the walls, announcing the dissolution of the National Assembly and the Council of State, the reintroduction of universal suffrage and the placing of the Seine department in a state of siege. Shortly afterwards he inserted a false announcement in the *Moniteur*, according to which influential parliamentary names had formed themselves into a Council of State around him.

The rump Parliament, which had gathered in the municipal offices of the tenth arrondissement and which consisted principally of Legitimists and Orléanists, resolved, to repeated cries of 'Long live the Republic,' on the deposition of Bonaparte, vainly harangued the gaping masses outside the building and was finally dragged off by an escort of African riflemen first to the d'Orsay barracks and later, packed into Black Marias, to the prisons of Mazas, Ham and Vincennes. Thus ended the Party of Order, the Legislative Assembly and the February Revolution. Before we hurry to our conclusion here is a brief table of its history:

I. *First period.* From 24 February to 4 May 1848. February period. Prologue. Universal brotherhood swindle.

II. *Second period.* Period of formation of the Republic and the Constituent National Assembly.

   1. 4 May to 25 June 1848. Struggle of other classes combined against the proletariat; defeat of the latter in the June Days.

   2. 25 June to 10 December 1848. Dictatorship of the pure bourgeois republicans. Drafting of the Constitution. Proclamation of martial law in Paris. The bourgeois dictatorship replaced on 10 December by the election of Bonaparte as President.

   3. 20 December 1848 to 28 May 1849. Struggle of the Constituent Assembly with Bonaparte and his allies, the Party of Order; defeat of the former and fall of the republican bourgeoisie.

III. *Third period.* Period of the *constitutional Republic* and the *Legislative National Assembly.*

   1. 28 May to 13 June 1849. Struggle of the petty bourgeoisie against the bourgeoisie and Bonaparte. Defeat of petty-bourgeois democracy.

   2. 13 June 1849 to 31 May 1850. Parliamentary dictatorship of the Party of Order, which secures its control by abolition of universal suffrage, but loses the parliamentary ministry.

   3. 31 May 1850 to 2 December 1851. Struggle between the parliamentary bourgeoisie and Bonaparte.

      a) 31 May 1850 to 12 January 1851. Parliament loses supreme command of the army.

b) 12 January to 11 April 1851. It is defeated in its attempts to regain control of the administrative authority. The Party of Order loses its independent parliamentary majority and forms a coalition with the Republicans and the Montagne.

c) 11 April to 9 October 1851. Attempts at revision, fusion, prorogation. The Party of Order breaks up into its separate parts. The break of the bourgeois parliament and press with the bourgeois masses is consolidated.

d) 9 October to 2 December 1851. Open breach between Parliament and the executive authority. The former makes its last testament and succumbs, deserted alike by its own class, by the army and by all other classes. Downfall of the parliamentary regime and of bourgeois rule. Victory of Bonaparte. Parody of imperalist restoration.

VII

The *social republic* appeared as a phrase, a prophecy, on the threshold of the February revolution. In the June Days of 1848 it was choked by the blood of the Paris proletariat, but it wanders like a ghost through the subsequent acts of the drama. The *democratic republic* announced its arrival. On 13 June 1849 it collapsed, together with its *petty bourgeois* deserters, but as it fled scattered doubly boastful claims in its wake. The *parliamentary republic* with the bourgeoisie then took over the whole stage, and enjoyed its life to the full but on 2 December 1851 it was buried to the terrified cries of 'Long live the republic!' from the royalist coalition.

The French bourgeoisie, recoiling from the rule of the working proletariat, has brought the *Lumpenproletariat* to power, led by the head of the Society of 10 December. The bourgeoisie kept France in a state of panic by anticipating the terrors of red anarchy; Bonaparte rescued it from this fate when, on 4 December, he allowed the Army of Order, in drunken enthusiasm, to shoot down from their windows the polite citizens of the Boulevard Montmartre and the Boulevard des Italiens. It made a god of the sword; the sword is its master. It destroyed the revolutionary press; its own press is wiped out. It placed public assemblies under police supervision; its private gatherings are supervised by the police. It disbanded the democratic National Guard; its own National Guard is now disbanded. It proclaimed a state of siege; martial law now threatens it. It supplanted the juries with military commissions; its juries are replaced by military commissions. It handed over popular education to the priests; the priests impose their own education upon it. It transported without trial; now it is being transported without trial. It used the power of the state to suppress every movement of society; every impulse of its society is now crushed by the power of the state. It rebelled against its own politicians and intellectuals out of enthusiasm for its moneybags; its politicians and intellectuals have been done away with but its moneybags are robbed, its mouth gagged and its pen broken. The bourgeoisie tirelessly exhorted the revolution, in the words of St. Arsenius to the Christians: '*Fuge, tace, quiesce!* Flee, be silent, keep still!' Bonaparte urges the bourgeoisie to '*Fuge, tace, quiesce!* Flee, be silent, keep still!'

The French bourgeoisie had long since solved Napoleon's dilemma: '*Dans cinquante ans l'Europe sera républicaine ou cosaque*' [in fifty years Europe will be either republican or Cossack]. It had found the solution in the '*république cosaque*' [Cossack republic]. No Circe has by evil spells transformed that artistic creation, the bourgeois republic, into a monstrosity. That republic has lost nothing but its appearance of respectability. Present-day France existed complete within the parliamentary republic. Only a bayonet-thrust was needed to burst the bubble and reveal the atrocity within.

Why did the proletariat of Paris not revolt after 2 December?

The fall of the bourgeoisie had then only been decreed but the decree had not been carried out. Any serious revolt by the proletariat would immediately have reanimated the bourgeoisie, reconciled it with the army and ensured for the workers a second June defeat.

On 4 December the proletariat was goaded on to fight by bourgeois and *épicier* [tradesman]. On the evening of the same day several legions of the National Guard promised to appear, armed and accoutred, at the scene of battle. For both bourgeois and tradesman had discovered that Bonaparte, in one of his decrees of 2 December, had abolished the secret vote and required them to record their 'Yes' or 'No' after their names in the official registers. The opposition of 4 December alarmed Bonaparte. During the night he had posters stuck on all street corners in Paris, announcing the restoration of the secret vote. Bourgeois and tradesman believed they had achieved their aim. It was the tradesman and bourgeois who did not show up the next day.

The proletariat of Paris was robbed by Bonaparte of its leaders, the barricade commanders, in a sudden attack on the night of 1–2 December. As an army without officers, and disinclined by reason of the memories of June 1848 and 1849 and of May 1850 to fight under the Montagnard banner, it left it to its vanguard, the secret societies, to rescue the insurrectionist honour of Paris, which the bourgeoisie so feebly surrendered to the soldiery that Bonaparte was later able to disarm the National Guard with the sneering excuse that he feared its weapons might be misused against it by the anarchists!

'*C'est le triomphe complet et définitif du socialisme*' [It is the complete and definitive triumph of socialism] was how Guizot described the 2 December. But if the downfall of the parliamentary republic does contain within itself the germs of the triumph of the proletarian revolution, its immediate tangible result was *the victory of Bonaparte over Parliament, of the executive over the legislature, of wordless power over the power of empty talk.* In Parliament the general will was elevated to law by the nation, that is, it adopted the law of the ruling class as its general will. It abdicated every will of its own in face of the executive and submitted itself to the despotic commands of an alien will, to authority. The contrast between executive and legislature expresses the contrast between the heteronomy and the autonomy of a nation. France thus seems to have escaped from the despotic rule of a class only to fall victim to the despotism of an individual, indeed to the authority of an individual without authority. The struggle seems to have been settled in such a way that all classes, equally powerless and speechless, bend the knee before the rifle-butt.

But the revolution is radical. It is still making its way through purgatory. It carries out its business methodically. Up to 2 December 1851 it had completed half of its preparations and it is now completing the other half. It began by perfecting parliamentary authority in order to be able to overthrow it. Now that this has been achieved, it is perfecting executive power, reducing it to its purest expression, isolating it, making it an exclusive object of study, in order to concentrate against it all its destructive powers. And when it has completed this second part of its preparatory work, Europe will leap up from its seat and cry in triumph: Well burrowed, old mole!

This executive authority with its monstrous bureaucratic and military organization, its vast and ingenious machinery of state, an army of officials numbering half a million beside a military force of a further half million, this horrible parasitic growth which wraps itself round the body of French society like a caul, stopping up all its pores, this arose in the era of absolute monarchy with the decline of the feudal system, which it helped to accelerate. The seignorial privileges of landowners and towns were metamorphosed into as many attributes of state authority, feudal dignitaries became paid officials, and the many-coloured pattern of conflicting medieval plenary authorities changed to the regulated plan of a state authority whose functions are shared out and centralized as in industry. The first French revolution, whose task it was to break up all local, territorial, civic and provincial special powers in order to form the nation into a civil unity, had to develop further the process of centralization begun by the absolute monarchy but, together with this, the extent, attributes and subordinate staff of government authority. Napoleon completed this machinery of state. The Legitimist and July monarchies added only a greater division of labour, increasing proportionately as division of labour within bourgeois society created new interest groups and therefore new material for the state administration. Every *common* interest was immediately detached from society, set over against it as a higher *general* interest, wrested from the spontaneous involvement of individual members of society and made the subject of government action, whether it was a bridge, a schoolhouse, the communal property of a village community, or the railways, the national estate or the national university of France. The parliamentary republic, in its struggle against the revolution, was finally forced to strengthen the resources and centralization of government authority by means of repressive measures. All upheavals only improved this machine instead of breaking it. The parties, competing in turn for mastery, regarded the possession of this monstrous edifice of state as the principal spoil of the victor.

But under the absolute monarchy, during the first revolution and under Napoleon, the bureaucracy was only a means of preparing for the class-rule of the bourgeoisie. Under the Restoration, Louis Philippe and the parliamentary republic it became the instrument of the ruling class, strive as it might for independent power.

Only under the second Bonaparte does the state seem to

have become completely autonomous. The state machine has established itself so securely, as against bourgeois society, that it needs as leader only the head of the Society of 10 December, a fortune-hunter from foreign parts, chosen as leader by a drunken soldiery bought with drams and sausages, whom he must ever and again bribe with more sausage. Thence derive the dejection and despair, the feeling of frightful humiliation and degradation which oppresses the French breast and robs it of breath. France feels itself dishonoured.

Nevertheless, the authority of the state is not suspended in mid-air. Bonaparte represents a class, indeed the most numerous class in French society, the peasant smallholders.

As the Bourbons were the dynasty of great landed estates and the Orléans the dynasty of money, so the Bonapartes are the dynasty of the peasants, that is, of the mass of the French people. Not the Bonaparte who subjected himself to the bourgeois parliament, but the Bonaparte who broke up the bourgeois parliament, is the chosen leader of the peasants. For three years the towns had succeeded in falsifying the significance of the election of 10 December and cheating the peasants of the restoration of the empire. The election of 10 December 1848 was not completed until the *coup d'état* of 2 December 1851.

The peasant smallholders form an immense body, whose members live in identical situations but without making many contacts with each other. Their mode of production isolates them from one another instead of bringing them into closer connection. The isolation is increased by the poor French systems of communication and the poverty of the peasants. Their sphere of production, the smallholding, allows of no division of labour in its cultivation, no application of science and therefore no diversity of development, no variation of talent, no abundance of social relationships. Every individual peasant family is more or less self-sufficient, directly producing the greater part of what it consumes and winning its bread more by exchange with nature than by intercourse with society. The smallholding, the peasant and his family; next to it another smallholding, another peasant and another family. A number of these make a village and a number of villages a department. In this way the greater part of the French nation is formed by the simple addition of units of corresponding size, much as many potatoes in a sack make up a sack of potatoes. In so far as millions of families live under economic conditions which divide their way of life, their interests and their cultural level from those of other classes and foster hostility towards them, they form a single class. In so far as a purely local connection only exists among the smallholders and the identity of their interests fosters no community spirit, no national association and no political organization among them, they do not form a class. Thus they are incapable of asserting their class interests in their own name, whether in Parliament or in a convention. They cannot represent themselves and must be represented. Their representative must appear to them both as their lord and master and as a ruling being of unlimited power who protects them from the other classes and sends down rain and sunshine from above. The political influence of the smallholders is therefore finally expressed in the subordination of society to the executive authority.

Historical tradition gave rise to the French peasant's miracle-working faith that a man named Napoleon would restore all their former grandeur. And an individual did turn up, who pretends to be this man because he too bears the name Napoleon, according to the *Code Napoléon* which lays down that '*la recherche de la paternité est interdite*' [inquiry into paternity is forbidden]. After twenty years of vagrant life and a series of grotesque adventures the saying is fulfilled and the man becomes Emperor of the French. The nephew's obsession came to pass because it coincided with the obsession of the most numerous class among the French people.

But, it may be objected, what about the peasant risings in half of France, the army's battles against the peasants, their wholesale imprisonment and transportation?

Since the days of Louis XIV France has known no such persecution of the peasants 'for demagogic agitation.'

Let it be clearly understood, however. The Bonaparte dynasty represents not the revolutionary but the conservative peasant, not the peasant who wants to force his way out of his social sphere of existence, the smallholding, but one who rather wishes to consolidate it; it represents not the country people who by their own efforts and in conjunction with the towns hope to overthrow the old order, but on the contrary those who, apathetically imprisoned in this old order, hope to see themselves together with their smallholdings rescued and raised to honour by the ghost of Empire. It represents not the enlightenment of the peasant but his superstition, not his judgement but his prejudice, not his future but his past, not a present-day Cévennes but rather another Vendée.[6]

Three years of oppressive rule by the parliamentary republic had freed a part of the French peasantry from Napoleonic illusion and had revolutionized them, however superficially; but they were forcibly driven back by the bourgeoisie whenever they began to act. Under the parliamentary republic the modern consciousness of the French peasant fought with the traditional. The process developed as a ceaseless struggle between schoolmasters and priests. The bourgeoisie struck down the schoolmasters. The peasants for the first time made strenuous efforts to retain their independence in face of the government's ac-

---

6. The Cévennes were the scene of an anti-feudal peasant rising in the early eighteenth century; the Vendée was the centre of a counter-revolutionary rising in 1793. [E.K.]

tions. This was apparent in the continued conflict between mayors and prefects. The bourgeoisie dismissed the mayors. Finally in the time of the parliamentary republic the peasants in various districts rose up against their own offspring, the army. The bourgeoisie punished them with states of siege and executions. And the same bourgeoisie now cries out against the stupidity of the masses, the 'vile multitude,' which has betrayed it to Bonaparte. It had itself forcibly strengthened the imperialism of the peasantry, and maintained the conditions which bred this peasant religion. The bourgeoisie must in any case fear the stupidity of the masses as long as they remain conservative, and the judgement of the masses as soon as they become revolutionary.

In the risings after the *coup d'état* part of the French peasantry protested, weapons in hand, against its own vote of 10 December 1848. The schooling they had undergone since 1848 had sharpened their wits. They had, however, enrolled themselves in the nether world of history and history held them to their word, while the majority was still so deluded that in the reddest departments the peasant population openly voted for Bonaparte. The National Assembly thought it had impeded his actions. He had now simply broken the bonds which the towns had placed upon the will of the country. They even, in places, entertained the grotesque notion that it was possible for a Napoleon and a convention to co-exist.

After the first revolution had changed the peasants from semi-bondmen into free landed proprietors, Napoleon established and regulated the conditions under which they might exploit undisturbed the soil of France, their newly acquired prize, and satisfy their youthful enjoyment of possession. But what is now ruining the French peasant is this same smallholding, the division of land and form of tenure established in France by Napoleon. It is these material conditions, after all, which made of the French feudal peasant a smallholder and of Napoleon an emperor.

Two generations have sufficed to produce the inevitable result: a progressive deterioration of agriculture and an ever increasing load of debt for the husbandman. The 'Napoleonic' form of tenure, which in the early nineteenth century was a condition for the liberation and enrichment of the French country folk has developed in the course of this century as the legal source of their slavery and their poverty. And just this law is the first of the *'idées napoléoniennes'* which the second Bonaparte has to maintain. Even if he shares the peasants' illusion that not in the smallholdings themselves but rather externally, in the influence of secondary circumstances, are to be sought the causes of their downfall, his experiments will collapse like soap bubbles on contact with the relationships of production.

The economic development of the smallholding has totally altered the relationship of the peasants to the other classes of society. Under Napoleon the division of all land in the rural districts supplemented free competition and the beginning of big industry in the towns. The peasant class was the ever-present protest against the recently overthrown landed aristocracy. The roots which smallholding struck in French soil deprived feudalism of all sustenance. Its boundary fences formed a natural fortification for the bourgeoisie against every attack by their former overlords. But in the course of the nineteenth century the urban moneylender replaced the feudal lord, the mortgage replaced the feudal obligations attaching to land, and bourgeois capital replaced aristocratic ownership of land. The peasant's smallholding is simply an excuse, allowing the capitalist to draw profit, interest and rents from the soil while leaving it to the husbandman himself to discover how to extract from it a wage for his labour. The mortgage debt burdening the soil of France lays upon the French peasantry a tax as great as the annual interest on the whole of the British national debt. In this capitalist state of slavery, to which its development inescapably leads, the smallholding system has turned the greater part of the French nation into troglodytes. Sixteen million peasants, including women and children, live in caves, of which most have only one opening, others only two and the most fortunate only three. Windows are to a house what the five senses are to the head. The bourgeois system, which at the beginning of the century placed the state as sentinel before the newly-created smallholding and manured the latter with laurels, has become a vampire sucking out its blood and brains and throwing them into the alchemist's cauldron of capital. The *Code Napoléon* is now no more than a register of conveyances, sheriffs and bankruptcy sales. To the four million (including children, etc.) official paupers, vagrants, criminals and prostitutes whom France can number must be added another five million who are tottering on the brink of life's abyss and either subsist on the land itself or wander continually, with their rags and their children, from the country to the town or from the towns to the country. The interests of the peasants no longer, as under Napoleon, accord with those of the bourgeoisie but are opposed to them and to capital. They therefore find their natural allies and leaders among the *proletariat of the towns*, whose task it is to overthrow the bourgeois order. But the *strong* and *unrestrained government*—and this is the second '*idée napoléonienne*' to be carried out by Bonaparte—has been summoned to the defence by force of this 'material' order. This '*ordre matériel*' also supplies the catchword in all Bonaparte's proclamations against rebellious peasants.

As well as the mortgage with which capital burdens it, the smallholding is weighed down by taxes. Taxation is the source of life for the bureaucracy, the army, the clergy and the court, in short for the whole executive machinery. Strong government and heavy taxes are the same thing. The smallholding system is by its nature designed as the foundation of an all-powerful and multitudinous bureaucracy. It creates a similar level of living conditions and population over the whole surface of the country. Thus it also permits of an equal influence, from one supreme centre, upon all points of this uniform mass. It destroys the aristocratic intermediate stages between the mass of the people and the authority of the state. From all sides, that is, it calls forth direct action by the state power and the introduction of its agents without intermediaries. In the end it breeds an unemployed surplus population, which can find room neither on the land nor in the towns and therefore seizes upon posts in state service as a kind of respectable charity, thereby provoking the creation of such posts. Napoleon repaid compulsory taxation with interest, in the new markets he opened with the bayonet and in the plundering of the continent. Then such taxation was an incentive to peasant industry, whereas now it robs that industry of its last remaining source of help and leaves the peasant defenceless against pauperism. And an enormous bureaucracy, decked in gold lace and well-nourished, is the *'idée napoléonienne,'* which the second Bonaparte finds most congenial. This was inevitable since he has been forced to create, alongside the real classes of society, an artificial caste for whom the maintenance of his regime will be a bread-and-butter matter. Therefore one of his first financial operations was to increase official salaries to their old level and to create new sinecures.

Another *'idée napoléonienne'* is the rule of the *priests* as a means of government. But even if the newly created smallholding, in its harmony with society, its dependence on natural forces, its subjection to a higher protective authority, was naturally religious, the smallholding which is debt-ridden, at odds with society and with authority, driven beyond its own narrow limits, is naturally irreligious. Heaven was quite a nice addition to the newly-won narrow piece of ground, especially since it also made the weather; it becomes an insult when it is forced upon one as a substitute for the smallholding. The priest is then seen as merely the anointed bloodhound of the earthly police forces—another '*idée napoléonienne.*' The expedition to Rome will happen next time in France itself, but in a sense contrary to Monsieur de Montalembert's.

Finally, the culminating point of the '*idées napoléoniennes*' is the ascendancy of the *army.* The army was the smallholders' point of honour, transforming them into heroes, defending their new possession against external foes, glorifying their newly-won nationality, plundering and revolutionizing the world. The uniform was their gala dress, war was their poetry, the smallholding itself, extended and rounded off in imagination, was their fatherland, and patriotism the ideal form of the sense of ownership. But the enemies against whom the French peasant has now to defend his property are no longer Cossacks but *huissiers* [bailiffs] and tax-collectors. The smallholding no longer lies in a so-called fatherland but in a mortgage-register. The army itself is no longer the flower of peasant youth but the bog-plant of a peasant *Lumpenproletariat.* It largely consists of *remplaçants*, of substitutes, just as the second Bonaparte is merely a *remplaçant*, a substitute for Napoleon. Its heroic deeds now consist of hunting the peasants like chamois or other game, of police duties, and, when the inner contradictions of his system drive the head of the Society of 10 December over the French border, it will, after a few acts of banditry, win for itself not laurels but thrashings.

Thus it is clear that all '*idées napoléoniennes*' *are ideas of the undeveloped, fresh and youthful smallholding;* they are senseless for the worn-out smallholding. They are merely the hallucinations of its death struggle, words turned into phrases, spirits into ghosts. But the parody of imperialism was needed, to free the mass of the French nation from the burden of tradition and to work out clearly the opposition of the power of the state to society. With the progressive destruction of the smallholding system the state structure founded upon it collapses too. The political centralization required by modern society can

only be built upon the ruins of the military and bureaucratic machinery of government which was forged in opposition to feudalism. [The destruction of the machinery
of state will not endanger centralization. Bureaucracy is
merely the mean and brutal form of a centralization which
is still encumbered with its opposite, feudalism. In despair
regarding the Napoleonic restoration, the French peasant
abandons his faith in his smallholding, thereby bringing
down the whole edifice of state erected upon it, and *preserves the chorus of the proletarian revolution, without
which its solo melody will become a requiem in all peasant nations.*][7]

The condition of the French peasantry explains the riddle of the *general elections of 20 and 21 December*, which
led the second Bonaparte to Mount Sinai, not to receive
laws but to give them.

The bourgeoisie had clearly now no other choice but to
elect Bonaparte. When the Puritans at the Council of
Constance complained of the sacrilegious lives of the
Popes and wailed about the need for moral reform, Cardinal Pierre d'Ailly thundered at them: 'Only the devil
himself could save the Catholic Church now, and you demand angels.' In the same way the French bourgeoisie,
after the *coup d'état*, cried: Now only the head of the Society of 10 December can save bourgeois society! Only
theft can save property; perjury religion; bastardy the
family; disorder, order!

Bonaparte, as the independent power of executive authority, feels himself called on to secure 'bourgeois order.'
But the strength of this bourgeois order is the middle
class, wherefore he sees himself as the representative of
the middle class and issues decrees as such. Yet he has
achieved his present position only by breaking the political power of this middle class and daily breaking it anew.

---

7. The bracketed sentences, part of the original 1852 text, were
omitted by Marx from the 1869 edition. [E.K.]

In this he sees himself as the opponent of the political and literary power of the middle class. But in protecting its material strength he regenerates its political power. The cause must therefore be kept alive, but its effect must be wiped out wherever it shows itself. This however cannot be achieved without minor confusions of cause and effect, since in interaction both lose their distinguishing marks. New decrees wipe out the boundary between the two. Bonaparte sees himself as defender both of the peasants and of the nation as a whole against the bourgeoisie, as the benefactor, within bourgeois society, of the lower classes. New decrees cheat the 'true socialists' of their statecraft in advance. But, above all, Bonaparte sees himself as the head of the Society of 10 December, the representative of the *Lumpenproletariat* to which he himself, his entourage, his administration and his army belong and whose first concern is to benefit itself and draw California lottery prizes from the Treasury. And he establishes himself as head of the Society of 10 December by decrees, without decrees, in spite of decrees.

This contradictory task of his explains the contradictions of the man's government, the uncertain groping backwards and forwards which seeks now to win, now to humiliate one or another class, and rouses them all equally against itself, whose uncertainty in practice forms a highly comic contrast to the dictatorial categorical style of the government's official acts, obediently copied from the uncle.

Industry and trade, that is middle-class businesses, are to blossom under the strong government as in a forcing-house. Innumerable railway concessions are granted. But the Bonapartist *Lumpenproletariat* must enrich itself. Jobbery in railway concessions on the stock exchange by these already in the secret. But no capital is available for the railways. The Bank is enjoined to advance money on railway shares. But the Bank is to be both personally exploited and for this reason cajoled. The Bank is relieved of the obligation to publish a weekly report. A leonine compact between Bank and government.[8] The people must be given employment. State building programs are begun. But these public buildings increase the people's burden of taxation. Therefore the taxes are cut by attacking the *rentiers*, by converting the five-per-cent rate of interest into four-and-a-half-per-cent. But the middle class must in turn receive a sweetener. So the tax on wine is doubled for the masses, who buy it retail, and halved for the middle class, who drink it wholesale. Dissolution of the real workers' associations, but a promise of future marvels of association. The peasants are to be helped. Mortgage banks are set up which increase their indebtedness and hasten the concentration of property. But these banks must be used to make money out of the confiscated estates of the House of Orléans. No capitalist will consent to this condition, which is not contained in the decree, and the mortgage bank remains an empty decree, and so on and so on.

Bonaparte would like to figure as the patriarchal benefactor of all classes but he cannot give to one without taking from another. As was said of the Duc de Guise in the time of the Fronde—that he was the most obliging man in France because he had turned all his estates into bond-debts of his supporters to himself—so Bonaparte would like to be the most obliging man in France by turning all property, all labour, in France into a personal obligation to himself. He would like to rob all France in order to give it back to France, or rather in order to buy back France with French money, for as head of the Society of 10 December he must buy all that he is to possess. So all state institutions, the Senate, the Council of State, the legislative body, the Legion of Honour, the military medals, the wash-houses, public works, railways, the General Staff of the National Guard, excluding privates, the confiscated

8. A reference to Aesop's fable of the lion. [E.K.]

estates of the House of Orléans, all become the Institute of the Marketplace. All places in the army and in government become means of purchase. Most important of all in this process of taking from France in order to give back to France are the percentages which are wasted on the head and members of the Society of 10 December in the course of the turnover. The pun by which Countess L., the mistress of M. de Morny, described the confiscation of the Orléans estates: '*C'est le premier vol de l'aigle*' [It is the first flight of the eagle][9] fits every flight of this *eagle* who is more a *raven*. He himself and his hangers-on daily call to each other, in the words of that Carthusian monk of Italy to the miser who ostentatiously enumerated the estates on which he proposed to live for years: '*Tu fai conto sopra i beni, bisogna prima far il conto sopra gli anni.*'[10] In order to make no mistake with years, they count up by minutes. At court, in the ministries, at the head of the government and the army a swarm of fellows pushes its way in, of the best of whom it can only be said that no man knows whence he comes, a rowdy, infamous, rapacious bohemian crew, crawling into gold-laced coats with the same grotesque ceremony as the high dignitaries of Soulouque.[11] One can form some idea of this upper stratum of the Society of 10 December when one considers that *Véron-Crevel*[12] is its moralist and *Granier de Cassagnac* its thinker. When Guizot, during his ministry, used this Granier in an obscure local newspaper against the dynastic opposition, he used to extol him in the phrase: '*C'est le roi des drôles,*' 'That is the king of jesters.' It would not be right to recall the Regency [during the minority of Louis

---

9. *Vol* means flight and theft. [Footnote by Marx.]
10. 'You are counting up your estates, you should rather count up your years.' [Footnote by Marx.]
11. President, later Emperor of Haiti. [E.K.]
12. Balzac, in *La Cousine Bette*, portrays the thoroughly dissolute Parisian philistine in Crevel, based on Dr. Véron, the owner of *Le Constitutionnel*. [Footnote by Marx.]

XV] or Louis XV in connection with the court and the lineage of Louis Bonaparte. For 'France has often suffered a government by mistresses but never yet a government of kept men.'[13]

Swept on by the contradictory demands of his position, Bonaparte, like a conjuror who must by constant surprises, that is, by a miniature *coup d'état* each day, keep the eyes of the public upon himself as replacement for Napoleon, throws the whole bourgeois economy into confusion, attacks everything which the revolution of 1848 held inviolable, makes some men patient of revolution, others eager for it, and breeds anarchy itself in the name of order. At the same time he strips the halo from the whole machinery of state, profanes it, making it at once disgusting and ridiculous. He repeats the cult of the Holy Tunic at Trier in the cult of the imperial cloak of Napoleon in Paris. But when the imperial cloak finally rests on the shoulders of Louis Bonaparte, the bronze statue of Napoleon will crash down from the top of the Vendôme Column.

MEW 8, 115–23, 159–62, 190–207.

---

13. Remark by Madame Girardin. [Footnote by Marx.]

4. Journalism and Politics: 1853–1864

EDITOR'S NOTE

The years 1852 up to 1864, when he received the legacies from the death of his mother and his friend Wilhelm Wolff, were years of considerable financial distress for Marx. He turned to popular journalism besides continuing his 'scientific'—i.e., economic—studies and reading, as ever, voraciously to keep up with new knowledge and world affairs. His direct involvement in political organization ceased in 1852 with his decision to dissolve the Communist League after the Cologne arrests had wiped out continental activity; it did not resume until he was drawn, almost by accident, into the formation of the First International in 1864. For all that, they were not unproductive years, though it is in this crucial period of his maturity that Marx displays most clearly his consistent inability to finish a major piece of work, to set out his system, or part of his system, in a comparatively complete and self-standing form. His intensive and wide-ranging economic studies, excerpted in Section 5, cover an enormous amount of ground and involved extensive note-taking, drafting, and rewriting running into thousands of pages. But the draft

Outlines (*Grundrisse*) of the Critique of Political Economy set out in seven notebooks in 1857–1858; *The Contribution to the Critique of Political Economy*, published in 1859; and even the first volume of *Capital*, finally sent to the printer at Engels's insistence in 1867, are all unfinished sections of the study of modern capitalism and its economic foundations, which he planned but never completed. He no doubt found some relief in indulging his passion for invective. There was the 'vindication of his honour' in the pamphlet *Herr Vogt* (1860), replying *in extenso* to accusations of blackmail and forgery. There was his hatred, during this period, for Russia as the cornerstone of European reaction, culminating in his Russophobic *Secret Diplomatic History of the Eighteenth Century* and his attacks, in newspaper articles, on Lord Palmerston as a Russian agent. Revealing as these works may be of aspects of Marx's character, they have no other permanent value.

Marx's journalism in the 1850s and 1860s was principally forced upon him by financial need. From 1852 to 1862 he contributed to the *New York Daily Tribune*, edited by Charles Dana, beginning with a series of articles written for him by Engels on revolution and counter-revolution in Germany, but then himself commenting regularly on European affairs—events in India, China, Turkey, and the Middle East, British foreign policy, Austrian and English economic affairs, the Greek insurrection, etc. In a series of articles between September 1861 and February 1862 he reported on day-to-day English reactions to the American Civil War and the Trent Affair. In 1861 he also began to write for the Viennese paper *Die Presse*, continuing, with considerable help from Engels on the military side, to report critically on the progress of the war in America.

Marx had no exaggerated opinion of the importance of his journalism. It enabled him to disseminate a point of view—not always congenial to the newspapers he wrote for. He made effective use of his wide reading, of his interest in economic and financial matters, and his capacity for 'mugging up' a subject and seeing the thrust of a historical development. The nature of world affairs in the 1850s and 1860s was such that much of his writing is concerned with questions of what we today would call imperialism and the problems of modernization. He believed, in broad terms, in the historically progressive role of capitalism and imperialism in underdeveloped, Oriental despotic, feudal, and slaveholding economies, even if he was anxious to expose the hypocritically concealed greed and self-interest that drove the capitalist into his so-called civilizing mission. But while his journalistic articles display a general attitude and will be of interest to the scholar tracing in detail Marx's reactions to the events of his time, they are generally so much tied to those specific events, written with the perspective of the week rather than the year, that they are not easily excerpted. The three articles on India and the article on China presented here are among the better known and less narrow in scope, and display his journalism at its best.

The International Working Men's Association (the First International) was founded in September 1864 at a meeting in St Martin's Hall in London, attended by English, Italian, French, Swiss, and Polish workers and members of the Communist German Workers' Educational Association. Marx had taken no part in planning the meeting or the formation of such an organization, but was invited to attend and elected to a sub-committee to draft the organization's rules and principles. He did so and quickly became the Association's dominating and outstanding theoretical mind, drafting addresses and reports to its congresses, including the famous *Address on the Civil War in France* (excerpted in Section 6). Here we reproduce the *Inaugural Address and Provi-*

sional Rules of the International drafted by Marx during the last week of October 1864, adopted by the General Council on November 1, and immediately published as a pamphlet in London.

THE BRITISH RULE IN INDIA

London, 10 June 1853

Hindustan is an Italy of Asiatic dimensions, the Himalayas for the Alps, the Plains of Bengal for the Plains of Lombardy, the Deccan for the Apennines, and the Isle of Ceylon for the Island of Sicily. The same rich variety in the products of the soil, and the same dismemberment in the political configuration. Just as Italy has, from time to time, been compressed by the conqueror's sword into different national masses, so do we find Hindustan, when not under the pressure of the Mohammedan, or the Mogul, or the Briton, dissolved into as many independent and conflicting states as it numbered towns, or even villages. Yet, in a social point of view, Hindustan is not the Italy, but the Ireland of the East. And this strange combination of Italy and Ireland, of a world of voluptuousness and a world of woes, is anticipated in the ancient traditions of the religion of Hindustan. That religion is at once a religion of sensualist exuberance, and a religion of self-torturing asceticism; a religion of the Lingam and of the Juggernaut; the religion of the monk, and of the bayadere.

I share not the opinion of those who believe in a golden age of Hindustan, without recurring, however, like Sir Charles Wood, for the confirmation of my view, to the authority of Khuli Khan. But take, for example, the times of Aurungzeb; or the epoch when the Mogul appeared in the north and the Portuguese in the south; or the age of Mohammedan invasion, and of the heptarchy in southern India; or, if you will, go still more back to antiquity, take the mythological chronology of the Brahmin himself, who places the commencement of Indian misery in an epoch even more remote than the Christian creation of the world.

There cannot, however, remain any doubt but that the misery inflicted by the British on Hindustan is of an essentially different and infinitely more intensive kind than all Hindustan had to suffer before. I do not allude to European despotism, planted upon Asiatic despotism, by the British East India Company, forming a more monstrous combination than any of the divine monsters startling us in the Temple of Salsette. This is no distinctive feature of British colonial rule, but only an imitation of the Dutch, and so much so that in order to characterize the working of the British East India Company, it is sufficient to literally repeat what Sir Stamford Raffles, the *English* Governor of Java, said of the old Dutch East India Company.

The Dutch Company, actuated solely by the spirit of gain, and viewing their Javan subjects with less regard or consideration than a West India planter formerly viewed the gang upon his estate, because the latter had paid the purchase money of human property, which the other had not, employed all the pre-existing machinery of despotism to squeeze from the people their utmost mite of contribution, the last dregs of their labour, and thus aggravated the evils of a capricious and semi-barbarous government, by working it with all the practised ingenuity of politicians, and all the monopolizing selfishness of traders.[1]

All the civil wars, invasions, revolutions, conquests, famines, strangely complex, rapid and destructive as the successive action in Hindustan may appear, did not go deeper than its surface. England has broken down the entire framework of Indian society, without any symptoms

---

1. Sir Stamford Raffles, *The History of Java*, 2 vols., London, 1817, I, p. 151. [E.K.]

of reconstitution yet appearing. This loss of his old world, with no gain of a new one, imparts a particular kind of melancholy to the present misery of the Hindu, and separates Hindustan, ruled by Britain, from all its ancient traditions, and from the whole of its past history.

There have been in Asia, generally, from immemorial times, but three departments of government: that of finance, or the plunder of the interior; that of war, or the plunder of the exterior; and, finally, the department of public works. Climate and territorial conditions, especially the vast tracts of desert, extending from the Sahara, through Arabia, Persia, India and Tartary, to the most elevated Asiatic highlands, constituted artificial irrigation by canals and waterworks the basis of Oriental agriculture. As in Egypt and India, inundations are used for fertilizing the soil of Mesopotamia, Persia, etc.; advantage is taken of a high level for feeding irrigative canals. This prime necessity of an economical and common use of water, which in the Occident drove private enterprise to voluntary association, as in Flanders and Italy, necessitated in the Orient, where civilization was too low and the territorial extent too vast to call into life voluntary association, the interference of the centralizing power of government. Hence an economical function devolved upon all Asiatic governments, the function of providing public works. This artificial fertilization of the soil, dependent on a central government, and immediately decaying with the neglect of irrigation and drainage, explains the otherwise strange fact that we now find whole territories barren and desert that were once brilliantly cultivated, as Palmyra, Petra, the ruins in Yemen, and large provinces of Egypt, Persia and Hindustan; it also explains how a single war of devastation has been able to depopulate a country for centuries, and to strip it of all its civilization.

Now, the British in East India accepted from their predecessors the departments of finance and of war, but they have neglected entirely that of public works. Hence the deterioration of an agriculture which is not capable of being conducted on the British principle of free competition, of *laissez-faire* and *laissez-aller*. But in Asiatic empires we are quite accustomed to see agriculture deteriorating under one government and reviving again under some other government. There the harvests correspond to good or bad governments, as they change in Europe with good or bad seasons. Thus the oppression and neglect of agriculture, bad as it is, could not be looked upon as the final blow dealt to Indian society by the British intruder, had it not been attended by a circumstance of quite different importance, a novelty in the annals of the whole Asiatic world. However changing the political aspect of India's past must appear, its social condition has remained unaltered since its remotest antiquity, until the first decennium of the nineteenth century. The hand-loom and the spinning-wheel, producing their regular myriads of spinners and weavers, were the pivots of the structure of that society. From immemorial times Europe received the admirable textures of Indian labour, sending in return for them her precious metals, and furnishing thereby his material to the goldsmith, that indispensable member of Indian society, whose love of finery is so great that even the lowest class, those who go about nearly naked, have commonly a pair of golden earrings and a gold ornament of some kind hung round their necks. Rings on the fingers and toes have also been common. Women as well as children frequently wore massive bracelets and anklets of gold or silver, and statuettes of divinities in gold and silver were met with in the households. It was the British intruder who broke up the Indian hand-loom and destroyed the spinning-wheel. England began with driving the Indian cottons from the European market; it then introduced twist into Hindustan and in the end inundated the very mother country of cotton with cottons. From 1818 to 1836 the export of twist from Great Britain to India rose in the proportion of 1 to 5,200. In 1824 the export of British muslins to India hardly amounted to 1,000,000 yards, while in 1837 it surpassed 64,000,000 yards. But at the same time the population of Dacca decreased from 150,000 inhabitants to 20,000. This decline of Indian towns celebrated for their fabrics was by no means the worst consequence. British steam and science uprooted, over the whole surface of Hindustan, the union between agriculture and manufacturing industry.

These two circumstances—the Hindu, on the one hand, leaving, like all Oriental peoples, to the central government the care of the great public works, the prime condition of his agriculture and commerce, dispersed, on the other hand, over the surface of the country, and agglomerated in small centres by the domestic union of agricultural and manufacturing pursuits—these two circumstances had brought about, since the remotest times, a social system of particular features—the so-called *village system*, which gave to each of these small unions their independent organization and distinct life. The peculiar character of this system may be judged from the following description, contained in an old official report of the British House of Commons on Indian affairs:

A village, geographically considered, is a tract of country comprising some hundred or thousand acres of arable and waste lands; politically viewed it resembles a corporation or township. Its proper establishment of officers and servants consists of the following descriptions: the *potail*, or head inhabitant, who has generally the superintendence of the affairs of the village, settles the disputes of the inhabitants, attends to the police, and performs the duty of collecting the revenue within his village, a duty which his personal influence and minute acquaintance with the situation and concerns of the people render him the best qualified for this charge. The *kurnum* keeps the accounts of cultivation, and registers everything connected with it. The *tallier* and the *totie,* the duty of the former of which consists in gaining information of crimes and offences, and in escorting and protecting persons travelling from one village to another; the province of the latter appearing to be more immediately confined to the village, consisting, among other duties, in guarding the crops and assisting in measuring them. The *boundaryman,* who preserves the limits of the village, or gives evidence respecting them in cases of dispute. The superintendent of tanks and watercourses distributes the water for the purposes of agriculture. The Brahmin, who performs the village worship. The schoolmaster, who is seen teaching the children in a village to read and write in the sand. The calendar-Brahmin, or astrologer, etc. These officers and servants generally constitute the establishment of a village; but in some parts of the country it is of less extent; some of the duties and functions above described being united in the same person; in others it exceeds the above-named number of individuals. Under this simple form of municipal government, the inhabitants of the country have lived from time immemorial. The boundaries of the villages have been but seldom altered; and though the villages themselves have been sometimes injured, and even desolated by war, famine or disease, the same name, the same limits, the same interests, and even the same families, have continued for ages. The inhabitants gave themselves no trouble about the breaking up and divisions of kingdoms; while the village remains entire, they care not to what power it is transferred, or to what sovereign it devolves; its internal economy remains unchanged. The *potail* is still the head inhabitant, and still acts as the petty judge or magistrate, and collector or rentor of the village.[2]

These small stereotype forms of social organism have been to the greater part dissolved, and are disappearing, not so much through the brutal interference of the British

---

2. Cf. G. Campbell, *Modern India,* London, 1852, pp. 84–85. [E.K.]

tax-gatherer and the British soldier, as to the working of English steam and English free trade. Those family-communities were based on domestic industry in that peculiar combination of hand-weaving, hand-spinning and hand-tilling agriculture which gave them self-supporting power. English interference having placed the spinner in Lancashire and the weaver in Bengal, or sweeping away both Hindu spinner and weaver, dissolved these small semi-barbarian, semi-civilized communities, by blowing up their economical basis, and thus produced the greatest, and, to speak the truth, the only *social* revolution ever heard of in Asia.

Now, sickening as it must be to human feeling to witness those myriads of industrious patriarchal and inoffensive social organizations disorganized and dissolved into their units, thrown into a sea of woes, and their individual members losing at the same time their ancient form of civilization and their hereditary means of subsistence, we must not forget that these idyllic village communities, inoffensive though they may appear, had always been the solid foundation of Oriental despotism, that they restrained the human mind within the smallest possible compass, making it the unresisting tool of superstition, enslaving it beneath traditional rules, depriving it of all grandeur and historical energies. We must not forget the barbarian egotism which, concentrating on some miserable patch of land, had quietly witnessed the ruin of empires, the perpetration of unspeakable cruelties, the massacre of the population of large towns, with no other consideration bestowed upon them than on natural events, itself the helpless prey of any aggressor who deigned to notice it at all. We must not forget that this undignified, stagnatory, and vegetative life, that this passive sort of existence evoked on the other part, in contradistinction, wild, aimless, unbounded forces of destruction, and rendered murder itself a religious rite in Hindustan. We must not forget that these little communities were contaminated by distinctions of caste and by slavery, that they subjugated man to external circumstances instead of elevating man to be the sovereign of circumstances, that they transformed a self-developing social state into never-changing natural destiny, and thus brought about a brutalizing worship of nature, exhibiting its degradation in the fact that man, the sovereign of nature, fell down on his knees in adoration of Hanuman, the monkey, and Sabbala, the cow.

England, it is true, in causing a social revolution in Hindustan was actuated only by the vilest interests, and was stupid in her manner of enforcing them. But that is not the question. The question is, can mankind fulfil its destiny without a fundamental revolution in the social state of Asia? If not, whatever may have been the crimes of England she was the unconscious tool of history in bringing about that revolution.

Then, whatever bitterness the spectacle of the crumbling of an ancient world may have for our personal feelings, we have the right, in point of history, to exclaim with Goethe:

> *Sollte diese Qual uns quälen,*
> *Da sie unsre Lust vermehrt,*
> *Hat nicht Myriaden Seelen*
> *Timurs Herrschaft aufgezehrt?*[3]

New York Daily Tribune, June 25, 1853.

---

3. 'Should this torture cause us anguish since it increases our pleasure; did not Timur's power consume a myriad souls?'—From Goethe's *Westöstlicher Diwan. An Suleika*. [E.K.]

From 'THE FUTURE RESULTS OF BRITISH RULE IN INDIA'

London, 22 July 1853

England has to fulfil a double mission in India: one destructive, the other regenerating—the annihilation of old Asiatic society, and the laying of the material foundations of Western society in Asia.

Arabs, Turks, Tartars, Moguls, who had successively overrun India, soon became Hinduized, the barbarian conquerors being, by an eternal law of history, conquered themselves by the superior civilization of their subjects. The British were the first conquerors superior and therefore inaccessible to Hindu civilization. They destroyed it by breaking up the native communities, by uprooting the native industry, and by levelling all that was great and elevated in the native society. The historic pages of their rule in India report hardly anything beyond that destruction. The work of regeneration hardly transpires through a heap of ruins. Nevertheless it has begun.

The political unity of India, more consolidated, and extending further than it ever did under the Great Moguls, was the first condition of its regeneration. That unity, imposed by the British sword, will now be strengthened and perpetuated by the electric telegraph. The native army, organized and trained by the British drill-sergeant, was the *sine qua non* of Indian self-emancipation, and of India ceasing to be the prey of the first foreign intruder. The free press, introduced for the first time into Asiatic society, and managed principally by the common offspring of Hindus and Europeans, is a new and powerful agent of reconstruction. The zemindari and ryotwari themselves, abominable as they are, involve two distinct forms of private property in land—the great desideratum of Asiatic society. From the Indian natives, reluctantly and sparingly educated at Calcutta, under English superintendence, a fresh class is springing up, endowed with the requirements for government and imbued with European science. Steam has brought India into regular and rapid communication with Europe, has connected its chief ports with those of the whole south-eastern ocean, and has re-vindicated it from the isolated position which was the prime law of its stagnation. The day is not far distant when, by a combination of railways and steam vessels, the distance between England and India, measured by time, will be shortened to eight days, and when that once fabulous country will thus be actually annexed to the Western world.

The ruling classes of Great Britain have had, till now, but an accidental, transitory and exceptional interest in the progress of India. The aristocracy wanted to conquer it, the moneyocracy to plunder it, and the millocracy to undersell it. But now the tables are turned. The millocracy have discovered that the transformation of India into a reproductive country has become of vital importance to them, and that, to that end, it is necessary, above all, to gift her with means of irrigation and of internal communication. They intend now drawing a net of railways over India. And they will do it. The results must be inappreciable.

It is notorious that the productive powers of India are paralysed by the utter want of means for conveying and exchanging its various produce. Nowhere more than in India do we meet with social destitution in the midst of natural plenty, for want of the means of exchange. It was proved before a Committee of the British House of Commons, which sat in 1848, that 'when grain was selling from 6s. to 8s. a quarter at Khandesh, it was sold at 64s. to 70s. at Poona, where the people were dying in the streets of famine, without the possibility of gaining supplies from Khandesh, because the clay roads were impracticable.'

The introduction of railways may be easily made to subserve agricultural purposes by the formation of tanks, where ground is required for embankment, and by the conveyance of water along the different lines. Thus irrigation, the *sine qua non* of farming in the East, might be greatly extended, and the frequently recurring local famines, arising from the want of water, would be averted. The general importance of railways, viewed under this head, must become evident when we remember that irrigated lands, even in the districts near Ghauts, pay three times as much in taxes, afford ten or twelve times as much employment, and yield twelve or fifteen times as much profit, as the same area without irrigation.

Railways will afford the means of diminishing the amount and the cost of the military establishments. Col. Warren, Town Major of the Fort St William, stated before a Select Committee of the House of Commons: 'The practicability of receiving intelligence from distant parts of the country in as many hours as at present it requires days and even weeks, and of sending instructions with troops and stores, in the more brief period, are considerations which cannot be too highly estimated. Troops could be kept at more distant and healthier stations than at present, and much loss of life from sickness would by this means be spared. Stores could not to the same extent be required at the various depots, and the loss by decay, and the destruction incidental to the climate, would also be avoided. The number of troops might be diminished in direct proportion to their effectiveness.'

We know that the municipal organization and the economical basis of the village communities have been broken up, but their worst feature, the dissolution of society into stereotype and disconnected atoms, has survived their vitality. The village isolation produced the absence of roads in India, and the absence of roads perpetuated the village isolation. On this plan a community existed with a given scale of low conveniences, almost without intercourse with other villages, without the desires and efforts indispensable to social advance. The British having broken up this self-sufficient *inertia* of the villages, railways will provide the new want of communication and intercourse. Besides, 'one of the effects of the railway system will be to bring into every village affected by it such knowledge of the contrivances and appliances of other countries, and such means of obtaining them, as will first put the hereditary and stipendiary village artisanship of India to full proof of its capabilities, and then supply its defects.'[1]

I know that the English millocracy intend to endow India with railways with the exclusive view of extracting at diminished expenses the cotton and other raw materials for their manufacturers. But when you have once introduced machinery into the locomotion of a country which possesses iron and coals, you are unable to withhold it from its fabrication. You cannot maintain a net of railways over an immense country without introducing all those industrial processes necessary to meet the immediate and current want of railway locomotion, and out of which there must grow the application of machinery to those branches of industry not immediately connected with railways. The railway system will therefore become, in India, truly the forerunner of modern industry. This is the more certain as the Hindus are allowed by British authorities themselves to possess particular aptitude for accommodating themselves to entirely new labour, and acquiring the requisite knowledge of machinery. Ample proof of this fact is afforded by the capacities and expertness of the native engineers in the Calcutta mint, where they have been for years employed in working the steam machinery, by the natives attached to the several steam-engines in the Hurdwar coal districts, and by other instances. Mr Campbell himself, greatly influenced as he is by the prejudices of the East India Company, is obliged to avow 'that the great mass of the Indian people possesses a

---

1. J. Chapman, *The Cotton and Commerce of India*, London, 1851, p. 91. [E.K.]

great *industrial energy*, is well fitted to accumulate capital, and remarkable for a mathematical clearness of head and talent for figures and exact sciences.' 'Their intellects,' he says, 'are excellent.'[2]

Modern industry, resulting from the railway system, will dissolve the hereditary divisions of labour, upon which rest the Indian castes, those decisive impediments to Indian progress and Indian power.

All the English bourgeoisie may be forced to do will neither emancipate nor materially mend the social condition of the mass of the people, depending not only on the development of the productive powers, but on their appropriation by the people. But what they will not fail to do is to lay down the material premises for both. Has the bourgeoisie ever done more? Has it ever effected a progress without dragging individuals and peoples through blood and dirt, through misery and degradation?

The Indians will not reap the fruits of the new elements of society scattered among them by the British bourgeoisie till in Great Britain itself the now ruling classes shall have been supplanted by the industrial proletariat, or till the Hindus themselves shall have grown strong enough to throw off the English yoke altogether. At all events, we may safely expect to see, at a more or less remote period, the regeneration of that great and interesting country. . . .

New York Daily Tribune, August 8, 1853; reprinted in *Karl Marx on Colonialism and Modernization*, edited with introduction by Shlomo Avineri, New York, 1968, pp. 125–30.

---

2. Campbell, *Modern India*, London, 1852, pp. 59–60.

1853

REVOLUTION IN CHINA AND IN EUROPE

A most profound yet fantastic speculator on the principles which govern the movements of Humanity was wont to extol as one of the ruling secrets of nature what he called the law of the contact of extremes. The homely proverb that "extremes meet" was, in his view, a grand and potent truth in every sphere of life; an axiom with which the philosopher could as little dispense as the astronomer with the laws of Kepler or the great discovery of Newton.

Whether the "contact of extremes" be such a universal principle or not, a striking illustration of it may be seen in the effect the Chinese revolution seems likely to exercise upon the civilized world. It may seem a very strange, and a very paradoxical assertion that the next uprising of the people of Europe, and their next movement for republican freedom and economy of Government, may depend more probably on what is now passing in the Celestial Empire—the very opposite of Europe—than on any other political cause that now exists—more even than on the menaces of Russia and the consequent likelihood of a general European war. But yet it is no paradox, as all may understand by attentively considering the circumstances, of the case.

Whatever be the social causes, and whatever religious, dynastic, or national shape they may assume, that have brought about the chronic rebellions subsisting in China for about ten years past, and now gathered together in one formidable revolution, the occasion of this outbreak has unquestionably been afforded by the English cannon forcing upon China that soporific drug called opium. Before the British arms the authority of the Manchu dynasty fell to pieces; the superstitious faith in the Eternity of the Celestial Empire broke down; the barbarous and hermetic isolation from the civilized world was infringed; and an opening was made for that intercourse which has since proceeded so rapidly under the golden attractions of California and Australia. At the same time the silver coin of the Empire, its life-blood, began to be drained away to the British East Indies.

Up to 1830, the balance of trade being continually in favour of the Chinese, there existed an uninterrupted importation of silver from India, Britain and the United States into China. Since 1833, and especially since 1840, the export of silver from China to India has become almost exhausting for the Celestial Empire. Hence the strong decrees of the Emperor against the opium trade, responded to by still stronger resistance to his measures. Besides this immediate economical consequence, the bribery connected with opium smuggling has entirely demoralized the Chinese State officers in the Southern provinces. Just as the Emperor was wont to be considered the father of all China, so his officers were looked upon as sustaining the paternal relation to their respective districts. But this patriarchal authority, the only moral link embracing the vast machinery of the State, has gradually been corroded by the corruption of those officers, who have made great gains by conniving at opium smuggling. This has occurred principally in the same Southern provinces where the rebellion commenced. It is almost needless to observe that, in the same measure in which opium has obtained the sovereignty over the Chinese, the Emperor and his staff of pedantic mandarins have become dispossessed of their own sovereignty. It would seem as though history had first to make this whole people drunk before it could rouse them out of their hereditary stupidity.

Though scarcely existing in former times, the import of English cottons, and to a small extent of English woollens, has rapidly risen since 1833, the epoch when the monopoly of trade with China was transferred from the East India Company to private commerce, and on a much greater scale since 1840, the epoch when other nations, and especially our own, also obtained a share in the Chinese trade. This introduction of foreign manufactures has had a similar effect on the native industry to that which it formerly had on Asia Minor, Persia and India. In China the spinners and weavers have suffered greatly under this foreign competition, and the community has become unsettled in proportion.

The tribute to be paid to England after the unfortunate war of 1840, the great unproductive consumption of opium, the drain of the precious metals by this trade, the destructive influence of foreign competition on native manufactures, the demoralized condition of the public administration, produced two things: the old taxation became more burdensome and harassing, and new taxation was added to the old. Thus in a decree of the Emperor, dated Pekin, Jan. 5, 1853, we find orders given to the viceroys and governors of the southern provinces of Woo-Chang and Hun-Yang to remit and defer the payment of taxes, and especially not in any case to exact more than the regular amount; for otherwise, says the decree, "how will the poor people be able to bear it?" And "Thus, perhaps," continues the Emperor, "will my people, in a period of general hardship and distress, be exempted from the evils of being pursued and worried by the tax-gatherer." Such language as this, and such concessions we remember to have heard from Austria, the China of Germany, in 1848.

All these dissolving agencies acting together on the finances, the morals, the industry, and political structure of China, received their full development under the English cannon in 1840, which broke down the authority of the Emperor, and forced the Celestial Empire into contact with the terrestrial world. Complete isolation was the prime condition of the preservation of Old China. That isolation having come to a violent end by the medium of England, dissolution must follow as surely as that of any mummy carefully preserved in a hermetically sealed coffin, whenever it is brought into contact with the open air. Now, England having brought about the revolution of China, the question is how that revolution will in time react on England, and through England on Europe. This question is not difficult of solution.

The attention of our readers has often been called to the unparalleled growth of British manufactures since 1850. Amid the most surprising prosperity, it has not been difficult to point out the clear symptoms of an approaching industrial crisis. Notwithstanding California and Australia, notwithstanding the immense and unprecedented emigration, there must ever, without any particular accident, in due time arrive a moment when the extension of the markets is unable to keep pace with the extension of British manufactures, and this disproportion must bring about a new crisis with the same certainty as it has done in the past. But, if one of the great markets suddenly becomes contracted, the arrival of the crisis is necessarily accelerated thereby. Now, the Chinese rebellion must, for the time being, have precisely this effect upon England. The necessity for opening new markets, or for extending the old ones, was one of the principal causes of the reduction of the British tea-duties, as, with an increased importation of tea, an increased exportation of manufactures to China was expected to take place. Now, the value of the annual exports from the United Kingdom to China amounted, before the repeal in 1834 of the trading monopoly possessed by the East India Company, to only £600,-000; in 1836, it reached the sum of £1,326,388; in 1845, it had risen to £2,394,827; in 1852 it amounted to about £3,-000,000. The quantity of tea imported from China did not exceed, in 1793, 16,167,331 lbs.; but in 1845, it amounted to 50,714,657 lbs.; in 1846, to 57,584,561 lbs.; it is now above 60,000,000 lbs.

The tea crop of the last season will not prove short, as shown already by the export lists from Shanghai, of 2,000,000 lbs. above the preceding year. This excess is to be accounted for by two circumstances. On one hand, the state of the market at the close of 1851 was much depressed, and the large surplus stock left has been thrown into the export of 1852. On the other hand, the recent accounts of the altered British legislation with regard to imports of tea, reaching China, have brought forward all the available teas to a ready market, at greatly enhanced prices. But with respect to the coming crop, the case stands very differently. This is shown by the following extracts from the correspondence of a large tea firm in London:

In Shanghai the terror is extreme. Gold has advanced in value upwards of 25 per cent, *being eagerly sought for hoarding;* silver had so far disappeared that *none could be obtained* to pay the Chinese dues on the British vessels requiring port clearance; and in consequence of which Mr. [Consul] Alcock has consented to become responsible to the Chinese authorities for the payment of these dues, on receipt of East India Company's bills, or other approved securities. *The scarcity of the precious metals* is one of the most unfavourable features, when viewed in reference to the immediate future of commerce, as this abstraction occurs precisely at that period when their use is most needed, to enable the tea and silk buyers to go into the interior and effect their purchases, for which a *large portion of bullion is paid in advance, to enable the producers to carry on their operations.*

... At this period of the year it is usual to begin making arrangements for the new teas, whereas at present nothing is talked of but the means of protecting persons and property, all transactions being at a stand. ... If the means are not applied to secure the leaves in April and May, the early crop, which includes all the finer descriptions, both of black and green teas, will be as much lost as unreaped wheat at Christmas.[1]

Now the means for securing the tea leaves will certainly not be given by the English, American or French squadrons stationed in the Chinese seas, but these may easily, by their interference, produce such complications as to cut off all transactions between the tea-producing interior and the tea-exporting sea ports. Thus, for the present crop, a rise in the prices must be expected—speculation has already commenced in London—and for the crop to come a large deficit is as good as certain. Nor is this all. The Chinese, ready though they may be, as are all people in periods of revolutionary convulsion, to sell off to the foreigner all the bulky commodities they have on hand, will, as the Orientals are used to do in the apprehension of great changes, set to hoarding, not taking much in return for their tea and silk, except hard money. England has accordingly to expect a rise in the price of one of her chief articles of consumption, a drain of bullion, and a great contraction of an important market for her cotton and woollen goods. Even the *Economist,* that optimist conjurer of all things menacing the tranquil minds of the mercantile community, is compelled to use language like this:

> We must not flatter ourselves with finding as extensive a market as formerly for our exports to China. . . . It is more probable, therefore, that our export trade to China should suffer, and that there should be a diminished demand for the produce of Manchester and Glasgow.[2]

It must not be forgotten that the rise in the price of so indispensable an article as tea, and the contraction of so important a market as China, will coincide with a deficient

1. *The Economist,* May 21, 1853. Marx's italics. [E.K.]
2. *The Economist,* May 21, 1853.

harvest in Western Europe, and, therefore, with rising prices of meat, corn, and all other agricultural produce. Hence contracted markets for manufacturers, because every rise in the prices of the first necessities of life is counter-balanced, at home and abroad, by a corresponding reduction in the demand for manufactures. From every part of Great Britain complaints have been received on the backward state of most of the crops. The *Economist* says on this subject:

> In the South of England "not only will there be left much land unsown, until too late for a crop of any sort, but much of the sown land will prove to be foul, or otherwise in a bad state for corn-growing." On the wet or poor soils destined for wheat, signs that mischief is going on are apparent. "The time for planting mangel-wurzel may now be said to have passed away, and very little has been planted, while the time for preparing land for turnips is rapidly going by, without any adequate preparation for this important crop having been accomplished ... oat-sowing has been much interfered with by the snow and rain. Few oats were sown early, and late-sown oats seldom produce a large crop."[3]

In many districts losses among the breeding flocks have been considerable. The price of other farm-produce than corn is from 20 to 30, and even 50 per cent higher than last year. On the Continent, corn has risen comparatively more than in England. Rye has risen in Belgium and Holland a full 100 per cent. Wheat and other grains are following suit.

Under these circumstances, as the greater part of the regular commercial circle has already been run through by British trade, it may safely be augured that the Chinese revolution will throw the spark into the overloaded mine

3. *The Economist*, May 14, 1853.

of the present industrial system and cause the explosion of the long-prepared general crisis, which, spreading abroad, will be closely followed by political revolutions on the Continent. It would be a curious spectacle, that of China sending disorder into the Western World while the Western Powers, by English, French and American war-steamers, are conveying "order" to Shanghai, Nankin and the mouths of the Great Canal. Do these order-mongering Powers, which would attempt to support the wavering Manchu dynasty, forget that the hatred against foreigners and their exclusion from the Empire, once the mere result of China's geographical and ethnographical situation, have become a political system only since the conquest of the country by the race of the Manchu Tartars? There can be no doubt that the turbulent dissensions among the European nations who, at the later end of the 17th century, rivaled each other in the trade with China, lent a mighty aid to the exclusive policy adopted by the Manchus. But more than this was done by the fear of the new dynasty, lest the foreigners might favor the discontent existing among a large proportion of the Chinese during the first half-century or thereabouts of their subjection to the Tartars. From these considerations, foreigners were then prohibited from all communication with the Chinese, except through Canton, a town at a great distance from Pekin and the tea-districts, and their commerce restricted to intercourse with the Hong merchants, licensed by the Government expressly for the foreign trade, in order to keep the rest of its subjects from all connection with the odious strangers. In any case an interference on the part of the Western Governments at this time can only serve to render the revolution more violent, and protract the stagnation of trade.

At the same time it is to be observed with regard to India that the British Government of that country depends for full one seventh of its revenue on the sale of opium to the Chinese while a considerable proportion of the Indian demand for British manufactures depends on the production of that opium in India. The Chinese, it is true, are no more likely to renounce the use of opium than are the Germans to forswear tobacco. But as the new Emperor is understood to be favorable to the culture of the poppy and the preparation of opium in China itself, it is evident that a death-blow is very likely to be struck at once at the business of opium-raising in India, the Indian revenue, and the commercial resources of Hindustan. Though this blow would not immediately be felt by the interests concerned, it would operate effectually in due time, and would come in to intensify and prolong the universal financial crisis whose horoscope we have cast above.

Since the commencement of the eighteenth century there has been no serious revolution in Europe which had not been preceded by a commercial and financial crisis. This applies no less to the revolution of 1789 than to that of 1848. It is true, not only that we every day behold more threatening symptoms of conflict between the ruling powers and their subjects, between the State and society, between the various classes; but also the conflict of the existing powers among each other gradually reaching that height where the sword must be drawn, and the *ultima ratio* of princes be recurred to. In the European capitals, every day brings despatches big with universal war, vanishing under the despatches of the following day, bearing the assurance of peace for a week or so. We may be sure, nevertheless, that to whatever height the conflict between the European powers may rise, however threatening the aspect of the diplomatic horizon may appear, whatever movements may be attempted by some enthusiastic fraction in this or that country, the rage of princes and the fury of the people are alike enervated by the breath of prosperity. Neither wars nor revolutions are likely to put Europe by the ears, unless in consequence of a general commercial and industrial crisis, the signal of which has, as usual, to be given by England, the representative of European industry in the market of the world.

It is unnecessary to dwell on the political consequences such a crisis must produce in these times, with the unprecedented extension of factories in England, with the utter dissolution of her official parties, with the whole State machinery of France transformed into one immense swindling and stockjobbing concern, with Austria on the eve of bankruptcy, with wrongs everywhere accumulated to be revenged by the people, with the conflicting interests of the reactionary powers themselves, and with the Russian dream of conquest once more revealed to the world.

New York Daily Tribune, June 14, 1853; reprinted in *Karl Marx on Colonialism and Modernization*, ed. Avineri, op. cit., pp. 62–70.

1857

THE INDIAN REVOLT

London, September 4, 1857

The outrages committed by the revolted sepoys in India are indeed appalling, hideous, ineffable—such as one is prepared to meet only in wars of insurrection, of nationalities, of races, and above all of religion; in one word, such as respectable England used to applaud when perpetrated by the Vendeans on the "Blues," by the Spanish guerrillas on the infidel Frenchmen, by Serbians on their German and Hungarian neighbours, by Croats on Viennese rebels, by Cavaignac's Garde Mobile or Bonaparte's Decembrists on the sons and daughters of proletarian France. However infamous the conduct of the sepoys, it is only the reflex, in a concentrated form, of England's own conduct in India, not only during the epoch of the foundation of her Eastern

Empire, but even during the last ten years of a long-settled rule. To characterize that rule, it suffices to say that torture formed an organic institution of its financial policy. There is something in human history like retribution; and it is a rule of historical retribution that its instrument be forged not by the offended, but by the offender himself.

The first blow dealt to the French monarchy proceeded from the nobility, not from the peasants. The Indian revolt does not commence with the ryots, tortured, dishonoured and stripped naked by the British, but with the sepoys, clad, fed and petted, fatted and pampered by them. To find parallels to the sepoy atrocities, we need not, as some London papers pretend, fall back on the middle ages, nor even wander beyond the history of contemporary England. All we want is to study the first Chinese war, an event, so to say, of yesterday. The English soldiery then committed abominations for the mere fun of it; their passions being neither sanctified by religious fanaticism nor exacerbated by hatred against an overbearing and conquering race, nor provoked by the stern resistance of a heroic enemy. The violations of women, the spittings of children, the roasting of whole villages, were then mere wanton sports, not recorded by mandarins, but by British officers themselves.

Even at the present catastrophe it would be an unmitigated mistake to suppose that all the cruelty is on the side of the sepoys, and all the milk of human kindness flows on the side of the English. The letters of the British officers are redolent of malignity. An officer writing from Peshawar gives a description of the disarming of the 10th Irregular Cavalry for not charging the 55th Native Infantry when ordered to do so. He exults in the fact that they were not only disarmed, but stripped of their coats and boots, and after having received 12d. per man, were marched down to the riverside, and there embarked in boats and sent down the Indus, where the writer is delighted to expect every mother's son will have a chance of

being drowned in the rapids. Another writer informs us
that some inhabitants of Peshawar having caused a night
alarm by exploding little mines of gunpowder in honour
of a wedding (a national custom), the persons concerned
were tied up next morning, and "received such a flogging
as they will not easily forget." News arrived from Pindee
that three native chiefs were plotting. Sir John Lawrence
replied to a message ordering a spy to attend to the meeting. On the spy's report, Sir John sent a second message,
"Hang them." The chiefs were hanged. An officer in the
civil service, from Allahabad, writes: "We have power of
life and death in our hands, and we assure you we spare
not." Another from the same place: "Not a day passes
but we string up from ten to fifteen of them (non-
combatants)." One exulting officer writes: "Holmes is
hanging them by the score, like a 'brick.' " Another, in al-
lusion to the summary hanging of a large body of the natives: "Then our fun commenced." A third: "We hold
court-martials on horseback, and every nigger we meet we
either string up or shoot." From Benares we are informed
that thirty zemindars were hanged on the mere suspicion
of sympathizing with their own countrymen, and whole
villages were burned down on the same plea. An officer
from Benares, whose letter is printed in the London
Times, says: "The European troops have become fiends
when opposed to natives."

And then it should not be forgotten that, while the
cruelties of the English are related as acts of martial vigour, told simply, rapidly, without dwelling on disgusting
details, the outrages of the natives, shocking as they are,
are still deliberately exaggerated. For instance, the cir-
cumstantial account first appearing in *The Times*, and
then going the rounds of the London press, of the atrocities perpetrated at Delhi and Meerut, from whom did it
proceed? From a cowardly parson residing at Bangalore,
Mysore, more than a thousand miles, as the bird flies, distant from the scene of action. Actual accounts of Delhi

evince the imagination of an English parson to be capable of breeding greater horrors than even the wild fancy of a Hindu mutineer. The cutting of noses, breasts, etc., in one word, the horrid mutilations committed by the sepoys, are of course more revolting to European feeling than the throwing of red-hot shell on Canton dwellings by a Secretary of the Manchester Peace Society, or the roasting of Arabs pent up in a cave by a French Marshal, or the flaying alive of British soldiers by the cat-o'-nine-tails under drum-head court-martial, or any other of the philanthropical appliances used in British penitentiary colonies. Cruelty, like every other thing, has its fashion, changing according to time and place. Caesar, the accomplished scholar, candidly narrates how he ordered many thousand Gallic warriors to have their right hands cut off. Napoleon would have been ashamed to do this. He preferred dispatching his own French regiments, suspected of republicanism, to Santo Domingo, there to die of the blacks and the plague.

The infamous mutilations committed by the sepoys remind one of the practices of the Christian Byzantine Empire, or the prescriptions of Emperor Charles V's criminal law, or the English punishments for high treason, as still recorded by Judge Blackstone. With Hindus, whom their religion has made virtuosi in the art of self-torturing, these tortures inflicted on the enemies of their race and creed appear quite natural, and must appear still more so to the English, who, only some years since, still used to draw revenues from the Juggernaut festivals, protecting and assisting the bloody rites of a religion of cruelty.

The frantic roars of the "bloody old *Times*," as Cobbett used to call it—its playing the part of a furious character in one of Mozart's operas, who indulges in most melodious strains in the idea of first hanging his enemy, then roasting him, then quartering him, then spitting him, and then flaying him alive—its tearing the passion of revenge to tatters and to rags—all this would appear but silly if under the pathos of tragedy there were not distinctly perceptible the tricks of comedy. The London *Times* overdoes its part, not only from panic. It supplies comedy with a subject even missed by Molière, the Tartuffe of Revenge. What it simply wants is to write up the funds and to screen the Government. As Delhi has not, like the walls of Jericho, fallen before mere puffs of wind, John Bull is to be steeped in cries for revenge up to his very ears, to make him forget that his Government is responsible for the mischief hatched and the colossal dimensions it had been allowed to assume.

New York Daily Tribune, September 16, 1857; reprinted in *Karl Marx on Colonialism and Modernization*, edited by Avineri, op. cit., pp. 212–15.

1864

INAUGURAL ADDRESS AND PROVISIONAL RULES OF THE INTERNATIONAL WORKING MEN'S ASSOCIATION

Fellow working men,

It is a great fact that the misery of the working masses has not diminished from 1848 to 1864, and yet this period is unrivalled for the development of its industry and the growth of its commerce. In 1850, a moderate organ of the British middle class, of more than average information, predicted that if the exports and imports of England were to rise fifty per cent, English pauperism would sink to zero. Alas! On 7 April 1864 the Chancellor of the Exchequer delighted his parliamentary audience by the statement that the total import and export trade of England had grown in 1863 'to £443,955,000, that astonishing sum about three times the trade of the comparatively recent epoch of 1843'. With all that, he was eloquent upon 'poverty'. 'Think,' he exlaimed, 'of those who are on the border of that region,' upon 'wages ... not increased'; upon 'human life ... in nine cases out of ten but a struggle of existence'. He did not speak of the people of Ireland, gradually replaced by machinery in the north, and by sheepwalks in the south, though even the sheep in that unhappy country are decreasing, it is true, not at so rapid a rate as the men. He did not repeat what then had been just betrayed by the highest representatives of the upper ten thousand in a sudden fit of terror. When the garotte panic had reached a certain height, the House of Lords caused an inquiry to be made into, and a report to be published upon, transportation and penal servitude. Out came the murder in the bulky blue book of 1863, and proved it was, by official facts and figures, that the worst of the convicted criminals, the penal serfs of England and Scotland, toiled much less and fared far better than the agricultural labourers of England and Scotland. But this was not all. When, consequent upon the civil war in America, the operatives of Lancashire and Cheshire were thrown upon the streets, the same House of Lords sent to the manufacturing districts a physician commissioned to investigate into the smallest possible amount of carbon and nitrogen, to be administered in the cheapest and plainest form, which on an average might just suffice to 'avert starvation diseases'. Dr Smith, the medical deputy, ascertained that 28,000 grains of carbon and 1,330 grains of nitrogen were the weekly allowance that would keep an average adult just over the level of starvation diseases, and he found furthermore that quantity pretty nearly to agree with the scanty nourishment to which the pressure of extreme distress had actually reduced the cotton operatives. But now mark! The same learned doctor was later on again deputed by the Medical Officer of the Privy Council to inquire into the nourishment of the poorer labouring classes. The results of his researches are embodied in the *Sixth Report on Public Health*, published by order of Parliament in the course of the present year. What did the doctor discover? That the silk weavers, the needle women, the kid glovers, the stocking weavers, and so forth, received, on an average, not even the distress pittance of the cotton operatives, not even the amount of carbon and nitrogen 'just sufficient to avert starvation diseases'. 'Moreover,' we quote from the report,

> as regards the examined families of the agricultural population, it appeared that more than a fifth were with less than the estimated sufficiency of carbonaceous food, that more than one-third were with less than the estimated sufficiency of nitrogenous food, and that in three counties (Berkshire, Oxfordshire, and Somersetshire) insufficiency of nitrogenous food was the average local diet.

'It must be remembered,' adds the official report,

> that privation of food is very reluctantly borne, and that, as a rule, great poorness of diet will only come when other privations have preceded it. . . . Even cleanliness will have been found costly or difficult, and if there still be self-respectful endeavours to maintain it, every such endeavour will represent additional pangs of hunger . . . These are painful reflections, especially when it is remembered that the poverty to which they advert is not the deserved poverty of idleness; in all cases it is the poverty of working populations. Indeed, the work which obtains the scanty pittance of food is for the most part excessively prolonged.

The report brings out the strange, and rather unexpected fact, 'that of the divisions of the United Kingdom', England, Wales, Scotland, and Ireland, 'the agricultural population of England', the richest division, 'is considerably the worst fed'; but that even the agricultural labourers of Berkshire, Oxfordshire, and Somersetshire, fare better than great numbers of skilled indoor operatives of the east of London.

Such are the official statements published by order of Parliament in 1864, during the millennium of free trade, at a time when the Chancellor of the Exchequer told the House of Commons that: 'The average condition of the British labourer has improved in a degree we know to be extraordinary and unexampled in the history of any country or any age.'

Upon these official congratulations jars the dry remark of the official *Public Health Report:* 'The public health of a country means the health of its masses, and the masses will scarcely be healthy unless, to their very base, they be at least moderately prosperous.'

Dazzled by the 'Progress of the Nation' statistics dancing before his eyes, the Chancellor of the Exchequer exclaims in wild ecstasy: 'From 1842 to 1852 the taxable income of the country increased by 6 per cent; in the eight years from 1853 to 1861, it has increased from the basis taken in 1853 20 per cent. The fact is so astonishing to be almost incredible . . .' 'This intoxicating augmentation of wealth and power,' adds Mr Gladstone, 'is entirely confined to classes of property'.

If you want to know under what conditions of broken health, tainted morals, and mental ruin, that 'intoxicating augmentation of wealth and power entirely confined to classes of property' was, and is being, produced by the classes of labour, look to the picture hung up in the last *Public Health Report* of the workshops of tailors, printers, and dressmakers! Compare the *Report of the Children's Employment Commission* of 1863, where it is stated, for instance, that:

> The potters as a class, both men and women, represent a much degenerated population, both physically

and mentally . . . The unhealthy child is an unhealthy parent in his turn . . . A progressive deterioration of the race must go on . . . The degenerescence of the population of Staffordshire would be even greater were it not for the constant recruiting from the adjacent country, and the intermarriages with more healthy races.

Glance at Mr Tremenheere's blue book on *The Grievances Complained of by the Journeymen Bakers!* And who has not shuddered at the paradoxical statement made by the inspectors of factories, and illustrated by the Registrar General, that the Lancashire operatives, while put upon the distress pittance of food, were actually improving in health because of their temporary exclusion by the cotton famine from the cotton factory, and that the mortality of the children was decreasing, because their mothers were now at last allowed to give them, instead of Godfrey's cordial, their own breasts.

Again reverse the medal! The Income and Property Tax Returns laid before the House of Commons on 20 July 1864 teach us that the persons with yearly incomes valued by the tax-gatherer at £50,000 and upwards, had, from 5 April 1862 to 5 April 1863, been joined by a dozen and one, their number having increased in that single year from 67 to 80. The same returns disclose the fact that about 3,000 persons divide amongst themselves a yearly income of about £25,000,000 sterling, rather more than the total revenue doled out annually to the whole mass of the agricultural labourers of England and Wales. Open the Census of 1861, and you will find that the number of the male landed proprietors of England and Wales had decreased from 16,934 in 1851, to 15,066 in 1861, so that the concentration of land had grown in 10 years 11 per cent. If the concentration of the soil of the country in a few hands proceeds at the same rate, the land question will become singularly simplified, as it had become in the

Roman empire, when Nero grinned at the discovery that half the province of Africa was owned by six gentlemen.

We have dwelt so long upon these 'facts so astonishing to be almost incredible', because England heads the Europe of commerce and industry. It will be remembered that some months ago one of the refugee sons of Louis Philippe publicly congratulated the English agricultural labourer on the superiority of his lot over that of his less florid comrade on the other side of the Channel. Indeed, with local colours changed, and on a scale somewhat contracted, the English facts reproduce themselves in all the industrious and progressive countries of the Continent. In all of them there has taken place, since 1848, an unheard-of development of industry, and an undreamed-of expansion of imports and exports. In all of them 'the augmentation of wealth and power entirely confined to classes of property' was truly 'intoxicating'. In all of them, as in England, a minority of the working classes got their real wages somewhat advanced; while in most cases the monetary rise of wages denoted no more a real access of comforts than the inmate of the metropolitan poor-house or orphan asylum, for instance, was in the least benefited by his first necessaries costing £9 15s. 8d. in 1861 against £7 7s. 4d. in 1852. Everywhere the great mass of the working classes were sinking down to a lower depth, at the same rate, at least, that those above them were rising in the social scale. In all countries of Europe it has now become a truth demonstrable to every unprejudiced mind, and only denied by those whose interest it is to hedge other people in a fool's paradise, that no improvement of machinery, no appliance of science to production, no contrivances of communication, no new colonies, no emigration, no opening of markets, no free trade, nor all these things put together, will do away with the miseries of the industrious masses; but that, on the present false base, every fresh development of the productive powers of labour must tend to deepen social contrasts and point social antagonisms.

Death of starvation rose almost to the rank of an institution, during this intoxicating epoch of economical progress, in the metropolis of the British empire. That epoch is marked in the annals of the world by the quickened return, the widening compass, and the deadlier effects of the social pest called a commercial and industrial crisis.

After the failure of the revolutions of 1848, all party organizations and party journals of the working classes were, on the Continent, crushed by the iron hand of force, the most advanced sons of labour fled in despair to the transatlantic republic, and the short-lived dreams of emancipation vanished before an epoch of industrial fever, moral marasmus, and political reaction. The defeat of the continental working classes, partly owed to the diplomacy of the English government, acting then as now in fraternal solidarity with the cabinet of St Petersburg, soon spread its contagious effects on this side of the Channel. While the rout of their continental brethren unmanned the English working classes, and broke their faith in their own cause, it restored to the landlord and the money-lord their somewhat shaken confidence. They insolently withdrew concessions already advertised. The discoveries of new goldlands led to an immense exodus, leaving an irreparable void in the ranks of the British proletariat. Others of its formerly active members were caught by the temporary bribe of greater work and wages, and turned into 'political blacks'. All the efforts made at keeping up, or remodelling, the Chartist movement, failed signally; the press organs of the working class died one by one of the apathy of the masses, and, in point of fact, never before seemed the English working class so thoroughly reconciled to a state of political nullity. If, then, there had been no solidarity of action between the British and the continental working classes, there was, at all events, a solidarity of defeat.

And yet the period passed since the revolutions of 1848

has not been without its compensating features. We shall here only point to two great facts.

After a thirty years' struggle, fought with most admirable perseverance, the English working classes, improving a momentaneous split between the landlords and moneylords, succeeded in carrying the Ten Hours Bill. The immense physical, moral, and intellectual benefits hence accruing to the factory operatives, half-yearly chronicled in the reports of the inspectors of factories, are now acknowledged on all sides. Most of the continental governments had to accept the English Factory Act in more or less modified forms, and the English Parliament itself is every year compelled to enlarge its sphere of action. But besides its practical import, there was something else to exalt the marvellous success of this working men's measure. Through their most notorious organs of science, such as Dr Ure, Professor Senior, and other sages of that stamp, the middle class had predicted, and to their heart's content proved, that any legal restriction of the hours of labour must sound the death knell of British industry, which vampire-like, could but live by sucking blood, and children's blood, too. In olden times, child murder was a mysterious rite of the religion of Moloch, but it was practised on some very solemn occasions only, once a year perhaps, and then Moloch had no exclusive bias for the children of the poor. This struggle about the legal restriction of the hours of labour raged the more fiercely since, apart from frightened avarice, it told indeed upon the great contest between the blind rule of the supply and demand laws which form the political economy of the middle class, and social production controlled by social foresight, which forms the political economy of the working class. Hence the Ten Hours Bill was not only a great practical success; it was the victory of a principle; it was the first time that in broad daylight the political economy of the middle class succumbed to the political economy of the working class.

But there was in store a still greater victory of the political economy of labour over the political economy of property. We speak of the cooperative movement, especially the cooperative factories raised by the unassisted efforts of a few bold 'hands'. The value of these great social experiments cannot be overrated. By deed, instead of by argument, they have shown that production on a large scale, and in accord with the behests of modern science, may be carried on without the existence of a class of masters employing a class of hands; that to bear fruit, the means of labour need not be monopolized as a means of dominion over, and of extortion against, the labouring man himself; and that, like slave labour, like serf labour, hired labour is but a transitory and inferior form, destined to disappear before associated labour plying its toil with a willing hand, a ready mind, and a joyous heart. In England, the seeds of the cooperative system were sown by Robert Owen; the working men's experiments, tried on the Continent, were, in fact, the practical upshot of the theories, not invented, but loudly proclaimed, in 1848.

At the same time, the experience of the period from 1848 to 1864 has proved beyond doubt that, however excellent in principle, and however useful in practice, cooperative labour, if kept within the narrow circle of the casual efforts of private workmen, will never be able to arrest the growth in geometrical progression of monopoly, to free the masses, nor even to perceptibly lighten the burden of their miseries. It is perhaps for this very reason that plausible noblemen, philanthropic middle-class spouters, and even keen political economists, have all at once turned nauseously complimentary to the very cooperative labour system they had vainly tried to nip in the bud by deriding it as the utopia of the dreamer, or stigmatizing it as the sacrilege of the socialist. To save the industrious masses, cooperative labour ought to be developed to national dimensions, and, consequently, to be fostered by national means. Yet the lords of land and the lords of capital will always use their political privileges for the defence and perpetuation of their economical monopolies. So far from promoting, they will continue to lay every possible impediment in the way of the emancipation of labour. Remember the sneer with which, last session, Lord Palmerston put down the advocates of the Irish Tenants' Right Bill. The House of Commons, cried he, is a house of landed proprietors.

To conquer political power has therefore become the great duty of the working classes. They seem to have comprehended this, for in England, Germany, Italy and France there have taken place simultaneous revivals, and simultaneous efforts are being made at the political reorganization of the working men's party.

One element of success they possess—numbers; but numbers weigh only in the balance, if united by combination and led by knowledge. Past experience has shown how disregard of that bond of brotherhood which ought to exist between the workmen of different countries, and incite them to stand firmly by each other in all their struggles for emancipation, will be chastised by the common discomfiture of their incoherent efforts. This thought prompted the working men of different countries assembled on 28 September 1864, in public meeting at St Martin's Hall, to found the International Association.

Another conviction swayed that meeting.

If the emancipation of the working classes requires their fraternal concurrence, how are they to fulfil that great mission with a foreign policy in pursuit of criminal designs, playing upon national prejudices, and squandering in piratical wars the people's blood and treasure? It was not the wisdom of the ruling classes, but the heroic resistance to their criminal folly by the working classes of England, that saved the west of Europe from plunging headlong into an infamous crusade for the perpetuation and propagation of slavery on the other side of the Atlantic. The shameless approval, mock sympathy, or idiotic indifference, with which the upper classes of Europe have witnessed the mountain fortress of the Caucasus falling a prey to, and heroic Poland being assassinated by, Russia; the immense and unresisted encroachments of that barbarous power, whose head is at St Petersburg, and whose hands are in every cabinet of Europe, have taught the working classes the duty to master themselves the mysteries of international politics; to watch the diplomatic acts of their respective governments; to counteract them, if necessary, by all means in their power; when unable to prevent, to combine in simultaneous denunciations, and to vindicate the simple laws of morals and justice, which ought to govern the relations of private individuals, as the rules paramount of the intercourse of nations.

The fight for such a foreign policy forms part of the general struggle for the emancipation of the working classes.

Proletarians of all countries, unite!

PROVISIONAL RULES

Considering,

That the emancipation of the working classes must be conquered by the working classes themselves; that the struggle for the emancipation of the working classes means not a struggle for class privileges and monopolies, but for equal rights and duties, and the abolition of all class rule;

That the economical subjection of the man of labour to the monopolizer of the means of labour, that is, the sources of life, lies at the bottom of servitude in all its forms, of all social misery, mental degradation, and political dependence;

That the economical emancipation of the working classes is therefore the great end to which every political movement ought to be subordinate as a means;

That all efforts aiming at that great end have hitherto failed from the want of solidarity between the manifold divisions of labour in each country, and from the absence of a fraternal bond of union between the working classes of different countries;

That the emancipation of labour is neither a local nor a national, but a social problem, embracing all countries in which modern society exists, and depending for its solution on the concurrence, practical and theoretical, of the most advanced countries;

That the present revival of the working classes in the most industrious countries of Europe, while it raises a new hope, gives solemn warning against a relapse into the old errors and calls for the immediate combination of the still disconnected movements;

For these reasons—

The undersigned members of the committee, holding its powers by resolution of the public meeting held on 28 September 1864, at St Martin's Hall, London, have taken the steps necessary for founding the Working Men's International Association;

They declare that this International Association and all societies and individuals adhering to it, will acknowledge truth, justice, and morality, as the basis of their conduct towards each other, and towards all men, without regard to colour, creed, or nationality;

They hold it the duty of a man to claim the rights of a man and a citizen, not only for himself, but for every man who does his duty. No rights without duties, no duties without rights;

And in this spirit they have drawn up the following provisional rules of the International Association:

1. This association is established to afford a central medium of communication and cooperation between working men's societies existing in different countries, and aiming at the same end, viz., the protection, advancement, and complete emancipation of the working classes.

2. The name of the society shall be: 'The Working Men's International Association'.

3. In 1865 there shall meet in Belgium a general working men's Congress, consisting of representatives of such working men's societies as may have joined the International Association. The Congress will have to proclaim before Europe the common aspirations of the working classes, decide on the definitive rules of the International Association, consider the means required for its successful working, and appoint the Central Council of the Association. The General Congress is to meet once a year.

4. The Central Council shall sit in London, and consist of working men belonging to the different countries represented in the International Association. It shall from its own members elect the officers necessary for the transaction of business, such as a president, a treasurer, a general secretary, corresponding secretaries for the different countries, etc.

5. On its annual meetings, the General Congress shall receive a public account of the annual transactions of the Central Council. The Central Council, yearly appointed by the Congress, shall have power to add to the number of its members. In cases of urgency, it may convoke the General Congress before the regular yearly term.

6. The Central Council shall form an international agency between the different cooperating associations, so that the working men in one country be constantly informed of the movements of their class in every other country; that an inquiry into the social state of the different countries of Europe be made simultaneously, and under a common direction; that the questions of general interest mooted in one society be ventilated by all; and that when immediate practical steps should be needed, as, for instance, in case of international quarrels, the action of the associated societies be simultaneous and uniform. Whenever it seems opportune, the Central Council shall

take the initiative of proposals to be laid before the different national or local societies.

7. Since the success of the working men's movement in each country cannot be secured but by the power of union and combination, while, on the other hand, the usefulness of the international Central Council must greatly depend on the circumstance whether it has to deal with a few national centres of working men's associations, or with a great number of small and disconnected local societies, the members of the International Association shall use their utmost efforts to combine the disconnected working men's societies of their respective countries into national bodies, represented by central national organs. It is self-understood, however, that the appliance of this rule will depend upon the peculiar laws of each country, and that, apart from legal obstacles, no independent local society shall be precluded from directly corresponding with the London Central Council.

8. Until the meeting of the first Congress, the committee chosen on 28 September 1864 will act as a Provisional Central Council, try to connect the different national working men's associations, enlist members in the United Kingdom, take the steps preparatory to the convocation of the 'General Congress, and discuss with the national and local societies the main questions to be laid before that Congress.

9. Each member of the International Association, on removing his domicile from one country to another, will receive the fraternal support of the associated working men.

10. While united in a perpetual bond of fraternal cooperation, the working men's societies, joining the International Association, will preserve their existent organizations intact.

Address and Provisional Rules of the Working Men's International Association, London, 1864.

5. 'Wading Through Economic Filth': Economic Writings, 1857–1867

EDITOR'S NOTE

'The devastating effects of English industry, when contemplated with regard to India,' Karl Marx wrote in one of his articles on Indian affairs (*New York Daily Tribune*, August 5, 1853), '... are palpable and confounding. But we must not forget that they are only the organic results of the whole system of production as it is now constituted. That production rests on the supreme rule of capital. The centralization of capital is essential to the existence of capital as an independent power. The destructive influence of that centralization upon the markets of the world does but reveal, in the most gigantic dimensions, the inherent organic laws of political economy now at work in every civilized town. The bourgeois period of history has to create the material basis of the new world—on the one hand the universal intercourse founded upon the mutual dependency of mankind, and the means of that intercourse; on the other hand the development of the productive powers of man and the transformation of material production into a scientific domination of natural agencies. Bourgeois industry and commerce create these material conditions of a new world in the same way as geological revolutions have created the surface of the earth. When a great social revolution shall have mastered the results of the bourgeois epoch, the market of the world and the modern powers of production, and subjected them to the common control of the most advanced peoples, then only will human progress cease to resemble that hideous pagan idol, who would not drink the nectar but from the skulls of the slain.'

The understanding of the process of material production (in modern times primarily of 'commodities' for distribution and exchange), the analysis of 'the inherent organic laws of political economy', unquestionably stood at the center of Marx's system. The materialist interpretation of history proclaimed that this process of production provides the key to an understanding of human history and of human society. It is that through which these can be understood. The great categories of bourgeois economic thought—labour, capital, and rent—were for Marx living protagonists in a great contemporary drama that would end in the collapse of capitalism and of its way of viewing and organizing the world. The contradiction between labour and capital, the theory of surplus value, the distinction between constant and variable capital, the allied beliefs that capitalism was confronted by a falling rate of profit and ever-sharpening economic crises resulting from inherent tendencies to overproduction and underconsumption, the doctrine of the growing (absolute or relative) immiserization of the proletariat: all these were crucial to Marx's claim that he was neither a defiant romantic nor a moralizing prophet, but a *scientist* of revolution, a man showing the present world its inevitable but also higher and better future.

In 1857, while wading conscientiously but with great effort of will through what he called 'economic filth,' Marx drafted the first outline plan of his proposed great work on political economy. This work, he believed, would lay bare the laws of capitalist society and show clearly and 'scientifically' its inescapable tendencies and its ultimate necessary transformation into a free society of producers. The plan read as follows:

I.   THE BOOK ON CAPITAL
    a) Capital in general
      1. Production process of capital
      2. Circulation process of capital
      3. Profit and interest
    b) Section on Competition
    c) Section on the Credit System
    d) Section on Share-Capital
II.   THE BOOK ON LANDED PROPERTY
III. THE BOOK ON WAGE-LABOUR
IV.   THE BOOK ON THE STATE
V.   THE BOOK ON FOREIGN TRADE
VI.   THE BOOK ON THE WORLD MARKET AND CRISES

The seven notebooks of 1857 and 1858, containing drafts for this intended critique of political economy, were first published as Marx's *Grundrisse der Kritik der politischen Ökonomie* (the editor's title) in Moscow in 1939, where the discovery of the manuscript—apparently unknown to Engels—had been announced in 1925. Their gradual permeation into the consciousness of Marx scholars in the 1950s and 1960s has first been fully reflected only in the 1970s. It has profoundly affected much of the detailed discussion of Marx's methodology and of his relation to Hegel, of Marx's view of pre-capitalist formations and of the nature and role of property; it has affected the discussion of his economics more generally. The drafts do not contain what many political theorists would have wished for—any outlines or materials for Marx's proposed books on the state, on foreign trade, or on the world market. Those books in fact were never written. In 1859 Marx published, under pressure from Engels and the publishers, a summary introduction to his main economic thought as the *Contribution to the Critique of Political Economy* (apart from the Preface reproduced earlier in the present volume, it is of little intrinsic interest, being superseded by *Capital*). In 1866, drawing near the completion of his first proper volume, published in 1867 as *Capital, Volume I*, he had produced a new outline for the work, now entitled *Capital—A Critique of Political Economy*. This outline read as follows:

BOOK I   PRODUCTION PROCESS OF
           CAPITAL
BOOK II   CIRCULATION PROCESS OF
           CAPITAL
BOOK III   FORMS OF THE PROCESS
           AS A WHOLE
BOOK IV   THE HISTORY OF THEORY

Only the first volume—indeed subtitled 'the production process of capital'—was published in Marx's lifetime, though it appeared in a number of editions, in the original German, and in English, French, and Russian translations with revisions or new prefaces by Marx. Volumes II—'the circulation process'—and III—'the process as a whole'—were compiled, in accordance with the new outline, by Engels, from drafts left by Marx, and published after Marx's death. Volume IV, also compiled from drafts left by Marx, was published even later by Karl Kautsky under the title *Theories of Surplus Value*, in three separate volumes.

These massive but incomplete portions of Marx's in-

tended *magnum opus*—the critique of political economy—were for him his most important scientific and
scholarly legacy. Nevertheless, they have understandably
not commended themselves to a general public, even of
Marxist activists and believers. They are too massive, too
complex, too demanding. And if we succeed in wading
through what appears to be the rigorous logical analysis of
the capitalist process of production in Volume I as a study
of the process of the production of value, of surplus value,
of capital, and of the constant production and reproduction of basic antagonistic social relations, we are liable to
be discouraged by the discovery that the whole of that
volume is perhaps best treated as an abstract model to be
amended and supplemented by the recognition of further
complexities and countervailing trends in Volumes II and
III. It takes a very serious economist to work through all
this; at least until recently the vast majority of contemporary Western economists have regarded Marx's economic
analysis as a historical curiosity, and many still hold this
view. For them it is an able and in many ways prescient
attempt to deal with problems in a dated and quite inap-
posite Ricardian theoretical framework, and therefore of
no contemporary interest. On that question, of course,
there is and will long be hot debate—but it is debate for
the economically literate. For the general reader, even for
the most serious reader of this selection, one can only hope
to give some of the flavour and some important themes of
Marx's economic writing. The selections that follow are
from the famous methodological introduction with which
the drafts known as the *Grundrisse* open; from the talk
Value, Price and Profit, which Marx wrote in 1865 for a
debate in the General Council of the First International on
the effects of demanding rises in wages; and from the first
volume of *Capital*. *Value, Price and Profit* presents in
simple language, for a lay audience, some of the central
economic notions in *Capital*. The selections from *Capital*

are meant to give an indication of the style and range of Marx's writing rather than to present an argument that cannot be summarized in selections. To convey the flavour of the writing, his usually long and frequent footnotes are retained in the selection from Chapter 1.

FROM *GRUNDRISSE*

~~~~~~

INTRODUCTION: PRODUCTION, CONSUMPTION, DISTRIBUTION, EXCHANGE (CIRCULATION)

(1) PRODUCTION

Independent Individuals. Eighteenth-century ideas.
The subject matter here, first of all, *material production.*

Individuals producing in society—therefore socially determined production by individuals—is naturally the starting point. The single, isolated hunter and fisherman, with whom Smith and Ricardo begin, belongs to the unimaginative fancies of eighteenth-century Robinsonades [Utopias on the lines of Defoe's *Robinson Crusoe*], which certainly do not, as cultural historians believe, express simply a reaction to over-refinement and a return to a misconceived natural life. As little as Rousseau's *Contrat social*, whereby naturally independent subjects are brought into association and relationship by contract, is based on such naturalism. This is illusion, the purely aesthetic illusion of small and great Robinsonades. It is, on the contrary, the anticipation of 'bourgeois society,' which, since the sixteenth century, has been preparing itself for, and, in the eighteenth has made giant strides towards, maturity. In this freely competitive society the individual appears as released from the natural ties, etc. which, in earlier epochs of history, made him an appendage of a distinct, limited human conglomerate. For the prophets of the eighteenth century, on whose shoulders Smith and Ricardo still firmly stand, this eighteenth-century individual—the product, on the one hand, of the breaking up of feudal social patterns and, on the other, of the new productive powers developed since the sixteenth century—hovers as an ideal of a past existence. Not as a historical result but as the starting point of history. Because as Natural Man, conformable to their idea of human nature, not as arising historically but as determined by nature. This illusion has occurred in each successive epoch up till now. Steuart, who in many respects, as aristocrat and in contrast to the eighteenth century, stands on firmer historical ground, has avoided such naïveté.

The further back in history we go, the more does the individual, and thus also the productive individual, appear as dependent, as part of a greater whole: first still quite naturally in the family and, expanding thence, in the tribe; later in the various forms of community resulting from opposition between and amalgamation of tribes. Not until the eighteenth century, in 'bourgeois society,' do the various forms of association in society appear to the individual simply as means to his private ends, as external necessity. But the epoch producing this position, that of the individualized individual, is precisely the epoch of the hitherto most highly developed social (from this point of view, general) conditions. Man, in the most literal sense, is a ζῶον πολιτιχόν [zoon politikon—a political animal], not just a social animal but an animal which can achieve individuation only in society. The production of the isolated individual outside society—a rare event which may perhaps occur where a civilized man, already possessing dynamic social powers within himself, is driven by chance into the wilderness—is as much as impossibility as the development of language without individuals living *together* and talking to one another. This should detain us no longer. It need not have been mentioned at all if the nonsense, which seemed sensible and reasonable to people in the eighteenth century, had not been seriously reintroduced, by Bastiat, Carey, Proudhon, etc., into the latest economic theory. Proudhon among others naturally finds it pleasant to give a historico-philosophical explanation of the origins of an economic relation of whose historical formation he is ignorant, by turning to the myth that Adam or Prometheus hit upon the idea ready-made and it was then introduced, etc. Nothing is more tediously dry than a *locus communis* having fantasies.

Perpetuation of historic relations of production.—Production and distribution in general. Property.

Now when we speak of production, it is always of production at a particular stage of social development—or production by individuals in society. Hence it might appear that, in order to speak of production at all, we must either trace the historical development in its various phases or declare at once that we are dealing with a specific historical epoch, as for example with modern bourgeois production, which in fact is our particular subject. Only, all epochs of production have certain features and definitions in common. *Production in general* is an abstraction, but a reasonable abstraction inasmuch as it really calls attention to and fixes the common element, saving us recapitulation. Nevertheless this *universality*, or the common element distinguished through comparison, is itself organized into manifold subdivisions and numerous divergent definitions. Some belong to all epochs, some are common to only a few. [Some] definitions will be common to the most modern epoch and to the earliest. No production will be conceivable without them; but when the most highly developed languages have rules and definitions in common with the least developed, then it is necessary to distinguish what determines their development, its difference from the universal and common element, the definitions which are valid for production in general, in order that their essential diversity is not forgotten in this unity—which after all derives from the fact that the subject, mankind, and the object, nature, are the same. In this forgetfulness, for example, lies the whole wisdom of modern economists who demonstrate the everlasting and harmonious character of existing social conditions. For example. No production possible without an instrument of production, even though this instrument were merely the hand. None possible without previous accumulated labour, even if this labour were only the skill acquired by and concentrated in the hand of the savage through repeated practice. Capital is among other things also an instrument of production, the objectification of past labour. Therefore capital is a universal and perpetual condition of nature; that is, if I omit just that specific quality which alone makes capital out of 'instrument of production,' out of 'accumulated labour.' The whole history of the relations of production thus appears, as for instance in Carey, as a malevolent falsification on the part of governments.

If there is no such thing as production in general, there is also no such thing as general production. Production is always a *particular* branch of production—e.g., agriculture, stock-farming, manufacture, etc.—or it is *totality*. Political economy, however, is not technology. The relationship of general conditions of production at a given social level to particular forms of production will be developed elsewhere (later). Finally too, production is not just particular: It is, rather, a stable substance of society, a social subject, which is active in a greater or lesser totality of branches of production. The relationship which scientific representation bears to the actual movement does not belong here either. Production in general. Particular branches of production. Totality of production.

It is customary to provide a work on the economy with a general introduction—and it is just this which appears under the title 'Production' (see, for example, J. S. Mill), in which the *general conditions* of all production are dealt with. This general section consists or ostensibly consists of: 1) the conditions failing which production is impossible. That is, in fact, merely to indicate the essential motives of all production. This actually reduces itself, as we shall see, to a few very simple definitions, which can be expressed in shallow tautologies; 2) the conditions which, to a greater or lesser degree, advance production, such as, for instance, Adam Smith's progressive and stagnant state of society. In order to raise this perceptive observation of his to scientific significance, investigations would be necessary concerning the periods of *degrees of production* in the development of individual nations—an investigation which properly lies outside the limits of our subject, but inasmuch as it does belong to it, should be considered with the development of competition, accumulation, etc. In a general context the answer amounts to the generalization that an industrial nation achieves the peak of its production at the moment when, in general, it reaches its historical peak. In fact.[1] The industrial peak of a nation, when still not the gain itself but the process of gaining is its main concern. So far the Yankees outstrip the English. Or again, that, for example, certain races, situations, climates, natural conditions such as access to the sea, fertility of the soil, etc., are more favourable to production than others. This again leads to the tautology that wealth is more easily produced to the degree that its elements are subjectively and objectively more abundant.

But all this is not the economists' true concern in this general area. Rather, production—see, for instance, Mill—is to be represented, in distinction from distribution, etc., as bound by historically independent eternal natural laws, thus providing an opportunity for the underhand introduction of *bourgeois* situations as irreversible natural laws of society in the abstract. This is the more or less conscious aim of the whole process. In the matter of distribution, on the other hand, people are supposed to have allowed themselves, in point of fact, all kinds of options. Quite apart from this crude severance of

---

1. English in the original. [E.K.]

production and distribution and their true relationship, it must be evident from the beginning that, however varied distribution may be at different stages of social development, it must be just as possible, in this case as in the case of production, to pick out common definitions, just as possible to confound or obliterate all historical differences in *universal human* laws. For example, the slave, the serf and the wage labourer all receive an amount of food which enables them to exist as slave, serf or wage labourer. The conqueror living from tribute, the official living from taxes, the landowner from rent, the monk from alms, the Levite from tithes, all receive a share of social production, determined by other laws than that determining the share of the slave, etc. The two cardinal points made under this heading by all economists are: 1) property; 2) protection of the same by courts, police, etc. These may be briefly answered:

on 1) All production is appropriation of nature by the individual within and by means of a particular form of society. In this sense it is tautologous to say that property (appropriation) is a condition of production. It is, however, nonsensical to make a jump from that to a specific form of property, e.g., private property. (Which additionally supposes an opposite form, that of *non-property*, as an equal condition.) History on the contrary shows common property (e.g., among the Indians, Slavs, early Celts, etc.) to be the more primitive form, a form which, in the guise of communally held property, long continues to play a significant role. The question whether wealth will develop more successfully under this form of ownership or that is not under discussion here. But that no discussion of production and hence of society is possible where no form of ownership exists, is tautologous. Appropriation which makes nothing its own is a *contradictio in subjecto*.

on 2) Safeguarding of gains, etc. When these trivialities are reduced to their true value they express more than their advocates realize. That is to say that every form of production breeds its own legal systems, forms of government, etc. Their crudity and conceptual barrenness are evident in attempts to bring together in a casual relationship, a merely reflexive connection, things which belong together organically. Bourgeois economists delude themselves with the notion that better production is possible under a modern police system than under the law of the mailed fist, for example. They simply forget that the latter is also a law and that the right of might still lives on, in another form, in their 'constitutional state.'

When the social conditions representing a certain stage of production first arise, or when they are already withering away, disturbances of production naturally occur, though to different degrees and with different results.

To sum up: Definitions common to all stages of production exist, which are established by thought as universal; but the so-called *general conditions* of all production are merely these abstract impulses which relate to no actual historical stage of production.

(2) *The general relation of production to distribution, exchange, consumption.*

Before embarking on a more extensive analysis of production it is necessary to examine the various headings which economists set against them.

The obvious presentation: in production members of society adapt (produce, fashion) the products of nature to human needs; distribution determines the proportion in which the individual shares in these products; exchange makes available to him the specific products into which he wants to convert the share allotted him in distribution; finally, in consumption the products become objects of enjoyment, of individual application. Production brings forth the objects corresponding to requirements; distribution shares them out according to social laws; exchange further distributes what has been shared out, according to individual need; lastly, in consumption the product leaves this social movement, becomes a direct object and servant of individual need which it satisfies in use. Production thus appears as the starting point, consumption as the end, distribution and exchange as the middle which is itself again twofold, since distribution is determined as the impetus deriving from society, exchange as that deriving from the individual. In production, the person is objectified; in the person the thing is subjectified; in distribution society, in the form of universal, governing definitions, takes over mediation between production and consumption; in exchange they are mediated by the accidental constitution of the individual.

Distribution determines the proportion (share) in which products fall to individuals; exchange determines production, in which the individual claims the share allotted to him in distribution.

Production, distribution, exchange, consumption thus form a regular syllogism; production the universal, distribution and exchange the particular, consumption the singular in which the whole is locked together.[2] This is, of course, a connection, but a superficial one. Production is determined by universal natural laws, distribution by accident of society, for which reason it can further produc-

---

2. Marx's conception of the syllogism here is inaccurate: if the major premise is universal and the minor particular, the conclusion will be particular. To reach a singular conclusion we would require a singular minor premise. Marx's conception is aided by the ambiguity between universality and particularity as applied to propositions, and universality and particularity as applied to terms, and the uncertainty and the controversy concerning singular propositions in traditional formal logic. He may be thinking that 'all men are mortal' is a universal proposition, that 'Socrates is a man' is a particular proposition because it elevates a particular feature or refers to a particular (whereas it is in fact a singular proposition), and that the conclusion 'Socrates is mortal' is truly singular because it focuses attention on the singular subject, a proper name. But all this is confusion. More plausibly, Marx may be thinking of the conclusion bringing together into a (single or singular) unity the major and the minor premise. [E.K.]

tion to a greater or lesser degree; exchange lies between the two as a formal social movement, and the concluding act of consumption, conceived not only as objective but also as purpose, really lies outside the economy, except in so far as it reacts upon the starting point and introduces the whole process afresh.

Opponents of the political economists—whether from within or outside their sphere—who reproach them with barbarically sundering what belongs together, stand either on the same ground as they do or below them. Nothing is more common than the charge that the political economists focus too exclusively on production as an end in itself. Distribution is equally important. This change is based on the economic idea that distribution occupies a self-sufficient, independent sphere beside production. Or the motives would not be conceived in their unity. As though this severance had forced its way not from reality into the textbooks but conversely from the textbooks into reality, and as though this was a question of the dialectical matching of concepts and not of the comprehension of actual conditions! . . .

Ultimate Exchange and Circulation

. . . The inference at which we arrive is not that production, distribution, exchange and consumption are identical but that they are all members of a totality, differences within a unity. Production encroaches not only on itself in the contrary definition of production but on the other moments[3] determining action as well. From it the process always starts again anew. It is self-evident that exchange and consumption cannot outstrip it. So, too, distribution as distribution of products. As distribution of the agents of production, however, it is itself a moment of production. A specific production thus determines specific con-

---

3. A Hegelian term indicating a specific constituent impulse or logico-historical tendency within a whole. Cf. *momentum.* [E.K.]

sumption, distribution, exchange, and the *specific inter-relationships of these moments*. Admittedly, production too, *in its one-sided form*, is for its part determined by the other moments. For example, when the market, that is the sphere of exchange, expands, production grows to fill the new area and its divisions are deeper. Any alteration of distribution alters production; e.g., from concentration of capital, an altered distribution of population between town and country, etc. Lastly, the requirements of consumption determine production. There is interaction between the various moments. This is the case with every organic whole.

(3) *The Method of Political Economy*

In considering a given country politico-economically, we begin with its population, its distribution by classes, between town and country and the coast, the different branches of production, exports and imports, annual production and consumption, the prices of goods, etc.

It seems right to start with the real and concrete, the actual presuppositions, thus, for example, in economics with the population, which is the basis for and the subject of the whole social act of production. But upon closer examination this is seen to be false. Population, if, for example, I omit the classes of which it consists, is an abstraction. These classes, again, are empty terms if I do not know the elements on which they depend. For example, wage labour, capital, etc. These control exchange, division of labour, prices, etc. Capital, for example, is nothing without wage labour, without value, money, prices, etc. If, therefore, I were to begin with the population it would be a chaotic representation of the whole, and by means of more exact definitions I would arrive analytically at ever simpler ideas; from the postulated concrete to ever thinner abstractions, till I had reached the simplest definitions. From that point it would be necessary to retrace my steps until I finally arrived once more at population, but this time not as the chaotic representation of a

whole but as a rich totality of many definitions and relations. The first path is the one followed, historically, by
economics from its genesis. The seventeenth-century
economists, for example, always begin with the living
whole, the population, the nation, state, a number of
states, etc.; they always end by bringing out, through
analysis, a few determining, abstract, universal relations
such as division of labour, money, value, etc. As soon as
these individual moments had been more or less established and abstracted, economic systems began, moving
upward from the simple relations such as labour, division
of labour, need, exchange value to the state, exchange between nations and world trade. The latter is manifestly
the scientifically correct method. The concrete is concrete
because it is the sum-total of many determinations, i.e.,
unity of the manifold. In thought, therefore, it appears
as a process of pulling together, as result not as starting
point, although it is the actual starting point and thus
also the starting point for perception and representation.
On the first path, the whole representation dissolved in
abstract definitions; on the second, abstract definitions
lead to a reproduction of the concrete in the course
of thinking. Hegel thus fell into the illusion of conceiving the real as the result of thought concentrated and absorbed in itself, itself its own motive power, whereas
the method of mounting from the abstract to the concrete is only that whereby thought appropriates the
concrete, to reproduce it as intellectually concrete. In no
way the genesis of the concrete itself. Take, for example,
the simplest economic category, e.g., exchange value; to
this is subordinated population, a population which produces in given conditions; also particular types of family,
community or state, etc. It can never exist except as an
abstract, one-sided relation of an already given concrete
living whole. As a category, on the other hand, exchange
value leads an antediluvian existence. Hence, for that
consciousness—and the philosophical consciousness is

determined in this way—for which conceptual thought is the real person and thus the conceptual world as such the true reality—the movement of categories seems the true act of production—which, unfortunately only gets its impulse from outside—whose result is the world; and this—but this again is tautologous—is correct in so far as concrete totality, a thought totality, a thought *concretum*, is in fact a product of thought, of understanding; in no way however a product of the self-creating idea, which thinks itself outside or beyond perception and imagination, but the working-out of perception and imagination into concepts. The whole, as it comes into the head as a totality of thought, is a product of the thinking brain, which assimilates the world to itself in the only way possible to it, a way which differs from the artistic, religious, practical and intellectual assimilation of this world. The real subject continues to exist independently outside the mind; as long, that is, as the mind operates only speculatively, theoretically. Hence even in the theoretical method the subject, society, must always be kept in mind as a presupposition.

But do these simple categories not also have an independent historical or natural existence prior to the more concrete ones? *Ça dépend*. Hegel, for example, correctly starts the philosophy of law with possession, as the simplest legal relation of the subject [person]. But possession does not exist before family or master-and-servant relationships which are much more concrete. Against this it would be correct to say that families or kinship groups exist which simply *possess*, but own no *property*. The simpler category thus appears as a relation of simple family or kinship groups with respect to property. In a more highly developed society it appears as the simpler relation of a developed organization. The concrete substratum, whose point of reference is property, is however always presupposed. One can imagine a single savage possessing something. In that case, however, possession is not a legal relationship. It is not correct that possession evolves historically together with the family. Rather does it always subsume this 'concrete legal category.' Meanwhile there would always remain thus much, that simple categories are expressions of relations in which the less developed concrete can have realized itself without having yet posited the more many-sided connection or relation which is intellectually expressed in the more concrete category; while the more developed concrete retains the same category as a subordinate relation. Money can exist, and historically did exist, before capital existed, or banks, wage labour, etc. In this regard it may therefore be said that the simpler category may express prevailing relations of a more developed whole, already existing historically before the whole developed in the direction expressed by a more concrete category. To that degree the progress of abstract thought, rising from the simplest to the combination, would represent the true historical process.

On the other hand it may be said that highly developed but historically less mature forms of society exist, in which the highest forms of economic organization, e.g., cooperation, a developed division of labour, occur without the existence of money in any form, for example, Peru. In Slav communities, too, money, and the exchange process necessitating it, never or seldom emerges within individual communities, but on their boundaries, in dealings with other groups, so that it is entirely wrong to make exchange central to the community, as its original constituent element. It appears, at first, in the inter-connections between the various communities rather than in the relations between members of one and the same community. Furthermore, although money plays an early and universal part, nevertheless in ancient times it was a dominant feature only of those nations of somewhat one-sided determination, trading nations. Even in the most cultivated sectors of antiquity, among the Greeks and Romans, its full development, which is assumed in modern bourgeois society, only appears in the period of their dissolution. Thus this perfectly simple category does not appear historically in its most thoroughgoing form except in the most highly developed social conditions. Nor does it at all make its way through all economic relations. For example, in the Roman Empire at its highest point of development, taxes and payments in kind remained fundamental. The money system really only fully developed there in the army. Nor did it ever seize the whole of labour. Therefore, although the simpler category may have existed historically before the more concrete one, it can belong in its full intensive and extensive development precisely to a complex form of society, whereas the more concrete category was more fully developed in a less developed form of society.

Labour appears a perfectly simple category. Even its representation in this general form—as labour as such—is age-old. Yet, conceived of economically in this simple form, 'labour' is a category just as modern as the circumstances that give rise to this simple abstraction. The monetary system, for example, places wealth quite objectively outside itself in money. In contrast with this point of view, it was a great advance when the manufacturing or commercial system located the source of wealth not in the object but in subjective activity—commerce and manufacture—while nevertheless still conceiving this activity, in a limited way, as money-making. Over against this system stands the physiocratic, taking a particular form of labour—agriculture—as the producer of wealth and [seeing] the object itself no longer in the disguise of money but as product in general, as the universal result of labour. This product, in conformity with the limitations of activity, [still seen] as a product determined by nature—a product of agriculture, fruit of the soil *par excellence*.

It was a colossal step forward for Adam Smith to discard every specificity of wealth-generating activity—just labour, not manufacturing, or commercial or agricultural labour alone, but each of these as much as the others. With the abstract general concept of wealth-generating activity now also the general concept of the object defined as wealth, the product in general or again labour in general, but as past, objectified, labour. How difficult and important this transition was comes out in Adam Smith's own occasional lapses back into the physiocratic system. Now it might seem as if this had discovered only the abstract expression for the simplest and earliest relationship in which men—in whatever form of society—appear as producers. In one way this is correct, in another not. Indifference towards a particular kind of labour presupposes a highly developed totality of actual kinds of labour, none of which is supreme. Thus the most universal abstractions are generally formed by the richest concrete development, where one thing seems common to many, common to all. Then it ceases to be conceivable only in a particular form. On the other hand, this abstract idea of labour in general is not just the intellectual result of a concrete totality of labour-tasks. Indifference to a specific labour-task corresponds to a form of society in which individuals readily move from one task to another and the particular kind of task is to them fortuitous and so a matter of indifference. Here labour, not merely as category but in reality, has become a means for the creation of wealth in general and has ceased to be joined, as definition, in a special relation with individuals. Such a state of affairs is most highly developed in the most modern example of bourgeois society—the United States. Here, then, the abstraction of the category 'labour,' 'labour in general,' labour unadorned, the starting point of modern economy, is first realized in practice. The simplest abstraction, that is, that to which the modern economy gives pre-eminence, and which expresses a primeval relation valid for all forms of society, realizes itself practically as a category of the most modern society only in this abstraction. It might be said that what appears in the United States as historical product—this indifference to specific forms of labour—could appear to the Russians, for example, as a natural tendency. But again, whether barbarians have the capacity to be used for everything or whether civilized men themselves undertake everything makes the devil of a difference. Furthermore, in practice this Russian indifference to the precise nature of labour indicates a traditional tendency to settle in the rut of one particular task, from which they can only be wrenched by external influences.

This example of labour strikingly illustrates how even the most abstract categories, in spite of their validity for all epochs—because of their abstract nature—are yet in the precise terms of this abstraction themselves as much the product of historical conditions and possess their full validity only in respect of and within these conditions.

Bourgeois society is the most advanced and complex historical organization of production. The categories in which its conditions [relations] are expressed, the understanding of its structure, thus at the same time afford insight into the structure and relations of production of all past and gone forms of society, from the ruins and elements of which it has built itself up, and fragments of which, in part still unvanquished, are dragged along in it, while the merest suggestions have attained a mature significance, etc. The anatomy of men holds a key to the anatomy of the ape. Indications of higher possibilities in the lower animal orders can, however, only be understood where the higher development is already known. Bourgeois economy thus supplies the key to the economy of the ancient world, etc. By no means in the manner of those economists who obliterate all historical differences and recognize bourgeois characteristics in all forms of society. One can understand tribute, tithes, etc., if one is familiar with ground-rents. But one must not make them identical. Moreover, since bourgeois society is itself only a form of development through contradiction, conditions of earlier societies encountered there will often be very stunted or even travesties of themselves. Take for example communal property. If, then, it is true that the categories of bourgeois economy are true for all other forms of society, this must be taken with a grain of salt. They may contain them in a developed, stunted or caricatured form but always essentially altered. So-called historical development is really based on the fact that the latest form regards earlier forms as stages on the way to itself and, since it is rarely and only under quite specific conditions capable of self-criticism—there is naturally no question here of such historical periods as see themselves as periods of decay—always conceives them one-sidedly. Christianity was not capable of promoting the objective understanding of earlier mythologies until its own power of self-criticism had attained a certain level, as it were δυγάμει [dynamei, dative form of dynamis—power]. So bourgeois economy only came to understand the feudal, ancient and oriental systems when self-criticism of bourgeois society began. To the extent that bourgeois economy did not in myth-making fashion simply identify itself with the past, its critique of earlier, that is feudal, systems with which it was still directly battling, resembled the critique by Christianity of paganism or that by Protestantism of Catholicism.

As generally with every historical social science, so with the operation of economic categories it must always be remembered that, in reality as in the head, the subject, here modern bourgeois society, is given, and that the categories therefore express forms of being, definitions of existence, often only single aspects, of this particular society. This subject, which therefore *in a scientific sense* in no way begins only at the point at which it is now discussed *as such*. This must be remembered because it is immediately decisive for their classification. Nothing, for instance, seems more natural than to start with ground-rent, with ownership of land, since it is bound to the soil, the source of all production and all existence and to the first form of production in all moderately settled societies—agriculture. But nothing would be more mistaken. In all forms of society it is one specific [form of] production which itself and so likewise in its relations determines the position and influence of all the rest. It is a general illumination which bathes all other colours and modifies their particularity. It is a special ether which determines the specific gravity of all existence which is conspicuous in it. For example, with pastoral peoples (mere hunters and fishermen lie beyond the point at which true development begins). Among these is found a certain sporadic type of agriculture. This determines land ownership. It is common ownership and preserves this form more or less to the same degree in which these peoples maintain their traditions, as for example with the communal ownership of the Slavs. Among established agricultural peoples—such a settled state is already a great step—where this prevails, as in ancient and feudal society, industry itself and its organization together with the corresponding forms of ownership have more or less the character of land ownership; it is either totally dependent upon it, as in ancient Rome or, as in the Middle Ages, copies regional organization in the town and its relations. Capital itself—inasmuch as it is not simply capital in monetary form—has in medieval times, as traditional manual tool, etc., this character of land ownership. In bourgeois society the situation is reversed. Agriculture increasingly becomes a mere branch of industry, wholly controlled by capital. So too with ground-rents. In all forms governed by land ownership the natural relationship is still dominant. In those governed by capital, the social, historically created element. Ground-rent cannot be understood apart from capital, though capital may be apart from ground-rent. Capital is the all powerful economic force of bourgeois society. It must form both the starting point and the conclusion and must evolve before land ownership. After both have been specially examined their inter-relationship must be examined.

It would thus be impracticable and wrong to let the economic categories follow one another in the same order in which they were historically decisive. Rather is their order determined by the relationship in which they stand to each other in modern bourgeois society, which is exactly the reverse of what seems to be natural to them or what corresponds to the order of historical development. It is not a question of the historical position occupied by economic conditions in the sequence of different forms of society, still less of their order 'in the Idea' (Proudhon) (a hazy conception of historical movement), but of their organization within modern society.

The purity (abstract specificity), with which trading nations—Phoenicians, Carthaginians—appear in the ancient world is simply the result of the dominance of agricultural peoples. Capital, as trading-capital or money-capital, appears in this abstraction precisely where capital is not yet the controlling element of societies. Lombards and Jews occupy the same position *vis-à-vis* medieval agricultural societies.

As a further instance of the different positions which the same categories may assume at different stages of society: one of the last forms of bourgeois society, *joint-stock companies.* These, however, also appear at its inception, in the shape of the great trading companies granted privileges and monopolies.

The concept of national wealth insinuates itself into the work of the seventeenth-century economists—a conception which partly continues on into the eighteenth—in the idea that wealth is created only for the state, whose power, however, is related to this wealth. In this still unconsciously hypocritical form wealth itself and the production of the same proclaimed themselves the goal of modern states and regarded them thereafter solely as means for the production of wealth.

The argument must evidently be organized thus: 1) Universal abstract definitions, more or less applicable to all forms of society in the sense analysed above. 2) The categories forming the inner structure of bourgeois society, on which the fundamental classes are based, capital, wage labour, land ownership; their relationship to each other; town and country; the three great social classes; exchange between them; circulation; credit system (private). 3) Summary of bourgeois society in the form of the state; considered in relation to itself; the 'unproductive' classes; taxes; national debt; public credit; population; colonies; emigration. 4) International conditions of production; international division of labour; international exchange; export and import; rate of exchange. 5) The world market and crises.

Karl Marx, *Grundrisse der Kritik der politischen Ökonomie* (*Rohentwurf*), 1857–1858, Berlin, 1953, pp. 5–11, 20–29.

1865

From VALUE, PRICE AND PROFIT

VI. *[VALUE AND LABOUR]*

Citizens, I have now arrived at a point where I must enter upon the real development of the question. I cannot promise to do this in a very satisfactory way, because to do so I should be obliged to go over the whole field of political economy. I can, as the French would say, but *effleurer la question*, touch upon the main points.

The first question we have to put is: What is the *value* of a commodity? How is it determined?

At first sight it would seem that the value of a commodity is a thing quite *relative*, and not to be settled without considering one commodity in its relations to all other commodities. In fact, in speaking of the value, the value in exchange of a commodity, we mean the proportional quantities in which it exchanges with all other commodities. But then arises the question: How are the proportions in which commodities exchange with each other regulated?

We know from experience that these proportions vary infinitely. Taking one single commodity, wheat, for instance, we shall find that a quarter of wheat exchanges in almost countless variations of proportion with different commodities. Yet, *its value remaining always the same*, whether expressed in silk, gold, or any other commodity, it must be something distinct from, and independent of, these *different rates of exchange* with different articles. It must be possible to express, in a very different form, these various equations with various commodities.

Besides, if I say a quarter of wheat exchanges with iron in a certain proportion, or the value of a quarter of wheat is expressed in a certain amount of iron, I say that the value of wheat and its equivalent in iron are equal *to some third thing*, which is neither wheat nor iron, because I suppose them to express the same magnitude in two different shapes. Either of them, the wheat or the iron, must, therefore, independently of the other, be reducible to this third thing which is their common measure.

To elucidate this point I shall recur to a very simple geometrical illustration. In comparing the areas of triangles of all possible forms and magnitudes, or comparing triangles with rectangles, or any other rectilinear figure, how do we proceed? We reduce the area of any triangle whatever to an expression quite different from its visible form. Having found from the nature of the triangle that its area is equal to half the product of its base by its height, we can then compare the different values of all sorts of triangles, and of all rectilinear figures whatever, because all of them may be resolved into a certain number of triangles.

The same mode of procedure must obtain with the values of commodities. We must be able to reduce all of them to an expression common to all, distinguishing them only by the proportions in which they contain that identical measure.

As the *exchangeable values* of commodities are only *social functions* of those things, and have nothing at all to do with their *natural* qualities, we must first ask, What is the common *social substance* of all commodities? It is *Labour*. To produce a commodity a certain amount of labour must be bestowed upon it, or worked up in it. And I say not only *Labour*, but *social Labour*. A man who produces an article for his own immediate use, to consume it himself, creates a *product*, but not a *commodity*. As a self-sustaining producer he has nothing to do with society. But to produce a *commodity*, a man must not only produce an article satisfying some *social* want, but his labour itself must form part and parcel of the total sum of labour expended by society. It must be subordinate to the *Division of Labour within Society*. It is nothing without the other divisions of labour, and on its part is required to *integrate* them.

If we consider *commodities as values*, we consider them exclusively under the single aspect of *realised, fixed*, or, if you like, *crystallised social labour*. In this respect they can *differ* only by representing greater or smaller quantities of labour, as, for example, a greater amount of labour may be worked up in a silken handkerchief than in a brick. But how does one measure *quantities of labour?* By the *time the labour lasts*, in measuring the labour by the hour, the day, etc. Of course, to apply this measure, all sorts of labour are reduced to average or simple labour as their unit.

We arrive, therefore, at this conclusion. A commodity has a *value*, because it is a *crystallisation of social labour*. The *greatness* of its value, of its *relative* value, depends upon the greater or less amount of that social substance contained in it; that is to say, on the relative mass of labour necessary for its production. The *relative values of commodities* are, therefore, determined by the *respective*

Amount of labour = value of commodity (handwritten annotation)

quantities or amounts of labour, worked up, realised, fixed in them. The *correlative* quantities of commodities which can be produced in the *same time of labour* are *equal.* Or the value of one commodity is to the value of another commodity as the quantity of labour fixed in the one is to the quantity of labour fixed in the other.

I suspect that many of you will ask, Does then, indeed, there exist such a vast, or any difference whatever, between determining the values of commodities by *wages*, and determining them by the *relative quantities of labour* necessary for their production? You must, however, be aware that the *reward* for labour, and *quantity* of labour, are quite disparate things. Suppose, for example, *equal quantities of labour* to be fixed in one quarter of wheat and one ounce of gold. I resort to the example because it was used by Benjamin Franklin in his first Essay published in 1729, and entitled, *A Modest Enquiry into the Nature and Necessity of a Paper Currency*, where he, one of the first, hit upon the true nature of value. Well. We suppose, then, that one quarter of wheat and one ounce of gold are *equal values* or *equivalents*, because they are *crystallisations of equal amounts of average labour*, of so many days' or so many weeks' labour respectively fixed in them. In thus determining the relative values of gold and corn, do we refer in any way whatever to the *wages* of the agricultural labourer and the miner? Not a bit. We leave it quite *indeterminate how* their day's or week's labour was paid, or even whether wages labour was employed at all. If it was, wages may have been very unequal. The labourer whose labour is realised in the quarter of wheat may receive two bushels only, and the labourer employed in mining may receive one-half of the ounce of gold. Or, supposing their wages to be equal, they may deviate in all possible proportions from the values of the commodities produced by them. They may amount to one-half, one-third, one-fourth, one-fifth, or any other proportional part of the one quarter of corn or the one ounce of gold. Their *wages* can, of course, not *exceed*, not be *more* than the values of the commodities they produced, but they can be *less* in every possible degree. Their *wages* will be *limited* by the *values* of the products, but the *values of their products* will not be limited by the wages. And above all, the values, the relative values of corn and gold, for example, will have been settled without any regard whatever to the value of the labour employed, that is to say, to *wages*. To determine the values of commodities by the *relative quantities of labour fixed in them*, is, therefore, a thing quite different from the tautological method of determining the values of commodities by the value of labour, or by *wages*. This point, however, will be further elucidated in the progress of our inquiry.

In calculating the exchangeable value of a commodity we must add to the quantity of labour *last* employed the quantity of labour *previously* worked up in the raw material of the commodity, and the labour bestowed on the implements, tools, machinery, and buildings, with which such labour is assisted. For example, the value of a certain amount of cotton-yarn is the crystallisation of the quantity of labour added to the cotton during the spinning process, the quantity of labour previously realised in the cotton itself, the quantity of labour realised in the coal, oil, and other auxiliary substances used, the quantity of labour fixed in the steam engine, the spindles, the factory building, and so forth. Instruments of production properly so-called, such as tools, machinery, buildings, serve again and again for a longer or shorter period during repeated processes of production. If they were used up at once, like the raw material, their whole value would at once be transferred to the commodities they assist in producing. But as a spindle, for example, is but gradually used up, an average calculation is made, based upon the average time it lasts, and its average waste of wear and tear during a certain period, say a day. In this way we calculate how much of the value of the spindle is transferred to the yarn daily spun, and how much, therefore, of the total amount of labour realised in a pound of yarn, for example, is due to the quantity of labour previously realised in the spindle. For our present purpose it is not necessary to dwell any longer upon this point.

It might seem that if the value of a commodity is determined by the *quantity of labour bestowed upon its production*, the lazier a man, or the clumsier a man, the more valuable his commodity, because the greater the time of labour required for finishing the commodity. This, however, would be a sad mistake. You will recollect that I used the word "*Social* labour," and many points are involved in this qualification of "*Social.*" In saying that the value of a commodity is determined by the *quantity of labour* worked up or crystallised in it, we mean *the quantity of labour necessary* for its production in a given state of society, under certain social average conditions of production, with a given social average intensity, and average skill of the labour employed. When, in England, the power-loom came to compete with the hand-loom, only one half of the former time of labour was wanted to convert a given amount of yarn into a yard of cotton or cloth. The poor hand-loom weaver now worked seventeen or eighteen hours daily, instead of the nine or ten hours he had worked before. Still the product of twenty hours of his labour represented now only ten social hours of labour, or ten hours of labour socially necessary for the conversion of a certain amount of yarn into textile stuffs. His product of twenty hours had, therefore, no more value than his former product of ten hours.

If then the quantity of socially necessary labour realised in commodities regulates their exchangeable values, every increase in the quantity of labour wanted for the production of a commodity must augment its value, as every diminution must lower it.

If the respective quantities of labour necessary for the production of the respective commodities remained constant, their relative values also would be constant. But such is not the case. The quantity of labour necessary for the production of a commodity changes continuously with the changes in the productive powers of the labour employed. The greater the productive powers of labour, the more produce is finished in a given time of labour: and the smaller the productive powers of labour, the less produce is finished in the same time. If, for example, in the progress of population it should become necessary to cultivate less fertile soils, the same amount of produce would be only attainable by a greater amount of labour spent, and the value of agricultural produce would consequently rise. On the other hand, if with the modern means of production, a single spinner converts into yarn, during one working day, many thousand times the amount of cotton which he could have spun during the same time with the spinning wheel, it is evident that every single pound of cotton will absorb many thousand times less of spinning labour than it did before, and, consequently, the value added by spinning to every single pound of cotton will be a thousand times less than before. The value of yarn will sink accordingly.

Apart from the different natural energies and acquired working abilities of different peoples, the productive powers of labour must principally depend:

Firstly. Upon the *natural* conditions of labour, such as fertility of soil, mines, and so forth;

Secondly. Upon the progressive improvement of the *Social Powers of Labour*, such as are derived from production on a grand scale, concentration of capital and combination of labour, subdivision of labour, machinery, improved methods, appliance of chemical and other natural agencies, shortening of time and space by means of communication and transport, and every other contrivance by which science presses natural agencies into the service of labour, and by which the social or co-operative character of labour is developed. The greater the productive powers of labour, the less labour is bestowed upon a given amount of produce; hence the smaller the value of this produce. The smaller the productive powers of labour, the more labour is bestowed upon the same amount of produce; hence the greater its value. As a general law we may, therefore, set it down that:—

The values of commodities are directly as the times of labour employed in their production, and are inversely as the productive powers of the labour employed.

Having till now only spoken of *Value*, I shall add a few words about *Price*, which is a peculiar form assumed by value.

Price, taken by itself, is nothing but the *monetary expression of value*. The values of all commodities of this country, for example, are expressed in gold prices, while on the Continent they are mainly expressed in silver prices. The value of gold or silver, like that of all commodities, is regulated by the quantity of labour necessary for getting them. You exchange a certain amount of your national products, in which a certain amount of your national labour is crystallised, for the produce of the gold and silver producing countries, in which a certain quantity of *their* labour is crystallised. It is in this way, in fact by barter, that you learn to express in gold and silver the values of all commodities, that is, the respective quantities of labour bestowed upon them. Looking somewhat closer into the *monetary expression of value*, or what comes to the same, the conversion of value into price, you will find that it is a process by which you give to the *values* of all commodities an *independent* and *homogeneous form*, or by which you express them as quantities of equal social labour. So far as it is but the monetary expression of value, price has been called *natural price* by Adam Smith, *"prix nécessaire"* by the French physiocrats.

What then is the relation between *value* and *market*

Natural price = value

Market Price = Supply & demand.

prices, or between *natural prices* and *market prices?* You all know that the *market price* is the *same* for all commodities of the same kind, however the conditions of production may differ for the individual producers. The market price expresses only the *average amount of social labour* necessary, under the average conditions of production, to supply the market with a certain mass of a certain article. It is calculated upon the whole lot of a commodity of a certain description.

So far the *market price* of a commodity coincides with its *value.* On the other hand, the oscillations of market prices, rising now over, sinking now under the value or natural price, depend upon the fluctuations of supply and demand. The deviations of market prices from values are continual, but as Adam Smith says:

> The natural price . . . is the central price, to which the prices of all commodities are continually gravitating. Different accidents may sometimes keep them suspended a good deal above it, and sometimes force them down even somewhat below it. But whatever may be the obstacles which hinder them from settling in this centre of repose and continuance they are constantly tending towards it.

I cannot now sift this matter. It suffices to say that *if* supply and demand equilibrate each other, the market prices of commodities will correspond with their natural prices, that is to say, with their values, as determined by the respective quantities of labour required for their production. But supply and demand *must* constantly tend to equilibrate each other, although they do so only by compensating one fluctuation by another, a rise by a fall, and *vice versa.* If instead of considering only the daily fluctuations you analyse the movement of market prices for longer periods, as Mr. Tooke, for example, has done in his *History of Prices,* you will find that the fluctuations of market prices, their deviations from values, their ups and downs, paralyse and compensate each other; so that, apart from the effect of monopolies and some other modifications I must now pass by, all descriptions of commodities are, on the average, sold at their respective *values* or natural prices. The average periods during which the fluctuations of market prices compensate each other are different for different kinds of commodities, because with one kind it is easier to adapt supply to demand than with the other.

If then, speaking broadly, and embracing somewhat longer periods, all descriptions of commodities sell at their respective values, it is nonsense to suppose that profit, not in individual cases, but that the constant and usual profits of different trades spring from *surcharging* the prices of commodities, or selling them at a price over and above their *value*. The absurdity of this notion becomes evident if it is generalised. What a man would constantly win as a seller he would as constantly lose as a purchaser. It would not do to say that there are men who are buyers without being sellers, or consumers without being producers. What these people pay to the producers, they must first get from them for nothing. If a man first takes your money and afterwards returns that money in buying your commodities, you will never enrich yourselves by selling your commodities too dear to that same man. This sort of transaction might diminish a loss, but would never help in realising a profit.

To explain, therefore, the *general nature of profits*, you must start from the theorem that, on an average, commodities are *sold at their real value*, and that *profits are derived from selling them at their values*, that is, in proportion to the quantity of labour realised in them. If you cannot explain profit upon this supposition, you cannot explain it at all. This seems paradox and contrary to everyday observation. It is also paradox that the earth moves round the sun, and that water consists of two highly inflammable gases. Scientific truth is always paradox, if judged by everyday experience, which catches only the delusive appearance of things.

VII. LABOURING POWER

Having now, as far as it could be done in such a cursory manner, analysed the nature of *Value*, of the *Value of any commodity whatever*, we must turn our attention to the specific *Value of Labour*. And here, again, I must startle you by a seeming paradox. All of you feel sure that what they daily sell is their Labour; that, therefore, Labour has a Price, and that, the price of a commodity being only the monetary expression of its value, there must certainly exist such a thing as the *Value of Labour*. However, there exists no such thing as the *Value of Labour* in the common acceptance of the word. We have seen that the amount of necessary labour crystallised in a commodity constitutes its value. Now, applying this notion of value, how could we define, say, the value of a ten hours' working day? How much labour is contained in that day? Ten hours' labour. To say that the value of a ten hours' working day is equal to ten hours' labour, or the quantity of labour contained in it, would be a tautological and, moreover, a nonsensical expression. Of course, having once found out the true but hidden sense of the expression "*Value of Labour*," we shall be able to interpret this irrational, and seemingly impossible application of value, in the same way that, having once made sure of the real movement of the celestial bodies, we shall be able to explain their apparent or merely phenomenal movements.

What the working man sells is not directly his *Labour*, but his *Labouring Power*, the temporary disposal of which he makes over to the capitalist. This is so much the case that I do not know whether by the English laws, but certainly by some Continental Laws, the *maximum time* is fixed for which a man is allowed to sell his labouring power. If allowed to do so for any indefinite period whatever, slavery would be immediately restored. Such a sale, if it comprised his lifetime, for example, would make him at once the lifelong slave of his employer.

One of the oldest economists and most original philosophers of England—Thomas Hobbes—has already, in his *Leviathan*, instinctively hit upon this point overlooked by all his successors. He says:

> *The value or worth of a man* is, as in all other things, his *price:* that is, so much as would be given for the *Use of his Power.*

Proceeding from this basis, we shall be able to determine the *Value of Labour* as that of all other commodities.

But before doing so, we might ask, how does this strange phenomenon arise, that we find on the market a set of buyers, possessed of land, machinery, raw material, and the means of subsistence, all of them, save land in its crude state, the *products of labour*, and on the other hand, a set of sellers who have nothing to sell except their labouring power, their working arms and brains? That the one set buys continually in order to make a profit and enrich themselves, while the other set continually sells in order to earn their livelihood? The inquiry into this question would be an inquiry into what the economists call *"Previous, or Original Accumulation,"* but which ought to be called *Original Expropriation*. We should find that this so-called *Original Accumulation* means nothing but a series of historical processes, resulting in a *Decomposition of the Original Union* existing between the Labouring Man and his Instruments of Labour. Such an inquiry, however, lies beyond the pale of my present subject. The *Separation* between the Man of Labour and the Instruments of Labour once established, such a state of things will maintain itself and reproduce itself upon a constantly increasing scale, until a new and fundamental revolution in the mode of production should again overturn it, and restore the original union in a new historical form.

What, then, is the *Value of Labouring Power?*

Like that of every other commodity, its value is determined by the quantity of labour necessary to produce it. The labouring power of a man exists only in his living individuality. A certain mass of necessaries must be consumed by a man to grow up and maintain his life. But the man, like the machine, will wear out, and must be replaced by another man. Beside the mass of necessaries required for *his own* maintenance, he wants another amount of necessaries to bring up a certain quota of children that are to replace him on the labour market and to perpetuate the race of labourers. Moreover, to develop his labouring power, and acquire a given skill, another amount of values must be spent. For our purpose it suffices to consider only *average* labour, the costs of whose education and development are vanishing magnitudes. Still I must seize upon this occasion to state that, as the costs of producing labouring powers of different quality differ, so must differ the values of the labouring powers employed in different trades. The cry for an *equality of wages* rests, therefore, upon a mistake, is an *insane* wish never to be fulfilled. It is an offspring of that false and superficial radicalism that accepts premises and tries to evade conclusions. Upon the basis of the wages system the value of labouring power is settled like that of every other commodity; and as different kinds of labouring power have different values, or require different quantities of labour for their production, they *must* fetch different prices in the labour market. To clamour for *equal or even equitable retribution* on the basis of the wages system is the same as to clamour for *freedom* on the basis of the slavery system. What you think just or equitable is out of the question. The question is: What is necessary and unavoidable with a given system of production?

After what has been said, it will be seen that the *value of labouring power* is determined by the *value of the necessaries* required to produce, develop, maintain, and perpetuate the labouring power.

VIII. PRODUCTION OF SURPLUS VALUE

Now suppose that the average amount of the daily necessaries of a labouring man require *six hours of average labour* for their production. Suppose, moreover, six hours of average labour to be also realised in a quantity of gold equal to 3*s.* Then 3*s.* would be the *Price*, or the monetary expression of the *Daily Value* of that man's *Labouring Power.* If he worked daily six hours he would daily produce a value sufficient to buy the average amount of his daily necessaries, or to maintain himself as a labouring man.

But our man is a wages labourer. He must, therefore, sell his labouring power to a capitalist. If he sells it at 3*s.* daily, or 18*s.* weekly, he sells it at its value. Suppose him to be a spinner. If he works six hours daily he will add to the cotton a value of 3*s.* daily. This value, daily added by him, would be an exact equivalent for the wages, or the price of his labouring power, received daily. But in that case *no surplus value* or *surplus produce* whatever would go to the capitalist. Here, then, we come to the rub.

In buying the labouring power of the workman, and paying its value, the capitalist, like every other purchaser, has acquired the right to consume or use the commodity bought. You consume or use the labouring power of a man by making him work as you consume or use a machine by making it run. By paying the daily or weekly value of the labouring power of the workman, the capitalist has, therefore, acquired the right to use or make that labouring power work during the *whole day or week*. The working day or the working week has, of course, certain limits, but those we shall afterwards look more closely at.

For the present I want to turn your attention to one decisive point.

Upkeep

The *value* of the labouring power is determined by the quantity of labour necessary to maintain or reproduce it, but the *use* of that labouring power is only limited by the active energies and physical strength of the labourer. The daily or weekly *value* of the labouring power is quite distinct from the daily or weekly exercise of that power, the same as the food a horse wants and the time it can carry the horseman are quite distinct. The quantity of labour by which the *value* of the workman's labouring power is limited forms by no means a limit to the quantity of labour which his labouring power is apt to perform. Take the example of our spinner. We have seen that, to daily reproduce his labouring power, he must daily reproduce a value of three shillings, which he will do by working six hours daily. But this does not disable him from working ten or twelve or more hours a day. But by paying the daily or weekly *value* of the spinner's labouring power, the capitalist has acquired the right of using that labouring power during *the whole day or week*. He will, therefore, make him work say, daily, *twelve* hours. *Over and above* the six hours required to replace his wages, or the value of his labouring power, he will, therefore, have to work *six other hours*, which I shall call hours of *surplus labour*, which surplus labour will realise itself in a *surplus value* and a *surplus produce*. If our spinner, for example, by his daily labour of six hours, added three shillings' value to the cotton, a value forming an exact equivalent to his wages, he will, in twelve hours, add six shillings' worth to the cotton, and produce *a proportional surplus of yarn*. As he has sold his labouring power to the capitalist, the whole value or produce created by him belongs to the capitalist, the owner *pro tem.* of his labouring power. By advancing three shillings, the capitalist will, therefore, realise a value of six shillings, because, advancing a value in which six hours of labour are crystallised, he will receive in return a value in which twelve hours of labour are crystallised. By repeating this same process daily, the capitalist will daily advance three shillings and daily pocket six shillings, one-half of which will go to pay wages anew, and the other half of which will form *surplus value,* for which the capitalist pays no equivalent. It is this *sort of exchange between capital and labour* upon which capitalistic production, or the wages system, is founded, and which must constantly result in reproducing the working man as a working man, and the capitalist as a capitalist.

The rate of surplus value, all other circumstances remaining the same, will depend on the proportion between that part of the working day necessary to reproduce the value of the labouring power and the *surplus time* or *surplus labour* performed for the capitalist. It will, therefore, depend on the *ratio in which the working day is prolonged over and above that extent,* by working which the working man would only reproduce the value of his labouring, or replace his wages.

IX. *VALUE OF LABOUR*

We must now return to the expression, "*Value, or Price of Labour.*"

We have seen that, in fact, it is only the value of the labouring power, measured by the values of commodities necessary for its maintenance. But since the workman receives his wages *after* his labour is performed, and knows, moreover, that what he actually gives to the capitalist is his labour, the value or price of his labouring power necessarily appears to him as the *price* or *value of his labour itself.* If the price of his labouring power is three shillings, in which six hours of labour are realised, and if he works twelve hours, he necessarily considers these three shillings as the value or price of twelve hours of labour, although these twelve hours of labour realise themselves in a value of six shillings. A double consequence flows from this.

Firstly. *The value or price of the labouring power* takes the semblance of the *price or value of labour itself,* although, strictly speaking, value and price of labour are senseless terms.

Secondly. Although one part only of the workman's daily labour is *paid,* while the other part is *unpaid,* and while that unpaid or surplus labour constitutes exactly the fund out of which *surplus value* or *profit* is formed, it seems as if the aggregate labour was paid labour.

This false appearance distinguishes *wages labour* from other *historical* forms of labour. On the basis of the wages system even the *unpaid* labour seems to be *paid* labour. With the *slave,* on the contrary, even that part of his labour which is paid appears to be unpaid. Of course, in order to work the slave must live, and one part of his working day goes to replace the value of his own maintenance. But since no bargain is struck between him and his master, and no acts of selling and buying are going on between the two parties, all his labour seems to be given away for nothing.

Take, on the other hand, the peasant serf, such as he, I might say, until yesterday existed in the whole East of Europe. This peasant worked, for example, three days for himself on his own field or the field allotted to him, and the three subsequent days he performed compulsory and gratuitous labour on the estate of his lord. Here, then, the paid and unpaid parts of labour were sensibly separated, separated in time and space; and our Liberals overflowed with moral indignation at the preposterous notion of making a man work for nothing.

In point of fact, however, whether a man works three days of the week for himself on his own field and three days for nothing on the estate of his lord, or whether he works in the factory or the workshop six hours daily for himself and six for his employer, comes to the same, although in the latter case the paid and unpaid portions of labour are inseparably mixed up with each other, and the nature of the whole transaction is completely masked by the *intervention of a contract* and the *pay* received at the end of the week. The gratuitous labour appears to be voluntarily given in the one instance, and to be compulsory in the other. That makes all the difference.

In using the expression *"value of labour,"* I shall only use it as a popular slang term for *"value of labouring power."*

X. PROFIT IS MADE BY SELLING A COMMODITY AT ITS VALUE

Suppose an average hour of labour to be realised in a value equal to sixpence, or twelve average hours of labour to be realised in six shillings. Suppose, further, the value of labour to be three shillings or the produce of six hours' labour. If, then, in the raw material, machinery, and so forth, used up in a commodity, twenty-four hours of average labour were realised, its value would amount to twelve shillings. If, moreover, the workman employed by the capitalist added twelve hours of labour to those means of production, these twelve hours would be realised in an additional value of six shillings. The *total value of the product* would, therefore, amount to thirty-six hours of realised labour, and be equal to eighteen shillings. But as the value of labour, or the wages paid to the workman, would be three shillings only, no equivalent would have been paid by the capitalist for the six hours of surplus labour worked by the workman, and realised in the value of the commodity. By selling this commodity at its value for eighteen shillings, the capitalist would, therefore, realise a value of three shillings, for which he had paid no equivalent. These three shillings would constitute the surplus value or profit pocketed by him. The capitalist would consequently realise the profit of three shillings, not by selling his commodity at a price *over and above* its value, but by selling it *at its real value*.

The value of a commodity is determined by the *total quantity of labour* contained in it. But part of that quantity of labour is realised in a value for which an equivalent has been paid in the form of wages; part of it is realised in a value for which *no* equivalent has been paid. Part of the labour contained in the commodity is *paid* labour; part is *unpaid* labour. By selling, therefore, the commodity *at its value*, that is, as the crystallisation of the *total quantity of labour* bestowed upon it, the capitalist must necessarily sell it at a profit. He sells not only what has cost him an equivalent, but he sells also what has cost him nothing, although it has cost his workman labour. The cost of the commodity to the capitalist and its real cost are different things. I repeat, therefore, that normal and average profits are made by selling commodities not *above* but *at their real values*.

XI. THE DIFFERENT PARTS INTO WHICH SURPLUS VALUE IS DECOMPOSED

The *surplus value*, or that part of the total value of the commodity in which the *surplus labour* or *unpaid labour* of the working man is realised, I call *Profit*. The whole of that profit is not pocketed by the employing capitalist. The monopoly of land enables the landlord to take one part of that *surplus value*, under the name of *rent*, whether the land is used for agriculture, buildings or railways, or for any other productive purpose. On the other hand, the very fact that the possession of the *instruments of labour* enables the employing capitalist to produce a *surplus value*, or, what comes to the same, to *appropriate to himself a certain amount of unpaid labour*, enables the owner of the means of labour, which he lends wholly or partly to the employing capitalist—enables, in one word, the money-lending capitalist to claim for himself under the name of *interest* another part of that surplus value, so that there remains to the employing capitalist *as such* only what is called *industrial* or *commercial profit*.

By what laws this division of the total amount of surplus value amongst the three categories of people is regulated is a question quite foreign to our subject. This much, however, results from what has been stated.

Rent, Interest, and Industrial Profit are only *different names for different parts* of the *surplus value* of the commodity, or the *unpaid labour enclosed in it,* and they are *equally derived from this source, and from this source alone.* They are not derived from *land* as such or from *capital* as such, but land and capital enable their owners to get their respective shares out of the surplus value extracted by the employing capitalist from the labourer. For the labourer himself it is a matter of subordinate importance whether that surplus value, the result of his surplus labour, or unpaid labour, is altogether pocketed by the employing capitalist, or whether the latter is obliged to pay portions of it, under the name of rent and interest, away to third parties. Suppose the employing capitalist to use only his own capital and to be his own landlord, then the whole surplus value would go into his pocket.

It is the employing capitalist who immediately extracts from the labourer this surplus value, whatever part of it he may ultimately be able to keep for himself. Upon this relation, therefore, between the employing capitalist and the wages labourer the whole wages system and the whole present system of production hinge. Some of the citizens who took part in our debate were, therefore, wrong in trying to mince matters, and to treat this fundamental relation between the employing capitalist and the working man as a secondary question, although they were right in stating that, under given circumstances, a rise of prices might affect in very unequal degrees the employing capitalist, the landlord, the moneyed capitalist, and, if you please, the tax-gatherer.

Another consequence follows from what has been stated.

That part of the value of the commodity which represents only the value of the raw materials, the machinery, in one word, the value of the means of production used up, forms *no revenue* at all, but replaces *only capital*. But, apart from this, it is false that the other part of the value of the commodity *which forms revenue*, or may be spent in the form of wages, profits, rent, interest, is *constituted* by the value of wages, the value of rent, the value of profits, and so forth. We shall, in the first instance, discard wages, and only treat industrial profits, interest, and rent. We have just seen that the *surplus value* contained in the commodity or that part of its value in which *unpaid labour* is realised, resolves itself into different fractions, bearing three different names. But it would be quite the reverse of the truth to say that its value is *composed* of, or *formed* by, the *addition* of the *independent values of these three constituents*.

If one hour of labour realises itself in a value of sixpence, if the working day of the labourer comprises twelve hours, if half of this time is unpaid labour, that surplus labour will add to the commodity a *surplus value* of three shillings, that is, a value for which no equivalent has been paid. This surplus value of three shillings constitutes the *whole fund* which the employing capitalist may divide, in whatever proportions, with the landlord and the moneylender. The value of these three shillings constitutes the limit of the value they have to divide amongst them. But it is not the employing capitalist who adds to the value of the commodity an arbitrary value for his profit, to which another value is added for the landlord, and so forth, so that the addition of these arbitrarily fixed values would constitute the total value. You see, therefore, the fallacy of the popular notion, which confounds the *decomposition of a given value* into three parts, with the *formation* of that value by the addition of three *independent* values, thus converting the aggregate value, from which rent, profit, and interest are derived, into an arbitrary magnitude.

If the total profit realised by a capitalist be equal to £100, we call this sum, considered as *absolute* magnitude, the *amount of profit.* But if we calculate the ratio which those £100 bear to the capital advanced, we call this *relative* magnitude, the *rate of profit.* It is evident that this rate of profit may be expressed in a double way.

Suppose £100 to be the capital *advanced in wages.* If the surplus value created is also £100—and this would show us that half the working day of the labourer consists of *unpaid* labour—and if we measured this profit by the value of the capital advanced in wages, we should say that the *rate of profit* amounted to one hundred per cent, because the value advanced would be one hundred and the value realised would be two hundred.

If, on the other hand, we should not only consider the *capital advanced in wages,* but the *total capital* advanced, say, for example, £500, of which £400 represented the value of raw materials, machinery, and so forth, we should say that the *rate of profit* amounted only to twenty per cent, because the profit of one hundred would be but the fifth part of the *total* capital advanced.

The first mode of expressing the rate of profit is the only one which shows you the real ratio between paid and unpaid labour, the real degree of the *exploitation* (you must allow me this French word) *of labour.* The other mode of expression is that in common use, and is, indeed, appropriate for certain purposes. At all events, it is very useful for concealing the degree in which the capitalist extracts gratuitous labour from the workman.

In the remarks I have still to make I shall use the word *Profit* for the whole amount of the surplus value extracted by the capitalist without any regard to the division of the surplus value between different parties, and in using the words *Rate of Profit*, I shall always measure profits by the value of the capital advanced in wages.

XII. GENERAL RELATION OF PROFITS, WAGES AND PRICES

Deduct from the value of a commodity the value replacing the value of the raw materials and other means of production used upon it, that is to say, deduct the value representing the *past* labour contained in it, and the remainder of its value will resolve into the quantity of labour added by the working man *last* employed. If that working man works twelve hours daily, if twelve hours of average labour crystallise themselves in an amount of gold equal to six shillings, this additional value of six shillings is the *only* value his labour will have created. This given value, determined by the time of his labour, is the only fund from which both he and the capitalist have to draw their respective shares or dividends, the only value to be divided into wages and profits. It is evident that this value itself will not be altered by the variable proportions in which it may be divided amongst the two parties. There will also be nothing changed if in the place of one working man you put the whole working population, twelve million working days, for example, instead of one.

Since the capitalist and workman have only to divide this limited value, that is, the value measured by the total labour of the working man, the more the one gets the less will the other get, and *vice versa*. Whenever a quantity is given, one part of it will increase inversely as the other decreases. If the wages change, profits will change in an opposite direction. If wages fall, profits will rise; and if wages rise, profits will fall. If the working man, on our former supposition, gets three shillings, equal to one half of the value he has created, or if his whole working day consists half of paid, half of unpaid labour, the *rate of profit* will be 100 per cent, because the capitalist would also get three shillings. If the working man receives only two shillings, or works only one-third of the whole day for himself, the capitalist will get four shillings, and the rate of profit will be 200 per cent. If the working man receives four shillings, the capitalist will only receive two, and the rate of profit would sink to 50 per cent, but all these variations will not affect the value of the commodity. A general rise of wages would, therefore, result in a fall of the general rate of profit, but not affect values.

But although the values of commodities, which must ultimately regulate their market prices, are exclusively determined by the total quantities of labour fixed in them, and not by the division of that quantity into paid and unpaid labour, it by no means follows that the values of the single commodities, *or* lots of commodities, produced during twelve hours, for example, will remain constant. The *number* or mass of commodities produced in a given time of labour, or by a given quantity of labour, depends upon the *productive power* of the labour employed, and not upon its *extent* or length. With one degree of the productive power of spinning labour, for example, a working day of twelve hours may produce twelve pounds of yarn, with a lesser degree of productive power only two pounds. If then twelve hours' average labour were realised in the value of six shillings, in the one case the twelve pounds of yarn would cost six shillings, in the other case the two pounds of yarn would also cost six shillings. One pound of yarn would, therefore, cost sixpence in the one case, and three shillings in the other. This difference of price would result from the difference in the productive powers of the labour employed. One hour of labour would be realised in one pound of yarn with the greater productive power, while with the smaller productive power, six hours of labour would be realised in one pound of yarn. The price of a pound of yarn would, in the one instance, be only sixpence, although wages were relatively high and the rate of profit low; it would be three shillings in the other instance, although wages were low and the rate of profit high. This would be so because the price of the pound of yarn is regulated by the *total amount of labour worked up in it*, and not by the *proportional division of that total amount into paid and unpaid labour*. The fact I have before mentioned that high-priced labour may produce cheap, and low-priced labour may produce dear commodities, loses, therefore, its paradoxical appearance. It is only the expression of the general law that the value of a commodity is regulated by the quantity of labour worked up in it, and that the quantity of labour worked up in it depends altogether upon the productive powers of the labour employed, and will, therefore, vary with every variation in the productivity of labour.

reread last chapter

XIII. MAIN CASES OF ATTEMPTS AT RAISING WAGES OR RESISTING THEIR FALL

Let us now seriously consider the main cases in which a rise of wages is attempted or a reduction of wages resisted.

1. We have seen that the *value of the labouring power*, or in more popular parlance, the *value of labour*, is determined by the value of necessaries, or the quantity of labour required to produce them. If, then, in a given country the value of the daily average necessaries of the labourer represented six hours of labour expressed in three shillings, the labourer would have to work six hours daily to produce an equivalent for his daily maintenance. If the whole working day was twelve hours, the capitalist

would pay him the value of his labour by paying him three shillings. Half the working day would be unpaid labour, and the rate of profit would amount to 100 per cent. But now suppose that, consequent upon a decrease of productivity, more labour should be wanted to produce, say, the same amount of agricultural produce, so that the price of the average daily necessaries should rise from three to four shillings. In that case the *value of labour* would rise by one-third, or 33⅓ per cent. Eight hours of the working day would be required to produce an equivalent for the daily maintenance of the labourer, according to his old standard of living. The surplus labour would therefore sink from six hours to four, and the rate of profit from 100 to 50 per cent. But in insisting upon a rise of wages, the labourer would only insist upon getting the *increased value of his labour*, like every other seller of a commodity, who, the costs of his commodities having increased, tries to get its increased value paid. If wages did not rise, or not sufficiently rise, to compensate for the increased values of necessaries, the *price* of labour would sink below the *value of labour*, and the labourer's standard of life would deteriorate. ˍ ⟨cost of living⟩

But a change might also take place in an opposite direction. By virtue of the increased productivity of labour, the same amount of the average daily necessaries might sink from three to two shillings, or only four hours out of the working day, instead of six, be wanted to reproduce an equivalent for the value of the daily necessaries. The working man would now be able to buy with two shillings as many necessaries as he did before with three shillings. Indeed, the *value of labour* would have sunk, but that diminished value would command the same amount of commodities as before. Then profits would rise from three to four shillings, and, the rate of profit from 100 to 200 per cent. Although the labourer's absolute standard of life would have remained the same, his *relative* wages, and therewith his *relative social position*, as compared with that of the capitalist, would have been lowered. If the working man should resist that reduction of relative wages, he would try to get some share in the increased productive powers of his own labour, and to maintain his former relative position in the social scale. Thus, after the abolition of the Corn Laws, and in flagrant violation of the most solemn pledges given during the anti-corn law agitation, the English factory lords generally reduced wages ten per cent. The resistance of the workmen was at first baffled, but, consequent upon circumstances I cannot now enter upon, the ten per cent lost were afterwards regained.

2. The *values* of necessaries, and consequently the *value of labour*, might remain the same, but a change might occur in their *money prices*, consequent upon a previous change in the *value of money*.

By the discovery of more fertile mines and so forth, two ounces of gold might, for example, cost no more labour to produce than one ounce did before. The *value* of gold would then be depreciated by one half, or fifty per cent. As the *values* of all other commodities would then be expressed in twice their former *money prices*, so also the same with the *value of labour*. Twelve hours of labour, formerly expressed in six shillings, would now be expressed in twelve shillings. If the working man's wages should remain three shillings, instead of rising to six shillings, the *money price of his labour* would only be equal to *half the value of his labour*, and his standard of life would fearfully deteriorate. This would also happen in a greater or lesser degree if his wages should rise, but not proportionately to the fall in the value of gold. In such a case nothing would have been changed, either in the productive powers of labour, or in supply and demand, or in values. Nothing could have changed except the money *names* of those values. To say that in such a case the workman ought not to insist upon a proportionate rise of wages, is to say that he must be content to be paid with names, instead of with things. All past history proves that whenever such a depreciation of money occurs the capitalists are on the alert to seize this opportunity for defrauding the workman. A very large school of political economists assert that, consequent upon the new discoveries of gold lands, the better working of silver mines, and the cheaper supply of quicksilver, the value of precious metals has been again depreciated. This would explain the general and simultaneous attempts on the Continent at a rise of wages.

3. We have till now supposed that the *working day* has given limits. The working day, however, has, by itself, no constant limits. It is the constant tendency of capital to stretch it to its utmost physically possible length, because in the same degree surplus labour, and consequently the profit resulting therefrom, will be increased. The more capital succeeds in prolonging the working day, the greater the amount of other people's labour it will appropriate. During the seventeenth and even the first two-thirds of the eighteenth century a ten hours' working day was the normal working day all over England. During the anti-Jacobin war, which was in fact a war waged by the British barons against the British working masses, capital celebrated its bacchanalia, and prolonged the working day from ten to twelve, fourteen, eighteen hours. Malthus, by no means a man whom you would suspect of a maudlin sentimentalism, declared in a pamphlet, published about 1815, that if this sort of thing was to go on the life of the nation would be attacked at its very source. A few years before the general introduction of the newly-invented machinery, about 1765, a pamphlet appeared in England under the title, *An Essay on Trade*. The anonymous author, an avowed enemy of the working classes, declaims on the necessity of expanding the limits of the working day. Amongst other means to this end, he proposes *working houses*, which, he says, ought to be "Houses of Terror." And what is the length of the working day he

prescribes for these "Houses of Terror"? *Twelve hours,* the very same time which in 1832 was declared by capitalists, political economists, and ministers to be not only the existing but the necessary time of labour for a child under twelve years.

By selling his labouring power, and he must do so under the present system, the working man makes over to the capitalist the consumption of that power, but within certain rational limits. He sells his labouring power in order to maintain it, apart from its natural wear and tear, but not to destroy it. In selling his labouring power at its daily or weekly value, it is understood that in one day or one week that labouring power shall not be submitted to two days' or two weeks' waste or wear and tear. Take a machine worth £1,000. If it is used up in ten years it will add to the value of the commodities in whose production it assists £100 yearly. If it be used up in five years it would add £200 yearly, or the value of its annual wear and tear is in inverse ratio to the time in which it is consumed. But this distinguishes the working man from the machine. Machinery does not wear out exactly in the same ratio in which it is used. Man, on the contrary, decays in a greater ratio than would be visible from the mere numerical addition of work.

In their attempts at reducing the working day to its former rational dimensions, or, where they cannot enforce a legal fixation of a normal working day, at checking overwork by a rise of wages, a rise not only in proportion to the surplus time exacted, but in a greater proportion, working men fulfil only a duty to themselves and their race. They only set limits to the tyrannical usurpations of capital. Time is the room of human development. A man who has no free time to dispose of, whose whole lifetime, apart from the mere physical interruptions by sleep, meals, and so forth, is absorbed by his labour for the capitalist, is less than a beast of burden. He is a mere machine for producing Foreign Wealth, broken in body and brutalised in mind. Yet the whole history of modern industry shows that capital, if not checked, will recklessly and ruthlessly work to cast down the whole working class to the utmost state of degradation.

In prolonging the working day the capitalist may pay *higher wages* and still lower the *value of labour*, if the rise of wages does not correspond to the greater amount of labour extracted, and the quicker decay of the labouring power thus caused. This may be done in another way. Your middle-class statisticians will tell you, for instance, that the average wages of factory families in Lancashire have risen. They forget that instead of the labour of the man, the head of the family, his wife and perhaps three or four children are now thrown under the Juggernaut wheels of capital, and that the rise of the aggregate wages does not correspond to the aggregate surplus labour extracted from the family.

Even with given limits of the working day, such as now exist in all branches of industry subjected to the factory laws, a rise of wages may become necessary, if only to keep up the old standard *value of labour*. By increasing the *intensity* of labour, a man may be made to expend as much vital force in one hour as he formerly did in two. This has, to a certain degree, been effected in the trades, placed under the Factory Acts, by the acceleration of machinery, and the greater number of working machines which a single individual has now to superintend. If the increase in the intensity of labour or the mass of labour spent in an hour keeps some fair proportion to the decrease in the extent of the working day, the working man will still be the winner. If this limit is overshot, he loses in one form what he has gained in another, and ten hours of labour may then become as ruinous as twelve hours were before. In checking this tendency of capital, by struggling for a rise of wages corresponding to the rising intensity of labour, the working man only resists the depreciation of his labour and the deterioration of his race.

4. All of you know that, from reasons I have not now to explain, capitalistic production moves through certain periodical cycles. It moves through a state of quiescence, growing animation, prosperity, overtrade, crisis, and stagnation. The market prices of commodities, and the market rates of profit, follow these phases, now sinking below their averages, now rising above them. Considering the whole cycle, you will find that one deviation of the market price is being compensated by the other, and that, taking the average of the cycle, the market prices of commodities are regulated by their values. Well! During the phase of sinking market prices and the phases of crisis and stagnation, the working man, if not thrown out of employment altogether, is sure to have his wages lowered. Not to be defrauded, he must, even with such a fall of market prices, debate with the capitalist in what proportional degree a fall of wages has become necessary. If, during the phases of prosperity, when extra profits are made, he did not battle for a rise of wages, he would, taking the average of one industrial cycle, not even receive his *average wages*, or the *value* of his labour. It is the utmost height of folly to demand that while his wages are necessarily affected by the adverse phases of the cycle, he should exclude himself from compensation during the prosperous phases of the cycle. Generally, the *values* of all commodities are only realised by the compensation of the continuously changing market prices, springing from the continuous fluctuations of demand and supply. On the basis of the present system labour is only a commodity like others. It must, therefore, pass through the same fluctuations to fetch an average price corresponding to its value. It would be absurd to treat it on the one hand as a commodity, and to want on the other hand to exempt it from the laws which regulate the prices of commodities. The slave receives a permanent and fixed amount of maintenance; the wages labourer does not. He must try to get a rise of wages in the one instance, if only to compensate for a fall of wages in

the other. If he resigned himself to accept the will, the dictates of the capitalist as a permanent economical law, he would share in all the miseries of the slave, without the security of the slave.

5. In all the cases I have considered, and they form ninety-nine out of a hundred, you have seen that a struggle for a rise of wages follows only in the track of *previous* changes, and is the necessary offspring of previous changes in the amount of production, the productive powers of labour, the value of labour, the value of money, the extent or the intensity of labour extracted, the fluctuations of market prices, dependent upon the fluctuations of demand and supply, and consistent with the different phases of the industrial cycle; in one word, as reactions of labour against the previous action of capital. By treating the struggle for a rise of wages independently of all these circumstances, by looking only upon the change of wages, and overlooking all the other changes from which they emanate, you proceed from a false premise in order to arrive at false conclusions.

XIV. THE STRUGGLE BETWEEN CAPITAL AND LABOUR AND ITS RESULTS

1. Having shown that the periodical resistance on the part of the working men against a reduction of wages, and their periodical attempts at getting a rise of wages, are inseparable from the wages system, and dictated by the very fact of labour being assimilated to commodities, and therefore subject to the laws regulating the general movement of prices; having, furthermore, shown that a general rise of wages would result in a fall in the general rate of profit, but not affect the average prices of commodities, or their values, the question now ultimately arises, how far, in this incessant struggle between capital and labour, the latter is likely to prove successful.

I might answer by a generalisation, and say that, as with all other commodities, so with labour, its *market price* will, in the long run, adapt itself to its *value;* that, therefore, despite all the ups and downs, and do what he may, the working man will, on an average, only receive the value of his labour, which resolves into the value of his labouring power, which is determined by the value of the necessaries required for its maintenance and reproduction, which value of necessaries finally is regulated by the quantity of labour wanted to produce them.

But there are some peculiar features which distinguish the *value of the labouring power, or the value of labour*, from the values of all other commodities. The value of the labouring power is formed by two elements—the one merely physical, the other historical or social. Its *ultimate limit* is determined by the *physical* element, that is to say, to maintain and reproduce itself, to perpetuate its physical existence, the working class must receive the necessaries absolutely indispensable for living and multiplying. The *value* of those indispensable necessaries forms, therefore, the ultimate limit of the *value of labour*. On the other hand, the length of the working day is also limited by ultimate, although very elastic boundaries. Its ultimate limit is given by the physical force of the labouring man. If the daily exhaustion of his vital forces exceeds a certain degree, it cannot be exerted anew, day by day. However, as I said, this limit is very elastic. A quick succession of unhealthy and short-lived generations will keep the labour market as well supplied as a series of vigorous and long-lived generations.

Besides this mere physical element, the value of labour is in every country determined by a *traditional standard of life.* It is not mere physical life, but it is the satisfaction of certain wants springing from the social conditions in which people are placed and reared up. The English standard of life may be reduced to the Irish standard; the standard of life of a German peasant to that of a Livonian peasant. The important part which historical tradition and social habitude play in this respect, you may learn from Mr. Thornton's work on *Over-population*, where he shows that the average wages in different agricultural districts of England still nowadays differ more or less according to the more or less favourable circumstances under which the districts have emerged from the state of serfdom.

This historical or social element, entering into the value of labour, may be expanded, or contracted, or altogether extinguished, so that nothing remains but the *physical limit*. During the time of the anti-Jacobin war, undertaken, as the incorrigible tax-eater and sinecurist, old George Rose, used to say, to save the comforts of our holy religion from the inroads of the French infidels, the honest English farmers, so tenderly handled in a former chapter of ours, depressed the wages of the agricultural labourers even beneath that *mere physical minimum*, but made up by Poor Laws the remainder necessary for the physical perpetuation of the race. This was a glorious way to convert the wages labourer into a slave, and Shakespeare's proud yeoman into a pauper.

By comparing the standard wages or values of labour in different countries, and by comparing them in different historical epochs of the same country, you will find that the *value of labour* itself is not a fixed but a variable magnitude, even supposing the values of all other commodities to remain constant.

A similar comparison would prove that not only the *market rates* of profit change but its *average* rates.

But as to *profits*, there exists no law which determines their *minimum*. We cannot say what is the ultimate limit of their decrease. And why cannot we fix that limit? Because, although we can fix the *minimum* of wages, we cannot fix their *maximum*. We can only say that, the limits of the working day being given, the *maximum* of profit corresponds to the *physical minimum of wages*; and that wages being given, the *maximum of profit* corresponds to such a prolongation of the working day as is compatible with the physical forces of the labourer. The maximum of profit is, therefore, limited by the physical minimum of wages and the physical maximum of the working day. It is evident that between the two limits of this *maximum rate of profit* an immense scale of variations is possible. The fixation of its actual degree is only settled by the continuous struggle between capital and labour, the capitalist constantly tending to reduce wages to their physical minimum, and to extend the working day to its physical maximum, while the working man constantly presses in the opposite direction.

The matter resolves itself into a question of the respective powers of the combatants.

2. As to the *limitation of the working day* in England, as in all other countries, it has never been settled except by *legislative interference*. Without the working men's continuous pressure from without that interference would never have taken place. But at all events, the result was not to be attained by private settlement between the working men and the capitalists. This very necessity of *general political action* affords the proof that in its merely economic action capital is the stronger side.

As to the *limits* of the *value of labour*, its actual settlement always depends upon supply and demand, I mean the demand for labour on the part of capital, and the supply of labour by the working men. In colonial countries the law of supply and demand favours the working man. Hence the relatively high standard of wages in the United States. Capital may there try its utmost. It cannot prevent the labour market from being continuously emptied by the continuous conversion of wages labourers into independent, self-sustaining peasants. The position of wages labourer is for a very large part of the American people but a probational state, which they are sure to leave within a longer or shorter term. To mend this colonial state of things, the paternal British Government accepted for some time what is called the modern colonisation theory, which consists in putting an artificial high price upon colonial land, in order to prevent the too quick conversion of the wages labourer into the independent peasant.

But let us now come to old civilised countries, in which capital domineers over the whole process of production. Take, for example, the rise in England of agricultural wages from 1849 to 1859. What was its consequence? The farmers could not, as our friend Weston would have advised them, raise the value of wheat, nor even its market prices. They had, on the contrary, to submit to their fall. But during these eleven years they introduced machinery of all sorts, adopted more scientific methods, converted part of arable land into pasture, increased the size of farms, and with this the scale of production, and by these and other processes diminishing the demand for labour by increasing its productive power, made the agricultural population again relatively redundant. This is the general method in which a reaction, quicker or slower, of capital against a rise of wages takes place in old, settled countries. Ricardo has justly remarked that machinery is in constant competition with labour, and can often be only introduced when the price of labour has reached a certain height, but the appliance of machinery is but one of the many methods for increasing the productive powers of labour. This very same development which makes common labour relatively redundant simplifies on the other hand skilled labour, and thus depreciates it. *Industrialized labor*

The same law obtains in another form. With the development of the productive powers of labour the accumulation of capital will be accelerated, even despite a relatively high rate of wages. Hence, one might infer, as Adam Smith, in whose days modern industry was still in its infancy, did infer, that the accelerated accumulation of capital must turn the balance in favour of the working man, by securing a growing demand for his labour. From this same standpoint many contemporary writers have wondered that English capital having grown in the last twenty years so much quicker than English population, wages should not have been more enhanced. But simultaneously with the progress of accumulation there takes place a *progressive change* in the *composition of capital.* That part of the aggregate capital which consists of fixed capital, machinery, raw materials, means of production in all possible forms, progressively increases as compared with the other part of capital, which is laid out in wages or in the purchase of labour. This law has been stated in a more or less accurate manner by Mr. Barton, Ricardo, Sismondi, Professor Richard Jones, Professor Ramsay, Cherbuliez, and others.

If the proportion of these two elements of capital was originally one to one, it will, in the progress of industry, become five to one, and so forth. If of a total capital of 600, 300 is laid out in instruments, raw materials, and so forth, and 300 in wages, the total capital wants only to be doubled to create a demand for 600 working men instead of for 300. But if of a capital of 600, 500 is laid out in machinery, materials, and so forth, and 100 only in wages, the same capital must increase from 600 to 3,600 in order to create a demand for 600 workmen instead of 300. In the progress of industry the demand for labour keeps, therefore, no pace with accumulation of capital. It will still increase, but increase in a constantly diminishing ratio as compared with the increase of capital.

These few hints will suffice to show that the very development of modern industry must progressively turn the scale in favour of the capitalist against the working man, and that consequently the general tendency of capitalistic production is not to raise, but to sink the average standard of wages, or to push the *value of labour* more or less to its *minimum limit.* Such being the tendency of *things* in this system, is this saying that the working class ought to renounce their resistance against the encroachments of capital, and abandon their attempts at making the best of the occasional chances for their temporary improvement? If they did, they would be degraded to one level mass of broken wretches past salvation. I think I have shown that their struggles for the standard of wages are incidents inseparable from the whole wages system, that in ninety-nine cases out of a hundred their efforts at raising wages are only efforts at maintaining the given value of labour, and that the necessity of debating their price with the capitalist is inherent in their condition of having to sell themselves as commodities. By cowardly giving way in their everyday conflict with capital, they would certainly disqualify themselves for the initiating of any larger movement.

At the same time, and quite apart from the general servitude involved in the wages system, the working class ought not to exaggerate to themselves the ultimate working of these everyday struggles. They ought not to forget that they are fighting with effects, but not with the causes of those effects; that they are retarding the downward movement, but not changing its direction; that they are applying palliatives, not curing the malady. They ought, therefore, not to be exclusively absorbed in these unavoidable guerrilla fights incessantly springing up from the never-ceasing encroachments of capital or changes of the market. They ought to understand that, with all the miseries it imposes upon them, the present system simultaneously engenders the *material conditions* and the *social forms* necessary for an economical reconstruction of society. Instead of the *conservative* motto, *"A fair day's wage for a fair day's work!"* they ought to inscribe on their banner the *revolutionary* watchword, *"Abolition of the wages system!"*

After this very long and, I fear, tedious exposition which I was obliged to enter into to do some justice to the subject-matter, I shall conclude by proposing the following resolutions:

Firstly. A general rise in the rate of wages would result in a fall of the general rate of profit, but, broadly speaking, not affect the prices of commodities.

Secondly. The general tendency of capitalist production is not to raise, but to sink the average standard of wages.

Thirdly. Trade Unions work well as centres of resistance against the encroachments of capital. They fail partially from an injudicious use of their power. They fail generally from limiting themselves to a guerrilla war against the effects of the existing system, instead of simultaneously trying to change it, instead of using their organised forces as a lever for the final emancipation of the working class, that is to say, the ultimate abolition of the wages system.

Karl Marx, *Value, Price and Profit: Addressed to Working Men,* edited by Eleanor Marx Aveling, London, 1898, pp. 41–94; reprinted as *Wages, Price and Profit* in Karl Marx and Frederick Engels, *Selected Works,* 3 vols., Moscow, 1969, Vol. II, pp. 48–76.

1867

From CAPITAL, VOLUME I

FROM THE PREFACE TO THE FIRST GERMAN EDITION

The work, the first volume of which I now submit to the public, forms the continuation of my *Zur Kritik der Politischen Ökonomie* (*A Contribution to the Critique of Political Economy*) published in 1859. The long pause between the first part and the continuation is due to an illness of many years' duration that again and again interrupted my work. . . .

Every beginning is difficult, holds in all sciences. To

understand the first chapter, especially the section that contains the analysis of commodities, will, therefore, present the greatest difficulty. That which concerns more especially the analysis of the substance of value and the magnitude of value, I have, as much as it was possible, popularised. The value-form, whose fully developed shape is the money-form, is very elementary and simple. Nevertheless, the human mind has for more than 2000 years sought in vain to get to the bottom of it, whilst on the other hand, to the successful analysis of much more composite and complex forms, there has been at least an approximation. Why? Because the body, as an organic whole, is more easy of study than are the cells of that body. In the analysis of economic forms, moreover, neither microscopes nor chemical reagents are of use. The force of abstraction must replace both. But in bourgeois society the commodity-form of the product of labour—or the value-form of the commodity—is the economic cell-form. To the superficial observer, the analysis of these forms seems to turn upon minutiae. It does in fact deal with minutiae, but they are of the same order as those dealt with in microscopic anatomy.

With the exception of the section on value-form, therefore, this volume cannot stand accused on the score of difficulty. I presuppose, of course, a reader who is willing to learn something new and therefore to think for himself.

The physicist either observes physical phenomena where they occur in their most typical form and most free from disturbing influence, or, wherever possible, he makes experiments under conditions that assure the occurrence of the phenomenon in its normality. In this work I have to examine the capitalist mode of production, and the conditions of production and exchange corresponding to that mode. Up to the present time, their classic ground is England. That is the reason why England is used as the chief illustration in the development of my theoretical ideas. If, however, the German reader shrugs his shoulders at the condition of the English industrial and agricultural labourers, or in optimist fashion comforts himself with the thought that in Germany things are not nearly so bad, I must plainly tell him: '*De te fabula narratur!*' ['It is of you that the story is told!']

Intrinsically, it is not a question of the higher or lower degree of development of the social antagonisms that result from the natural laws of capitalist production. It is a question of these laws themselves, of these tendencies working with iron necessity towards inevitable results. The country that is more developed industrially only shows, to the less developed, the image of its own future.

But apart from this: Where capitalist production is fully naturalised among the Germans (for instance, in the factories proper) the condition of things is much worse than in England, because the counterpoise of the Factory Acts is wanting. In all other spheres, we, like all the rest of Continental Western Europe, suffer not only from the development of capitalist production, but also from the incompleteness of that development. Alongside of modern evils, a whole series of inherited evils oppress us, arising from the passive survival of antiquated modes of production, with their inevitable train of social and political anachronisms. We suffer not only from the living, but from the dead. . . .

The social statistics of Germany and the rest of Continental Western Europe are, in comparison with those of England, wretchedly compiled. But they raise the veil just enough to let us catch a glimpse of the Medusa head behind it. We should be appalled at the state of things at home, if, as in England, our governments and parliaments appointed periodically commissioners of enquiry into economic conditions; if these commissions were armed with the same plenary powers to get at the truth; if it was possible to find for this purpose men as competent, as free from artisanship and respect of persons as are the English factory-inspectors, her medical reporters on public health, her commissioners of enquiry into the exploitation of women and children, into housing and food. Perseus wore a magic cap that the monsters he hunted down might not see him. We draw the magic cap down over eyes and ears as a make-believe that there are no monsters.

Let us not deceive ourselves on this. As in the eighteenth century, the American War of Independence sounded the tocsin for the European middle class, so in the nineteenth century, the American civil war sounded it for the European working-class. In England the progress of social disintegration is palpable. When it has reached a certain point, it must react on the Continent. There it will take a form more brutal or more humane, according to the degree of development of the working-class itself. Apart from higher motives, therefore, their own most important interests dictate to the classes that are for the nonce the ruling ones, the removal of all legally removable hindrances to the free development of the working-class. For this reason, as well as others, I have given so large a space in this volume to the history, the details, and the results of English factory legislation. One nation can and should learn from others. And even when a society has got upon the right track for the discovery of the natural laws of its movement—and it is the ultimate aim of this work to lay bare the economic law of motion of modern society—it can neither clear by bold leaps, nor remove by legal enactments, the obstacles offered by successive phases of its normal development. But it can shorten and lessen the birth-pangs.

To prevent possible misunderstanding, a word. I paint the capitalist and the landlord in no sense *couleur de rose*. But here individuals are dealt with only in so far as they are the personifications of economic categories, embodiments of particular class-relations and class-interests. My standpoint, from which the evolution of the economic formation of society is viewed as a process of natural history, can less than any other make the individual responsible for relations whose creature he socially remains, however much he may subjectively raise himself above them.

In the domain of Political Economy, free scientific enquiry meets not merely the same enemies as in all other domains. The peculiar nature of the material it deals with, summons as foes into the field of battle the most violent, mean and malignant passions of the human breast, the Furies of private interest. The English Established Church, e.g., will more readily pardon an attack on 38 of its 39 articles than on 1/39 of its income. Nowadays atheism itself is *culpa levis* [light offence], as compared with criticism of existing property relations. Nevertheless, there is an unmistakeable advance. I refer, e.g., to the Blue Book published within the last few weeks: "Correspondence with Her Majesty's Missions Abroad, regarding Industrial Questions and Trades Unions." The representatives of the English Crown in foreign countries there declare in so many words that in Germany, in France, to be brief, in all the civilised states of the European continent, a radical change in the existing relations between capital and labour is as evident and inevitable as in England. At the same time, on the other side of the Atlantic Ocean, Mr. Wade, Vice-President of the United States, declared in public meetings that, after the abolition of slavery, a radical change of the relations of capital and of property in land is next upon the order of the day. These are signs of the times, not to be hidden by purple mantles or black cassocks. They do not signify that tomorrow a miracle will happen. They show that, within the ruling-classes themselves, a foreboding is dawning, that the present society is no solid crystal, but an organism capable of change, and is constantly changing.

The second volume of this work will treat of the process of the circulation of capital (Book II.), and of the varied forms assumed by capital in the course of its development (Book III.), the third and last volume (Book IV.), the history of the theory. . . .

CHAPTER 1: 'COMMODITIES'

Section 1. The Two Factors of a Commodity: Use-Value and Value (The Substance of Value and the Magnitude of Value).

The wealth of those societies in which the capitalist mode of production prevails, presents itself as 'an immense accumulation of commodities,'[1] its unit being a single commodity. Our investigation must therefore begin with the analysis of a commodity.

A commodity is, in the first place, an object outside us, a thing that by its properties satisfies human wants of some sort or another. The nature of such wants, whether, for instance, they spring from the stomach or from fancy, makes no difference.[2] Neither are we here concerned to know how the object satisfies these wants, whether directly as means of subsistence, or indirectly as means of production.

Every useful thing, as iron, paper, etc., may be looked at from the two points of view of quality and quantity. It is an assemblage of many properties, and may therefore be of use in various ways. To discover the various uses of things is the work of history.[3] So also is the establishment of socially-recognised standards of measure for the quan-

---

1. Karl Marx, *Zur Kritik der Politischen Ökonomie*, Berlin, 1859, p. 4.
2. 'Desire implies want; it is the appetite of the mind, and as natural as hunger to the body.... The greatest number (of things) have their value from supplying the wants of the mind'(Nicholas Barbon: *A Discourse on Coining the New Money Lighter. In Answer to Mr Locke's Considerations etc.*, London, 1696, pp. 2, 3).
3. 'Things have an intrinsick vertue' (this is Barbon's special term for value in use) 'which in all places have the same vertue; as the loadstone to attract iron' (*op. cit.*, p. 6). The property which the magnet possesses of attracting iron, became of use only after by means of that property the polarity of the magnet had been discovered.

tities of these useful objects. The diversity of these measures has its origin partly in the diverse nature of the objects to be measured, partly in convention.

The utility of a thing makes it a use-value.[4] But this utility is not a thing of air. Being limited by the physical properties of the commodity, it has no existence apart from that commodity. A commodity, such as iron, corn, or a diamond, is therefore, so far as it is a material thing, a use-value, something useful. This property of a commodity is independent of the amount of labour required to appropriate its useful qualities. When treating of use-value, we always assume to be dealing with definite quantities, such as dozens of watches, yards of linen, or tons of iron. The use-values of commodities furnish the material for a special study, that of the commercial knowledge of commodities.[5] Use-values become a reality only by use or consumption: they also constitute the substance of all wealth, whatever may be the social form of that wealth. In the form of society we are about to consider, they are, in addition, the material depositories of exchange value.

Exchange value, at first sight, presents itself as a quantitative relation, as the proportion in which values in use of one sort are exchanged for those of another sort,[6] a rela-

---

4. 'The natural worth of anything consists in its fitness to supply the necessities, or serve the conveniencies of human life' (John Locke, 'Some Considerations on the Consequences of the Lowering of Interest' [1691], in *Works*, London, 1777, vol. 2, p. 28). In English writers of the seventeenth century we frequently find 'worth' in the sense of value in use, and 'value' in the sense of exchange value. This is quite in accordance with the spirit of a language that likes to use a Teutonic word for the actual thing, and a Romance word for its reflection.

5. In bourgeois societies the economical *fictio juris* prevails, that everyone, as a buyer, possesses an encyclopaedic knowledge of commodities.

6. 'Value consists in the exchange relationship which exists between a thing and any other, between a certain quantity of a product and a certain quantity of any other' (Le Trosne, *De l'interêt social*, in *Physiocrates*, ed. Daire, Paris, 1846, p. 889).

tion constantly changing with time and place. Hence exchange value appears to be something accidental and purely relative, and consequently an intrinsic value, i.e., an exchange value that is inseparably connected with, inherent in commodities, seems a contradiction in terms.[7] Let us consider the matter a little more closely.

A given commodity, e.g., a quarter of wheat is exchanged for x blacking, y silk, or z gold, etc.—in short, for other commodities in the most different proportions. Instead of one exchange value, the wheat has, therefore, a great many. But since x blacking, y silk, or z gold, etc., each represent the exchange value of one quarter of wheat, x blacking, y silk, z gold, etc., must, as exchange values, be replaceable by each other, or equal to each other. Therefore, first: the valid exchange values of a given commodity express something equal; secondly, exchange value, generally, is only the mode of expression, the phenomenal form, of something contained in it, yet distinguishable from it.

Let us take two commodities, e.g., corn and iron. The proportions in which they are exchangeable, whatever those proportions may be, can always be represented by an equation in which a given quantity of corn is equated to some quantity of iron: e.g., 1 quarter corn = x cwt. iron. What does this equation tell us? It tells us that in two different things—in 1 quarter of corn and x cwt. of iron—there exists in equal quantities something common to both. The two things must therefore be equal to a third, which in itself is neither the one nor the other. Each of them, so far as it is exchange value, must therefore be reducible to this third.

A simple geometrical illustration will make this clear. In order to calculate and compare the areas of rectilinear fig-

---

7. 'Nothing can have an intrinsick value' (Barbon, *op. cit.*, p. 6), or as Butler says:

> 'The value of a thing
> Is just as much as it will bring.'

ures, we decompose them into triangles. But the area of the triangle itself is expressed by something totally different from its visible figure, namely, by half the product of the base into the altitude. In the same way the exchange values of commodities must be capable of being expressed in terms of something common to them all, of which thing they represent a greater or less quantity.

This common 'something' cannot be either a geometrical, a chemical, or any other natural property of commodities. Such properties claim our attention only in so far as they affect the utility of those commodities, make them use-values. But the exchange of commodities is evidently an act characterised by a total abstraction from use-value. Then one use-value is just as good as another, provided only it be present in sufficient quantity. Or, as old Barbon says, 'One sort of wares is as good as another, if the values be equal. There is no difference or distinction in things of equal value. . . . An hundred pounds' worth of lead or iron, is of as great value as one hundred pounds' worth of silver or gold.'[8] As use-values, commodities are, above all, of different quantities, and consequently do not contain an atom of use-value.

If then we leave out of consideration the use-value of commodities, they have only one common property left, that of being products of labour. But even the product of labour itself has undergone a change in our hands. If we make abstraction from its use-value, we make abstraction at the same time from the material elements and shapes that make the product a use-value; we see in it no longer a table, a house, yarn, or any other useful thing. Its existence as a material thing is put out of sight. Neither can it any longer be regarded as the product of the labour of the joiner, the mason, the spinner, or of any other definite kind of productive labour. Along with the useful qualities

---

8. Barbon, *op. cit.*, pp. 53,7.

of the products themselves, we put out of sight both the useful character of the various kinds of labour embodied in them, and the concrete forms of that labour; there is nothing left but what is common to them all; all are reduced to one and the same sort of labour, human labour in the abstract.

Let us now consider the residue of each of these products; it consists of the same unsubstantial reality in each, a mere congelation of homogeneous human labour, of labour-power expended without regard to the mode of its expenditure. All that these things now tell us is, that human labour-power has been expended in their production, that human labour is embodied in them. When looked at as crystals of this social substance, common to them all, they are—Values.

We have seen that when commodities are exchanged, their exchange value manifests itself as something totally independent of their use-value. But if we abstract from their use-value, there remains their Value as defined above. Therefore, the common substance that manifests itself in the exchange value of commodities, whenever they are exchanged, is their value. The progress of our investigation will show that exchange value is the only form in which the value of commodities can manifest itself or be expressed. For the present, however, we have to consider the nature of value independently of this, its form.

A use-value, or useful article, therefore, has value only because human labour in the abstract has been embodied or materialised in it. How, then, is the magnitude of this value to be measured? Plainly, by the quantity of the value-creating substance, the labour, contained in the article. The quantity of labour, however, is measured by its duration, and labour-time in its turn finds its standard in weeks, days and hours.

Some people might think that if the value of a commodity is determined by the quantity of labour spent on it; the more idle and unskilful the labourer, the more valuable would his commodity be, because more time would be required in its production. The labour, however, that forms the substance of value, is homogeneous human labour, expenditure of one uniform labour-power. The total labour-power of society, which is embodied in the sum total of the values of all commodities produced by that society, counts here as one homogeneous mass of human labour-power, composed though it be of innumerable individual units. Each of these units is the same as any other, so far as it has the character of the average labour-power of society, and takes effect as such; that is, so far as it requires, for producing a commodity, no more time than is needed on an average, no more than is socially necessary. The labour-time socially necessary is that required to produce an article under the normal conditions of production, and with the average degree of skill and intensity prevalent at the time. The introduction of power looms into England probably reduced by one half the labour required to weave a given quantity of yarn into cloth. The hand-loom weavers, as a matter of fact, continued to require the same time as before; but for all that, the product of one hour of their labour represented after the change only half an hour's social labour, and consequently fell to one-half its former value.

We see then that that which determines the magnitude of the value of any article is the amount of labour socially necessary, or the labour-time socially necessary for its production.[9] Each individual commodity, in this connec-

---

9. 'The value of them [the necessaries of life] when they are exchanged the one for another, is regulated by the quantity of labour necessarily required, and commonly taken in producing them' (*Some Thoughts on the Interest of Money in General, and Particularly in the Publick Funds*, London, p. 36). This remarkable anonymous work, written in the last century, bears no date. It is clear, however, from internal evidence, that it appeared in the reign of George II, about 1739 or 1740.

tion, is to be considered as an average sample of its class.[10] Commodities, therefore, in which equal quantities of labour are embodied, or which can be produced in the same time, have the same value. The value of one commodity is to the value of any other, as the labour-time necessary for the production of the one is to that necessary for the production of the other. 'As values, all commodities are only definite masses of congealed labour-time.'[11]

The value of a commodity would therefore remain constant, if the labour-time required for its production also remained constant. But the latter changes with every variation in the productiveness of labour. This productiveness is determined by various circumstances, amongst others, by the average amount of skill of the workmen, the state of science, and the degree of its practical application, the social organisation of production, the extent and capabilities of the means of production, and by physical conditions. For example, the same amount of labour in favourable seasons is embodied in eight bushels of corn and, in unfavourable, only in four. The same labour extracts from rich mines more metal than from poor mines. Diamonds are of very rare occurrence on the earth's surface, and hence their discovery costs, on an average, a great deal of labour-time. Consequently much labour is represented in a small compass. Jacob doubts whether gold has ever been paid for at its full value. This applies still more to diamonds. According to Eschwege, the total produce of the Brazilian diamond mines for the eighty years, ending in 1823, had not realized the price of one-and-a-half year's average produce of the sugar and coffee plantations of the same country, although the diamonds cost much more labour and therefore represented

---

10. 'All products of one kind really form a single mass, whose price is generally determined, without reference to particular circumstances' (Le Trosne, *op. cit.*, p. 893).
11. Marx, *Zur Kritik*, p. 6.

more value. With richer mines, the same quantity of labour would embody itself in more diamonds, and their
value would fall. If we could succeed, at a small expenditure of labour, in converting carbon into diamonds, their
value might fall below that of bricks. In general, the
greater the productiveness of labour, the less is the labour-
time required for the production of an article, the less is
the amount of labour crystallized in that article, and the
less is its value; and *vice versa*, the less the productiveness
of labour, the greater is the labour-time required for the
production of an article, and the greater is its value. The
value of a commodity, therefore, varies directly as the
quantity, and inversely as the productiveness, of the labour incorporated in it.

A thing can be a use-value, without having value. This
is the case whenever its utility to man is not due to labour.
Such are air, virgin soil, natural meadows, etc. A thing can
be useful, and the product of human labour, without
being a commodity. Whoever directly satisfies his wants
with the produce of his own labour creates, indeed, use-
values, but not commodities. In order to produce the latter, he must not only produce use-values, but use-values
for others, social use-values. Lastly, nothing can have
value without being an object of utility. If the thing is
useless, so is the labour contained in it; the labour does not
count as labour, and therefore creates no value. . . .

Section 4. The Fetishism of Commodities and the Secret Thereof

A commodity appears, at first sight, a very trivial thing,
and easily understood. Its analysis shows that it is, in reality, a very queer thing, abounding in metaphysical subtle-
ties and theological niceties. So far as it is a value in use,
there is nothing mysterious about it, whether we consider
it from the point of view that by its properties it is capable
of satisfying human wants, or from the point that those

properties are the product of human labour. It is as clear as noon-day, that man, by his industry, changes the forms of the materials furnished by nature, in such a way as to make them useful to him. The form of wood, for instance, is altered by making a table out of it. Yet, for all that the table continues to be that common, every-day thing, wood. But, so soon as it steps forth as a commodity, it is changed into something transcendent. It not only stands with its feet on the ground, but, in relation to all other commodities, it stands on its head, and evolves out of its wooden brain grotesque ideas, far more wonderful than if it were to start dancing of its own accord.[12]

The mystical character of commodities does not originate, therefore, in their use-value. Just as little does it proceed from the nature of the determining factors of value. For, in the first place, however varied the useful kinds of labour, or productive activities, may be, it is a physiological fact, that they are functions of the human organism, and that each such function, whatever may be its nature or form, is essentially the expenditure of human brain, nerves, muscles, etc. Secondly, with regard to that which forms the groundwork for the quantitative determination of value, namely, the duration of that expenditure, or the quantity of labour, it is quite clear that there is a palpable difference between its quantity and quality. In all states of society, the labour-time that it costs to produce the means of subsistence must necessarily be an object of interest to mankind, though not of equal interest in different stages of development.[13] And lastly, from the moment that men in

---

12. One is reminded that china and the tables began to dance when the rest of the world seemed to stand still—*pour encourager les autres*.

13. Among the ancient Germans the unit for measuring land was what could be worked in a day and was therefore known as *Tagwerk*, *Tagwanne* (*jurnale* or *terra jurnalis* or *diornalis*), *Mannwerk*, *Mannskraft*, *Mannsmaad*, *Mannshauet*, etc. See G. L.

any way work for one another, their labour assumes a social form.

Whence, then, arises the enigmatical character of the product of labour, so soon as it assumes the form of commodities? Clearly from this form itself. The equality of all sorts of human labour is expressed objectively by their products all being equally values; the measure of the expenditure of labour-power by the duration of that expenditure, takes the form of the quantity of value of the products of labour; and finally, the mutual relations of the producers, within which the social character of their labour affirms itself, take the form of a social relation between the products.

A commodity is therefore a mysterious thing, simply because in it the social character of men's labour appears to them as an objective character stamped upon the product of that labour; because the relation of the producers to the sum total of their own labour is presented to them as a social relation, existing not between themselves, but between the products of their labour. This is the reason why the products of labour become commodities, social things whose qualities are at the same time perceptible and imperceptible by the senses. In the same way the light from an object is perceived by us not as the subjective excitation of our optic nerve, but as the objective form of something outside the eye itself. But, in the act of seeing, there is at all events an actual passage of light from one thing to another, from the external object to the eye. There is a physical relation between physical things. But it is different with commodities. There, the existence of the things *qua* commodities, and the value relation between the products of labour which stamps them as commodities, have absolutely no connection with their physical properties and with the material relations arising therefrom.

---

von Maurer, *Einleitung zur Geschichte der Mark-, Hof-, usw. Verfassung*, Munich, 1854, pp. 129–59.

There it is a definite social relation between men, that assumes, in their eyes, the fantastic form of a relation between things. In order, therefore, to find an analogy, we must have recourse to the mist-enveloped regions of the religious world. In that world the productions of the human brain appear as independent beings endowed with life, and entering into relation both with one another and the human race. So it is in the world of commodities with the products of men's hands. This I call the Fetishism which attaches itself to the products of labour, so soon as they are produced as commodities, and which is therefore inseparable from the production of commodities.

This fetishism of commodities has its origin, as the foregoing analysis has already shown, in the peculiar social character of the labour that produces them.

As a general rule, articles of utility become commodities only because they are products of the labour of private individuals or groups of individuals who carry on their work independently of each other. The sum total of the labour of all these private individuals forms the aggregate labour of society. Since the producers do not come into social contact with each other until they exchange their products, the specific social character of each producer's labour does not show itself except in the act of exchange. In other words, the labour of the individual asserts itself as a part of the labour of society only by means of the relations which the act of exchange establishes directly between the products, and indirectly, through them, between the producers. To the latter, therefore, the relations connecting the labour of one individual with that of the rest appear, not as direct social relations between individuals at work, but as what they really are, material relations between persons and social relations between things. It is only by being exchanged that the products of labour acquire, as values, one uniform social status distinct from their varied forms of existence as objects of utility. This division of a product into a useful thing and a value becomes practically important only when exchange has acquired such an extension that useful articles are produced for the purpose of being exchanged, and their character as values has therefore to be taken into account, beforehand, during production. From this moment the labour of the individual producer acquires socially a two-fold character. On the one hand, it must, as a definite useful kind of labour, satisfy a definite social want, and thus hold its place as part and parcel of the collective labour of all, as a branch of a social division of labour that has sprung up spontaneously. On the other hand, it can satisfy the manifold wants of the individual producer himself, only in so far as the mutual exchangeability of all kinds of useful private labour is an established social fact, and therefore the private useful labour of each producer ranks on an equality with that of all others. The equalisation of the most different kinds of labour can be the result only of an abstraction from their inequalities, or of reducing them to their common denominator, viz., expenditure of human labour power or human labour in the abstract. The two-fold social character of the labour of the individual appears to him, when reflected in his brain, only under those forms which are impressed upon that labour in everyday practice by the exchange of products. In this way, the character that his own labour possesses of being socially useful takes the form of the condition, that the product must be not only useful, but useful for others, and the social character that his particular labour has, of being the equal of all other particular kinds of labour, takes the form that all the physically different articles that are the products of labour have one common quality, viz., that of having value.

Hence, when we bring the products of our labour into relation with each other as values, it is not because we see in these articles the material receptacles of homogeneous human labour. Quite the contrary: whenever, by an exchange, we equate as values our different products, by that very act we also equate, as human labour, the different kinds of labour expended upon them. We are not aware of this, nevertheless we do it.[14] Value, therefore, does not stalk about with a label describing what it is. It is value, rather, that converts every product into a social hieroglyphic. Later on, we try to decipher the hieroglyphic, to get behind the secret of our own social products; for to stamp an object of utility as a value is just as much a social product as language. The recent scientific discovery that the products of labour, so far as they are values, are but material expressions of the human labour spent in their production, marks, indeed, an epoch in the history of the development of the human race, but by no means dissipates the mist through which the social character of labour appears to us to be an objective character of the products themselves. The fact, that in the particular form of production with which we are dealing, viz., the production of commodities, the specific social character of private labour carried on independently consists in the equality of every kind of that labour, by virtue of its being human labour, which character, therefore, assumes in the product the form of value—this fact appears to the producers, notwithstanding the discovery above referred to, to be just as real and final as the fact, that, after the discovery by science of the component gases of air, the atmosphere itself remained unaltered.

What, first of all, practically concerns producers when they make an exchange is the question, how much of some other product they get for their own. In what proportions are the products exchangeable? When these proportions have, by custom, attained a certain stability, they appear

---

14. When, therefore, Galiani says, 'Value is a relation between persons'— *La Ricchezza è una ragione tra due persone*—he should have added 'disguised as a relation between things' (Galiani, *Della Moneta* in Vol. 3 of Custodi's collection *Scrittori classici italiani di economia politica, Parte moderna*, Milan, 1803, p. 220).

to result from the nature of the products, so that, for instance, one ton of iron and two ounces of gold appear as naturally to be of equal value, as a pound of gold and a pound of iron in spite of their different physical and chemical qualities appear to be of equal weight. The character of having value, when once impressed upon products, obtains fixity only by reason of their acting and re-acting upon each other as quantities of value. These quantities vary continually, independently of the will, foresight and action of the producers. To them, their own social action takes the form of the action of objects, which rule the producers instead of being ruled by them. It requires a fully developed production of commodities before, from accumulated experience alone, the scientific conviction springs up, that all the different kinds of private labour, which are carried on independently of each other, and yet as spontaneously developed branches of the social division of labour, are continually being reduced to the quantitative proportions in which society requires them. And why? Because, in the midst of all the accidental and ever fluctuating exchange-relations between the products, the labour-time socially necessary for their production forcibly asserts itself like an over-riding law of nature. The law of gravity thus asserts itself when a house falls about our ears.[15] The determination of the magnitude of value by labour-time is therefore a secret, hidden under the apparent fluctuations in the relative values of commodities. Its discovery, while removing all appearance of mere accidentality from the determination of the magnitude of the values of products, yet in no way alters the mode in which that determination takes place

15. 'What is one to think of a law which can only succeed by means of periodic revolutions? It is simply a law of nature depending on the unawareness of the participants' (F. Engels, 'Umrisse zu einer Kritik der Nationalökonomie' in *Deutsch-französische Jahrbücher*, edited by Arnold Ruge and Karl Marx, Paris, 1844).

Man's reflections on the forms of social life, and consequently also his scientific analysis of those forms, take a course directly opposite to that of their actual historical development. He begins, *post festum*, with the results of the process of development ready to hand before him. The characters that stamp products as commodities, and whose establishment is a necessary preliminary to the circulation of commodities, have already acquired the stability of natural, self-understood forms of social life, before man seeks to decipher, not their historical character, for in his eyes they are immutable, but their meaning. Consequently it was the analysis of the prices of commodities that alone led to the determination of the magnitude of value, and it was the common expression of all commodities in money that alone led to the establishment of their characters as values. It is, however, just this ultimate money form of the world of commodities that actually conceals, instead of disclosing, the social character of private labour, and the social relations between the individual producers. When I state that coats or boots stand in a relation to linen, because it is the universal incarnation of abstract human labour, the absurdity of the statement is self-evident. Nevertheless, when the producers of coats and boots compare those articles with linen, or, what is the same thing, with gold or silver, as the universal equivalent, they express the relation between their own private labour and the collective labour of society in the same absurd form.

The categories of bourgeois economy consist of suchlike forms. They are forms of thought expressing with social validity the conditions and relations of a definite, historically determined mode of production, viz., the production of commodities. The whole mystery of commodities, all the magic and necromancy that surrounds the products of labour as long as they take the form of commodities, vanishes therefore, so soon as we come to other forms of production.

Since Robinson Crusoe's experiences are a favourite theme with political economists,[16] let us take a look at him on his island. Moderate though he be, yet some few wants he has to satisfy, and must therefore do a little useful work of various sorts, such as making tools and furniture, taming goats, fishing and hunting. Of his prayers and the like we take no account, since they are a source of pleasure to him, and he looks upon them as so much recreation. In spite of the variety of his work, he knows that his labour, whatever its form, is but the activity of one and the same Robinson and, consequently, that it consists of nothing but different modes of human labour. Necessity itself compels him to apportion his time accurately between his different kinds of work. Whether one kind occupies a greater space in his general activity than another depends on the difficulties, greater or less as the case may be, to be overcome in attaining the useful effect aimed at. This our friend Robinson soon learns by experience, and having rescued a watch, ledger, and pen and ink from the wreck, commences, like a true-born Briton, to keep a set of books. His stock-book contains a list of the objects of utility that belong to him, of the operations necessary for their production; and lastly, of the labour-time that definite quantities of those objects have, on an average, cost him. All the relations between Robinson and the objects that form this wealth of his own creation, are here so simple and clear as to be intelligible without exertion, even to Mr. Sedley Taylor. And yet those relations contain all that is essential to the determination of value.

---

16. Even Ricardo is not without his 'Robinsonade.' 'He straightway makes the primitive fisherman and the primitive hunter, as commodity owners, exchange fish and game proportionately to the labour-time incorporated in these exchange values. In this way he commits the anachronism of making his primitive fisherman and hunter calculate their implements by means of annuity tables in use on the London Stock Exchange in 1817. The "parallelograms of Mr. Owen" seem to be the only form of society, apart from the bourgeois, with which he was familiar' (Marx, *Zur Kritik*, pp. 38–39).

Let us now transport ourselves from Robinson's island bathed in light to the European middle ages shrouded in darkness. Here, instead of the independent man, we find everyone dependent, serfs and lords, vassals and suzerains, laymen and clergy. Personal dependence here characterises the social relations of production just as much as it does the other spheres of life organised on the basis of that production. But for the very reason that personal dependence forms the groundwork of society, there is no necessity for labour and its products to assume a fantastic form different from their reality. They take the shape, in the transactions of society, of services in kind and payments in kind. Here the particular and natural form of labour, and not, as in a society based on production of commodities, its general abstract form, is the immediate social form of labour. Compulsory labour is just as properly measured by time as commodity-producing labour; but every serf knows that what he expends in the service of his lord is a definite quantity of his own personal labour-power. The tithe to be rendered to the priest is more matter of fact than his blessing. No matter, then, what we may think of the parts played by the different classes of people themselves in this society, the social relations between individuals in the performance of their labour appear at all events as their own mutual personal relations, and are not disguised under the shape of social relations between the products of labour.

For an example of labour in common or directly associated labour, we have no occasion to go back to that spontaneously developed form which we find on the threshold of the history of all civilised races.[17] We have one close at

---

17. 'A ridiculous presumption has latterly got abroad that common property in its primitive form is specifically a Slavonian, or even exclusively Russian, form. It is the primitive form that we can prove to have existed amongst Romans, Teutons, and Celts, and even to this day we find numerous examples, ruins though they be, in India. A more exhaustive study of Asiatic, and especially of Indian forms of

hand in the patriarchal industries of a peasant family, that produces corn, cattle, yarn, linen and clothing for home use. These different articles are, as regards the family, so many products of its labour, but as between themselves they are not commodities. The different kinds of labour, such as tillage, cattle tending, spinning, weaving and making clothes, which result in the various products, are in themselves, and such as they are, direct social functions, because functions of the family, which, just as much as a society based on the production of commodities, possesses a spontaneously developed system of division of labour. The distribution of the work within the family, and the regulation of the labour-time of the several members, depend as well upon differences of age and sex as upon natural conditions varying with the seasons. The labour-power of each individual, by its very nature, operates in this case merely as a definite portion of the whole labour-power of the family and, therefore, the measure of the expenditure of individual labour-power by its duration appears here by its very nature as a social character of their labour.

Let us now picture to ourselves, by way of change, a community of free individuals, carrying on their work with the means of production in common, in which the labour-power of all the different individuals is consciously applied as the combined labour-power of the community. All the characteristics of Robinson's labour are here repeated but with this difference, that they are social, instead of individual. Everything produced by him was exclusively the result of his own personal labour, and therefore simply an object of use for himself. The total product of our community is a social product. One por-

---

common property, would show how, from the different forms of primitive common property, different forms of its dissolution have been developed. Thus, for instance, the various original types of Roman and Teutonic private property are deducible from different forms of Indian common property' (Marx, *Zur Kritik*, p. 10).

tion serves as fresh means of production and remains social. But another portion is consumed by the members as means of subsistence. A distribution of this portion amongst them is consequently necessary. The mode of this distribution will vary with the productive organisation of the community, and the degree of historical development attained by the producers. We will assume, but merely for the sake of a parallel with the production of commodities, that the share of each individual producer in the means of subsistence is determined by his labour-time. Labour-time would, in that case, play a double part. Its apportionment in accordance with a definite social plan maintains the proper proportion between the different kinds of work to be done and the various wants of the community. On the other hand, it also serves as a measure of the portion of the common labour borne by each individual, and of his share in the part of the total product destined for individual consumption. The social relations of the individual producers, with regard both to their labour and to its products, are in this case perfectly simple and intelligible, and that with regard not only to production but also to distribution.

The religious world is but the reflex of the real world. And for a society based upon the production of commodities, in which the producers in general enter into social relations with one another by treating their products as commodities and values, whereby they reduce their individual private labour to the standard of homogeneous human labour—for such a society, Christianity with its *cultus* of abstract man, more especially in its bourgeois developments, Protestantism, Deism, etc., is the most fitting form of religion. In the ancient Asiatic and other ancient modes of production, we find that the conversion of products into commodities, and therefore the conversion of men into producers of commodities, holds a subordinate place, which, however, increases in importance as the primitive communities approach nearer and nearer to their dissolution. Trading nations, properly so called, exist in the ancient world only in its interstices, like the gods of Epicurus in the *intermundia*, or like Jews in the pores of Polish society. Those ancient social organisms of production are, as compared with bourgeois society, extremely simple and transparent. But they are founded either on the immature development of man individually, who has not yet severed the umbilical cord that unites him with his fellow men in a primitive tribal community, or upon direct relations of subjection. They can arise and exist only when the development of the productive power of labour has not risen beyond a low stage, and when, therefore, the social relations within the sphere of material life, between man and man, and between man and Nature, are correspondingly narrow. This narrowness is reflected in the ancient worship of Nature, and in the other elements of the popular religions. The religious reflex of the real world can, in any case, only then finally vanish, when the practical relations of everyday life offer to man none but perfectly intelligible and reasonable relations with regard to his fellow men and to nature.

The life-process of society, which is based on the process of material production, does not strip off its mystical veil until it is treated as production by freely associated men, and is consciously regulated by them in accordance with a settled plan. This, however, demands for society a certain material groundwork or set of conditions of existence which in their turn are the spontaneous product of a long and painful process of development.

Political economy has indeed analysed, however incompletely,[18] value and its magnitude, and has discovered

---

18. The inadequacy of Ricardo's analysis of the magnitude of value—and it is the best—will appear from the third and fourth books of this work. As regards value in general, the classical school of political economy nowhere distinguishes positively and with full conviction between labour as expressed in the value of a product

what lies beneath these forms. But it has never once asked the question why labour is represented by the value of its product and labour-time by the magnitude of that value.[19]

---

and the same labour expressed as the use-value of that product. It makes the distinction in practice, of course, treating labour at times quantitatively and at times qualitatively. But it does not occur to this school that a purely quantitative differentiation of kinds of labour presupposes their qualitative unity or equality. For instance, Ricardo declares himself in agreement with Destutt de Tracy when he says: 'As it is certain that our physical and moral faculties are alone our original riches, the employment of those faculties, labour of some kind, is our original treasure, and it is always from this employment that all those things are created, which we call riches. . . . It is certain, too, that all those things only represent the labour which has created them, and if they have a value, or even two distinct values, they can only derive them from that [the value] of the labour from which they emanate' (Ricardo, *The Principles of Political Economy*, 3rd edition, London, 1821, p. 334). We would here only point out that Ricardo imputes his own more profound interpretation to Destutt. The latter actually says, on the one hand that all things which constitute wealth 'represent the labour which has created them', but on the other that 'they acquire their two different values' (use-value and exchange value) from 'the value of labour'. He thus falls into the commonplace error of the vulgar economists, who assume the value of one commodity (here, of labour) in order to determine thereafter from it the values of others. But Ricardo understands him as saying that labour (not the value of labour) is represented both by use-value and exchange value. Nevertheless Ricardo himself so little distinguishes the two-fold character of the labour thus doubly represented, that he devotes the whole of his chapter on 'Value and Riches, their Distinctive Properties' to the laborious examination of the trivialities of a J. B. Say. At the end he is therefore quite astonished to find that Destutt agrees with him on the one hand as to labour being the source of value, and with J. B. Say on the other hand as to the notion of value.

19. It is one of the basic failings of classical political economy that it never succeeded in discovering, through its analysis of commodities and especially of their value, that form of value which in fact constitutes its exchange value. Even its best representatives, Adam Smith and Ricardo, treat the form of value as something of no importance, or external to the nature of the commodity itself. The reason for this is not only that the analysis of the magnitude of value absorbs their whole attention, it lies deeper. The value-form of the product of labour is both the most abstract and the most universal form of the

These formulae, which bear stamped upon them in un-mistakeable letters that they belong to a state of society, in which the process of production has the mastery over man instead of being controlled by him—such formulae appear to the bourgeois intellect to be as much a self-evident necessity imposed by nature as productive labour itself. Hence forms of social production that preceded the bourgeois form are treated by the bourgeoisie in much the same way as the Fathers of the Church treated pre-Christian religions.[20]

---

bourgeois method of production, which is thereby characterised as both a particular kind of social production and at the same time historical in context. If, then, it is mistakenly treated as the eternal natural form of social production, the specific characteristics of the value-form, and thus of the commodity-form and its developments of money-form, capital-form, etc., are necessarily overlooked. We consequently find that economists, who completely agree about labour-time being the measure of the magnitude of value, have the most strange and contradictory ideas about money, the finished form of the universal equivalent. This is conspicuously so, for example, in their treatment of banking, where the commonplace definitions of money are no longer adequate. Thus there arose in opposition a restored mercantilist system (Ganilh, etc.), which sees in value merely a social form, or its insubstantial ghost. Once for all may I here state that by classical political economy I understand all economists since W. Petty who investigate the internal relationship of bourgeois conditions of production, as against the vulgar economists who only concern themselves with apparent relationships, ceaselessly regurgitating the materials long since supplied by the scholarly economists, in an attempt to find a plausible explanation of the grossest phenomena for bourgeois domestic consumption, and who further confine themselves to the pedantic systematization of the banal and complacent ideas of the bourgeois agents of production and their proclamation as eternal truths.
20. 'Economists have a singular method of procedure. There are only two kinds of institutions for them, artificial and natural. The institutions of feudalism are artificial, those of the bourgeoisie are natural institutions. In this they resemble theologians who also establish two kinds of religion. Every religion which is not theirs is an invention of men, while their own is an emanation from God' (Karl Marx, *Misère de la philosophie*, Brussels-Paris, 1847, p. 113). Truly comical is M. Bastiat, who imagines that the ancient Greeks and Romans lived by plunder alone. But if one is to live for hundreds of

To what extent some economists are misled by the fetishism inherent in commodities, or by the objective appearance of the social characteristics of labour, is shown, amongst other ways, by the dull and tedious quarrel over the part played by nature in the formation of exchange value. Since exchange value is a definite social manner of expressing the amount of labour bestowed upon an object, nature has no more to do with it than it has in fixing the course of exchange.

The mode of production in which the product takes the

---

years by plunder, there must always be something at hand to plunder, the objects of plunder must be continually renewed. It therefore appears that Greeks and Romans also had some process of production, consequently an economy, which as much constituted the material foundation of their world as the bourgeois economy does of the modern world. Or perhaps Bastiat believes that a method of production based on slave labour must be based on a system of plunder? There he is on dangerous ground. If an intellectual giant like Aristotle erred in his estimation of slave labour, how should a pigmy economist like Bastiat be correct in his appreciation of wage labour? I seize this opportunity of briefly answering an objection, made by a German paper in America, to my work *Zur Kritik der politischen Ökonomie*, 1859. It claimed that my view that each special mode of production and the relations of production corresponding to it, in short the 'economic basis of society, is the true foundation of the legal and political superstructure to which definite forms of social consciousness correspond,' that 'The mode of production of material life determines the general character of social, political and intellectual life'—that all this was indeed true of the contemporary world where material interests predominate but for neither the Middle Ages ruled by Catholicism nor for Athens and Rome which politics controlled. In the first place it is strange that anyone should suppose that these universally familiar phrases concerning the Middle Ages and the ancient world could be unknown to anyone else. This much, however, is clear, that the Middle Ages could not live by Catholicism nor the ancients from politics. On the contrary, the methods by which they gained their living explain why in one case politics, in the other Catholicism, played the chief part. Moreover, little acquaintance with the history of the Roman republic, for example, is required, to be aware that its secret history is the history of landed property. Then again Don Quixote has already paid the penalty for imagining knight-errantry to be compatible with all economic forms of society.

form of a commodity, or is produced directly for exchange, is the most general and most embryonic form of bourgeois production. It therefore makes its appearance at an early date in history, though not in the same predominating and characteristic manner as nowadays. Hence its fetish character is comparatively easy to see through. But when we come to more concrete forms, even this appearance of simplicity vanishes. Whence arose the illusions of the monetary system? To it gold and silver, when serving as money, did not represent a social relation between producers, but were natural objects with strange social properties. And modern economy, which looks down with such disdain on the monetary system, does not its superstition come out as clear as noon-day, whenever it treats of capital? How long is it since economy discarded the physiocratic illusion that rents grow out of the soil and not out of society?

But not to anticipate, we will content ourselves with yet another example relating to the commodity form. Could commodities themselves speak, they would say: Our use-value may be a thing that interests men. It is no part of us as objects. What, however, does belong to us as objects, is our value. Our natural intercourse as commodities proves it. In the eyes of each other we are nothing but exchange values. Now listen how those commodities speak through the mouth of the economist. 'Value' (i.e., exchange value) 'is a property of things, riches' (i.e., use-value) 'of men. Value, in this sense, necessarily implies exchange, riches do not.'[21] 'Riches' (use-value) 'are the attribute of man, value is the attribute of commodities. A man or a community is rich, a pearl or a diamond is valuable. . . . A pearl or a diamond is valuable as a pearl or diamond.'[22] So far no

21. *Observations on Certain Verbal Disputes in Political Economy, Particularly Relating to Value, and to Demand and Supply*, London, 1821, p. 16.
22. [S. Bailey], *A Critical Dissertation on the Nature, Measures, and Causes of Value*, London, 1825, p. 165.

chemist has ever discovered exchange value either in a pearl or a diamond. The economical discoverers of this chemical element, who by-the-bye lay special claim to critical acumen, find however that the use-value of objects belongs to them independently of their material properties, while their value, on the other hand, forms a part of them as objects. What confirms them in this view, is the peculiar circumstance that the use-value of objects is realised without exchange, by means of a direct relation between the objects and man, while, on the other hand, their value is realised only by exchange, that is, by means of a social process. Who fails here to call to mind our good friend Dogberry, who informs the nightwatchman Sea-coal that 'To be a well-favoured man is the gift of fortune; but reading and writing comes by nature'? . . .[23]

CHAPTER 26: 'THE SECRET OF PRIMITIVE ACCUMULATION'

We have seen how money is changed into capital; how through capital surplus-value is made, and from surplus-value more capital. But the accumulation of capital presupposes surplus-value; surplus-value presupposes capitalistic production; capitalistic production presupposes the pre-existence of considerable masses of capital and of labour-power in the hands of producers of commodities. The whole movement, therefore seems to turn

---

23. The author of the *Observations* and S. Bailey accuse Ricardo of converting exchange value from something relative into something absolute. The opposite is the case. He has reduced the apparent relativity which these objects, for example diamonds and pearls, possess as exchange value, to the true relationship concealed behind the appearance, to their relativity as mere expressions of human labour. If the followers of Ricardo answer Bailey roughly but not convincingly, this is only because they could find in Ricardo's own works no key to the inner connection between value and value-form or exchange value.

in a vicious circle, out of which we can only get by supposing a primitive accumulation (previous accumulation of Adam Smith) preceding capitalistic accumulation; an accumulation not the result of the capitalist mode of production, but its starting-point.

This primitive accumulation plays in political economy about the same part as original sin in theology. Adam bit the apple, and thereupon sin fell on the human race. Its origin is supposed to be explained when it is told as an anecdote of the past. In times long gone by there were two sorts of people; one, the diligent, intelligent, and, above all, frugal élite; the other, lazy rascals, spending their substance, and more, in riotous living. The legend of theological original sin tells us certainly how man came to be condemned to eat his bread in the sweat of his brow; but the history of economic original sin reveals to us that there are people to whom this is by no means essential. Never mind! Thus it came to pass that the former sort accumulated wealth, and the latter sort had at last nothing to sell except their own skins. And from this original sin dates the poverty of the great majority that, despite all its labour, has up to now nothing to sell but itself, and the wealth of the few that increases constantly although they have long ceased to work. Such insipid childishness is every day preached to us in the defence of property. M. Thiers, for example, had the assurance to repeat it with all the solemnity of a statesman, to the French people, once so *spirituel*. But as soon as the question of property crops up, it becomes a sacred duty to proclaim the intellectual food of the infant as the one thing fit for all ages and for all stages of development. In actual history it is notorious that conquest, enslavement, robbery, murder, briefly force, play the great part. In the tender annals of political economy, the idyllic reigns from time immemorial. Right and 'labour' were from all time the sole means of enrichment, the present year of course always excepted. As a matter of fact, the methods of primitive accumulation are anything but idyllic.

In themselves, money and commodities are no more capital than are the means of production and of subsistence. They want transforming into capital. But this transformation itself can only take place under certain circumstances that centre in this, viz., that two very different kinds of commodity-possessors must come face to face and into contact; on the one hand, the owners of money, means of production, means of subsistence, who are eager to increase the sum of values they possess, by having other people's labour-power; on the other hand, free labourers, the sellers of their own labour-power, and therefore the sellers of labour. Free labourers, in the double sense that neither they themselves form part and parcel of the means of production, as in the case of slaves, bondsmen, etc., nor do the means of production belong to them, as in the case of peasant-proprietors; they are, therefore, free from, unencumbered by, any means of production of their own. With this polarisation of the market for commodities, the fundamental conditions of capitalist production are given. The capitalist system presupposes the complete separation of the labourers from all property in the means by which they can realise their labour. As soon as capitalist production is once on its own legs, it not only maintains this separation, but reproduces it on a continually extending scale. The process, therefore, that clears the way for the capitalist system can be none other than the process which takes away from the labourer the possession of his means of production; a process that transforms, on the one hand, the social means of subsistence and of production into capital, on the other, the immediate producers into wage-labourers. The so-called primitive accumulation, therefore, is nothing else than the historical process of divorcing the producer from the means of production. It appears as primitive, because it forms the pre-historic stage of capital and of the mode of production corresponding with it.

The economic structure of capitalistic society has grown out of the economic structure of feudal society. The dissolution of the latter set free the elements of the former.

The immediate producer, the labourer, could only dispose of his own person after he had ceased to be attached to the soil and ceased to be the slave, serf, or bondman of another. To become a free seller of labour-power, who carries his commodity wherever he finds a market, he must further have escaped from the regime of the guilds, their rules for apprentices and journey-men, and the impediments of their labour regulations. Hence, the historical movement which changes the producers into wage-workers, appears, on the one hand, as their emancipation from serfdom and from the fetters of the guilds, and this side alone exists for our bourgeois historians. But, on the other hand, these new freedmen became sellers of themselves only after they had been robbed of all their own means of production, and of all the guarantees of existence afforded by the old feudal arrangements. And the history of this, their expropriation, is written in the annals of mankind in letters of blood and fire.

The industrial capitalists, these new potentates, had on their part not only to displace the guild masters of handicrafts, but also the feudal lords, the possessors of the sources of wealth. In this respect their conquest of social power appears as the fruit of a victorious struggle both against feudal lordship and its revolting prerogatives, and against the guilds and the fetters they laid on the free development of production and the free exploitation of man by man. The *chevaliers d'industrie*, however, only succeeded in supplanting the chevaliers of the sword by making use of events of which they themselves were wholly innocent. They have risen by means as vile as those by which the Roman freed-man once on a time made himself the master of his *patronus*.

The starting point of the development that gave rise to the wage-labourer as well as to the capitalist, was the servitude of the labourer. The advance consisted in a change of form of this servitude, in the transformation of feudal exploitation into capitalist exploitation. To understand its march, we need not go back very far. Although we come across the first beginnings of capitalist production as early as the fourteenth or fifteenth century, sporadically, in certain towns of the Mediterranean, the capitalistic era dates from the sixteenth century. Wherever it appears, the abolition of serfdom has been long effected, and the highest development of the middle ages, the existence of sovereign towns, has been long on the wane.

In the history of primitive accumulation, all revolutions are epoch-making that act as levers for the capitalist class in course of formation; but, above all, those moments when great masses of men are suddenly and forcibly torn from their means of subsistence, and hurled as free and 'unattached' proletarians on the labour market. The expropriation of the agricultural producer, of the peasant, from the soil, is the basis of the whole process. The history of this expropriation, in different countries, assumes different aspects, and runs through its various phases in different orders of succession, and at different periods. In England alone, which we take as our example, has it the classic form.

From CHAPTER 27: 'THE EXPROPRIATION OF THE AGRICULTURAL POPULATION FROM THE LAND'

In England, serfdom had practically disappeared in the last part of the fourteenth century. The immense majority of the population consisted then, and to a still larger extent in the fifteenth century, of free peasant proprietors, whatever was the feudal title under which their right of property was hidden. In the larger seignorial domains, the old bailiff, himself a serf, was displaced by the free farmer. The wage-labourers of agriculture consisted partly of peasants, who utilised their leisure time by working on the large estates, partly of an independent special class of wage-labourers, relatively and absolutely few in numbers. The latter also were practically at the same time peasant farmers, since, besides their wages, they had alloted to them arable land to the extent of four or more acres, together with their cottages. Besides they, with the rest of the peasants, enjoyed the usufruct of the common land, which gave pasture to their cattle, furnished them with timber, fire-wood, turf, &c. In all countries of Europe, feudal production is characterised by division of the soil amongst the greatest possible number of sub-feudatories. The might of the feudal lord, like that of the sovereign, depended not on the length of his rent roll, but on the number of his subjects, and the latter depended on the number of peasant proprietors. Although, therefore, the English land, after the Norman conquest, was distributed in gigantic baronies, one of which often included some 900 of the old Anglo-Saxon lordships, it was bestrewn with small peasant properties, only here and there interspersed with great seignorial domains. Such conditions, together with the prosperity of the towns so characteristic of the fifteenth century, allowed of that wealth of the people which Chancellor Fortescue so eloquently paints in his *De laudibus legum Angliae*, but it excluded the possibility of capitalist wealth.

The prelude of the revolution that laid the foundation of the capitalist mode of production, was played in the last third of the fifteenth, and the first decade of the sixteenth century. A mass of free proletarians was hurled on the labour-market by the breaking-up of the bands of feudal retainers, who, as Sir James Steuart well says, 'everywhere uselessly filled house and castle.' Although the royal power, itself a product of bourgeois development, in its strife after absolute sovereignty forcibly hastened on the dissolution of these bands of retainers, it was by no means the sole cause of it. In insolent conflict with king and parliament, the great feudal lords created an incomparably larger proletariat by the forcible driving of the peasantry from the land, to which the latter had the same feudal right as the lord himself, and by the usurpation of the common lands. The rapid rise of the Flemish wool manufactures, and the corresponding rise in the price of wool in England, gave the direct impulse to these evictions. The old nobility had been devoured by the great feudal wars. The new nobility was the child of its time, for which money was the power of all powers. Transformation of arable land into sheep-walks was, therefore, its cry. Harrison, in his *Description of England,* prefixed to Holinshed's Chronicle, describes how the expropriation of small peasants is ruining the country. 'What care our great encroachers?' The dwellings of the peasants and the cottages of the labourers were razed to the ground or doomed to decay. 'If,' says Harrison, 'the old records of euerie manour be sought ... it will soon appear that in some manour seventeene, eighteene, or twentie houses are shrunk ... that England was neuer less furnished with people than at the present ... Of cities and townes either utterly decaied or more than a quarter or half diminished, though some one be a little increased here or there; of townes pulled downe for sheepe-walks, and no more but the lordships now standing in them ... I could saie somewhat.' The complaints of these old chroniclers are always exaggerated, but they reflect faithfully the impression made on contemporaries by the revolution in the conditions of production. A comparison of the writings of Chancellor Fortescue and Thomas More reveals the gulf between the fifteenth and sixteenth century. As Thornton rightly has it, the English working-class was precipitated without any transition from its golden into its iron age.

Legislation was terrified at this revolution. It did not yet stand on that height of civilisation where the 'wealth of the nation' (i.e., the formation of capital, and the reckless exploitation and impoverishing of the mass of the people) figure as the *ultima Thule* of all state-craft. In his history of Henry VII, Bacon says: 'Inclosures at that time (1489) began to be more frequent, whereby arable land (which could not be manured without people and families) was turned into pasture, which was easily rid by a few herdsmen; and tenancies for years, lives, and at will (whereupon much of the yeomanry lived) were turned into demesnes. This bred a decay of people, and (by consequence) a decay of towns, churches, tithes, and the like. . . . In remedying of this inconvenience the king's wisdom was admirable, and the parliament's at that time . . . they took a course to take away depopulating inclosures, and depopulating pasturage.' An Act of Henry VII, 1489, cap. 19, forbad the destruction of all 'houses of husbandry' to which at least twenty acres of land belonged. By an Act, 25 Henry VIII, the same law was renewed. It recites, among other things, that many farms and large flocks of cattle, especially of sheep, are concentrated in the hands of a few men, whereby the rent of land has much risen and tillage has fallen off, churches and houses have been pulled down, and marvellous numbers of people have been deprived of the means wherewith to maintain themselves and their families. The Act, therefore, ordains the rebuilding of the decayed farmsteads, and fixes a proportion between corn land and pasture land, &c. An Act of 1533 recites that some owners possess 24,000 sheep, and limits the number to be owned to 2000. The cry of the people and the legislation directed, for 150 years after Henry VII, against the expropriation of the small farmers and peasants, were alike fruitless. The secret of their inefficiency Bacon, without knowing it, reveals to us. 'The device of King Henry VII,' says Bacon in his *Essays, Civil and Moral,* Essay 29, 'was profound and admirable, in making farms and houses of husbandry of a standard; that is, maintained with such a proportion of land unto them as may breed a subject to live in convenient plenty, and no servile condition, and to keep the plough in the hands of the owners and not mere hirelings.' What the capitalist system demanded was, on the other hand, a degraded and almost servile condition of the mass of the people, the transformation of them into mercenaries, and of their means of labour into capital. During this transformation period, legislation also strove to retain the four acres of land by the cottage of the agricultural wage-labourer, and forbad him to take lodgers into his cottage. In the reign of James I, 1627 [James I died in 1625.-E.K.], Roger Crocker of Front Mill was condemned for having built a cottage on the manor of Front Mill without four acres of land attached to the same in perpetuity. As late as Charles I's reign, 1638, a royal commission was appointed to enforce the carrying out of the old laws, especially that referring to the four acres of land. Even in Cromwell's time, the building of a house within four miles of London was forbidden unless it was endowed with four acres of land. As late as the first half of the eighteenth century complaint is made if the cottage of the agricultural labourer has not an adjunct of one or two acres of land. Nowadays he is lucky if it is furnished with a little garden, or if he may rent, far away from his cottage, a few roods. 'Landlords and farmers,' says Dr. Hunter, 'work here hand in hand. A few acres to the cottage would make the labourers too independent.'

The process of forcible expropriation of the people received in the sixteenth century a new and frightful impulse from the Reformation, and from the consequent colossal spoliation of the church property. The Catholic church was, at the time of the Reformation, feudal proprietor of a great part of the English land. The suppression of the monasteries, &c., hurled their inmates into the proletariat. The estates of the church were to a large extent given away to rapacious royal favourites, or sold at a nominal price to speculating farmers and citizens, who drove out, *en masse*, the hereditary sub-tenants and threw their holdings into one. The legally guaranteed property of the poorer folk in a part of the church's tithes was tacitly confiscated. '*Pauper ubique jacet*,' cried Queen Elizabeth, after a journey through England. In the forty-third year of her reign the nation was obliged to recognise pauperism officially by the introduction of a poor-rate. 'The authors of this law seem to have been ashamed to state the grounds of it, for [contrary to traditional usage] it has no preamble whatever.' By the 16th of Charles I, ch. 4, it was declared perpetual, and in fact only in 1834 did it take a new and harsher form. These immediate results of the Reformation were not its most lasting ones. The property of the church formed the religious bulwark of the traditional conditions of landed property. With its fall these were no longer tenable.

Even in the last decade of the seventeenth century, the yeomanry, the class of independent peasants, were more numerous than the class of farmers. They had formed the backbone of Cromwell's strength, and, even according to the confession of Macaulay, stood in favourable contrast to the drunken squires and to their servants, the country clergy, who had to marry their masters' cast-off mistresses. About 1750, the yeomanry had disappeared, and so had, in the last decade of the eighteenth century, the last trace of the common land of the agricultural labourer. We leave on one side here the purely economic causes of the agricultural revolution. We deal only with the forcible means employed.

After the restoration of the Stuarts, the landed proprietors carried, by legal means, an act of usurpation, effected everywhere on the Continent without any legal formality. They abolished the feudal tenure of land, i.e., they got rid of all its obligations to the state, 'indemnified' the state by taxes on the peasantry and the rest of the mass of the people, vindicated for themselves the rights of modern private property in estates to which they had only a feudal title, and, finally, passed those laws of settlement, which, *mutatis mutandis*, had the same effect on the English agricultural labourer, as the edict of the Tartar Boris Godunov on the Russian peasantry.

The 'Glorious Revolution' brought into power, along with William of Orange, the landlord and capitalist appropriators of surplus-value. They inaugurated the new era by practising on a colossal scale thefts of state lands, thefts that had been hitherto managed more modestly. These estates were given away, sold at a ridiculous figure, or even annexed to private estates by direct seizure. All this happened without the slightest observation of legal etiquette. The crown lands thus fraudulently appropriated, together with the robbery of the Church estates, as far as these had not been lost again during the republican revolution, form the basis of the present princely domains of the English oligarchy. The bourgeois capitalists favoured the operation with the view, among others, to promoting free trade in land, to extending the domain of modern agriculture on the large farm-system, and to increasing their supply of the free agricultural proletarians ready to hand. Besides, the new landed aristocracy was the natural ally of the new bankocracy, of the newly-hatched *haute finance*, and of the large manufacturers, then depending on protective duties. The English bourgeoisie acted for its own interest quite as wisely as did the Swedish bourgeoisie who, reversing the process, hand in hand with their economic allies, the peasantry, helped the kings in the forcible resumption of the Crown lands from the oligarchy. This happened since 1604 under Charles X and Charles XI.

Communal property—always distinct from the state property just dealt with—was an old Teutonic institution which lived on under cover of feudalism. We have seen how the forcible usurpation of this, generally accompanied by the turning of arable into pasture land, begins at the end of the fifteenth and extends into the sixteenth century. But, at that time, the process was carried on by means of individual acts of violence against which legislation, for a hundred and fifty years, fought in vain. The advance made by the eighteenth century shows itself in this, that the law itself becomes now the instrument of the theft of the people's land, although the large farmers make use of their little independent methods as well. The parliamentary form of the robbery is that of Acts for enclosures of Commons, in other words, decrees by which the landlords grant themselves the people's land as private property, decrees of expropriation of the people. Sir F. M. Eden refutes his own crafty special pleading, in which he tries to represent communal property as the private property of the great landlords who have taken the place of the feudal lords, when he, himself, demands a 'general Act of Parliament for the enclosure of Commons' (admitting thereby that a parliamentary *coup d'état* is necessary for its transformation into private property), and moreover calls on the legislature for the indemnification for the expropriated poor.

While the place of the independent yeoman was taken by tenants at will, small farmers on yearly leases, a servile rabble dependent on the pleasure of the landlords, the systematic robbery of the communal lands helped especially, next to the theft of the state domains, to swell those large farms, that were called in the eighteenth century capital farms or merchant farms, and to 'set free' the agricultural population as proletarians for manufacturing industry.

The eighteenth century, however, did not yet recognise as fully as the nineteenth, the identity between national wealth and the poverty of the people. Hence the most vigorous polemic, in the economic literature of that time, on the 'enclosure of commons.' From the mass of materials that lie before me, I give a few extracts that will throw a strong light on the circumstances of the time. 'In several parishes of Hertfordshire,' writes one indignant person, '24 farms, numbering on the average 50–150 acres, have been melted up into three farms.' 'In Northamptonshire and Leicestershire the enclosure of common lands has taken place on a very large scale, and most of the new lordships, resulting from the enclosure, have been turned into pasturage, in consequence of which many lordships have not now 50 acres ploughed yearly, in which 1500 were ploughed formerly. The ruins of former dwelling-houses, barns, stables, &c.' are the sole traces of the former inhabitants. 'An hundred houses and families have in some open field villages ... dwindled to eight or ten. ... The landholders in most parishes that have been enclosed only 15 or 20 years, are very few in comparison of the numbers who occupied them in their open-field state. It is no uncommon thing for 4 or 5 wealthy graziers to engross a large enclosed lordship which was before in the hands of 20 or 30 farmers, and as many smaller tenants and proprietors. All these are hereby thrown out of their livings with their families and many other families who were chiefly employed and supported by them.' It was not only the land that lay waste, but often land cultivated either in common or held under a definite rent paid to the community, that was annexed by the neighbouring landlords under pretext of enclosure. I have here in view enclosures of open fields and lands already improved. It is acknowledged by even the writers in defence of enclosures that these diminished villages increase the monopolies of farms, raise the prices of provisions, and produce depopulation ... and even the enclosure of waste lands (as now carried on) bears hard on the poor, by depriving them of a part of their subsistence, and only goes towards increasing farms already too large. 'When,' says Dr. Price, 'this land gets into the hands of a few great farmers, the consequence must be that the little farmers [earlier designated by him 'a multitude of little proprietors and tenants, who maintain themselves and families by the produce of the ground they occupy, by sheep kept on a common, by poultry, hogs, &c., and who therefore have little occasion to purchase any of the means of subsistence'] will be converted into a body of men who earn their subsistence by working for others, and who will be under a necessity of going to market for all they want. . . . There will, perhaps, be more labour, because there will be more compulsion to it. . . . Towns and manufacturers will increase, because more will be driven to them in quest of places and employment. This is the way in which the engrossing of farms naturally operates. And this is the way in which, for many years, it has been actually operating in this kingdom.' He sums up the effect of the enclosures thus: 'Upon the whole, the circumstances of the lower ranks of men are altered in almost every respect for the worse. From little occupiers of land, they are reduced to the state of daylabourers and hirelings; and, at the same time, their subsistence in that state has become more difficult.' In fact, usurpation of the common lands and the revolution in agriculture accompanying this told so acutely on the agricultural labourers that, even according to Eden, between 1765 and 1780, their wages began to fall below the minimum, and to be supplemented by official poor-law relief. Their wages, he says 'were not more than enough for the absolute necessaries of life'. . . .

In the nineteenth century, the very memory of the connection between the agricultural labourer and the communal property had, of course, vanished. To say nothing of more recent times, have the agricultural population received a farthing of compensation for the 3,511,770 acres of common land which between 1801 and 1831 were stolen from them and by parliamentary devices presented to the landlords by the landlords?

The last process of wholesale expropriation of the agricultural population from the soil is, finally, the so-called clearing of estates, i.e., the sweeping men off them. All the English methods hitherto considered culminated in 'clearance.' As we saw in the picture of modern conditions given in a former chapter, where there are no more independent peasants to get rid of, the 'clearance' of cottages begins; so that the agricultural labourers do not find on the soil cultivated by them even the spot necessary for their own housing. But what 'clearance of estates' really and properly signifies we learn only in the promised land of modern romance, the Highlands of Scotland. There the process is distinguished by its systematic character, by the magnitude of the scale on which it is carried out at one blow (in Ireland landlords have gone to the length of sweeping away several villages at once; in Scotland areas as large as German principalities are dealt with), finally by the peculiar form of property, under which the embezzled lands were held.

The Highland Celts were organised in clans, each of which was the owner of the land on which it was settled. The representative of the clan, its chief or 'great man,' was only the titular owner of this property, just as the Queen of England is the titular owner of all the national soil. When the English government succeeded in suppressing the intestine wars of these 'great men,' and their constant incursions into the Lowland plains, the chiefs of the clans by no means gave up their time-honoured trade as robbers; they only changed its form. On their own authority they transformed their nominal right into a right of private property, and as this brought them into collision with their clansmen, resolved to drive them out by open force. 'A king of England might as well claim to drive his subjects into the sea,' says Professor Newman. This revolution, which began in Scotland after the last rising of the followers of the Pretender, can be followed through its first phases in the writings of Sir James Steuart and James Anderson. In the eighteenth century the hunted-out Gaels were forbidden to emigrate from the country, with a view to driving them by force to Glasgow and other manufacturing towns. As an example of the method obtaining in the nineteenth century, the 'clearance' made by the Duchess of Sutherland will suffice here. This person, well instructed in economy, resolved, on entering upon her government, to effect a radical cure, and to turn the whole country, whose population had already been, by earlier processes of the like kind, reduced to 15,000, into a sheepwalk. From 1814 to 1820 these 15,000 inhabitants, about 3000 families, were systematically hunted and rooted out. All their villages were destroyed and burnt, all their fields turned into pasturage. British soldiers enforced this eviction, and came to blows with the inhabitants. One old woman was burnt to death in the flames of the hut, which she refused to leave. Thus this fine lady appropriated 794,-000 acres of land that had from time immemorial belonged to the clan. She assigned to the expelled inhabitants about 6000 acres on the sea-shore—two acres per family. The 6000 acres had until this time lain waste, and brought in no income to their owners. The Duchess, in the nobility of her heart, actually went so far as to let these at an average rent of 2s. 6d. per acre to the clansmen, who for centuries had shed their blood for her family. The whole of the stolen clan-land she divided into twenty-nine great sheep farms, each inhabited by a single family, for the most part imported English farm-servants. In the year 1835 the 15,000 Gaels were already replaced by 131,000 sheep. The remnant of the aborigines flung on the sea-shore, tried to live by catching fish. They became amphibious and lived, as an English author says, half on land and half on water, and withal only half on both.

But the brave Gaels must expiate yet more bitterly their idolatry, romantic and of the mountains, for the great men of the clan. The smell of their fish rose to the noses of the great men. They scented some profit in it, and let the sea-shore to the great fishmongers of London. For the second time the Gaels were hunted out.

But, finally, part of the sheep-walks are turned into deer preserves. Every one knows that there are no real forests in England. The deer in the parks of the great are demurely domestic cattle, fat as London aldermen. Scotland is therefore the last refuge of the 'noble passion.' 'In the Highlands,' says Somers in 1848, 'new forests are springing up like mushrooms. Here, on one side of Gaick, you have the new forest of Glenfeshie; and there on the other you have the new forest of Ardverikie. In the same line you have the Black Mount, an immense waste also recently erected. From east to west—from the neighbourhood of Aberdeen to the crags of Oban—you have now a continuous line of forests; while in other parts of the Highlands there are the new forests of Loch Archaig, Glengarry, Glenmoriston, &c. Sheep were introduced into glens which had been the seats of communities of small farmers; and the latter were driven to seek subsistence on coarser and more sterile tracks of soil. Now deer are supplanting sheep; and these are once more dispossessing the small tenants, who will necessarily be driven down upon still coarser land and to more grinding penury. Deer forests and the people cannot co-exist. One or other of the two must yield. Let the forests be increased in number and extent during the next quarter of a century, as they have been in the last, and the Gaels will perish from their native soil. . . . This movement among the Highland proprietors is with some a matter of ambition . . . with some love of sport . . . while others, of a more practical cast, follow the trade in deer with an eye solely to profit. For it is a fact, that a mountain range laid out in forest is, in many cases, more profitable to the proprietor than when let as a sheep walk. . . . The huntsman who wants a deer-forest limits his offers by no other calculation than the extent of his purse. . . . Sufferings have been inflicted in the Highlands scarcely less severe than those occasioned by the policy of the Norman kings. Deer have received extended ranges, while men have been hunted within a narrower and still narrower circle. . . . One after one the liberties of the people have been cloven down. . . . And the oppressions are daily on the increase. . . . The clearance and dispersion of the people is pursued by the proprietors as a settled principle, as an agricultural necessity, just as trees and brushwood are cleared from the wastes of America or Australia; and the operation goes on in a quiet, business-like way, &c.'

The spoliation of the church's property, the fraudulent alienation of the state domains, the robbery of the common lands, the usurpation of feudal and clan property, and its transformation into modern private property under circumstances of reckless terrorism, were just so many idyllic methods of primitive accumulation. They conquered the field for capitalistic agriculture, made the soil part and parcel of capital, and created for the town industries the necessary supply of a 'free' and outlawed proletariat. . . .

CHAPTER 31: 'THE GENESIS OF THE INDUSTRIAL CAPITALIST'

The genesis of the industrial capitalist did not proceed in such a gradual way as that of the farmer. Doubtless many small guild-masters, and yet more independent small artisans, or even wage-labourers, transformed themselves into small capitalists, and (by gradually extending exploitation of wage-labour and corresponding accumulation) into full-blown capitalists. In the infancy of capitalist production, things often happened as in the infancy of medieval towns, where the question, which of the escaped serfs should be master and which servant, was in great part decided by the earlier or later date of their flight. The snail's-pace of this method corresponded in no wise with the commercial requirements of the new world-market that the great discoveries of the end of the fifteenth century created. But the middle ages had handed down two distinct forms of capital, which mature in the most different economic social formations, and which, before the era of the capitalist mode of production, are considered as capital *quand même*—usurer's capital and merchant's capital.

'At present, all the wealth of society goes first into the possession of the capitalist . . . he pays the landowner his rent, the labourer his wages, the tax and tithe gatherer their claims, and keeps a large, indeed the largest, and a continually augmenting share, of the annual produce of labour for himself. The capitalist may now be said to be the first owner of all the wealth of the community, though no law has conferred on him the right to this property . . . this change has been effected by the taking of interest on capital . . . and it is not a little curious that all the lawgivers of Europe endeavoured to prevent this by statutes, viz., statutes against usury . . . The power of the capitalist over all the wealth of the country is a complete change in the right of property, and by what law, or series of laws, was it effected?' The author should have remembered that revolutions are not made by laws.

The money capital formed by means of usury and commerce was prevented from turning into industrial capital, in the country by the feudal constitution, in the towns by the guild organisation. These fetters vanished with the dissolution of feudal society, with the expropriation and partial eviction of the country population. The new manufactures were established at sea-ports, or at inland points beyond the control of the old municipalities and their guilds. Hence in England an embittered struggle of the corporate towns against these new industrial nurseries

The discovery of gold and silver in America, the extirpation, enslavement and entombment in mines of the aboriginal population, the beginning of the conquest and looting of the East Indies, the turning of Africa into a warren for the commercial hunting of black-skins, signal-

.ised the rosy dawn of the era of capitalist production. These idyllic proceedings are the chief moments of primitive accumulation. On their heels treads the commercial war of the European nations, with the globe for a theatre. It begins with the revolt of the Netherlands from Spain, assumes giant dimensions in England's anti-Jacobin war, and is still going on in the opium wars against China, &c.

The different momenta of primitive accumulation distribute themselves now, more or less in chronological order, particularly over Spain, Portugal, Holland, France, and England. In England at the end of the seventeenth century, they arrive at a systematical combination, embracing the colonies, the national debt, the modern mode of taxation, and the protectionist system. These methods depend in part on brute force, for example, the colonial system. But they all employ the power of the state, the concentrated and organised force of society, to hasten, hothouse fashion, the process of transformation of the feudal mode of production into the capitalist mode, and to shorten the transition. Force is the midwife of every old society pregnant with a new one. It is itself an economic power.

Of the Christian colonial system, W. Howitt, a man who makes a specialty of Christianity, says: 'The barbarities and desperate outrages of the so-called Christian race, throughout every region of the world, and upon every people they have been able to subdue, are not to be paralleled by those of any other race, however fierce, however untaught, and however reckless of mercy and of shame, in any age of the earth.' The history of the colonial administration of Holland—and Holland was the head capitalistic nation of the seventeenth century—'is one of the most extraordinary relations of treachery, bribery, massacre, and meanness.' Nothing is more characteristic than their system of stealing men, to get slaves for Java. The men stealers were trained for this purpose. The thief, the interpreter, and the seller, were the chief agents in this trade, native princes the chief sellers. The young people stolen were thrown into the secret dungeons of Celebes, until they were ready for sending to the slave-ships. An official report says: 'This one town of Macassar, e.g., is full of secret prisons, one more horrible than the other, crammed with unfortunates, victims of greed and tyranny fettered in chains, forcibly torn from their families.' To secure Malacca, the Dutch corrupted the Portuguese governor. He let them into the town in 1641. They hurried at once to his house and assassinated him, to 'abstain' from the payment of £21,875, the price of his treason. Wherever they set foot, devastation and depopulation followed. Banjuwangi, a province of Java, in 1750 numbered over 80,000 inhabitants, in 1811 only 18,000. Sweet commerce!

The English East India Company, as is well known, obtained, besides the political rule in India, the exclusive monopoly of the tea-trade, as well as of the Chinese trade in general, and of the transport of goods to and from Europe. But the coasting trade of India and between the islands, as well as the internal trade of India, were the monopoly of the higher employees of the company. The monopolies of salt, opium, betel and other commodities, were inexhaustible mines of wealth. The employees themselves fixed the price and plundered at will the unhappy Hindus. The Governor-General took part in this private traffic. His favourites received contracts under conditions whereby they, cleverer than the alchemists, made gold out of nothing. Great fortunes sprang up like mushrooms in a day; primitive accumulation went on without the advance of a shilling. The trial of Warren Hastings swarms with such cases. Here is an instance. A contract for opium was given to a certain Sullivan at the moment of his departure on an official mission to a part of India far removed from the opium district. Sullivan sold his contract to one Binn for £40,000; Binn sold it the same day for £60,000, and the ultimate purchaser who carried out the contract declared that after all he realised an enormous gain. According to one of the lists laid before Parliament, the Company and its employees from 1757–1766 got £6,000,000 from the Indians as gifts. Between 1769 and 1770, the English manufactured a famine by buying up all the rice and refusing to sell it again, except at fabulous prices.

The treatment of the aborigines was, naturally, most frightful in plantation-colonies destined for export trade only, such as the West Indies, and in rich and well-populated countries, such as Mexico and India, that were given over to plunder. But even in the colonies properly so-called, the Christian character of primitive accumulation did not belie itself. Those sober virtuosi of Protestantism, the Puritans of New England, in 1703, by decrees of their assembly set a premium of £40 on every Indian scalp and every captured red-skin: in 1720 a premium of £100 on every scalp; in 1744, after Massachusetts Bay had proclaimed a certain tribe as rebels, the following prices: for a male scalp of twelve years and upwards £100 (new currency), for a male prisoner £105, for women and children prisoners £50, for scalps of women and children £50. Some decades later, the colonial system took its revenge on the descendants of the pious pilgrim fathers, who had grown seditious in the meantime. At English instigation and for English pay they were tomahawked by red-skins. The British Parliament proclaimed blood-hounds and scalping as 'means that God and Nature had given into its hand.'

The colonial system ripened, like a hot-house, trade and navigation. The 'Monopolia Companies' of Luther were powerful levers for concentration of capital. The colonies secured a market for the budding manufactures, and, through the monopoly of the market, an increased accumulation. The treasures captured outside Europe by undisguised looting, enslavement, and murder, floated back to the mother-country and were there turned into capital. Holland, which first fully developed the colonial system,

in 1648 stood already in the acme of its commercial greatness. It was 'in almost exclusive possession of the East Indian trade and the commerce between the south-east and
north-west of Europe. Its fisheries, marine, manufactures,
surpassed those of any other country. The total capital of
the Republic was probably more important than that of all
the rest of Europe put together.' Gülich forgets to add that
by 1648, the people of Holland were more overworked,
poorer and more brutally oppressed than those of all the
rest of Europe put together.

Today industrial supremacy implies commercial supremacy. In the period of manufacture properly so-called,
it is, on the other hand, the commercial supremacy that
gives industrial predominance. Hence the preponderant
role that the colonial system plays at that time. It was 'the
strange God' who perched himself on the altar cheek by
jowl with the old gods of Europe, and one fine day with a
shove and a kick chucked them all of a heap. It proclaimed
surplus-value making as the sole end and aim of humanity.

The system of public credit, i.e., of national debts,
whose origin we discover in Genoa and Venice as early as
the middle ages, took possession of Europe generally
during the manufacturing period. The colonial system
with its maritime trade and commercial wars served as a
forcing-house for it. Thus it first took root in Holland.
National debts, i.e., the alienation of the state—whether
despotic, constitutional or republican—marked with its
stamp the capitalistic era. The only part of the so-called
national wealth that actually enters into the collective possessions of modern peoples is—their national debt. Hence,
as a necessary consequence, the modern doctrine that a
nation becomes the richer the more deeply it is in debt.
Public credit becomes the *credo* of capital. And with the
rise of national debt-making, want of faith in the national
debt takes the place of the blasphemy against the Holy
Ghost, which may not be forgiven.

The public debt becomes one of the most powerful

levers of primitive accumulation. As with the stroke of an enchanter's wand, it endows barren money with the power of breeding and thus turns it into capital, without the necessity of its exposing itself to the troubles and risks inseparable from its employment in industry or even in usury. The state-creditors actually give nothing away, for the sum lent is transformed into public bonds, easily negotiable, which go on functioning in their hands just as so much hard cash would. But further, apart from the class of lazy annuitants thus created, and from the improvised wealth of the financiers, middlemen between the government and the nation—as also apart from the tax-farmers, merchants, private manufacturers, to whom a good part of every national loan renders the service of a capital fallen from heaven—the national debt has given rise to joint-stock companies, to dealings in negotiable effects of all kinds, and to stock-jobbing, in a word to stock-exchange gambling and the modern bankocracy.

At their birth the great banks, decorated with national titles, were only associations of private speculators, who placed themselves by the side of governments, and, thanks to the privileges they received, were in a position to advance money to the state. Hence the accumulation of the national debt has no more infallible measure than the successive rise in the stock of these banks, whose full development dates from the founding of the Bank of England in 1694. The Bank of England began with lending its money to the Government at 8%; at the same time it was empowered by Parliament to coin money out of the same capital, by lending it again to the public in the form of bank-notes. It was allowed to use these notes for discounting bills, making advances on commodities, and for buying the precious metals. It was not long ere this credit-money, made by the bank itself, became the coin in which the Bank of England made its loans to the state, and paid, on account of the state, the interest on the public debt. It was not enough that the bank gave with one hand

and took back more with the other; it remained, even while receiving, the eternal creditor of the nation down to the last shilling advanced. Gradually it became inevitably the receptacle of the metallic hoard of the country, and the centre of gravity of all commercial credit. What effect was produced on their contemporaries by the sudden uprising of this brood of bankocrats, financiers, rentiers, brokers, stock-jobbers, &c., is proved by such writings of the time as Bolingbroke's.

With the national debt arose an international credit system, which often conceals one of the sources of primitive accumulation in this or that people. Thus the villainies of the Venetian thieving system formed one of the secret bases of the capital-wealth of Holland to whom Venice in her decadence lent large sums of money. So also was it with Holland and England. By the beginning of the eighteenth century the Dutch manufactures were far outstripped. Holland had ceased to be the nation preponderant in commerce and industry. One of its main lines of business, therefore, from 1701 to 1776, is the lending out of enormous amounts of capital, especially to its great rival England. The same thing is going on today between England and the United States. A gread deal of capital, which appears today in the United States without any certificate of birth, was yesterday, in England, the capitalised blood of children.

As the national debt finds its support in the public revenue, which must cover the yearly payments for interest, &c., the modern system of taxation was the necessary complement of the system of national loans. The loans enable the government to meet extraordinary expenses, without the tax-payers feeling it immediately, but they necessitate, as a consequence, increased taxes. On the other hand, the raising of taxation caused by the accumulation of debts contracted one after another, compels the government always to have recourse to new loans for new extraordinary expenses. Modern fiscality, whose pivot is formed by taxes on the most necessary means of subsistence (thereby increasing their price), thus contains within itself the germ of automatic progression. Overtaxation is not an incident, but rather a principle. In Holland, therefore, where this system was first inaugurated, the great patriot, De Witt, has in his *Maxims* extolled it as the best system for making the wage-labourer submissive, frugal, industrious, and overburdened with labour. The destructive influence that it exercises on the condition of the wage-labourer concerns us less however, here, than the forcible expropriation, resulting from it, of peasants, artisans, and in a word, all elements of the lower middle-class. On this there are not two opinions, even among the bourgeois economists. Its expropriating efficacy is still further heightened by the system of protection, which forms one of its integral parts.

The great part that the public debt, and the fiscal system corresponding with it, have played in the capitalisation of wealth and the expropriation of the masses, has led many writers, like Cobbett, Doubleday and others, to seek in this, incorrectly, the fundamental cause of the misery of the modern peoples.

The system of protection was an artificial means of manufacturing manufacturers, of expropriating independent labourers, of capitalising the national means of production and subsistence, of forcibly abbreviating the transition from the medieval to the modern mode of production. The European states tore one another to pieces about the patent of this invention, and, once entered into the service of the surplus-value makers, did not merely lay under contribution in the pursuit of this purpose their own people, indirectly through protective duties, directly through export premiums. They also forcibly rooted out, in their dependent countries, all industry, as, for example, England did with the Irish woollen manufacture. On the continent of Europe, after Colbert's example, the process was much simplified. The primitive industrial capital, here, came in part directly out of the state treasury. 'Why,' cried Mirabeau, 'why go so far to seek the cause of the manufacturing glory of Saxony before the war? 180,000,000 of debts contracted by the sovereigns!'

Colonial system, public debts, heavy taxes, protection, commercial wars, &c., these children of the true manufacturing period, increase gigantically during the infancy of Modern Industry. The birth of the latter is heralded by a great slaughter of the innocents. Like the royal navy, the factories were recruited by means of the press-gang. Blasé as Sir F. M. Eden is as to the horrors of the expropriation of the agricultural population from the soil, from the last third of the fifteenth century to his own time; with all the self-satisfaction with which he rejoices in this process 'essential' for establishing capitalistic agriculture and 'the due proportion between arable and pasture land'—he does not show, however, the same economic insight in respect to the necessity of child-stealing and child-slavery for the transformation of manufacturing exploitation into factory exploitation, and the establishment of the 'true relation' between capital and labour-power. He says: 'It may, perhaps, be worthy the attention of the public to consider, whether any manufacture, which, in order to be carried on successfully, requires that cottages and workhouses should be ransacked for poor children; that they should be employed by turns during the greater part of the night and robbed of that rest which, though indispensable to all, is most required by the young; and that numbers of both sexes, of different ages and dispositions, should be collected together in such a manner that the contagion of example cannot but lead to profligacy and debauchery; will this add to the sum of individual or national felicity?'

'In the counties of Derbyshire, Nottinghamshire, and more particularly in Lancashire,' says Fielden, 'the newly-invented machinery was used in large factories built on the sides of streams capable of turning the water-wheel. Thousands of hands were suddenly required in these places, remote from towns; and Lancashire, in particular, being, till then, comparatively thinly populated and barren, a population was all that she now wanted. The small and nimble fingers of little children being by very far the most in request, the custom instantly sprang up of procuring *apprentices* from the different parish workhouses of London, Birmingham, and elsewhere. Many, many thousands of these little, hapless creatures were sent down into the north, being from the age of 7 to the age of 13 or 14 years old. The custom was for the master to clothe his apprentices and to feed and lodge them in an "apprentice house" near the factory; overseers were appointed to see to the works, whose interest it was to work the children to the utmost, because their pay was in proportion to the quantity of work that they could exact. Cruelty was, of course, the consequence. . . . In many of the manufacturing districts, but particularly, I am afraid, in the guilty county to which I belong [Lancashire], cruelties the most heart-rending were practised upon the unoffending and friendless creatures who were thus consigned to the charge of master manufacturers; they were harassed to the brink of death by excess of labour . . . were flogged, fettered and tortured in the most exquisite refinement of cruelty; . . . they were in many cases starved to the bone while flogged to their work and . . . even in some instances . . . were driven to commit suicide. . . . The beautiful and romantic valleys of Derbyshire, Nottinghamshire and Lancashire, secluded from the public eye, became the dismal solitudes of torture, and of many a murder. The profits of manufactures were enormous; but this only whetted the appetite that it should have satisfied, and therefore the manufacturers had recourse to an expedient that seemed to secure to them those profits without any possibility of limit; they began the practice of what is termed "night-working," that is, having tired one set of hands, by working them throughout the day, they had another set ready to go on working throughout the night; the day-set getting into the beds that the night-set had just quitted, and in their turn again, the night-set getting into the beds that the day-set quitted in the morning. It is a common tradition in Lancashire, that the beds *never get cold.*'

With the development of capitalist production during the manufacturing period, the public opinion of Europe had lost the last remnant of shame and conscience. The nations bragged cynically of every infamy that served them as a means of accumulating capital. Read, for example, the naïve *Annals of Commerce* of the worthy A. Anderson. Here it is trumpeted forth as a triumph of English statecraft that at the Peace of Utrecht, England extorted from the Spaniards by the Asiento Treaty the privilege of being allowed to ply the negro-trade, until then only carried on between Africa and the English West Indies, between Africa and Spanish America as well. England thereby acquired the right of supplying Spanish America until 1743 with 4800 negroes yearly. This threw, at the same time, an official cloak over British smuggling. Liverpool waxed fat on the slave-trade. This was its method of primitive accumulation. And, even to the present day, Liverpool 'respectability' is the Pindar of the slave-trade which—compare the work of Aikin already quoted [J. Aikin, *Description of the Country from 30 to 40 Miles Round Manchester*, London, 1795]—'has coincided with that spirit of bold adventure which has characterised the trade of Liverpool and rapidly carried it to its present state of prosperity; has occasioned vast employment for shipping and sailors, and greatly augmented the demand for the manufactures of the country' (p. 339). Liverpool employed in the slave-trade, in 1730, 15 ships; in 1751, 53; in 1760, 74; in 1770, 96; and in 1792, 132.

While the cotton industry introduced child-slavery in England, it gave in the United States a stimulus to the transformation of the earlier, more or less patriarchal slavery, into a system of commercial exploitation. In fact, the veiled slavery of the wage-workers in Europe needed, for its pedestal, slavery pure and simple in the new world.

Tantae molis erat, to establish the 'eternal laws of Nature' of the capitalist mode of production, to complete the process of separation between labourers and conditions of labour, to transform, at one pole, the social means of production and subsistence into capital, at the opposite pole, the mass of the population into wage-labourers, into 'free labouring poor,' that artificial product of modern society. If money, according to Augier, 'comes into the world with a congenital blood-stain on one cheek,' capital comes dripping from head to foot, from every pore, with blood and dirt.

CHAPTER 32:
'THE HISTORICAL TENDENCY OF CAPITALIST ACCUMULATION'

What does the primitive accumulation of capital, i.e., its historical genesis, resolve itself into? In so far as it is not immediate transformation of slaves and serfs into wage-labourers, and therefore a mere change of form, it only means the expropriation of the immediate producers, i.e., the dissolution of private property based on the labour of its owner. Private property, as the antithesis to social, collective property, exists only where the means of labour and the external conditions of labour belong to private individuals. But according as these private individuals are labourers or not labourers, private property has a different character. The numberless shades that it at first sight presents correspond to the intermediate stages lying between these two extremes. The private property of the labourer in his means of production is the foundation of petty industry, whether agricultural, manufacturing, or both; petty industry, again, is an essential condition for the development of social production and of the free individuality of the labourer himself. Of course, this petty mode of production exists also under slavery, serfdom, and other states of dependence. But it flourishes, it lets loose its whole energy, it attains its adequate classical form, only where the labourer is the private owner of his own means of labour set in action by himself: the peasant of the land which he cultivates, the artisan of the tool which he handles as a virtuoso. This mode of production pre-supposes parcelling of the soil, and scattering of the other means of production. As it excludes the concentration of these means of production, so also it excludes co-operation, division of labour within each separate process of production, the control over, and the productive application of the forces of nature by society, and the free development of the social productive powers. It is compatible only with a system of production, and a society, moving within narrow and more or less primitive bounds. To perpetuate it would be, as Pecqueur rightly says, 'to decrease universal mediocrity.' At a certain stage of development it brings forth the material agencies for its own dissolution. From that moment new forces and new passions spring up in the bosom of society; but the old social organisation fetters them and keeps them down. It must be annihilated; it is annihilated. Its annihilation, the transformation of the individualised and scattered means of production into socially concentrated ones, of the pigmy property of the many into the huge property of the few, the expropriation of the great mass of the people from the soil, from the means of subsistence, and from the means of labour, this fearful and painful expropriation of the mass of the people forms the prelude to the history of capital. It comprises a series of forcible methods, of which we have passed in review only those that have been epoch-making as methods of the primitive accumulation of capital. The expropriation of the immediate producers was accomplished with merciless vandalism, and under the stimulus of passions the most infamous, the most sordid, the pettiest, the most meanly odious. Self-earned private property, that is based, so to say, on the fusing together of the isolated, independent labouring-individual with the conditions of his labour, is supplanted by capitalistic private property, which rests on exploitation of the nominally free labour of others, i.e., on wage-labour.

As soon as this process of transformation has sufficiently decomposed the old society from top to bottom, as soon as the labourers are turned into proletarians, their means of labour into capital, as soon as the capitalist mode of production stands on its own feet, then the further socialisation of labour and further transformation of the land and other means of production into socially exploited and, therefore, common means of production, as well as the further expropriation of private proprietors, takes a new form. That which is now to be expropriated is no longer the labourer working for himself, but the capitalist exploiting many labourers. This expropriation is accomplished by the action of the immanent laws of capitalistic production itself, by the centralisation of capital. One capitalist always kills many. Hand in hand with this centralisation, or this expropriation of many capitalists by few, develop, on an ever extending scale, the co-operative form of the labour-process, the conscious technical application of science, the methodical cultivation of the soil, the transformation of the instruments of labour into instruments of labour only usable in common, the economising of all means of production by their use as the means of production of combined, socialised labour, the entanglement of all peoples in the net of the world-market, and with this, the international character of the capitalistic régime. Along with the constantly diminishing number of the magnates of capital, who usurp and monopolise all advantages of this process of transformation, grows the mass of misery, oppression, slavery, degradation, exploitation; but with this too grows the revolt of the working-class, a class always increasing in numbers, and disciplined, united, organised by the very mechanism of the process of capitalist production itself. The monopoly of capital becomes a fetter upon the mode of production, which has sprung up and flourished along with, and under it. Centralisation of the means of production and socialisation of labour at last reach a point where they become incompatible with their capitalist integument. This integument is burst asunder. The knell of capitalist private property sounds. The expropriators are expropriated.

The capitalist mode of appropriation, the result of the capitalist mode of production, produces capitalist private property. This is the first negation of individual private property, as founded on the labour of the proprietor. But capitalist production begets, with the inexorability of a law of nature, its own negation. It is the negation of negation. This does not re-establish private property for the producer, but gives him individual property based on the acquisitions of the capitalist era: i.e., on co-operation and the possession in common of the land and of the means of production.

The transformation of scattered private property, arising from individual labour, into capitalist private property is, naturally, a process, incomparably more protracted, violent, and difficult, than the transformation of capitalistic private property, already practically resting on socialised production, into socialised property. In the former case, we had the expropriation of the mass of the people by a few usurpers; in the latter, we have the expropriation of a few usurpers by the mass of the people.

CHAPTER 33:
'THE MODERN THEORY OF COLONISATION'

Political economy confuses on principle two very different kinds of private property, of which one rests on the producers' own labour, the other on the employment of the labour of others. It forgets that the latter not only is the direct antithesis of the former, but absolutely grows on its tomb only. In Western Europe, the home of political economy, the process of primitive accumulation is more or less accomplished. Here the capitalist régime has either directly conquered the whole domain of national production, or, where economic conditions are less developed, it, at least, indirectly controls those strata of society which, though belonging to the antiquated mode of production, continue to exist side by side with it in gradual decay. To this ready-made world of capital, the political economist applies the notions of law and of property inherited from a pre-capitalistic world with all the more anxious zeal and all the greater unction, the more loudly the facts cry out in the face of his ideology. It is otherwise in the colonies. There the capitalist régime everywhere comes into collision with the resistance of the producer, who, as owner of his own conditions of labour, employs that labour to enrich himself, instead of the capitalist. The contradiction of these two diametrically opposed economic systems, manifests itself here practically in a struggle between them. Where the capitalist has at his back the power of the mother-country, he tries to clear out of his way by force, the modes of production and appropriation, based on his independent labour of the producer. The same interest, which compels the sycophant of capital, the political economist, in the mother-country, to proclaim the theoretical identity of the capitalist mode of production with its contrary, that same interest compels him in the colonies to make a clean breast of it, and to proclaim aloud the antagonism of the two modes of production. To this end he proves how the development of the social productive power of labour, co-operation, division of labour, use of machinery on a large scale, &c., are impossible without the expropriation of the labourers, and the corresponding transformation of their means of production into capital.

In the interest of the so-called national wealth, he seeks for artificial means to ensure the poverty of the people. Here his apologetic armour crumbles off, bit by bit, like rotten touchwood. It is the great merit of E. G. Wakefield to have discovered, not anything new about the colonies, but to have discovered in the colonies the truth as to the conditions of capitalist production in the mother-country. As the system of protection at its origin attempted to manufacture capitalists artificially in the mother-country, so Wakefield's colonisation theory, which England tried for a time to enforce by Acts of Parliament, attempted to effect the manufacture of wage-workers in the colonies. This he calls 'systematic colonisation.'

First of all, Wakefield discovered that in the colonies, property in money, means of subsistence, machines, and other means of production, does not as yet stamp a man as a capitalist if there be wanting the correlative—the wage-worker, the other man who is compelled to sell himself of his own free-will. He discovered that capital is not a thing, but a social relation between persons, established by the instrumentality of things. Mr. Peel, he moans, took with him from England to Swan River, West Australia, means of subsistence and of production to the amount of £50,000. Mr. Peel had the foresight to bring with him, besides, 3000 persons of the working-class, men, women, and children. Once arrived at his destination, 'Mr. Peel was left without a servant to make his bed or fetch him water from the river.' Unhappy Mr. Peel who provided for everything except the export of English modes of production to Swan River!

For the understanding of the following discoveries of Wakefield, two preliminary remarks: We know that the means of production and subsistence, while they remain the property of the immediate producer, are not capital. They become capital, only under circumstances in which they serve at the same time as means of exploitation and subjection of the labourer. But this capitalist soul of theirs

is so intimately wedded, in the head of the political economist, to their material substance, that he christens them
capital under all circumstances, even when they are its
exact opposite. Thus is it with Wakefield. Further: the
splitting up of the means of production into the individual
property of many independent labourers, working on
their own account, he calls equal division of capital. It is
with the political economist as with the feudal jurist. The
latter stuck on to pure monetary relations the labels supplied by feudal law.

'If,' says Wakefield, 'all the members of the society are
supposed to possess equal portions of capital ... no man
would have a motive for accumulating more capital than
he could use with his own hands. This is to some extent
the case in new American settlements, where a passion for
owning land prevents the existence of a class of labourers
for hire.' So long, therefore, as the labourer can accumulate for himself—and this he can do so long as he remains
possessor of his means of production—capitalist accumulation and the capitalistic mode of production are impossible. The class of wage-labourers, essential to these, is
wanting. How, then, in old Europe, was the expropriation
of the labourer from his conditions of labour, i.e., the co-
existence of capital and wage-labour, brought about? By a
social contract of a quite original kind. 'Mankind have
adopted a ... simple contrivance for promoting the accumulation of capital,' which, of course, since the time of
Adam, floated in their imagination as the sole and final
end of their existence: 'they have divided themselves into
owners of capital and owners of labour. . . . This division
was the result of concert and combination.' In one word:
the mass of mankind expropriated itself in honour of the
'accumulation of capital.' Now, one would think that this
instinct of self-denying fanaticism would give itself full
fling especially in the colonies, where alone exist the men
and conditions that could turn a social contract from a
dream to a reality. But why, then, should 'systematic col-

onisation' be called in to replace its opposite, spontaneous, unregulated colonisation? But—but—'In the Northern States of the American Union, it may be doubted whether so many as a tenth of the people would fall under the description of hired labourers. . . . In England . . . the labouring class compose the bulk of the people.' Nay, the impulse to self-expropriation, on the part of labouring humanity, for the glory of capital, exists so little, that slavery, according to Wakefield himself, is the sole natural basis of colonial wealth. His systematic colonisation is a mere *pis aller*, since he unfortunately has to do with free men, not with slaves. 'The first Spanish settlers in Saint Domingo did not obtain labourers from Spain. But, without labourers, their capital must have perished, or, at least, must soon have been diminished to that small amount which each individual could employ with his own hands. This has actually occurred in the last Colony founded by Englishmen—the Swan River Settlement—where a great mass of capital, of seeds, implements, and cattle, has perished for want of labourers to use it, and where no settler has preserved much more capital than he can employ with his own hands.'

We have seen that the expropriation of the mass of the people from the soil forms the basis of the capitalist mode of production. The essence of a free colony, on the contrary, consists in this—that the bulk of the soil is still public property, and every settler on it therefore can turn part of it into his private property and individual means of production, without hindering the later settlers in the same operation. This is the secret both of the prosperity of the colonies and of their inveterate vice—opposition to the establishment of capital. 'Where land is very cheap and all men are free, where every one who so pleases can easily obtain a piece of land for himself, not only is labour very dear, as respects the labourer's share of the produce, but the difficulty is to obtain combined labour at any price.'

As in the colonies the separation of the labourer from

the conditions of labour and their root, the soil, does not yet exist, or only sporadically, or on too limited a scale, so neither does the separation of agriculture from industry exist, nor the destruction of the household industry of the peasantry. Whence then is to come the internal market for capital? 'No part of the population of America is exclusively agricultural, excepting slaves and their employers who combine capital and labour in particular works. Free Americans, who cultivate the soil, follow many other occupations. Some portion of the furniture and tools which they use is commonly made by themselves. They frequently build their own houses, and carry to market, at whatever distance, the produce of their own industry. They are spinners and weavers; they make soap and candles, as well as, in many cases, shoes and clothes for their own use. In America the cultivation of land is often the secondary pursuit of a blacksmith, a miller or a shopkeeper.' With such queer people as these, where is the field of abstinence for the capitalists?

The great beauty of capitalist production consists in this—that it not only constantly reproduces the wage-worker as wage-worker, but produces always, in proportion to the accumulation of capital, a relative surplus population of wage-workers. Thus the law of supply and demand of labour is kept in the right rut, the oscillation of wages is penned within limits satisfactory to capitalist exploitation, and lastly, the social dependence of the labourer on the capitalist, that indispensable requisite, is secured; an unmistakeable relation of dependence, which the smug political economist, at home, in the mother-country, can transmogrify into one of free contract between buyer and seller, between equally independent owners of commodities, the owner of the commodity capital and the owner of the commodity labour. But in the colonies this pretty fancy is torn asunder. The absolute population here increases much more quickly than in the mother-country, because many labourers enter this world as ready-made adults, and yet the labour-market is always understocked. The law of the supply and demand of labour falls to pieces. On the one hand, the old world constantly throws in capital, thirsting after exploitation and 'abstinence'; on the other, the regular reproduction of the wage-labourer as wage-labourer comes into collision with impediments the most impertinent and in part invincible. What becomes of the production of wage-labourers, supernumerary in proportion to the accumulation of capital? The wage-worker of today is tomorrow an independent peasant, or artisan, working for himself. He vanishes from the labour-market, but not into the workhouse. This constant transformation of the wage-labourers into independent producers, who work for themselves instead of for capital, and enrich themselves instead of the capitalist gentry, reacts in its turn very perversely on the conditions of the labour-market. Not only does the degree of exploitation of the wage-labourer remain indecently low. The wage-labourer loses into the bargain, along with the relation of dependence, also the sentiment of the dependence on the abstemious capitalist. Hence all the inconveniences that our E. G. Wakefield pictures so doughtily, so eloquently, so pathetically.

The supply of wage-labour, he complains, is neither constant, nor regular, nor sufficient. 'The supply of labour is always, not only small, but uncertain.' 'Though the produce divided between the capitalist and the labourer be large, the labourer takes so great a share that he soon becomes a capitalist. . . . Few, even of those whose lives are unusually long, can accumulate great masses of wealth.' The labourers most distinctly decline to allow the capitalist to abstain from the payment of the greater part of their labour. It avails him nothing, if he is so cunning as to import from Europe, with his own capital, his own wageworkers. They soon 'cease . . . to be labourers for hire; they . . . become independent landowners, if not competitors with their former masters in the labour market.'

Think of the horror! The excellent capitalist has imported bodily from Europe, with his own good money, his own competitors! The end of the world has come! No wonder Wakefield laments the absence of all dependence and of all sentiment of dependence on the part of the wage-workers in the colonies. On account of the high wages, says his disciple, Merivale, there is in the colonies 'the urgent desire for cheaper and more subservient labourers—for a class to whom the capitalist might dictate terms, instead of being dictated to by them. . . . In ancient civilised countries the labourer, though free, is by a law of nature dependent on capitalists; in colonies this dependence must be created by artificial means.'

What is now, according to Wakefield, the consequence of this unfortunate state of things in the colonies? A 'barbarising tendency of dispersion' of producers and national wealth. The parcelling-out of the means of production among innumerable owners, working on their own account, annihilates, along with the centralisation of capital, all the foundations of combined labour. Every long-winded undertaking, extending over several years and demanding outlay of fixed capital, is prevented from being carried out. In Europe, capital invests without hesitating a moment, for the working-class constitutes its living appurtenance, always in excess, always at disposal. But in the colonies! Wakefield tells an extremely doleful anecdote. He was talking with some capitalists of Canada and the state of New York, where the immigrant wave often becomes stagnant and deposits a sediment of 'supernumerary' labourers. 'Our capital,' says one of the characters in the melodrama, 'was ready for many operations which require a considerable period of time for their completion; but we could not begin such operations with labour which, we knew, would soon leave us. If we had been sure of retaining the labour of such emigrants, we should have been glad to have engaged it at once, and for a high price: and we should have engaged it, even though we had been sure it would leave us, provided we had been sure of a fresh supply whenever we might need it.'

After Wakefield has contrasted the English capitalist agriculture and its 'combined' labour with the scattered cultivation of American peasants, he unwittingly gives us a glimpse at the reverse of the medal. He depicts the mass of the American people as well-to-do, independent, enterprising and comparatively cultured, while 'the English agricultural labourer is a miserable wretch, a pauper. . . . In what country, except North America and some new colonies, do the wages of free labour employed in agriculture, much exceed a bare subsistence for the labourer? . . . Undoubtedly, farm-horses in England, being a valuable property, are better fed than English peasants.' But never mind, national wealth is, once again, by its very nature, identical with misery of the people.

How, then, to heal the anti-capitalistic cancer of the colonies? If men were willing, at a blow, to turn all the soil from public into private property, they would destroy certainly the root of the evil, but also—the colonies. The trick is how to kill two birds with one stone. Let the Government put upon the virgin soil an artificial price, independent of the law of supply and demand, a price that compels the immigrant to work a long time for wages before he can earn enough money to buy land, and turn himself into an independent peasant. The funds resulting from the sale of land at a price relatively prohibitory for the wage-workers, this fund of money extorted from the wages of labour by violation of the sacred law of supply and demand, the Government is to employ, on the other hand, in proportion as it grows, to import have-nothings from Europe into the colonies, and thus keep the wage-labour market full for the capitalists. Under these circumstances, *tout sera pour le mieux dans le meilleur des mondes possibles* [everything will be for the best in the best of all possible worlds]. This is the great secret of 'systematic colonisation.' By this plan, Wakefield cries in triumph, 'the supply of labour *must* be constant and regular, because, first, as no labourer would be able to procure land until he had worked for money, all immigrant labourers, working for a time for wages and in combination, would produce capital for the employment of more labourers; secondly, because every labourer who left off working for wages and became a landowner, would, by purchasing land, provide a fund for bringing fresh labour to the colony.' The price of the soil imposed by the state must, of course, be a 'sufficient price'—i.e., so high 'as to prevent the labourers from becoming independent landowners until others had followed to take their place.' This 'sufficient price for the land' is nothing but a euphemistic circumlocution for the ransom which the labourer pays to the capitalist for leave to retire from the wage-labour market to the land. First, he must create for the capitalist 'capital,' with which the latter may be able to exploit more labourers; then he must place, at his own expense, a *locum tenens* on the labour-market, whom the Government forwards across the sea for the benefit of his old master, the capitalist.

It is very characteristic that the English Government for years practised this method of 'primitive accumulation,' prescribed by Mr. Wakefield expressly for the use of the colonies. The fiasco was, of course, as complete as that of Sir Robert Peel's Bank Act. The stream of emigration was only diverted from the English colonies to the United States. Meanwhile, the advance of capitalistic production in Europe, accompanied by increasing Government pressure, has rendered Wakefield's recipe superfluous. On the one hand, the enormous and ceaseless stream of men, year after year driven upon America, leaves behind a stationary sediment in the east of the United States, the wave of immigration from Europe throwing men on the labour-market there more rapidly than the wave of emigration westwards can wash them away. On the other hand, the American Civil War brought in its train a colossal national debt, and, with it, pressure of taxes, the rise of the vilest financial aristocracy, the squandering of a huge part of the public land on speculative companies for the exploitation of railways, mines, &c., in brief, the most rapid centralisation of capital. The great republic has, therefore, ceased to be the promised land for emigrant labourers. Capitalistic production advances there with giant strides, even though the lowering of wages and the dependence of the wage-worker are yet far from being brought down to the normal European level. The shameless lavishing of uncultivated colonial land on aristocrats and capitalists by the Government, so loudly denounced even by Wakefield, has produced, especially in Australia, in conjunction with the stream of men that the gold-diggings attract, and with the competition that the importation of English commodities causes even to the smallest artisan, an ample 'relative surplus labouring population,' so that almost every mail brings the Job's news of a 'glut of the Australian labour-market,' and prostitution in some places there flourishes as wantonly as in the London Haymarket.

However, we are not concerned here with the condition of the colonies. The only thing that interests us is the secret discovered in the new world by the political economy of the old world, and proclaimed on the house-tops: that the capitalist mode of production and accumulation, and therefore capitalist private property, have for their fundamental condition the annihilation of self earned private property; in other words, the expropriation of the labourer.

MEW, 23, 11–17, 49–55, 85–98, 741–55, 756–61, 777–802, as translated by S. Moore and E. Aveling (authorized English edition, London, 1887).

6. The Paris Commune and the Future of Socialism: 1870–1882

~~~~~~~~~~~~~~~~~~~~~~~~~~~~~~~~~~~

EDITOR'S NOTE

Not the publication of the first volume of *Capital*, but the proclamation of the Paris Commune in 1871—falsely attributed to the secret influence of Karl Marx and the London headquarters of the International—was the immediate cause of a major breakthrough in Marx's bid for world attention. His name figured in *The Times*, the long-neglected *Communist Manifesto* was quickly republished, while the mere existence of *Capital, Volume I*, no matter how few its serious readers, gave weight to his standing as the leading socialist thinker. But while Marx's last dozen years were years of much greater comfort, security, and recognition, and of a certain mellowing of character, they were also years of illness, of a growing awareness that he would not finish his great scientific work—years of that comparative loss of energy that comes upon us all. In letters and in occasional comments on other people's work and proposals, he showed an awareness of changing conditions, of the growth of organized mass parties of labour; he also took an increasingly sympathetic interest in the Russian revolutionary movement, which had shown interest in and an appreciation of his work. Essentially, between 1870 and his death in 1883 he produced only one proper work—the Addresses of the First International on the Franco-Prussian War and the proclamation and defeat of the Paris Commune, published under the title *The Civil War in France*. Written from London in considerable ignorance, in common with the rest of the world, of what was actually happening in Paris, they are nevertheless vintage Marx—powerful, incisive, and infused with general theoretical conceptions and standpoints. As Marx's only serious grappling with the relationship of the proletariat to the modern state, they have commanded renewed attention through their emphasis on decentralization, and the more anarchist portions of Marx's drafts for the Addresses, excluded from the final version, were pointedly republished in cheap and popular editions, by the Foreign Languages Press in Peking in the period of the Great Proletarian Cultural Revolution. Selections from the Third Address and from the drafts are presented below.

Marx's *Critique of the Gotha Programme*—a unity programme meant to bring together the antagonistic Marxian and Lassallean wings of German socialism when they met in Gotha in May 1875—is hardly a work; it is a quick and hostile reaction in the form of critical annotations to the Programme. But its distinction between the stages of socialism/communism has become central to orthodox Marxism, and anyone who has not read Marx's *Critique* has missed a vital component in the systematized creed.

Marx's last published writing is a Preface to the Russian edition of the *Communist Manifesto*. Its view of the possibility of revolution in Russia should be supplemented, by a careful student, with a consideration of the important three separate and lengthy answers which Marx drafted but never sent, to the

Russian populist exile Vera Zasulich, who asked whether the traditional peasant commune was doomed to disappear, and of the brief and ambivalent reply that he did finally send. But for this volume, the Preface serves as sufficient reminder, and it is fitting that Marx's own last published writing should point to Russia as the site of the first revolution to be proclaimed in Marx's name and on the basis of his theories.

From THE CIVIL WAR IN FRANCE

ADDRESS OF THE GENERAL COUNCIL OF THE INTERNATIONAL WORKING MEN'S ASSOCIATION

III

On the dawn of the 18th of March, Paris arose to the thunderburst of "Vive la Commune!" What is the Commune, that sphinx so tantalizing to the bourgeois mind?

"The proletarians of Paris," said the Central Committee in its manifesto of the 18th March, "amidst the failures and treasons of the ruling classes, have understood that the hour has struck for them to save the situation by taking into their own hands the direction of public affairs. . . . They have understood that it is their imperious duty and their absolute right to render themselves masters of their own destinies, by seizing upon the governmental power." But the working class cannot simply lay hold of the ready-made state machinery, and wield it for its own purposes.

The centralized State power, with its ubiquitous organs of standing army, police, bureaucracy, clergy, and judicature—organs wrought after the plan of a systematic and hierarchic division of labour,—originates from the days of absolute monarchy, serving nascent middle-class society as a mighty weapon in its struggles against feudalism. Still, its development remained clogged by all manner of mediaeval rubbish, seignorial rights, local privileges, municipal and guild monopolies and provincial constitutions. The gigantic broom of the French Revolution of the eighteenth century swept away all these relics of bygone times, thus clearing simultaneously the social soil of its last hindrances to the superstructure of the modern State edifice raised under the First Empire, itself the offspring of the coalition wars of the old semi-feudal Europe against modern France. During the subsequent *régimes* the Government, placed under parliamentary control—that is, under the direct control of the propertied classes—became not only a hotbed of huge national debts and crushing taxes; with its irresistible allurements of place, pelf, and patronage, it became not only the bone of contention between the rival factions and adventurers of the ruling classes; but its political character changed simultaneously with the economic changes of society. At the same pace at which the progress of modern industry developed, widened, intensified the class antagonism between capital and labour, the State power assumed more and more the character of the national power of capital over labour, of a public force organized for social enslavement, of an engine of class despotism. After every revolution marking a progressive phase in the class struggle, the purely repressive character of the State power stands out in bolder and bolder relief. The Revolution of 1830, resulting in the transfer of Government from the landlords to the capitalists, transferred it from the more remote to the more direct antagonists of the working men. The bourgeois Republicans, who, in the name of the Revolution of February, took the State power, used it for the June massacres, in order to convince the working class that "social" republic meant the republic ensuring their social subjection, and in order to convince the royalist bulk of the bourgeois and landlord class that they might safely leave the cares and emoluments of government to the bourgeois "Republicans." However, after their one heroic exploit of June, the bourgeois Republicans had, from the front, to fall back to the rear of the "Party of Order"—a combination formed by all the rival fractions and factions of the appropriating class in their now openly declared antagonism to the producing classes. The proper form of their joint-stock Government was the *Parliamentary Republic*, with Louis Bonaparte for its President. Theirs was a *régime* of avowed class terrorism and deliberate insult towards the "vile multitude." If the Parliamentary Republic, as M. Thiers said, "divided them (the different fractions of the ruling class) least," it opened an abyss between that class and the whole body of society outside their spare ranks. The restraints by which their own divisions had under former *régimes* still checked the State power, were removed by their union; and in view of the threatening upheaval of the proletariat, they now used that State power mercilessly and ostentatiously as the national war-engine of capital against labour. In their uninterrupted crusade against the producing masses they were, however, bound not only to invest the executive with continually increased powers of repression, but at the same time to divest their own parliamentary stronghold—the National Assembly—one by one, of all its own means of defence against the Executive. The Executive, in the person of Louis Bonaparte, turned them out. The natural offspring of the "Party-of-Order" Republic was the Second Empire.

The empire, with the *coup d'état* for its certificate of birth, universal suffrage for its sanction, and the sword for its sceptre, professed to rest upon the peasantry, the large mass of producers not directly involved in the struggle of capital and labour. It professed to save the working class by breaking down Parliamentarism, and, with it, the undisguised subserviency of Government to the propertied classes. It professed to save the propertied classes by upholding their economic supremacy over the working class; and, finally, it professed to unite all classes by reviving for all the chimera of national glory. In reality, it was the only form of government possible at a time when the bourgeoisie had already lost, and the working class had not yet acquired, the faculty of ruling the nation. It was acclaimed throughout the world as the saviour of society. Under its sway, bourgeois society, freed from political cares, attained a development unexpected even by itself. Its industry and commerce expanded to colossal dimensions; financial swindling celebrated cosmopolitan orgies; the misery of the masses was set off by a shameless display of gorgeous, meretricious and debased luxury. The State power, apparently soaring high above society, was at the same time itself the greatest scandal of that society and the very hotbed of all its corruptions. Its own rottenness, and the rottenness of the society it had saved, were laid bare by the bayonet of Prussia, herself eagerly bent upon transferring the supreme seat of that *régime* from Paris to Berlin. Imperialism is, at the same time, the most prostitute and the ultimate form of the State power which nascent middle-class society had commenced to elaborate as a means of its own emancipation from feudalism, and which full-grown bourgeois society had finally transformed into a means for the enslavement of labour by capital.

The direct antithesis to the empire was the Commune. The cry of "social republic," with which the Revolution of February was ushered in by the Paris proletariat, did but express a vague aspiration after a Republic that was not only to supersede the monarchical form of class rule, but class rule itself. The Commune was the positive form of that Republic.

Paris, the central seat of the old governmental power, and, at the same time, the social stronghold of the French working class, had risen in arms against the attempt of Thiers and the Rurals to restore and perpetuate that old governmental power bequeathed to them by the empire. Paris could resist only because, in consequence of the siege, it had got rid of the army, and replaced it by a National Guard, the bulk of which consisted of working men.

This fact was now to be transformed into an institution. The first decree of the Commune, therefore, was the suppression of the standing army, and the substitution for it of the armed people.

The Commune was formed of the municipal councillors, chosen by universal suffrage in the various wards of the town, responsible and revocable at short terms. The majority of its members were naturally working men, or acknowledged representatives of the working class. The Commune was to be a working, not a parliamentary, body, executive and legislative at the same time. Instead of continuing to be the agent of the Central Government, the police was at once stripped of its political attributes, and turned into the responsible and at all times revocable agent of the Commune. So were the officials of all other branches of the Administration. From the members of the Commune downwards, the public service had to be done at *workmen's wages.* The vested interests and the representation allowances of the high dignitaries of State disappeared along with the high dignitaries themselves. Public functions ceased to be the private property of the tools of the Central Government. Not only municipal administration, but the whole initiative hitherto exercised by the State was laid into the hands of the Commune.

Having once got rid of the standing army and the police, the physical force elements of the old Government, the Commune was anxious to break the spiritual force of repression, the "parson-power," by the disestablishment and disendowment of all churches as proprietary bodies. The priests were sent back to the recesses of private life, there to feed upon the alms of the faithful in imitation of their predecessors, the Apostles. The whole of the educational institutions were opened to the people gratuitously, and at the same time cleared of all interference of Church and State. Thus, not only was education made accessible to all, but science itself freed from the fetters which class prejudice and governmental force had imposed upon it.

The judicial functionaries were to be divested of that sham independence which had but served to mask their abject subserviency to all succeeding governments to which, in turn, they had taken, and broken, the oaths of allegiance. Like the rest of public servants, magistrates and judges were to be elective, responsible and revocable.

The Paris Commune was, of course, to serve as a model to all the great industrial centres of France. The communal *régime* once established in Paris and the secondary centres, the old centralized Government would in the provinces, too, have to give way to the self-government of the producers. In a rough sketch of national organization which the Commune had no time to develop, it states clearly that the Commune was to be the political form of even the smallest country hamlet, and that in the rural districts the standing army was to be replaced by a national militia, with an extremely short term of service. The rural communes of every district were to administer their common affairs by an assembly of delegates in the central town, and these district assemblies were again to send deputies to the National Delegation in Paris, each delegate to be at any time revocable and bound by the *mandat impératif* (formal instructions) of his constituents. The few but important functions which still would remain for a central government were not to be suppressed, as has been intentionally mis-stated, but were to be discharged by Communal, and therefore strictly responsible agents. The unity of the nation was not to be broken, but, on the contrary, to be organized by the Communal Constitution, and to become a reality by the destruction of the State power which claimed to be the embodiment of that unity independent of, and superior to, the nation itself, from which it was but a parasitic excrescence. While the merely repressive organs of the old governmental power were to be amputated, its legitimate functions were to be wrested from an authority usurping pre-eminence over society itself, and restored to the responsible agents of society. Instead of deciding once in three or six years which member of the ruling class was to misrepresent the people in Parliament, universal suffrage was to serve the people, constituted in Communes, as individual suffrage serves every other employer in the search for the workmen and managers in his business. And it is well known that companies, like individuals, in matters of real business generally know how to put the right man in the right place, and, if they for once make a mistake, to redress it promptly. On the other hand, nothing could be more foreign to the spirit of the Commune than to supersede universal suffrage by hierarchic investiture.

It is generally the fate of completely new historical creations to be mistaken for the counterpart of older and even defunct forms of social life, to which they may bear a certain likeness. Thus, this new Commune, which breaks the modern State power, has been mistaken for a reproduction of the mediaeval Communes, which first preceded, and afterwards became the substratum of, that very State power. The Communal Constitution has been mistaken for an attempt to break up into a federation of small States, as dreamt of by Montesquieu and the Girondins that unity of great nations which, if originally brought about by political force, has now become a powerful coefficient of social production. The antagonism of the Commune against the State power has been mistaken for an exaggerated form of the ancient struggle against over-centralization. Peculiar historical circumstances may have prevented the classical development, as in France, of the bourgeois form of government, and may have allowed, as in England, to complete the great central State organs by corrupt vestries, jobbing councillors, and ferocious poor-law guardians in the towns, and virtually hereditary magistrates in the counties. The Communal Constitution would have restored to the social body all the forces hitherto absorbed by the State parasite feeding upon, and clogging the free movement of, society. By this one act it would have initiated the regeneration of France. The provincial French middle class saw in the Commune an attempt to restore the sway their order had held over the country under Louis Philippe, and which, under Louis Napoleon, was supplanted by the pretended rule of the country over the towns. In reality, the Communal Constitution brought the rural producers under the intellectual lead of the central towns of their districts, and there secured to them, in the working men, the natural trustees of their interests. The very existence of the Commune involved, as a matter of course, local municipal liberty, but no longer as a check upon the, now superseded, State power. It could only enter into the head of a Bismarck, who, when not engaged on his intrigues of blood and iron, always likes to resume his old trade, so befitting his mental calibre, of contributor to *Kladderadatsch* (the Berlin *Punch*), it could only enter into such a head, to ascribe to the Paris Commune aspirations after that caricature of the old French municipal organization of 1791, the Prussian municipal constitution which degrades the town governments to mere secondary wheels in the police-machinery of the Prussian State. The Commune made that catchword of bourgeois revolutions, cheap government, a reality, by destroying the two greatest sources of expenditure—the standing army and State functionarism. Its very existence presupposed the non-existence of monarchy, which, in Europe at least, is the normal incumbrance and indispensable cloak of class rule. It supplied the Republic with the basis of really democratic institutions. But neither cheap government nor the "true Republic" was its ultimate aim; they were its mere concomitants.

The multiplicity of interpretations to which the Commune has been subjected, and the multiplicity of interests which construed it in their favour, show that it was a thoroughly expansive political form, while all previous forms of government had been emphatically repressive.

Its true secret was this. It was essentially a working-class government, the produce of the struggle of the producing against the appropriating class, the political form at last discovered under which to work out the economic emancipation of labour.

Except on this last condition, the Communal Constitution would have been an impossibility and a delusion. The political rule of the producer cannnot coexist with the perpetuation of his social slavery. The Commune was therefore to serve as a lever for uprooting the economical foundations upon which rests the existence of classes, and therefore of class rule. With labour emancipated, every man becomes a working man, and productive labour ceases to be a class attribute.

It is a strange fact. In spite of all the tall talk and all the immense literature, for the last sixty years, about Emancipation of Labour, no sooner do the working men anywhere take the subject into their own hands with a will than uprises at once all the apologetic phraseology of the mouth-pieces of present society with its two poles of Capital and Wage-slavery (the landlord now is but the sleeping partner of the capitalist), as if capitalist society was still in its purest state of virgin innocence, with its antagonisms still undeveloped, with its delusions still unexploded, with its prostitute realities not yet laid bare. The Commune, they exclaim, intends to abolish property, the basis of all civilization! Yes, gentlemen, the Commune intended to abolish that class-property which makes the labour of the many the wealth of the few. It aimed at the expropriation of the expropriators. It wanted to make individual property a truth by transforming the means of production, land and capital, now chiefly the means of enslaving and exploiting labour, into mere instruments of free and associated labour.—But this is Communism, "impossible" Communism! Why, those members of the ruling classes who are intelligent enough to perceive the impossibility of continuing the present system—and they are many—have become the obtrusive and full-mouthed apostles of co-operative production. If co-operative production is not to remain a sham and a snare; if it is to supersede the Capitalist system; if united co-operative societies are to regulate national production upon a common plan, thus taking it under their own control, and putting an end to the constant anarchy and periodical convulsions which are the fatality of Capitalist production—what else, gentlemen, would it be but Communism, "possible" Communism?

The working class did not expect miracles from the Commune. They had no ready-made utopias to introduce *par décret du peuple*. They know that in order to work out their own emancipation, and along with it that higher form to which present society is irresistibly tending by its own economical agencies, they will have to pass through long struggles, through a series of historic processes, transforming circumstances and men. They have no ideals to realize, but to set free the elements of the new society with which old collapsing bourgeois society itself is pregnant. In the full consciousness of their historic mission, and with the heroic resolve to act up to it, the working class can afford to smile at the coarse invective of the gentlemen's gentlemen with the pen and inkhorn, and at the didactic patronage of well-wishing bourgeois-doctrinaires, pouring forth their ignorant platitudes and sectarian crotchets in the oracular tone of scientific infallibility.

When the Paris Commune took the management of the revolution in its own hands; when plain working men for the first time dared to infringe upon the governmental privilege of their "natural superiors," and, under circumstances of unexampled difficulty, performed their work modestly, conscientiously, and efficiently,—performed it at salaries the highest of which barely amounted to one-fifth of what, according to high scientific authority, is the minimum required for a secretary to a certain metropolitan school-board,—the old world writhed in convulsions of rage at the sight of the Red Flag, the symbol of the Republic of Labour, floating over the Hôtel de Ville.

And yet, this was the first revolution in which the working class was openly acknowledged as the only class capable of social initiative, even by the great bulk of the Paris middle class—shopkeepers, tradesmen, merchants—the wealthy capitalists alone excepted. The Commune had saved them by a sagacious settlement of that ever-recurring cause of dispute among the middle classes themselves—the debtor and creditor accounts. The same portion of the middle class, after they had assisted in putting down the working men's insurrection of June, 1848, had been at once unceremoniously sacrificed to their creditors by the then Constituent Assembly. But this was not their only motive for now rallying round the working class. They felt that there was but one alternative—the Commune, or the Empire—under whatever name it might reappear. The Empire had ruined them economically by the havoc it made of public wealth, by the wholesale financial swindling it fostered, by the props it lent to the artificially accelerated centralization of capital, and the concomitant expropriation of their own ranks. It had suppressed them politically, it had shocked them morally by its orgies, it had insulted their Voltairianism by handing over the education of their children to the *frères Ignorantins,* it had revolted their national feeling as Frenchmen by precipitating them headlong into a war which left only one equivalent for the ruins it made—the disappearance of the Empire. In fact, after the exodus from Paris of the high Bonapartist and capitalist *bohème,* the true middle-class Party of Order came out in the shape of the "Union Républicaine," enrolling themselves under the colours of the Commune and defending it against the wilful misconstruction of Thiers. Whether the gratitude of this great body of the middle class will stand the present severe trial, time must show. . . .

IV

... The conspiracy of the ruling class to break down the Revolution by a civil war carried on under the patronage of the foreign invader—a conspiracy which we have traced from the very 4th of September down to the entrance of MacMahon's praetorians through the gate of St. Cloud—culminated in the carnage of Paris. Bismarck gloats over the ruins of Paris, in which he saw perhaps the first instalment of that general destruction of great cities he had prayed for when still a simple Rural in the Prussian *Chambre introuvable* of 1849. He gloats over the cadavers of the Paris proletariat. For him this is not only the extermination of revolution, but the extinction of France, now decapitated in reality, and by the French Government itself. With the shallowness characteristic of all successful statesmen, he sees but the surface of this tremendous historic event. When ever before has history exhibited the spectacle of a conqueror crowning his victory by turning into, not only the gendarme, but the hired bravo of the conquered Government? There existed no war between Prussia and the Commune of Paris. On the contrary, the Commune had accepted the peace preliminaries, and Prussia had announced her neutrality. Prussia was, therefore, no belligerent. She acted the part of a bravo, a cowardly bravo, because incurring no danger; a hired bravo, because stipulating beforehand the payment of her blood-money of 500 millions on the fall of Paris. And thus, at last, came out the true character of the war, ordained by Providence as a chastisement of godless and debauched France by pious and moral Germany! And this unparalleled breach of the law of nations, even as understood by the old-world lawyers, instead of arousing the "civilized" Governments of Europe to declare the felonious Prussian Government, the mere tool of the St. Petersburg Cabinet, an outlaw amongst nations, only incites them to consider whether the few victims who escape the double cordon around Paris are not to be given up to the hangman at Versailles!

That after the most tremendous war of modern times, the conquering and the conquered hosts should fraternize for the common massacre of the proletariat—this unparalleled event does indicate, not, as Bismarck thinks, the final repression of a new society upheaving, but the crumbling into dust of bourgeois society. The highest heroic effort of which old society is still capable is national war; and this is now proved to be a mere governmental humbug, intended to defer the struggle of classes, and to be thrown aside as soon as that class struggle bursts out into civil war. Class rule is no longer able to disguise itself in a national uniform; the national Governments are *one* as against the proletariat!

After Whit-Sunday, 1871, there can be neither peace nor truce possible between the working men of France and the appropriators of their produce. The iron hand of a mercenary soldiery may keep for a time both classes tied down in common oppression. But the battle must break out again and again in ever-growing dimensions, and there can be no doubt as to who will be the victor in the end— the appropriating few, or the immense working majority. And the French working class is only the advanced guard of the modern proletariat.

While the European governments thus testify, before Paris, to the international character of class rule, they cry down the International Working Men's Association— the international counter-organization of labour against the cosmopolitan conspiracy of capital—as the head fountain of all these disasters. Thiers denounced it as the despot of labour, pretending to be its liberator. Picard ordered that all communications between the French Internationals and those abroad should be cut off; Count Jaubert, Thiers' mummified accomplice of 1835, declares it the great problem of all civilized governments to weed it out. The Rurals roar against it, and the whole European press joins the chorus. An honourable French writer, completely foreign to our Association, speaks as follows:—"The members of the Central Committee of the National Guard, as well as the greater part of the members of the Commune, are the most active, intelligent, and energetic minds of the International Working Men's Association; . . . men who are thoroughly honest, sincere, intelligent, devoted, pure, and fanatical in the *good* sense of the word." The police-tinged bourgeois mind naturally figures to itself the International Working Men's Association as acting in the manner of a secret conspiracy, its central body ordering, from time to time, explosions in different countries. Our Association is, in fact, nothing but the international bond between the most advanced working men in the various countries of the civilized world. Wherever, in whatever shape, and under whatever conditions the class struggle obtains any consistency, it is but natural that members of our Association should stand in the foreground. The soil out of which it grows is modern society itself. It cannot be stamped out by any amount of carnage. To stamp it out, the Governments would have to stamp out the despotism of capital over labour—the condition of their own parasitical existence.

Working men's Paris, with its Commune, will be for ever celebrated as the glorious harbinger of a new society. Its martyrs are enshrined in the great heart of the working class. Its exterminators history has already nailed to that eternal pillory from which all the prayers of their priests will not avail to redeem them.

MEW 17, 335–44, 360–62, as translated in Karl Marx, *The Civil War in France*, Peking, 1966, pp. 63–75, 96–99.

FROM THE FIRST DRAFT: 'THE CHARACTER OF THE COMMUNE'

The centralized state machinery which, with its ubiquitous and complicated military, bureaucratic, ecclesiastical and judicial organizations, wraps itself around (entangles)[1] the vital civil society like a boa constrictor, was first forged in the days of absolute monarchy as a weapon of developing modern society in its struggle for emancipation from feudalism. The seignorial privileges of the medieval lords, cities and clergy were transformed into the attributes of a single state power, which replaced feudal dignitaries by salaried state officials and transferred arms from the medieval retainers of feudal lords and the city guilds to a standing army; for the checkered (particolored) anarchy of conflicting medieval powers was substituted the regulated plan of a state authority, with a systematic and hierarchic division of labor. The first French Revolution with its task of establishing national unity (of creating a nation) had to break down all local, territorial, civic and provincial independence. It was, therefore, forced to develop what absolute monarchy had begun, the centralization and organization of state power, and to extend the compass and attributes of state power, the number of its tools, its independence and its supernatural dominion over actual society, which indeed took the place of the medieval supernatural Heaven with its saints. Every minor individual interest engendered by the interrelation of social groups was separated from society itself, fixed and made independent of it and set in opposition to it in the form of state interest, administered by state priests with precisely determined hierarchical functions.

This parasitic growth upon civil society, claiming to be its ideal image, developed fully under the rule of the first

---

1. The variants in parentheses occur in Marx's original draft. [E.K.]

Bonaparte. The Restoration and the July monarchy added nothing to it but a greater division of labor, increasing in proportion as the division of labor within civil society created new interest groups and thus new material for state action. In their struggle against the revolution of 1848, the parliamentary republic of France and all the governments of continental Europe were forced to strengthen the means of action and the centralization of government power by repressive measures against the popular movement. All revolutions thus only perfected the state machinery instead of throwing off this deadening incubus. The factions and parties of the ruling classes which alternately struggled for supremacy, viewed the seizure (control) (usurpation) and direction of this immense machinery of government as the principal spoils of victory. Their activity centred on the creation of immense standing armies, a host of state parasites and huge national debts. During the time of the absolute monarchy the machinery of state was a weapon of modern society against feudalism, a struggle crowned by the French revolution; under the first Bonaparte it served not only to suppress the revolution and annihilate all the liberties of the people, but it was also an instrument for the French revolution to strike outwards, to create on the Continent, in the French interest, instead of feudal monarchies numerous states after the French image. Under the Restoration and the July monarchy it [the machinery of state] became not only a means for the forcible class domination by the bourgeoisie but also a means of adding a second exploitation of the people to direct economic exploitation by assuring to bourgeois families all the good places in the State organization. At the time of the revolutionary struggle of 1848, finally, it was the means of destroying that revolution and all attempts at the emancipation of the masses. But this parasite only achieved its final stage of development under the Second Empire. The power of the government, with its standing army, its all-directing bureaucracy, its brutalizing clergy and its servile judicial hierarchy, had grown so independent of society itself, that a grotesquely mediocre adventurer with a greedy band of desperadoes behind him sufficed to manipulate it. It no longer needed the pretext of an armed coalition of old Europe against the modern world founded by the revolution of 1789. It no longer appeared as a means of class domination, subordinate to a parliamentary ministry or legislature. It injured in its rule even the interests of the ruling classes, whose parliamentary parade it replaced with self-elected legislative bodies and self-paid senates; it sanctioned its absolute authority by universal suffrage, and the acknowledged necessity of maintaining "order," that is the rule of the landowner and the capitalist over the producer; it hid, under the rags of a masquerade of the past, the orgies of corruption of the present and the victory of the parasitic faction of financial swindlers; thus, in giving way to all the *excesses* of the reactionary influences of the past—a pandemonium of infamy—the power of the state attained its final and supreme expression under the Second Empire. At first sight this seemed to be the final victory of the power of government over society but it was in fact the orgy of all corrupt elements of that society. To the uninitiated it appeared to be the victory of the executives over the legislature, of the final defeat of that form of class rule which pretends to be the self-government of society brought about by another of its forms pretending to be a power superior to society. In fact it was only the most degenerate, the only possible form of that class domination which was as humiliating to the ruling classes as to the working classes whom they kept in chains by their authority.

The 4 September was only the restoration of the republic against the grotesque adventurer who had strangled it. The true antithesis to the *Empire itself*—that is to the power of the state, the centralized executive power, of which the Second Empire was only the exhaustive form—was *the Commune.* That state power is in fact the creation of the bourgeoisie, first a means of breaking down feudalism, then a means of crushing the aspirations towards freedom of the producers, of the working class. All reactions and all revolutions have only served to transfer this organized might—this organized power for the enslavement of labor—from one hand to the other, from one faction of the ruling classes to another. It has served the ruling classes as a means of subjugation and self-enrichment. It has sucked new strengths from each new change. It has served as the instrument for crushing every popular rising and for suppressing the working classes after they had fought and had been made use of to secure the transfer of power from one group of their oppressors to another. Thus the Commune was not a revolution against this or that—legitimate, constitutional, republican or imperial—form of state power. It was a revolution against the *State* itself, against this unnatural abortion of society; it was a popular revival of the true social life of the people. It was not a revolution aimed at transferring authority from one faction of the ruling classes to another, but a revolution meant to destroy the abominable machinery of class-domination itself. It was not one of those petty struggles between the executive and parliamentary forms of class domination, but a revolt against both these forms which complement each other and of which the parliamentary form was only the deceptive appendage of the executive. The Second Empire was the final form of this state usurpation. The Commune was the definite negation of this state power and therefore the beginning of the social revolution of the 19th century. Whatever its fate has been in Paris, it will make *le tour du monde.* It was acclaimed both by the working classes of Europe and by those of the United States as the magic formula for freedom. The glories and the antediluvian deeds of the Prussian conqueror seemed only phantoms of a bygone age.

Only the working class could formulate this new aspiration in the word "Commune" and initiate it by the struggles of the Commune of Paris. Even the final expression of that state power—in the Second Empire—although it humbled the pride of the ruling classes and swept away their parliamentary pretensions to self-government, had been only the last possible form of their class rule. While politically dispossessing them, the Second Empire was the orgiastic culmination of all the economic and social infamies of their rule. The middle and lower ranks of the bourgeoisie were by their economic living conditions excluded from initiating a new revolution and compelled to follow in the wake of the ruling classes or to become the allies of the working class. The peasants were the passive economic foundation of the Second Empire, of that last triumph of a *State* separate from and independent of society. Only the proletariat, fired by the new social task which it has to accomplish for society as a whole, that of doing away with all classes and all class rule, were in a position to destroy the instrument of that class rule—the state—that centralized and organized authority claiming to be the master instead of the servant of society. The Second Empire, at once the last coronation and the most signal prostitution of the state, which had taken over the place of the medieval church, arose out of the active struggle of the ruling classes, passively supported by the peasants, against the proletariat. It had sprung to life against them. And by them it was destroyed, not as a special form of (centralized) authority, but as its fullest and most powerful expression of apparent independence from society, and thus also its basest reality, covered in shame from head to foot, whose essence was absolute corruption at home and absolute powerlessness abroad.

But this one form of class rule had only broken down to make executive power, the state machinery of government, the great and single object of attack by the revolution.

Parliamentary government in France had come to an

end. Its last term and fullest authority was in the parliamentary republic from May 1848 to the *coup d'état*. The Empire that killed it was its own creation. Under the Empire with its *corps législatif* and its senate—and in this form it has been reproduced in the military monarchies of Prussia and Austria—parliamentary government was a mere farce, a mere appendage of despotism in its crudest form. Parliamentarianism thus was dead in France and the workers' revolution certainly did not mean to restore it to life.

The *Commune* is the resumption of the authority of the state by society as its own living power instead of as a power controlling and subduing society; it is the resumption of authority by the masses themselves, forming their own power in place of the organized power of their oppression; it is the political form of their social emancipation instead of being an artificial power (appropriated by their oppressors) (their own power opposed to and organized against their oppressors) of society manipulated for oppression by their enemies. The form was simple like all great things. In contrast to earlier revolutions—where the time necessary for any historical development had in the past always been lost and where in the first days of popular victory, as soon as the people had laid down their arms, these had been turned against them—the Commune began by replacing the army by the National Guard. "For the first time since 4 September the republic has been liberated from *the government of its enemies* . . . in the city a national militia defends the citizens against authority (the government) *instead of a standing army defending the government against the citizens.*" (*Proclamation* of the Central Committee of 22 March.)

(The people had only to organize this militia on a national scale, to do away with the standing army; this is the first economic *conditio sine qua non* for all social improvements, abolishing at once this source of taxes and state debt, and this constant danger of government usurpation by class rule—either of regular class rule or that of an adventurer pretending to save all the classes.) At the same time it is the safest guarantee against foreign aggression which actually makes a costly military apparatus impossible in all other states; it is the emancipation of the peasant from bloodtax and [from being] the most productive source of all state taxation and state debts. This is already the point at which the Commune is an *incentive to the peasant* and the first word of his emancipation. The "independent police-force" is abolished and its ruffians replaced by servants of the Commune. Universal suffrage, till now abused either as parliamentary sanction of the Holy Authority of the State, or as a toy in the hands of the ruling classes, and only employed by the people once in many years to sanction (choose the instruments of) parliamentary class rule, is put to its proper use: the choice by communities of their own administrative and legislative officers. The removal of the delusion that administration and political direction were mysteries, transcendental functions only to be entrusted to the hands of a trained caste—state parasites, richly paid sycophants and sinecurists in the higher posts, who absorb the educated members of the masses and turn them against themselves in the lower places of the hierarchy. The abolition of the state hierarchy altogether and the replacement of the haughty rulers of the nation by its servants, who can be dismissed at any time, of the appearance of responsibility by a real responsibility, since they act under constant public supervision. Paid like skilled workmen, 12 pounds a month, the highest salary not exceeding 240 pounds a year—a salary, according to a great scientific authority Professor Huxley, rather more than one fifth of what would satisfy a clerk of the Metropolitan School Board. The whole deception of state mysteries and state claims was abolished by a Commune which is largely composed of simple working men, who are organizing the defence of Paris, waging war against the Bonapartist Praetorian Guard, ensuring supplies for this immense city, filling all positions hitherto divided between government, police, and prefecture; they do their work openly, simply, under the most difficult and complicated circumstances, and do it, as Milton wrote his *Paradise Lost*, for a few pounds; they act publicly, with no pretensions to infallibility, not hiding themselves behind official evasions, and are not ashamed to confess blunders while at the same time correcting them. At one stroke they make public duties—military, administrative, political—*real workmen's duties*, instead of the hidden attributes of a trained caste; (keep order in the turbulence of civil war and revolution) (initiate measures of general restoration). Whatever the merits of individual measures of the Commune may be, its greatest measure was the creation of the Commune itself, born at a time when the foreign enemy stood at one door and the class enemy at the other; it demonstrates its vitality by its existence and confirms its theories by its actions. Its appearance was a victory over the victors of France. Captive Paris took back in one bold move the leadership of Europe, not through dependence on brute force, but by leading a social movement embodying the aspirations of the working classes of all countries.

If all great towns organized themselves into Communes on the Parisian model, no government could suppress this movement by the sudden advance of reaction. Just through this preparatory step, time for inner development, the guarantee of the movement, would be won. All France would organize itself into spontaneous self-governing communes, the standing army would be replaced by a national militia, the army of state-parasites removed, the ecclesiastical hierarchy replaced by schoolmasters, the state courts transformed into organs of the Commune; the elections of national representatives not a conjuring display by an all-powerful government but the deliberate expression of organized communes; the offices of state would be reduced to a few only for general national purposes.

Such is the *Commune—the political form of social emancipation*, of the liberation of labor from usurpation (slavery) by the monopolists of the means of labor which were created by the laborers themselves or are the gift of nature. Just as the state machinery and parliamentary government are not the real life of the ruling classes, but only the organized general organs of their rule, the political guarantees, forms and expressions of the old order of things, so the Commune is not the social movement of the working class and consequently of a general regeneration of mankind, but its organized means of action. The Commune does not do away with the class struggle, through which the working classes strive for the abolition of all classes and, therefore, of all [class rule] (because it represents no special interest. It represents the liberation of "labor," that is of the fundamental and natural conditions of individual and social life which can only be imposed by the minority upon the majority through usurpation, fraud, and artificial contrivances) but it creates the rational intermediate stage in which this class struggle can pass through its different phases in the most rational and humane way. The Commune can arouse violent reactions and just as violent revolutions. It begins the *emancipation of labor*—its great goal—by doing away with the unproductive and harmful operations of state parasites, on the one hand by removing the causes for the sacrifice of an immense part of the national product to the satisfaction of the state monster and on the other by performing the actual work of administration, local and national, for workingmen's wages. It begins therefore with an immense saving, with economic reform as well as political transformation.

Once communal organization is firmly established on a national scale, the catastrophes it might still have to undergo, sporadic slave-owners' rebellions while momentarily interrupting the work of peaceful progress, would really only accelerate the movement, by giving a sword into the hand of the Social Revolution.

The working class knows that it has to pass through different phases of the class struggle. It knows that replacing the economic conditions of class labor by the conditions of free and cooperative labor can only be the progressive work of time, that this (economic transformation) requires not only a change in distribution, but also a new organization of production or, better still, the liberation (setting free) from the chains of slavery, from its present class character, of the social forms of production in labor as at present organized (produced by contemporary industry) and their harmonious national and international coordination. The working class know that this work of regeneration will be repeatedly delayed and impeded by the resistance of vested interests and class egoisms. They know that the present "spontaneous action of the natural laws of capital and landed property" can only be superseded by "the spontaneous action of the laws of the social economy of free and associated labor" through a long process of development of new conditions, just as the "spontaneous action of the economic laws of slavery" and the "spontaneous action of the economic laws of serfdom" were. But at the same time they know that great strides may be made immediately through the communal form of political organization and that the time has come to begin that movement for themselves and for mankind.

MEW 17, 538–49.

MARGINAL NOTES TO THE PROGRAMME OF THE GERMAN WORKERS' PARTY [Critique of the Gotha Programme]

I

1. "Labour is the source of all wealth and all culture, *and since* useful labour is possible only in society and through society, the proceeds of labour belong undiminished with equal right to all members of society."

First Part of the Paragraph: "Labour is the source of all wealth and all culture."

Labour is *not the source* of all wealth. *Nature* is just as much the source of use values (and it is surely of such that material wealth consists!) as labour, which itself is only the manifestation of a force of nature, human labour power. The above phrase is to be found in all children's primers and is correct in so far as it is *implied* that labour is performed with the appurtenant subjects and instruments. But a socialist programme cannot allow such bourgeois phrases to pass over in silence the *conditions* that alone give them meaning. And in so far as man from the beginning behaves towards nature, the primary source of all instruments and subjects of labour, as an owner, treats her as belonging to him, his labour becomes the source of use values, therefore also of wealth. The bourgeois have very good grounds for falsely ascribing *supernatural creative power* to labour; since precisely from the fact that labour depends on nature it follows that the man who possesses no other property than his labour power must, in all conditions of society and culture, be the slave of other men who have made themselves the owners of the material conditions of labour. He can work only with their permission, hence live only with their permission.

Let us now leave the sentence as it stands, or rather limps. What would one have expected in conclusion? Obviously this:

"Since labour is the source of all wealth, no one in society can appropriate wealth except as the product of labour. Therefore, if he himself does not work, he lives by the labour of others and also acquires his culture at the expense of the labour of others."

Instead of this, by means of the verbal rivet *"and since"* a second proposition is added in order to draw a conclusion from this and not from the first one.

Second Part of the Paragraph: "Useful labour is possible only in society and through society."

According to the first proposition, labour was the source of all wealth and all culture; therefore no society is possible without labour. Now we learn, conversely, that no "useful" labour is possible without society.

One could just as well have said that only in society can useless and even socially harmful labour become a branch of gainful occupation, that only in society can one live by being idle, etc., etc.—in short, one could just as well have copied the whole of Rousseau.

And what is "useful" labour? Surely only labour which produces the intended useful result. A savage—and man was a savage after he had ceased to be an ape—who kills an animal with a stone, who collects fruits, etc., performs "useful" labour.

Thirdly. The Conclusion: "And since useful labour is possible only in society and through society, the proceeds of labour belong undiminished with equal right to all members of society."

A fine conclusion! If useful labour is possible only in society and through society, the proceeds of labour belong to society—and only so much therefrom accrues to the individual worker as is not required to maintain the "condition" of labour, society.

In fact, this proposition has at all times been made use

of by the champions of the *state of society prevailing at any given time*. First come the claims of the government and everything that sticks to it, since it is the social organ for the maintenance of the social order; then come the claims of the various kinds of private property, for the various kinds of private property are the foundations of society, etc. One sees that such hollow phrases can be twisted and turned as desired.

The first and second parts of the paragraph have some intelligible connection only in the following wording:

"Labour becomes the source of wealth and culture only as social labour," or, what is the same thing, "in and through society."

This proposition is incontestably correct, for although isolated labour (its material conditions presupposed) can create use values, it can create neither wealth nor culture.

But equally incontestable is this other proposition:

"In proportion as labour develops socially, and becomes thereby a source of wealth and culture, poverty and destitution develop among the workers, and wealth and culture among the non-workers."

This is the law of all history hitherto. What, therefore, had to be done here, instead of setting down general phrases about "labour" and "society," was to prove concretely how in present capitalist society the material, etc., conditions have at last been created which enable and compel the workers to lift this social curse.

In fact, however, the whole paragraph, bungled in style and content, is only there in order to inscribe the "Lassallean catchword of the "undiminished proceeds of labour" as a slogan at the top of the party banner. I shall return later to the "proceeds of labour," "equal right," etc., since the same thing recurs in a somewhat different form further on.

2. "In present-day society, the instruments of labour are the monopoly of the capitalist class: the re-

sulting dependence of the working class is the cause of misery and servitude in all its forms."

This sentence, borrowed from the Rules of the International, is incorrect in this "improved" edition.

In present-day society the instruments of labour are the monopoly of the landowners (the monopoly of property in land is even the basis of the monopoly of capital) *and* the capitalists. In the passage in question, the Rules of the International do not mention either the one or the other class of monopolists. They speak of the *"monopoliser of the means of labour,* that is, *the sources of life."* The addition, *"sources of life,"* makes it sufficiently clear that land is included in the instruments of labour.

The correction was introduced because Lassalle, for reasons now generally known, attacked *only* the capitalist class and not the landowners. In England, the capitalist is usually not even the owner of the land on which his factory stands.

3. "The emancipation of labour demands the promotion of the instruments of labour to the common property of society and the co-operative regulation of the total labour with a fair distribution of the proceeds of labour."

"Promotion of the instruments of labour to the common property" ought obviously to read their "conversion into the common property"; but this only in passing.

What are "proceeds of labour"? The product of labour or its value? And in the latter case, is it the total value of the product or only that part of the value which labour has newly added to the value of the means of production consumed?

"Proceeds of labour" is a loose notion which Lassalle has put in the place of definite economic conceptions.

What is "a fair distribution"?

Do not the bourgeois assert that the present-day distribution is "fair"? And is it not, in fact, the only "fair" distribution on the basis of the present-day mode of production? Are economic relations regulated by legal conceptions or do not, on the contrary, legal relations arise from economic ones? Have not also the socialist sectarians the most varied notions about "fair" distribution?

To understand what is implied in this connection by the phrase "fair distribution," we must take the first paragraph and this one together. The latter presupposes a society wherein "the instruments of labour are common property and the total labour is co-operatively regulated," and from the first paragraph we learn that "the proceeds of labour belong undiminished with equal right to all members of society."

"To all members of society"? To those who do not work as well? What remains then of the "undiminished proceeds of labour?" Only to those members of society who work? What remains then of the "equal right" of all members of society?

But "all members of society" and "equal right" are obviously mere phrases. The kernel consists in this, that in this communist society every worker must receive the "undiminished" Lassallean "proceeds of labour."

Let us take first of all the words "proceeds of labour" in the sense of the product of labour; then the co-operative proceeds of labour are the *total social product*.

From this must now be deducted:

First, cover for replacement of the means of production used up.

Secondly, additional portion for expansion of production.

Thirdly, reserve or insurance funds to provide against accidents, dislocations caused by natural calamities, etc.

These deductions from the "undiminished proceeds of labour" are an economic necessity and their magnitude is to be determined according to available means and forces, and partly by computation of probabilities, but they are in no way calculable by equity.

There remains the other part of the total product, intended to serve as means of consumption.

Before this is divided among the individuals, there has to be deducted again, from it:

First, the general costs of administration not belonging to production.

This part will, from the outset, be very considerably restricted in comparison with present-day society and it diminishes in proportion as the new society develops.

Secondly, that which is intended for the common satisfaction of needs, such as schools, health services, etc.

From the outset this part grows considerably in comparison with present-day society and it grows in proportion as the new society develops.

Thirdly, funds for those unable to work, etc., in short, for what is included under so-called official poor relief today.

Only now do we come to the "distribution" which the programme, under Lassallean influence, alone has in view in its narrow fashion, namely, to that part of the means of consumption which is divided among the individual producers of the co-operative society.

The "undiminished proceeds of labour" have already unnoticeably become converted into the "diminished" proceeds, although what the producer is deprived of in his capacity as a private individual benefits him directly or indirectly in his capacity as a member of society.

Just as the phrase of the "undiminished proceeds of labour" has disappeared, so now does the phrase of the "proceeds of labour" disappear altogether.

Within the co-operative society based on common ownership of the means of production, the producers do not exchange their products; just as little does the labour employed on the products appear here *as the value* of these products, as a material quality possessed by them, since now, in contrast to capitalist society, individual labour no longer exists in an indirect fashion but directly as a component part of the total labour. The phrase "proceeds of labour," objectionable also today on account of its ambiguity, thus loses all meaning.

What we have to deal with here is a communist society, not as it has *developed* on its own foundations, but, on the contrary, just as it *emerges* from capitalist society; which is thus in every respect, economically, morally and intellectually, still stamped with the birth marks of the old society from whose womb it emerges. Accordingly, the individual producer receives back from society—after the deductions have been made—exactly what he gives to it. What he has given to it is his individual quantum of labour. For example, the social working day consists of the sum of the individual hours of work; the individual labour time of the individual producer is the part of the social working day contributed by him, his share in it. He receives a certificate from society that he has furnished such and such an amount of labour (after deducting his labour for the common funds), and with this certificate he draws from the social stock of means of consumption as much as costs the same amount of labour. The same amount of labour which he has given to society in one form he receives back in another.

Here obviously the same principle prevails as that which regulates the exchange of commodities, as far as this is exchange of equal values. Content and form are changed, because under the altered circumstances no one can give anything except his labour, and because, on the other hand, nothing can pass to the ownership of individuals except individual means of consumption. But, as far as the distribution of the latter among the individual producers is concerned, the same principle prevails as in the exchange of commodity-equivalents: a given amount of labour in one form is exchanged for an equal amount of labour in another form.

Hence, *equal right* here is still in principle—*bourgeois right*, although principle and practice are no longer at loggerheads, while the exchange of equivalents in commodity exchange only exists *on the average* and not in the individual case.

In spite of this advance, this *equal right* is still constantly stigmatised by a bourgeois limitation. The right of the producers is *proportional* to the labour they supply; the equality consists in the fact that measurement is made with an *equal standard*, labour.

But one man is superior to another physically or mentally and so supplies more labour in the same time, or can labour for a longer time; and labour, to serve as a measure, must be defined by its duration or intensity, otherwise it ceases to be a standard of measurement. This *equal* right is an unequal right for unequal labour. It recognises no class differences, because everyone is only a worker like everyone else; but it tacitly recognises unequal individual endowment and thus productive capacity as natural privileges. *It is, therefore, a right of inequality, in its content, like every right.* Right by its very nature can consist only in the application of an equal standard; but unequal individuals (and they would not be different individuals if they were not unequal) are measurable only by an equal standard in so far as they are brought under an equal point of view, are taken from one *definite* side only, for instance, in the present case, are regarded *only as workers* and nothing more is seen in them, everything else being ignored. Further, one worker is married, another not; one has more children than another, and so on and so forth. Thus, with an equal performance of labour, and hence an equal share in the social consumption fund, one will in fact receive more than another, one will be richer than another, and so on. To avoid all these defects, right instead of being equal would have to be unequal.

But these defects are inevitable in the first phase of communist society as it is when it has just emerged after prolonged birth pangs from capitalist society. Right can never be higher than the economic structure of society and its cultural development conditioned thereby.

In a higher phase of communist society, after the en-slaving subordination of the individual to the division of labour, and therewith also the antithesis between mental and physical labour, has vanished; after labour has be-come not only a means of life but life's prime want; after the productive forces have also increased with the all-round development of the individual, and all the springs of co-operative wealth flow more abundantly—only then can the narrow horizon of bourgeois right be crossed in its entirety and society inscribe on its banners: From each according to his ability, to each according to his needs!

I have dealt more at length with the "undiminished proceeds of labour," on the one hand, and with "equal right" and "fair distribution," on the other, in order to show what a crime it is to attempt, on the one hand, to force on our Party again, as dogmas, ideas which in a cer-tain period had some meaning but have now become ob-solete verbal rubbish, while again perverting, on the other, the realistic outlook, which it cost so much effort to instil into the Party but which has now taken root in it, by means of ideological nonsense about right and other trash so common among the democrats and French Socialists.

Quite apart from the analysis so far given, it was in gen-eral a mistake to make a fuss about so-called *distribution* and put the principal stress on it.

Any distribution whatever of the means of consump-tion is only a consequence of the distribution of the con-ditions of production themselves. The latter distribution, however, is a feature of the mode of production itself. The capitalist mode of production, for example, rests on the fact that the material conditions of production are in the hands of non-workers in the form of property in capital and land, while the masses are only owners of the personal condition of production, of labour power. If the elements of production are so distributed, then the present-day distribution of the means of consumption results automatically. If the material conditions of production are the co-operative property of the workers themselves, then there likewise results a distribution of the means of consumption different from the present one. Vulgar socialism (and from it in turn a section of the democracy) has taken over from the bourgeois economists the consideration and treatment of distribution as independent of the mode of production and hence the presentation of socialism as turning principally on distribution. After the real relation has long been made clear, why retrogress again?

4. "The emancipation of labour must be the work of the working class, relatively to which all other classes are *only one reactionary mass*."

The first strophe is taken from the introductory words of the Rules of the International, but "improved." There it is said: "The emancipation of the working class must be the act of the workers themselves"; here, on the contrary, the "working class" has to emancipate—what? "Labour." Let him understand who can.

In compensation, the antistrophe, on the other hand, is a Lassallean quotation of the first water: "relatively to which (the working class) all other classes are *only one reactionary mass*."

In the *Communist Manifesto* it is said: "Of all the classes that stand face to face with the bourgeoisie today, the proletariat alone is a *really revolutionary class*. The other classes decay and finally disappear in the face of Modern Industry; the proletariat is its special and essential product."

The bourgeoisie is here conceived as a revolutionary class—as the bearer of large-scale industry—relatively to the feudal lords and the lower middle class, who desire to maintain all social positions that are the creation of obsolete modes of production. Thus they do not form *together* with the *bourgeoisie* only one reactionary mass.

On the other hand, the proletariat is revolutionary relatively to the bourgeoisie because, having itself grown up on the basis of large-scale industry, it strives to strip off from production the capitalist character that the bourgeoisie seeks to perpetuate. But the *Manifesto* adds that the "lower middle class" is becoming revolutionary "in view of [its] impending transfer into the proletariat."

From this point of view, therefore, it is again nonsense to say that it, together with the bourgeoisie, and with the feudal lords into the bargain, "forms only one reactionary mass" relatively to the working class.

. Has one proclaimed to the artisans, small manufacturers, etc., and *peasants* during the last elections: Relatively to us you, together with the bourgeoisie and feudal lords, form only one reactionary mass?

Lassalle knew the *Communist Manifesto* by heart, as his faithful followers know the gospels written by him. If, therefore, he has falsified it so grossly, this has occurred only to put a good colour on his alliance with absolutist and feudal opponents against the bourgeoisie.

In the above paragraph, moreover, his oracular saying is dragged in by main force without any connection with the botched quotation from the Rules of the International. Thus it is here simply an impertinence, and indeed not at all displeasing to Herr Bismarck, one of those cheap pieces of insolence in which the Marat of Berlin deals.

5. "The working class strives for its emancipation first of all *within the framework of the present-day national state*, conscious that the necessary result of its efforts, which are common to the workers of all civilised countries, will be the international brotherhood of peoples."

Lassalle, in opposition to the *Communist Manifesto* and to all earlier socialism, conceived the workers' movement from the narrowest national standpoint. He is being followed in this—and that after the work of the International!

It is altogether self-evident that, to be able to fight at all, the working class must organise itself, at home *as a class* and that its own country is the immediate arena of its struggle. In so far its class struggle is national, not in substance, but, as the *Communist Manifesto* says, "in form." But the "framework of the present-day national state," for instance, the German Empire, is itself in its turn economically "within the framework" of the world market, politically "within the framework" of the system of states. Every businessman knows that German trade is at the same time foreign trade, and the greatness of Herr Bismarck consists, to be sure, precisely in his pursuing a kind of *international* policy.

And to what does the German Workers' Party reduce its internationalism? To the consciousness that the result of its efforts will be *"the international brotherhood of peoples"*—a phrase borrowed from the bourgeois League of Peace and Freedom, which is intended to pass as equivalent to the international brotherhood of the working classes in the joint struggle against the ruling classes and their governments. Not a word, therefore, *about the international functions* of the German working class! And it is thus that it is to challenge its own bourgeoisie—which is already linked up in brotherhood against it with the bourgeois of all other countries—and Herr Bismarck's international policy of conspiracy!

In fact, the internationalism of the programme stands *even infinitely below* that of the Free Trade Party. The latter also asserts that the result of its efforts will be "the international brotherhood of peoples." But it also *does* something to make trade international and by no means contents itself with the consciousness—that all peoples are carrying on trade at home.

The international activity of the working classes does

not in any way depend on the existence of the *International Working Men's Association*. This was only the first attempt to create a central organ for that activity; an attempt which was a lasting success on account of the impulse which it gave but which was no longer realisable in its *first historical form* after the fall of the Paris Commune.

Bismarck's *Norddeutsche* was absolutely right when it announced, to the satisfaction of its master, that the German Workers' Party had sworn off internationalism in the new programme.

II

"Starting from these basic principles, the German Workers' Party strives by all legal means for the *free state—and—*socialist society; the abolition of the wage system *together with* the *iron law of wages—* and—exploitation in every form; the elimination of all social and political inequality."

I shall return to the "free" state later.

So, in future, the German Workers' Party has got to believe in Lassalle's "iron law of wages"! That this may not be lost, the nonsense is perpetrated of speaking of the "abolition of the wage system" (it should read: system of wage labour) *"together with* the iron law of wages." If I abolish wage labour, then naturally I abolish its laws also, whether they are of "iron" or sponge. But Lassalle's attack on wage labour turns almost solely on this so-called law. In order, therefore, to prove that Lassalle's sect has conquered, the "wage system" must be abolished *"together with* the iron law of wages" and not without it.

It is well known that nothing of the "iron law of wages" is Lassalle's except the word "iron" borrowed from Goethe's "great, eternal iron laws." The word *iron* is a label by which the true believers recognise one another.

But if I take the law with Lassalle's stamp on it and, consequently, in his sense, then I must also take it with his substantiation for it. And what is that? As Lange already showed, shortly after Lassalle's death, it is the Malthusian theory of population (preached by Lange himself). But if this theory is correct, then again I *cannot* abolish the law even if I abolish wage labour a hundred times over, because the law then governs not only the system of wage labour but *every* social system. Basing themselves directly on this, the economists have been proving for fifty years and more that socialism cannot abolish poverty, *which has its basis in nature*, but can only make it *general*, distribute it simultaneously over the whole surface of society!

But all this is not the main thing. *Quite apart* from the *false* Lassallean formulation of the law, the truly outrageous retrogression consists in the following:

Since Lassalle's death there has asserted itself in *our* Party the scientific understanding that wages are not what they *appear* to be, namely, the *value*, or *price*, *of labour*, but only a masked form for the *value*, or *price*, *of labour power*. Thereby the whole bourgeois conception of wages hitherto, as well as all the criticism hitherto directed against this conception, was thrown overboard once for all and it was made clear that the wage-worker has permission to work for his own subsistence, that is, *to live*, only in so far as he works for a certain time gratis for the capitalist (and hence also for the latter's co-consumers of surplus value); that the whole capitalist system of production turns on the increase of this gratis labour by extending the working day or by developing the productivity, that is, increasing the intensity of labour power, etc.; that, consequently, the system of wage labour is a system of slavery, and indeed of a slavery which becomes more severe in proportion as the social productive forces of labour develop, whether the worker receives better or worse payment. And after this understanding has gained more and more ground in our Party, one returns to Lassalle's dogmas although one must have known that Lassalle *did not know* what wages were, but following in the wake of the bourgeois economists took the appearance for the essence of the matter.

It is as if, among slaves who have at last got behind the secret of slavery and broken out in rebellion, a slave still in thrall to obsolete notions were to inscribe on the programme of the rebellion: Slavery must be abolished because the feeding of slaves in the system of slavery cannot exceed a certain low maximum!

Does not the mere fact that the representatives of our Party were capable of perpetrating such a monstrous attack on the understanding that has spread among the mass of our Party prove by itself with what criminal levity and with what lack of conscience they set to work in drawing up this compromise programme!

Instead of the indefinite concluding phrase of the paragraph, "the elimination of all social and political inequality," it ought to have been said that with the abolition of class distinctions all social and political inequality arising from them would disappear of itself.

III

"The German Workers' Party, in order *to pave the way to the solution of the social question,* demands the establishment of producers' co-operative societies *with state aid under the democratic control of the toiling people.* The producers' co-operative societies *are to be called into being* for industry and agriculture on such a scale *that the socialist organisation of the total labour will arise from them.*"

After the Lassallean "iron law of wages," the physic of the prophet. The way to it is "paved" in worthy fashion. In place of the existing class struggle appears a newspaper scribbler's phrase: "the social *question*," to the "*solution*" of which one "paves the way." Instead of arising from the revolutionary process of transformation of society, the "socialist organisation of the total labour" "arises" from the "state aid" that the state gives to the producers' co-operative societies and which the *state*, not the worker, "*calls into being.*" It is worthy of Lassalle's imagination that with state loans one can build a new society just as well as a new railway!

From the remnants of a sense of shame, "state aid" has been put—under the democratic control of the "toiling people."

In the first place, the majority of the "toiling people" in Germany consists of peasants, and not of proletarians.

Secondly, "democratic" means in German "*volksherrs-chaftlich*" ["by the rule of the people"]. But what does "control by the rule of the people of the toiling people" mean? And particularly in the case of a toiling people which, through these demands that it puts to the state, ex-presses its full consciousness that it neither rules nor is ripe for ruling!

It would be superfluous to deal here with the criticism of the recipe prescribed by Buchez in the reign of Louis Philippe in *opposition* to the French Socialists and ac-cepted by the reactionary workers of the *Atelier*. The chief offence does not lie in having inscribed this specific nostrum in the programme, but in taking, in general, a ret-rograde step from the standpoint of a class movement to that of a sectarian movement.

That the workers desire to establish the conditions for co-operative production on a social scale, and first of all on a national scale, in their own country, only means that they are working to revolutionise the present conditions of production, and it has nothing in common with the foun-dation of co-operative societies with state aid. But as far as the present co-operative societies are concerned, they are of value *only* in so far as they are the independent crea-tions of the workers and not protégés either of the govern-ments or of the bourgeois.

IV

I come now to the democratic section.

A. *The free basis of the state.*

First of all, according to II, the German Workers' Party strives for "the free state."

Free state—what is this?

It is by no means the aim of the workers, who have got rid of the narrow mentality of humble subjects, to set the state free. In the German Empire the "state" is almost as "free" as in Russia. Freedom consists in converting the state from an organ superimposed upon society into one completely subordinate to it, and today, too, the forms of state are more free or less free to the extent that they restrict the "freedom of the state."

The German Workers' Party—at least if it adopts the programme—shows that its socialist ideas are not even skin-deep; in that, instead of treating existing society (and this holds good for any future one) as the *basis* of the existing state (or of the future state in the case of future society), it treats the state rather as an independent entity that possesses its own *intellectual, ethical and libertarian bases.*

And what of the riotous misuse which the programme makes of the words *"present-day state," "present-day society,"* and of the still more riotous misconception it creates in regard to the state to which it addresses its demands?

"Present-day society" is capitalist society, which exists in all civilised countries, more or less free from medieval admixture, more or less modified by the particular historical development of each country, more or less developed. On the other hand, the "present-day state" changes with a country's frontier. It is different in the Prusso-German

Empire from what it is in Switzerland, and different in England from what it is in the United States. "The present-day state" is, therefore, a fiction.

Nevertheless, the different states of the different civilised countries, in spite of their motley diversity of form, all have this in common, that they are based on modern bourgeois society, only one more or less capitalistically developed. They have, therefore, also certain essential characteristics in common. In this sense it is possible to speak of the "present-day state," in contrast with the future, in which its present root, bourgeois society, will have died off.

The question then arises: what transformation will the state undergo in communist society? In other words, what social functions will remain in existence there that are analogous to present state functions? This question can only be answered scientifically, and one does not get a flea-hop nearer to the problem by a thousandfold combination of the word people with the word state.

Between capitalist and communist society lies the period of the revolutionary transformation of the one into the other. Corresponding to this is also a political transition period in which the state can be nothing but *the revolutionary dictatorship of the proletariat.*

Now the programme does not deal with this nor with the future state of communist society.

Its political demands contain nothing beyond the old democratic litany familiar to all: universal suffrage, direct legislation, popular rights, a people's militia, etc. They are a mere echo of the bourgeois People's Party, of the League of Peace and Freedom. They are all demands which, in so far as they are not exaggerated in fantastic presentation, have already been *realised.* Only the state to which they belong does not lie within the borders of the German Empire, but in Switzerland, the United States, etc. This sort of "state of the future" is a present-day state, although existing outside the "framework" of the German Empire. But one thing has been forgotten. Since the German Workers' Party expressly declares that it acts within "the present-day national state," hence within *its own* state, the Prusso-German Empire—its demands would indeed otherwise be largely meaningless, since one only demands what one has not got—it should not have forgotten the chief thing, namely, that all those pretty little gewgaws rest on the recognition of the so-called sovereignty of the people and hence are appropriate only in a *democratic republic*.

Since one has not the courage—and wisely so, for the circumstances demand caution—to demand the democratic republic, as the French workers' programmes under Louis Philippe and under Louis Napoleon did, one should not have resorted, either, to the subterfuge, neither "honest" nor decent, of demanding things which have meaning only in a democratic republic from a state which is nothing but a police-guarded military despotism, embellished with parliamentary forms, alloyed with a feudal admixture, already influenced by the bourgeoisie and bureaucratically carpentered, and then to assure this state into the bargain that one imagines one will be able to force such things upon it "by legal means."

Even vulgar democracy, which sees the millennium in the democratic republic and has no suspicion that it is precisely in this last form of state of bourgeois society that the class struggle has to be fought out to a conclusion—even it towers mountains above this kind of democratism which keeps within the limits of what is permitted by the police and not permitted by logic.

That, in fact, by the word "state" is meant the government machine, or the state in so far as it forms a special organism separated from society through division of labour, is shown by the words "the German Workers' Party demands *as the economic basis of the state:* a single progressive income tax," etc. Taxes are the economic basis of the government machinery and of nothing else. In the state of the future, existing in Switzerland, this demand has been pretty well fulfilled. Income tax presupposes various sources of income of the various social classes, and hence capitalist society. It is, therefore, nothing remarkable that the Liverpool financial reformers, bourgeois headed by Gladstone's brother, are putting forward the same demand as the programme.

B. The German Workers' Party demands as the intellectual and ethical basis of the state:
1. Universal and *equal elementary education* by the state. Universal compulsory school attendance. Free instruction.

Equal elementary education? What idea lies behind these words? Is it believed that in present-day society (and it is only with this one has to deal) education can be *equal* for all classes? Or is it demanded that the upper classes also shall be compulsorily reduced to the modicum of education—the elementary school—that alone is compatible with the economic conditions not only of the wage-workers but of the peasants as well?

"Universal compulsory school attendance. Free instruction." The former exists even in Germany, the second in Switzerland and in the United States in the case of elementary schools. If in some states of the latter country higher educational institutions are also "free" that only means in fact defraying the cost of the education of the upper classes from the general tax receipts. Incidentally, the same holds good for "free administration of justice" demanded under A. 5. The administration of criminal justice is to be had free everywhere; that of civil justice is concerned almost exclusively with conflicts over property and hence affects almost exclusively the possessing classes.

Are they to carry on their litigation at the expense of the national coffers?

The paragraph on the schools should at least have demanded technical schools (theoretical and practical) in combination with the elementary school.

"Elementary education by the state" is altogether objectionable. Defining by a general law the expenditures on the elementary schools, the qualifications of the teaching staff, the branches of instruction, etc., and, as is done in the United States, supervising the fulfilment of these legal specifications by state inspectors, is a very different thing from appointing the state as the educator of the people! Government and Church should rather be equally excluded from any influence on the school. Particularly, indeed, in the Prusso-German Empire (and one should not take refuge in the rotten subterfuge that one is speaking of a "state of the future"; we have seen how matters stand in this respect) the state has need, on the contrary, of a very stern education by the people.

But the whole programme, for all its democratic clang, is tainted through and through by the Lassallean sect's servile belief in the state, or, what is no better, by a democratic belief in miracles, or rather it is a compromise between these two kinds of belief in miracles, both equally remote from socialism.

"Freedom of science" says a paragraph of the Prussian Constitution. Why, then, here?

"Freedom of conscience"! If one desired at this time of the *Kulturkampf* to remind liberalism of its old catchwords, it surely could have been done only in the following form: Everyone should be able to attend to his religious as well as his bodily needs without the police sticking their noses in. But the workers' party ought at any rate in this connection to have expressed its awareness of the fact that bourgeois "freedom of conscience" is nothing but the toleration of all possible kinds of *religious*

freedom of conscience, and that for its part it endeavours rather to liberate the conscience from the witchery or religion. But one chooses not to transgress the "bourgeois" level.

I have now come to the end, for the appendix that now follows in the programme does not constitute a characteristic component part of it. Hence I can be very brief here.

2. *Normal working day.*

In no other country has the workers' party limited itself to such an indefinite demand, but has always fixed the length of the working day that it considers normal under the given circumstances.

3. "Restriction of female labour and prohibition of child labour."

The standardisation of the working day must include the restriction of female labour, in so far as it relates to the duration, intermissions, etc., of the working day: otherwise it could only mean the exclusion of female labour from branches of industry that are especially unhealthy for the female body or are objectionable morally for the female sex. If that is what was meant, it should have been said so.

"*Prohibition of child labour.*" Here it was absolutely essential to state the age limit.

A *general prohibition* of child labour is incompatible with the existence of large-scale industry and hence an empty, pious wish. Its realisation—if it were possible—would be reactionary, since, with a strict regulation of the working time according to the different age groups and other safety measures for the protection of children, an early combination of productive labour with education is one of the most potent means for the transformation of present-day society.

4. "State supervision of factory, workshop and domestic industry."

In consideration of the Prusso-German state it should definitely have been demanded that the inspectors are to be removable only by a court of law; that any worker can have them prosecuted for neglect of duty; that they must belong to the medical profession.

5. "Regulation of prison labour."

A petty demand in a general workers' programme. In any case, it should have been clearly stated that there is no intention from fear of competition to allow ordinary criminals to be treated like beasts, and especially that there is no desire to deprive them of their sole means of betterment, productive labour. This was surely the least one might have expected from Socialists.

6. "An effective liability law."

It should have been stated what is meant by an "effective" liability law.

Be it noted, incidentally, that in speaking of the normal working day the part of factory legislation that deals with health regulations and safety measures, etc., has been overlooked. The liability law only comes into operation when these regulations are infringed.

In short, this appendix also is distinguished by slovenly editing.

Dixi et salvavi animam meam. [I have spoken and saved my soul.]

MEW 19, 15–32, as translated in Karl Marx and Frederick Engels, *Selected Works*, 3 vols., Moscow, 1969, Vol. III, pp. 13–30.

1882

PREFACE TO THE RUSSIAN EDITION OF THE *COMMUNIST MANIFESTO*

The first Russian edition of the *Manifesto of the Communist Party*, translated by Bakunin, was published early in the sixties by the printing office of the *Kolokol*. Then the West could see in it (the *Russian* edition of the Manifesto) only a literary curiosity. Such a view would be impossible today.

What a limited field the proletarian movement still occupied at that time (December 1847) is most clearly shown by the last section of the Manifesto: the position of the Communists in relation to the various opposition parties in the various countries. Precisely Russia and the United States are missing here. It was the time when Russia constituted the last great reserve of all European reaction, when the United States absorbed the surplus proletarian forces of Europe through immigration. Both countries provided Europe with raw materials and were at the same time markets for the sale of its industrial products. At that time both were, therefore, in one way or another, pillars of the existing European order.

How very different today! Precisely European immigration fitted North America for a gigantic agricultural production, whose competition is shaking the very foundations of European landed property—large and small. In addition it enabled the United States to exploit its tremendous industrial resources with an energy and on a scale that must shortly break the industrial monopoly of Western Europe, and especially of England, existing up to now. Both circumstances react in revolutionary manner upon America itself. Step by step the small and middle landownership of the farmers, the basis of the whole political constitution, is succumbing to the competition of giant farms; simultaneously, a mass proletariat and a fabulous concentration of capital are developing for the first time in the industrial regions.

And now Russia! During the Revolution of 1848–49 not only the European princes, but the European bourgeois as well, found their only salvation from the proletariat, just beginning to awaken, in Russian intervention. The tsar was proclaimed the chief of European reaction. Today he is a prisoner of war of the revolution, in Gatchina, and Russia forms the vanguard of revolutionary action in Europe.

The Communist Manifesto had as its object the proclamation of the inevitably impending dissolution of modern bourgeois property. But in Russia we find, face to face with the rapidly developing capitalist swindle and bourgeois landed property, just beginning to develop, more than half the land owned in common by the peasants. Now the question is: can the Russian *obshchina* [village community], though generally undermined, yet a form of the primeval common ownership of land, pass directly to the higher form of communist common ownership? Or, on the contrary, must it first pass through the same process of dissolution as constitutes the historical evolution of the West?

The only answer to that possible today is this: If the Russian Revolution becomes the signal for a proletarian revolution in the West, so that both complement each other, the present Russian common ownership of land may serve as the starting-point for a communist development.

MEW, 4, 575–76, as translated in Karl Marx and Frederick Engels, *Selected Works*, 3 vols., Moscow, 1969, Vol. I, pp. 99–101.

READER'S GUIDE

~~~~~~~~~~~~~~~~~~~~~~~~~~~~~~~~~~~~~

The principal concepts and conceptions in Marx's thought, with appropriate page references to material in this volume.

ALIENATION

Marx's concept of alienation builds on the work of his predecessors, the German idealist philosophers Fichte and Hegel, who argued that the mind comes to recognize its powers and itself by projecting those powers outside itself (*Entäusserung*, externalization or alienation) and then allowing the externalizations to confront it as independent powers and dominate it (*Entfremdung* or estrangement). Marx, putting no special weight on the distinction between the two stages, which he sees as part of a single process, gives this philosophical category social content by substituting, as Feuerbach did, man for mind and seeing alienation as lying in man's subjugation to social idols, ends, and institutions he has himself created. Man, instead of determining the conditions of social production and social organization, becomes determined by them. As history moves through the stages of slave-owning society, feudalism, and capitalism, alienation becomes more pervasive, more abstract, and more intense. It had begun with man's dependence on nature—or rather on his conceptions of nature and of natural forces, deified to confront him as man-made idols—and moved through man's dependence on and subjugation by other men in slave-owning and feudal societies to the pervasive alienation of capitalism, in which man is estranged from nature, from other men confronting him as exploiters or competitors, from the products of his work, that are not part of his purposes and satisfactions but belong to another, and from the very activity of working itself, which he separates from his life and sells by the hour on the labour market. The concept of alienation is central in Marx's development from Left Hegelianism through Feuerbachian humanism to communism. It continues in a less philosophical guise to inform his later work, where Marx uses the allied concepts of dehumanization, exploitation, and fetishism of commodities and sees man as losing sight or control of social purposes through the abstraction, alienation, and mystification made possible by money. Pages xxii–xxxiv; xxxviii–xliii; 75–163; 177–78; 232–33; 444–61.

See also: Eugene Kamenka, *Marxism and Ethics,* London and New York, 1969, pp. 4–30; Eugene Kamenka, *The Ethical Foundations of Marxism,* London and Boston, 1962, 2nd ed. 1972, pp. 17–47; Bertell Ollman, *Alienation: Marx's Conception of Man in Capitalist Society,* London and New York, 1971, 2nd ed. 1976; John Plamenatz, *Karl Marx's Philosophy of Man,* Oxford, 1975, pp. 87–172.

ASIATIC MODE OF PRODUCTION

A form of public slavery which, according to Marx, succeeded primitive communism, or perhaps an early form of feudalism, in such great civilizations of the East as India and China, but not Japan. In the Asiatic mode of production private property and the classes based upon it failed to develop, allowing the state to become the main organizer of production and appropriator of surplus value. Marx believed that the aridity of the Orient and the scattered nature of population there required, at an early stage, the centralized organizing power of the state to secure the foundations of agriculture through irrigation and flood control, requiring large-scale public works. This allowed the state to become dominant over the rest of society and resulted in the absence or comparative unimportance of independent trade or economic activity, of cities dependent on such trade, and of classes and class struggles. Like Hegel and some political economists including James Mill, Marx thought that the Asiatic mode of production lacks the internal dynamic for change provided by class interest and class struggle and he therefore believed that progress required the societies of Oriental despotism to be revolutionized by capitalist intrusion. In Russia, with the Tatar invasion, Marx believed, there had been an intrusion of Oriental despotic forms. Pages 161; 329–36; 455–56.

See also: K. A. Wittfogel, *Oriental Despotism: A Comparative Study of Total Power*, New Haven, 1959; Marian Sawer, *Marxism and the Question of the Asiatic Mode of Production*, The Hague, 1977.

BOURGEOISIE

The ruling class under capitalism, owners of capital and of means of production (factories) engaged in production for a large-scale commercial market. Pages 184; 203–28; 235–36; 390–91.

See also entries on: *Capitalism, Classes, Class Struggle.*

CAPITALISM

The mode of production based on private property in the means of production, production for a market, and the use of money as pervasive features of the economy and on the rule of the bourgeoisie. Marx distinguishes between the big bourgeoisie, international in character, owning and developing the major means of production and creating an international market and a world in its own image, and a petty bourgeoisie of small shopkeepers, professional men, etc., destined to be proletarianized by the inherent tendency of capitalism to sharpen and simplify all social conflicts and relationships into the contrast between the owners of the means of production (the bourgeoisie) and those who own nothing but their labour power (the proletariat). The inherent contradictions of capitalism, which will bring about its collapse, lie not only in the fundamental and inescapable contradiction between the interests of a small owning class and a large labouring class. They lie also in what Marx sees as an inescapable fall in the rate of profit as the proportion of investment in machinery increases; this leads to necessarily increasingly vicious exploitation of the proletariat and to a growing army of the unemployed. The unplanned nature of capitalist production based on private profit leads, in these circumstances, to over-production and underconsumption and to the consequent recurrence of ever more serious economic crises. The extent to which Marx recognizes countervailing trends which do not make the collapse of capitalism economically inevitable, or which make possible a gradual socialization of capitalism from within, as the result of economic forces or of political democratic development, is a matter of controversy. Pages xxvi–xxxviii; 464–503.

See also: J. A. Schumpeter, *Capitalism, Socialism, and Democracy*, London, 1943, 3rd ed. 1950, pp. 9–44; M. C. Howard and J. E. King, *The Political Economy of Marx*, Harlow, 1975; Leszek Kolakowski, *Main Currents of Marxism: Its Rise, Growth, and Dissolution*, 3 vols., Oxford, 1978, Vol. 1, pp. 262–334; Roman Rosdolsky, *The Making of Marx's 'Capital,'* translated from German, London, 1977, pp. 167–313.

CIVIL SOCIETY

Marx follows the usage of Adam Ferguson rather than the more complex discussion in Hegel in treating civil society as the world of industry and trade, the pre- or extra-political world of the egoistic self-seeking individual standing in a relationship of competition and antagonism to all other individuals. Civil society, which displays Hobbes's war of all against all, is contrasted by Marx with the pretended universalism of the state: the two require each other but stand in fundamental conflict. After 1845, when Marx "discovered" the materialist conception of history, he sees civil society as the real source and theatre of all historical development and the state as overcoming civil society only in fantasy, as in fact dominated by it. The sharp separation of the economic, the moral and the political, the dualism of civil society and the state, according to Marx, reaches its apogee in bourgeois society. Pages 89; 102–14; 179–80.

See also: Kamenka, *The Ethical Foundations of Marxism, supra*, pp. 51–86; Shlomo Avineri, *The Social and Political Thought of Karl Marx*, Cambridge, 1968, pp. 17–27;

George Lichtheim, *Marxism: An Historical and Critical Study*, London, 1961, 2nd ed. with corrections 1971, pp. 154–61; John Plamenatz, *Man and Society: A Critical Examination of Some Important Social and Political Theories from Machiavelli to Marx*, 2 vols., London, 1963, vol. 2, pp. 216–68; and entries on: *Class, State, infra.*

CLASS, CLASS STRUGGLE

Society, for Marx, is divided into classes which are defined by their relationship to the principal means of production, not by their income, status, or pretensions. Every age since primitive communism, according to Marx, has seen the division of society into exploiters, who own or appropriate the means of production and the surplus value produced by those means, and the exploited, who are forced to work them. There are thus slave owners and slaves, feudal lords and serfs, bourgeois and proletarians. There are also intermediate classes described by more specific aspects of their economic activity or their relationship to major factors of production—artisans, peasants, merchants, and, in modern times, professional men and public servants whom Marx, following a wider usage, does call, at times, the middle classes. Marx treats these intermediate classes as essentially dependent and transitional in relation to the more central groupings, especially under capitalism. The peasantry forms a class only in the sense in which potatoes in a sack form a sack of potatoes.

Classes, for Marx, at the political and ideological level and to some degree at the economic, are the motive power of history. Each ruling class comes to power as the carrier of economic development, of progress, though it later becomes an obstacle to further economic progress. The conflict between the ruling class and other (exploited) classes is the central and dominant fact in the political and ideological history of each mode of production or epoch. Classes, consciously or unconsciously, pursue their own interests and see the world from their specific social vantage point—they have a distorted, partial, self-interested perception that is the class ideology. Classes that have such an objective common interest and perception are classes in themselves; when, as a result of their situation, they become conscious of their interests and work out a coherent ideology, they are classes not only in themselves but also for themselves.

Marx's theory of class is an attempt to develop a dynamic explanatory model that will account for change, not a static description like that of stratification theory. Critics, however, have pointed to the vagueness and inconsistency of Marx's use of class, to the dubious Marxist character of the conception of a middle class and the falsity of Marx's view that it will disappear, to his neglect of explanatory conceptions, especially important for revolution, like nationalism, race, religion, and the class of intellectuals. Pages xxxiv–xxxvi; 121–24; 166–70; 193–94; 203–17; 257–323.

See also: Ralph Dahrendorf, *Class and Class Conflict in Industrial Society*, London, 1959, especially ch. I, pp. 3–35; Plamenatz, *Man and Society, supra,* vol. 2, pp. 293–322; Kolakowski, *supra,* vol. 1, pp. 335–75; Lichtheim, *supra,* pp. 380–92; Henri Lefebvre, *The Sociology of Marx,* translated from French by N. Guterman, Harmondsworth, 1972, pp. 89–122; entries on *Civil Society, State.*

COMMUNISM

The state of society, according to Marx, in which there is no private property, no socially significant division of labour or exclusive ownership of tools and means of production, and no use of money as a substitute for the social control of production, and in which production is directly for use. This stage will be achieved as a result of the internal collapse of capitalism when the proletariat comes to expropriate the expropriators and places into social ownership the means of production, distribution, and exchange. Marx envisages capitalist habits and the use of money not being abolished overnight after such a revolution. Politically, the revolution will be accompanied by a temporary repressive dictatorship of the proletariat, which will then be the vast majority of mankind, preventing the old ruling class and its agents from regaining power. Economically, the first stage of communism, often called socialism by Marx's followers, will be based on the

continuation of a money economy and of democratized labour discipline according to the principle "From each according to his capacity, to each according to his contribution." When such socialized production has caused the
springs of wealth to flow more freely, when labour has become highly educated and versatile, and when the vestiges of
bourgeois habits and self-seeking have been eliminated,
money will cease to play a significant role and the principle of
society will become "From each according to his capacity, to
each according to his need." Pages xxxv–xxxvi; 94; 127;
146–52; 177–79; 189–95; 218–28; 242–44; 454–55; 547–55.

In the 1860s, when Marx and Engels had become aware of
the researches of Haxthausen and Maurer pointing to communal ownership of land as the original form of agriculture,
they postulated at the beginning of human history a period of
primitive communism in which ownership and production
were in common, in which there was no class differentiation,
and in which only a rudimentary (sexual) division of labour
existed. Such primitive communism, however, in which
human capacities are only weakly developed, leaves man a
prey to hostile natural forces and a slave of his environment.
Pages 453–54.

DIALECTICAL MATERIALISM

Marx took over from Hegel the conception that change is
the result of dialectical contradictions, of the inevitable conflict of opposites which results in their mutual destruction together with their preservation (or "sublation," *Aufhebung*)
at a higher level in a new synthesis in which these contradictions are overcome. The opposites—thesis and antithesis—
require each other, cannot exist without bringing each other
into being, and the dialectic is thus not fortuitous and not to
be grasped without seeing the wider whole of which these
opposites are part. The dialectic also implies that historical
development is not a matter of gradual change in the relative
weight of social forces, but that such gradual changes of
quantity result in sudden leaps or transformations of quality.
Subsequent, principally Soviet, interpreters have formalized
the laws of the dialectic, basing themselves on pronounce-

ments by Engels, into three laws: the law of the transformation of quantity into quality; the law of the interpenetration and conflict of opposites; and the law of the negation of the negation, which requires the antithesis as well as the thesis to be "negated" and overcome in the new synthesis. An initially reasonably plausible example to be found in Marx is the necessary conflict and contradiction accompanied by mutual logical dependence between capitalist and proletarian, the existence of each of which presupposes and requires the existence of the other. The synthesis provided by communism in abolishing private ownership in the means of production abolishes or "negates" both capitalist and proletarian. Other examples of dialectical interpenetration and conflict in Marx are state and civil society, and interpreters seeking to overcome implausibities in Marx's separation of social elements—classes, productive forces, and relations of production, economic base, and superstructure—often insist that these must be treated "dialectically," i.e., as mutually dependent, interpenetrating, not to be understood in isolation but only as part of a wider whole.

Marx's "dialectical method," never set out clearly or extensively by Marx himself, has been the subject of much sympathetic interpretation and much criticism. Non-dialectical philosophers commonly complain that the "contradiction" referred to in the dialectic is not the logical contradiction between a true proposition and its contradictory. It is rather a conflict of opposite tendencies, which can and do coexist without logical "contradiction" or any necessary collapse of the system. The terms "dialectic of nature" and "dialectical materialism" are not found in Marx at all.

See also: Kamenka, *The Ethical Foundations of Marxism*, *supra*, pp. 17–25; Ollman, *supra*, pp. 3–69; H. B. Acton, *The Illusion of the Epoch: Marxism-Leninism as a Philosophical Creed*, London, 1955, pp. 71–104; Richard Norman and Sean Sayers, *Hegel, Marx and Dialectic: A Debate*, Brighton, 1980; Z. A. Jordan, *The Evolution of Dialectical Materialism: A Philosophical and Sociological Analysis*, London and New York, 1967.

EXPLOITATION

The process by which the appropriators of the means of production extract surplus value (see *Labour Theory of Value*) from the labour of those who work these means, thus appropriating what is not theirs. Marx does not mean by exploitation taking more or paying less than "is reasonable." What is reasonable, fair, or just, according to Marx, is always a relative concept depending on the state of the market; exploitation is an objective, nonrelative concept bringing out that one class appropriates the labour and the creations of another. Pages 415; 533–41.

FETISHISM OF COMMODITIES

The process, characteristic of capitalism, in which commodities cease to be produced for social use and become absolute ends in themselves, dominating man instead of serving him, becoming the ultimate values in the system of production. Pages 444–61. *See also* ALIENATION.

FEUDALISM

The stage of society based on serfdom and the manorial system, in which the economic, the religious and the political, the private and the public, are not yet sharply separated and where men are held in bondage as whole men not abstracted into free citizens on the one hand and wage slaves on the other. Marx, and especially Engels, stressed the comparative complexity of feudalism, the multifariousness of classes and subclasses within it; they see capitalism as the simplifying society. Towns, with their merchants, runaway serfs, and demands for "liberties," are seen by Marx as standing in fundamental tension with feudalism and helping to bring about its downfall, as does the creation of a money economy and of production for a market, requiring mobility of labour and hence liberation from serfdom. Pages 111–13; 466–71; 479.

IDEOLOGY

Marx sees classes as producing ideologies, views of the world and of social, political, moral, aesthetic, etc., problems which serve the interests of that class and express its partial and incomplete point of view. Ideologies, to that extent, are treated as "false consciousness," not mere fantasies but rather distorted perspectives. It is a matter of controversy whether the "ideology" of the proletariat surmounts this narrowness and distortion to become true or correct consciousness. Pages 162–86; 203–41; 455–56.

See also: Plamenatz, *Man and Society, supra,* vol. 2, pp. 323–50; John Plamenatz, *Ideology* (Key Concepts in Political Science), London, 1970; John McMurtry, *The Structure of Marx's World-View,* Princeton, 1978, pp. 123–44; Martin Seliger, *The Marxist Conception of Ideology: A Critical Essay,* Cambridge, 1977.

LABOUR THEORY OF VALUE, SURPLUS VALUE

The labour theory of value, which Marx adopted from Ricardo, states that labour is the source of all value—a proposition which is as much a declaration of moral principle as an attempted definition for purposes of economic analysis. According to Marx, in given conditions man can produce more than he needs to consume in order to continue working; he therefore produces surplus value. This surplus value is appropriated by those who command labour and own the means of production—before capitalism, by openly appropriating the surplus product; in the monetary economy of capitalism, by paying the worker less than the value of what he produces, by paying him enough for his subsistence as opposed to the value of the products he creates. Pages xxxvi; 219; 394–444; 461–65.

MATERIALISM (PHILOSOPHICAL)

Marx, from 1845 onward, professes himself a materialist. The claim is best understood in relation to Hegel and the idealist tradition in philosophy. Marx insists that being determines consciousness, and not vice versa, and—with less clarity and consistency—that "the world," i.e., what is known, is independent of the knower. He attacks, however, "passive" materialism, which treats the mind as merely receiving impressions from outside; he is anxious to stress the active, creative role of mind and he never speaks of objects of knowledge save *as they are known*. The precise character of Marx's "materialism" has therefore been the subject of varying interpretation and much dispute. Pages 155–58; 170–71.

See also: Acton, *supra*, pp. 9–70; Jordan, *supra*, pp. 16–64; Alfred Schmidt, *The Concept of Nature in Marx*, translated from German by Ben Fowkes, London, 1971, pp. 95–126; Thomas J. Blakeley, *Soviet Theory of Knowledge*, Dordrecht, 1964.

MATERIALIST CONCEPTION OF HISTORY (HISTORICAL MATERIALISM)

Marx's materialist conception of history is both a method for studying the general trend of historical events and a broad summation of the principal stages through which, according to Marx, history has moved. Logically, the method begins with the proposition that social being, the material productive life of men lived in relation with each other in society, determines social consciousness, i.e., ideologies and forms of state and social organization. Marx therefore divides social life into an economic or material base, seeing society as an organization for production and reproduction, and an ideological superstructure which "reflects" that base. The economic base consists of productive forces and relations of production. The productive forces are the tools and skills, including knowledge, all of them socially conditioned, which are available at any given period for the purposes of material production. The relations of production are the manner in which factors of production, tools, and the social product are owned and distributed in any given mode of production. A principal line in Marx's writing suggests that the state of productive forces at a given stage of development determines the relations of production at that stage—a particular form of relations being the most economically efficient for the utilization of the productive forces available. Productive forces, however, develop steadily, incrementally, while relations of production are comparatively fixed at any given stage. This produces the possibility and reality of a growing time lag between the stage of development of productive forces and the relations of production or class-structure of a given society. The irresistible growth of the productive forces then bursts through the integument of the relations of production which have become a fetter on the productive forces. Social and political revolution takes place and a new set of relations of production, a new mode of production, is born.

The superstructure, in Marx's principal line of reasoning, is entirely derivative, to be explained in terms of the economic base. It consists of political and legal forms of state and, at a level still further removed from the material, of political, legal, philosophical, ethical, aesthetic, etc., ideologies. The state and its political and legal structure, according to Marx, represent the will of the ruling class and its method of organizing and securing the relations of production advantageous to it. The state is born with the division of society into classes as a result of the appropriation of tools by one section of society which forces another section to labour and secures a disproportionate part of the return—a line of thought developed by Engels in his *Origin of the Family, Private Property and the State* rather than by Marx. Ideologies (q.v.), according to Marx, reflect the outlook and interest of specific classes of society, often with a certain time lag. The ruling or dominant ideology of any social period is the ideology of its ruling class.

The language Marx uses in setting out the materialist conception of history as a historical method is not precise and his work contains many concessions and admissions of countervailing influences. Marx speaks of the economic base "determining" or "conditioning" the superstructure. Some read this to assert causal determination, others a functional relationship of concomitant variability between superstructure and base without any claim of temporal or causal priority. Yet a third view, allied with structuralism, sees the causality involved as not mechanistic but structural, the causality of a whole determining the nature of its parts. There is further disagreement whether, on the mechanistic causal view, the productive forces determine relations of production, which in turn determine the superstructure, or whether the productive forces and the relations of production must be taken together as causal factors. Critics suggest that Marx cannot maintain a one-way determinism from productive forces through relations of production to superstructure, but that his and Engels's conceiving a reaction back (i.e., in a two-way determinism) destroys the long-run predictability or inevitability that his theory requires. At the logical level, critics have argued further that superstructural elements—e.g., scientific knowledge in the case of productive forces and legal provisions in the case of relations of production—are required for the very definition and characterization of elements in the base, thus destroying Marx's attempt to separate these elements for the purpose of causal relationships. Pages 115–18; 155–58; 375–81; 434–36; 459; 490–98.

As a general summation of the development of history, the materialist conception of history argues that society moves, inexorably, through the following stages: primitive communism, the Asiatic mode of production (or public slavery) or classical slave owning (private slavery), feudalism, and capitalism, to be followed by communism. Each stage has been linked by interpreters with a particular stage of the development of productive forces: stone tools, accompanied by nomadic hunting and food-gathering ways of life and some agriculture for primitive communism; iron tools, accompanied by war and mining for slave-owning societies; the hand mill and the development of more skilled agriculture generally for feudalism; the steam mill and factory production for a market for capitalism, with an earlier mercantile capitalism based on artisan production for a commodities market preceding it. Communism arises from the contradiction between the increasingly social nature of production under capitalism and the private organization of ownership at one level and from the class struggle between bourgeois and proletariat ending in the victory of the proletariat at another.

The *Communist Manifesto* presents a unilinear and, critics say, Euro-centric model in which the Asiatic mode of production is omitted and in which all humanity appears to move from slave owning through feudal to bourgeois modes of production. In the *Grundrisse* and elsewhere, there is a more complex multilinear development in which the growth of individualism and of private property is greatly emphasized for northwest European societies and in which war and conquest often replace what the *Communist Manifesto* presents as an internal dynamic. Interpreters have constructed from this a multilinear schematism in which there are separate accounts of development for northwestern (Germanic or Frankish) Europe, where the movement is from primitive communism to a form of manorial society and early feudalism, with slave owning playing no significant economic part; for the Graeco-Roman world, where slave owning shows some tendency to move toward feudalism, but is converted into feudalism only by Frankish conquest; for Slav civilization, which begins with Germanic feudalism through the Norse origins of the Russian state but succumbs to the Asiatic mode of production with the Tatar conquest and later becomes capitalized through European intrusion; and for the Oriental world (India and China), which moves from a primitive communism through perhaps a short and unsuccessful feudal stage to the Asiatic mode of production, being undermined in the nineteenth century by European expansion. Pages 161; 165–68; 183–84; 203–17.

See also: Plamenatz, *Man and Society, supra,* vol. 2, pp. 268–93; Gerald A. Cohen, *Karl Marx's Theory of History: A Defence,* Oxford, 1978; Melvin Rader, *Marx's Interpretation of History,* New York, 1979; William H. Shaw, *Marx's Theory of History,* London, 1978; Sawer, *supra,* pp. 188–227.

REVOLUTION

The social and political upheaval in which a new class overthrows a former ruling class and ushers in a new set of relations of production and a new mode of production. Revolutions for Marx are always the result of economic developments which make the old ruling class incapable of carrying on the further economic development of society. In past revolutions, the class which stands at the head of the revolutionary movement tends to act, at the beginning, as the representative of the whole of the rest of society challenging the ruling class, and therefore to have a comparatively "universal" soul; as the revolution progresses, its own particularistic interests reassert themselves. Marx sees the French Revolution as displaying this phenomenon and suggests, on that basis, a strategy of revolution, even of bourgeois revolutions, in the future in which a proletariat and a truly revolutionary party can seek constantly to radicalize the revolution, to make revolution "permanent." Pages 119–24; 160; 182–83; 197–298.

See also: Avineri, *supra*, pp. 134–201; Lichtheim, *supra*, pp. 51–62; Plamenatz, *Karl Marx's Philosophy of Man, supra*, pp. 173–201; Robert C. Tucker, *The Marxian Revolutionary Idea*, New York, 1969; E. Kamenka and F. B. Smith (eds.), *Intellectuals and Revolution: Socialism and the Experience of 1848*, London and New York, 1979.

STATE

The political power of society, separated from the rest of society and controlled by the ruling class of that society in its own interest. The completed abstraction of the state from society is the work of the bourgeoisie. The claim of the state bureaucracy to be a "universal" class serving public interest and not sectional interest is false. Marx does not emphasize the independent power of the state, although his conception of the Asiatic mode of production concedes that such independent power, in certain conditions, is possible. His analysis of the regime of Napoleon III suggests that a stalemate in the class struggle made it possible for an adventurer to capture and use the state. Pages 87–114; 118–19; 152–55; 174–75; 184–85; 308–23; 525–55.

See also: Plamenatz, *Man and Society, supra*, vol. 2, pp. 351–408; McMurtry, *supra*, pp. 100–127; Lefebvre, *supra*, pp. 123–85; entries on: *Civil Society, Class*.

INDEX

of the most important names, institutions, works, and places mentioned by Marx

~~~~~~~~~~~~~~~~~~~~~~~~~~~~~~~~~~~~~~~